"The challenges within the commercial space market are often perceived as technical. And while it is indeed a technical challenge, for example, to land and re-use a rocket booster, or to understand how to perform 3D printing and additive manufacturing in space, the more intractable hurdles may well be economic, financial, regulatory, political, and cultural. In this excellent compilation of writing from experts in the global space sector's legal and regulatory community, Dr. Lesley Jane Smith and co-editors have assembled a 'must-read' for practitioners and scholars alike. The frameworks of Apollo and other large, monolithic, government-driven space programs have given way to a new, multi-variate, and extremely dynamic private-sector, that is moving faster than many of the legal and policy frameworks can adapt. Consequently, this timely compendium from the world's best thinkers on where the market is headed, challenges that we all face, and regulatory frameworks that must be navigated, is an essential read for our entire community."

John M. Horack, PhD, *Professor and Neil Armstrong Chair in Aerospace Policy, The Ohio State University*

"The economic growth of emerging ecosystems relies wholly on a legal framework that protects the interests of investors, operators and nation states. Without innovative legal frameworks such as those outlined in this book by thought-leading legal scholars in this space, the private space sector would have no basis for growth. This Handbook is essential reading and reference for those executives, policy makers and investors who wish to venture into the growing opportunity of the space sector with clarity on where and how they are best able to contribute to and unlock success in this exciting field."

Prof. Sinead O'Sullivan, *Institute for Strategy and Competitiveness, Harvard Business School*

"Given the rapid growth of the global space economy with projections of a trillion-dollar space economy by the year 2040, *The Handbook on Commercial Space Law – Legal Practice(s) for New Space* is an extremely timely publication that is certain to become an invaluable reference tool for many years to come to commercial practitioners, policymakers and academics addressing the market changes brought about by NewSpace. In a series of well-structured chapters written by a global cross-section of space specialists, Lesley Jane Smith, Ingo Baumann and Susan-Gale Wintermuth have collected a strong set of contributions that highlight, in a comparative fashion: the main legal challenges posed by NewSpace, how different countries are adapting their national regulatory frameworks, as well as adopting different approaches to foster innovation and support NewSpace."

Lucy Stojak, *Chair, Canadian Space Council Directrice exécutive, Mosaic - Pôle créativité et innovation, Montréal (Québec)*

"The Space economy is entering the Industrial Revolution phase of its rapid development, with both private and public sector investment and satellite launches going exponential, as are the uses for space tech in putting industries such as data centres in space, sourcing solar power from space and observing the earth in new ways. I also believe firmly that a planet of 10 billion people will never achieve net zero without space industrialisation.
That is why this book is so timely and useful. As Chair of the world's first publicly quoted investment trust for space tech I want answers to lots of questions on global commercial space law and here they are. We are in an age of rapid change with consequent instability and in that context the rule of law and its rapid adaptation to technological change is crucial, so I intend to keep my copy of *The Routledge Handbook on Commercial Space Law* close by."

Will Whitehorn, *Chancellor of Napier University, Edinburgh, Former Virgin Galactic, Chair, Seraphim Venture Capital Trust, FRAeS FCILT FMS, Chair, Seraphim Space Investment Trust PLC, Member, UK Space Agency Space Exploration Advisory Committee*

"This Handbook covers all relevant issues and trends in today's revolutionary transition from traditional space governance to commercial and privatised NewSpace. The impressive team of editors and contributors provides outstanding insight and guidance for navigating in this new universe of space becoming indispensable for our economies and societies on national levels as well as on a global scale."

Dr. Kai-Uwe Schrogl, *President, International Institute of Space Law (IISL), Head of strategy, European Space Agency, Paris*

"As the space economy gallops ahead with private sector participation extending the earlier generation national space programs, the regulatory landscape that was aligned with the earlier sector construct, starts getting outdated and the need for the regulations to keep pace with the technological and economic developments seems both urgent and important. The value, that this development of private sector participation brings, is demonstrated both with respect to technology disruption and socio-economic impact. The players themselves are rearing to be on the tracks, however as the space activities are unbound by geographical boundaries, the treatment in terms of permissions, issues of commerce, patents, liabilities and rights, social responsibility etc take on a meaning that is not facilitated by the existing national and international construct of laws.
This book is more of treatise on this subject and carefully highlights issues and the attempts by some nations to address these. Not all of these are optimal in a fast developing and expanding sector and each new attempt needs to build on the success and concerns that these attempts raise. Equally important is the fact that the private sector needs to be facilitated by these attempts, and have a significant role in not just the outcomes of these deliberations, but also play a constructive role in these developing regulatory landscape. In this direction the book, while being a comprehensive asset to the policy makers is also a significant input for the private sector players themselves to understand the developing regulatory ecosystem, under which they need to survive and thrive.

I thank the various experts for sharing the knowledge that stems from their deep engagement in understanding and steering the international deliberations, especially Dr. Ranjana Kaul who helps us see the situation from the India lens. I also thank the Lesley Jane Smith, Ingo Baumann and Susan-Gale Wintermuth for bringing out this compendium of thoughts from all the internationals experts."

Dr. Subba Rao Pavuluri, *President, Satcom Industry Association (SIA -India) and CMD Ananth Technologies Ltd*

"60 years ago, President John F Kennedy addressed Rice University (Texas) on the moon-shot programme. And during that historical speech he determined that 'The greater our knowledge increases, the greater our ignorance unfolds'. The Editor and Authors of this vanguard Routledge Handbook have delivered a timely compendium of lessons learnt, knowledge gained and the critical challenges and opportunities around the future. And it is genuinely global in perspective yet precise in detail and understanding. It is entirely relevant. The document's unquestionable strength is the spectrum of contributors and the intelligent fusing of the value that they each add, building knowledge and addressing ignorance. Space today, and as it was 60 years ago, is really hard. But because of the thoughtful, consolidated and extensive approach taken during the compilation of this Handbook, the space practitioner has a comprehensive handrail to the present and the future on which they can confidently rely."

James CMcG Johnston, *OBE BSc MIoD FCMI, Director, Transcend Change Limited (commercial and secure government satellite consultant, ex RAF)*

"Space today offers one of cutting edge and fast-growing opportunity for taking technology into new business. In comparison to well established business areas, such as IT or transport law, the newcomers' investors in space enterprises might be confused in discovering incomplete legal frameworks depending on where they are based, an apparent maze of regulatory conditions to become applicable, the dispersed availability of proven legal expertise in each jurisdiction. The representatives of the legal community who have undertaken this work are showing how to transition such impressions from complex or frustrating to reassuring and attractive. For both State actors and entrepreneurs, this volume tries to provide a mapping and to illustrate the legal landscape that space investors and operators will find, so to help an understanding of the challenges and opportunities offered by the space business. In this respect this publication is a useful example of how to foster the progressive and beneficial growth of laws and regulations, so to be experienced and leveraged by all kind of space actors and their endeavours. We wish to this collective work a long-term success of followers and so to continue developing our legal practice and business knowledge for using space."

Marco Ferrazzani, *Senior Legal Counsel, European Space Agency (ESA)*

"This innovative book belongs on the shelf of any commercial space lawyer and those seeking to enter this exciting field. This well-researched treatise delves into major new developments in commercial space law such as in-orbit servicing, large constellations, artificial intelligence, big data, private spaceflight, and space resource exploitation. I believe all commercial space lawyers will benefit from the authors' insight as we draft and review agreements for the novel space activities before us and on the horizon. I certainly will be consulting this book as I wrestle with the challenges of first-of-their-kind commercial space agreements and their national and international implications."

Milton "Skip" Smith, *Chair, Aerospace Practice Group, Sherman & Howard, Denver, CO, legal Counsel to the private Dragon Crew*

ROUTLEDGE HANDBOOK OF COMMERCIAL SPACE LAW

The *Routledge Handbook of Commercial Space Law* provides a definitive survey of the transitions and adjustments across the stakeholder community contributing to outer space activities. The interaction between NewSpace, traditional aerospace industrials, and non-traditional space-related technologies is driving market changes which will affect state practice in what has until now been a government dominated market. Greater private commercial participation will lead to new economic approaches to risk-sharing models driven by a space services dominated market. This handbook is a detailed reference source of original articles which analyse and critically evaluate the scope of the current paradigm change, and explain why space contracts and risk apportionment as currently known will change in tune with ongoing market transitions. Reference is made to the scope of best practices across various leading states involved in space activities. With contributions from a selection of highly regarded and leading scholars and practitioners in the Commercial Space Law field, and the inclusion of salient documents, regulatory and contractual documents, the *Routledge Handbook of Commercial Space Law* is an essential resource for students, scholars, and practitioners who are interested in the field of Commercial Space Law.

Lesley Jane Smith is Professor of International Economic Law at the Leuphana University, Germany, is partner in Weber-Steinhaus & Smith, Bremen, and Vice President of the International Institute of Space Law. A member of the International Academy of Astronautics and Corresponding Fellow at the Royal Society Edinburgh, she served the International Astronautical Federation as General Counsel, and currently acts as Alternate Ombudsman to the European Space Agency.

Ingo Baumann is a founding partner of BHO Legal, a technology law firm based in Cologne, Germany. He is member of the International Institute of Space Law, the European Centre for Space Law and various space industry associations. He is active in several programmes as mentors for start-ups in the space sector.

Susan-Gale Wintermuth is Professor in the China-EU Law School at China University of Political Science and Law, Beijing, China. She is a lecturer at the Stockholm School of Economics Riga, where she instructs on international business law. She also contributes on the same subject to the Executive MBA at the Stockholm School of Economics Riga.

Routledge Handbooks in Law Series

About the Series

Routledge Handbooks in Law present state-of-the-art surveys of important and emerging topics in Law and Legal Studies, providing accessible yet thorough assessments of key fields, themes and recent developments in research.

All chapters for each volume are specially commissioned, and written by leading and emerging scholars in the field. Carefully edited and organized, Routledge Handbooks in Law provide indispensable reference tools for students and researchers seeking a comprehensive overview of new and exciting topics in the relevant subject areas. They are also valuable teaching resources as accompaniments to textbooks, anthologies, and research-orientated publications.

Routledge Handbook of Commercial Space Law
Edited by Lesley Jane Smith, Ingo Baumann, and Susan-Gale Wintermuth

For more details, visit – Routledge Handbooks in Law – Book Series – Routledge & CRC Press

ROUTLEDGE HANDBOOK OF COMMERCIAL SPACE LAW

Edited by Lesley Jane Smith, Ingo Baumann, and Susan-Gale Wintermuth

Routledge
Taylor & Francis Group
LONDON AND NEW YORK

Cover design image: Wirestock, Inc. / Alamy Stock Photo

First published 2024
by Routledge
Park Square, Milton Park, Abingdon, Oxon OX14 4RN

and by Routledge
605 Third Avenue, New York, NY 10158

Routledge is an imprint of the Taylor & Francis Group, an informa business

British Library Cataloguing-in-Publication Data
A catalogue record for this book is available from the British Library

ISBN: 978-1-032-10074-6 (hbk)
ISBN: 978-1-032-21447-4 (pbk)
ISBN: 978-1-003-26847-5 (ebk)

DOI: 10.4324/9781003268475

Typeset in Times New Roman
by Deanta Global Publishing Services, Chennai, India

DISCLAIMER

Dear Reader, please note:

Space law is fast moving and in flux. The editors would like to call your attention to the fact that all attempts have been made to ensure that the information in the following chapters is current as of 31 October 2022. Moreover, due to the Covid-caused delay in finalising this book, chapters were submitted at different times. These chapters give you a good, in depth look at various issues. Nonetheless, we urge you to determine if there are updates, were you interested in pursuing a particular topic.

Additionally, all opinions are those of the individual authors and not of any state, organisation or business for whom they may work or be associated.

CONTENTS

FIGURES

CONTRIBUTORS

Olga Batura is a public policy consultant and visiting scholar at the Leuphana University Lüneburg, Germany, and Duke University, US/China, with a background in public international law and EU law focusing on telecommunications and digital economy.

Ingo Baumann is a founding partner of BHO Legal, a technology law firm based in Cologne, Germany. He is member of the International Institute of Space Law, the European Centre for Space Law and various space industry associations. He is active in several programmes as mentor for start-ups in the space sector.

P.J. Blount is a Lecturer in Law in the School of Law and Politics at Cardiff University, UK. Blount currently serves as the Executive Secretary of the International Institute of Space Law (IISL) and is an editor of the IISL Proceedings.

Ulrike M. Bohlmann is a German Attorney working for the European Space Agency, where she leads the Section for Director General Support and Member States Relations. A Member of IAA and IISL, as well as FRSA, she has held positions in ESA's Legal Department advising on space programmes, international cooperation and internal policy.

Kamlesh Brocard studied law as an undergraduate in the United Kingdom, and at graduate level in Germany and France, before joining the Swiss Space Office, State Secretariat for Education, Research and Innovation (SERI), as Scientific adviser.

Philippe Clerc is Chief Officer of Compliance and Corporate Ethics at the French Space Agency (CNES) and former Head of CNES' legal department. His career spans key legal positions within CNES, the French Ministry of Research and Space and Arianespace, which gives him a complete perspective and understanding of space-related legal affairs.

Matthias Creydt is an attorney in Munich, Germany, and founding partner of the law firm, CREYDT.LAW. He advises clients on all aspects of export control law, including compliance, sanctions and embargoes, and US re-export control law. Prior to this, he was Head of Export Control Germany with a leading global European aerospace company.

Laura Cummings is the Regulatory Affairs Counsel for Astroscale US, contributing to space policy development and overseeing licensing of the commercial geostationary servicing spacecraft LEXI. She is President of the Commercial Smallsat Spectrum Management Association, and a prospective member of the International Institute of Space Law.

Gerhard Deiters is a lawyer and partner at BHO Legal in Cologne. He specialises in IT, data, and data protection law, as well as in the areas of aviation and space. He also works as an external data protection officer.

Joel A. Dennerley is a management consultant and co-edited the book *Risk Management in Outer Space Activities* as part of the Springer Space Law and Policy series.

Giulia De Rossi graduated in "International Security" and "Space Policies and Institutions" prior to becoming a Space Consultant at Partners4Innovation. She authored the first research paper on Albania's potential for developing a Space economy for its socio-financial sector, together with EPOKA University and the Economic Society of Albania.

Catherine Doldirina is General Counsel at D-Orbit SpA, Italy.

Stefano M. Fiorilli is the Head of the Procurement and EU Administration Department at the European Space Agency (ESA). After private practice in Brussels in the field of Corporate Law and Merging and Acquisitions, he held a number of management positions at ESA, thereafter assuming his current position within the Executive.

Jason Forshaw is the Head of Future Business (Europe) at Astroscale. A recognised leader in the field of space debris, Jason has worked on several of the world's pioneering missions: SOADR (Envisat), RemoveDebris, ELSA-d and ELSA-M. Jason's alma maters include Sheffield University, Virginia Tech, Surrey Space Centre, and Stanford University.

Cécile Gaubert is Attorney registered at the Paris Bar, specializing in space law. Cécile has published several articles relating to space legal issues and regularly gives speeches at international colloquia. She is also involved in space-related associations and she is the Chairwoman of the Space Committee of the Société Française de Droit Aérien et Spatial.

Allison Genco is a Senior Attorney Advisor within the National Aeronautics and Space Administration (NASA) Office of the General Counsel in Washington, DC. She holds various awards in recognition of her legal work in support of human spaceflight exploration. She was previously senior procurement attorney within the Department of the Navy Office of the General Counsel.

Hamza Hameed is a Legal Consultant at the International Institute for the Unification of Private Law (UNIDROIT) and Co-Chair, Space Generation Advisory Council (SGAC). He leads UNIDROIT's work on the Space Protocol of the Cape Town Convention and teaches spacecraft financing at Leiden University. He is a member of the International Institute for Space Law (IISL).

Oliver Heinrich is co-founder and partner with BHO Legal. He earned his doctorate at the German Institute for Air and Space Law on questions of state aid and public procurement law for national and European research funding.

Julie Jiru was a Judge Advocate General (JAG) with the US Air Force prior to joining SpaceX (Space Exploration Technologies Corp.), where she managed legal and contractual aspects of SpaceX's NASA portfolio for 13 years. She is a member of the International Institute of Space Law.

Christopher Johnson is the Space Law Advisor at the Secure World Foundation and Professor of Law (Adjunct) at Georgetown University Law Center, USA.

Ranjana Kaul is a Partner at Dua Associates, Law Offices, New Delhi, India, with a BA (Bombay University, India); MA, PhD (University of Poona, India); LLB (University of Delhi, India) and LLM (Institute of Air and Space Law, McGill University, Canada).

Souichirou Kozuka is Professor of Law at Gakushuin University, Tokyo. He served as co-chair of the Space Law Committee of the International Bar Association (IBA) in 2016 and 2017. He is correspondent of UNIDROIT (the International Institute for the Unification of Private Law), and Associate Member of the International Academy of Comparative Law (IACL).

Holger Krag is the Head of the Space Safety Programme Office for the European Space Agency that is responsible for the Agency's Space Debris, Space Weather and Planetary Defence Activities. He represents ESA in the IADC (Inter Agency Debris Coordination Committee), and is a lecturer at the Technical University of Darmstadt.

Ruairidh J.M. Leishman is a solicitor at Shepherd and Wedderburn LLP, a Scottish headquartered, UK law firm. Since 2016 he has been an undergraduate tutor at the University of Strathclyde, Glasgow and is a Member of the IISL. He has a particular interest in the UK space legislation and Scotland's emerging "space glen".

Adriana Marais's PhD and postdoctoral work in quantum biology focused on photosynthesis and origins of prebiotic molecules in space. Adriana is currently director at Foundation for Space Development Africa, scientific moderator on space resources with Geneva Science and Diplomacy Anticipator, also faculty at Singularity University. In 2019, Adriana founded Proudly Human's Off-World Project, in preparation for extreme conditions on Earth and beyond.

Tanja Masson-Zwaan is Assistant Professor and Deputy Director of the International Institute of Air and Space Law (IIASL), Leiden University, the Netherlands, and President Emerita of the International Institute of Space Law (IISL).

Catrina Melograna is an aerospace professional and holds a JD and an LLM in Air and Space Law from Leiden University, the Netherlands, and is a member of the International Institute of Space Law.

Jan Helge Mey is a partner at BHO Legal. His main areas of expertise include public procurement law, public commercial law, subsidy and foreign trade law as well as air and space law. He studied in Cologne (Germany) and Qingdao (PR China), receiving his LLM degree from McGill University in Montréal, Canada. He subsequently worked at the Institute for Air and Space Law in Cologne.

Erik Pellander has been a research fellow at BHO Legal, a technology law firm based in Cologne, Germany, since 2011. Before joining BHO in 2011 he worked at the Institute of Air and Space Law, Cologne, as well as at the legal department of the German Space Agency (DLR).

Regina Peldszus works on Space Security and Space Situational Awareness in the European space sector. She is a space policy officer on special leave from German Space Agency at DLR, where she co-chaired EU Space Surveillance & Tracking, and with ESA. She is a member of the IAF Committee on Space Traffic Management

Gina Petrovici works at the UN-Affairs Department of the German Space Agency at DLR. She is currently the German Delegation's member at COPUOS and ESA IRC. Gina formerly worked as a Junior Lawyer at ESA (DLR fellowship). She is Space Law Lecturer and member of IISL, ECSL, WIA-E, SGAC, and DGVN.

Kevin Pomfret is a partner at the Williams Mullen Law firm and is based in the Washington, DC area. He began his career as a satellite imagery analyst with the National Photographic Interpretation Center.

Maria A. Pozza is the Director and Principal of Gravity Lawyers, a law firm that specialises in New Zealand's space law, international space law, cybersecurity compliance over data, IT and system frameworks, as well as providing commercial and corporate in-house legal support.

Ruth Pritchard-Kelly is the Senior Advisor for Regulatory and Space Policy at OneWeb where she advises a global team of legal & technical policy analysts. She is a member of the International Institute of Space Law and the Space and Satellite Professionals International, as well as being on the Advisory Committee for the Secure World Foundation and on the Board of the US Telecommunications Training Institute.

Maria Rhimbassen is Associate Researcher with Chaire SIRIUS at the University of Toulouse, France.

Bernhard Schmidt-Tedd, Honorary Professor of Law, Leuphana University, Germany, is the former Head of Department, UN Affairs at DLR, the German Space Agency. He was Chair of the Working Group on the Status and Application of the five UN treaties (2016 -2022) within the Legal Subcommittee, LSC, United Nations Committee on the Peaceful use of Outer Space, COPUOS.

Lesley Jane Smith is Professor of International Economic Law at the Leuphana University, Germany, is partner in Weber-Steinhaus & Smith, Bremen, and Vice President of the International Institute of Space Law. A member of the International Academy of Astronautics and *Corresponding* Fellow at the Royal Society Edinburgh, she served the International Astronautical Federation as General Counsel, and currently acts as Alternate Ombudsman to the European Space Agency.

Mark J. Sundahl is Professor of Law and Director of the Global Space Law Center (GSLC), Cleveland State University, USA.

Mizuki Tani-Hatakenaka has dealt with legal affairs and policy recommendations in Japan Aerospace Exploration Agency (JAXA) since 2008, and drafted space-related bills at the Ministry of Education, Culture, Sports, Science and Technology (MEXT). She holds an Advanced LL.M. in Air and Space Law from Leiden University as a Leiden Excellence Scholarship awardee in 2018.

Jenni Tapio is Chief Specialist at the Ministry of Economic Affairs and Employment of Finland, specializing in space law and policy. She spearheads the team responsible for licensing and supervision of national space activities. Ms. Tapio is the Secretary General of the Finnish Space Committee, chairing its division on space situational awareness. She has been elected as First Vice-Chair of COPUOS (2022–2023).

Alan Thompson is Head of Government Affairs in Skyrora and is responsible for managing and engaging with all key stakeholders across industry and Government, including the Parliamentary Space Committee, UK Space, Space Scotland and direct engagement with all government authorities and the Space flight regulators – UKSA and CAA. Alan's international trade experience gives a new perspective to Space industry development.

Anna Veneziano is the Deputy Secretary-General of the International Institute for the Unification of Private Law (UNIDROIT), and a Professor of Comparative Law at the University of Teramo, Italy. Before joining UNIDROIT, she was part of the Italian delegation that negotiated the Cape Town Convention and its Aircraft and Space Protocols.

Olga Volynskaya is Assistant Professor in the Space Research Department at the Lomonosov Moscow State University, Russia, and Academician of the Tsiolkovsky Russian Academy of Cosmonautics.

Lisa Gräfin von der Schulenburg is an attorney at CREYDT.LAW in Hamburg, Germany. She advises on German, European and US export control law and compliance. She has worked with US federal agencies, and her expertise lies in US re-export control, sanctions and embargoes, compliance management, and organisational consulting.

Susan-Gale Wintermuth is Professor in the China-EU Law School, at China University of Political Science and Law, Beijing, China. She is a lecturer at the Stockholm School of Economics Riga, where she instructs on international business law. She also contributes on the same subject to the Executive MBA at the Stockholm School of Economics Riga, Latvia.

Yun Zhao is Henry Cheng Professor in International Law and Head of the Department of Law at the University of Hong Kong.

FOREWORD

In May 2022, I returned from my Cosmic Kiss Mission to the International Space Station ISS.

I spent 175 days on the ISS, a symbol of international cooperation and the peaceful use of space for more than 20 years. It is based on an intergovernmental agreement and we astronauts are members of our respective astronaut corps.

The participating governments had the foresight required to enable this to take place. Nevertheless, the rapid increase in commercialisation of space has not passed unnoticed. My Crew and I launched in November 2021 in the Crew Dragon Endurance, built as part of NASA's Commercial Crew Programme, on a Falcon 9 rocket. More and more experiments on the station are now being serviced by space logistics companies, and the number of commercial experiments is constantly increasing. The European company, Airbus, operates the Bartolomeo platform, which can be used for applications in Earth observation, robotics, materials science, or astrophysics.

From the ISS, we can see not only the Earth, but also the growth of commercial space objects, especially those flying large constellations. It is truly impressive to see the capabilities of the commercial industry and how rapidly it is developing. Soon, individuals will be travelling to space as passengers of space tourism companies. Numerous companies are planning to develop a lunar economy, and some are already looking towards Mars.

This handbook comes at the right time. Further developments in space activities require reliable regulations at both international and national level. While advancing commercial space activities, the safety of space operations and the sustainability of the space environment are essential and must be ensured. We need appropriate rules and standards to make this possible. Nor should we not forget that the family of the United Nations, when developing international space law, designated the exploration and use of space as the province of all humankind. We should – and must – continue to advance this joint exploration and use within a system of peaceful cooperation. International cooperation has enabled us to achieve tremendous goals. Space travel is only one, and there is much more to come.

Dr. Matthias Maurer
Astronaut, European Space Agency ESA

Cologne, Germany
31 October 2022

EDITORS' PREFACE

Lesley Jane Smith, Ingo Baumann, and Susan-Gale Wintermuth

This book was inspired by the remarkable technological and market developments that have taken place in the space sector over the past decade. The work was originally designed to become the second edition of our first volume relating to contracts and procurement in the European space sector, *Contracting for Space – Contract Practice in the European Space Sector*, eds Smith, Baumann, Ashgate (fn: ISBN 978-1-4094-1923-5). We published that volume in 2011, as a reference handbook for practitioners in the European space industry. At the time, the European Union had stepped up its space ambitions with the GNSS programme, Galileo and EGNOS, as well as with GMES, renamed thereafter as Copernicus, its satellite programme on Earth Observation. All this required specific provision for accompanying procurements and contracts, and a new system of governance between the relevant stakeholders. As editors, we invited a team of well-respected practitioners and academic colleagues with whom we mapped out and analysed various legal, contractual, procurement, and regulatory subjects that accompanied these programmes as they were rolled out across the triangle of national space agencies, the European Space Agency (ESA) and the European Union (EU).

The results were presented during a dedicated conference in Bremen, with almost one hundred participants. The first edition sold out much faster than expected. When requests for translations of the work into other languages appeared, we reflected on preparing a second edition. As with all other aspects of life, the project was interrupted, and subsequently delayed through the challenges we all faced in managing daily life throughout the pandemic. Despite initial attempts at earlier publication, collaboration on this volume only took off from the end of 2021.

A challenge in itself, the publishers advised that this new volume, to become one of the Routledge handbooks selected for publication every decade, should provide insight into developments in the commercial space sector from a global, and not a regional European perspective. The increase in commercially driven space activities, even if not a new development, has created new dynamics across all major space faring nations, and beyond. New business models and applications lead to equally new legal and regulatory questions and challenges. This volume does not therefore contain a mere update of our Contracting for Space volume, but offers a new approach, by examining the global "NewSpace" phenomenon.

Coordinating our authors across the globe was another challenge, but their commitment, enthusiasm, and support have been reassuring. With the contributions brought together in this work, we offer our readers a sound and robust foundation about how the space economy and its stakeholders are moving into an exciting new era. The book is prospective in its outlook, even if market and technology evolution is faster than ever. The volume provides a guide to the global space industry for practitioners, in their daily dealings with regulatory, procurement, and contractual matters.

We would like to express our sincere thanks to all our authors, and particularly to our commissioning editor, Siobhan Poole, and her collaborator, Sanjo Joseph of Taylor & Francis. Our greatest thanks are directed in particular to Professor Dr. Bernhard Schmidt-Tedd and Dr. Olga Volynskaya, members of our advisory board, who worked patiently and assiduously to guide and support us. The author and the team also wish to express their appreciation to Marie Lucy Stojak. Further thanks go to Tina Hess for her outstanding assistance, oversight and wisdom in keeping our global author team on track and schedule. A special word of thanks goes to our young space law professionals, Lukas Jung, Klara Maria Toepfer, Katharina Prall, as well as Leonie Enderle for their contributions and their ability to see us through in finalising the volume.

INTRODUCTION

Lesley Jane Smith, Ingo Baumann, and Susan-Gale Wintermuth

Space activities in recent years are generally portrayed in the media with images of exciting commercial advances, featuring a new generation of entrepreneurs that has emerged to join the traditional aerospace and defence industrial community. These entrepreneurs are embracing the development of new markets in space services, and attracting unprecedented interest and volume of private investment. They are also inspiring a generation of young engineers to found their own companies, some of whom are dedicated to contributing to the United Nations Sustainability Goals (UNSG).

As illustrated by SpaceX's *Dragon*, the first reusable private space vehicle designed to bring crew and cargo to the International Space Station (ISS), or with newer lighter, small-scale, and reusable launchers under development, the space market is undergoing a major transition. New business models are being adopted from the digital economy, including all forms of "*service*" provision. Space companies are increasingly relying on the latest information and communications technologies, such as blockchain, or artificial intelligence. Others are making use of bespoke products from other industry sectors (COTS), and producing components with additive manufacturing (3-D Printing). This, alongside miniaturization, enables faster production of satellites, launchers and their components in higher quantities. In satellite communications, high-throughput communications satellites enable broadband services, and new satellite constellations in low earth orbit (LEO) aim at providing global data solutions, including those designed to support Internet of Things (IoT) and Machine-to-Machine (M2M) communications. In Earth observation (EO), cloud computing enables the archiving of and access to massive data sets, and supports online workflows for data search, analytics and value-adding. This goes hand in hand with a change in business model, from bespoke services, to automated online services. Launchers with reusable components are reducing costs and increasing launch rates. At the time of writing, more than one hundred new concepts for launchers are under development, as a result of the predicted demand for small satellite launches. The community is opening to new horizons and visions, from in-space manufacturing, development of a lunar economy to future missions to Mars, and mining planetary space resources.

Commercial space is not new, and commercial industry has built and participated in public space programmes from the outset. The ongoing wave of commercialisation is, however, steering a transition in the traditional relationship between public and private stakeholders. New concepts of public-private partnerships are underway, responding to 'first buyer' and 'anchor customer' approaches. Space agencies are adopting more agile rules of procurement, opening them to participation by small and start-up companies. Founders of new businesses are met with differing forms of support, from business incubators, accelerators, mentor programs, to prize funding and public co-investment.

Society's dependence on space-based services is at an all-high.[1] Positioning, timing and navigation (PNT) are the backbone of global logistics and transport.[2] Communication links provide us with television, internet and new data services for the Internet of Things, autonomous driving or precision farming. Earth Observation systems generate key information on climate change, and support rapid action in the event of natural disasters. Space-based services deliver essential input and back-up to our societies at all levels, public and private.[3]

At the time of writing, society is emerging from a crippling and, initially, underestimated global pandemic, the likes of which were last witnessed at the end of WWI, if at a different level of magnitude.[4] The twenty-first century is witness to other crises relating to climate change, natural disaster, food and energy security, accompanied by human suffering and strife. Responsible ecological behaviour, largely reusability and alternative energy resources, such as solar power, are also considerations for space activities. Not only do we witness the vulnerability of planet earth and mankind; the vulnerability of outer space is seriously endangered through uncontrolled debris and an unprecedented growth of new satellite launches. Increasing efforts are devoted to creating a system of international space traffic management and practices are updated to mitigate space debris. National space legislation is under review, to improve requirements for safe and sustainable space operations.

The editors of this volume have brought together a work, compiled with contributions from outstanding legal and regulatory experts in the global space sector, sharing their wealth of practical experience and knowledge. This volume provides an insight into the new types of business and applications, such as on-orbiting servicing, large constellations, or space resource exploitation, and the legal challenges that accompany them. A significant part is devoted to most recent developments in selected national space legislation, and the increased regulatory efforts towards ensuring a safe and sustainable space environment. The volume concludes with a perspective on human space activities, forty years from now.

Bremen, Cologne, Luneburg 31 October 2022

1 Economist Feb 19, 2022; Organization for Economic Cooperation and Development, OECD G20 Forum, *Space Economy for People and Planet*, Rome, September 2021, available online. The perception that space activities are relatively low is not shared by the general public, who remain unaware of the benefits and activities derived from space activities.

2 These are meanwhile self-understood, as standard attributes of satellite system technology. Aircraft, trains, commercial, including private vehicles, and shipping vessels are equipped with tracking devices serving the interests of owners, insurers and not least, civil aviation authorities, to track and trace their location.

3 Airbus delivered the earth observation satellite PeruSat to Peru on 2016 to support its own geospatial management, see its own website relating to earth observation products and services.

4 The outbreak of Spanish flu crippled various nations over the period 1918–1919, leading to the death of 50 million.

PART I

General framework and boundary conditions

A

Changing institutional roles in space policy

1

TOWARDS A NEW LEGAL ECOSYSTEM FOR THE EXPLOITATION OF SPACE

Philippe Clerc

Introduction

A new space economy has emerged since the beginning of the XXI century. This new space economy is commonly referred to as NewSpace.

This introductory chapter addresses issues that this new situation may raise on the evolution of space law, or more generally the law of all human activities in any place related to space exploration, use, and conquest. The analysis highlights an evolution of the traditional space policy and law towards a new generation of economic law that has taken up the challenge of reconciling the principles of competition and cooperation[1] between public and private interests, taking into account the preserving terrestrial and extra-terrestrial environments in the interest of future generations. It addresses how this new model of economic law emerged, how the great space powers focused once again on space policy, and, following a legal prospective approach, what the future looks like.

It is organised into three major parts: the emergence of new private actors and new intervention patterns for agencies; the return of ambitions of the great space powers; and the advent of new disruptive and shared systems of the future.

This chapter ends with a section entitled "Convergences", which brings the three main topics together with a view to addressing common principles they raise for the development of space law.

1.1 The emergence of new private actors and new intervention patterns for agencies

The new private actors and the new intervention patterns for agencies first appeared at the beginning of the current century. So, first let us review some of the innovations coming from the United States, then proceed to discuss European achievements.

1 The famous concept of "coopetition" by Jean-Jacques Dordain, former Director General of the European Space Agency (2003–2015), in *L'espace un laboratoire de cooperation*, La Tribune, No. 6005, 16 July 2016.

DOI: 10.4324/9781003268475-3

1.1.1 New entrants from the digital economy

This discussion must start with a recognition of the new entrants into the field of space. These new entrants are the face of the NewSpace phenomenon. It is manifested by the rise of new wealthy entrepreneurs who had already proven their worth in the digital economy, culture, or leisure. Among the most iconic are Elon Musk,[2] Greg Wyler,[3] Jeff Bezos,[4] and Richard Branson.[5] They have now entered the markets for launch services for high-speed internet satellite constellations, cargo refueling, transport to the International Space Station (ISS), and space tourism.[6] They are also positioning themselves for future exploration programmes and permanent inhabited bases on the Moon and Mars. These include NASA's Artemis programme, as suppliers but also as partners developing an autonomous capacity that should enable them, in due course, to build and manage their own private and commercial infrastructures. The newcomers positioned themselves from the outset, vis-à-vis space agencies, as the technical and design authority for innovative systems that must be developed in order to satisfy both commercial and public needs, whether civil or military, for space services or their terrestrial applications. They propose substantial reductions in user costs through technical simplifications, production optimisation, system reusability or resilience, and – importantly – they display a greater tolerance for failure in the demonstration phase.

1.1.2 Changes in the way space agencies operate towards the private sector

The technological, industrial, and economic disruption by this wave of visionary entrepreneurs, hardened by market forces, is commonly cited as one of the positive consequences of the 1990s' privatisation movement of the space and intercommunication sectors. Is this disruption simply an effect of the "invisible hand", according to the economic theory of Adam Smith,[7] or the outcome of changes by public agencies to favour new private sector entrants? Former NASA Administrator Jim Bridenstine[8] said that "NewSpace is all about a new way of contracting".[9] To better appreciate this turning point (discussed in more detail *infra.* at 1.3 and 1.4), let us look back at the pre-existing way of operating public-private relations for space activities.

The major Western space agencies[10] appeared in the world from the 1960s onwards, mostly following the same model as NASA, to propose and implement the political ambitions of their countries. They acted as organisations with the mission of specifying the design of space systems to be developed, manufactured, and implemented in response to a space policy decided at the high-

2 He founded Paypal and Tesla, then in 2002, Space Exploration Technologies Corp. (SpaceX).

3 Founder in 2007 of 03b Networks, which he sold to the satellite operator SES in 2016, then founder in 2015 of OneWeb deploying a mega-constellation of broadband internet satellites, being taken over by the operator Eutelsat (September 2022).

4 Founder of Amazon and in the space sector of Blue Origin.

5 Virgin Group is expanding into space under the name Virgin Galactic.

6 Launchers: Falcon 9, Super Heavy, Starship (and Raptor engines) for SpaceX, New Shepard and New Glenn (heavy launcher) for Blue Origin. Constellations, Starlink for SpaceX. Services: Crew Dragon operations for SpaceX.

7 A theory according to which all individual actions of economic actors, guided solely by the personal interest of each one, contribute to the wealth and common good.

8 Jim Bridenstine's term of office was from April 2018 to January 2021.

9 Comments reported by Géraldine Naja in *L'espace est-il à vendre*? Air et Cosmos, No. 2768, 4 February 2022, p. 32, signed by Pierre-François Mouriaux.

10 NASA (1958), CNES (1961), ELDO (launchers, 1962) or ESRO (satellites, 1962) are the precursors in Europe of the European Space Agency (1975). In the USSR, the state body responsible for space activities, *Minobshchemash* (Ministry of General Engineering), was established in 1955, succeeded by Roscosmos.

est level. They acted as a principal when contracting with the private industry. This method applied to all their programmes, whether scientific, civil, commercial, or defence. In this way, the agencies supported the necessary private sector investments in research and technological development from a public budget and managed the associated risks until the prototype was produced and qualified in orbit, which generally followed the inaugural launch. Industry, for its part, benefited from the technologies acquired, which then enabled it to exploit space services and applications.

This division of roles was well understood between government agencies and an emerging space industry, which was, and is, well versed in public procurement and its strategic interests. It has not been fundamentally challenged following the privatisation and globalisation of this industry at the end of the last century.

1.1.3 Development of new systems supported by pre-purchase of services rather than funding of prototypes

In the early 2000s, it became necessary for NASA to encourage the development of new players in order to free itself, for its launch service needs, from the monopoly of the United Launch Alliance (ULA).[11] This joint venture between Boeing and Lockheed Martin, which uses the Delta IV and Delta II heavy and medium launchers and Atlas V, had become the main beneficiary of protectionist legislation, derived from the Buy American Act, which obliges the administration, and in its turn NASA, to buy exclusively from national launch operators. However, prices had become unreasonable for the public budget.[12]

It is in this context that NASA, in the early 2000s, initiated new intervention schemes favouring the private sector. The most characteristic of these are the Commercial Orbital Transportations Services (COTS), with their Commercial Resupply Services (CRS 1 and 2) contracts for the resupply of cargo to the ISS, and the Commercial Crew Program (CRP) for crew transport. The advantage of such contracts is that they allow the public authorities to specify their needs and the criteria for selecting manufacturers and their projects in terms of results, performance, or innovation, without prejudging the technical means of achieving them. The objective is also to limit to the strictest possible extent the norms, specifications, standards, and processes for verifying and reviewing the technical progress of the space agency. These new contracts involve the advance purchase by the public authorities, several years in advance, of services at a fixed or determinable price, which will be provided using space vehicles to be developed under the legal responsibility and at the risk of the industrialist.

Contractually (and fiscally), the agency ultimately receives a *service* and not, as before, the delivery or sale of a *good*.[13] As a side benefit, NASA can make its own facilities, launch bases, test facilities, and the technical expertise of its employees available to the private sector for a small fee under the Space Act Agreements (SAAs).[14]

11 A joint venture between Boeing and Lockheed Martin formed in 2004.

12 Among these rules derived from the Buy American Act for space are: the US Space Transportation Policy of 6 January 2005, section V; the National Space Policy of 19 September 1996, Inter-sector Guidelines – Space Transportation, §2.a iii and §2.b; the National Space Transportation Policy of 5 August 1994, section IV, §1, and finally the Commercial Space Act of 28 October 1998, title II, section 201, §a.

13 It should also be noted that the difference in legal qualification between goods and services is not neutral, because it can impact the accounting and tax treatment of the operation.

14 The relevant guide can be found on the open NASA website: *Space Agreement Guide – NASA Advisor Implementation – Instruction NAII 1050 -1-C last update 11/08/2014.*

The NewSpace proponents seem to have achieved their initial objectives, and the balance sheet remains a win-win for both the public and private sectors. As an example, NASA has been able to regain, thanks to SpaceX's low-cost Falcon 9 launcher and its operational reuse capacity, a leading position in the commercial launch market, which it had abandoned at the end of the 1980s to the benefit of the European operator Arianespace and the Ariane system. NASA was also able to resume resupplying the ISS with the same launcher and the Dragon capsule,[15] thus ending its dependence on its geopolitical rival Russia, which uses Soyuz launchers and capsules for this purpose, two symbols of the great space epics of the former Union of Soviet Socialist Republics.

By the same token, the private proponents of NewSpace have built their economic development model around these public-private partnership (PPP) offers, and more particularly Elon Musk's SpaceX company is currently its main beneficiary. Thanks to the tens of billions of US dollars in the pre-financing acquired through the COTS and CRP programmes, SpaceX has been able to amortise the research and development costs of its entire range of vehicles and to release funds that can be used for its own exploration projects. The main loser might appear to be the traditional space industry as a result of this US industrial policy adjustment driven by a longer-term objective of preserving competition and multiple sources of supply internally. The success of SpaceX has seemed to turn the tide in favour of the private sector.[16]

1.1.4 The contribution of Europeans to NewSpace

Europe, for its part, in its various components,[17] has also turned to such schemes, and has often even anticipated them.

1.1.4.1 The first privatisations carried out by space agencies in Europe

Europe, well before the United States, began privatising and marketing launch services by creating the limited company Arianespace in 1980 after the first successful qualification launch of the Ariane launcher. This privatisation was supported by a *sui generis* trans-European legal framework established by the states participating in the European Space Agency (ESA) programme.[18] Arianespace quickly became the leader in the commercial launch market until around 2010, when it was dethroned by SpaceX.

15 This is evidenced by Crew-2's service to the ISS, launched on 23 April 2021 from the Kennedy Space Center (Cape Canaveral) in Florida, with French ESA astronaut Thomas Pesquet on board.

16 There has nonetheless been some resistance from Congress, as illustrated in the Artemis-1 lunar exploration programme, wherein the development and construction of the future American heavy-lift launcher SLS, the most powerful launcher ever built, was entrusted in 2010 to a consortium made up of Boeing, United Launch Alliance (ULA), Northrop Grumman, and Aerojet Rocketdyne. Despite delays, cost overruns, an alternative bid from SpaceX, and strong criticism in Congress in 2018, the programme was upheld by the Senate for industrial policy reasons and to maintain jobs in the southern United States.

17 Namely, ESA, the European Union, and their respective Member States.

18 In the framework of a concession-type scheme granted by the participating states of ESA according to a treaty known as the "Declaration of certain States participating in the Ariane production phase", a declaration that has been renewed in its structure to the present day. ESA was designated as the trustee in this treaty and is responsible for ensuring its proper implementation.

Following this example, CNES, thanks to its EPIC[19] status, has embarked on a policy of spinning off commercial companies dedicated to the exploitation of its operational projects, not to generate dividends, but to stimulate the start-up of the corresponding markets. The aim is to accelerate production and promote the recurrent exploitation of its systems by accompanying the incubation period and preparing the privatisation of these companies in an orderly fashion. This has led to the creation of Intespace (test facilities), Spot Image (Earth observation), Scot Conseil (Earth observation applications consultancy), CLS (location, messaging, downstream services), etc. Nowadays, all these companies have been successfully privatised. There were, of course, some failures at the start, but they also served as a learning experience.[20]

Today, the development programme for the next Ariane 6 launch system also marks a break with previous versions.[21] The launcher contract is awarded directly by ESA to a single European prime contractor, Arianegroup.[22] The agency no longer imposes its technical or management specifications on the company, but rather "High-Level Requirements" relating to the expected performance of a generic launch system concept. Public funding is granted in return for an expected preferential price for future European institutional launches to be procured by ESA, the European Union, and their Member States, subject to purchase volume. Space agency experts can be seconded (embedded) to the industry to provide technical assistance.

1.1.4.2 Europe – a forerunner of PPPs for satellites and multi-purpose applications

It was also in Europe that a voluntary policy of PPP emerged at the end of the 1990s to support the development and operation of public, civil, defensive, and commercial multi-user space assets. These include, at France's initiative:[23] the Proteus multi-mission platform, the Skybridge internet constellation, the Argos alert locator system from CLS, the Pleiade multi-user observation system, Athena-Fidus in defence telecommunications, and the Vegetation instrument on board Spot 4. The Vegetation project,[24] designed to monitor agriculture, involving France, Belgium, Italy, Sweden, and the European Commission, was to become the precursor of the European Union's intervention in the space sector, on the legal basis of its research framework programme.[25] The Paradigm project, in the United Kingdom, also paved the way for PPPs for government and defence uses of telecom satellites designed, built, and owned exclusively by the private sector.

19 Acronym for "*établissement public industriel et commercial*" (French) – public institution of an industrial and commercial nature.

20 In particular, Locstar (developing an eponymous geostationary satellite navigation and messaging project for transport) was liquidated in the mid-1990s, and Skybridge LP (a low-Earth orbit internet constellation), in partnership with European and American industries, was liquidated in the early 2000s.

21 Where the responsibilities of project owner or contracting authority were assumed by ESA, and those of design authority and prime contractor delegated to CNES, the French space agency.

22 Originally, the joint venture Airbus Safran Launcher, resulting from the merger of the launchers and missiles branches of the two groups, then renamed as Arianegroup after absorbing the launch operator Arianespace, following the purchase of the blocking minority and the Ariane brand from CNES, which had been a shareholder since its creation in 1980. CNES remains the prime contractor for the ground segment in French Guiana.

23 This new partnership policy was set out in a "guide" finalised in 1988 in consultation with the various partners of CNES, and in particular those of the *Groupement des industries françaises aéronautiques et spatiales* (GIFAS). Cf. Clerc P. *Partnership between CNES and Industry: a New Market Oriented Approach*, in New Space Market, edited by G. Haskell and M. Rycroft, International Space University. Edition Kluwer Academic Publishers, The Netherlands, 1997, pp. 13–22.

24 The project started in the early 1990s, and the satellite was launched in 1998.

25 Treaty on the Functioning of the European Union (TFEU), Art. 179 *et seq*.

In this context, ESA and the national agencies in Europe have reviewed their legal and contractual methods of intervention by proposing simplified and faster selection processes upstream, using competitive dialogue formulas and pre-purchases. They are also resorting to subsidies, in a break with their culture of "giving orders", and are proposing incubation solutions, the provision of test facilities, laboratories, or public expertise, support for the creation of seed funds or dedicated venture capital, or even a return to targeted equity investments. Finally, they are lightening their standards and technical progress reviews to adapt them to the specificities of the new systems and to the risk taken by the NewSpace players.

1.2 The return of the ambitions of the great space powers

The NewSpace is also the return of state interventionism, intergovernmental cooperation, and rivalry in the conquest of space. Over the past three decades, China, India, and Japan have become space powers alongside the United States, Russia, and Europe. Thus, strategic and dominance issues emerged in the 1990s, firstly in relation to the use of space-based data (see *infra.* 1.2.1). Then, at the beginning of our millennium, a new race has begun among states to explore and exploit space orbits and celestial bodies, bringing about a new generation of international agreements (see *infra.* 1.2.2).

In this context, it should be pointed out that European governments have shown a capacity to coordinate their space policies and programmes (see *infra.* 1.2.3). We discuss below the emergence of this return to space by the great space powers.

1.2.1 Sovereign needs related to global information literacy

The success of the first satellite applications quickly demonstrated capacity in real time, and on a global scale, to exchange, broadcast, capture, listen, locate, observe, and process any kind of information or phenomenon observable on Earth. As a result, at the end of the last century, a preoccupation with informational sovereignty led to a strong return of states to space policy. Various doctrines were then theorised, for example, in the United States under the names of "Space Control" or "Space Power",[26] which argued for the state to retain control over such sources and means of global information exchange, despite a contemporary context of global privatisation of the telecommunications, industry, and space operations sectors.

These theories point in particular to the historical parallel of the mastery of the seas in the XIX century by the United Kingdom. This control ensured its supremacy over the entire world economy during that period. The argument follows that the XXI century will be the century of economic domination through global information literacy. This prediction seems to have been confirmed at the dawn of our millennium following the rise of the internet and then of the digital services industry by the tech giants. We can thus subsume, under the name of "spatial info-dominance", a synthesis of the two concepts of space power and info-dominance.[27]

26 The doctrine of space control, which is at the origin of the space power and space dominance doctrines, appeared for the first time in 1988, theorised by the US Air Force Lieutenant Colonel D. E. Lupton, see *A Space Warfare: On Space Power Doctrine*, Maxwell Air Force Base, Air University Press, June 1988, p. 99. For an analysis of this policy, see E. C. Dolmann, *Astropolitik, classical Geopolitics in the Space Age*, London, Frank Cass, 2002, p. 222.

27 For an updated European vision, see X. Pasco, *Towards a 'territorial' policy of space? Le renouveau américain*, Géopolitique, No. 98, April 2007 ; P. Gros and N. Vilboux, *Les forces spatiales américaines – modernisation et*

It is in this context that new forms of warfare are emerging.[28] They combine disparate means and actions, military or otherwise, with conventional and irregular forces (pirates or privateers). They are fed by the capacities of different land, air, and naval weapons, capacities increased by the relay of terrestrial internet or satellite networks, be they military, civil, governmental, or commercial. We now speak of "cyber space and information warfare", or more simply of "hybrid warfare".

These prospects are reshuffling the deck in terms of the legislative environment, programmes, and defence doctrines of states *vis-à-vis* space activities. They give rise to a worldwide increase in the adoption of national legislation to authorise and control the conduct of space operations at all levels, firstly in application of international space law for launch operations, control of vehicles in orbit, and their possible return to Earth, but also for access to frequencies, and downstream for the deployment of telecommunications and satellite broadcasting services – all in compliance with the rules applying to the services concerned and with ordinary competition and public aid law.[29]

On the programmatic level, states maintain their interventionism in new forms, but at the same level of support for research and industrial development, or even in the interest of economic equilibrium,[30] of competitive or pre-competitive space sectors deemed to be of strategic importance.

At the strategic level, a taboo has been lifted, that of preserving space from all forms of military activity. Many states are developing, or even proclaiming, space defence doctrines that aim to integrate at the highest level public and private space capabilities under national jurisdiction. In this sense, France is one of the first nations to have officially announced its intention to adopt a "space strategy for active defence".[31] This strategy was disclosed in more detail by the Minister of the Armed Forces, Florence Parly.[32] While taking care not to engage in an arms race or the deployment of weapons of mass destruction,[33] this so-called "active" defence, considering the risks of a creeping weaponisation of space,[34] must enable the country to face, in a proportionate manner, any threat to space vehicles, under national control or in European or international cooperation.

1.2.2 The new superpower race to the Moon and Mars

Another competition is underway between the major powers for the conquest of the Moon, then Mars, with a view to setting up permanent human bases and conducting scientific and industrial

restructuration, Observatoire de la politique de défense américaine, Fondation de la recherche stratégique, Report No. 3, September 2019.

28 As a first manifestation of such "hybrid war", a round table of experts (Colonel Thierry Bauer, head of the COMCYBER operations division, Colonel Guillaume Bourdeloux, commander of space operations for the French Air Force, and General Pascal Ianni, communications advisor and spokesman for the Chief of Staff of the French Armed Forces) mentions in June 2022 that of the Crimea in 2014 (not to be confused with the more conventional one in Ukraine following the invasion of Russia on 24 February 2022). See C. Helen Chachaty, *Guerre cyber, spatiale, informationnelle: la France est-elle prête à faire face à une guerre hybride?* La Tribune, 16 June 2022.

29 For example, a €60-million state guarantee for private operators in the event of damage to third parties, as was enshrined in French law in 2008, was previously notified to the European Commission for validation, see *C (2007) 5093 final – Brussels, 23.X.2007 – State aid N 208/2007 – France State guarantee for damage caused to third parties in the context of space operations*.

30 Like ESA's EGAS (European Guaranteed Access to Space) programme in 2004.

31 Public announcement on 13 July 2019.

32 Speech by Florence Parly, *The new defence space strategy*, on 25 July 2019 at the Lyon Mont-Verdun air base.

33 Such measures would be incompatible with Article IV of the Outer Space Treaty.

34 Satellites can be designed or equipped to spy on, jam, dazzle, hinder, disable, or destroy strategic space capabilities, whether military, civilian, or commercial.

activities there. This race is organised around two blocks: the first led by the United States, via bilateral agreements for its Artemis lunar programme, the other by a Sino-Russian alliance for its International Lunar Research Station (ILRS) programme.

1.2.2.1 The Artemis Accords supported by bilateral agreements with the United States

The Artemis Accords provide for bilateral governmental agreements, or Artemis agreements, with the US government. These Artemis agreements address high-level issues raised by the 1967 Outer Space Treaty with respect to planetary environment and the delicate issue of resource extraction and appropriation. This step should be seen in the tense context of the failure of the 1979 Moon Agreement.[35] The method proposed by the United States is to negotiate such agreements with each of its future partners on a case-by-case basis, and based on a model project.[36] The implementation of these agreements towards national industries for the development, manufacturing, and operation of spacecraft and other space assets is to be assigned under NASA coordination to the contracting authority of each participating agency. Generally speaking, it is a major challenge for the negotiation of contracts and the evolution of the associated legal framework. It will indeed be necessary to deal with the diversity of procedures for competition and negotiation of public contracts, concessions, PPPs, or space legislation in force in each country, either towards the existing players or new entrants. It should also be noted that this new integrated space, services, and digital industry, which competes aggressively on the international scene, is fully subject to the rules of competition and control of public aid, in other words to the regular public economic law.

1.2.2.2 The Sino-Russian International Lunar Research Station (ILRS) project

For their part, China and Russia signed a memorandum of understanding on 9 March 2021 via their space agencies, CNSA and Roscosmos, for the creation of an International Lunar Research Station, inviting any interested country to join the project.[37] The construction here is based on a bilateral agreement between two major space powers, delegated to agency level, in the more flexible form of a best-efforts memorandum. The two partners propose to open their cooperation to other participants in a multilateral framework to be defined.

1.2.2.3 Europe and the exploration of the Moon and Mars

Europe, for its part, has never had its own manned exploration programme, either towards the Moon or orbital stations, at intergovernmental level or at the level of one of its states. Its approach

35 The failure of the Moon Agreement results firstly from the lack of its ratification among the major space powers (especially USA, USSR/Russia, China), this deficiency impairing its enforceability as international treaty; secondly as to the content of such agreement (especially under its article 11), from uncertainties on the terms and conditions of setting up the competent international body, and the legal criteria to be used by the latter, in order to authorise future mining and appropriation of resources from the Moon or other extra-terrestrial soils.

36 A first group of seven countries signed these agreements on 13 October 2020, on the occasion of the International Astronautical Congress (IAC). They were the United Arab Emirates, Australia, Japan, Canada, Italy, Luxembourg, and the United Kingdom.

37 They formulated a joint declaration in this sense on 23 May 2021 in Nanjing, in front of several foreign diplomatic representations on the eve of the 2021 edition of the China Space Day Conference. According to Roscosmos, the *draft* declaration on ILRS was finalised only at the end of September 2021.

is to come together in a structured framework in order to have a significant impact on achieving the most ambitious, universal, and collegiate cooperation possible.

Before the current ISS, Europe initially joined, via ESA, the very Western project of the Freedom station, supported by US President Ronald Reagan; then, in the midst of the Cold War, cooperated with the Soviet Union. After the collapse of this union following the fall of the Berlin Wall, Europe accompanied the American policy of opening the ISS to the Russian Federation within the multilateral framework of the intergovernmental agreement (IGA) signed in 1998. For the purists, it will be remembered that from that time onwards the multilateral framework was reduced to the level of general principles. The operational implementation of the ISS project and its industrial realisation are under the overall supervision of NASA, which enters into bilateral agreements with each participating space agency, including ESA on behalf of all participating European states.[38]

Europe's position has become more delicate in the face of the two rival initiatives and taking into account other disturbances such as the withdrawal of the United Kingdom from the EU (which however remains a member of ESA), and above all the war between Russia and Ukraine, and the tensions with China over Taiwan.

There is no more equivocation today, after the beginning of the war in Ukraine. The majority of European states, bilaterally or within ESA, or the EU, have signed or expressed their intention to sign the Artemis Accords, in line with their historical Western alliances (NATO in particular). The approach of the European stakeholders is however to obtain tangible counterparts, guarantees, or assurances from the US Government, obviously in terms of industrial and scientific return, but also regarding the respect of the non-appropriation of land and planetary protection principles of the Outer Space Treaty. It also aims at the commitments of the United States in other international agreements on related topics in the service of the Earth and humanity, as for example its adhesion to the Space Climate Observatory (SCO)[39] in the wake of the Paris Agreement on climate change of 2015.[40] On the other hand, the cooperation with Russia was stopped instantly in Europe, a phenomenon that had never been observed at the height of the Cold War, even with France which had always maintained a scientific and commercial space cooperation since 1966.[41]

38 For a contradictory study on the appropriateness of creating an intergovernmental structure for such projects, see Clerc P. *Imaginer une organisation multilatérale de l'espace extra-atmosphérique*, colloquium of the Société française pour le droit international, Faculté de droit de Toulouse, 6–7 May 2021, Editions Pedone, Paris, 2021, pp. 221–248.

39 Regarding the SCO, just after the signature by France of the Artemis Accords at the French Embassy in Washington on 7 June 2022, Richard Spinrad, Under-Secretary of Commerce for Oceans and Atmosphere and Administrator of the US National Oceanic and Atmospheric Administration (NOAA), signed the SCO Charter. The SCO is an initiative of the One Planet Summit under the leadership of CNES to combine satellite and *in situ* data with scientific research to model and track climate change and its impacts at global-to-local scales. It is also working to establish indicators and decision-support tools in a coordinated and cross-disciplinary fashion, including with social and economic sciences, to enhance the global community's collective ability to mitigate the impacts of climate change. One Planet Summit is an international meeting on climate change that was held on 12 December 2017 in Paris organised by France, the United Nations, and the World Bank, bringing together nearly 4,000 participants including about 50 heads of state and government.

40 COP21 (Paris Climate Change Conference) resulted in an agreement signed on 12 December 2015 committing 195 states and the European Union to reduce their greenhouse gas emissions. The Paris Agreement is an instrument for implementing the United Nations Framework Convention on Climate Change.

41 France indeed, for its part, occupies a singular position historically. While it has always favoured close and ambitious cooperation with the United States since the creation of CNES (cf. cooperation agreement signed on 21 March 1961 with NASA), it has also developed long-term cooperation with Russia since 1966, following the Brezhnev–De Gaulle meeting of 1966 (signature of the agreement of 30 June 1966 on cooperation in the exploration and use of

Since then, more than 30 launches have taken place despite the crisis in Georgia and the first crisis with Ukraine over the Crimea. However, this cooperation in French Guiana was frozen with the Russian invasion of Ukraine in February 2022.

1.2.3 The inspiring model of European governance

1.2.3.1 The rise of the European Union

In contrast to the apparent competition between the two superpower blocks, Europe has been able to enter into a collaborative effort. In addition to, or as an extension of, the action of its Member States and ESA, the European effort today benefits fully from the reinforcement of the policies and programmes of the European Union, which has had explicit space competence since December 2007, following the enactment of the Lisbon Treaty.[42]

This competence is exercised upstream in the conduct of research and technological development projects relating to space systems, and downstream for data programmes of general European interest with an operational vocation[43] or recurring[44] such as Galileo (the equivalent and complement to the American GPS), Copernicus (civil Earth observation), or for space surveillance, space traffic management, and space situational awareness for collision prevention.[45] The EU is also preparing, at the instigation of the European Commissioner for the Internal Market, Thierry Breton, to launch a constellation for secure connectivity, now named IRIS2 (Infrastructure for Resilience, Interconnectivity and Security by Satellite) to maintain its sovereignty and autonomy.[46] For the purpose of implementing its programmes, the European Union set up its own agency – the European Union Space Programme Agency (EUSPA) – in May 2021.[47]

space for peaceful purposes). This agreement was renewed and opened to economic issues by the agreement of 26 November 1996. This cooperation took concrete form with the flight of the first French astronaut, Jean-Loup Chrétien, on board the Soviet Salyut-7 station in July 1982, in the midst of the Cold War following the USSR's invasion of Afghanistan in December 1979. It took a long-term operational and commercial turn in 1996 with the creation of Starsem, a Russian-European subsidiary registered in France, to market Soyuz launcher services from Baikonur (Kazakhstan), and then the setting up of this launch range system at Kourou, in French Guiana following an intergovernmental agreement of 7 November 2003. This project was Europeanised by agreement signed on 19 January 2005 with the ESA relating to the Soyuz launch complex at the Guiana Space Center.

42 Competence enshrined in the TFEU: its Art. 189 defines the contours of this spatial competence, and Art. 4.3 specifies the specific regime of shared competence that applies to it *vis-à-vis* the Member States.

43 And more particularly programmes serving its sectoral competences such as agriculture, fisheries, economic, social, and territorial cohesion (spatial planning and structural funds), essential infrastructure, trans-European networks, transport, environment, telecommunications, the necessary extensions of its framework programme for research and technological development (Art. 179 et seq. of the TFEU), or its common foreign and security policy (Art. 23 *et seq.* of the Treaty on European Union (TEU)).

44 This is in contrast to projects conducted upstream, under the responsibility of the space agencies, which are generally referred to as the probationary, prototype, demonstration, pre-competitive development, or promotion phases.

45 Concepts referred to as space surveillance and tracking (SST), space traffic management (STM), and space situational awareness (SSA).

46 The Commission published on 15 February 2022, on the eve of the informal meeting of European space ministers in Toulouse under the French Presidency, a draft Regulation for a secure connectivity constellation. The ministers all supported this initiative. In addition, the Commission and the European External Action Service (EEAS) published a Communication on Space Traffic Management on the same date.

47 Regulation (EU) 2021/696 of the European Parliament and of the Council of 28 April 2021 establishing the European Space Programme and the European Space Programme Agency and recalling Regulations (EU) No 912/2010, (EU) No 1285/2013 and (EU) No 377/2014 and Decision No 541/2014/EU (OJ L 170, 12.5.2021, p. 69).

The EU also has a transverse legislative competence which, although it does not apply directly to space operations and objects that fall under the jurisdiction and the international liability of the Member States concerned,[48] covers everything that affects their services and derived uses on Earth, in other words, everything that affects a satellite's payload.[49]

1.2.3.2 Enhanced European convergence

Competences among states, ESA, and the EU are therefore cooperative and complementary, rather than competitive. This also stimulates exchanges, innovation, and excellence. It is acknowledged that many observers have questioned this pointing to the "handicap" of scattered or duplicated resources among the various government agencies, existing or emerging companies, ESA, and the European Union. However much truth there may be to this observation, this risk seems to be contained, at least on paper, because of the fairly clear division in their respective founding treaties. Space and research are listed as a "shared competence", not to say "complementary or parallel", in that it is specified that the exercise of this competence by the Union "may not have the effect of preventing Member States from exercising theirs" and vice versa.[50]

States thus retain all their prerogatives within their national framework, in international cooperation, or via the intergovernmental extension of ESA,[51] to conduct their own civil or defence space policy. They also retain exclusive competence for the development of space law, both nationally and internationally, as a law targeted at operations on space vehicles or infrastructure. This exclusive competence derives from the Outer Space Treaty.[52] It is also justified by the fact that it is the same states, and only them, that bear international liability for damage caused by objects under their jurisdiction, registration, or control. There is parallel with the Law of the Sea, which remains a competence of the states (via the jurisdiction of the flag) even if the EU can regulate the services under its competences such as transport, fishing, trade, etc.

Last but not least, the coordination and complementarity of the various European public intervention levers is based on dialogue and concerted action at the level of the national agencies whose mission[53] is to represent[54] or assist their government in the various European bodies concerned.

48 Article 189.2 of the TFEU expressly prohibits it: "[…] in order to contribute to the achievement of the objectives […], the European Parliament and the Council, acting in accordance with the ordinary legislative procedure, shall adopt the necessary measures […] excluding any harmonisation of the laws and regulations of the Member States".

49 The payload of a satellite is the on-board instrument, sensor, transmitter, receiver, or transponder that determines its mission, its usefulness in terms of services, and therefore its economic interest. It differs from the bus, which contains all the elements or services necessary for the operation of the vehicle (and its payload) in orbit or for its passivation at the end of its life (telemetry, attitude and trajectory control, propellants, solar panels, batteries, antennas, energy and thermal propulsion, etc.).

50 To this extent, for "shared competence", Art. 4.3 of the TFEU (for Research and Space) does not have the same meaning as in Art. 4.3 for other EU competences (listed in (a) to (k)) where use by the Union gives it precedence over that of the states and ultimately contributes to eroding their national legislative competence in this area.

51 In this respect, Art. 189(3) of the TFEU explicitly states that the Union shall establish any useful link with ESA.

52 This situation results from the Outer Space Treaty, which in its Art. VI (and XIII for international intergovernmental organisations) places the responsibility for authorisation and control of space activities under their jurisdiction solely on the signatory states. It is also the launching states that are financially liable for damage caused to third parties by space objects for which they are responsible, and in particular those of their private sector. Article 189.2 of the TFEU prohibits the EU from legislating or coordinating the legislation of Member States in this area.

53 For CNES, this competence is enshrined in its founding law of 19 December 1961, now codified in Art. L331-2 of the Research Code.

54 Within the Council and the Programme Boards of ESA.

It should also be noted that despite the difficulties linked to its ongoing construction and its own divergences, Europe in space knows how to equip itself with the financial, institutional, technological, and industrial means to meet the challenges of the new global situation. Its remobilisation seems to be well underway today.[55]

1.3 The advent of new, disruptive, and shared systems of the future

This new approach to space, both on private and government levels, is inseparable from the emergence of innovative vehicles and systems. These systems, which are technologically disruptive and offer new services, are shaking up the established order in this sector.

The focus here is on three major developments in recent years, and the issues they raise: high-speed mega-constellations of satellites in low-Earth orbit; future reusable systems and in-orbit services; and, finally, the establishment of human bases on extra-terrestrial soil.

1.3.1 Mega-constellations of satellites in low-Earth orbit

Constellations of mini-satellites for telecommunications in orbit are not NewSpace innovations. The current[56] constellations designed to provide high-speed internet access in all parts of the world are on a different scale than those early ones. They consist of several hundred, or even tens of thousands, of smaller, less expensive satellites, but less safe and less manoeuvrable, and therefore more damaging to the space environment, both in terms of debris generation and collision risks, and in terms of light pollution. They call for a harmonised adaptation of national technical regulations to authorise and control such systems.

Furthermore, on Earth, the fact that these extra-terrestrial infrastructures are produced, owned, operated, and controlled by private giants of the digital economy, fuels the risk of global informational dominance driven from the Silicon Valley ecosystem. Another pitfall is that this multiplication of constellations affects the availability of frequencies in these orbits for the latest entrants,[57] and in particular for European government and commercial needs.

Faced with this sovereignty issue, the EU has initiated the IRIS2 programme for secure satellite connectivity. One third of the investment would be covered by the Commission, another third by the Member States, and the final third by the private sector. The system would be operated under a public-private concession scheme.[58] This project, if it comes to fruition, raises interesting questions for lawyers in terms of its novel governance framework, traditional European Union com-

55 See footnote 47.

56 These include Elon Musk's SpaceX's Starlink (42,000 satellites planned), in non-exclusive partnership with Microsoft (and its Azur Space project, which is the marriage of cloud and space data), Jeff Bezos's Kuiper (3,200 satellites), Guo Wang for China (13,000 satellites) or OneWeb (650 satellites). The OneWeb company initiated by Greg Wyler was taken over after its bankruptcy in October 2021 by a consortium composed of the Indian group Bharti Enterprises (CEO Sunil Mittal), the French operator Eutelsat, and the British Government.

57 According to the rules of the International Telecommunication Union, access to international radio spectrum capacity is based on the "first come, first served" principle. Subsequent operators must "coordinate" with the first to avoid interfering with their transmissions and receptions, which is not always technically possible or economically acceptable.

58 See footnote 47.

petition law and public aid to the space sector,[59] in the sublimated context of a digital economy, liberalised on a global scale and highly judicialised between its competitors.

1.3.2 Future reusable systems and in-orbit services

1.3.2.1 Technical and economic credibility of "R systems"[60]

There are unavoidable rules in physics and space, then as now. An object must reach a speed of eight kilometres per second[61] to achieve the balance of forces that frees it from the Earth's attraction, its own gravity, and which keeps it on a stable trajectory in orbit around the Earth. It then becomes a space object in the physical and legal sense.[62]

To meet this challenge, it is necessary to lighten the structures as much as possible. This weight reduction leads the launcher to eject its useless engine and fairing components. In order not to weigh down the launcher, a satellite carries just the right amount of consumables on. After having exhausted its resources, the vehicle becomes non-functional, i.e. debris – an economic non-value, but also a risk of inconvenience, collision, or pollution for others on its orbital trajectory.

The possibility of reusing spacecraft, resupplying and repairing systems in orbit[63] was opened up by the US Shuttle programme in 1981 but, in the 30 years of its operation, it has failed to demonstrate its economic viability. Experience has shown that the cost of deploying and restoring the elements concerned has remained higher than the gains made by the operation while maintaining the same safety objectives for goods and people.

One of the indisputable contributions of NewSpace is to have been able to demonstrate the technical and then economic feasibility of recovering launch vehicle stages, and more particularly on Space X's Falcon 9 launcher.

In addition, operational and commercial projects are emerging for "space tugs"[64] designed to re-orbit, resupply, or repair satellites or to place them in graveyard orbits at the end of their mission, or even to rehabilitate them into operational vehicles. This is the challenge of "R systems". A first mission was successfully flown in October 2020 by Northrop Grumman's MEV-1 space tanker to extend the life of an Intelsat 901 commercial satellite by several years. ESA has launched an Active Debris Removal In-Orbit Servicing (ADRIOS) programme, which includes an orbit-cleaning mission[65] ClearSpace-1, to be operated in 2025. Elon Musk also

59 On the issue of the legality of public support to the aerospace sector, see O. Blin, *Le financement du secteur aérospatial à l'épreuve du droit: la position de l'Union européenne*, Colloque de la Société française pour le droit international, Faculté de droit de Toulouse, 6–7 May 2021, Editions Pedone, Paris 2021, pp. 425–438.

60 Reuse, Repair, Resupply, Recycle, Re-orbit; Rehabilitation, Restoration, Refurbishment, Removal, etc.

61 By comparison, the speed of a rifle bullet varies from 600 to 1,300 m/s, i.e. 13 to six times slower than a satellite. This is how the bullet always ends up falling back to the ground, succumbing to the deceleration linked to the Earth's attraction (gravity) and to the friction of the atmosphere, if it has not already encountered an obstacle.

62 In the legal sense, based on the physical parameters of registration provided for in Article IV of the 1975 Convention on Registration of Objects Launched into Outer Space (Registration Convention).

63 The Hubble Telescope launched in 1990 was designed to be repaired in orbit by the Shuttle. This possibility was used in 1993 to correct the anomaly in its optical part. Four other missions, in 1997, 1999, 2002, and 2009, were used to modernise its scientific instruments, replace its faulty or obsolete equipment, and refuel it.

64 And since they have already been launched, they are already available at a lower cost in space. These tugs can rely on their on-board or in-orbit energy (solar energy, or even propellants from other in-orbit refueling) to fulfil their mission.

65 The terms "orbit restoration", "debris destruction", or "active debris removal" are also used to define such activities.

plans to use these stage recovery and on-orbit propellant supply technologies for his Starship Mars coloniser.

All these new systems call for a substantial evolution of the technical regulations which have so far been designed exclusively on a national basis and for single-use systems.

1.3.2.2 An upheaval in the authorisation and control regimes and in the responsibilities towards third parties

The licences that states currently issue under the Outer Space Treaty (Article VI) all relate to predictable and standardised operations around a single space object or their series (constellations). They are applied in a linear and sequenced manner, following predefined phases of responsibility between the launch, placement, and maintenance in orbit (control) of the space object (or satellite), and then its end-of-life with its movement into an assigned orbit or Earth re-entry. All operations on this object are "remotely controlled" from the ground by radio means in connection with the only functions available on board the object.

The new in-orbit services propose to involve a third-party vehicle, physically intervening in orbit by docking or in a close field of vision or communication. This intervener has its own authorisation, control, radio frequency, and liability regimes. It may also be of another nationality.

It will therefore first be necessary for each licence in force on a vehicle applying for assistance to be amended to authorise such risky and unanticipated operations. These licences will also have to be reconciled with those of the assistance vehicle, whether it is national or foreign. Each licence should also prescribe in a coherent and predictable way, between the parties and with regard to third parties, at each moment and during each manoeuvre,[66] who is the operator contractually responsible or potentially "at fault" with regard to these third parties.

There is therefore a challenge at national and international levels to develop a consensual licensing standard that allows the development of these critical systems and services. More specifically, it will be a question of technically promoting the interconnection of systems and vehicles and clarifying the concept of liability for fault in space arising from the 1972 Convention on International Liability for Damage Caused by Space Objects (Liability Convention). Obviously, these reflections will have to be conducted in coherence with the work in progress, at the technical, legal, and institutional levels, for the development of universal STM and SSA systems.

Finally, it should be noted that these new services, in addition to the industrial and commercial development stakes they represent, contribute to a genuine public interest mission of rescue and preservation of the space environment. This public utility could also justify the setting up of a specific regime of reduced or detailed fault or the taking of a specific guarantee by the state,[67] following the example of what already applies for the benefit of firemen, forces of law and order, or environmental protection.

1.3.2.3 New contractual standards for a "Space to Space" economy

In order to secure commercial transactions, new contractual standards should be devised for these services between and among different space vehicles already installed. This activity is part of a

66 Approach, docking, filling, repair, re-orbiting, undocking, etc.

67 Namely, in France, an extension of the state guarantee for damage to third parties exceeding €60M, under the law of 3 June 2008, which currently only applies to damage caused during the launch phase on the ground or in the air.

new economic order, that of "Space to Space", the current one being either "Earth to Space"[68] or "Space to Earth".[69]

Standard clauses should be considered to deal with the transfer of risk, and possible limitations of contractual liability, warranty of latent defects, and their effects on insurance contracts. In fact, it would be a matter of creating, as it were, a "special contract" regime for these services within the meaning of the domestic civil codes and relaying it on an international scale by means of a system comparable to that of the INCOTERMS used for cross-border sales.

1.3.2.4 The programmed end of the absolutism of limitation of liability or waivers clauses in the space industry

Such an exercise of harmonisation by means of "special contracts" will necessarily lead to a reconsideration of the systematic application of the clauses currently in force concerning waivers, exemption from liability, or limitation of guarantee for hidden defects, and consequently the non-subrogation of insurers. Such clauses have been established in practice, for the benefit of the supplier or service provider, among industrialists, operators,[70] and their public or private customers, and then recognised by national legislation[71] to avoid the multiplication of chain litigation within the production line (on Earth) in the event of damage caused to a third party by a defective space object, badly piloted or out of control.

Thus, for a space launch, the transfer of risk at the contractual level, between the industrialist, the operator, and the customer, is generally fixed at the same moment, at the time of lift-off, when the launch becomes irreversible.[72] This same moment coincides with the moment fixed by national law to define the beginning of the space operation,[73] i.e. the changeover of the liability regimes between those of domestic and common law, for all production activities carried out on the ground, and those derived from international law and specific to space operations and objects (space law). Finally, this event also coincides with the transfer of ownership between the launch vehicle manufacturer and the launch operator.

This appropriation currently has no economic consequences for a launcher that will be completely destroyed a few moments later. But the same cannot be said for a reusable or repairable system.

This context of spacecraft reuse, combined with the possibility of services investigating the cause of its failure in orbit, or repairing or re-orbiting the object launched into orbit, will encourage customers and insurers to refuse or limit the scope of these clauses exonerating the liability of

68 Launch operations or services (rocket flight), satellite remote controls (station keeping operations), satellite mission-related communications and uplink signals, etc.

69 All the information services delivered to earthlings by satellite payloads (communications, observation, navigation, etc.) and their applications.

70 And, where applicable, their shareholders, when these are the industrial manufacturers of the system operated (cf. the situation of Arianespace from the outset with its shareholding comprising the supplier(s) of the Ariane launcher, excluding the case of CNES).

71 In France, according to Art. 20 of the above-mentioned law of 3 June 2008 on space operations. The validation of these clauses by the law was imperative.

72 That is, depending on the type of launcher, at the ignition of the solid rocket boosters or the release of the propellant supply cords following the opening of the launch tower hooks.

73 In France, the launch phase is clearly defined (Art. 1.4 of the 2008 law).

suppliers. Suppliers are already beginning to disregard them in the United States[74] by waiving their protection when offering reusable systems or their services for sale.

1.3.2.5 Towards new international (public) services to assist or remove systems from orbit

In particular, these in-orbit service capabilities pave the way for new activities such as assistance, rescue or removal of vehicles or debris from orbit.[75] This opportunity raises a number of legal requirements under both private and public law to ensure the prior consent, express or implied, of the owner, operator, or licensing or registration state of the distressed vehicle or of debris taken into care by such services.

It would require no more and no less than to introduce an obligation to compensate the owner-operator or the state of registration, inspired by the theory of quasi-contracts, following the example of solutions already validated for salvage and rescue activities[76] or the disposal of maritime wrecks.[77] It could also be based on the principles of the Rescue Agreement,[78] as being specifically extended to include such assistance, return, and reimbursement obligations to active debris removal and other services on space objects. The extension would then take place, under a dedicated instrument, to space objects in distress, at the end of their planned life or to identified space debris.

Finally, it will be necessary to adapt the current technical regulations for docking, taking, and returning to the controls at international level, initially favouring mutual recognition and shared common standards. In this respect, government agencies could draw on methodologies already tried and tested elsewhere. Reference may usefully be made to those that have enabled the construction of the Space Debris Mitigation Guidelines (SDMG) within the Inter-Agency Space Debris Coordination Committee (IADC)[79] or, in the aviation field, to the Standards and Recommended Practices (SARPs) of the International Civil Aviation Organization (ICAO).[80]

1.3.3 The establishment of human bases on extra-terrestrial soil

Current plans for permanent inhabited bases on the Moon or Mars raise further critical legal issues of technical regulations, public-private partnerships, and geopolitical issues of intergovernmental cooperation. Among these, let us first consider the most publicised one, which can be related to the private occupation of spaces and territories, and its corollary, the appropriation of spatial resources.

74 This is the case with SpaceX *vis-à-vis* the US administration according to their agreements that were made public.

75 Valentin Degrange, *Les éboueurs de l'espace: service public, ruée vers l'or ou les deux*, Colloque de la Société française pour le droit international, Faculté de droit de Toulouse, 6–7 May 2021, Editions Pedone, Paris 2021, pp. 439–452.

76 In both civil and common law, the regime of "quasi-contracts" or their equivalents in public law according to the theory of the occasional collaborator in a public service, is to ensure a fair right to remuneration.

77 Nairobi International Convention on the Removal of Wrecks, concluded on 18 May 2007.

78 Agreement on the Rescue of Astronauts, the Return of Astronauts, and the Return of Objects Launched into Outer Space, adopted on 19 December 1967.

79 SDMG were formalised by the IADC and endorsed by UNGA Resolution 62/217 para. 26.

80 See G. Doucet, *SARPs: A Step Towards Harmonization of National Regulations for the Enhancement of Sustainability of the Space Environment*, IAC Congress 2018, Bremen, Germany, IAC-18, E7,7-B3.8,8X46324.

Another, more fundamental, question is the degree or limit of the capacities of our land and human rights to move to permanent installations, to govern increasingly autonomous activities, conducted in a perennial way in hostile and remote environments.

1.3.3.1 The appropriation of spatial resources

This topic is treated in more detail in the chapter by Masson-Zwann and Sundahl. However, it is mentioned here as an important issue to be resolved as it becomes more and more likely that private entities will have the technology to lay claim to extra-territorial resources.[81]

1.3.3.2 A relative autonomy for the law regarding far remote facilities and operations

Following the example of the great maritime expeditions of the Renaissance, and then of the (public-private) Eastern India companies in Europe in the XVII century (albeit not for colonisation),[82] any activity carried out by means of transport and in remote areas inevitably leads to the *elasticity of the law* in relation to its terrestrial anchorage. These explorers or entrepreneurs were able to benefit from a broad delegation of sovereignty for their missions to Asia, in the regalian and economic domains, on condition that they gave a regular account of their activities upon their return to their home territory.

Such delegations do not appear necessary at the beginning of the conquest of space as long as the vehicles remain controlled in real time from a terrestrial base and that this base comes under a national (and territorial) jurisdiction which is imposed on the operator concerned, and consequently on the owner of the space object. The on-board control system remains largely automated and even in manned vehicles, the power of initiative and autonomy of the commander and his crew in relation to the ground is limited to emergency situations and the most sensitive manoeuvres.[83]

81 This issue is also the subject of a study by P. Clerc in *Extra-terrestrial Human Bases at the Crossroads of Economic and Space Law* in Outer Space Future for Humankind, Essential Air and Space Law No. 26, edited by M. Benkö and K.-U. Schrogl, Eleven, The Netherlands, 2021, pp. 69–91.

82 This is a very sensitive point in our analysis. We will only note here that the original economic and political model of the three Eastern India companies in Europe (for Asia) in the XVII century, in view of their contemporary status (cf. *Déclaration du Roy*, 1 September 1664 in France), unlike those of the Western India companies (for North America), was not based *a priori* on colonisation or the territorial appropriation of the countries from which the goods were to be purchased (spices, textiles, etc.). It was based on territorial and commercial concessions granted, limited to seaports and trading posts, according to agreements made with fully sovereign local authorities. It also allowed the company to be granted diplomatic protection (flag), administrative powers from their jurisdiction state, with accountability upon return to the country, and exclusive licensing of products marketing in Europe in order to promote a fair return on investment regarding the risks and the domestic policy of development of a higher level maritime industry. It should not be confused with the movement of colonisation and land appropriation of these same countries that began at the end of the XVIII century, notably with the occupation of India by the United Kingdom. Of course, none of the above can elude or excuse slavery and other crimes against local populations and humanity that can have been generated by such companies. For a historical overview of the three major European companies in the XVII century (the Netherlands, the United Kingdom, and France) see P. Haudrere, G. Le Bouëdec, *Les compagnies des Indes*, Rennes, Éditions Ouest-France, 2015, p. 146, and J. Sottas, *Histoire de la compagnie royale des Indes Orientales*, 1905, republished by SIA.

83 One illustration has remained historic in this respect: the changes of control over the Apollo 13 spacecraft between NASA's control centre in Houston and the crew following the damage that occurred during its mission between 11 April and 17 April 1970. See the film Apollo 13 by Ron Howard, released in 1995, adapted from the book "Lost Moon: the Perious Voyage of Apollo 13" by James "Jim" Lowel (commander of the mission) and Jeffrey Kluger.

The situation is quite different when the vehicles are away from their earthly control centre, and even more so when they are permanently manned and operated on lunar or Martian soil. It is therefore necessary to define the conditions under which states relocate or delegate part of their sovereignty and economic power to public and private actors operating in distant, hostile, and environmentally sensitive spaces.[84]

In this respect, the decentralised (or elastic) national model of the administration of the French Southern Territories (TAF) for the Kerguelen Islands archipelago between the mainland or office (Paris) and these faraway activities, or on an international scale, that of Spitzbergen (Svalbard) in the Arctic,[85] and to a lesser extent the Antarctic Treaty,[86] could be used as a model.

1.4 Convergences

It is not possible in this introductory chapter and for such a book to conclude on subjects that are destined to be developed in depth by eminent specialists.

Therefore, this last section retains only three concepts or principles likely to gather a fair consensus among the actors who will contribute to the future discussions on the evolution of the legal framework of space activities.

The first is based on the principle of *responsibility*. It can be defined as the capacity and duty of any space actor, whether public or private, to conduct its activity in a peaceful, useful, and safe manner for itself, others, the terrestrial and extra-terrestrial environments, and then to answer for its action to those to whom it causes harm.

This responsibility is inseparable from the *freedom of exploration and use* of space for states, but also from the *freedom of enterprise* for the private sector.

Legally, the principle of responsibility finds its source in the various treaties and agreements of the United Nations, beginning with the Outer Space Treaty. It requires private space activities to be subject to authorisation and supervision of the state concerned.[87] It induces the *liability for fault or without fault in case of damage* towards a third victim,[88] and can even oblige actors, outside of any prior agreement under the *quasi-contractual responsibility*, to interfere in the affairs of others in an act of rescue, assistance, or restitution, and consequently to obtain from the second a reimbursement of the useful expenses incurred.[89] It also guides the new contractual relations to

84 See footnote 81.

85 The latter recognises a delocalised administrative sovereignty to Norway while opening the economic exploitation of the territories to an organisation of international signatories.

Transposed to outer space economic activities, the sovereign authority granting licences to the private actors could consist in a multilateral organisation or agreement between states having originally jurisdiction, responsibility, and liability for these activities under Arts VI, VII, and VIII of the Outer Space Treaty. Thus, for instance, regarding economic exploitation of launchers in Europe see the "Declaration by certain European governments on the launcher exploitation phase of Ariane, Vega and Soyuz from the Guiana Space center", effective date 26 November 2009 (first version of 14 April 1980 for Ariane production).

86 The Antarctic Treaty, signed on 1 December 1959 in Washington, D.C., in the United States, offers an interesting model for an international regime of delocalised administration over remote, hostile, and unappropriable spaces, but it is limited to civil and scientific activities, since it does not provide for the economic exploitation of the continent's resources. Indeed, the 1991 Madrid Protocol on the protection of the environment in Antarctica makes the continent a natural reserve dedicated to peace and science.

87 Article VI of the Outer Space Treaty, the Registration Convention, and national legislations.

88 Articles VII, IX, and X of the Liability Convention.

89 The Rescue Agreement or basic legal principles of the *negotiorum gestio*, of the occasional collaborator of public service, of the Good Samaritan, etc.

be standardised between service operators whether they act between Earth and space, on-orbit, or on celestial bodies.

It is thus at the heart of the issues concerning the management of collision risks in orbit or linked to debris, the development of suborbital flights, new services in orbit, assistance between spacecraft or ADR, and the international framework of the STM and SSA.

The second, to be carried by the states, following a dedicated agreement or by mutual recognition, consists in elaborating an *international regime for the protection of space investments* that would apply to all responsible activities in the sense defined above.[90] This path would make it possible to go beyond the ideological and divisive debate on the appropriation of land and resources of extra-terrestrial soils, the latter often presented as a necessary and preliminary step for any private investment. The first objective of this regime could be to secure the development of commercial exploitation in a targeted domain, over a reasonable limited period of time, in the respect of planetary protection, under a *framework of concession* granted by the states of jurisdiction concerned, and recognised by all, including in matters of competition law and taxation. This solution would be aimed in particular at services in orbit and public-private projects for human installations on the Moon and other celestial bodies.

Finally, the third solution consists in the *relaunching of transversal international negotiations* for an extension of space law to economic and competitive activities. States could invite the legal and technical subcommittees of the UNCOPUOS to open their instances of reflection, create bridges, or coordinate rounds with other international organisations on subjects of common interest. These include the ICAO for suborbital transport, the International Telecommunication Union on the management of the frequency spectrum for constellations, the World Trade Organization and the Organization for Economic Cooperation and Development on public aid and procurement, tax harmonisation, investment protection, and international trade in products and services resulting from the exploitation of space resources.

This approach should then be opened to the representatives of private companies that carry out these new activities in order to find concerted solutions between states, the actors in place and those of NewSpace, industrial manufacturers, and operators of space systems or of data and value-added services.

This wish for a responsible and organised contribution of the private sector to the emergence of a new economic space law will perhaps be the most audacious challenge to take up for the next steps of the NewSpace!

90 On the legal aspects of this protection, see A. de Nanteuil, *Droit international de l'investissement*, Editions Pedone, 2020, 3rd edition.

2

THE EU REGULATION FOR THE SPACE PROGRAMME

A new framework

Kamlesh Brocard

2.1 Introduction

European states have never been so undivided, and in agreement on so many topics at the same time: recent global events have forced moments of reflection such that the general consensus is to invest in technologies that can be leveraged not only to improve daily life, but also to help respond to the societal challenges we face, help avoid them, and assist in recovery. The European institutions indicate space is one of the sectors contributing to the resilience of those critical entities that provide essential services.[1] In the framework of its new industrial strategy,[2] the European Union (EU) is promoting the competitiveness of its space industries, both as a prerequisite for a safe and autonomous access to space, and as a way to stimulate the uptake of space applications and data.

This recognition stems from the strengthening commitment of the EU to space-related activities, linking various sectoral policies such as environment, transport, agriculture, and security – and the wider socio-economic benefits derived from the downstream services. Hence, national and regional authorities recognise space as an enabler, a tool to implement an array of policies from agriculture to defence via economy and environment. This trio of the EU, the European Space Agency (ESA), and their respective Member States has collectively achieved many successes in its ongoing efforts to ensure an ever-more coherent approach to space at the global level.

The capabilities which Europe's public and private sectors have developed helped position it as a global leader in the sector. With the European economy and society increasingly reliant on space services, more needed to be done at the political level. So, on 28 April 2021, Regulation (EU) No 696/2021[3] of the European Parliament and of the Council ("EU Space Regulation") was adopted, establishing the new Union Space Programme 2021–2027 ("EU Space Programme") and

1 On 28 June 2022, the European Commission welcomed the political agreement between the European Parliament and the Council on the Directive on the resilience of critical entities (CER Directive) COM(2020) 829 final, proposed by the Commission in December 2020.

2 "European industrial strategy", European Commission, Internal Market, Industry, Entrepreneurship and SMSEs.

3 Regulation (EU) 2021/696 of the European Parliament and of the Council of 28 April 2021 establishing the Union Space Programme and the European Union Agency for the Space Programme and repealing Regulations (EU) No.

 DOI: 10.4324/9781003268475-4

the European Union Agency for the Space Programme ("EUSPA"). The EU Space Regulation unifies in one document various rules that were previously in distinct regulations, while retaining the goals. The extent to which the new framework enables Europe to leverage its technological capabilities to boost commercialisation and investments for space ventures and consolidate its leadership in the current global context remains to be seen. This chapter examines the steps taken in Europe to achieve and retain its place in the global market of space through its "framework of space activities".

2.2 Constructing European space

European cooperation in space emerged with the foundations laid by the creation of the European Space Research Organisation and the European Launcher Development Organisation at the start of the 1960s. When in 1975 the two European institutions merged to create the intergovernmental European Space Agency (ESA), it not only signaled a new dawn for European cooperation in space, but also highlighted the ten founding Member States'[4] commitment to space research and development for peaceful purposes.[5] In 1979 the European Parliament adopted a first resolution[6] on European Community participation in space research, focusing on the socio-economic and industrial benefits. In spite of the significant challenges presented by operating within different legal and institutional bodies, a strengthening of the ties and coordination between the organisations, including their Member States, ensued over the following decades, underpinned by a commitment to foster space activities for the benefit of Europe. The European Space Policy "unveiled on 22 May 2007 by twenty-nine European countries and unifying the approach of ESA with those of the individual European Union Member States"[7] constituted a determining milestone in this journey and was later followed by the "Joint Statement on shared vision and goals for the future of Europe in space by the EU and ESA" in 2016.

2.2.1 EU competence for a Space Regulation

The EU Space Regulation is the latest and to date the most significant piece of legislation in the implementation of a European space policy. It marks a new phase in European legislation and governance for space. A binding legislative act, it must be applied in its entirety across the EU Member States. With its entry into force on 1 January 2021, the EU Space Regulation repealed Regulations (EU) No. 912/2010 setting up the European GNSS Agency, (EU) No. 1285/2013 on the implementation and exploitation of European satellite navigation systems, (EU) No. 377/2014 on the establishment of the Copernicus Programme and Decision No. 541/2014/EU on the establishment of a Framework for Space Surveillance and Tracking Support.

The foundational building blocks of the legislative structure leading to the EU Space Regulation were put in place sometime earlier, starting with the adoption in 1986 of the Single European Act. Although without explicit references to space, Title VI of the Treaty on European Union (TEU)

912/2010, (EU) No. 1285/2013 and (EU) No. 377/2014 and Decision No. 541/2014/EU entered into force on 12 May 2021 with retroactive effect from 1 January 2021 ("Space Regulation").

4 Belgium, Germany, Denmark, France, the United Kingdom, Italy, the Netherlands, Sweden, Switzerland, and Spain.

5 Article II Convention of 30 May 1975 on the Establishment of a European Space Agency ("ESA Convention").

6 European Parliament resolution on Community participation in space research, OJ C 127, pp. 42–43, 21 May 1979.

7 Resolution on the European Space Policy: ESA Director General's Proposal for the European Space Policy, The European Space Agency (ESA), available online.

"Research and Technological Development" represented an initial step in the common endeavour by EU Member States: setting priorities aligned with strategic and commercial benefits of space activities. The evolution of the treaties over the years has led to the gradual extension of the EU's competences to fields closely linked to space, setting the scene for a European Union space policy. In 2007, the Lisbon Treaty[8] provided new Art. 189 of the Treaty on the Functioning of the European Union (TFEU), making space a European policy by attributing a more direct EU competence, with Title XIX "Research and Technological Development and Space".

2.2.2 Constitutional limitations of Art. 189 TFEU

Article 189(1) TFEU provides that "to promote scientific and technical progress, industrial competitiveness and the implementation of its policies, the Union shall draw up a European space policy. To this end, it may promote joint initiatives, support research and technological development and coordinate the efforts needed for the exploration and exploitation of space". While this new competence may seem extensive, it remains a shared competence between the EU and its Member States, and has its limits. Pursuant to Art. 189(2) TFEU, "any harmonisation of the laws and regulations" of EU Member States in relation to space is excluded. It entails that, while the European Parliament and the Council acting in accordance with the ordinary legislative procedure are to establish the necessary measures to attain the objectives set out in Art. 189(1) TFEU, which may be in the form of a European space programme, there can be no attempt at harmonising rules across Member States. Thus, the EU does not have the legislative tools for the implementation of a coherent and harmonised space programme or policy for Member States. In relation to the space sector, both the Member States and the EU may in fact adopt legally binding rules, but since the EU rules cannot replace national legislative provisions, Member States retain full sovereignty. Given that not all EU Member States have enacted space legislation, and that divergences can be found not only in the reading of the legal provisions of existing national legal frameworks, but also in the national policies, the implementation of a common and coherent space policy would prove problematic at best. The Space Regulation thus provides the EU with a framework to implement a space policy and objectives only across Member States.

2.3 General scope of the Regulation

The EU Space Regulation enables the establishment of EUSPA and defines a renewed and unified Space Programme for the period 2021–2027, seeking to simplify the legal framework for the existing EU programmes. It proposes streamlined and simpler ways of cooperation between all institutional actors, without fundamentally altering the balance of responsibilities between all actors involved. It lays down the objectives, the budget for the period 2021–2027, the forms of funding, the rules for providing such funding, as well as the rules for the implementation of the EU Space Programme.[9] With the Programme's duration of seven years aligned on the Multiannual Financial Framework 2021–2027, the Regulation gives a useful financial perspective. In addition to the Regulation itself, the components of the EU Programme must also meet the objectives of the

8 For a reconstruction of the regulatory context and framework of the space sector prior to the Lisbon Treaty: M. Benkö, K.U. Schrogl (eds.), Space Law: Current Problems and Perspectives for Future Regulation, Utrecht, 2005; M. Lachs, The Law of Outer Space: An Experience in Contemporary Law Making, Leiden-Boston, 2010.

9 Article 1, Space Regulation.

European Green Deal and the digital transformation on the continent.[10] An overview of the provisions should allow for a better understanding of the Programme's objectives and components, its governance, and the functioning of EUSPA.

The EU Space Programme has three overarching missions: Earth Observation, Navigation and Protection, and Secure Communication. Article 3 lists the five components – or flagship programmes – implemented to fulfil the missions: (i) Galileo, (ii) the European Geostationary Navigation Overlay Service (EGNOS), (iii) Copernicus, (iv) Space Situational Awareness (SSA) and its three sub-components Space Surveillance and Tracking (SST), Space Weather (SWE), and Near Earth Object (NEO), and (v) GOVSATCOM.

The purposes of the five components of the Programme are as follows:

- the Galileo programme, the European GNSS global navigation satellite system, is aimed at providing improved positioning and timing information;
- EGNOS, the regional satellite augmentation system, is used to improve the performance of Galileo and other GNSS used for air traffic management, air navigation services, and other transport systems. It consists of a set of systems that collect and process data from multiple sources, such as satellites and *in situ* sensors, e.g., ground stations and air and/or maritime sensors.

These purposes were already initiated by the previous European entities, which operated before the creation of EUSPA, namely the Galileo Joint Undertaking, the European GNSS Supervisory Authority, and the European GNSS Agency. More specifically, today we have:

- Copernicus, the Earth observation system providing reliable, real-time data and geo-information services;
- the SSA programme, and its three sub-components, for
  - space surveillance system and tracking of space objects orbiting the Earth;
  - observation parameters related to space weather events; and
  - risk monitoring of near and approaching Earth objects.
- the GOVSATCOM programme, an EU governmental satellite communication service for the national security management of individual Member States and the entire European Union.

These five Programme components support the objectives of the Programme, through:

- the provision of quality data that can support EU priorities, notably in the areas of climate change, transport, and security;
- the promotion of the economic development of SMEs and start-ups in the sector, upstream, and the re-use of data provided by EU programmes, downstream;
- the strengthening of European strategic autonomy and Europe's place in global space diplomacy; and
- enhancing the safety and sustainability of space missions, for example by ensuring better debris removal in orbit.

10 As per the speech of Thierry Breton, the current European Commissioner for the Internal Market, responsible for European space policy at the 14th European Space Conference on 25 January 2022.

In addition, the Programme "shall also include additional measures to ensure efficient and autonomous access to space, namely to strengthen the Union space ecosystem and to reinforce the Union as a global player as specified in art. 3(2). The subject of launchers being inseparable from the principle of autonomous access to space, there have been talks of an Alliance on Space Launchers."[11]

The Regulation allocates financial resources to each individual Programme component, with Art. 10 presenting the general breakdown of €14.880 billion earmarked for the period 2021–2027.

2.3.1 Governance of the Programme

The EU Space Regulation expands governance further than previous regulations by bringing more programmes under the management of the Commission. It provides the Commission with the power to coordinate and supervise the different components, define the high-level objectives (budget, security, and schedule) as well as the long-term evolution of the Programme together with regulating the work between the different organisations, in conjunction with fostering the European market the data and services. Title IV "Programme Governance"' sets out in Arts. 26–32 the tasks and responsibilities of the Member States, the Commission, EUSPA, ESA, the European Organisation for the Exploitation of Meteorological Satellites (EUMETSAT), and other entities involved in the implementation of the Programme.

It is to be noted, in accordance with Art. 27(1), that Member States may participate in the Programme, but have no obligation to do so. They do however have the obligation to take all measures necessary to ensure the smooth functioning of the Programme as per Art. 27(4). They shall contribute to the implementation of the programme by offering their expertise and knowledge, in particular in the field of safety and security; they also contribute by making available to the Union the data, information, services, and infrastructure in their possession or located on their territory, including by ensuring the accessibility and use of Copernicus *in situ* data; finally, they shall cooperate with the Commission in order to improve the availability and reliability of Copernicus *in situ* data required by the Programme, taking into account applicable licences and obligations. The final element relates to the need to agree on licensing conditions for third-party data in order to facilitate their use for Copernicus.

Article 28 of the Regulation entrusts the Commission with the role of coordinating and supervising the activities of the various actors involved in the Programme, so that they always act in the interest of the Union and in accordance with the provisions of the Regulation. Finally, it has overall responsibility for the implementation of the Programme, without prejudice to the prerogatives of the Member States in matters of national security.

For the implementation of the objectives of the Space Regulation, the EU concluded in June 2021 the Financial Framework Partnership Agreement (FFPA)[12] with ESA and EUSPA, covering the period until end 2027.[13] Defining the roles, responsibilities, and obligations of the Commission,

11 "Updating the 2020 Industrial Strategy: towards a stronger Single Market for Europe's recovery", press release, European Commission, 5 May 2021.

12 Article 31, Space Regulation. Article 189(3) TFEU provides the basis for the EU-ESA cooperation. This institutional collaboration is governed by the 2004 Framework Agreement [2004] OJ L261/64 and more concretely implemented primarily for GNSS via several agreements, including Delegation Agreements giving authority to ESA to act on the EU's behalf in specific contexts.

13 Article 31, Space Regulation.

EUSPA, and ESA with regard to each component of the Space Programme and to the necessary coordination and control mechanisms, the FFPA brings into play the unique and complementary functions and competences the partners have in the conduct of European space activities.

Article 29 assigns EUSPA with its own tasks generally concerning the communication, market development, and promotion activities relating to the Galileo, EGNOS, and Copernicus services, as well as security accreditation of all Programme components, in accordance with Title V, Chapter II of the Regulation. The Commission delegates additional tasks to EUSPA related to Galileo, EGNOS, Copernicus, and GOVSATCOM, which are explicitly mentioned. The Commission may entrust other tasks, insofar as this delegation improves efficiency and does not cause duplication of activities carried out by other organisations under the Programme. An example of the delegation from the Commission is its decision of 3 June 2022 for EUSPA to take responsibility for the Programme's SST Front Desk operations service. The service is transferred from the European Satellite Centre (SatCen) to EUSPA's Galileo Security Monitoring Centre (GSMC), selected "on the basis of the best expertise in security issues and in service promotion" (Art. 59).

Subject to given criteria, EUSPA may also entrust, by means of contribution agreements, specific activities to other entities, in areas of their respective competence, under the conditions of indirect management applying to the Commission (Art. 29(5)).

Article 30 defines the role of ESA, which remains the main partner and is responsible for the following, provided the EU's interests are protected:

- Galileo and EGNOS: systems evolution, development of the ground segment, and the design and development of satellites, including testing and validation;
- Copernicus: development, design, and construction of the Copernicus space infrastructure, including the operations of that infrastructure and location;
- all the components of the Space Programme with upstream research and development activities in its fields of expertise; and
- technical expertise as requested by the Commission or EUSPA, without prejudice to the FFPA.

In this context, ESA has to apply the EU's security rules, in particular with regard to the processing of classified information.

The signature of the FFPA was hailed as anchoring the European Union's leadership in space as it establishes, under the umbrella of the Regulation, a balanced working relationship of the two organisations underpinned by the recognition of their complementarity. The negotiations leading to the agreement were intense[14] and were reportedly complicated by "frictions regarding budget management and responsibilities breakdown, in particular with regards to the role of EUSPA".[15] Its conclusion, which was also an ESA priority,[16] brought much-needed clarity of roles to, for instance, minimise overlaps between the key EU entities and ESA and maximise efficiency for Member States' funding, based on two principles: the complementarity of the actors and a balanced EU/ESA relationship.

Article 32 refers to the tasks of EUMETSAT and of any other entities that might be involved in the implementation of the Programme. The provision states that the Commission, through con-

14 ESA Agenda 2025: Make space for Europe, the FFPA, 2021.

15 ESPI Insights for November 2021 is out!, Space Sector Watch, November 2021.

16 ESA Agenda 2025: Make space for Europe (search for: "The year is 2035").

tribution agreements, may entrust EUMETSAT, or other agencies, bodies, and organisations other than those referred to in Arts. 29 and 30, provided that they are located in the Union, for instance the European Environment Agency, Frontex, the European Maritime Safety Agency, SatCen, and the European Centre for Medium-Range Weather Forecasts (ECMWF), with the task of enhancing the Copernicus infrastructure.

2.3.2 Functioning of EUSPA

The organisation and functioning of EUSPA are detailed in Arts. 72–83 of the Regulation.

Article 72 states that the administrative and management structure of EUSPA consists of the Administrative Board, the Executive Director, and the Security Accreditation Board. The Administrative Board is chaired by a chairperson chosen from among its members and is composed of one representative of each Member State and three members of the Commission. A member designated by the European Parliament also participates in the meetings without any voting rights. Furthermore, it is specified that the Executive Director, the Chairperson or Deputy Chairperson of the Security Accreditation Board, a representative of the Council, a representative of the High Representative, and a representative of the ESA may also participate in the meetings of the Administrative Board without voting rights. The Administrative Board, in the exercise of its functions under Art. 77, shall ensure that the Agency carries out the tasks entrusted to it and that it performs them in accordance with the terms and conditions laid down in the Regulation.

As per Arts. 78 and 79, the Executive Director leads and represents EUSPA, manages its day-to-day administration, implements the decisions of the Administrative Board and the multiannual and annual work programmes, with the exception of those parts implemented by the Chairperson of the Security Accreditation Board, prepares the annual report on the Agency's activities, progress, and prospects, with the exception of the section for which the Security Accreditation Board is responsible, and takes all necessary measures to ensure its functioning and to protect the interests of the EU.

Articles 80–83 detail the tasks and functioning of the Security Accreditation Board which, together with actors and entities indicated in the Regulation, has the task of ensuring the security level of the Programme. This is in order to avert any physical or cyber threats that could jeopardise the ground or space infrastructure, and thus prevent the implementation of the Programme and its individual components, described under Title V, "Program Security". The Board may also establish special subordinate bodies to which it entrusts specific tasks.

2.3.3 Role of ESA in the context of the Programme

ESA as a sovereign agency is composed of 22 Member States and further cooperating states, conducts research and development missions encompassing many areas including science, launchers, robotic and human exploration, navigation, Earth observation, and telecommunications. It does so with an annual budget of €7.15 billion for 2022, with the EU being the largest single contributor with €1,336 billion for the implementation of designated tasks.

The European institutions and ESA have not evolved totally independent of one another in fostering space in Europe. However, it is thanks to the cooperation among its organisations and their respective Member States that Europe has become one the global leaders in space. For instance, it is by relying on the technical expertise of ESA, that the EU has developed the series of major programmes extending its capabilities in space, in particular to become a global leader in acquiring space data for Earth Observation with Copernicus.

2.4 The new framework for space activities – Programme components

The full responsibility of financing, owning, and managing the tangible and intangible assets created or developed under the Programme's components lies with the EU, and subject to certain conditions, as defined in Art. 9. Article 10, introduces a new element of "warranty", warning users that "without prejudice to the obligations imposed by legally binding provisions, the services, data, and information provided by the Programme's components shall be provided without any express or implied warranty as regards their quality, accuracy, availability, reliability, speed, and suitability for any purpose. The Commission shall ensure that the users of those services, data, and information are duly informed". Simply explained, the aim of such exclusion of warranty is to act as a risk-related balancing mechanism between the end-user and the EU. This is especially relevant in a context where the EU is striving to increase user uptake and foster new downstream services and businesses. Acting as the EU's programme manager, the Commission has the overall responsibility for implementation of the Programme, including in the field of security.

2.4.1 The existing components – Galileo, EGNOS, Copernicus

With the heritage of the European GNSS Agency, EUSPA now has increased responsibilities in managing the exploitation of Galileo and EGNOS, including their service provision and operations security.[17] Operational since 2016, the constellation of 30 satellites in Medium Earth Orbit is considered to be the most accurate radio navigation system in the world, and is used for many applications. As at end 2021, there have been about 2.4 billion Galileo-compatible smartphones which have been sold worldwide, and its benefits can be seen in different areas for society, including in road and rail transport, location-based services, and emergency services. Galileo is accompanied by EGNOS, which augments and corrects its open signals.

The Space Regulation specifies that EGNOS provides, free of direct user charge, three types of user services and covers the direct area of the EU Member States. Technically, it is possible to extend coverage to other regions for other countries. Should this be agreed and implemented with other countries the associated costs of extension and functioning of EGNOS will be financed through means other than the Programme's budget, upon decision of the Commission.[18]

The new framework has brought some added clarity to the designation and description of the six Galileo services which was not the case in the repealed regulation of 2013.[19] There are no major changes and the financing means are fundamentally the same. Since it is a working combination, it is probably by design, affording the flexibility required to adapt to technological progress.

In contrast, concerning the Copernicus Earth Observation programme (including the Copernicus Contributing Missions), which is managed by the Commission and implemented in collaboration with Member States, ESA, EUMETSAT, ECMWF, Mercator Océan, and EU Agencies,[20] the Space Regulation (Title VII) has introduced more visible changes when compared to the previous 2014 regulation.[21] The new framework indicates that the Copernicus programme consists of the following: (i) data acquisition, which includes the development and functioning of the Sentinels,

17 "Space on a new trajectory with launch of EUSPA", EUSPA (under "Newsroom"), 2021.

18 Article 43(2)(3), Space Regulation.

19 See footnote 3 above.

20 "Europe's Eyes on Earth: Looking at our planet and its environment for the benefit of Europe's citizens", Copernicus .eu (Highlights).

21 See footnote 3 above.

access to third-party space-based Earth observation data, and to *in situ* and other auxiliary data; (ii) Copernicus Services, which process the collected data and information; (iii) infrastructure and services for data access and distribution in a user-friendly manner; and (iv) user uptake, market development, and capacity building. The old regulation only indicated (i) and (ii) above.

The Regulation also addresses the outcome of preceding evaluations[22] and consultation which highlighted *inter alia* the need to strengthen the integration of space data into other policy areas and economic sectors through increased focus on user uptake. The addition in particular of elements such as user uptake, market development, and capacity building emphasises the objectives of the EU to stimulate uptake by the private sector and promote data and services to maximise socio-economic benefits.

The Copernicus data and information policy provisions are contained in Art. 53. The key elements of which are no restrictions on either the use, be it commercial or non-commercial, or on users be they European or non-European; a free of charge version of any dataset is always available on the Copernicus dissemination platforms; and data and information are available worldwide without limitation in time.

Copernicus users may, on a free and worldwide basis, reproduce, distribute, communicate to the public, adapt, modify all Copernicus data and information and combine them with other data and information. Limitations applicable to the free, full, and open data policy are related to registration, dissemination formats, and access restrictions.

The Regulation introduces "Copernicus Services" as a new definition (Art. 2(21)): "value-added services of general and common interest to the European Union and member states, which are financed by the Programme and which transform Earth Observation data, *in situ* data and other ancillary data into processed, aggregated and interpreted information tailored to the needs of Copernicus users." This new definition, read in conjunction with the warranty provision in Art. 10, is an indication of the shift to use Copernicus data and information towards market-oriented services and to limit the associated liability risks.

The limitations to the full, free, and worldwide access are formulated in the Delegated Regulation 1159/2013[23] as on legal grounds such as international agreements, IPR, and protection of personal data, on the protection of security interests subject to an assessment of the sensitivity of the data and information to be undertaken by the Commission, or for technical reasons, namely if the capacities of the dissemination systems are not sufficient to serve all user requests, the "integrity of the Copernicus system". The Delegated Regulation also includes specific access conditions with which Copernicus online platform managers need to comply. In order to access and download data and information free of charge, "users shall be required to register only once and shall be accepted automatically" as per Art. 18 and have the possibility of declining to register but still being eligible "for discovery services and view services".

With the emergence of new commercial actors and ventures resulting from the evolution of the six Copernicus Expansions[24] being studied to address EU policy and gaps in Copernicus user needs and to expand the current capabilities of the Copernicus space component, it remains to be

22 E.g., "Copernicus Market Report – February 2019", European Commission.

23 Commission Delegated Regulation (EU) No. 1159/2013 of 12 July 2013 supplementing Regulation (EU) No. 911/2010 of the European Parliament and of the Council on the European Earth monitoring programme (GMES) by establishing registration and licensing conditions for GMES users and defining criteria for restricting access to GMES dedicated data and GMES service information.

24 The aim is to address EU policy and gaps in Copernicus user needs, and to expand the current capabilities of the Copernicus space component.

seen whether the current data policy continues to safeguard the Programme component objectives or if new mechanisms will be required.

2.4.2 The new components – SSA and GOVSATCOM

The Space Situational Awareness (SSA) programme is designed to ensure that extraterrestrial activities are safe and sustainable. Article 3(1)(d) specifies that it consists of three sub-components: SST, SWE, and NEO. As an SST system, its aim is to improve, operate, and provide data, information, and services related to the surveillance and tracking of space objects that orbit the Earth.[25] In particular, it endeavours to carry out a European inventory of objects in space and assesses the risks of collisions between different spacecraft, their debris, and NEOs, those naturally occurring elements in the solar system that may approach the Earth.[26] This monitoring includes the observation of meteorological phenomena such as solar flares.

The programme is intended to ensure the safety of Galileo and Copernicus satellites, among other things. The number of space debris larger than 1 cm is estimated at 780,000 and SST monitors space objects on different orbits to detect a risk of collision or re-entry to Earth. Satellites operators and civil protection authorities are informed accordingly to protect satellites. More than 140 user organisations benefit from free services for over 290 satellites, based on the information provided by a growing sensor network, currently comprising of 40 radars, telescopes, and laser ranging stations, which remain under the authority of the Member States. Thanks to the programme, the Commission estimates that more than 430 collisions were avoided in 2021.[27] It is worth highlighting that, akin to Galileo and Copernicus services, those related to SST are free of charge and will be available to European as well as non-European users.[28]

With its inclusion in the Regulation, the legal instrument for SSA has changed: prior to 1 January 2021, this Programme component was regulated by a Decision,[29] binding only in specific cases and upon those to whom they are directed. With its inclusion in the Regulation, the provisions pertaining to SSA are binding and apply in their entirety across the EU. It must also be noted that the previous decision dealt only with one sub-component (SST), with the provisions remaining essentially unchanged. The other two sub-components SWE and NEO are new and are relatively lightly regulated, likely to cater for the upcoming technological developments in this area.

The final component of the Space Programme is a government satellite communications initiative (GOVSATCOM) which aims to provide a secure communications service. Unlike the aforementioned Galileo, Copernicus, and SST, which comprise of infrastructure and hardware and have been operational for some years, the initiative is yet to be implemented. Article 3(1)(e) states it is a "satellite communications service under civil and governmental control enabling the provision of satellite communications capacities and services to Union and Member State authorities managing security critical missions and infrastructures". It is a special infrastructure designed for military or security-sensitive operations and planned to be more secure and resilient, guaranteeing availability even during critical events when networks might be disabled due to natural or man-made disasters.

25 Article 3(1)(d)(i), Space Regulation.
26 Ibid, Art. 54 (1)(a) and (b).
27 EU Space Surveillance and Tracking, eusst.eu.
28 Article 8, Space Regulation.
29 Decision No. 541/2014/EU of the European Parliament and of the Council of 16 April 2014 establishing a Framework for Space Surveillance and Tracking Support.

Designed to ensure an autonomous European service of secured satellites communication, GOVSATCOM has been on the EU's agenda in space and defence-related activities for a number of years[30] and is in response to the need for a new solution combining the advantages of commercial and military satellite systems in order to address both civil and military needs through European cooperation. Overall, it is part of the EU Global Strategy, the Space Strategy for Europe, as well as the European Defence Action Plan and will contribute to the EU response to hybrid threats as well as support numerous EU policy domains, in particular the EU Maritime Security Strategy, the EU Arctic Policy, and the EU Cyber Defence Policy Framework.[31]

The Regulation identifies four categories of subjects in the implementation of this component, namely GOVSATCOM authorities, participants, providers, and users and regulates – via the adoption of implementing acts by the Commission – the sharing and prioritisation of capacities, services, and user equipment.[32]

The Regulation's aim by pooling Member States' capacities in satellite communication services through GOVSATCOM is to consolidate and strengthen the operational capacities of public authorities. The development of this component of the Space Programme is significant for security in EU space activities.

2.4.3 Initiatives outside of the Regulation – Secure Connectivity and Space Traffic Management (STM)

The "Action Plan on Synergies between civil, defence and space industries", presented by the Commission in February 2021, established Secure Connectivity and STM as EU flagship projects. One year later, the Commission presented a proposal for a regulation establishing the Union secure connectivity programme for the period 2023–2027[33] and published with the EU High Representative for Foreign Affairs and Security Policy, the Joint Communication "An EU Approach for Space Traffic Management – An EU contribution addressing a global challenge".[34] Although not part of the EU Space Regulation itself, they must be mentioned in the context of the larger framework of space activities in Europe.

The proposal for EU space-based secure connectivity is in response to the growing demand for satellite communications. The goal is to develop a multi-orbital space-based connectivity system that will provide for a resilient connectivity system and high-speed connectivity based on quantum encryption. It will support the protection of critical infrastructures, surveillance, external actions, crisis management, and applications that are critical for Member States' economy, security, and defence. Reinforcing the role and capabilities of the private sector, the aim is to enable the provision of commercial services for advanced, reliable, and fast connections to citizens and businesses across Europe, including in communication dead zones ensuring cohesion across Member States. The service shall also ensure continuity of communication in the event of a cyberattack. "Our new infrastructure will provide high-speed internet access, serve as a back-up to our current internet

30 On the initiative of the European Defence Agency with 15 MS and Norway, later followed by the EC space strategy for Europe and European Defence Action Plan, GOVSATCOM Preparatory Action.

31 European Commission, Objectives and Benefits of GOVSATCOM.

32 Article 66, Space Regulation.

33 Proposal for a Regulation of the European Parliament and of the Council establishing the Union Secure Connectivity Programme for the period 2023–2027, COM(2022) 57 final.

34 Joint Communication: An EU Approach for Space Traffic Management – An EU contribution addressing a global challenge, European Commission, 15 February 2022.

infrastructure, increase our resilience and cyber security, and provide connectivity to the whole of Europe and Africa", summarised Internal Market Commissioner Thierry Breton on 15 February 2022 when the initiative was tabled. Estimated at €6 billion and financed by the EU, Member States, and the private sector, the project is due to reach full capacity in 2028.

In March 2023, Regulation (EU) 2023/588 establishing the Union Secure Connectivity Programme for 2023-2027 came into force, setting the goals for the deployment of an Infrastructure for Resilience, Interconnectivity and Security by Satellite" 'IRIS²'. IRIS² will be a multi-orbital satellite constellation covering the needs of European governments for secure communication services.

STM relates *inter alia* to SSA activities, debris mitigation, launch, and in-orbit operations and encompasses the means and the rules to access, conduct activities in, and return from outer space safely, sustainably, and securely. The joint initiative[35] focuses mainly on assessment of the STM requirements and impacts on the EU; enhancement of EU operational capabilities to support STM; establishment of STM regulatory aspects; promoting the EU STM approach at an international level. The joint communication stating in particular that the EU SST is the key operational capability for future EU STM as a first step for a common approach to STM in Europe and for establishing a regulatory framework for a common level playing field at the EU level in STM matters. In this context, the inaugural event in April 2022 of the EU industry and start-up forum constitutes one of the recent actions aimed at a timely involvement of the private sector. DG DEFIS in collaboration with the EU SST Consortium aimed to establish a forum to foster the innovation and competitiveness of the SSA's commercial sector to achieve a higher level of strategic autonomy in Europe.

2.5 The new framework for space activities – procurement and funding mechanisms

Some of the EU Space Programme components precedes the Regulation. Additionally, the implementation of new ones will lead to the fulfilment of the objectives set out in its Art. 4, namely to provide secure and reliable space services, information, and data that can meet EU political priorities and the needs of European citizens; to maximise socio-economic benefits, in particular by fostering innovation, development, and competitiveness of the European upstream and downstream sectors; to support the creation, growth, and development of SMEs, start-ups, and all companies operating in the space industrial sector to support an autonomous, secure, and efficient space access capability taking into account the Union's essential security interests; to strengthen the security of the Union and the Member States; to create a "European space ecosystem" by improving the competitiveness, autonomy, development, and technological independence of the Union and the Member States; to promote the role of the Union as a global player in space, encourage international cooperation, strengthen European space diplomacy; and enhance the sustainability of all outer-space activities related to space objects and space debris proliferation.

2.5.1 Budget

The European Parliament and the Council have allocated a total budget of €14.880 billion for the period 2021–2027. The distribution among the components is such that the largest share of €9.017 billion is intended for the Galileo and EGNOS programmes, €5.421 billion to Copernicus, and

35 "An EU Approach for Space Traffic Management", European Commission, Defence Industry and Space, 2021 ("EU Space Policy").

€0.442 billion to SSA and GOVSATCOM. This unprecedented level of funding underpins the EU's commitment to boosting the sector and to the role it wishes to play on the regional and global levels. Article 11 provides that the Commission can still exercise some discretion since it can reallocate funds between the different components under the condition that the reallocated funds do not exceed 7.5% of the category of expenditure that receives the funds or the category that receives it. In the event that the reallocated funds exceed the calculated 7.5%, the reallocation warrants the adoption of an implementing act via a special procedure (Art. 11(2)).

The Regulation provides for some much-needed budgetary flexibility in the implementation of the Programme. Although the level of complexity involved in the different components can be largely anticipated, not all contingencies can be predicted. Hence, it further provides that the funds can be allocated to Member States under shared management or can be transferred to the Programme at the request of a Member State and be used for the benefit of the Member State concerned (Art. 11(7)). Member States also have the possibility to add funds to the Programme to finance additional elements but only if such elements have no negative impact on the Programme. Here too, the Commission's decision is by way of an implementing act and the additional funds are processed as external assigned revenue (Art. 12).

2.5.2 Funding mechanisms

Title III of the Regulation (Financial Provisions) encompasses procurement and grants and prizes. These constitute the mechanisms for the European Space Programme to strengthen existing European space assets and services while targeting start-ups and SMEs which develop innovative solutions based on space technologies, data, and services. The EU Space Programme seeks to foster entrepreneurship and innovation via existing and new funding opportunities in support of the European space industry and the emergence of a diversified European "NewSpace" ecosystem fostering.

a) Procurement

The largest slice of financing will be via procurement procedures. In order to fulfil the EU's objective of enabling as many private actors as possible to participate, Art. 14(1) details the requirements for conducting the procedures, including the promotion throughout the supply chain, the widest and most open participation possible by economic operators, in particular start-ups, and to ensure effective competition and avoiding reliance on a single provider in order to promote the autonomy of the Union and satisfying the security criteria. In order to preserve the security, integrity, and resilience of the operational systems of the Union, the Commission shall apply eligibility and participation conditions (Art. 24).

Article 15 and 16 set out two special types of contracts, the "conditional stage-payment contract" and the "cost-reimbursement contract" respectively. The conditional stage-payment contract determines a fixed stage which is the subject of the contract, and for which the contractor offers a firm commitment. The contract also consists of one or more stages which are conditional in terms of budget and performance. However, the stages are not independent of each other but rather constitute a whole and must be executed if the criteria are met, upon decision of the contracting authority.

The second type of contract is the "cost-reimbursement contract", which is applicable in two different cases, namely where the contract has "very complex features or which includes a significant number of technical risks due to the required use of new technology" or "when the activities subject to the contract must, for operational reasons, start immediately, even though it is not yet possible to determine an accurate fixed price because of significant risks or because the performance of the contract in question is dependent on the performance of other contracts".

This description likely describes the majority of space projects-related contracts and they can be expected to represent the bulk of the agreements. In this case, it is the contracting authority which decides whether to opt for a full or a partial cost-reimbursement contract. The decision, regarding the level of reimbursement, including all direct costs incurred by the contractor in performing the contract, indirect costs, a fixed profit, and an appropriate incentive fee based on achieving the established goals, is reached in coordination with the contractor. Article 16(4) stipulates that a maximum ceiling price must be indicated, notwithstanding that it can be modified in accordance with Art. 172 of the Financial Regulation.[36]

Reinforcing the goal of increasing the types of collaboration or consortia as well as the number of newcomers in the space sector, Art. 17 provides that the contracting authority can request that the tenderer subcontracts part of the contract to companies which do not belong to the tenderer's group, especially when the contracting amounts exceed €10 million. In such cases, the contracting authority will aim to ensure that at least 30% of the value of the contract is subcontracted.

b) Grants and prizes

In addition, the EU Space Regulation includes grants and prizes as a way of financing certain space-related projects. There are different applicable criteria, all gearing towards attracting and fostering the entrepreneurial spirit within the research and innovation communities as well as private sectors across the EU Member States. For instance, in application of Art. 18(1), the Union can cover up to 100% of the eligible costs in spite of the application of the co-funding principle. Grants and prizes awarded can reach up to a maximum of €200,000. Article 20 enables assigning grants for pre-commercial procurement and procurement of innovative solutions. In such cases, the contractor shall own at least the intellectual property rights attached to the results. Moreover, "the contracting authorities shall enjoy at least royalty-free access rights to the results for their own use and the right to the right to grant, or require the contractor to grant, non-exclusive licences to third parties to exploit the results for the contracting authority under fair and reasonable conditions without any right to sub-licence".

Article 21 provides for the possibility to use "blending operations" to finance projects under the EU Space Programme. "Blending is the strategic use of a limited amount of grants to mobilise financing from partner financial institutions and the private sector to enhance the development impact of investment projects."[37] One of the main objectives of this instrument is to combine EU grants to mobilise private investments to get capital-intensive projects off the ground with a faster start. The private sector stakeholders can have a variety of roles in a project, since they can contribute to the financing either at the project level or in specific fund structures; they can benefit from EU support in order to access finance not available in the market or at the needed terms; and, in many cases, they will act as agents in the implementation of projects.[38]

A further financing possibility is the use of the "cumulative and alternative funding" mechanism provided by Art. 22, which provides that "an action that has received a contribution under the Programme may also receive a contribution from another Union programme". This is understandably under the condition that these do not cover the same costs, and that the rules of the relevant

36 Regulation (EU, Euratom) 2018/1046 of the European Parliament and of the Council of 18 July 2018 on the financial rules applicable to the general budget of the Union.

37 See European Commission's "Guidelines on EU blending operations", Publications Office of the European Union, November 2015.

38 Ibid.

Union Programme apply to the corresponding action. The cumulative financing available must not exceed the total eligible costs of the action. This mechanism aims at maximising the impact of funding possibilities made available across the EU's programmes and for different segments of the same space project since these tend to be capital and resource intensive. Additionally, Art. 23 indicates the possibility for the Commission or for EUSPA to conduct joint procurement procedures with ESA or other international organisations involved in the Programme components.

In light of the projects and ultimate Programme components at stake, the financing mechanisms made available for projects are key, if not the key to successful implementation. In comparison with the previous legal frameworks for Galileo and EGNOS and Copernicus, grouping the various possibilities of access to EU funding under the Regulation dedicated to the EU Space Programme indicates that the significance of financing mechanisms for such capital-intensive projects is recognised. While the maximum ceilings indicated for grants and prizes are unlikely to make or break a project by themselves, they are a tangible sign: they signal the public sector expert organisation's vote of confidence for a given project and provide the private stakeholders with a stepping stone to move closer to market.

2.5.3 Eligibility and participation conditions

Article 24 specifically addresses the eligibility and participation conditions for the procurement, grants, and prizes for the preservation of the security, integrity, and resilience of operational systems of the Union. It is understood that the overall aim of this article is to attempt to balance efforts to stimulate participation via the different calls and fund projects with promoting technological sovereignty of the EU and protecting its interest in this strategic domain. Before applying the eligibility and participation conditions, it is proposed that the Commission informs the Programme committee[39] and that it "shall take utmost account of the Member States' views on the scope of application of and the justification for those eligibility and participation conditions".

The provisions of Art. 24 further place a strong focus on the location of the legal entity, with requirements of (a) establishment and executive management structures being in the same Member State, (b) the work being carried out within Member States, and (c) the absence of decisive influence by a third country entity. The likely consequence from the outset is that a subsidiary of a company from outside the EU would have slim chances of being found eligible. The Commission may waive condition (c) if the Member State provides the guarantees that the controlling third country refrain from exercising controlling rights over or imposing reporting obligations on the legal entity in relation to the procurement, grant, or prize, and that the latter is not restricted in any manner in fulfilling the corresponding activities Art. 24(4).

In given cases where the specific technologies, goods, or services needed are not readily available within the EU, a legal entity with its management structures established in an EEA or EFTA member having concluded an agreement as per Art. 7, proposes to carry out the activities in such a country, the requirements of (a) or (b) above may be waived. In such cases, it must be shown that sufficient measures are implemented to ensure the protection of EU classified information (EUCI), in line with Art. 43 and that of the integrity, security, and resilience of the Programme's components, their operation, and their services. A legal entity from a third country could be eligible for procurements, grants, or prizes and on the condition that no substitute is readily available within the EU and provided that the EUCI provisions are met. It falls under the respon-

39 Article 107(1)(e), Space Regulation.

sibility of the Member State in which the legal entity is established to assess the guarantees of non-interference by a third country entity and the compliance with EUCI provisions. It is specified that the Commission shall comply with that assessment.

The above eligibility and participation conditions as well as the waiver conditions may create additional barriers for certain legal entities present within the territory of the EU but which have a parent company from a third country insofar as the security, integrity, and resilience of operational systems of the Union are concerned. It is clear that the innovating financing programmes, initiatives, and policies which are implemented to stimulate private sector participation are being balanced with the need to protect the EU's interests in the strategic domain of space in particular, to promote the technological sovereignty of the Union, its leadership, and its competitiveness.

2.6 Fostering the European space economy

The framework crafted by the EU Space Regulation is one expected to promote the open participation by new and established economic actors alike in the upstream and downstream sectors. Spurred by EU financial means and mechanisms, SMEs and start-ups are encouraged to exploit the huge potential of space data and services to develop value-adding applications. These means and mechanisms have been implemented in response also to the significant investments being made by the EU's global partners and competitors to stimulate their respective private sectors.

The "NewSpace" economy is not new *per se*. Private space companies have been heavily involved since the start of space exploration and utilisation over 60 years ago: NASA's Saturn V rocket was built by Boeing, McDonell Douglas, and North American[40] and ESA's ATV involved dozens of companies from ten European countries. What has boosted business and involvement of the private sector in space activities is the relatively recent significant reduction in the costs of access to space. The reduction in launch costs in the USA was the result of the involvement of private companies in the launch business, following a bill passed by the US Congress in 2010 about commercialisation and instructing NASA to buy launch services, post retirement of the Space Shuttle. The involvement of private actors in space spread to Europe although to a lesser extent than it did in the USA. It is the very involvement of the private sector in space that has resulted in a significant decrease of the costs of access to space. The decrease in itself attracts more commercial companies in many areas of the space business. Cheaper access to space means more private companies wish to get involved and coupled with the technological shifts happening, the costs are kept low or are further reduced. In the present situation, space is no longer just a publicly funded sector but is also a privately funded sector.

The current budget of €14.88 billion allocated by the Regulation does exceed the previous MFF budget and it must be recognised that within 20 years, the budgetary contribution to space policy has increased fourfold.[41] The increase in the budget for the years 2021–2027 underlines the EU expectations for space as an economic enabler with a positive spillover effect across various industries. According to EUSPA, the new EU Space Programme will generate an even higher return-on-investment through the creation of value-adding, safe and secure space-based services for the EU citizens, business, and governments alike. By 2025, space-related jobs across the Union should increase to 400,000.[42] Notwithstanding that in a regional and international comparison, ESA secured €16.9 bil-

40 For a recapitulation of entities involved, see Saturn Illustrated Chronology – Part 1: January 1966 through December 1966, January 1966.

41 €4.6bn from 2007 to 2013; €11.1bn from 2014 to 2020, MFF 2014–2020.

42 "The new European Union Space Programme a successful European cooperation paradigm" (2021) EUSPA, 22 June 2022.

lion at its 2022 Ministerial Council for projects over three years (a 17% increase compared to the 2019 Ministerial Council) and NASA had an annual budget of US$32.35 billion in 2023,[43] the different EU initiatives developed to incentivise private sector participation are gathering momentum.

2.6.1 Measures foreseen – the European approach

Globally, there is a significant rise in opportunities for the private sector, in the fields of Satellite Communications, Earth Observation, Microgravity Research, all underpinned by the availability of ever-advancing technologies, including edge computing and Artificial Intelligence for both ground and space segments. The different technologies, products, and services envisaged also mean that there are a number of existing and new categories of actors to consider: Academia, Start-ups, Space companies, Non-space companies, Institutions, and Investors, which calls for a "European approach" on many fronts.[44]

The Cassini (Competitive Space Start-ups for Innovation) space entrepreneurship initiative is an important element of this approach, to support innovative entrepreneurs, start-ups, and SMEs in the space industry, including NewSpace, during 2021–2027. All areas of the EU Space Programme are concerned and the initiative covers both upstream and downstream products and services. Cassini caters for a €1 billion EU seed and growth fund, also implementing hackathons and mentoring, prizes, business accelerator, partnering, and business matchmaking. One action under Cassini of particular interest is "Cassini Facility", directed at access to finance, in order to enable more space companies to raise risk capital. It provides capital to venture capital funds to be invested into EU-based companies developing and marketing space technology and digital services using space data. The aim is to get the start-ups access to the funding they need to scale up in the EU itself, and encourage more venture capital funds to invest in space and de-risk their investment. The Cassini fund is developed under the InvestEU umbrella, designed to stimulate capital markets in the EU. More specifically the European Commission can use the InvestEU Fund to address "sub-optimal investment situations and reduce the investment gap in targeted sectors", with space being eligible for financing and investment operations, particularly if in line with the objectives of the Space Strategy for Europe, which include "underpinning space entrepreneurship".[45]

Another financial measure is for the EU to lay the groundwork and facilitate procedures so that start-ups can have access to loans. Such an approach can be envisaged in conjunction with the European Investment Bank (EIB) and national commercial banks, so that the banks would be willing to take some of the risk. The EIB's investments in space-related projects date back to the 1980s and were then logically linked to legacy or traditional players. In recent times, it has also supported NewSpace projects.[46] Effective mechanisms must be implemented so that access to eligible entities, especially SMEs, is facilitated, which may well translate into an effective boost across the European sector.

The Commission's role *vis-à-vis* the private companies is also significant in the contractual relationship. Procurement of contracts will represent a large part of the business relationship between the Commission and the private actors. It is thought that a more constructive approach

43 See NASA figures, "The official source of government spending data", USASPENDING.gov.

44 See footnote 10 above.

45 European Parliament and European Council, Regulation (EU) 2021/523 of the European Parliament and of the Council of 24 March 2021 establishing the InvestEU Programme and amending Regulation (EU) 2015/1017.

46 European Investment Bank Announces first direct financing for a start-up in the European "New Space" sector – €20 million venture loan for Spire Global, European Commission, 3 December 2020.

would be for the Commission to act as an anchor-customer, buying services rather than to impose specific and strict requirements. Such an approach would be feasible for many of the Programme components as well as for programmes outside of the Regulation, such as Secure Connectivity, new launcher systems,[47] or synergies with the defence sector. In parallel, it would mean a significant change for the Commission which has relatively complex procurement rules.

The Horizon Europe funding programme for research and innovation for the period 2021–2027 includes the new European Innovation Council (EIC) and has a dedicated component dedicated to space projects, aiming to foster a globally competitive and innovative space sector. The EIC initiative itself consists of various programmes offering different funding possibilities, e.g. via blended finance, grants, and prizes, depending on given criteria. An additional tool as part of the overall European GNSS strategy for market uptake led by EUSPA is Fundamental Elements. It offers further complementary funding mechanisms for the development of downstream markets and to foster innovation based on Galileo, EGNOS, and the commercial users of Copernicus Fundamental Elements projects.[48]

2.7 Conclusion

The European space industry is exposed to competition mainly from the US and China, where the respective industries are largely sustained by the state. For the EU, the Space Regulation's objectives are to secure its leadership in space activities, foster innovative industries, safeguard autonomous access to space, and simplify governance via implementation of the Programme. These goals signal that Europe can and must acquire its share of the general growth in the global space economy. Viewed as a fundamental resource for the future of the EU economy, the commercial downstream space sector holds partly untapped potential. It is up to Europe to craft an efficient framework enabling access to this resource to use the substantial amount of data generated by space infrastructure for commercial activities. A European Investment Bank's report[49] indicates that in comparison with the USA in what is considered a race to attract and facilitate private investment and promote the downstream space sector, Europe is lagging behind partly due to a lesser availability of venture capital funds for early-stage start-ups. The various current and planned publicly funded initiatives to foster both demand and supply – from the EU and partners – of downstream services confirm that commercialisation is of strategic significance for Europe.

Legislative action, in the form of the EU Space Regulation, is being implemented as an enabling tool: it conveys more structure and clarity in the contents and governance of its Space Programme, enhanced competition stimulus to EU-wide (and beyond) research organisations and industry, and stimulates boundary conditions for established and new businesses to progress and be viable for the market and sustainable. The Regulation, in establishing synergies with other available funding sources and mechanisms of the EU, brings much-needed novelty and flexibility for the private sector. The key to success lies for the most part in the granular specifications of the applied funding mechanisms. These need to ensure streamlined and prompt access to funds and must be accompanied by overall demand creation and development of specific profitable markets.

47 At the time the Commission proposed the new Space Programme in 2008, it announced plans to aggregate the launch service needs of EU programmes and act as a smart customer of European reliable and cost-effective launch solutions building on actions started under the current budget period.

48 EUSPA, Fundamental Elements (updated 9 September 2022).

49 European Investment Bank: The future of the European space sector: How to leverage Europe's technological leadership and boost investments for space ventures (22 January 2019) (DOI: 10.2867/484965).

3

COMMERCIAL SPACE ACTIVITIES IN THE US

An overview of the current policy and regulatory framework

Catrina Melograna and Christopher Johnson[1]

Introduction

In the United States of America, commercial space activities are guided by and regulated through policies, laws, and regulations across the federal government. Shaped and informed by international treaty obligations, the US regulatory framework has evolved over decades and continues to develop as the space industry and the commercial sector grow. Given the prevalence of US space activities and how much US citizens and people worldwide rely on space services daily, it is not surprising that many government sectors touch space activities in some way. Given the robust and complex regulatory framework covering military, national security, civil, and commercial sectors, this chapter focuses only on commercial space activities, as opposed to government space activities.

Understanding the genesis of national space law in the US requires familiarity with the Outer Space Treaty and the international space law regime. As a signatory to the Outer Space Treaty,[2] the US implements its treaty obligations through national space legislation and regulation. As it applies to commercial activities, Article VI of the Outer Space Treaty obligates the US to authorise and continuously supervise the space activities of its *non-governmental* entities. Additionally, Article VI requires that states bear international responsibility for assuring that all national activities (governmental and non-governmental) conform with the Outer Space Treaty.[3] The US implements these obligations by creating a framework for licensing commercial space activities and

1 The authors would like to thank Audrey Allison, Mick Gleason, Diane Howard, and James Vedda for their suggestions on the topics in this chapter, and Jessica Noble for her contributions to an earlier version of this chapter.

2 Treaty on Principles Governing the Activities of States in the Exploration and Use of Outer Space, including the Moon and Other Celestial Bodies (1967) ("Outer Space Treaty").

3 Convention on International Liability for Damage Caused by Space Objects (1972) and Convention on Registration of Objects Launched into Outer Space (1975); see also Dempsey, Paul S., *The Emergence of National Space Law*, Annals Air & Space L. (2013).

 DOI: 10.4324/9781003268475-5

ensuring compliance and monitoring. While focusing on safety and promoting innovation as the space industry and space technologies mature, the US continuously develops its laws and regulations.

US space policy is prioritising the commercial sector and working to create a regulatory environment that promotes and fosters creativity and innovation, while also ensuring public safety. The commercial space sector has become more of a focus in US space policy as the federal government recognises its benefits, advantages, and utility. The importance of the commercial sector to all aspects of the US space enterprise is evident, and the regulatory framework is evolving.

While this chapter is only a broad survey of the vast US regulatory system, it strives to provide a helpful overview for commercial actors and a broader look at the relevant sources of national legislation in the US. It also touches on very recent space policies and regulations. US space law and regulation are rapidly changing and could look quite different in the coming months and years. It is an exciting time for the US space industry and space lawyers. This chapter is current as of Fall 2022. However, regulatory revisions are ongoing, and given the speed of innovation in the commercial sector and the growing need for stable and certain regulations, the rules will likely change accordingly. Research of the relevant US government websites and the Federal Register is recommended to keep up with the current rules. This chapter cites websites to help guide the reader to the official and most current governmental sources.

3.1 National space policy

3.1.1 The National Space Policy 2020

Current commercial space policy in the US is driven by the National Space Policy, the Space Priority Framework, and recent space policy directives. The 2020 National Space Policy[4] establishes principles and calls on all US government departments, agencies, and offices to implement them.[5] It states:

> The National Space Policy sets out the nation's commitment to leading in the responsible and constructive use of space, promoting a robust commercial space industry, returning Americans to the Moon and preparing for Mars, leading in exploration, and defending United States and allied interests in space.
>
> The National Space Policy recognizes that a robust, innovative, and competitive commercial space sector is foundational to economic development, continued progress, and sustained American leadership in space. It commits the United States to facilitating growth of an American commercial space sector that supports the nation's interests, is globally competitive, and advances American leadership in the generation of new markets and innovation-driven entrepreneurship.[6]

The US National Space Policy establishes the following principles related to commercial space:

4 Trump Administration, *National Space Policy of the United States of America*, 9 Dec. 2020, replacing the 2010 National Space Policy and reemphasised implementing the various Trump administration Space Policy Directives, 85 Federal Register 242, 81755, 16 Dec. 2020.

5 A year later, in 2021, the Biden-Harris Administration built upon and developed this policy with its Space Priorities Framework.

6 *Id.*

- A robust, innovative, and competitive commercial space sector is the source of continued progress and sustained United States leadership in space. The United States remains committed to encouraging and facilitating the continued growth of a domestic commercial space sector that is globally competitive, supports national interests, and advances United States leadership in the generation of new markets and innovation-driven entrepreneurship.
- As established in international law, outer space, including the Moon and other celestial bodies, is not subject to national appropriation by claim of sovereignty, by means of use or occupation, or by any other means. The United States will pursue the extraction and utilization of space resources in compliance with applicable law, recognizing those resources as critical for sustainable exploration, scientific discovery, and commercial operations.[7]

Importantly for the commercial sector, the National Space Policy calls for the government to incentivise the commercial space industry, and commercial industry involvement is woven throughout many of the principles, goals, and cross-sector guidelines. The Policy also calls for the strengthening of interagency and commercial partnerships to be facilitated by the National Space Council's Executive Secretary and agency heads.[8] The Policy also provides goals and guidelines relating to international cooperation, space environment, and export controls. The National Space Policy reemphasises the Space Policy Directives released during the Trump Administration and are discussed in subsequent sections.[9]

Since the release of the latest National Space Policy and various Space Policy Directives, government agencies and offices have been working to achieve the various listed principles, goals, and guidelines but rely on Congress for authorisation and funding. Indeed, implementation can be limited due to budget constraints as Congress authorises and appropriates specific funds which are guided by annual budgets.

3.1.2 United States Space Priority Framework

At the end of 2021, the Biden Administration released the US Space Priority Framework ("the Framework").[10] As mentioned above, this Framework elaborated on the previous Administration's National Space Policy. These documents build upon each other providing foundation and guidance and allowing subsequent policies to improve upon the ones before them. In a time where space innovation and technology are outpacing regulation and space mission timelines are counting down, it is critical that the fundamental principles remain consistent as leadership changes. This Framework is an example of this process.

Heavily focused on the commercial space industry, innovation, sustainability, and national security, the Framework provides an important mandate for the US government to the commercial industry. "The United States will foster a policy and regulatory environment that enables a competitive and burgeoning US commercial space sector."[11] It adds:

> U.S. regulations must provide clarity and certainty for the authorization and continuing supervision of non-governmental space activities, including for novel activities such as

7 *Id.*, 3–4.
8 *Id.*, 11.
9 *See* 85 FR 81755, *supra.*
10 Biden-Harris Administration, *United States Space Priorities Framework*, 9 Dec. 2021.
11 *Id.*, 5.

> on-orbit servicing, orbital debris removal, space-based manufacturing, commercial human spaceflight, and recovery and use of space resources. To create free and fair market competition internationally, the United States will work with allies and partners to update and harmonize space policies, regulations, export controls, and other measures that govern commercial activities worldwide.[12]

Additionally, the Framework laid out goals for strengthening international rules by engaging with international partners, allies, and the commercial sector to "promote the implementation of existing measures and lead in the development of new measures that contribute to the safety, stability, security, and long-term sustainability of space activities".[13] Finally, the Framework discussed space situational awareness sharing and sustainability.[14]

3.1.3 Presidential directives

US presidents establish space policies through presidential directives.[15] The directives prescribe goals and priorities for the government to implement through programs and regulations. Several of the government organisations currently involved in implementing commercial space policy include the Office of Science and Technology Policy (OSTP), National Security Council (NSC), National Space Council (NSpC), National Oceanic and Atmospheric Administration (NOAA) and the Department of Commerce (DoC)'s Office of Space Commerce (OSC), Office of Space and Advanced Technology in the Department of State, Federal Communications Commissions (FCC), National Aeronautics and Space Administration (NASA), and the Federal Aviation Administration (FAA)'s Office of Commercial Space Transportation (AST). In sum, space policy directives provide tasks and goals for federal agencies to achieve, and agencies amend or draft regulations and programs to implement them.

From 2017 to 2021, the Trump administration released seven space policy directives relating to issues from commercial space to nuclear power and propulsion. As discussed above, on 9 December 2020, the Trump administration issued the latest National Space Policy directive, replacing the 2010 National Space Policy.[16]

Additionally, presidents can issue a type of directive called an Executive Order.[17] Executive Orders are legally binding and published on the Federal Register. They direct the federal government to act in certain ways or accomplish particular tasks but do not require congressional approval.[18] The Trump Administration issued several important Executive Orders, including reviving the National Space Council and the use of space resources. The following sections describe the recent Space Policy Directives and Executive Orders.

12 *Id.*

13 *Id.*, 7.

14 *Id.*

15 *See* Congressional Research Service, *Presidential Directives: An Introduction*, 13 Nov. 2019.

16 Trump, Donald J., *National Space Policy Directive*, 9 Dec. 2020.

17 Congressional Research Service, *Presidential Directives: An Introduction, supra.*

18 *Id.* Note that Congress can vote on legislation to make it difficult to carry out Executive Orders, like eliminating funding. The President "manages the operations of the Executive branch of Government through Executive orders. After the President signs an Executive order, the White House sends it to the Office of the Federal Register (OFR)". American Bar Association, *What is an Executive Order?*, 25 Jan. 2021.

3.1.4 Space Policy Directives

Starting in 2017, the Trump Administration released the following Space Policy Directives (SPDs). Since the release of SPD-1, the US Government has been working on implementation in various ways.

SPD-1 – Reinvigorating America's Human Space Exploration Program

On 11 December 2017, SPD-1 called on the US government to

> [l]ead an innovative and sustainable program of exploration with commercial and international partners to enable human expansion across the solar system and to bring back to Earth new knowledge and opportunities. Beginning with missions beyond low-Earth orbit, the United States will lead the return of humans to the Moon for long-term exploration and utilization, followed by human missions to Mars and other destinations.[19]

This policy brought a focus on US-led exploration of the Moon, Mars, and beyond with commercial and international partners. On 13 October 2020, NASA, along with several other countries, signed the Artemis Accords. The Artemis Accords, building on SPD-1, incorporate the principles in the Outer Space Treaty and aim to send humans back to the Moon.

SPD-2 – Streamlining Regulations on Commercial Use of Space

On 28 May 2018, SPD-2 called on the executive agencies to review and implement regulations consistent with the recent space policy and to work with the National Space Council in these reviews. Specifically, SPD-2 directed the DoT to review commercial launch and reentry spaceflight regulations on licensing and to consider:

> (i) requiring a single license for all types of commercial space flight launch and re-entry operations; and
> (ii) replacing prescriptive requirements in the commercial space flight launch and re-entry licensing process with performance-based criteria.[20]

Further, Section 3 directed the Secretary of Commerce to:

> in coordination with the Secretary of State and the Secretary of Defense, shall transmit to the Director of the Office of Management and Budget a legislative proposal to encourage expansion of the licensing of commercial remote sensing activities.[21]

As part of its SPD-2 implementation, the FAA published a Notice of Proposed Rulemaking (NPRM) to streamline its launch licence process and regulations. It received comments from the industry and eventually released its Streamlined Licensing regulations in Part 450. The new rule

19 Trump, Donald J., *SPD-1 Reinvigorating America's Human Space Exploration Program*, 11 Dec. 2017.
20 Trump, Donald J., *SPD-2, Streamlining Regulations on Commercial Use of Space*, 28 May 2018.
21 *Id.*

"amends 14 CFR parts 415, 417, 431, and 435 by consolidating, updating, and streamlining all launch and reentry regulations into a single part 450".[22]

Another important aspect of SPD-2 is the call to reorganise the DoC to "consolidate in the Office of the Secretary of Commerce the responsibilities of the Department of Commerce with respect to the Department's regulation of commercial space flight activities".[23] Further, it directed the Secretary of Commerce to "transmit to the Director of the Office of Management and Budget a legislative proposal to create within the Department of Commerce an entity with primary responsibility for administering the Department's regulation of commercial space flight activities".[24]

SPD-3 – National Space Traffic Management Policy

On 18 June 2018, SPD-3 called on executive departments and agencies to pursue the following goals:

> Advance Space Situational Awareness (SSA) and Space Traffic Management (STM) Science and Technology; mitigate the effect of orbital debris on space activities; encourage and facilitate US commercial leadership in science and technology, SSA, and STM; provide US Government-supported basic SSA data and basic STM services to the public; improve SSA data interoperability and enable greater SSA data sharing; SSA data must be timely and accurate; develop STM standards and best practices; prevent unintentional radio frequency interference; improve the US domestic space object registry; develop policies and regulations for future US orbital operations.[25]

SPD-3 directs the departments and agencies to follow specific guidelines for "Managing the Integrity of the Space Operating Environment, Operating in a Congested Space Environment, and Strategies for Space Traffic Management in a Global Context".[26] Importantly for the commercial industry, SPD-3 calls for growing the commercial space industry with the encouragement and facilitation of commercial leadership in SSA, STM, and the related science and technology.[27]

Over the past several years, the United States Government has continued implementing SPD-3. For example, in 2021, the OSC was developing an Open Architecture Data Repository as one of the steps to providing "US Government-supported basic SSA data and basic STM services" to the public.[28]

SPD-4 – Establishment of the United States Space Force

On 19 February 2019, SPD-4 and the Fiscal Year 2020 National Defense Authorization Act established a new armed service, the US Space Force (USSF), within the Department of the US Air Force.[29] The USSF "organizes, trains, and equips space forces in order to protect US and allied

22 14 CFR Parts 401, 404, 413, 414, 415, 417, 420, 431, 433, 435, 437, 440, 450, and 460, Streamlined Launch and Reentry License Requirements, 2020.

23 SPD-2, *supra*.

24 *Id.*

25 Trump, Donald J., *SPD-3 National Space Traffic Management Policy*, 18 June 2018.

26 *Id.*

27 *Id.*

28 See SPD-3; see also Smith, Marcia, SpacePolicyOnline, *Biden Administration Embraces Office of Space Commerce in FY2023 Budget*, 29 Mar. 2022; see also the Aerospace Corporation, *Paving an Integrated Approach for Space's Traffic Jam Problem*, 30 Mar. 2022.

29 Trump, Donald J., *SPD-4, Establishment of US Space Force*, 19 Feb. 2019.

interests in space and to provide space capabilities to the joint force. USSF responsibilities will include developing Guardians, acquiring military space systems, maturing the military doctrine for space power, and organizing space forces to present to our Combatant Commands".[30] Although the USSF was established, the US Space Command is still active as the "warfighting component that actively employs forces from the US Army, Marine Corps, Navy, Air Force and Space Force to accomplish the mission in space".[31]

SPD-5 – Cybersecurity Principles for Space Systems

On 4 September 2020, President Trump signed SPD-5 requesting that "[c]ybersecurity principles and practices that apply to terrestrial systems also apply to space systems",[32] but that due to the nature of space systems, like physical inaccessibility and remote incidents, there are particular things that are more important when dealing with space systems and space activities. The effect on commercial space operators is the need to implement cybersecurity and protection measures into their systems to help ensure, among other things, their "ability to verify the integrity, confidentiality, and availability of critical functions and the missions, services, and data they enable and provide".[33]

SPD-6 – National Strategy for Space Nuclear Power and Propulsion (SNPP)

On 16 December 2020, President Trump signed SPD-6 establishing a "national strategy to ensure the development and use of SNPP systems when appropriate to enable and achieve the scientific, exploration, national security, and commercial objectives of the United States" with commercial industry and international partners.[34] Importantly for the commercial sector, SPD-6 directs the Secretary of Commerce to:

> promote responsible United States commercial SNPP investment, innovation, and use, and shall, when consistent with the authorities of the Secretary, ensure the publication of clear, flexible, performance-based rules that are applicable to use of SNPP and are easily navigated. Under the direction of the Secretary of Commerce, the Department of Commerce (DOC) shall ascertain and communicate the views of private-sector partners and potential private-sector partners to relevant agency partners in order to facilitate public-private collaboration in SNPP development and use.[35]

SPD-7 – The United States Space-Based Positioning, Navigation, and Timing Policy

On 15 January 2021, President Trump signed SPD-7 calling for "implementation actions and guidance for United States space-based positioning, navigation, and timing (PNT) programs and activities for United States national and homeland security, civil, commercial, and scientific purposes".[36]

30 *Id.*
31 US Space Command, *Frequently Asked Questions.*
32 Trump, Donald J., *SPD-5 Cybersecurity Principles for Space Systems*, 4 Sept. 2020.
33 *Id.*
34 Trump, Donald J., *SPD-6 National Strategy for Space Nuclear Power and Propulsion*, 16 Dec. 2020.
35 *Id.*
36 Trump, Donald J., *SPD-5 The United States Space-Based Positioning, Navigation, and Timing Policy*, 15 Jan. 2021.

3.1.5 Executive Orders

As mentioned above, presidents can issue Executive Orders to further their policy objectives. President Trump issued two important Executive Orders between 2017 and 2020, *Reviving the National Space Council* and *Encouraging International Support for the Recovery and Use of Space Resources*, discussed in the following sections.

3.1.6 US policy councils

There are several councils dedicated to advising the president and Executive Branch on space issues and policies. The National Aeronautics and Space Act of 1958 established the National Aeronautics and Space Council.[37] Operating from 1958 until 1973, it tracked aeronautical and space activities. It was also tasked to create a US space program. An updated council was established in 1989 by President George H. W. Bush.[38] This new council reviewed and advised the president on space policy and strategy and made recommendations to the president. It also "monitored and coordinated implementation" of the president's space policy objectives.[39]

More recently, on 30 June 2017, President Trump, through Executive Order, revived the National Space Council (NSpC) from 1989.[40] Regarding commercial policy, Section 3 provides:

> (a) The Council shall advise and assist the President regarding national space policy and strategy, and perform such other duties as the President may, from time to time, prescribe.
> (b) In particular, the Council is directed to:
>
> ...
>
> (iv) foster close coordination, cooperation, and technology and information exchange among the civil, national security, and commercial space sectors.

The current National Space Council is made up of government agency leaders and is chaired by the Vice President. In 2021, President Biden's Executive Order expanded the NSpC to include a more diverse set of members, including members from the Departments of Labor, Education, Agriculture, Interior, and the National Climate Advisor.[41] Further, it includes more robust participation by the Office of Management and Budget and now sits within the Office of the Vice President.

Several other policy councils advise the Executive Branch on space matters. In 1976, Congress, through the National Science and Technology Policy, Organization, and Priorities Act of 1976, created the White House Office of Science and Technology Policy (OSTP) to "consider prob-

37 Title II Coordination of Aeronautical and Space Activities National Aeronautics and Space Council. Sec. 201(a).

38 Bush, G.H.W., *Executive Order 12675 Establishing the National Space Council*, 20 April 1989.

39 *Id.* at Sec. 2 (b)(1)–(4).

40 Trump, Donald. J., *Executive Order 13803 Reviving the National Space Council*, 30 June 2017, 82 FR 31429, amended membership with *Executive Order Amending Executive Order 13803 – Reviving the National Space Council*, 13 Feb. 2020.

41 The White House, *Executive Order on the National Space Council*, 1 Dec. 2021. The new members join the Secretaries of State, Defense, Commerce, Transportation, Energy and Homeland Security; the Directors of National Intelligence; Office of Management and Budget; and Office of Science and Technology Policy; NASA Administrator; Assistants to the President for National Security Affairs, Economic Policy, and Domestic Policy; and the Chairman of the Joint Chiefs of Staff.

lems and developments in the fields of science, engineering, and technology and related activities affecting more than one Federal agency, and shall recommend policies and other measures".[42] Today the OSTP advises the Executive Branch on space issues and policy in addition to other science and technology policy issues.

In 1993, President Bill Clinton established the National Science and Technology Council, an interagency body to, among other things, "coordinate the science and technology policy-making process" and integrate policy across the federal government through implementing programs.[43]

3.1.7 Other important documents

3.1.7.1 Encouraging International Support for the Recovery and Use of Space Resources

In November 2015, President Barack Obama signed into law the US Commercial Space Launch Competitiveness Act allowing US companies to legally own and sell space resources they mine.[44] Building upon the 2015 Act, President Trump issued an Executive Order on *Encouraging International Support for the Recovery and Use of Space Resources*.[45] This order made it clear that the US views the recovery and use of space resources as legal, and that US citizens have the right to engage in these activities. Additionally, the order clarifies that the US is not a party to the Moon Agreement,[46] nor does it view the Moon Agreement to be an "effective or necessary instrument to guide nation states regarding the promotion of commercial participation in the long-term exploration, scientific discovery, and use of the Moon, Mars, or other celestial bodies".[47]

Despite the apparent purpose of the order to encourage commercial growth in this area of the space industry, internationally and domestically, some viewed this order as controversial.[48] However, it laid the groundwork for the subsequent Artemis Accords and its principles on resource extraction. Indeed, while the EO may have been viewed negatively by some when first released, countries continue to join the Artemis Accords, and as of this writing, 21 countries have signed.[49]

3.1.7.2 Orbital Debris Mitigation Standard Practices

In 2001, the United States Government Orbital Debris Mitigation Standard Practices (ODMSP) were created in response to the increasing amount of orbital debris.[50] NASA and others developed standard practices to "limit the generation of new, long-lived debris by the control of debris released during normal operations, minimizing debris generated by accidental explosions, the

42 42 USC 6651.

43 Clinton, W., *Executive Order 12881 Establishment of the National Science and Technology Council*, 23 Nov. 1993.

44 51 U.S. Code § 51302 Commercial exploration and commercial recovery.

45 Trump, Donald. J., *Executive Order on Encouraging International Support for the Recovery and Use of Space Resources*, 6 Apr. 2020.

46 Agreement Governing Activities of States on the Moon and Other Celestial Bodies, 18 Dec. 1979, 1363 UNTS 3 (The "Moon Agreement"). With only 18 signatories, the Moon Agreement is the least signed treaty in the international space law regime and is the only treaty addressing resource utilisation and discusses specifically lunar resources.

47 *Id.*

48 *See* Freeland, Steven & Annie Handmer, *Giant Leap for Corporations? The Trump Administration Wants to Mine Resources in Space, But is it Legal?*, The Conversation, 20 Apr. 2020.

49 DoS, Office of the Spokesperson, *First Meeting of Artemis Accords Signatories*, 19 Sept. 2022.

50 See U.S. Government Orbital Debris Mitigation Standard Practices, November 2019 Update, 1 ("ODMSP 2019").

selection of safe flight profile and operational configuration to minimize accidental collisions, and postmission disposal of space structures".[51] These standard practices apply not only to government missions but also to licensed commercial activities. The federal agencies with regulatory authority implement these standard practices into their licensing requirements. For example, the FCC requires an applicant to describe its debris mitigation strategy.[52]

In recent years, the orbital debris concern has grown, given the significant increase in debris. Indeed, there was a clear need for an update to the standard practices. In 2018, SPD-3 tasked NASA to lead a working group including the Sectaries of State, Defense, Commerce, Transportation, the Director of National Intelligence, and the Chairperson of the FCC to update the ODMSP and "establish new guidelines for satellite design and operation".[53] In 2019, NASA released the ODMSP update that included limiting the probability of debris generating events for missions, and clarified definitions of types of operations including "large constellations", "CubeSats", and "rendezvous, proximity operations, and satellite servicing" and designated standard practices for the different types.[54] While the update has been criticised for not decreasing the 25-year maximum de-orbit/disposal standard, the preamble provides for revisits to the standards: "[t]he USG intends to update and refine the ODMSP as necessary in the future to address advances in both technology and policy".[55]

3.2 US National law and regulation

3.2.1 Title 51 of the United States Code (USC)

Title 51 of the United States Code (USC) is the primary source of national space legislation regulating commercial space activities and includes the following regulatory topics: Devotion of Space Activities to Peaceful Purposes for the Benefit of Humankind; Aeronautical and Space Activities for Welfare and Security of the United States; Commercial Use of Space; Objectives of Aeronautical and Space Activities; Ground Propulsion Systems Research and Development; Bioengineering Research, Development, and Demonstration Programs; and Warning and Mitigation of Potential Hazards of Near-Earth Objects. Title 51 also includes the 1958 National Aeronautics and Space Act, the 1984 Commercial Space Launch Act, the 1992 Land Remote Sensing Policy Act, the Commercial Space Launch Act Amendments Act of 2004, and the 2015 Commercial Space Launch Competitiveness Act.

3.3 Overview of relevant regulatory authorities

Several separate US governmental agencies regulate US commercial space activities, and will be explored more later in this chapter.

3.3.1 The Federal Communications Commission

The Federal Communications Commission (FCC) is authorised to implement and enforce US satellite communications regulations.

51 *Id.*, 1.
52 Described in more detail in the FCC section.
53 Trump, SPD-3 Sec. 6(b), *supra*.
54 ODMSP 2019, 7, *supra*.
55 *Id.*, 1.

3.3.2 The Federal Aviation Administration

The Federal Aviation Administration (FAA) (under the Department of Transportation) is authorised to regulate commercial launch and reentry licences and commercial spaceport licences. The FAA's Office of Commercial Space Transportation (AST) works on these commercial space activities.

3.3.3 Department of Commerce

The National Oceanic and Atmospheric Association (NOAA) (under the Department of Commerce) regulates commercial remote sensing activities. Within NOAA is the Office of Space Commerce (OSC), which is the main office handling commercial space policy activities.[56]

3.4 Other government space organisations

3.4.1 Office of Space Affairs

The office handling international and diplomatic affairs relating to space is the Department of State Office of Space Affairs (SA), within the Department of State's Bureau of Oceans and International Environmental and Scientific Affairs (OES). Its mission is to carry "out diplomatic and public diplomacy efforts to strengthen American leadership in space exploration, applications, and commercialization by increasing understanding of, and support for, US national space policies and programs and to encourage the foreign use of US space capabilities, systems, and services".[57] SA is the head of the US delegation at the United Nations Committee on Peaceful Uses of Outer Space plenary sessions, the Department of State Legal is head of the delegation for the Legal Subcommittee, and NASA is the head of the US delegation for the Science and Technical Subcommittee. Additionally, SA maintains the national space object registry and leads the international consultations on space policy and law.[58]

3.4.2 The National Aeronautics and Space Administration

NASA is the most recognised name in space. The National Aeronautics and Space Act established NASA in 1958. It is a governmental organisation that collaborates closely with the commercial industry and partners with commercial space companies on many of its missions.[59]

3.4.3 Office of Emerging Security Challenges

Within the Department of State is the Bureau of Arms Control, Verification and Compliance (AVC) which works on United States security in space. Under the AVC is the Office of Emerging Security Challenges (ESC). Its mission is to "enhance America's space security and missile defense cooperation among America's allies and partners".

56 Office of Space Commerce Act Committee on Science, Space, and Technology House Report, 114–797, 28 Sept. 2016.

57 Office of Space Affairs, *Our Mission*.

58 *Id.*; US Mission UNVIE, *USA at the 2002 COPUOS Scientific and Technical Subcommittee*, 7 Feb. 2022.

59 NASA, *2019: A Year in Review – The State of NASA Procurement*, 2019.

3.5 Licensing commercial space activities

Currently, there are three main areas in which commercial space activities are licensed and supervised: spectrum use/allocation; launch and reentry; and remote sensing. Multiple federal agencies and internal offices handle these three areas. When working to obtain licences and authorisations, space companies may work with several different agencies and departments. Additionally, the law may require companies to obtain export control licences when their space activities use items or data found on the US munitions or commerce control lists.[60] The following sections are broken down into the three categories and discuss the relevant frameworks.

3.5.1 Spectrum allocation, coordination, management, and licensing

Satellites use radiofrequency spectrum (a region of the electromagnetic spectrum) to communicate with other satellites or to send and receive signals from ground stations. In the US, frequency bands are allocated for different radiocommunication services, and many operators share frequencies in those bands. Therefore, to avoid harmful interference during missions and ensure services can be delivered as planned, spectrum is allocated, coordinated, managed, and regulated. In the US the FCC and the National Telecommunications and Information Administration (NTIA) oversee these communications, including the allocations and licensing. Additionally, as this is an inherently international endeavour, the International Telecommunication Union facilitates the convening of nations to work together on spectrum use.

While not every commercial space operator needs to obtain a launch licence, nearly every company operating a satellite will need to use spectrum.[61] The necessity of applying, paying, and waiting for a spectrum licence is often overlooked by new space actors. Indeed, it is one of the first things operators should think and strategise about when planning operations. It can take years to get certain non-governmental spectrum licences or geostationary orbital slots, and if a company's mission is not deployed by a certain date, it risks losing the licence.[62][63] This section provides an overview of US spectrum management, licences, and relevant regulations.

3.5.1.1 Federal Communications Commission

The Communications Act of 1934 established the Federal Communications Commission ("FCC"). It provided the FCC with authority to regulate the communications sector as an "independent U.S.

60 22 CFR Part 121, The United States Munitions List.

61 FCC, *Further Streamlining Part 25 Rules Governing Satellite Services*, 5, 19 Nov. 2020, 35 FCC Rcd 13285 (16): "The Commission also extended the requirement for complete deployment of an authorized NGSO system from six years to nine years".

62 FCC "coordinates use of the spectrum with the National Telecommunications and Information Administration (NTIA), which consults with affected Federal agencies". FCC, *Allocation of Spectrum for Non-Federal Space Launch Operations; Amendment of Part 2 of the Commission's Rules for Federal Earth Stations Communicating with Non-Federal Fixed Satellite Service Space Stations; and Federal Space Station Use of the 399.9-400.05 MHz band*, FCC Fact Sheet, 1 Apr. 2021, FCC-CIRC2104-02, 4.

63 ITU, *ITU Members agree to new milestones for non-geostationary satellite deployment*, ITU News, 30 Jan. 2020. "Under the newly adopted regulatory regime, these systems will have to deploy 10% of their constellation within 2 years after the end of the current regulatory period for bringing into use, 50% within 5 years and complete the deployment within 7 years."

government agency overseen by Congress", and is "responsible for implementing and enforcing America's communications law and regulations".[64]

The process of regulating radiocommunications is complex, and with satellite communications, it includes many details and requirements for spectrum use licences. At a very high level, the FCC regulates by establishing domestic regulations through the Rulemaking Process and coordinates spectrum use and orbital slot placement internationally with the ITU.[65] The FCC manages spectrum allocation for governmental and commercial uses and can modify those frequency allocations.[66] This means, in the US, certain frequency bands are approved (or allocated) for certain uses. For example, when a commercial company seeks a licence to use a certain frequency band for a mission or for services, like providing satellite internet in the Ku-band, it must verify FCC allocation of that band for the desired use and duration. In certain circumstances, the FCC may need to go through the Rulemaking Process before commercial operators can obtain a licence for certain uses of certain bands.[67] Indeed, there are service and licensing rules for different radio services (i.e. Fixed-Satellite, Mobile-Satellite, etc.) in different frequency bands.

Therefore, to operate in the US, satellite operators must obtain a licence (or "market access" for systems licensed outside of the US). The International Bureau (IB) within the FCC oversees US licensing and market access.[68] Additionally, applicants pay filing fees, and once licensed, pay annual regulatory fees, and ITU fees.[69] In certain cases, the FCC requires additional fees.

Commercial operators can apply for licences under the commercial or experimental categories.[70][71] Part 25 provides the required authorisations and rules for two types of satellites, geostationary (GSO) and non-geostationary (NGSO),[72] and Subpart B provides the general licensing requirements. In 2018, the FCC proposed a third category of satellite licensing applicants in addition to geostationary satellites and non-geostationary satellites. Due to the increasing number of small satellite operators and their use of spectrum, this third new category for small satellites would streamline licensing but still require debris mitigation.[73] The goal was to "enable satellites that have shorter missions, less intensive spectrum use, and lower risk of producing orbital debris

64 FCC, *About the FCC*.

65 On 3 November 2022, FCC Chairwoman Rosenworcel announced plans to modernise the FCC by establishing a Space Bureau and Office of International Affairs. The International Bureau will "reorganize into Space Bureau and a standalone Office of International Affairs to better support the agency's statutory obligations". FCC, Commission Documents, *Chairwoman Rosenworcel Proposes Space Bureau*, 3 Nov. 2022.

66 *Id.*; 47 CFR Section 2.106. Within the FCC is the Office of Engineering and Technology (OET) which advises the FCC on technical and policy issues and tasks and maintains the US Table of Frequency Allocations. FCC, *Radio Spectrum Allocation*. The FCC handles non-government use and the NTIA (DOC) handles spectrum for government use. "Both agencies work together to ensure that policy decisions promote spectrum use consistent with both US economic interests and government user requirements." *Id.* See also FCC, Engineering & Technology.

67 See FCC, Significant Satellite Rulemakings; see also FCC, My IBFS.

68 See FCC, International Bureau Satellite Division.

69 See FCC, Fees.

70 47 CFR Part 25 (commercial licences); 47 CFR Part 5 (experimental licences).

71 FCC, Streamlining Licensing Procedures for Small Satellite, FCC Fact Sheet, 2018 and Report and Order, IB Docket 18–86.

72 47 CFR § 25.114 Applications for space station authorisations.

73 FCC Report and Order, IB Docket 18–86.

to be licensed on a streamlined basis".[74] The final rule provided the qualification requirements for the small satellite streamlined process.[75] [76]

Under Part 5 Experimental Radio Service covers licensing experimental spectrum use.[77] An experimental licence is temporary and is not typically allowed for commercial use.[78] Licences under Part 5 are for activities such as technical demonstrations, product development, or equipment testing.

The FCC is updating its regulations on spectrum licensing which will be discussed in the future developments section in this chapter.

3.5.1.2 Space station and Earth station licensing process

Satellite operators need to consider the entire satellite system in their plans, including components located in space and on the ground. They must also have "reasonable certainty while developing their satellite systems, that suitable locations will be available for the siting of gateway Earth stations that will connect and route user traffic".[79]

3.5.1.3 Orbital debris mitigation

In its licensing authorisation, the FCC includes orbital debris mitigation requirements, including end-of-life and decommissioning plans.[80] In 2020, the FCC's new rule Mitigation of Orbital Debris in the New Space Age was published.[81] It updated the orbital debris mitigation requirements and end-of-life disposal plans.[82]

3.5.1.4 The International Telecommunication Union

The ITU convenes the World Radiocommunication Conferences (WRC) at which international regulations called the Radio Regulations (RR) are revised and adopted.[83] The FCC, State Department,

74 *Id.*, 4–5.

75 See FCC Fact Sheet, *Further Streamlining Part 25 Rules Governing Satellite Services Report and Order* – IB Docket No. 18-314, 47 CFR Parts 1 and 25.

76 85 FR 43711, 47 CFR 1, 47 CFR 25 at III (B) (2020).

77 47 CFR Part 5; see also 47 CFR Part 5 § 5.64 Special provisions for satellite systems, (b) "Except where the satellite system has already been authorized by the FCC, applicants for an experimental authorization involving a satellite system must submit a description of the design and operational strategies the satellite system will use to mitigate orbital debris, including the following information".

78 47 CFR § 5.71 Licence period.

79 Citing 47 CFR § 25.114 and 47 CFR § 25.137(b). FCC, *Further Streamlining Part 25 Rules Governing Satellite Services*, 2, 19 Nov. 2020, 35 FCC 13285 (16).

80 47 USC §307 "public interest" authority from the Communications Act of 1934, as amended. "When the Commission adopted debris mitigation rules applying to satellites across all service types, the Commission concluded that its authority to review orbital debris mitigation plans fell within its responsibilities and obligations under the Act, derived from its authority with respect to authorizing radio communications." 85 FR 52422 A(1). However, the authority to set requirements and debris mitigation rules is not explicit. Indeed, some consider this subject to interpretation that has not yet been challenged. The FCC's recent announcement to change the 25-year rule to five years is discussed later in the "Recent developments" section.

81 *Id.*; 86 FR 52101.

82 47 CFR §25.114 (D)(1).

83 ITU Radio Regulations; ITU, World Radiocommunication Conferences; *see* NASA, *Spectrum 101 – An Introduction to National Aeronautics and Space Administration Spectrum Management*, Feb. 2016.

and NTIA represent the US at the ITU.[84] All ITU countries have a "notifying administration" and in the US it is the FCC.[85] Importantly, commercial operators play a critical role at the ITU and are involved in developing the international standards for satellite communications.[86]

3.5.2 Launch and reentry

A US citizen or commercial launch operator planning to launch a rocket anywhere in the world must obtain authorisation and a licence. Within the Department of Transportation, the Federal Aviation Administration's Office of Commercial Space Transportation (AST) is the licensing authority.

3.5.2.1 Federal Aviation Administration

Congress established the Department of Transportation in 1966 to foster a safe, efficient, and modern national transportation system. In 1926, Congress passed the Air Commerce Act, placing the Secretary of Commerce in charge of aviation matters like air commerce, air traffic, and aircraft certification. Over the years, these duties and authorities evolved. The FAA was established in 1958, separately from the DoT. Eventually, the FAA became part of the DoT, and the Office of Commercial Space Transportation (AST) was established, with its commercial licensing regulations taking effect in 1988.[87]

The FAA AST's goals are to:

- Regulate the U.S. commercial space transportation industry, to ensure compliance with international obligations of the United States, and to protect the public health and safety, safety of property, and national security and foreign policy interests of the United States;
- Encourage, facilitate, and promote commercial space launches and reentries by the private sector;
- Recommend appropriate changes in Federal statutes, treaties, regulations, policies, plans, and procedures; and
- Facilitate the strengthening and expansion of the United States space transportation infrastructure.[88]

President Trump's Space Policy Directive-2 in 2018 tasked the FAA to consider streamlining commercial regulations for licensing:[89]

The Secretary of Transportation shall consider the following:

(i) requiring a single license for all types of commercial space flight launch and re-entry operations; and

84 *Id.*
85 ITU, Notification Agency List.
86 ITU, Regulation of Satellite Systems.
87 FAA, *Regulatory Impact Analysis – Streamlined Launch and Reentry Licensing Requirements Final Rule 09-17-2020.*
88 51 U.S. Code § 50903 – General authority gives the Secretary of Transportation authority to regulate commercial launches and reentries.
89 The White House, *Space Policy Directive-2, Streamlining Regulations on Commercial Use of Space*, 24 May 2018.

(ii) replacing prescriptive requirements in the commercial space flight launch and re-entry licensing process with performance-based criteria.[90]

Subsequently, the FAA reorganised into the Office of Operational Safety and the Office of Strategic Management. Currently, the Office of Operational Safety (OOS) manages pre-application consultations, licences, permits, and waivers, while the Strategic Management Office works on guidance and research and manages the Office of Spaceports.

FAA regulations are in Title 14, Chapter III of the CFR. These regulations require a licence for commercial space launch and reentry activities, including operating commercial spaceports.[91] In 2020, the FAA updated the regulations, condensing the rules from four separate Parts into one Part. Additionally, the new rules allow a single licence for multiple launches. In October 2020, FAA published the final rule,[92] which went into effect on 10 March 2021.[93] It combined Parts 415, 417, 431, and 435 into Part 450.

3.5.2.2 Application process

FAA AST approves the following: Launch/Reentry Operator Licenses, Experimental Permits, and Spaceports. When a launch operator applies for a licence, it will submit all required information for review and approval listed in Part 450.[94] This includes a "compliance document list" and an "application compliance list". Additionally, potential applicants are required to schedule a consultation with the FAA prior to applying. It is intended to help with the applicants' time and cost by identifying regulatory issues earlier in the planning stages.[95]

Currently, for expendable and reusable launch vehicles, the application process includes the pre-application consultation, policy review and approval, safety review and approval, payload review and determination, financial responsibility determination, and environmental review. After the licence is approved, the FAA requires compliance monitoring, during which operators must allow access to the government to observe its activities.[96] Additionally, a launch operator must show it will comply with orbital debris guidelines.

90 *Id.*

91 14 CFR III.

92 *Id.*

93 Currently, there is a moratorium on regulating commercial human space flight; crew and participants partake in commercial spaceflight under "informed consent". The FAA's Regulatory Impact Analysis – Streamlined Launch and Reentry Licensing Requirements Final Rule 09-17-2020 discusses the purpose of the streamlining rule: "[t]o streamline and simplify the licensing of launch and reentry operations by relying on performance-based regulations rather than prescriptive regulations. This action consolidates and revises multiple commercial space launch and reentry regulations addressing licensing into a single regulatory part that states safety objectives to be achieved for the launch of suborbital and orbital launch vehicles, and the reentry of reentry vehicles. This action also enables flexible timeframes, addresses duplicative ground safety regulations, redefines when launch begins to allow specified pre-flight operations prior to license approval, and allows applicants to seek a single license to launch from multiple sites. This rule is necessary to reduce the need to file and process waivers, improve clarity of the regulations, and relieve administrative and cost burdens on industry and the FAA." *Id.*

94 See FAA, *2021 Application Letter Template*, updated 3 Nov. 2020.

95 See FAA, *Pre-Application Consultation Checklist*, updated 3 Nov. 2020.

96 14 CFR 450.209.

3.5.2.3 Environmental requirements

When regulating launch and reentry, the FAA must follow environmental regulations.[97] The National Environmental Policy Act (NEPA) requires the FAA to assess potential environmental impacts of space activities on Earth before licensing (i.e. Environmental Review for Licensed/Permitted Commercial Space Transportation Activities).[98] If after evaluation there is a determination that the potential for environmental impact exists, the applicant must take any action deemed necessary in order to proceed with the application process.[99] The FAA must also consider other laws when regulating: Clean Air Act, Clean Water Act, Endangered Species Act, Marine Mammal Protection Act, National Historic Preservation Act, US Department of Transportation Act, Section 4(f), Executive Order 11990, Protection of Wetlands, Executive Order 11988, Floodplain Management, Executive Order 12114, Environmental Effects Abroad of Major Federal Actions, Executive Order 12898, Federal Actions to Address Environmental Justice in Minority Populations and Low-Income Populations, and Executive Order 13045, Protection of Children from Environmental Health Risks and Safety Risks.[100]

3.5.2.4 Commercial spaceports

The FAA also licenses commercial spaceports in the United States.[101] Any US citizen or entity planning to operate a launch or reentry site, wherever it is in the world, must obtain a licence from the FAA. A non-US citizen or entity planning to operate a launch or reentry site in the US must also obtain an FAA licence.

3.5.2.5 The FAA and industry

The commercial sector is involved in advising and making recommendations to the FAA on commercial space regulations. In 1984, the DoT established the Commercial Space Transportation Committee (COMSTAC) "to provide information, advice, and recommendations to the FAA Administrator on critical matters concerning the U.S. commercial space transportation industry".[102] Members of this advisory board include commercial space company executives, manufacturers, customers, academia, and associations. Because COMSTAC is a Federal Advisory Committee, it is subject to certain rules such as committee management and member roles and responsibilities.[103]

97 42 USC Sec. 4321 Congressional Declaration of Purpose.

98 FAA AST, *Office of Commercial Space Transportation Environmental Policy*; 40 CFR §§ 1502.25 (a) and (b).

99 NEPA 42 USC § 4321 *et seq*.; Council on Environmental Quality Regulations 40 CFR Parts 1500–1508; FAA Order 1050.1F.

100 *Id.*

101 14 CFR Part 420 License to Operate a Launch Site; 14 CFR Part 433 License to Operate a Reentry Site.

102 FAA, COMSTAC Charter, 17 June 2021, "The Federal Advisory Committee Act (FACA) requires that certain procedures be followed whenever a Federal agency seeks the consensus advice of a group external to the Federal government. The purpose of Federal Advisory Committee (FAC) is to provide uniform standards for the operation of advisory committees used in the executive branch and to ensure public access to and knowledge of their deliberations". NOAA, *Federal Advisory Committees, Administrative Issuances*, 31 May 2022.

103 2001 Federal Advisory Committee Act (FACA) Final Rule.

3.5.3 Commercial remote sensing

Remote sensing is the collection of data and images of the "physical characteristics of an area by measuring its reflected and emitted radiation at a distance (typically from satellite or aircraft)".[104] The US government owns and operates remote sensing satellites like GOES-T, which monitors Earth's weather and environment. Commercial companies also own and operate remote sensing satellites, many of which take images of Earth (i.e. Earth observation). Collecting images of Earth or other satellites, or having the capability to do so, raises security concerns. Consequently, these activities are carefully regulated and closely monitored.

3.5.3.1 Department of Commerce

When a US commercial company wants to conduct remote sensing activities, whether it operates in the US or anywhere else, it must be authorised and licensed to do so.[105] The National and Commercial Space Programs Act (NCSPA)[106] provides that:

> [n]o person who is subject to the jurisdiction or control of the U.S. may operate any private remote sensing space system without a license, and authorized the Secretary of Commerce to license private sector parties to operate private remote sensing space systems. By law, the Secretary can grant a license only upon determining, in writing that the applicant (licensee) will comply with the requirements of the Act, any regulations issued pursuant to the Act and any applicable international obligations and national security concerns of the United States.[107]

However, the NCSPA delegates the private remote sensing licensing from the Secretary of Commerce to the NOAA National Environmental Satellite Data and Information (NESDIS).[108] NOAA, which sits within the Department of Commerce, has a mission "to provide daily weather forecasts, severe storm warnings, climate monitoring to fisheries management, coastal restoration, and the supporting of marine commerce".[109] NESDIS is focused on satellite data and "provides secure and timely access to global environmental data and information from satellites and other sources to promote and protect the nation's security, environment, economy, and quality of life".[110] Within NESDIS is the regulatory affairs office: NOAA Commercial Remote Sensing Regulatory Affairs (CRSRA), which licenses and handles compliance and monitoring of commercial remote

104 USGS, What is remote sensing and what is it used for?
105 51 USC § 60122. Conditions for operation.
106 51 USC § 60101, *et seq.* as amended.
107 NESDIS, *Commercial Remote Sensing Regulatory Affairs.*
108 51 USC §§ 60121–60126; NOAA, *NESDIS Regulatory Affairs.*
109 US Dept. of Commerce – Bureaus and Offices, *NOAA.* NOAA also currently operates 16 satellites, ten owned by NOAA.
110 NESDIS, *Our Mission.*

sensing activities.[111] According to CRSRA, a commercial remote sensing application can take up to 60 days to approve.[112] [113]

Another integral part of regulating commercial remote sensing is NOAA's Advisory Committee on Commercial Remote Sensing (ACCRES). Established in 2002, ACCRES provides "information, advice, and recommendations to the Under Secretary of Commerce for Oceans and Atmosphere relating to the US satellite commercial remote sensing industry" and NOAA's responsibilities provided in the NCSPA.[114]

In 2022, NOAA released its strategic plan to use and promote commercial space capabilities.[115] Strategic objective 1.7 provides the following strategies:

1. Coordinate regulatory functions across domestic and international stakeholders to promote competitiveness, and increase legal certainty for U.S. commercial space businesses;
2. Grow the customer base for U.S. commercial space goods and services;
3. Improve space safety and sustainability;
4. Promote commercial space innovation;
5. Advance development, use, and application of space-based Earth observation capabilities to empower better decision-making by the public and private sector.[116]

3.6 Export controls

Due to the nature of space products and technology, often commercial companies will be required to obtain export control licences. It is critical for US commercial companies to understand and comply with these regulations. All US citizens and companies must comply with export control regulations and are subject to criminal prosecution and fines for violations. Export control regulations impact most areas of a space company, including manufacturing, launch, and the hiring of employees.

Restrictions on the export (transfer of physical objects or knowledge transfer to other countries or citizens of other countries) of technology and data have changed over the years and, in some areas, have become less restrictive.[117] The International Traffic in Arms Regulations (ITAR) and the controlled exports are found on the US Munitions List (USML). The Arms Export Control

111 Licence requirements are found at 15 CFR Part 960. Currently, OSC sits under NESDIS; however, in the future, OSC may be moved out of NESDIS to "report directly to the Under Secretary of Commerce for Oceans and Atmosphere, who is also the NOAA Administrator". Smith, Marcia, *Congress Keeps NOAA's Office of Space Commerce in NESDIS*, Space Policy Online, 10 Mar. 2022.

112 NESDIS, *Regulatory Affairs Licensing*. The NESDIS website provides an application guide.

113 NESDIS, *Forms, References, & Workshops; see also* NOAA, *Memorandum of Understanding Among the Departments of Commerce, State, Defense, and Interior, and the Office of the Director of National Intelligence, Concerning the Licensing and Operations of Private Remote Sensing Satellite Systems*, 25 Apr. 2017.

114 ACCRES is also a FACA, discussed above. NESDIS, *Advisory Committee on Commercial Remote Sensing.*

115 DoC, *Space Commerce in DOC's Strategic Plan for 2022–2026.*

116 *Id.*

117 Amendment to the International Traffic in Arms Regulations: Revision of U.S. Munitions List Category XV, 13 May 2014, 79 FR 27180; Final Rule (Correction), 10 Nov. 2014, 79 FR 66608. See also DoC, *Introduction to US Export Controls for the Commercial Space Industry*, 8–10.

Act provides the president authority to control the export of defence items and services, and by Executive Order, is delegated to the Secretary of State.[118]

While ITAR regulates defense items on the USML, the Export Administration Regulations (EAR) regulate the commercial use and transfer of technology and data other countries or parties could acquire for military use ("dual-use" items or technology that could be used for commercial or military purposes). The Commerce Control List (CCL) identifies the technology and data requiring licences that commercial companies must obtain.[119] [120]

3.7 Recent developments

US space policy and law are rapidly changing to keep up with innovation, new challenges and threats, and emerging norms while ensuring safety to the public. Several recent developments may have a significant impact on the commercial space industry.

3.7.1 FCC five-year deorbiting rule for spectrum licences

A significant recent development for satellite operators operating in low-Earth orbit (LEO) is the FCC's new deorbit rules. On 29 September 2022, the FCC adopted rules for operators seeking an FCC licence changing the previous low-Earth orbit (LEO) space station deorbit requirement from 25 years down to five years.[121] The rule allows companies a two-year transition period. According to the FCC, the new rule requires:

> [S]atellites ending their mission in or passing through the low-Earth orbit region (below 2,000 kilometers altitude) to deorbit as soon as practicable but no later than five years after mission completion. This is the first concrete rule on this topic, replacing a long-standing guideline. These new rules will also afford satellite companies a transition period of two years. The mission length and deorbit timeline for any given satellite are established through its application process with the FCC's International Bureau.[122]

118 22 U.S. Code § 2778 – Control of arms exports and imports; see also Obama, Barack, Executive Order 13637 – Administration of Reformed Export Controls, 8 Mar. 2013.

119 Bureau of Industry, *Export Administration Regulations*. ("For remote sensing issues, the Act also grants the authority to the Secretary of State to determine conditions necessary to meet international obligations and foreign policies, and to the Secretary of Defense to determine conditions necessary to meet the national security concerns raised by any remote sensing license application submitted pursuant to the Act and applicable directives, or to any amendment, renewal, or successor thereto. In addition, pursuant to this MOU, NOAA shall also consult with the Director of National Intelligence (DNI) for the views of the Intelligence Community (IC) and with the Chairman of the Joint Chiefs of Staff for the views of the DOD joint operational community."); 51 U.S.C. 60124, Appendix D to Part 960, Title 15, *Memorandum of Understanding Among the Departments of Commerce, State, Defense, and Interior, and the Office of the Director of National Intelligence, Concerning the Licensing and Operations of Private Remote Sensing Satellite Systems*, 25 Apr. 2017.

120 See DoC, *Introduction to US Export Controls for the Commercial Space Industry*, *supra*, 4–6.

121 Space Innovation IB Docket No. 22-271 *Mitigation of Orbital Debris in the New Space Age* IB Docket No. 18-313, 30 Sept. 2022.

122 *Id.*

3.7.2 In-Space Servicing, Assembly, and Manufacturing (ISAM) National Strategy

Another recent development potentially impacting commercial space companies is the Biden Administration's In-Space Servicing, Assembly, and Manufacturing National Strategy released on 4 April 2022.[123]

Recognising the importance of ISAM technology, the White House established the following goals:

(1) advancing ISAM research and development;
(2) prioritizing the expansion of scalable infrastructure;
(3) accelerating the emerging ISAM commercial industry;
(4) promoting international collaboration and cooperation to achieve ISAM goals;
(5) prioritizing environmental sustainability as we move forward with ISAM capabilities; and
(6) inspiring a diverse future workforce as a potential outcome of ISAM innovation.[124]

The strategy recognised the following current challenges to ISAM the goals are intended to remedy:

(1) improving coordination and collaboration both within the USG, as well as among the USG, academia, industry, and international partners;
(2) sending a clear and consistent demand signal to private industry in order to stimulate investment, mitigate risk, and address investor confidence; and
(3) establishing and adopting ISAM standards to help promote growth.[125]

ISAM activities are still nascent, and current regulation is not necessarily up to the task of ensuring licences and/or safety. Given the speed of innovation and the clear need for new ways to mitigate and clean up space debris, recognising challenges and setting goals for ISAM is a positive development. Indeed, ISAM activities are contemplated to be part of the National Space Council efforts now underway for novel activities.[126]

123 The White House, *In-Space Servicing, Assembly, and Manufacturing National Strategy*, In-Space Servicing, Assembly, and Manufacturing National Strategy Working Group and the Manufacturing Interagency Working Group of the National Science & Technology Council, 4 Apr. 2022. ("ISAM is a suite of capabilities, which are used on-orbit, on the surface of celestial bodies, and in transit between these regimes. ISAM capabilities enable specific activities, in the areas of servicing—the in-space inspection, life extension, repair, or alteration of a spacecraft after its initial launch, which includes but is not limited to: visually acquire, rendezvous and/or proximity operations, docking, berthing, relocation, refueling, upgrading, repositioning, undocking, unberthing, release and departure, reuse, orbit transport and transfer, and timely debris collection and removal; assembly—the construction of space systems in space using pre-manufactured components; and manufacturing—the transformation of raw or recycled materials into components, products, or infrastructure in space.")

124 *Id.*, 5.

125 *Id.*

126 National Space Council Executive Office of the President, *Notice of In-space Authorization and Supervision Policy Listening Sessions – Request for Comments*, 87 FR 62845, 17 Oct. 2022; Foust, Jeff, Space News, *White House Requests Proposals for Regulating Novel Commercial Space Activities*, 12 Sept. 2022.

3.8 Conclusion

This chapter is not intended to provide a comprehensive analysis of how the US government regulates, licenses, and supervises the US commercial space sectors or of how it assures that the US commercial space activities comply with the obligations and restrictions of international law, including international space law. Rather, this chapter provides a broad survey of the relevant governmental authorities regulating commercial space and of their various legal bases for this regulation. It is also intended to inform commercial space companies and counsel about the various issues requiring consideration when planning space operations, as well as resources for research. As discussed in this chapter, US space law and regulation are rapidly changing and it is an exciting time for the space industry and space lawyers.

B

Fostering NewSpace

Finance models and favourable jurisdictions

4
NEWSPACE COMPANIES
Incorporating and financing operations

Catherine Doldirina and Susan-Gale Wintermuth

4.1 Introduction

Space activities are costly, especially for a start-up or a small to medium sized enterprise, primarily due to the expenses associated with the launch of the business, as well as the expenses necessary for research and development work related to prototyping, producing, testing, and making space technology market-ready products or services.[1] "Space technologies have low production rates, long development cycles and use specialised/unique materials and industrial processes which also have to satisfy stringent safety and quality requirements. This means that they are subjected to significantly more research and testing than other products."[2] This is particularly true for NewSpace companies which are often founded by engineers or space enthusiasts, who seek to develop new products and services and need to conduct all their activities from scratch, especially those related to transforming ideas and prototypes into the market-ready products or services, but who very often do not have necessary resources to carry out such activities.

The first missions of a space company's intended products or services are considered experimental and serve the purpose of in-orbit demonstration and validation of the relevant technology. Therefore, it is difficult to sell them at market price and hence they require investment. Thereafter, gaining and retaining customers depends to a great extent on the consistency and number of successfully launched missions. Winning government contracts is also a limited possibility until the companies can demonstrate a track record of some successes in testing and using their technologies in space. The road to profitability is rather long. These market specific circumstances result in the need to procure funds and resources by means of equity fundraising to manage such crucial tasks as technology advancement, product and business development, personnel attraction and retainment, tasks that are indispensable for start-ups' progress and the path to the market, breaking-even, and profitability.[3]

1 NASA, Systems Engineering Handbook, *3.0 NASA Program/Project Life Cycle*, available online.
2 A.R. Wilson et al., Ecospheric life cycle impacts of annual global space activities, *Science of the Total Environment*, vol. 834 (2022) 155305.
3 R. Nahata, Success is good but failure is not so bad either: Serial entrepreneurs and venture capital contracting. *Journal of Corporate Finance* vol. 58, October 2019, pp. 624–649, Introduction section.

DOI: 10.4324/9781003268475-7

This chapter covers the important aspect of positioning and preparing a start-up, or small to medium sized enterprise (SME), to seek that funding. The first part of the chapter covers corporate and other company forms that may facilitate access to financing. The focus is on Delaware, the favoured jurisdiction for incorporation by many companies, including notable NewSpace companies, and a unique jurisdiction with regard to company law.[4] This is not to say, however, that European states and the EU as a whole are not attractive, which is welcomed:[5] competition can bring about better ways and means. The second part of the chapter covers financing operations of NewSpace companies. It discusses various types of financing available to NewSpace companies and details organisational steps and contractual arrangements that need to be carried out and executed to perfect fundraising. It looks at critical aspects pertinent to different fundraising phases with a primary focus on venture capital (VC) private equity financing.

4.2 What makes a favourable jurisdiction?

Choosing wisely the jurisdiction of incorporation for a NewSpace start-up is not only critical for the life of a company but should also be taken into account from the financing operations perspective both in terms of potentially available financing and the regulatory framework applicable to preparation and execution of financing rounds. There are a number of considerations relevant to take into account when determining the jurisdiction of incorporation. From the company's perspective these include ease of setting up the business, obtaining necessary approvals, licences, permits, completion of required notifications and verifications, filing of certificates of incorporation, and meeting minimum capital requirements, as the case may be. Even when a start-up forms its business in other than a corporate form, at some point it will need to incorporate and, thus, selecting a jurisdiction where there is ease of changing from a simpler form to one that can raise capital is important. From the VC investor perspective, these include institutional aspects of economic systems and a "well-functioning legal system with strong protection of investor rights and effective, low-cost enforcement of contracts".[6] This section first looks at the US jurisdiction of Delaware, the favourite jurisdiction of many, including NewSpace companies. It then discusses the Securities and Exchange Commission's requirements that must be observed if an entity is US based.

4.2.1 US Delaware

More than 60% of the Fortune 500 companies have incorporated in Delaware, although their principal executive offices are elsewhere and they do business around the world.[7] Venture capital funds also favour the Delaware jurisdiction. The majority of the leading NewSpace launch providers follow suit. Space Exploration Technologies Corp (SpaceX)[8] and Virgin Galactic Holdings, Inc[9] elected to be incorporated in the US state of Delaware, although they do business elsewhere in the US and the world. A related entity, Virgin Orbit Holdings, Inc organised as a Delaware

4 Over half the Fortune 500 companies are incorporated in Delaware. C. Crail et al., Why Incorporate in Delaware? Benefits & Considerations, *Forbes Advisor*, 7 August 2022.

5 See this book, Section C, *The international legal framework for licensing space activities – innovative examples.*

6 A. Metrick, et al., *Venture Capital and the Finance of Innovation.* Wiley, 2021, p. 91; see also World Bank Group, Doing Business 2020 Report.

7 See Crail, *supra* note 4.

8 Space Exploration Technologies Corp, United States Securities and Exchange Commission (hereafter "SEC"), Form D Notice of Exempt Offering of Securities.

9 Virgin Galactic Holdings, Inc, SEC Form 10-Q (30 September 2022).

corporation,[10] even as it launches from the UK[11] (which allowed it to file for Chapter 11 bankruptcy reorganisation in Delaware). Rocket Lab USA, Inc, founded by New Zealander Peter Beck, is a publicly traded Delaware corporation with its principal executive in Long Beach, California.[12] Even the legacy company United Launch Alliance (ULA), a joint venture between the Boeing Company (a Delaware corporation) and Lockheed Martin Corporation (a Maryland corporation), is formed as a Delaware limited liability company.[13]

Is there something about Delaware? Each of the 50 states in the United States is sovereign in most areas of law, including company law.[14] However, once incorporated under a state's law, business can be conducted in any state in the US and the principal executive offices can be in any state. The significance of the state of incorporation or formation is that the business is anchored to it for purposes of filings and maintaining a registered agent for service of process.[15] And, the business can always be sued in Delaware regardless that it has no presence there other than a registered agent.[16] As a result of the fact that company law is exclusively state law, states have competed for the business of "forming businesses", presumably due to the income generated. Delaware has by far and away won the race.

The US system of harmonisation deserves some comment at this point. Although each state is largely sovereign on local matters, there is an effort to harmonise the laws among the states. This effort is carried out largely by the Uniform Law Commission, as well as by the American Bar Association. States are under no obligation to adopt a uniform or model law, and each state may make changes, if it does. The Model Business Corporations Act, for example, has been adopted by most states in one form or another. Delaware, however, wrote and updates its own, with the intent of maintaining its place as the jurisdiction of destination.

4.2.1.1 Forms of business entities: LLC and the corporation

The forms of business organisations in Delaware, as in other US jurisdictions, are varied but somewhat limited in number. Some of these business forms correspond to forms known elsewhere in the world and some do not; and the terms can at times be confusing. For example, an "LLC" (limited liability company), such as utilised by the joint venture United Launch Alliance, under both the Uniform Limited Liability Company Act and the Delaware Limited Liability Company Act, refers to an entity that has the advantage of corporate-type limited liability for the owner(s) and a single "flow through" partnership-style tax treatment. It has the advantage of allowing a more agile management than that of a corporation, and in fact, allows as few as one member. It has the disadvantage that it cannot "go public" as an LLC, but Delaware law has foreseen the need to

10 Virgin Orbit Holdings, Inc., SEC Form 10-Q (30 September 2022).

11 UK Space Agency, Virgin Orbit Mission success brings UK launch another step closer, Gov.Uk, 2 July 2022; Bachman, Justin, Richard Branson's Virgin Sends 7 Satellites to Space in First Launch Since IPO, Bloomberg, 14 January 2022.

12 Rocket Lab USA, Inc., SE CIK #0001849874.

13 United Launch Alliance LLC, State of Delaware, Department of State: Division of Corporations, Entity Details; see also United Launch Alliance, Joint Venture Master Agreement of 2 May 2005.

14 There is an effort to harmonise the laws of the states by the Uniform Law Commission, which promulgates model laws for adoption by the states. Some states adopt the model laws, some make changes and adopt the better part, others draft their own. See Uniform Law Commission.

15 See generally, Delaware Corporation Law, Title 8, § 101 *et seq*. There are commercial companies that serve as registered agents.

16 See, e.g., *Twitter, Inc. v. Elon R. Musk, et al.*, C.A. No. 2022-0613-KSJ, in the Court of Chancery of the State of Delaware.

convert, at some point in a start-up's trajectory, to a corporation and allows this conversion with relative ease.[17] posting the forms online. Additional capital for an LLC is generally limited to contributions by the member(s), buy-in of new members, or incurring debt, for which the member(s) will usually be required to be guarantor. In fact, Jeff Bezos formed Blue Origin as a Washington State LLC[18] (with similar but not identical LLC laws as Delaware).

Turning to the more commonly utilised business form, that of Delaware's General Corporation Law,[19] an important aspect for the space industry is a provision permitting stockholders to limit the liability of directors by appropriate language in the corporate charter. This is a response to the high cost of liability insurance for directors and officers that kept many from accepting these roles. Similarly, the statute allows corporations to indemnify these directors, officers, and employees.[20] The law also allows a broad range of "incorporators",[21] namely, "[a]ny person, partnership, association or corporation, singly or jointly with others, and without regard to such person's or entity's residence, domicile or state of incorporation".[22] This compares with other states, for example New York, which allows incorporation by "[o]ne or more natural persons of the age of eighteen years or over".[23] When the Delaware law states "without regard to such ... entity's ... state of incorporation" it is not limited to other states within the US, which are technically termed "foreign" as to Delaware law. "You do not have to live in, or even visit, the state of Delaware in order to form a Delaware company ... You do not have to be an American citizen to form and/or operate a Delaware company."[24] Importantly, similar to the LLC, Delaware law allows just one person to incorporate the company, hold the corporate roles of officer, director, and shareholder.[25]

4.2.1.2 Forms of business entities: alternative entities

Delaware also offers alternative entities, which can be very attractive to start-ups and SMEs. In addition to the limited liability company discussed above, a limited partnership[26] is available. This is an investment vehicle that allows funds to be raised without an IPO. A limited partnership "consist[s] of 2 or more persons and having 1 or more general partners and 1 or more limited partners".[27] The general partner runs the business; the limited partners invest. The general partner can be any legal entity. Because this is in the nature of a security, there must be a filing either with

17 Delaware Division of Corporations, Conversion of Entity Type.

18 Washington Secretary of State, Corporations and Charities Filing System, Business Information.

19 The Delaware Code Online, The General Corporation Law.

20 Delaware Corporation Code, § 102(b)(7) (2022).

21 Del. Code Ann. Tit. 8, § 101.

22 *Id.*

23 NY (Bus. Corp) § 401.

24 Harvard Business Services, Inc., DelawareInc.com, Delaware Company Formations for Non-Residents.

25 Delaware General Corporation Law: "§ 101. Incorporators; how corporation formed; purposes. (a) Any person, partnership, association or corporation, singly or jointly with others, and without regard to such person's or entity's residence, domicile or state of incorporation, may incorporate or organize a corporation under this chapter..."; "§ 141. Board of directors. (b) The board of directors of a corporation shall consist of 1 or more members, each of whom shall be a natural person; § 142. Officers (a)...Any number of offices may be held by the same person unless the certificate of incorporation or bylaws otherwise provide".

26 Delaware Limited Partnership Act, § 17-101 *et seq.*

27 *Id.* § 17-101(11).

the state, if the offering is intra-state, or with the SEC if interstate. Similar to the corporation, a limited partnership may limit the liability of its partners.[28]

4.2.1.3 Reports

State reporting for corporations is essentially the same in all US states. In Delaware, the (online) annual report for the prior year and the franchise tax are due on or before 1 March. Foreign corporations actually doing business in Delaware must file before 30 June. And, "[a]ll Domestic and Foreign Limited Liability Companies, Limited Partnerships, and General Partnerships formed or registered in Delaware are required to pay an annual tax of $300.00. *There is no requirement to file an Annual Report*".[29] Even if organised in Delaware, a company doing business in another US state must comply also with the laws of that jurisdiction, including any filings, such as a tax return for the state.

4.2.1.4 Other considerations: case law and courts

That which is advantageous about Delaware goes beyond the ease of incorporation, and the not-to-be-outdone service-oriented Delaware Division of corporations, which staffs a "hot line" 8:30 to 16:00 Eastern time zone, Monday through Friday excluding state holidays.[30] It includes the court system and the well-developed and well-defined body of case law, which lends clarity and predictability to the law in the form of precedent.

With regard to the court system, the Delaware Court of Chancery is a court of original and exclusive equity jurisdiction where all matters are heard by the court, not a jury. In its own words, Delaware has "unique competence in and exposure to issues of business law".[31] If issues of fact must be resolved (which is the role of the jury), the matter is referred to the Superior Court.[32] Moreover, Delaware has implemented a wide range of eServices relating to its Chancery Court.[33]

4.3 Securities and Exchange Commission

When fund-raising through the sale of securities, there are requirements to file with the federal Securities and Exchange Commission (SEC),[34] which informs us that "[a]ll companies, foreign and domestic, are required to file registration statements, periodic reports, and other forms electronically".[35] The SEC Rules, Regulation S-T, General Rules and Regulations for Electronic

28 *Id.* § 17-108: Subject to such standards and restrictions, if any, as are set forth in its partnership agreement, a limited partnership may, and shall have the power to, indemnify and hold harmless any partner or other person from and against any and all claims and demands whatsoever.

29 Emphasis added. Delaware Division of Corporations, Annual Report and Tax Instructions.

30 Delaware Division of Corporations, Contact Information.

31 Delaware Courts, Court of Chancery, Information and Services.

32 10 *Del. C.*, 369.

33 Delaware Courts, Best Practices and Procedures for eFiling/Filing with the Register in Chancery.

34 The SEC was established by the passage of the US Securities Act of 1933 and the Securities and Exchange Act of 1934, largely in response to the stock market crash of 1929 that led to the Great Depression. US Securities and Exchange Commission.

35 These are available through an online system called EDGAR. U.S. Securities and Exchange Commission, Filings & Forms.

Filings, explain which filings must be filed electronically, as there are some exceptions.[36] Your company may be a "reporting company" even if it is not listed on a stock exchange. A company is a "reporting company under Section 12 of the [1934 Securities and] Exchange Act if: 'it has more than $10 million in total assets and a class of equity securities, like common stock, that is held of record by either (1) 2,000 or more persons, or (2) 500 or more persons who are not accredited investors or it lists the securities on a U.S. exchange'".[37]

There is a long list of filings that a reporting company must faithfully observe when in the securities market.[38] They are the same regardless of the jurisdiction in which the business is formed. This requires full disclosure of market-related information, which investors can access freely and for free online through EDGAR, including access to registration statements, periodic financial reports, and other securities forms.[39] The information is provided so that the investing public can make informed decisions. And, indeed, full disclosure is a company's best defence if a disgruntled investor takes to litigation. Conversely, if a company does not comply with all SEC regulations, including full disclosure, the SEC can be ruthless.[40]

The SEC classifies securities into various categories, with different filing requirements, unless the offering falls within an exemption from registration, which is sometimes referred to as a "private offering". Exempt offerings can be found in Rule 506(b) for private placements, Rule 506(c) for some general solicitation offerings, Rule 504 for limited offerings. These allow eligible companies to raise up to a limited amount during a 12-month period.[41] If a company sells exempt securities, it must file with the SEC according to Regulation D within 15 days of the first sale.[42] Start-ups and SMEs are most likely to be interested in such exempt offerings, as they require less time and expense. Even if a company is exempt from filing with the SEC, it is still subject to strict federal (and state) laws against fraud, which generally includes any false, or even misleading, statement made either orally or in writing.

The SEC is making attempts to facilitate access to the capital market by start-ups and SMEs, including by having updated its rules in 2020 "to facilitate capital formation and increase opportunities for investors by expanding access to capital"[43] of such companies. The amendments simplify the ability of issuers to move from one offering exemption to another, set clear and consistent rules governing offering communications between issuers and investors, increase offering and investment limits for certain exemptions, harmonise certain disclosure requirements and bad actor disqualification provisions, and provide a revised confidential information standard applicable to certain exhibit filing requirements.[44] Companies wishing to avail themselves of exempt offerings under one of the three exempt categories available should consult the rules concerning limits and qualifications, as they are evolving in response to the needs of the market and the investor.

36 EDGAR Filer Manual, vol. II, sec. 3, *Index to Forms*.

37 US Securities and Exchange Commission, *Exchange Act Reporting and Registration*.

38 *Id.*

39 *Id.* "About EDGAR."

40 See, e.g., *SEC v. Musk*, Civil Action No. 1:18-cv-8865 (US District Court, Southern District of NY, 2018), *SEC v. Facebook, Inc.*, Case No. 19-cv-04241 (US District Court, Northern District of California, 2019).

41 See generally, SEC, Offering. There is also an exemption for "Regulation Crowdfunding", US Securities and Exchange Commission, Regulation Crowdfunding: A Small Entity Compliance Guide for Issuers.

42 US Securities and Exchange Commission, Filing a Form D Notice.

43 SEC, Facilitating Capital Formation and Expanding Investment Opportunities by Improving Access to Capital in Private Markets.

44 *Id.*

In contrast to exempt offerings, a "registered offering" allows an unlimited amount to be raised. There are strict regulations, starting with a registration statement, which must be approved by the SEC and effective *before any solicitation*. Thereafter there are reporting requirements even if no funds have been raised and no stock issued.[45] This category is unlikely to be attractive to a start-up or SME and is thus not further covered here.

4.4 Financing operations

4.4.1 Sources of financing

Companies can seek financing from both private and public sources. The forms of financing vary and include equity, loans, bank credit and borrowing, business expansion scheme funds, leasing, and franchising.[46] Private equity financing, with particular attention to venture capital (VC) funds, is the focus of this section.[47] Equity financing means that in exchange for money raised the company issues shares of business ownership to the investor(s).[48] More specifically, VC financing is characterised as an actively managed investment into a rapidly growing private company with few tangible assets, and at a relatively early stage of development in a dynamic industry.[49] Equity financing is normally raised over so-called "funding rounds" that include pre- and seed funding rounds, bridge funding round(s), Series A, B, C, and D funding rounds, and eventually initial public offering (IPO/SPAC),[50] and each is associated with various growth stages of a company.[51] A company may perfect multiple rounds within the same Series.[52]

While (early stage) funding opportunities have increased substantially over the course of past ten years in Europe[53] and worldwide and the investor landscape is diversifying,[54] the most financing opportunities for any sector of economic activity are offered in the United States.[55] The European VC industry is smaller, characterised by shorter track record, underdeveloped IPO market, and entrepreneurial ecosystem centred around scale-ups, lower fund sizes, and the fewer large late-stage VC funds.[56] However, in particular within the space sector, European start-ups now account

45 See generally, SEC, Financial Reporting Manual.

46 For a detailed overview of the various sources of financing see S. Carter et al., Basic finance for marketers. Food And Agriculture Organization of the United Nations 1997, chapter 7.

47 For core differences between public and private equity *see* S. Caselli, G. Negri, *Private Equity and Venture Capital in Europe: Markets, Techniques, and Deals*. Elsevier 2021. Chapter 1, Section 1.2.1, pp. 4–6.

48 Wolters Kluwer, Financing sources for your small business (21 June 2020).

49 R. J. Wooder, *Global Venture Capital Transactions: A Practical Approach*. Kluwer Law International, 2004, p. 3.

50 See also S. Caselli, G. Negri, *supra* Note 47, Chapter 6, Section 6.2.2.

51 S. Caselli, G. Negri, *supra* Note 47, Chapter 4, Section 4.4 and Chapter 5, Section 5.2.

52 Investor Updates, The Understandable Guide to Startup Funding Stages. Visible VC.

53 Y. Wijngaarde, J. Puls, G. Micajkov, The Journey to Series A in Europe. Fundraising benchmarks for founders of early-stage companies. Dealroom.com, April 2021.

54 L. Havermans, The State of European Early-Stage Investment, Dealroom.com, 12 October 2022, p. 6.

55 VC funding available in the US amounts to US$1.7 trillion compared to a combined Europe number of US$440.8 billion, while the number of the start-up companies is not so drastically different: 206,000 companies in the US and 169,000 in Europe. Exploring the most promising ecosystems, Global countries & regions, Dealroom.com.

56 EIF Business Angels Survey 2021/22: Market sentiment, EIF Working Paper 2022/81, p. 36. EIF's Research & Market Analysis. Other factors include smaller European VC industry/shorter track record, underdeveloped IPO market, underdeveloped entrepreneurial ecosystem centred around scale-ups, lower fund sizes due to insufficient funding from large investors, fewer large late-stage VC funds in Europe, insufficient follow-on financing leading companies to sell earlier, limited awareness about the importance of scale-ups in Europe, underdeveloped market

for a third of global space tech funding.[57] It is worth noting that the VC funding comes with its challenges, that include among others securing equity financing, securing liquidity, reduced exit opportunities, and rising inflation levels.[58] This means that the funded companies must work hard to achieve their business plan objectives and become profitable in order to reduce or overcome the impact of these challenges.

4.4.2 Organisational steps

In practice, largely independently of which funding round a company prepares to pursue, it needs to carry out several indispensable activities in order to attract investors and complete a funding round. This section provides an overview of such activities presented in principle in the chronological order of their execution within the timeline of a funding round. It should be noted however that a number of activities are carried out in parallel and satisfy various stages of the investment process as seen by the VC investors, that starts with the screening and preliminary due diligence, followed by the definition of the term sheet and final due diligence and concluded with the closing.[59]

4.4.2.1 Get the company story ready

Investors have a number of criteria that a company would need to meet in order for them to consider investing. The most significant include a strong management team, product value proposition, business model and scalability potential, technology maturity, financial criteria such as valuation and deal terms, cash generating capacity, and profitability.[60] The story (also transposed in the specific milestones within the business plan) must address these criteria and provide information as to how they are or will be met. It must present the company and its business and explain both its strengths and weaknesses. The company's valuation must also be determined, as it will affect the interest in the company and the possible maximum target amount of funds to be raised. The assess-

for venture debt, and lack of cross-over funds. An increased engagement by large institutional investors could be the most effective factor in bridging the late-stage financing gap, alongside public support for late-stage VC funds and the development of a European Sovereign Wealth Fund, *id.*, p. 37.

57 S. King, World-first space tech database, in partnership with the European Space Agency. Dealroom.com, 16 June 2022.

58 EIF VC Survey 2022: Market sentiment and impact of the current geopolitical & macroeconomic environment, p. 45. EIF Working Paper 2022/82, EIF's Research & Market Analysis. Shortage of skilled labour, rising labour costs, and supply chain disruptions are currently the three most important operational challenges for portfolio companies, p. 47.

59 For a comprehensive overview of these stages *see* A. Metrick, A. Yasuda, *Venture Capital and the Finance of Innovation*. Wiley, 2021, Chapter 7, Section 7.2.

60 EIF VC Survey 2022: Market sentiment and impact of the current geopolitical & macroeconomic environment, p.12 and 42. EIF Working Paper 2022/82, EIF's Research & Market Analysis. Full list of criteria (p. 75), in order of importance: Management team, Scalability of the business, Technology, Total size of the addressable market, Product's value proposition, Exit potential, Business model, Venture stage, Geographical location of venture, Revenue-generating capacity, Valuation and deal terms, Strategic fit in investment portfolio, ESG considerations, Industry, Ability to add value, Profitability/potential of the business, Past performance/track record, GPs/investors, Cash-generating capacity/potential, Diversity & inclusion considerations, Referral by other.

ment of the valuation is based on a number of factors, such as the company's management, proven track record, market size, and risks associated with business and corporate activities.[61]

4.4.2.2 Develop the company's business plan

The business plan provides the roadmap (forecast) of the company development based on the funds expected to be secured via financing round, and includes the company's actions directed towards maturation of technology, market offering, development of new products or services, growth of client base, number of signed contracts and their expected overall value, hiring new personnel, securing suppliers, business growth milestones, etc.[62] The business plan must be realistic and backed by the accurate assessment of the maturity of the offered products/services and the current position of the company on the market.[63] It should contain an executive summary, explain to potential investors the company's business opportunity and current financial situation, and current and future financing requirements.[64]

4.4.2.3 Get the company ready

The company must ensure compliance with the minimum obligatory requirements applicable to its operations, have all corporate and reporting documentation in order, and proof that the company has obtained any and all necessary licences, permits, or certifications. It should also ensure that prior to starting a funding round, if necessary and possible, the management team should be strengthened. More specifically, the company must have a management team whose members can effectively contribute to the fundraising process, e.g. qualified CFO, legal counsel, investor relations officer, compliance officer, chief operating officer, and other managerial figures. The company must also get qualified external financial, legal and other advisors, as may be necessary, since normally the internal personnel will not have a sufficient level of expertise and/or experience. In addition, the external advisors, often being multinational firms or offices with connections to experts in multiple jurisdictions,[65] are in the position to advise on legal, tax, financial, and other matters in countries other than in which the company is incorporated.

4.4.2.4 Execute necessary corporate governance steps

If the company has a board of directors within its corporate governance structure, depending on the country where the company is incorporated, such body will need to approve various documents or decisions related to the funding round. For example, it is standard practice that the board of directors approves the company's business plan, the term sheet, and any and all other subsequent documentation forming part of the contractual documentation implementing the funding round. In cases where a company has shareholders, certain matters will be subject to approval by the shareholders, including for example the relevant capital increase, execution of the relevant contractual

61 For an explanation, see N. Reif, Series A, B and C, Investopedia, 24 February 2022.

62 For a comprehensive overview of how to develop a business plan *see* R. Moro-Visconti, *Startup Valuation: From Strategic Business Planning to Digital Networking*. Springer International Publishing 2021, Chapter 2.

63 Cf. SPAC projections requirements recently updated in the relevant SEC regulations.

64 Entrepreneur, Business Strategy, Elements of a Business Plan.Fundera.com.

65 For the best rated law firms see Global Private Equity Legal Advisor Review. Full year 2021. 2022.

documentation, and performance of any necessary formal steps to implement the requirements set out in the contractual documentation.

4.4.2.5 Obtain necessary corporate/government approvals

NewSpace companies may need to acquire government approval in cases where a significant amount of financing raised comes from investors foreign to their country of incorporation. Governments across the world want to have some control over direct foreign investments in the companies that are their nationals and are considered strategic, or whose activities may have implications for national security.[66] A lot of space companies would qualify as such, and hence substantial financing they may seek from foreign investors may be subject to their government's scrutiny and approval.

For example, the European Union, via its Regulation related to the screening of direct foreign investments,[67] imposed the obligation to transpose the relevant provisions in the regulatory framework of its Member States. In Italy this was done by incorporating such provisions in the so-called "Golden Power Decree".[68] By virtue of its provisions, the Italian government has the right to exercise certain special powers to address significant threats to public interests, security, or public order related to companies operating in sectors such as defence, national security, transport, energy, communication, and high tech – and holding or managing strategic assets in those sectors. More specifically, in certain cases the government can impose specific requirements or conditions on the acquisition of stakes in companies operating in strategic areas; exercise a veto right over certain shareholders' and/or directors' resolutions concerning extraordinary transactions involving companies holding strategic assets;[69] forbid the acquisition of stakes of the companies holding strategic assets by entities capable of affecting the defence and/or national security interests.[70]

4.4.2.6 Define terms and conditions of the funding round

The material terms and conditions applicable to the investment sought in a funding round are usually referred to as the "term sheet". Their definition is usually a joint activity or rather a negotiation that involves company's funding objectives as outlined in the business plan and the proposal by the investor(s) or lead investor of the conditions under which the investment would be considered possible. Such terms and conditions normally identify the investment amount, the amount of the company equity an investor envisages to acquire as a result of the transaction, voting rights, as

66 Debevoise & Plimpton, Foreign Direct Investment Rules in Selected European Countries—An Overview, 16 June 2020. US regulatory framework: M. West, P. Luther, Foreign Direct Investment Regimes: USA. See also documentation released by the US Committee on Foreign Investment via US Treasury website.

67 Regulation (EU) 2019/452 of the European Parliament and of the Council of 19 March 2019 establishing a framework for the screening of foreign direct investments into the Union and the corresponding implementation legislation in the EU Member States.

68 Law Decree No. 21 of 15 March 2012 (converted with amendments into Law No. 56 of 11 May 2012), as amended by Law Decrees No. 179 of 18 December 2020, No. 180 of 23 December 2020, and No. 21 of 21 March 2022.

69 Such transactions include e.g. mergers & acquisitions, transfers of business, changes to the company's corporate purpose, transfer of the registered offices, issuance of securities over the company's assets.

70 Leonardo Base Prospectus for the EUR 4,000,000,000 Euro Medium Term Note Programme.

well as provisions related to anti-dilution, and liquidation preference.[71] The term sheet is then detailed and transposed into various provisions of the corresponding contractual documentation.[72]

4.4.2.7 Talk to investors

Usually, the company's financial advisor should help the company identify suitable potential investors and ideally make introductions to their representatives/teams. The investors need to be carefully assessed before approaching. For series rounds, especially B and C, attraction of a so-called lead investor is a critical step in securing the completion of the round and raising the targeted amount of capital. A lead investor is an individual or a company that will normally be the most significant investor of the funding round giving the company more confidence and a better position vis-a-vis other potential investors, as well as providing the company with relevant advice, making introductions, and negotiating investment contractual terms and conditions.[73] In the VC funding rounds, the companies must ensure, as the applicable law may require,[74] that they avoid use of general advertising or general solicitation in order to attract potential investors, i.e. the discussions must be held with those potential investors for which the company can prove it has a substantive and pre-existing relationship.[75]

4.4.2.8 Prepare for due diligence screening by the potential investors

Potential investors logically want to obtain as much useful information about the company as possible in order to make informed decisions regarding the potential investment.[76] The company must make available various documentation, including (i) corporate documents (bylaws, existing investment and shareholders agreements, other financing agreements that affect corporate governance; shareholders ledger; information about company's directors); (ii) financial documents (past financial statements of the company, cash-flows for various calendar periods, cash flow forecast and a profit forecast, capitalisation table, and financing history); (iii) business information (sales and procurement contracts, information about customers and competitors, information about company assets); (iv) intellectual property (company's IP portfolio, overview of filed and granted patents, trademarks, R&D activities, product development, etc.); (v) personnel (number of employees, contractors, the terms and conditions of employment, any disputes with current or former employees); insights about the market in which the company operates, including growth prospects and risks; (vi) certifications, licences, and permits the company is required to obtain/maintain in order to do business; (vii) insurance policies maintained; (viii) any additional information or documentation that may be requested by a potential investor.

The potential investors perform due diligence essentially to understand the probability of the return of their investment.[77] In the context of start-ups and early-stage development companies,

71 C. Giliker, What is a term sheet for investment? Harper James, 19.08.2022; see also Preparing a Venture Capital Term Sheet, Morgan Lewis, A. J. Berkeley and A. A. Parisi, Road Map for Undertaking a Private Offering. Practical Law Practice Note 4-501-6353, p. 20. 2022 Thomson Reuters.

72 See A. Metrick, A. Yasuda, *supra* Note 59, p. 138 and generally Chapter 8.

73 A. Cremades, How To Find A Lead Investor. Forbes, 2 October 2018.

74 As for example in the US, as further detailed in the "Securities and Exchange Commission" section of this chapter.

75 For the applicable US regulatory framework and requirements *see* A. J. Berkeley and A. A. Parisi, *supra* Note 71, p. 12.

76 Due Diligence: Investigation or audit of a potential deal or investment opportunity. Corporate Finance Institute, 10 February 2022.

77 For the VC due diligence purposes and structure *see* Venture Capital Due Diligence Guide, Wallstreet Prep. See also R. J. Wooder, *supra* Note 49, pp. 8–14.

due diligence is a critical process and must be prepared for and performed with utmost care, especially from the company's side, as its successful completion is often a pre-condition to making the decision to invest.[78] It is important to note that there is no "one fits all" solution for setting up the due diligence process, as apart from traditionally provided documentation, potential investors may request additional information or documentation that may not be readily available and the company will need to draw up such documentation. In addition, due diligence documentation must be up-to-date and hence it is almost impossible to "recycle" all documentation from, for instance, financing rounds the company completed in the past.

Once the commitment from potential investors to participate in a round is reached, the negotiation of the contractual documentation starts in order to achieve closing.

4.4.3 Contractual documentation

4.4.3.1 Disclosure letter

The disclosure letter to potential investors must provide information about any and all non-compliance instances that the company is experiencing, difficulties related to the conduct of the business, operations, etc., the situation with personnel, actual or potential lawsuits, and any other specific disclosures as requested by the investor(s) based on the outcomes of due diligence process. Disclosures must provide accurate and relevant information.[79] Failure to disclose any material information that may pose risks to the financing transaction or subsequent performance of the company may result in penalties under the "investment and shareholders agreement" (ISA) executed in relation to the financing. Accurate and complete disclosures, on the contrary, protect the company from breaching any representations and warranties it may need to make towards investors.[80]

4.4.3.2 Representations and warranties

Representation and warranties are given by the company and or its founders, as the case may be, to the investor(s) with regard to such categories as (i) truthfulness and accuracy of the information provided to investor(s) for the purpose of completing the financing round, including the information in the disclosure level; (ii) information about company founders and/or key management personnel; (iii) company financial statements; (iv) any events that may have occurred since the beginning of the financing round or are likely to occur by the time of its conclusion; (v) taxation; (vi) litigation; property, personal property, and products/services of the company; consents and compliance with any requirements applicable to company's business and operations; (vii) intellectual property critical for the company's operations, products/services; (viii) cybersecurity; (ix) the company's assets, debts, and stock; (x) any material conditions of employment that may have implications on the company's business and operations; (xi) existing capital commitments; (xii) company's insurance; (xiii) borrowings; (xiv) good standing in keeping company's records; (xv)

78 H. J. Kamps, The majority of early-stage VC deals fall apart in due diligence, TechCrunch+, 28 August 2022.

79 *Cf.* description of risk factors in the context of SPAC transaction and relevant documentation to be submitted to the authorities.

80 Cf. with the analysis of the disclosures in the context of the sale of the entire share capital of a company: A. Mills, Full disclosure: Is this warranted? M. J. Hudson. January 2019.

compliance, and others as may be required by the investor(s). These are normally related to any statements and information provided in the disclosure letter.[81]

A number of representations and warranties, usually limited to good standing and validity of their obligations under the ISA, may be required also from the company's shareholders and the investors, and in such case would also be included in the ISA contractual documentation. Indemnities for breach of the representations and warranties are normally included in the ISA.

4.4.3.3 Investment and shareholders agreement

The end of a funding round is the ISA, which is a complex set of contractual documentation that serves as the framework for perfecting the financing round and lays down any changes, corporate or otherwise, that the company undertakes to execute as the result of completing the financing round.[82] It contains provisions regarding, among others, (i) the formal steps necessary to carry out to enable the investment; (ii) the amount of financing; (iii) classes of shares, if applicable, dividends, conversion, anti-dilution, transfer of shares/interests, liquidation preference, redemption rights, lock-up and right of first refusal; (iv) management of the company, including composition of the board of directors and its committees, competences, reserved matters, quorum and voting rights; shareholders meeting's exclusive matters, quorum and voting rights; any requirements regarding company's key management personnel; (v) obligations of the company under ISA; (vi) exit conditions; obligations of company founders and/or key management personnel; (vii) additional future financing conditions. It normally contains as annexes or exhibits, e.g. (i) the disclosure letter, (ii) the representation and warranties document, (iii) any updated corporate documents, including bylaws; (iv) directors' agreements if such are necessary to be executed by new/incoming directors; (v) stock options regulation(s), if applicable; (vi) any financing or debt agreements/contracts that will survive the concluding of the financing round.[83]

Once the ISA is signed off by both the company and the investors, the next step is, hopefully, a successful partnership and company's growth.

4.5 Conclusion

NewSpace start-ups and SMEs must take into account the need for substantial funding from external sources to develop and make their products or services ready for the market, since even the most innovative or disruptive business ideas require a long period of research and development that such companies will not be able to finance internally. Hence, a careful assessment of the jurisdiction of incorporation should be made also from the perspective of availability and accessibility of financing. To date the US is the leader both in terms of being one of the preferred incorporation jurisdictions worldwide, in particular in Delaware, as highlighted in this chapter, as well as in terms of access to various sources of funding and its amount. Europe is trying to catch up, also by making political decision to prioritise development of space industry and attracting private actors, including start-ups and SMEs, to foster progress.

81 *See* R. J. Wooder, *supra* Note 49, pp. 16–18.

82 For a detailed overview of what ISA may contain see T. H. Maynard, D. M. Warren, S. Trevino, *Business Planning: Financing the Start-Up Business and Venture Capital Financing*. Wolters Kluwer, 2018, Chapter 10, Section B.

83 For a comprehensive overview of various ISA provisions see R. J. Wooder, *supra* Note 49, pp. 8–12.

It should be highlighted that, partly due to the global characteristics of the space industry and market, i.e. that the space market cannot be limited to the territories of individual countries or geographic regions, the companies developing promising technological solutions, products, and services, can be attractive for financing by investors not located in the incorporation country of such companies. This means that, subject to certain limitations related to e.g. national security concerns or availability of public funding, the financing of space companies also becomes "global" and investors from all over the world can consider financing of NewSpace companies independently of their jurisdiction of incorporation or operations. NewSpace companies can and do expand their presence by incorporating subsidiaries in various jurisdictions, increasing their possibilities to access various forms of financing to ensure successful growth.

Largely independently from the jurisdiction of incorporation the NewSpace companies should be aware of organisational steps that need to be carried out to attract financing and ensure successful completion of fundraising efforts. This activity is critical for such companies' success and must be taken very seriously, both in terms of securing a capable management team, working with the right consultants, ensuring compliance with the applicable regulatory framework, and of presenting the company and its business to potential investors. The success of securing financing does not depend both on the technology that a company develops and on the holistic assessment of the business, which is possible when potential investors become convinced that the company diligently carries out all aspects of its activities, including commercial, corporate, financial, human capital-related, and others.

5

THE SPACE PROTOCOL OF THE CAPE TOWN CONVENTION

A tool to promote greater commercialisation and private financing in the space sector

Hamza Hameed and Anna Veneziano

5.1 Introduction to the legal framework of the Space Protocol to the Cape Town Convention

Negotiated under the auspices of the International Institute for the Unification of Private Law (UNIDROIT) and adopted in Cape Town on 16 November 2001 at a diplomatic conference sponsored by UNIDROIT and the International Civil Aviation Organization (ICAO), the Convention on International Interests in Mobile Equipment (the "Cape Town Convention" or "Convention")[1] is regarded as one of the most ambitious, economically significant, and successful international treaties in the field of commercial and private law.[2] The Convention has 83 Contracting States, representing over 78.7% of global population and over 72% global nominal GDP.[3] The Convention has also been approved by the European Union.[4]

The Cape Town Convention is rightly described as "the most successful international secured transactions instrument ever adopted".[5] The treaty creates a comprehensive international legal regime promoting asset-based financing and leasing transactions to protect secured creditors, conditional sellers, and lessors in certain categories of high value mobile equipment. In doing so, the

1 Convention on International Interests in Mobile Equipment, 2307 UNTS 285.

2 For additional information on the Cape Town Convention see Roy Goode, Convention on International Interests in Mobile Equipment and Protocol thereto on Matters Specific to Aircraft Equipment, Official Commentary, 5th edition (2022).

3 Convention on International Interests in Mobile Equipment (Cape Town, 2001) – States Parties, available at the UNIDROIT website.

4 As of 25 July 2022. For most up-to-date status, see the UNIDROIT Website.

5 E.g., Charles W. Mooney, Cape Town Convention's Improbable-but-Possible Progeny Part One: An International Secured Transactions Registry of General Application, The Essay (2014) 55 Va J Int'l L 163, 166.

DOI: 10.4324/9781003268475-8

treaty provides greater legal certainty to holders of security and quasi-security interests in mobile assets, which is particularly relevant in situations when these assets cross national borders.[6]

The Cape Town Convention is supplemented by Protocols relating to high value equipment used in specific industries, and it is designed to apply in relation to each type of equipment in conjunction with the relevant Protocol.[7] Presently, there are four Protocols to the Convention: the Protocol on Matters Specific to Aircraft Equipment (2001);[8] the Luxembourg Protocol on Matters Specific to Railway Rolling Stock (2007);[9] the Protocol on Matters Specific to Space Assets (2012),[10] and the Protocol on Matters Specific to Mining, Agriculture and Construction Equipment (2019).[11]

The Space Protocol of the Cape Town Convention was adopted at a Diplomatic Conference attended by over 40 states and several intergovernmental organisations in Berlin in 2012. The Space Protocol extends the application of the Cape Town Convention and its rules to the space industry and includes specific practical and innovative provisions that cater to the unique circumstances created by the nature of space assets being located in orbit or on other celestial bodies.[12]

The need for an international system of secured transactions law, such as the Cape Town Convention, was identified in the 1980s and 1990s when there was a clear deficit in rules governing security interests in high value mobile goods in international transactions.[13] The starting point of the project that led to the adoption of the treaty was a growing global need for financing (including private capital) in the acquisition and use of high value mobile equipment. This was particularly evident, initially, in the aviation sector due to an exponential growth of air traffic and the aviation industry, coupled with a reduction of public financial support and the need to attract private capital, as well as positive externalities of acquisition and use of new equipment (e.g., greater safety of air travel).[14]

This increased demand for private capital was hindered by legal obstacles in using asset-based financing and leasing, particularly in cross-border transactions. The situation was without uniform law as there existed several issues in traditional conflict-of-laws approaches which were not always suited to movable assets. Moreover, the legal systems varied in their approach to recognition of security interests, the process for enforcement, and the remedies available when a creditor was looking to enforce its rights over an asset.[15]

Given this, the Cape Town Convention created a uniform legal regime by treaty to facilitate financing and leasing of certain types of uniquely identifiable, high value mobile equipment used

6 Roy Goode, From Acorn to Oak Tree: The Development of the Cape Town Convention and Protocols (2012) 17 Uniform Law Review – Revue de droit uniforme.

7 See Roy Goode, The Cape Town Convention on International Interests in Mobile Equipment: A Driving Force for International Asset-Based Financing (2002) 7 Uniform Law Review – Revue de droit uniforme; and Jeffrey Wool, Rethinking the Notion of Uniformity in the Drafting of International Commercial Law: A Preliminary Proposal for the Development of a Policy-Based Model (1997) Uniform Law Review – Revue de droit uniforme, 46.

8 See the Aircraft Protocol, which entered into force in 2006 together with the Convention; text available at the UNIDROIT website.

9 See Rail Protocol, text available at the UNIDROIT website.

10 See Space Protocol page at the UNIDROIT website.

11 See MAC Protocol page at the UNIDROIT website.

12 Roy Goode, Convention on International Interests in Mobile Equipment and Protocol thereto on Matters Specific to Space Assets, Official Commentary, 1st edition (UNIDROIT, 2013), 11.

13 For a detailed history of the Cape Town Convention, see Anton N. Didenko, The Cape Town Convention. A Documentary History (Bloomsbury Publishing 2021); see also Ron Cumming, Cape Town Convention and AEP Canadian Ratification Meeting, Transport Canada and Department of Justice Canada, Ottawa (January 2008).

14 *Ibid.*

15 See, e.g., Iwan Davies, The New Lex Mercatoria: International Interests in Mobile Equipment (2003) 52 ICLQ 151.

in specific industry sectors, with the key goal being to offer greater certainty to private financiers and creditors participating in secured lending activities.

The Cape Town Convention and all its Protocols have the following key features:

1. The International Interest: Parties can create an autonomous "international interest" over the equipment, deriving from a security agreement, a conditional sale, or a lease agreement.
2. The International Registry: A dedicated international asset-based and wholly electronic registry, specific to each Protocol, ensures transparency and predictability as well as effectiveness of creditors' rights as against competing creditors and in insolvency.
3. Clear Priority Rules: The registry provides a clear rule for determining priorities ("first-to-file rule"), including as against interests in domestic law, with limited and well-defined exceptions.
4. Effective Enforcement Measures Applicable also in Insolvency: The Cape Town Convention provides effective and swift enforcement measures, including out-of-court remedies if Contracting States so agree, and including advance relief pending final determination during court proceedings.
5. Flexibility through Declarations: States can make policy choices through declarations to the Convention and to the Protocols.
6. Enhanced Creditor Protection through Protocols: Protocols allow Contracting States to strengthen creditors' rights in enforcement and insolvency through declarations.

The Cape Town Convention and its Aircraft Protocol entered into force in 2006. Since then, the International Registry established under the Aircraft Protocol (which is presently in force in more than 80 states around the globe),[16] has recorded more than 1.3 million registrations over an estimated value of collateral of more than US$650 billion.[17] The operators of states that adopt the Convention and the Protocol may receive up to a ten percent (10%) discount on export credit premiums,[18] and have enjoyed improved rating in capital market lending operations. For example, it was calculated that the adoption of the Convention and the Protocol could enable an airline to save US$330,000 on the purchase of a new ATR 72 and US$2.5 million on the purchase of an Airbus A380.[19]

The Space Protocol to the Convention was drafted specifically to extend similar benefits to the space industry. The Protocol, which is designed to be applied together with the main Convention, consists of five parts: identification of the scope of application of the treaty in relation to the interests and transactions that are governed by the Cape Town Convention, the technical requirements for creating these interests, the specific remedies available to the parties, the specific priority rules that determine the rights of the parties, and the procedure for a party to ensure its priority through the registration of its interest.[20]

16 Protocol to the Convention on International Interests in Mobile Equipment on Matters Specific to Aircraft Equipment – States Parties, available at the UNIDROIT website.

17 See generally the website of the International Registry for Aircraft Objects; see also Celebrating One Million Registrations, Aviareto (2019).

18 Arrangement on Officially Supported Export Credits (OECD, 2022).

19 David Knibb, In Focus: How new export credit rules will change aircraft finances (FlightGlobal, 22 January 2013).

20 Mark J. Sundahl, The Cape Town Convention, Its Application to Space Assets and Relation to the Law of Outer Space (Martinus Nijhoff Publishers, 2013) 29.

Protection of an assignment of the debtor's rights to a creditor is achieved by provisions enabling such assignments to be recorded against the registration of the international interest to which they are related. The Space Protocol further assists creditors with capturing additional collateral sums payable to the debtor from third parties by way of rent, licence fees, etc. (collectively defined as "debtor's rights") payable for the lease of, or access to, the space asset.[21]

There are five underlying principles of the Convention which are equally applicable to the Space Protocol:

1. Firstly, the Protocol aims to achieve practicality, as it reflects the vital factors of asset-based financing and leasing transactions within the space sector.
2. Secondly, the treaty enhances party autonomy, which reflects the fact that all the parties to high value cross-border space transactions will be knowledgeable and experienced in such transactions and expertly represented to ensure that their agreements are respected and enforced.
3. Next, the Space Protocol will ensure predictability in the application of the legal regime. This is specifically referred to in the interpretation provisions of Art. 5(1) as well as in the priority rules of the Convention itself, which give pre-eminence to certainty and simplicity.
4. Furthermore, the Space Protocol furthers transparency, achieved by the fact that there are rules within the Convention, applied to the Protocol, which provide for publicity of an international interest through registration, in order to give notice of it to third parties and ensure the application of a transparent priority system.
5. The last principle is sensitivity to national legal cultures. Both the Convention and the Space Protocol allow a Contracting State to weigh the economic benefits of the uniform legal regime against established national laws, through declarations that can exclude select provisions of the treaty should they be considered incompatible. Alternatively, a Contracting State can opt into select provisions that will reinforce creditors' rights under the treaty, thereby reinforcing the economic benefits deriving from its application.[22]

In addition to the basic set of principles and rules contained in the Convention, the drafters of the Space Protocol explored several space industry-specific issues, and special rules were inserted into the Space Protocol to ensure that the nature of the space industry was accommodated. These special provisions are addressed in the following paragraphs.

5.1.1 Scope of the Space Protocol

The Space Protocol defines the term "space asset" as:

Any man-made uniquely identifiable asset in space or designed to be launched into space, and comprising:

(i) a spacecraft, such as a satellite, space station, space module, space capsule, space vehicle or reusable launch vehicle, whether or not including a space asset falling within (ii) or (iii) below;

21 These features are particularly important for the space sector. See Roy Goode, Convention on International Interests in Mobile Equipment and Protocol thereto on Matters Specific to Space Assets, Official Commentary, 1st edition (UNIDROIT, 2013) Part 2.

22 See Roy Goode, Convention on International Interests in Mobile Equipment and Protocol thereto on matters specific to Mining, Agricultural and Construction equipment, Official Commentary, 1st edition (UNIDROIT, 2021) 2.23.

(ii) a payload (whether telecommunications, navigation, observation, scientific or otherwise) in respect of which a separate registration may be effected in accordance with regulations; or
(iii) a part of a spacecraft or payload such as a transponder, in respect of which a separate registration may be effected in accordance with the regulations, together with all installed, incorporated or attached accessories, parts and equipment and all data, manuals and records relating thereto.[23]

The aforementioned definition is inclusive of all space objects which are commonly used by companies in the space industry. It is also cognisant of the high potential of technological advancements and developments within the space industry, and hence, has given discretion to the Regulations of the International Registry (hereinafter "Space Registry Regulations") to be established under the Space Protocol, to decide upon the inclusion of additional types of space assets, e.g., payloads, and parts, as appropriate, upon consultation with the industry, should there be a recognised need for independent financing of such assets.[24]

The current version of the Space Registry Regulations was finalised at the fourth session of the meetings of the Space Preparatory Commission, which was set up through Resolution 1 of the Diplomatic Conference in Berlin.[25]

This version distinguishes "transponders or other communication equipment" and other payloads and parts, namely "observation payload", "navigation payload", "scientific payload", and "other parts of a spacecraft or payload". For the fourth type of assets, Annex 1 to the Space Registry Regulations includes an Explanatory Note to the extent that the bankability of these types of assets is yet to be tested. This means that, for the time being, the Space Registry will start accepting registrations only in spacecraft and transponders or other communication equipment until revisions are made to the draft Space Registry Regulations. This corresponds with the current practice of financial leasing within the space industry, which is limited to satellites and satellite transponders; however, such a limited approach may be adjusted in the future as required through the Space Registry Regulations.[26]

5.1.2 Public service exemption

Noting that space assets are often used for the provision of important public services, the drafters of the Space Protocol ensured that such services are not unexpectedly terminated in the case of a

23 See Art. II of the Space Protocol. For a detailed discussion on the definition of a Space Asset under the Space Protocol see: Mark J. Sundahl, The Cape Town Convention: Its Application to Space Assets and Relation to the Law of Outer Space (2013) 35; Pai Zheng, Space Asset under the Space Protocol of the Cape Town Convention, Haiser Global Law School (2014). For a discussion of the early evolution of the term Space Asset in the Cape Town Convention, see Sylvia Ospina, The Concepts of Assets and Property: Similarities and Differences, and Their Applicability to Undertakings in Outer Space, Proceedings of the Forty-Fifth Colloquium on the Law of Outer Space (2003) Vol. 12; Olivier M. Ribbelink, The Protocol on Matters Specific to Space Assets, 12 European Rev. Private L. 37, 39 (2004).

24 For the Regulations see Appendix III of the Report of the Fourth Session of the Preparatory Commission for the Establishment of the International Registry for Space Assets Pursuant to the Space Protocol (UNIDROIT, 2015).

25 Members of the Space Preparatory Commission include Brazil, the People's Republic of China, the Czech Republic, France, Germany, India, Italy, the Russian Federation, Saudi Arabia, South Africa and the United States of America. Additional industry and regulatory such as the ITU are also actively involved in the meetings of this Commission.

26 See Rory McPhillips, Howard Rosen, Souchirou Kozuka, Stuard Kennedy, Comparative analysis of aircraft, rail and space international registries and their regulatory provisions, Cape Town Convention Journal, 5:1 (2017) 29-67.

default on part of the debtors to a financial agreement. As such, Art. XXVII of the Space Protocol contains a provision restricting the remedies available to a creditor with respect to a space asset that provides a public service.[27]

The underlying concept is that the state has a natural interest in ensuring that a creditor exercising its rights does not cause the abrupt termination of a service of public importance (e.g., a satellite system monitoring weather conditions or providing GPS public services). Article XXVII is triggered by the registration of a "public service notice", which can be done on agreement of the parties to the public service contract and the Contracting State.

The creditor's consent is not required to register a public service notice, however, since the debtor will be party to the public service contract, the creditor will be able to make a contractual provision restricting the debtor's right to consent to the registration of a public service notice.

Upon the registration of a public service notice, a creditor may not exercise remedies making the space asset unavailable during the "suspension period", which begins with the registration by the creditor of a default notice which states that it will or may exercise default remedies if the debtor does not cure its default within the registration period.

The length of the "suspension period" is confirmed by Contracting States through a mandatory declaration under Art. XXVII(4) and can be a period between three and six months. Article XXVII(9) provides an exception to suspension of remedies under a public service notice in the unusual circumstances that (1) the international interest is registered before the public service notice, (2) the creditor has no knowledge of the public service contract or the public service notice, and (3) the public service notice is not registered within six months after the initial launch of the space asset.[28]

5.1.3 Identification criteria for space assets

The International Registry is at the core of the Cape Town Convention system. Since it is an asset-based registry, it requires identification of the asset that is to be used as collateral. Besides providing for a broad definition of what may comprise as a space asset, the Space Protocol also addresses the identifiers for space assets that allow entering an interest into an object into the Registry. For this purpose, the Space Protocol refers to the Regulations that will bind the Registry upon its establishment.

The present version of the Regulations requires all assets to be associated to a "unique identification number". The process for the issuance of this number is detailed in Annex 2 of the Regulations. The owner of a space asset may request issuance of a unique identification number by providing the Registrar with (a) the name of the owner, (b) the name of the manufacturer, (c) the manufacturer's contract reference number, and (d) the category of space asset. If it appears that a unique identification number already exists for a particular asset, then the Registrar must use this.

Furthermore, the Registrar shall then create a "unique identification file" for each space asset for which the unique identification number is issued and record the unique identification number in the file. It is in this file that an international interest, when registered, is recorded. Additional

27 See Anna Veneziano and Hamza Hameed, The Space Protocol of the Cape Town Convention: An International Secured Transactions Regime for Space Assets, IAC-18,E7,2,4,x44273, Proceedings of the International Astronautical Congress 2018.

28 See Tugrul Cakir, The Public Service Exemption in the Space Protocol in light of that found in the Luxembourg Protocol, IAC-16,E7,1,9,x33965, Proceedings of the International Astronautical Congress (2016); Howard Rosen, Public service and the Cape Town Convention, Cape Town Convention Journal (2013) 131–147.

information to be used for reference in order to better identify the collateral, though not for determining priority, is also recorded in the same file.[29] Additional information such as the UTC time of the launch of the object, the frequency allotted to it, or any other COSPAR unique identifier associated to it may also be entered into the file.

5.1.4 Salvage

Salvage is a legal or contractual right or interest in, relating to, or derived from a space asset that vests in the insurer upon the payment of a loss relating to the space asset. Insurance is an important consideration in the financing of space assets and the Space Protocol seeks to ensure that this aspect of the industry is not significantly impacted by the Protocol. Article IV(3) provides that nothing in the Convention or Protocol can affect any legal or contractual rights of an insurer to salvage in accordance with the applicable law.

As such, salvage rights, including rights by subrogation, are not affected by the Convention or Protocol, so that any priority dispute between salvage rights and creditor rights will be resolved by the applicable law.[30]

5.1.5 TT&C enforcement mechanism

The Space Protocol was drafted specifically keeping in mind the current logistical impossibility of physical repossession of space assets. Hence, the drafters sought to address this by focussing on the Tracking, Telemetry and Control (TT&C) of space assets which can be found within the command codes associated to it. Satellite command codes are encryption keys which give control over the satellites. Article XIX allows the parties to an agreement to specifically agree to the placement of command codes and related data and materials with a third party to afford the creditor an opportunity to establish control over or operate the space asset to efficiently exercise its rights, as granted under the Space Protocol.[31]

However, Art. XXVI(2)(c) restricts Art. XIX in that laws and regulations of Contracting States can prohibit, restrict, or attach conditions to the placement of command codes with third parties.

5.1.6 Physically linked assets

Spacecraft can often be comprised of different modules that are physically linked together (e.g., the International Space Station). Article XVII(3) prescribes a significant restriction on the exercise of remedies related to physically linked assets. A creditor may not enforce an international interest in a space asset that is physically linked with another space asset so as to impair or interfere with

29 For the Regulations see Appendix III of the Report of the Fourth Session of the Preparatory Commission for the Establishment of the International Registry for Space Assets Pursuant to the Space Protocol (UNIDROIT, 2015). See also See McPhillips, Rosen, Kozuka, Kennedy, Comparative analysis of aircraft, rail and space international registries and their regulatory provisions.

30 For more on salvage rights see: Hughes, HFW Briefings, UNIDROIT Draft Space Assets Protocol (2012).

31 For more on the enforcement mechanism under the Space Protocol see: Martin Stanford, and Daniel Porras, Transfer of Possession and Control under the Protocol to the Convention on International Interests in Mobile Equipment on Matters Specific to Space Assets, in Corinne M. Jorgenson (ed), Proceedings of the International Institute of Space Law 2012 (Eleven International Publishing, 2013) 801–810; Michael Gerhard, Transfer of Operation and Control with Respect to Space Objects, Problems of Responsibility and Liability of States, German Journal of Air and Space Law (2002) 571–581.

the operation of the other space asset.[32] However, there are two limitations to the rule provided in Art. XVII(3):

- A creditor or buyer of the physically linked space asset must have registered its interest in the space asset before the interest of the enforcing creditor was registered;
- Article XVII(3) only takes effect subject to any agreement to the contrary between the two parties concerned (i.e., it is not a mandatory provision).

It has been noted that this rule does not, strictly speaking, address a priority issue, as the two interests relate to different space assets which are physically linked, rather than two interests in the same asset.[33]

5.2 The Space Protocol as a useful tool in space financing

5.2.1 Asset-based financing in the current industry landscape

The Space Protocol of the Cape Town Convention promotes the use of secured credit in the space industry and seeks to expand the amount of asset-based financing taking place.

The space sector is capital intensive and all participants in the industry, particularly those which are private companies, need a significant degree of investment in order to operate.[34] In trying to obtain financing, private space companies can generally rely on a number of different financial vehicles. This includes (i) equity finance, which refers to raising capital by selling a company's shares of stock; (ii) secured and unsecured lending, which refer to the borrowing of money either in exchange of rights in collateral, or based on a company's financial statements; or (iii) project finance, which refers to raising finance against a project's debt (or expected revenue), whereby lenders have the debt obligations satisfied with the revenue generated by a project.[35]

At this stage, it is important to draw a distinction between asset-based finance, which is a form of secured lending, and equity finance, unsecured lending, and project finance.[36] The Space Protocol, and the Cape Town Convention system in general, only apply to secured lending, and as such promote the use of secured lending on an asset-based model in the space sector. These treaties have no impact on all the other forms of finance, including the recent rise of venture capital and the use of special purpose acquisition vehicles, available for space companies.

Asset financing allows companies to leverage their assets and attain finance by giving creditors rights in those assets. The benefit of asset backed financing is that, in the case where the debtor cannot repay its debt to the creditor, the asset itself and its value may come under the ownership and/or control of the creditor. In this manner, the creditor will be ensured a higher degree of return

32 Paul B. Larsen, Berlin Space Protocol: Update, 64 German Journal of Air and Space Law (2015) 376.

33 See Roy Goode, Convention on International Interests in Mobile Equipment and Protocol thereto on Matters Specific to Space Assets, Official Commentary, 1st edition.

34 For example, apart from the construction and launch of a single satellite easily running into the hundreds of millions of dollars, the value of a transponder can easily range from five to twenty million dollars. See B. R. Elbert, Introduction to Satellite Communication, 3rd edition (Artech House, 2008) 141; and Anil K. Maini and Varsha Agrawal, Satellite Technology: Principles and Application, 3rd edition (Wiley, 2014) 203.

35 Edward R. Yescombe, Principles of Project Finance, 2nd edition (Academic Press, 2013) 1.

36 Michael C. Ehrhardt and Eugene F. Brigham, Corporate Finance: A Focused Approach, 6th edition (Cencage Learning, 2017) 693.

of the financing they have extended to the debtor.[37] This is more desirable to a creditor than offering the profits of the enterprise, especially when the enterprise fails, and the creditor would therefore receive little or no return on their outlay.[38]

Access to finance is among the three key pillars for the development of any industry, particularly one which has seen the emergence of a large number of small and medium sized entities.[39] Additionally, several institutions have identified access to credit as one of the prominent issues which needs to be addressed in continuing to support the growth of the NewSpace sector.[40] Asset-based lending, in the context of the commercial space industry, can be an important tool for improving the credit gap which exists in all capital-intensive sectors.

5.2.2 NewSpace and asset-based financing

The nature of companies in the space sector is rapidly changing, with a large amount of companies now categorised as "NewSpace" entering the industry. These companies are leaner, more business focussed, and often do not have the on-ground asset portfolios or founder support to continue to sustain their operations.

While start-up funding through venture capital is available up until a certain stage, many space companies face financial difficulties when trying to take their products to market. Asset-based financing allows for actors within the space industry to create a "new level of risk for financiers" and the Space Protocol greatly facilitates this. It creates "a uniform regulatory regime for the recognition and protection of security interests in space assets", – this ensures that issues such as those of conflict of laws or differing insolvency remedies, that are normally encountered in asset-based financing, are surpassed.

The Space Protocol facilitates transactions where assets serve as collateral, and by having a well-functioning legal framework in place, it reduces the riskiness of the extension of credit, by making it more likely that the amount loaned will be repaid if the debtor becomes insolvent. Additionally, the asset-based model also reduces the burden of a creditor as rather than monitoring the debtor absconding with the credit generally, the creditor now only has to monitor the asset securing the loan, and not the overall business and profitability of the debtor's enterprise.

By creating an international registry where interests in space assets can be recorded and perfected, the Space Protocol offers increased security and confidence to lenders to invest in the space industry. The fact that the Space Protocol additionally introduces a strong set of remedies in the case of a default further secures the investment and allows creditors from across the world to invest capital in space assets.[41]

The Space Protocol ensures that a standard set of international rules apply to such secured transactions. Therefore, the creditors do not have to be wary of a multiplicity of rules when internation-

37 Christopher D. Johnson, Financing for Commercial Space: Asset-Based Financing, International Space Law and UNIDROIT Draft Protocol on Space Assets (Advance LL.M. thesis, Leiden University, 2010).

38 Vadim Linetsky, Economic Benefits of the Cape Town Treaty (2009).

39 The other two pillars being Access to Markets and Access to Networks, see Mohini Malhotra and others, Expanding Access to Finance: Good Practices and Policies for Micro, Small, and Medium Enterprises (The International Bank for Reconstruction and Development/The World Bank, 2007).

40 See EIB Report; Alessandro de Concini and Jaroslav Toth, The future of the European space sector: How to leverage Europe's technological leadership and boost investments for space ventures (European Investment Bank, European Commission, 2019); OECD Handbook on Measuring the Space Economy, 2nd edition (2022).

41 Frans von der Dunk and Fabio Tronchetti (eds), Handbook on Space Law (Edward Elgar Publishing, 2015) 892.

ally investing in space industry projects. Moreover, this also ensures that the presence of the asset in space does not substantially affect the financing contract from a legal and risk perspective.[42]

The primacy and safety of interests in space assets, alongside the application of a strong system of remedies makes asset financing an attractive option for investors looking to contribute capital to the space industry. Moreover, the provisions of the Protocol also ensure that future creditors within the same asset can also easily search the online registry to check whether their investments are free of already existing third-party interests.[43]

Asset-based financing of space assets can only be effective and obtainable at affordable rates if creditors have confidence that their security rights in an asset will be enforced in the case where a debtor becomes insolvent.[44] The Space Protocol provides for this by giving creditors recognised property rights over the debtor's collateral, even in jurisdictions which might not have domestic law rules creating similar rights, which will be effective in all Contracting States of the treaty, thereby serving as "solid international legal framework to protect them [such rights and interests]".[45]

5.2.3 New technologies, secondary markets, and sustainable space finance

As new technologies develop, and the cost of access to space becomes cheaper and more affordable to a larger number of players, the importance of the availability of sustainable space financing grows. Additionally, as the space sector matures, acting sustainably in space also starts to become a priority for more companies.

In the past, space assets were purpose-built, with little to no secondary value as they could only deliver one type of service which was generally only useful to one particular company. However, several new technological developments are now making the case for a secondary market in space more foreseeable, which will certainly necessitate smooth mechanisms for the *in situ* transfer of space assets between parties. In terms of transfer of security rights and ownership interests, an efficient system of secured transactions law is important. Concurrently, there will also need to be standards and best practices for more public law related issues in this regard, which this chapter does not consider.[46]

Some of the new technologies which will enable a secondary market in space include:

a. In-orbit servicing – while in-orbit servicing can generally be divided into eight main categories,[47] improving technologies in the areas of satellite maintenance and repair for

42 Martin Stanford, The Availability of a New Form of Financing for Commercial Space Activities: The Extension of the Cape Town Convention to Space Assets, Cape Town Convention Journal (2012).

43 Mark J. Sundahl, The Cape Town Convention and the Law of Outer Space: Five Scenarios, 3 Cape Town Convention Journal (2014).

44 Mariam Yuzbashyan, Interaction Between Diverse Sources of Law Applicable to Legal Challenges Caused by Commercial Space Activities, Proceedings of the International Institute of Space Law (2012) 74, 82.

45 Álvaro Fabricio dos Santos, Financing of Space Assets, 19 SP (2003) 127.

46 For some of these matters, see Zhao Yun, Revisiting Selected Issues in the Draft Protocol to the Cape Town Convention on Matters Specific to Space Assets, 76 J. AIR L. & COM. (2011) 805.

47 See Joerg Kreisel, On-orbit Servicing of Satellites (OOS): Its Potential Market & Impact. (2002), which divides in orbit servicing into 1. Re-Orbiting: move of target to/in its target orbit; 2. De-Orbiting: move of target to graveyard orbit or initiation of destructive re-entry; 3. Salvage: salvage of target to e.g. orbital station or re-entry (non-destructive) to earth; 4. Maintenance: re-fueling or other re-supply of the target; 5. Repair: diagnosis and correction or repair of failures or faulty units of the target; 6. Retrofit: upgrade, update, or exchange of orbital replacement units

life extension, which presently makes up more than 50% of the in-orbit servicing market,[48] coupled with retrofitting space assets for different purposes, can greatly enhance their value on a secondary market where operators might look to derive additional value out of a space asset which has already served its primary purpose.[49]

b. In space manufacturing – in the past, the only mechanism through which assets were placed in orbit, or deployed on other celestial bodies, was through a launch from Earth. However, recently, there have been assets deployed into orbit from orbital outposts such as the International Space Station. Experiments have also been conducted for 3D printing in outer space, with plans to manufacture space assets in orbit, or on other celestial bodies rapidly being developed.[50]

   This gives rise to the potential for assets being built and deployed on demand in space, which subsequently creates a larger marketplace and thereby necessitates rules on issues such as rights of title, transfer of title, and financing.

c. Software deployed satellites and ground station as a service – another impediment for a secondary market in space was the fact that, historically, the launch of a space asset had to be coupled with the complementary establishment of a ground station which would be dedicated to communicating with the launched space asset. However, with more satellites now using standard off-the-shelf components in their assembly, it is possible to have ground stations as a service which can be purchased from service providers.[51]

   This allows for subsequent operators of a space asset to no longer have to go through issues such as proprietary communication links as an increasing number of space operators are moving towards the use of standardised protocols and tools. Additionally, with technological enhancements, the possibility to reconfigure a space asset through a software update which is installed via communication link can also allow subsequent acquirers of a space asset to use it for a purpose for which the object might not have originally been launched.

Secondary markets are a key driver towards the democratisation of any industry that has a high cost of entry and revolves around high value assets. It is also a key element in boosting sustainability, as assets have longer useful lives and deliver more value. Given that space applications have a role to play in helping accomplish almost all of the UN's Sustainable Development Goals,[52]

(ORUs) on the target; 7. Docked Inspection: system and fault diagnosis of the target using physical connectors; and 8. Remote Inspection: remote system and fault diagnosis of the target.

48 See Northern Sky Research report on 'In-orbit satellite servicing & space situational awareness represent a $6.2 billion opportunity' (2021).

49 Hamza Hameed, Secondary market for space assets – The economic case for on-orbit servicing as a mechanism to extend satellite life cycles and mitigate space debris, Proceedings of the International Astronautical Congress (Eleven International Publishing, 2021).

50 Prater T. Werkheiser, N., Ledbetter, F., and Morgan, K., In-Space Manufacturing at NASA Marshall Space Flight Center: A Portfolio of Fabrication and Recycling Technology for the International Space Station, AIAA SPACE 2018 Forum and Exposition (2018) 5364.

51 Hywel Curtis, Satellite Ground Station as a Service Provider, SatSearch.Co (2019).

52 Space4sdgs: How Space Can Be Used in Support of the 2030 Agenda For Sustainable Development, United Nations Office for Outer Space Affairs (2022).

most states are actively enhancing their space capacities and are looking to become more present in the space sector.

An instrument such as the Space Protocol can play a role in this by giving opportunities to parties from developing and emerging space economies to be able to acquire assets already in space, rather than having to launch their own. This might be a more attractive proposition for many, as the cost of the entry into the space industry is often the primary reason why participation from the developing world in the space industry is limited.

5.3 Conclusion

With many NewSpace companies being unable to get access to typical forms of space financing, especially at later stages in their development, the ability to leverage assets in exchange for favourable lending terms may prove to be very important to allow companies within the NewSpace sector to get access to capital. Furthermore, many small and medium sized companies in the space sector might only have their asset to leverage and set as collateral. An international secured transactions system such as the Space Protocol allows companies to rely upon their work and technology to secure financing – as opposed to divesting their stocks or securing loans with very high interest rates. This offers many benefits to NewSpace companies, and entrants into the space industry from developing countries who have trouble accessing the traditional types of funding available for space-related ventures.

The use of new technologies within NewSpace results in the production of innovative products meant for use in outer space, most of which will fall within the broad definition of "space asset" noted in the Space Protocol. The space industry has seen tremendous growth, which is expected to multiply in the near future, with Morgan Stanley estimating that the revenue generated by the global space industry will increase to US$1.1 trillion or more in 2040, up from US$350 billion in 2016.[53]

To facilitate this growth and allow for access to space to be open to all sorts of companies from developing and developed states, it is important to allow access to finance to companies of all sizes and capacities. The Space Protocol seeks to do this by allowing for capital to be injected into a company based primarily upon its work. Prior to the Space Protocol, there existed no international legal framework providing for asset-based financing within the space industry. To assist in the development of the space industry, an efficient international regime needed to be developed and this is exactly what the Space Protocol provides. The Space Protocol provides a stable and secure legal environment for transactions in space assets based on the tried and tested mechanism of asset-based financing.

At present, the Space Protocol has not yet entered into force, with the requirement for entry into force found in Art. XXXVIII of the Treaty.[54] Unidroit is actively working towards finalisation

53 Space: Investing in the Final Frontier, Morgan Stanley (2020).

54 Article XXXVIII reads: "1. – This Protocol enters into force between the States which have deposited instruments referred to in sub-paragraph (a) on the later of:

(a) the first day of the month following the expiration of three months after the date of the deposit of the tenth instrument of ratification, acceptance, approval or accession; and

(b) the date of the deposit by the Supervisory Authority with the Depositary of a certificate confirming that the International Registry is fully operational.

of the framework for the operation of the International Registry for the Space Protocol, as well as working with countries and stakeholders around the world to increase their understanding of the benefits that international secured transactions law can bring to the space industry, already today and increasingly so in the near future.

---

2. – For other States this Protocol enters into force on the first day of the month following the later of:
(a) the expiration of three months after the date of the deposit of their instrument of ratification, acceptance, approval or accession; and
(b) the date referred to in sub-paragraph (b) of the preceding paragraph."

C

The international legal framework for licensing space activities

Innovative examples

6

CANADA

Past, current, and future space law and policy perspectives

Maria Rhimbassen[1]

In the second century of Confederation,
the Fabric of Canadian society will be held together
by strands in space just as strongly as railway and telegraphy
held together the scattered provinces in the last century.

John H. Chapman, 1967

6.1 Introduction

Canada's early interest in the space sector reflects an identity interlinked with the vastness of its territory, the world's longest coastline, relatively small population, isolated communities, and its proximity to the North (and northern lights). The resulting interest in landmass monitoring, community connectivity, and science (ionosphere, ozone layer) made Canada a space pioneer. The current challenge resides in keeping up with this legacy, especially in regulatory terms, and channeling the Canadian space identity through a flourishing and competitive market, given the increasing commercialisation and privatisation of the sector worldwide.

The Canadian space sector generated CAN$5.5 billion in total revenues in 2019 (58% from domestic sources and 42% from exports), with a CAN$2.5 billion gross domestic product (2019), a domestic market share divided between government (11%) and non-government customers (89%), employing nearly 21,000 people throughout the economy.[2] Despite its legacy, Canada's space budget represents only 1% of the world's total funding for civil space activities,[3] and just 2% of the world's industry market share. The sector suffers from "brain drain",[4] mostly due to limited employment/funding opportunities (despite Canada's new centralising "Canada Business App"

1 The author and the team at *Routledge Handbook of Commercial Space Law* wish to express their appreciation to Marie Lucy Stojak.

2 *2020 State of the Canadian Space Sector Report, Facts and Figures*, 2019, CSA [CSA Report, 2020].

3 *Euroconsult Assessment of the Canadian Space Sector*, 2015, CSA, p. 4.

4 The co-founder of the US-based SWARM Tech company is Canadian and is an example of Canada losing talent since she co-created the world's lowest cost two-way satellite communications network.

DOI: 10.4324/9781003268475-10

Main Canadian Projects: Moon Exploration, BRITE Constellation, CASSIOPE (CSA), MOST (CSA), NEOSSat (CSA/DND), SCISAT (CSA)
International Partnerships: Explore Moon to Mars, International Space Station (ISS),
ASTROSAT (ISRO), CURIOSITY (NASA), James Webb Space Telescope (NASA), OSIRIS-REx (NASA), The Planck Space Telescope (ESA), PROBA-2 (ESA), Satellite Soil Moisture Ocean Salinity (ESA), THEMIS (NASA)
Applicable law: CISSAIA, The Cooperation Agreement between the Government of Canada and the European Space Agency,
Government Support: Strategic Innovation Fund (SIF), CSA (Space Technology Development Program (STDP), SmartEarth, Lunar Exploration Acceleration Plan (LEAP)), ESA, NASA
More at: https://ised-isde.canada.ca/site/canadian-space-industry/en/space-science-and-exploration

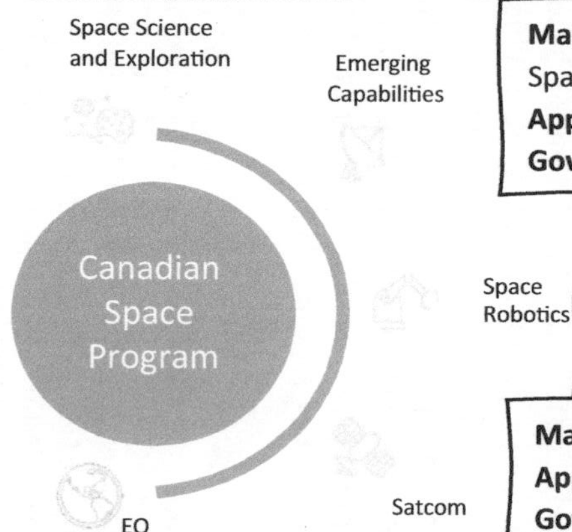

Main Canadian Projects: OSIRIS-Rex, Surveillance of Space 2, NorthStar Earth and Space (SIF), Quantum Encryption and Science Satellite (QEYSSat), Moon exploration
Applicable law: Radiocommunications Act, RSSSA,
Government Support: SIF, CSA (STDP, SmartEarth, LEAP), ESA

Main Canadian Projects: Canadarm3, Moon Exploration, Canadarm, Canadarm2, Lunar Exploration Light Rover (LELR), Dextre
Applicable law:
Government Support: CSA (STDP, SmartEarth, LEAP), ESA, NASA, ITB Policy

Main Canadian Projects: Telesat LEO; Spacebridge (Advanced Satellite Networks)
Applicable law: RSSSA
Government Support: SIF, CSA (STDP), ESA

Main Canadian Projects: RADARSAT-2, RADARSAT, Constellation, SCISAT
International Partnerships: CloudSat (NASA); Canada's Optical Spectrograph and InfraRed; Imaging System (OSIRIS) on the Odin satellite (Sweden); Soil, Moisture, Ocean, Salinity (SMOS) Satellite (ESA); Thermal Ion Imagers for the Swarm satellite (ESA); The Surface Water and Ocean Topography (SWOT) mission (NASA, CNES); Canadian instrument MOPITT
Applicable law: Telecommunications Act; RSSSA
Government Support: SIF, CSA (STDP, SmartEarth), ESA, NASA

Figure 6.1 Snapshot of the Canadian space sector, data compiled by the author from the CSA website

cross-departmental funding tool)[5] and a lack of long-term business predictability from government contracts. The industry has a lack of venture capital (VC), and several Canadian space companies have opened subsidiaries in VC-friendly jurisdictions (e.g., the US, the UK, Luxembourg). This explains efforts, primarily led by industry, to urge the Canadian government to provide stronger support for Canada's space sector, with regard to commercial space activities.

Canadian space legislation is scattered. Currently, stakeholders involved in NewSpace activities (e.g., space traffic management (STM), on-orbit servicing (OOS), active debris removal (ADR), space resources utilisation (SRU)) must navigate through a complex maze and a legal void. A new comprehensive legislation that centralises all space-related activities is needed. This chapter presents a brief overview of Canada's space-related technological achievements and a more substantive history and description of legislative/policy milestones to inform readers of the current state of space affairs in Canada.

6.2 The Canadian space programme: a historical bird's-eye view of major technological and scientific milestones

To better understand the regulatory context of Canadian space activities, it is necessary to present the major milestones that shaped Canada's involvement in the space sector. Indeed, this exercise demonstrates the nation's pioneering identity and legacy in the early days of the Space Age. According to the Canadian Space Agency's State of the Canadian Space Sector Report (2020),[6] Canada's activities in the space sector are divided into the following segments: satellite telecommunications (83%); navigation (8%); Earth observation (4%); space exploration (2%); space science (2%); and other (1%), whereas the proportion of space sector revenues by value-chain segment is divided this way: services (46%); products and applications (19%); satellite operations (18%); ground segment manufacturing (6%); space segment manufacturing (6%); and research, engineering, and consulting services (5%).

Canada's involvement in modern space activities started in 1957–1958, during the International Geophysical Year. Canada and the United States built suborbital launching facilities, the Churchill Research Range, in Northern Manitoba (shut down in 1989).[7] In 1957, the Space Age began with the launch of the Soviet Sputnik 1 satellite. Canadian scientists[8] were the first to record its beeping. In 1958, Canada became a charter member of the newly created United Nations *ad hoc* Committee on the Peaceful Uses of Outer Space (COPUOS) and, in 1959, NASA agreed to launch Canada's indigenous Alouette 1 satellite to study the Earth's ionosphere. Alouette 1 was successfully launched in September 1962, thus making Canada the third nation, after the Soviet Union and the US, to design and build its own satellite. The main purpose of Alouette 1 was to study the propagation of satellite-to-ground communications systems at high latitudes pertinent to the nation. In 1962, Canada installed its first telecommunications hardware on a US satellite and, in 1964, became a founding member of INTELSAT. In 1967, Canada ratified the Outer Space Treaty (OST) which entered into force that same year. In 1969, Mission Apollo 11 took place, enabling humanity to set foot on the Moon for the first time. The Eagle Module used during this mission relied on Canadian-built landing gear. This proved to be a very productive year for the Federal Government of Canada, which also announced the creation of Telesat Canada, a Crown

5 *Canada Business App*, Gov't of Canada.

6 CSA Report, 2020, supra, note 2.

7 *Canadian Space Milestones*, CSA, Gov't of Canada [CSA Milestones].

8 CSA Report, 2020, supra, note 2.

corporation. Telesat launched a Hughes Aircraft HS-333 communications satellite, named Anik A1, which was placed into geosynchronous orbit in November 1972, becoming the first national domestic satellite to be placed in orbit by a commercial organisation. As of this writing, Telesat, which was privatised in 1991, is the fourth largest global fixed satellite services operator in the world. It will launch Lightspeed, a network of low-Earth orbit (LEO) satellites to provide high-speed connectivity to all Canadian households by 2030,[9] thanks to the 2019 "High-Speed Access for All: Canada's Connectivity Strategy".[10]

The Anik satellite communications (satcom) programme has represented a series of consecutive world firsts (world's first domestic GEO satcom; interconnected satcoms on the same orbit; dual-use satellite; direct broadcast satellite for commercial use; largest commercial satcom communications satellite; etc.). In the 1980s, Canada became an Earth observation (EO) pioneer in synthetic aperture radar (SAR) technology thanks to its RADARSAT programme, approved in 1984, and launched RADARSAT-1 in 1995, providing the first-ever high-resolution image of the South Pole.

Another milestone was the Communications Technology Satellite (CTS), also known as Hermes, a joint effort between the Department of Communications, NASA, and the European Space Agency (ESA). Hermes became the most powerful communications satellite at the time. Canada also started to excel in space robotics, with the creation of the Canadarm, which launched in 1981 and was used on the Space Shuttle (Canadarm2, launched in 1999, served exclusively on the ISS, and Canadarm3, designed to operate without human intervention around the Moon, was announced in 2019 when Canada committed to the NASA Lunar Gateway programme). The Canadian astronaut Hansen will take part in the Artemis II mission.

Thanks to an agreement with ESA, Canada participated in the world's largest hybrid communications satellite at the time, Olympus; the ENVISAT programme, which in 2002 was the world's most advanced EO satellite; the Herschel Space Observatory (the largest most powerful infrared telescope ever flown in space); and the Planck Space Telescope (which, in 2013, unveiled the most precise map of the cosmos to date, showing the Universe's age and composition).

In the 1980s, the first search and rescue mission was conducted using a satellite-assisted system set in place by a partnership between the US, the Soviet Union, France, and Canada (the number of Canadian lives saved with this service totaled 1,500 in 2013,[11] while more than 2,200 Canadian lives are saved each year thanks to satellite technology).

Canada also started its astronaut programme and entered the International Space Station (ISS) dialogue in the 1980s. Since then, Canada has opened itself to bilateral agreements (Russia, Japan, China, India, UK, etc.) and, as of this writing, approximately 200 bilateral agreements have been signed.

In the 2000s, Canada joined the French National Centre for Space Studies (CNES) and ESA in creating the International Charter on Space and Major Disasters. Canada innovated once again with space robotics (drilling technology that could potentially be used on Mars; meteorological instruments for the NASA-led Phoenix mission, which discovered snow falling from Martian clouds; the APXS X-Ray instrument on the NASA-led Curiosity mission that helped to study the potential of the Martian environment to support microbial life; the Dextre on the ISS, a versatile robot to demonstrate key technologies that could lead to future robotic systems that can repair

9 *Government of Canada announces $1.44-billion investment in Telesat supporting the future of connectivity for rural and remote communities*, ISED, Gov't of Canada, 12 August 2021.

10 *High-speed Internet for all Canadians*, ISED, Gov't of Canada.

11 Government of Canada, *Comprehensive Socio-Economic Impact Assessment of the Canadian Space Sector*, Euroconsult, CSA, Final Report, 27 March 2015.

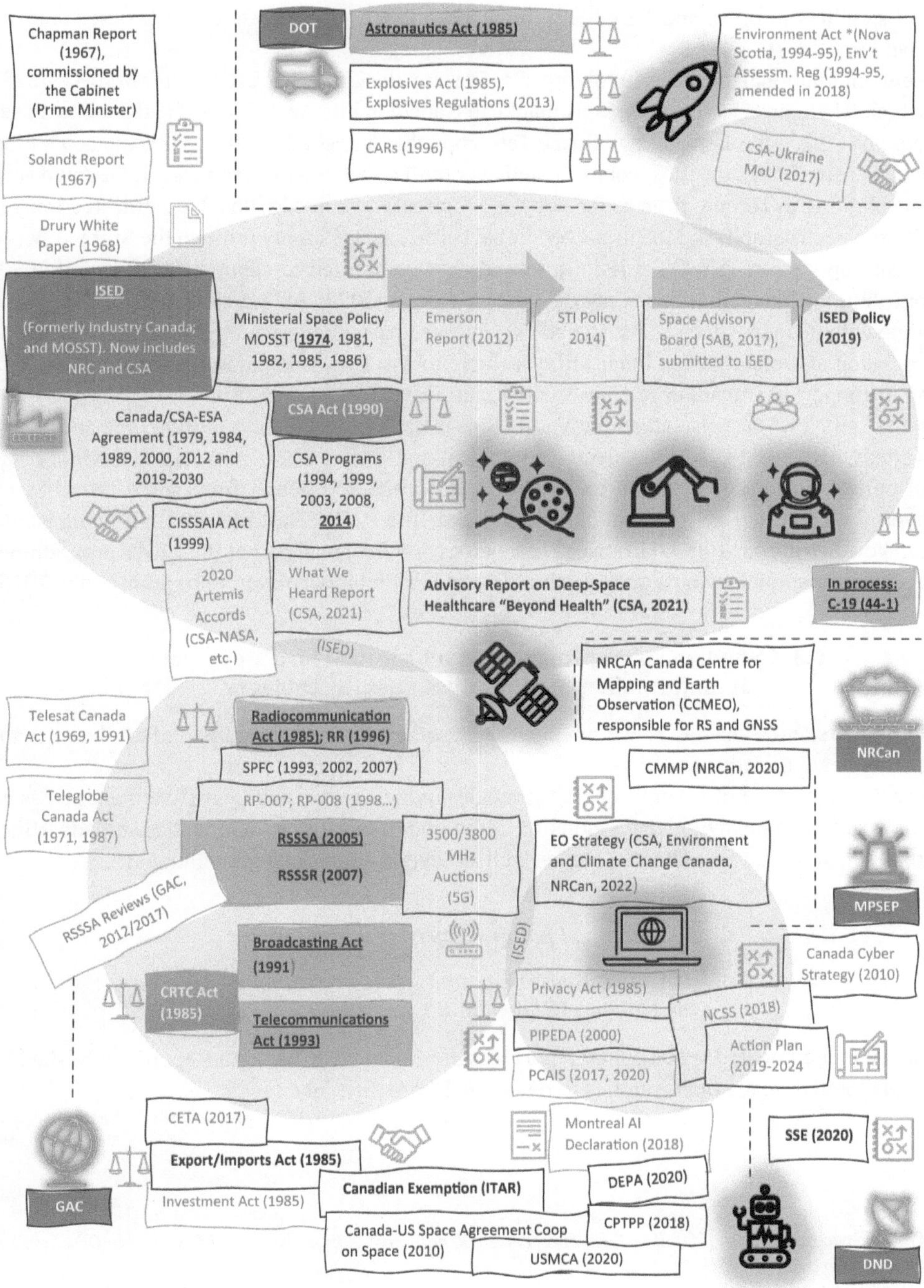

Figure 6.2 Map of Canada's space policy and law as compiled by the author

or refuel satellites in orbit; and NEOSSat, the world's first microsatellite to track space objects, debris, and satellites).

Recent international projects involving Canada are the 2014 NASA-led mission, OSIRIS-REx, which takes samples from asteroids thanks to Canadian high-tech lasers (OSIRIS-Rex Laser Altimeter, or OLA); the James Webb Space Telescope that launched in 2021, with Canada's Fine Guidance Sensor (FGS), the most sophisticated ever built on a telescope (so powerful it could spot someone blinking in Toronto from as far away as Montreal) combined with a Near-Infrared Imager and Slitless Spectrograph; and the first-ever global surface water survey through the Surface Water and Ocean Topography (SWOT mission). Canada has committed to support the ISS until 2030, and contribute to lunar missions. Canada's recent Budget 2023–2024 announced funding commensurate with its main space goals: Canada's continued participation in the ISS until 2030; funding to develop and contribute a lunar utility vehicle to assist astronauts on the moon; as well as funding in support of Canadian science on the Lunar Gateway station.

Most recent NewSpace private initiatives include missions to tackle monitoring methane (GHG Sat)[12] (after Quebec and California created a joint cap-and-trade carbon market) and the first commercial optical-sensor constellation to monitor LEO orbits and debris from space (NorthStar). Moreover, the Quantum Encryption and Science Satellite (QEYSSat) mission will demonstrate quantum key distribution (QKD) in space.[13] Canadensys Aerospace, part of the LEAP programme, heading an international team, is tasked to build Canada's first moon rover, to be launched in 2026.

6.3 Canadian space programme: a historical bird's-eye view of major policy and law milestones, by category

To better understand Canadian space policy, it is important to draw a roadmap of all the relevant strategic and legal documents.

These are comprised of several reports, strategies, policies, etc., and laws (five main pieces of legislation and accompanying regulations on radio-communications, aeronautics, broadcasting, telecommunications, and remote sensing, as well as several subordinate regulations).

6.3.1 Structural policy reports and legislation

6.3.1.1 Upper atmosphere and space programmes in Canada (Chapman Report, 1967)[14]

Canada's first documented space policy report was the so-called "Chapman Report". Published in 1967, it elaborated on the opportunities to be derived from the space sector.

12 GHGSAT, Spectra, *In terms of funding, GHGSat received 20 million $CA from the federal Sustainable Development Technology Canada (SDTC).*

13 "QKD is a technology that creates virtually unbreakable encryption codes and will provide Canada with secure communications in the age of quantum computing. QEYSSat will bring Canada a step closer to the realization of a truly secure communication infrastructure that will enable national and even global interconnection." Mission calendar: December 2017: Contract award to IQC; April 2018: Request for proposals presented to the space industry; August 2018: Contract award to COM DEV and Neptec to develop the mission concept and system requirements; June 2019: Contract award to Honeywell for design and implementation phases; May 2020: Preliminary design review. The lead science institution is the University of Waterloo's Institute for Quantum Computing (IQC).

14 Chapman, J., et al., *Upper Atmosphere and Space Programs in Canada*, Science Secretariat, Gov't of Canada, 1967.

The Chapman Report's key recommendations were to acknowledge the importance of connectivity for all Canadians (including those in remote areas) and of the socioeconomic benefits of space spin-offs. The report recommended the establishment of a centralised space programme for development and manufacturing, and of a national space agency (civilian/contracting with commercial sector) prioritising specialisation in certain space technologies and a balanced import/export profile, small satellite launch system, domestic satcom system, and industry involvement at all stages.

The recommendations in the Chapman Report were reiterated in "A Space Program for Canada", 1967 (Solandt Report)[15] – a well-respected document, although not an official government report, issued by the Science Council of Canada directly to the Prime Minister. Noticeably, only the Solandt Report, the 1968 Drury White Paper, and the recent 2019 New Space Strategy for Canada emphasise the need for regulatory reform. This is because space activities were initially less complex and were government-initiated. More recently, commercial activities have demanded new national governance approaches to ensure Canada remains competitive within an increasingly global space arena.

The Solandt report recommended that Canada create a space programme and space agency and take a leadership position in "unlocking the secrets and potentialities of space".[16] The report also acknowledged the importance of the law regarding space in response to the 1967 OST and its signature by Canada.

6.3.1.2 A domestic satellite communication system for Canada (Drury White Paper, 1968)[17]

This white paper from the Minister of Industry acknowledged the vital importance of a domestic communication system for Canada's growth, prosperity, and unity. This policy objective was achieved with the passing of the Telesat Canada Act.[18] Under this Act, Telesat Canada Corporation was established as a Crown corporation (a public-private partnership (PPP) approach). In 1971, another Crown Corporation, Teleglobe Canada, was created under the Teleglobe Canada Act[19] and was aimed at providing Canada with international satellite communication capabilities. This PPP approach reflects the government's desire to protect the national interest and ensure fair pricing, and competition. It should be noted that Telesat was privatised in 1991,[20] while Teleglobe was privatised in 1987.[21]

The White Paper also makes reference to the International Telecommunications Union (ITU) Radio Regulations (RR) and points out that radio frequencies (RFs) and the geosynchronous orbit are both limited resources. In view of this, the white paper recognised the urgency for Canada to plan its domestic satellite system due to the "first-come, first-served" basis used internationally for RF use.

15 Solandt, O., *A Space Program for Canada, Science Council of Canada*, Gov't of Canada, Jul 1967.

16 Kerkonian, A. D., *New Law for New Space: The Case for a Comprehensive Canadian Space Law*, (DCL thesis, McGill University, Institute of Air and Space Law, 2020), p. 99, 104–106.

17 Drury, C. A., *Whitepaper on A Domestic Satellite Communication System for Canada, Ministry of Industry*, Gov't of Canada, 1968.

18 Telesat Canada Act, RS 1969, c T-4.

19 Teleglobe Canada Act, RSC 1985 c T-6.

20 Telesat Canada Reorganization and Divestiture Act, SC 1991 c 52.

21 Teleglobe Canada Reorganization and Divestiture Act, SC 1987 c 12.

6.3.1.3 Canadian policy for space, the Ministry of State for Science and Technology (MOSST, 1974)

This is Canada's first space policy. It acknowledged the growing international sphere of space actors and emphasised the need for a long-term strategy to strengthen the Canadian economy while ensuring Canadian independence and increasing international cooperation and trade.

This led to the creation, in 1981, of an Interdepartmental Committee on Space (ICS), which had an advisory role and reviewed proposals submitted by several departments (e.g., Energy, Mines and Resources; Environment; Fisheries and Oceans).[22] The ICS were against the siloed approach to space governance in Canada, which they believed made space projects vulnerable to budget volatility.[23] They proposed new interdepartmental divisions and recommended cashing in on commercial opportunities and building a government-led (PPP) satcom system. In 1982, MOSST designated a prime contractor and expanded its foreign policy based on international partnerships. This enabled Canadian participation in major international space programmes and helped reduce costs. It also led to "beneficial commercial relationships" in the global space market.[24] In 1985, MOSST increased funding for satcom, remote sensing, and the ISS, and took steps to develop a viable space industry of satellite-based services by selecting niches most beneficial to the economic development of the country.[25]

In 1986, MOSST released "The Canadian Space Program: Long Term Initiatives",[26] which recommended building on existing expertise such as space technology, engineering, and applications. The document also discussed the significant socioeconomic benefits of the scientific exploration of space, and it established five areas where Canada could leverage an even more considerable return on investment. These were commercial mobile satcom/telco systems (MSAT); a remote sensing programme (e.g., RADARSAT, ESA RS programmes); hardware for the ISS and spin-ins/spin-offs by partnering up with the industry; microgravity research by the government, academia, and the industry for advanced manufacturing; and spin-offs (such as telemedicine) from the practices of astronauts.

6.3.1.4 Cooperation Agreement between Canada (later the CSA) and the European Space Agency (1979, in effect until 1 January 2030)[27]

Pursuant to this agreement, Canada can participate in programmes based on the principle of "*juste retour*" where the CSA pays an annual membership fee so Canadian space companies can bid on tenders for ESA contracts[28] outside of the two ESA core programmes – general budget and the mandatory science programme (e.g., satcom (ARTES)); EO (Copernicus, etc.); exploration (E3P); navigation (NAVISP); technology (GSTP)).[29]

22 *Ministry of State for Science and Technology, Background Paper: The Canadian Space Program Plan for 1981/82 – 1983/84, Gov't of Canada, Apr 1981*, in Kerkonian, *supra*. note 16, p. 108.

23 Kerkonian, *supra*. note 16, p. 110, citing AIAC's report.

24 Ibid., p. 114.

25 Ibid.

26 *The Canadian Space Program: New Initiatives, Government of Canada,* Ministry of State for Science and Technology, May 1986.

27 *Cooperation Agreement between the Government of Canada and the European Space Agency*, Treaty E105577, Gov't of Canada.

28 *Canada-European Space Agency Cooperation Agreement*, CSA, Gov't of Canada.

29 *Canada's areas of action in ESA programs*, CSA, Gov't of Canada.

6.3.1.5 The Canadian Space Agency (CSA) Act, 1990

The Act focuses on coordinating Canada's space policies and programmes, promoting the peaceful use and development of space through science and technology to provide socioeconomic benefits, encouraging commercial exploitation of space and technology transfer to industry, promoting outreach, etc. Though not formalised within the Act, the Minister of Industry (now Innovation, Science and Economic Development – ISED) is responsible for the CSA, which is not regulatory in nature[30] but rather acts as a facilitator (i.e. it does not issue licences, nor does it regulate the activities of its partners such as the private industry, but it issues funding for specific projects).[31]

6.3.1.6 The Canadian Space Programme: a new horizon (CSA, 1994)

This report recommended that the CSA be responsible for the coordination of all civilian space activities in order to prevent government space-related jurisdictional overlap. It also stressed strategic use of space to protect national security and sovereignty, and it mentioned the need for "innovative and flexible" financing mechanisms. Outreach to younger generations was also recommended.[32]

A report released by the CSA in 1999 entitled "The Canadian Space Program: A New Era for Canada in Space" restructured the Canadian space programme around five pillars: (1) Earth and the environment; (2) space sciences; (3) human presence in space; (4) satcom; and (5) commercialisation.[33]

Another report, "Canadian Space Strategy: Serving and Inspiring the Nation" (CSA, 2003), focused on recognising space as a national priority[34] that could improve the economic and social well-being of Canadians.[35]

In 2008, the CSA created a Long-Term Space Plan,[36] but the document was unreleased due to the financial crisis).[37]

6.3.1.7 Reaching Higher: Canada's Interests and Future in Space (Emerson Report, 2012)

This report's purpose was to "to conduct a comprehensive review of all policies and programs related to the aerospace and space industries to develop a federal policy framework to maximize the competitiveness of this export-oriented sector and the resulting benefits to Canadians".[38]

Key recommendations included protecting and developing the North, refining agricultural practices, studying transportation and urban planning, improving meteorology, addressing OOS (debris remediation, refueling, etc.), and developing future SRU activities such as space mining. The report also saw a need for strengthening cross-sectoral collaboration and establishing a perma-

30 Kerkonian, *supra.* note 16, p. 155.

31 *Funding programs and opportunities*, CSA, Gov't of Canada.

32 Kerkonian, *supra.* note 16, p. 119.

33 *CSA 1999 Program*, pp. 18–19, in Kerkonian, *supra.* note 16, p. 122.

34 Ibid.

35 *The Canadian Space Strategy: Serving and Inspiring the Nation*, CSA, p. 5.

36 Gibbs, G., *Rationale and Framework for a Canadian National Space Policy*, SpaceQ, 7 September 2017.

37 Kerkonian, *supra.* note 16, p. 124.

38 David Emerson, *Reaching Higher: Canada's Interests and Future in Space*, Aerospace Review, Government of Canada, Vol 2, Nov 2012 [Emerson Report].

nent Canadian Space Advisory Council that represents all stakeholders to provide a "representatively diverse and neutral" perspective to the Minister of ISED.[39]

The report also stated that global trends (climate change, the rebalancing of economic and geopolitical power, the need for increased resources, the rise in security threats, the digital revolution, the aging population, etc.) could be addressed by a robust space infrastructure. However, the report noted that there were obstacles in the way, citing Canada's space programme's "inadequate clarity of purpose".[40] Many other obstacles were mentioned, including restricted private sector competition, dependence on public spending, national policies that prohibit foreign competition for national security reasons, and a lack of indigenous launch capability.

6.3.1.8 Space policy framework: launching the next generation (CSA, 2014)

Eleven years after the previous 2003 ministerial space policy, the Minister of ISED issued CSA's new policy to "strategically coordinate its policies and commitments [...] and put its existing resources to best use",[41] although without defining the new policy and remaining "budget neutral" and silent on future policy.[42]

This policy report acknowledged that space is "congested, contested and competitive" and is transitioning from the public realm into a commercially driven one. It recommended targeting a "competitive position" for the public/private sectors and tackling new customers/markets using five principles: (1) Canadian sovereignty, security, and prosperity; (2) private sector importance; (3) international relations (IR) expansion; (4) Canadian specialisation and excellence; and (5) inspiration of future generations (STEM education). The report also identified four action areas: (1) commercialisation (national defence, weather forecasting, public safety, etc.); (2) R&D (satcom/telco, optics, robotics, etc.); (3) exploration (advanced systems, international partnerships, human presence in space, etc.); (4) stewardship, management, and accountability (e.g., a Space Advisory Council).

6.3.1.9 What we heard: report on consultations (Space Advisory Board (SAB), 2017)[43]

Innovation, Science, and Economic Development Canada (ISED) revitalised the SAB in 2017 for an initial three-year renewable mandate. The SAB was tasked by the Minister of ISED to consult with stakeholders on a new space strategy and to report its findings. The SAB conducted numerous roundtables with stakeholders (industry, academia, space associations, investments groups, governments, amateurs, and education groups) to provide recommendations to the Minister in relation to Canada's next space strategy.[44]

These consultations resulted in two main recommendations: (1) designating space as a "*national strategic asset*" to ensure, *inter alia*, that a "whole-of-government" approach is taken in the development and management of the national space programme; and (2) maintaining the SAB to provide independent advice on the implementation of the space strategy, maintain dialogue

39 Ibid., p. 32.

40 Ibid., p. 14.

41 *Canada Space Policy Framework: Launching the Next Generation,* CSA, Gov't of Canada, 2014, p. 7, in Kerkonian, *supra.* note 16, p. 128.

42 Ibid., p. 129.

43 *Consultations on Canada's Future in Space: What We Heard,* Space Advisory Board, August 2017 [SAB].

44 Ibid., p. 1.

with various stakeholders in the community, and generate metrics for evaluating the success of Canada's future space programme.[45]

6.3.1.10 Exploration, innovation, imagination: a new space strategy for Canada (ISED, 2019)

The Minister of ISED presented Canada's new ministerial-level space strategy.[46] It focused on cohesion, and addressed the "realities of the new and evolving space environment"[47] while committing to additional R&D funding to build and demonstrate space technology with future commercial applications[48] (e.g., draft policies government, provide academia and industry access to open space-based data). Space is described as a "strategic national asset" that "requires a whole-of-government effort to ensure that Canada can continue to rely on space to help meet national needs"[49] (e.g., space based EO data for climate change utilising the RADARSAT Constellation Mission).

Key recommendations included joining the US-led Lunar Orbital Platform Gateway (LOP-G) programme, which led to the signature of the 2020 NASA Artemis Accords, and to building the next-generation AI-enabled deep-space robotic systems (e.g., Canadarm3) and continuing the Canadian astronaut programme. The need for education and outreach was also emphasised, as well as a need to increase nation-wide broadband connectivity. The report also identified a need to encourage industry to contribute to economic growth and job creation[50] using a clear, simple, and modern regulatory framework (strategic oversight for national security, commercial growth, international partnerships, and business-to-business (B2B) exchanges).[51] It was also recommended that future EO capabilities be prioritised (data and analytics for climate change).[52] Further, the report recommends that Canada recognise the NewSpace environment as critical to future growth and adopt regulatory policies that support and encourage NewSpace entrepreneurship.

The 2019 Strategy was iterated in the CSA 2021–2022 Departmental Plan.[53] This was followed by "Resourceful, Resilient, Ready: Canada's Strategy for Satellite Earth Observation", which was released in early 2022 by the Minister of Innovation, Science and Industry, the Minister of Environment and Climate Change, and the Minister of Natural Resources. This report's aim was to provide a "whole-of-society" approach to climate change and to support "day-to-day evidence-based decision making and planning" while "recognizing social, economic, and environmental priorities here on Earth". The report has led to investment in Canada's High-altitude Aerosols, Water vapour and Clouds (HAWC) as part of the Atmosphere Observing System (AOS) mission led by NASA.

Key recommendations included ensuring that satellite EO data is free, open, and accessible to maximise innovation and scientific and economic development; harnessing satellite EO to generate solutions for the Arctic, air quality, water management, and forest fires, etc.; and strengthening the delivery of critical services to keep Canadians healthy, safe, and informed.

45 Ibid., pp. 12–14, in Kerkonian, *supra.* note 16, p. 130.

46 Ibid., p. 136.

47 *Exploration, Imagination, Innovation: A New Space Strategy for Canada*, ISED, Gov't of Canada, 2019 [ISED 2019].

48 Ibid., in Kerkonian, *supra.* note 16, p. 132.

49 ISED 2019, supra, note 47, p. 9.

50 *Announcement of Opportunity (AO) through CSA's smartEarth funding program for EO: Canadian Downstream Space Sector Delivering on Canada's Better Future*, CSA, Gov't of Canada.

51 ISED 2019, *supra.* note 48, p. 16, in Kerkonian, *supra.* note 16, p. 132; *Contributions, grants and contracts awarded*, CSA, Gov't of Canada.

52 Kerkonian, *supra.* note 16, p. 132.

53 *CSA Departmental Plan 2021–22*, CSA, Gov't of Canada.

6.3.1.11 What We Heard: consultations report (CSA, 2021)[54]

In planning for Canada's next space strategy, the CSA initiated public consultations in 2020–2021 to hear stakeholders' opinions (academic, non-governmental organisations, industry, SMEs, start-ups, and individual stakeholders) on space priorities (space exploration, PPPs for robotics, quantum technology, AI and in-space communications, SRU such as space mining, IP, space debris, climate change, cybersecurity, space launch, Canada's leadership in terms of international space governance, etc., to discuss regulatory reform, given the expanding evolution of the commercial ecosystem and activities that need regulation. A new "What We Heard" report dedicated to regulatory reform is expected to be issued later in 2023).

6.3.1.12 Beyond Health: report of the Advisory Council on deep-space healthcare (CSA, 2021)[55]

This report aims at establishing Canada as the leader in deep-space healthcare, based on the recommendations of the Deep-Space Healthcare Advisory Council set up by the CSA in 2019. The report identifies deep-space healthcare as a strategic priority for the Canadian Space Agency. It also underlines the importance of AI in the health sector and how Canada's expertise in AI can help develop remote healthcare solutions in space and on Earth. On that topic, Canada is devoting much effort to space-related AI research and innovation (e.g. AIxSpace, etc.).

6.3.2 Comprehensive national legislation and technical regulation directly applicable to space

6.3.2.1 Main national space law No. 1: Radiocommunication Act, 1985 (updated version)[56] *and complemented by the Radiocommunication Regulations, SOR/96-484 (1996)*[57]

In Canada, the RF spectrum is considered a public resource and is regulated by the Government in the public interest. Canada has jurisdiction over all RF within its borders and on board a variety of vessels, including spacecraft under the direction or control of a citizen or resident of Canada or a corporation incorporated or resident in Canada.[58] Prior to launching, all satellite systems relying on radio communication systems under Canadian jurisdiction must obtain a radio and/or wireless authorisation (licence) issued by the Minister of Innovation, Science, and Economic Development (ISED). More information can be found in the Client Procedures Circulars (CPCs) from the Government Canada.[59] Typically, Canadian satellites require two main licences: one for radiocommunications, and the other for the specific mission of the payload.

The Spectrum Policy Framework for Canada was first released in 1993, and has been renewed twice since then (in 2002 and 2007).[60] ISED's policy framework for the licensing of fixed-satellite

54 *What We Heard report*, CSA, 31 March 2021.

55 Thirsk, R. (Chair of the Advisory Council on Deep-Space Healthcare), *Beyond Health: Report of the Advisory Council on Deep-Space Healthcare*, June 15, 2021, CSA/ASC.

56 Radiocommunication Act, RA, R.S.C., 1985, c. R-2; 1989, c. 17, s. 2.

57 Radiocommunication Regulations, *RR, SOR/96-484*.

58 Radiocommunications Act, s. 3(3)(b).

59 Referring to guidelines and technical requirements, see Client Procedures Circulars (CPC), Gov't of Canada. One example is the *CPC-2-6-01 – Procedure for the Submission of Applications to License Fixed Earth Stations and to Approve the Use of Foreign Satellites in Canada*, or CPC-2-6-06 – *Guidelines for the Submission of Applications to Provide Mobile Satellite Services in Canada.*

60 *SPFC – Spectrum Policy Framework for Canada*, June 2007, Gov't of Canada.

service (FSS) and broadcasting-satellite service (BSS) on a first-come, first-served basis is provided by the Policy Framework for Fixed-Satellite Service (FSS) and Broadcasting-Satellite Service (BSS) (RP-008), and the Policy Framework for the Provision of Mobile Satellite Service (MSS) Via Regional and Global Satellite Systems in the Canadian Market (RP-007), both first issued in 1998. Licensing requires (1) the eligibility to hold a spectrum or radio licence, (2) Canadian direction and control of the space station, (3) compliance with Canadian spectrum allocations and utilisation policies, (4) Canadian capacity and coverage requirements, and (5) a technical plan, including the space debris mitigation plan, for the space station.

6.3.2.2 Main national space law No. 2: Aeronautics Act, 1985 (Transport Canada)

Except for the Churchill Research Range (now shut down) and an on-going commercial spaceport initiative, Maritime Launch Services (MLS) in Nova Scotia, there is no launching capability or infrastructure in Canada. Instead, Canada has chosen to rely on international partners. This is to the detriment of the domestic industry, and it aggravates the brain drain. Furthermore, existing legislation for launching activities is insufficient.[61] It includes rockets under "aircraft", requiring compliance with the Explosives Acts of 1985/Explosives Regulations of 2013[62] ("model vs high-power rocket motors"), or the 1996 Canadian Aviation Regulations (CARs), amended in 2021.

Current legislation fails to clarify the conditions of public interest, on top of not having provisions for rockets more powerful than 40,960 newton-seconds, which deters any commercial initiative. In short, there is currently no law for the launching of satellites in Canada. The lack of clarity concerning the Federal Government's role, as in the case of MLS, in Nova Scotia, as opposed to the scope of applicable environmental law, confirms the need for more transparency, given the planned MLS spaceport will rely on foreign rockets (2017 MoU between Canada and the Ukraine). The federal government has entered into a process designed to frame a regulatory framework adapted to commercial launches. The Minister of Transport has announced support for commercial space launch activities in Canada, working with other federal departments and agencies to develop robust regulatory requirements for commercial space launch and to ensure that any launch is considered and approved in a manner consistent with domestic legislation, international treaties and conventions, and national security and foreign policy interests of Canada.[63]

6.3.2.3 Main national space law No. 3: Broadcasting Act, 1991 (and the Canadian Radio-television and Telecommunications Commission (CRTC) Act, 1985)

These regulate broadcasting in Canada, and on any ship, vessel, or spacecraft under Canadian jurisdiction, as well as any broadcasting signal originating from or received on Canadian soil/jurisdiction.[64] The CRTC is an administrative tribunal that regulates and supervises broadcasting and implements the Canadian Broadcasting Policy which includes protecting Canadian culture. For space-based radio broadcasting sources, the operators must apply for licences from both the CRTC and ISED. However, future broadcasting enabled by space-based internet providers (ISPs) might fall

61 Kerkonian, *supra.* note 16, p. 144.

62 Explosives Regulations, *ER*, 2013 (SOR/2013-211), Gov't of Canada.

63 *Space Agencies of Ukraine and Canada signed a Memorandum of Understanding*, 1 November 2017, Gov't of Ukraine.

64 Broadcasting Act, SC 1991, c 11.

under telco law/services because it is the "access to the Internet service" that would be channeled and not "predetermined content itself",[65] as determined by the Supreme Court of Canada in 2012.[66]

6.3.2.4 Main national space law No. 4: Telecommunications Act, 1993

Telecommunication legislation in Canada dates to 1852 with the Telegraphs Act and the 1906 Railway Act before transferring the sector to the CRTC in 1976. Since then, there have been attempts to merge broadcasting ("broadcasting undertakings") and telco under the same Act, but constitution-related legal hurdles prevented it.[67] The Act defines telco as "the emission, transmission or reception of intelligence by any wire, cable, radio, optical or other electromagnetic system, or by another or by any similar technical system". Canadian Ownership and Control Rules prevent foreign takeover of Canadian carriers when contrary to Canada's national security interests. Further, CRTC requirements include protection of user privacy, access to emergency services, network neutrality, National Contribution Fund (universal service to ensure access to basic telco services), etc.

6.3.2.5 Main national space law No. 5: Remote Sensing and Space Systems Act (RSSSA, 2005)[68] and accompanying Remote Sensing and Space Systems Regulations (RSSSR, 2007)

These originate in a 2000 bilateral agreement between Canada and the US to collectively control RS for shared national security and foreign policy interests, especially once privatised.[69] The RSSSA defines a RS satellite as "a satellite that is capable of sensing the surface of the Earth through the use of electromagnetic waves", which is a broad definition that includes all satellites with imaging capabilities, whether they are designed to view Earth from deep space or not.[70] Operating a RS satellite without a licence by the Ministry of Foreign Affairs (MFA) (now Global Affairs Canada (GAC)) is prohibited. Licensing considers national security, the defence of Canada, the safety of Canadian Forces, and Canada's conduct with respect to international relations (IR), and distinguishes between raw data (non-transformed, which can be distributed to third parties only with permission from the MFA) vs processed data ("RS product" which, once transformed, can be distributed to third parties unless prohibited by the MFA). In short, the RSSSA does not limit RS *per se*, but rather restricts distribution (RS products, access prioritisation by the MFA, etc.). The exception to this is when the MFA requests interruptions of service ("shutter control") for security or IR reasons (other limitations can be added at the licensing level).

The RSSR requires, *inter alia*, a System Disposal Plan (as per the non-binding international Debris Mitigation Guidelines), a Command Protection Plan, and a Data Protection Plan.[71] Clear milestones must appear on the licence (e.g., construction contract must be signed within two years and the satellite must become operational within five years). The licensing fee regime is organised

65 Kerkonian, *supra.* note 16, p. 148.

66 *Reference re Broadcasting Act*, Supreme Court Judgments, 2012 SCC 4 [2012] 1 SCR 142.

67 *An Overview of the Telecommunications Act* (prepared by Hank Intven), Gov't of Canada.

68 *Space policy and the Remote Sensing Space Systems Act* (RSSSA), Gov't of Canada.

69 *Agreement Between the Government of Canada and the Government of the United States of America Concerning the Operation of Commercial Remote Sensing Satellite Systems*, CTS 2000 No 14, GAC, Government of Canada, 3 March 2014.

70 Kerkonian, *supra.* note 16, p. 151.

71 Remote Sensing Space Systems Act – Operating licence application guide *(RSSSA),* Version 1.0 – 26 October 2020 GAC.

by satellite service.[72] GAC has commissioned two independent external reviews of the RSSSA (2012/2017) and a third one is in progress as of this writing.[73] In 2022, Space Strategies Consulting Ltd. (SSCL) conducted an independent review of the RSSSA[74] and found that it inhibits technological development of remote sensing space systems and that "Canada is therefore becoming a less desirable place to conduct space remote sensing research and development, grow space remote sensing businesses, and exploit space systems to address global challenges like climate change". Further reviews are mandated every five years (s. 45.1 of the RSSSA).

6.3.2.6 Spectrum Policy Framework (SPFC) (ISED, 2007) (latest version)

Thanks to the Department of Industry Act, the Radiocommunication Act, Radiocommunication Regulations, and the Telecommunications Act, ISED is responsible for spectrum (a "critical resource") management in Canada. (See the Commercial Mobile Spectrum Outlook;[75] 2018–2022 Spectrum Outlook.)[76]

A government online portal (Spectrum management and telecommunications)[77] compiles useful data on broadcasting applications, licences, certificates, online registration, allocations, auctions, the Canadian Table of Frequency Allocations, tutorials, etc. ISED has been holding spectrum auctions since 1999. In 2021, it held auctions for the 3500 MHz Band, and announced a future auction for the 3800 MHz band, both supporting 5G capacity (2020 Decision on Revisions to the 3500 MHz Band to Accommodate Flexible Use and Preliminary Decisions on Changes to the 3800 MHz Band).[78] This provides Canadians with a greater choice of wireless networks and deployment of 5G networks, which is "essential to Canada becoming a global center for innovation" in critical areas such as autonomous vehicles, smart cities, clean energy, precision agriculture, advanced telemedicine, etc. Cross-border 5G data transfers are regulated under the US-Mexico-Canada Agreement (USMCA), effective since 2020, replacing NAFTA. In 2021, ISED announced consultations to plan improved spectrum access and a new licensing regime for unused spectrum.

6.3.3 National legislation and strategy including provisions applicable to space or agreements that can impact space

6.3.3.1 Export and Import Permits Act (MFA, 1985)

This authorises the Minister of Foreign Affairs (MFA)[79] to issue a permit to any resident of Canada to export items included on the Export Control List (military and strategic goods and technology, etc.)[80] or export to a country included on the Area Control List, subject to certain terms and conditions before these items can be exported legally. Strategic goods include global navigation satellite

72 *Consultation on Updates to the Licensing and Fee Framework for Earth Stations and Space Stations in Canada*, August 2021, Gov't of Canada.

73 *Review of the Remote Sensing Space Systems Act* (RSSSA), IASL, McGill, Institute of Air & Space Law.

74 *2022 Independent Review of the Remote Sensing Space Systems Act* (RSSSA), Space Strategies Consulting Ltd., 21 March 2022.

75 *Commercial Mobile Spectrum Outlook,* Gov't of Canada, 2013.

76 *Spectrum Outlook 2018–2022*, Gov't of Canada.

77 *Spectrum management and telecommunications*, Homepage, Gov't of Canada.

78 *Government of Canada launches consultation to ensure Canadians have access to high-quality wireless services*, ISED, Ottawa, Ontario, 17 December 2021.

79 *Export and Import Permits Act* (R.S.C., 1985, c. E-19).

80 *Export Control List*, SOR/89-202.

systems, propulsion and space-related equipment, payloads, ground stations for telemetry and tracking and control of space launch vehicles or spacecraft, etc. The Controlled Goods Program (CGP) is a federal industrial security programme administered by Public Works and Government Services Canada (PWGSC) to strengthen Canada's defence trade controls for satellite global positioning systems and communications equipment, military equipment, and IP. All items imported from the US require a permit. In terms of defence, the Canadian Exemption (ITAR §126.5) allows US suppliers to export license-free certain less sensitive, unclassified ITAR-controlled material and services to Canadian recipients registered under the CGP. One prerequisite for Canadian Industry to use the Canadian Exemption is to register with the Controlled Goods Directorate (CGD). Exports to Canada of more sensitive as well as classified ITAR-controlled items or services still require a licence, just like any other destination.[81] Also, the 2010 Framework Agreement Between the Government of Canada and the Government of the United States of America for Cooperation in the Exploration and Use of Outer Space for Peaceful Purposes contains further provisions on cross-border exchanges and applicable exemptions (trade, taxes and customs, cross-waivers of liability, IP, registration, dispute resolution, etc.).[82]

6.3.3.2 The Civil International Space Station Agreement Implementation Act (CISSAIA, 1999)

This implements the multilateral ISS agreement of which Canada is a state party. In return for Canada's contribution to the ISS, Canada has a specific share in the utilisation of the ISS (to fly astronauts or conduct scientific experiments). Private activities are not regulated by the CISSAIA, except if part of a scientific experiment on board of or launched from the ISS.[83] The Canadian Criminal Code includes provisions related to criminal activities carried out on the way to, on board of, or returning from the ISS. Section 7 (2.34) states that for any action or omission that would constitute an indictable offence if committed in Canada is committed during a space flight, the offence is deemed to have been committed in Canada. This provision is specific to activities related to the ISS rather than in space generally.

This is amended by the Civil Lunar Gateway Agreement Implementation Act, as part of the Budget Implementation Act of 2022 C-19 (44-1).[84] The proposed budget contains the Civil Lunar Gateway Agreement Implementation Act as an Amendment in part 5, s. 18, and was tabled in April 2022 in the House of Commons. The text has the purpose of clarifying the extension of the extra-territoriality principle of Canadian criminal jurisdiction, to cis-lunar space and the moon:

> A Canadian crew member who, during a space flight, commits an act or omission outside Canada that if committed in Canada would constitute an indictable offense is deemed to have committed that act or omission in Canada.[85]

81 *Export Controls*, Gov't of Canada.

82 Framework Agreement Between the Government of Canada and the Government of the United States of America for Cooperation in the Exploration and Use of Outer Space for Peaceful Purposes, E105172, Gov't of Canada.

83 Kerkonian, *supra.* note 16, p. 156.

84 C-19, 44th Parliament, 1st session, 22 November 2021, to present: An Act to implement certain provisions of the budget tabled in Parliament on 7 April 2022 and other measures. Short title: Budget Implementation Act, 2022, No. 1, status available online.

85 BILL C-19 An Act to implement certain provisions of the budget tabled in Parliament on 7 April 2022 and other measures, Part 5, s. 18.

As the second nation to opt into the Lunar Gateway mission and the Artemis Accords, with a committed budget of CAD$1.9 billion over the next 24 years, Canada is implementing the MoU between the Government of Canada and the Government of the United States of America concerning Cooperation on the Civil Lunar Gateway and other related amendments to other Acts. This is an important Act because it can significantly impact international criminal law given its provisions on national jurisdiction and extraterritoriality in the space sector. Although, arguably, through this attribution link, this extension is not substantially new, its clarification puts Canada in the legal forefront as a leader in specifying what a space crime could entail, and this is crucial in this commercially growing sector.

6.3.3.3 The Comprehensive Economic and Trade Agreement (CETA) (GAC, 2017)[86]

As a bilateral agreement between Canada and the European Union (EU) for trade, this Act also addresses space by specifically stating that, for the CSA, the procurement of covered goods and services is limited to those related to satcom, EO, and global navigation satellite systems (GNSS). Therefore, it can be argued that full access reciprocity (e.g., European protected procurement for defence reasons) is not achieved and Canada might pull out from the space part, based on a clause, after the first five years (i.e. Annex 19-A – Market access schedule of Canada).

6.3.3.4 The Canadian Minerals and Metals Plan (CMMP), (NRCan, 2020)

Canada is a global leader[87] in the terrestrial mining industry. The CMMP includes space-based technology for mining and space mining ("use of raw materials from asteroids or planetary bodies").[88] The minerals sector is taking advantage of space solutions such as robotics, remote sensing, and aerial and EO technology to create "safer, cleaner, and more efficient operations".[89] The CMMP recommends the federal government develop a policy approach for mining new frontiers such as space to foster investment and economic development.[90]

6.3.3.5 Strong, Secure, Engaged (SSE): Canada's Defence Policy (DND, 2020)

One of the most ambitious space-related government documents, this calls for increased space and cyberspace capabilities across the nation, which is significantly important for security and defence and affects the influence of non-state actors, Arctic security, and the changing nature of peace operations.[91] The Royal Canadian Air Force (RCAF) will, among others, operate the future SSA microsatellite Redwing (2027–2033), oversee the defence space programme (space domain)[92] by establishing the "3 Canadian Space Division",[93] and coordinating regional and international participation (NORAD, Five-Eyes, NATO, UN, etc.). The report notes that satellites provide support across all operations, and that space is "congested, competitive, and contested."[94]

86 *Text of the Comprehensive Economic and Trade Agreement* – Annex 19-A, GAC, Govt't of Canada.
87 Canadian Mineral and Metal Plan, *CMMP*, NRCan.
88 Ibid., p. 32.
89 Ibid.
90 Ibid., p. 28.
91 Strong, Secure, Engaged (SSE), Canada's Defence Policy, DND, Gov't of Canada [SSE].
92 Ibid., p. 38.
93 *Establishment of 3 Canadian Space Division, Government of Canada,* Gov't of Canada, 22 July 2022.
94 Ibid., p. 56.

The key recommendations from this report are: modernise space-based capabilities and protect these critical assets while promoting the peaceful use of outer space; acquire space capabilities for global coverage satcom, EO, maritime domain awareness, space situational awareness (SSA), surveillance (e.g., Sapphire) and targeting; work with partners (e.g., research, cooperation and coordination with academia, industry, governments and allies) for Canada's national interests on space issues;[95] and, finally, build resilience and provide leadership in shaping international norms for responsible behaviour in space. A recent example of Canada's involvement at the international level is its participation in the newly-launched 2022 Combined Space Operations Vision 2031 (CSpO) effort, in partnership with the US, UK, France, Germany, Australia and New Zealand.

6.4 Discussion

As demonstrated above, the laws, policies, and provisions that apply to the space sector in Canada are scattered among a wide variety of governmental departments and legal instruments (e.g., ISED, GAC, International Trade, Export Promotion, Natural Resources, Fisheries and Oceans, Transport, National Defence, Environment, and Climate Change). This makes it difficult for new entrants to navigate through the licensing process and can represent an obstacle to NewSpace in Canada. Moreover, what slows down NewSpace further is the lack of regulation on emerging space activities, such as suborbital tourism (only scientific high-altitude balloons take place in Canada,[96] or zero-G scientific campaigns by the NRC),[97] OOS, or SRU. While these activities are not regulated at the international level (i.e., in international law), Canada ought to provide domestic actors with regulatory, financial, and fiscal incentives and clarifications which would not only spur innovation, but also attract foreign commercial stakeholders and contribute to the national economy. This is a major impediment to the development of innovation and commercial activity in Canada, an issue that has been highlighted in several reports, despite the recent support announced by the government about regulating commercial launches.[98] For example, Canada is building a commercial spaceport, but has no launching regulation other than relying on the OST and the Liability Convention (1972) with regards to liability. This means that Canada has no policy on required insurance for launching activities and therefore the state, which must indemnify third parties at the international level under international law, has no legal means to seek compensation from private actors responsible for damages. Several new national space legislations in other countries have remedied that by providing a mandatory insurance beyond which the state's guarantee applies.

Another aspect that needs to be addressed by regulatory reform is interdepartmental coordination and cohesion. Indeed, Canada's Investment Act and the Canadian Competition Act are at odds in several cases of foreign mergers with, or takeovers of, Canadian companies (e.g., Canada's MDA merger with the US's DigitalGlobe in 2017, thus becoming the US-based MAXAR in 2018, before MAXAR sold it back to Canada (Northern Private Capital) for US$1 billion in 2019,[99] or COM DEV's purchase by US-based Honeywell in 2016). In those cases, the Government of Canada has the power to clear or block such mergers, based on its interpretation of the Canada Investment Act and its

95 Ibid., p. 111.

96 Thanks to an International Collaboration with the Centre national d'études spatiales (CNES), such experiments are conducted in Timmins, Ontario.

97 Canada's National Microgravity Facility (Parabolic Aircraft).

98 For example, see: Dooling, J. et al., Revitalizing Canada's Visions for Space, Canadian Global Affairs Institute, June 2022.

99 Murphy, J., *Canada's space sector set for a relaunch*, Space News, 19 April 2021. Moreover, on 1 April 2021, MDA raised CAN$400 million for its initial public offering (IPO) on the Toronto Stock Exchange.

assessment of the operation being a "net benefit for Canada", regardless of competition law (creating a monopoly, killing domestic competition, etc.). This is problematic because, when it comes to competition law, the discretion of the executive branch outweighs that of the judicial branch, resulting in unpredictability and uncertainty in terms of foreign mergers policy and Canadian companies' future.

To facilitate cohesion and coordination between federal government departments and between the federal government and industry would require the establishment of a permanent body akin to the US National Space Council. As recommended by Space Canada in Canada's 2034 Pre-Budget Consultations, such a body should report directly to the Prime Minister's office to ensure that space is prioritised at the highest level of government and that a coordinated "whole of government approach" is adopted.

A 2017 roundtable consisting of stakeholders from across the Canadian space community of practice determined key NewSpace priorities.[100] The stakeholders included industry associations such as the Canadian Space Commerce Association (CSCA) and Aerospace Industries Association of Canada (AIAC), space companies such as MDA, Urthecast, Planet, GHGSat, Deltion, Airbus Defence and Space, Mission Control, ABB Systems, Northstar and Magellan Aerospace, and support industry, such as Euroconsult, BMO Nesbitt-Burns, Quantius, Dentons Canada LLP, and government, such as the CSA, GAC, ISED, and NRC-IRAP. The miniaturisation of technology has lowered entry barriers and, as a result, the number of space companies has risen dramatically, thus flooding the (unprepared) authorities with licence applications. The process is outdated and needs to be adapted.

The Roundtable participants recommended that the application process be "synthesised" as opposed to applying to several Ministries, as is the case now, with mandatory applications to GAC and ISED, and, externally, to the ITU. On top of that challenge, companies have difficulties in leveraging financing without proper licensing. However, to commercialise their projects and build a business case, companies also need licensing, which creates a "chicken and egg" scenario that requires regulatory reform to help the commercialisation of the NewSpace sector. To illustrate this point, it is difficult for NewSpace companies to reach the required minimum threshold of CA$5 million to enter the "Accelerated Growth Strategy" (AGS) programme, which serves as a "force multiplier" to synthesise funding government agents and to provide "rapid response and rapid investment". In the same vein, it has been argued that the CSA Space Technology and Development Program (STDP) is unable to fund NewSpace companies that are too "early stage", and that small amounts of risk capital could fill this gap. There has been some progress in that direction due to a recent Request for Proposals and Announcement of Opportunity. It has been suggested that a "Regulatory Light" regime, as inspired by the one implemented in the US, be established in Canada as well, whereby innovators benefit from certain regulatory alleviation (e.g., cheaper licensing process, trial licences for a limited period, and blanket approvals with flexible parameters until final iteration). Other measures include establishing a continuous funding cycle for NewSpace in Canada, whereby there is a "defined ladder or route of funding to follow: seed, start-up, venture, Tier 1/Series, Tier2/Series B", and regulatory guidelines in terms of IP in the process (who retains IP during procurement, for example, or what is patentable or not). There is also increased interest in nourishing an entrepreneurial environment (e.g., funding space incubators and accelerators similar to the US Small Business Innovation Research Program (SBIR) or the UK's Innovate UK and UK Start Up Loan Scheme). Small companies and subcontractors can benefit from a mentorship-like programme (ISED Industrial and Technology Benefits Policy or ITB) whereby they partner up with heritage companies in defence-related contracts.

100 *Space 2.0: New Space Roundtable*, hosted by the Canadian Space Agency, St-Hubert, 24 February 2017.

In terms of government procurement, reform adapted to NewSpace is recommended given that the traditional procurement process is not well suited to the compressed phasing approach and development cycles characteristic of NewSpace companies (i.e., "speed" and "iterative process of innovation"). Canada does not use government procurement to demonstrate Canadian technologies (as all other nations do) and this hampers not only the development of new technologies, but also Canada's ability to sell in the export market, where the "stamp of government approval" is essential. Both exactEarth and UrtheCast have most of their sales in the export market. Their ability to sell in the export market is hampered by the fact that the Canadian government has not procured these services, and, in at least one instance, have procured the services from foreign companies rather than domestic ones. Furthermore, the Canadian regulatory process is slow and outdated. Canada is not keeping up with the NewSpace environment in which its companies must operate. Two of Canada's leading space system manufacturers, MDA and COM DEV, recognised that the Canadian government lacked direction and was not planning investment in space, so they moved their strategic centres to other countries. COM DEV, exactEarth, and Neptec all set up shop abroad (in the UK, among others) to take advantage of a more favourable environment for the development of space capabilities and related data analytics. Canadian companies investing in the UK can obtain matching ESA/UK funding on much larger scales than are available in Canada. Smaller-scale examples include NewSpace companies such as UrtheCast, Kepler Communications, and GHGSat raising significant funds from non-Canadian sources, which puts them at risk of eventually becoming foreign-owned. For example, NorthStar recently established its European HQ in Luxembourg.[101]

Many of the NewSpace companies in Canada have obtained substantial private sector funding to develop space-based services for commercial and military markets. In the area of Earth Observation these require massive data processing, AI, and big data analytics to produce timely products for these markets. The gap is in having the Canadian Government procure these services. Government should leverage current research centers in Canada that are involved in AI and big data analytics to partner with the space industry on R&D. NewSpace companies are now taking a lead role, developing the space systems and analytical tools for a wide range of potential commercial and government applications – the potential government role in this regard is to help define their requirements, to become an anchor customer for these new services (becoming a catalyst for exports), and to encourage/promote technology demonstrators. Also, several NewSpace companies (notably GHGSat) are underlining the huge opportunity for Canada to fund and have access to ESA's Copernicus data. Canada could/should fund (i) development of big data and AI applications based on Copernicus data, and (ii) contributions of Canadian satellite data to Copernicus to foster the development of big data and AI applications based on Canadian satellite data.

Lastly, all stakeholders expressed a wish for the government to clarify its stance on international law and agreements issues to enable companies to determine their rights and limitations in space commerce (e.g., Canada's take on the 1979 Moon Agreement with respect to lunar resources exploitation, and its recent adherence to the Artemis Accords, and how this changes the lunar ISRU perspective).

In short, the recommendations from the 2017 "Space 2.0" roundtable involving the CSA and commercial associations from the Canadian space sector can be summarised as such (p. 6):

101 The LFF (Luxembourg Future Fund) is investing ± US$ 55 million in North Star. For more, see: *Luxembourg Invests in Northstar Earth and Space That Establishes Its European Headquarters in the Grand Duchy of Luxembourg to Support Sustainable Space Activities,* LSA, 17 December 2021.

a. Reviewing the regulatory framework for operators' licensing requirements;
b. Reviewing international policies and treaties that may impact commercial rights;
c. Reviewing the implementation of IP policies;
d. Establishing the continuous funding cycle to graduate companies to the next technology readiness level (TRL) level or along the commercialization pathway; and
e. Accelerating a company's ability to work with heritage companies and delivering on contracts by linking NewSpace companies to large firms through ITB requirements.[102]

What is striking is that since the announcement of the 2019 Canadian Space Strategy, the government has yet to establish a long-term funded space programme with a clear implementation plan.

6.5 Conclusion

In conclusion, a space operator must, today, apply for licences at the ISED and the GAC for satellite operations, and in theory, at the DOT for launching (but current legislation does not provide licences for commercial rocket capacity). While this legal architecture could remain in place, much is expected to change in the very near future as emerging space activities (NewSpace) need regulation at a faster pace as the 2023 consultations led by the federal Government will tell. A commercial spaceport is being built in Canada and there is no law to regulate it. The void is being filled by provincial environmental law, which confirms the urgent need for reform, and has now found the Government's support for the introduction of a regulatory framework.

Several emerging space activities of interest to Canada and to Canadian companies such as space traffic management, space situational awareness, on-orbit serving, space mining, to name but a few, currently do not fall within the scope of any existing Canadian space law and therefore cannot be licensed.

The 2021 Minister of Innovation, Science and Industry Mandate Letter lays out several key priorities which have a direct impact on the space sector. These priorities highlight the key trends to watch for in the near future and focus on areas such as EO/RS data for climate change, quantum technology for cybersecurity, AI for space applications such as EO and healthcare, and other practical uses of space technology that benefit humanity, especially down on Earth.[103]

There is an urgent need for Canada to embrace the recommendations of the 2019 Space Strategy to recognise space as a "national strategic asset" and to adopt a "whole-of-government approach" to ensure that Canada can continue to rely on space to help meet its national needs. As of this writing, neither of these key elements has been embraced by the government, leading to its current siloed approach and its lack of leadership and cohesion. There is also an urgent need for Canada to rapidly review its legislative and regulatory frameworks (e.g., remote sensing, space mining) to determine if/how they support innovation business models paralleling efforts in other jurisdictions. Disruptive technologies are impacting the pace of change in the global space sector and Canadian policies and regulations need to keep up to support Canadian industries. It is possible that the realisation of such a legislative review would lead to the conclusion that Canada needs a comprehensive space law to oversee all current and future space activities.

102 *Space 2.0 Round Table, between the Aerospace Industries Association of Canada (AIAC)*, Old Space, and the Canadian Space Commerce Association (CSCA), CSA HQ, New Space, 24 February, in Boucher, M., The Canadian Space Commerce Association Releases Report From the Space 2.0 Roundtable, SpaceQ, 26 April 2017.

103 *Minister of Innovation, Science and Industry Mandate Letter*, Office of the Prime Minister, 16 December 2021.

In turn, once implemented, this new space legislation would enable Canada to better contribute to the global governance of the space ecosystem. Indeed, with this in mind, it is essential to highlight Canada's significant legacy in terms of international diplomacy (e.g. landmine treaty, UNCLOS, Montreal Protocol on the ozone layer, etc.) and therefore its true potential to further contribute to global space governance in the future (e.g., as illustrated by its role as an important member of the group that developed the COPUOS 21 Space Sustainability Guidelines in 2019) is a key source of both inspiration and vision to be shared. While Canada provides in its latest budget for financial resources to prioritise its leadership in space, as well as support for commercial space activities such as launching, it appears time now to consider national space legislation and enable Canada to fully embrace the New Space age.

Acknowledgements

The author wishes to thank Professor L.J. Smith and Dr. M. L. Stojak for their valuable feedback and comments. Moreover, the author wishes to acknowledge the value of Dr. A. Kerkonian's thesis which provided a solid basis for this chapter, the kind guidance of Dr. S. Wintermuth with the editing process, and Dr. D. Kendall's time, words of wisdom, and cardinal insight.

7

NATIONAL SPACE LAW AND LICENSING OF COMMERCIAL SPACE ACTIVITIES IN JAPAN

Souichirou Kozuka[1]

7.1 Introduction

Until 1990s, the Japanese space exploration was mostly either a national project carried out by the space agency, then named NASDA (National Space Development Agency), or the other governmental agency, ISAS (Institute of Space and Astronautical Science), the exceptions being the commercial operation of communication and broadcasting satellites.[2] The only statute relevant to space activities in those days was the NASDA law. Besides provisions on the structure and governance of NASDA as a semi-public body, it included a few important provisions on the agency's activities.[3]

Japan ratified the Outer Space Treaty in 1967 and acceded to three other treaties of the United Nations, namely the Astronaut Rescue and Return Agreement, Liability Convention, and Registration Convention in 1983. Even before acceding to these treaties, the Japanese government had examined carefully whether the domestic legislation was necessary to implement them, in particular concerning the rights of victims in case damages are caused on the surface of Japan by another state's space activity and compensation scheme for damages that the Japanese space activity causes in another state. They concluded that these domestic laws were not necessary under the conditions at that time.[4]

As a result, the government internally decided about the steps to be taken in these cases of damages from space activities. The procedure of demanding compensation for damages caused by the space activity of another state, in contrast to the procedure for making compensation due to Japan's space activity, was considered relevant to the people's rights and was published in the Official Gazette.[5] As regards the requirement of licensing and continued supervision under Art. VI

1 This chapter is based on the author's research supported by the Japan Society for the Promotion of Science, grant identifier no. 21H00687.

2 Setsuko Aoki, 'Current status and recent developments in Japan's national space law and its relevance to Pacific Rim space law and Activities' (2009) 35 J Space L 363, 367.

3 See Aoki (n 1), 400–403.

4 Aoki (n 1), 393.

5 Official Gazette (*Kampô*), 20 June 1983, Extra Issue no. 10, p. 16.

DOI: 10.4324/9781003268475-11

of the Outer Space Treaty, the government took the position that no special legislation is necessary, given that the government supervised NASDA as a semi-pubic body and that commercial telecom and broadcasting companies need a licence for the radio station in space under the Radio Act before operating a satellite.[6]

7.2 Current system of space law in Japan

The situation has changed during the last two decades. Beginning with the privatisation of launch of major rockets, as part of the privatisation of various national services in the early 2000s,[7] Japanese space exploration has gradually shifted to the commercial sector. Japan Aerospace Exploration Agency (JAXA), established in 2003 consolidating former NASDA, ISAS, and National Aerospace Laboratory (NAL), now concentrates on the scientific programmes and development of basic technologies, as well as the support of commercial activities. Furthermore, various universities and some engineering schools have developed programmes of small satellites, loosely coordinated by the network UNISEC (University Space Engineering Consortium). These private space activities, whether commercial or educational, have required the domestic legislation to properly supervise them.

In response to these developments, four laws have been enacted. The first was the Basic Space Act of 2008. It is one of the policy-oriented basic laws,[8] providing for the framework of space policy and the governmental organisation for its implementation. In fact, the enactment of the Basic Space Act was motivated more by the political intention to enable the military use of space assets, the need to address commercialisation of space activities being the subsidiary purpose.[9]

On the policy side, the Basic Space Act lists six "guiding principles" of Japan's space policy, namely:

- Peaceful use of the outer space;
- Enhancement of the people's life in the nation, including the national security;
- Promotion of the industry;
- Development of the human society;
- International cooperation; and
- Consideration for the environment.[10]

As regards the governmental organisation, the Basic Space Act establishes the Strategic Headquarters for National Space Policy.[11] The chairperson of the Headquarters is the Prime

6 Aoki (n 1), 394–396, 404–406.

7 Aoki (n 1), 368–370; Mamoru Endo, 'The Japanese space launch program' in: Kai-Uwe Schrogl et al (eds), 2 *Handbook of Space Security* (Springer 2015) 899, 917–918.

8 On another example of policy-oriented basic law, see Souichirou Kozuka and Hideyuki Nakamura, 'The law applicable on the continental shelf and in the exclusive economic zone: the Japanese perspective' in: Aldo Chircop et al. (eds), 25 *Ocean Yearbook* (Martinus Nijhoff 2011) 357.

9 Setsuko Aoki, 'Introduction to the Japanese Basic Space Law of 2008' (2008) 57 ZLW 585. On the background concerning the military use of space assets, see Kazuto Suzuki, 'Basic law for space activities: a new space policy for Japan for the 21st century', in: European Space Policy Institute (ed), *Yearbook on Space Policy 2006/2007* (Springer 2007) 225; Saadia M. Pekkanen and Paul Kallender-Umezu, *In Defence of Japan* (Stanford University Press 2010) 33–40.

10 Art. 2-7, Basic Space Act.

11 Art. 25, Basic Space Act.

Minister,[12] supported by the Chief Cabinet Officer and Minister for Space Policies as vice-chairs.[13] The Headquarters consists of all other members of the Cabinet.[14] Its secretariat is placed within the Cabinet Office,[15] currently the National Space Policy Secretariat (hereinafter "Secretariat").

In the very last provision, the Basic Space Act requires the government to work on the legislation to implement space law treaties and other relevant international agreements, giving due regard to the promotion of national interests in the international society and the facilitation of space exploration and utilisation by the private sector.[16] After having spent eight years, the Space Activities Act was enacted to introduce the licence scheme for the private launch and operation of space objects in 2016. At the same time, the Remote Sensing Act was introduced providing for the additional security measures for the collection and distribution of remote sensing data.

Just after the enactment of the two laws to regulate traditional space activities, the wave of "NewSpace" arrived in Japan. Start-ups have appeared with the ideas of novel types of activities, including the space resources exploration and on-orbit servicing. The government has faced the issue of how to deal with these new space activities. After the deliberations among space lawyers and industry representatives, some members of the Diet (Japanese Parliament) have decided that a new law is needed for space resources exploration. The Space Resources Act, which explicitly approves ownership in the extracted space resources among others, was enacted in 2021. For on-orbit servicing, no special legislation has been made, but the government has published guidelines for the issuance of a licence for such an activity under the Space Activities Act.

Commercial human spaceflight has been one of the most controversial issues in the space law in Japan. Japan has never had a mission of human spaceflight on its own. While several Japanese astronauts were sent to the International Space Station, their flights were part of the international program and the vehicles they used were either American or Russian. Exceptions were two private persons who flew on the Russian spacecraft, one on a flight to Mir in 1990 and the other on a commercial flight to ISS in 2021. When a few start-ups appeared with the ambition of offering suborbital human flights commercially, and others started considering inviting foreign suborbital flight operators to use Japanese airports as the spaceport, it became apparent that the current law lacks a system to licence and regulate human spaceflights. Deliberations are still going on, partly because the proposed programmes are making progress only slowly.

7.3 Legal framework over established space activities

In the following sections, the issues of Japanese space law, briefly described above, are examined. First, the overview of the licensing scheme under the Space Activities Act and Remote Sensing Act is given. Then the regulation of novel types of space activities, in particular space resources exploration and on-orbit servicing, is discussed. It is followed by the review of ongoing debates about the possible law for human spaceflights. The final section concludes this chapter by giving outlook for future developments.

12 Art. 28, Basic Space Act.
13 Art. 29, Basic Space Act.
14 Art. 27, Basic Space Act.
15 Art. 32, Basic Space Act.
16 Art. 35, Basic Space Act.

7.3.1 Types of activities subject to licence

The Space Activities Act provides for two types of licences: the licence for launch of a satellite and that for operation of a satellite. A non-governmental entity that intends to carry out either of these activities must apply for a licence from the government. The Secretariat is responsible for the examination of the application. Legally speaking, the Prime Minister, as minister in charge of the Cabinet Office of Japan (CAO), issues licences.

When the first round of deliberations on the Space Activities Act started in 2009, the Commercial Space Launch Act of the United States was closely studied. The Interim Summary of the deliberations listed five types of activities to be licensed, apparently following the US model.[17] They were launch of a space object, procurement of launch of a space object abroad, reentry of a space object, operation of a satellite, as well as operation of a space port. In the course of the second round of deliberations beginning in 2015, following the interruption partly due to the Great East Japan Earthquake and the incident at Fukushima Nuclear Power Plant in 2011, the structure has become simple.

Under the current Act, the reentry of a satellite is examined as part of the manner of its operation, not as an independent class of activity. Further, the idea of licensing the operation of a space port has been abandoned, given that the most important role of the space port operator is to ensure safety at the time of launch, which is examined as part of a licence for a launch. The procurement of launch of a satellite abroad is not regulated by the current Act, as a result of limiting the geographical scope of applications, discussed below in 7.2.2.

The Space Activities Act uses the term "satellite" instead of a "space object" used in the Interim Summary. However, the change of the term does not make any difference, as the "satellite" is broadly defined under the Space Activities Act as "an artificial object that is launched in the orbit around the Earth or beyond it, or placed and used on a celestial body other than the Earth".[18] The defined term may be equivalent to "space object" as used in the UN space law treaties.

7.3.2 Scope of application

Japan's Space Activities Act differs from the global standard of domestic space law in its narrow scope of application. The scope is limited geographically and the personal jurisdiction for space activities carried out by a Japanese national or corporation out of Japan's territory is not claimed.

To be more specific, an entity (natural or legal person)[19] must apply for a licence before launching a satellite from a facility located in the territory of Japan or on board a vessel or an aircraft of Japanese nationality.[20] This means that the licence scheme does not cover all the situations where Japan becomes the launching state under the space treaties. Procurement of launch by a foreign launch service provider is excluded from the scope of application because the Japanese government cannot enforce its power of investigation or sanction when the launch takes place in the territory of another state without infringing the sovereignty of the latter state. It also has the

17 Setsuko Aoki, 'Japanese Space Activities Act in the Making' (2012) 61 ZLW 111.

18 Art. 2(2), Space Activities Act.

19 In Japanese statutes, "者" (person) is a term covering both natural and legal person. An applicant for a licence under the Space Activities Act may usually be a legal person (corporation), though it is conceivable that a university professor as an individual might apply for a licence of operating a small satellite when his or her university does not wish to be a licensee.

20 Art. 4, Space Activities Act.

advantage to avoid duplicative regulation, which will be beneficial to the Japanese space industry.[21] However, the approach may be justifiable only when the launch service provider is located in a state equipped with the proper domestic space law.

Pursuant to the same approach, an entity must apply for a licence before operating a satellite from the control facility within Japan.[22] Receiving data from a satellite not controllable from the Earth (i.e., satellite without thrusters) requires no licence. If there are more than one facility to control the satellite, as is the case with non-geostationary satellites, whether a facility is considered as "controlling" the satellite may become an issue to be negotiated with the regulator.

As regards the entity to be covered, JAXA is also subject to the Space Activities Act as the non-governmental entity, though its nature as a national research and development agency is semi-public. It is the Japanese government's position that JAXA is the non-governmental entity under Art. VI of the Outer Space Treaty and that its activities are subject to authorisation and continued supervision of the government, as seen in the Memorandum of Understanding under the International Space Station Agreement, which treats JAXA (previously NASDA) as assisting the Ministry of Education, Culture, Sports and Technology (MEXT, previously the Science and Technology Agency).[23] In applying for a licence for a launch, JAXA may benefit from the simplified procedure.[24]

7.3.3 Licence for launch of a satellite

As already mentioned, an entity that intends to launch a satellite must be licensed by the Prime Minister. The licence is issued if (i) the design of the launch vehicle satisfies the safety requirements as specified in the Cabinet Office Order implementing the Space Activities Act, (ii) the launch facility satisfies the safety requirements as specified in the Cabinet Office Order, (iii) the launch plan properly ensures the public safety and the applicant is capable of carrying out the plan, and (iv) the satellite to be launched is used for the purpose and in the manner conforming to the guiding principles under the Basic Space Act, without interference with the implementation of the relevant international treaties and public safety.[25] The requirements are supplemented in the Cabinet Office Order and further elaborated by the Guidelines and Manuals.

The licence is required each time a launch is made. However, the applicant may apply for certification of the design of its launch vehicle in advance and be exempt from examination of the design against the safety requirements to be made every time.[26] Certification by a foreign state equivalent to Japan's certification is also acceptable if so designated in the Cabinet Office Order,[27] though currently the Cabinet Office Order designates no foreign certification. Similarly, the applicant may apply for certification of the suitability of launch facility to a certain type of the launch vehicle and be exempt from the examination of the launch facility to be made every time.[28]

21 Setsuko Aoki, 'Domestic legal conditions for space activities in Asia' (2019) 113 AJIL Unbound 103,105–106.
22 Art. 20, Space Activities Act.
23 Art. 1.3, the Memorandum of Understanding between the Government of Japan and the National Aeronautics and Space Administration of the United States of America Concerning Cooperation on the Civil International Space Station.
24 Art. 19, Space Activities Act.
25 Art. 6, Space Activities Act.
26 Art. 13, Space Activities Act.
27 See Art. 4(2), no. 2, Space Activities Act.
28 Art. 16, Space Activities Act.

The licensee shall build the launch vehicle in accordance with the licensed design.[29] It shall also ensure financial capability of compensating possible damages by liability insurance or otherwise.[30] The amount to be insured shall be determined by the Cabinet Office Order.[31] The Cabinet Office Order, as amended in August 2021, has delegated determination of the specific amount to the Prime Minister in consultation with the Minister of Finance.[32] The most recent decision of the Prime Minister set the amount ranging from 2.4 billion yen to 13.5 billion yen corresponding to the types of the launch vehicle.[33] It is the first time that the previous practice of applying the same amount (20 billion yen) to any type of launch vehicle was changed.[34]

7.3.4 Liability system for damages caused by the launch

The Space Activities Act provides for a unique liability system for damages to the surface of the Earth caused by the launch of a satellite, which is referred to as the "launch vehicle fall-down damages" in the Act.[35] It is a special rule to the general tort liability codified in the Civil Code. Article 709 of the Civil Code provides for the fault-based liability, comprehensively applicable to any kind of wrongful act or omission, unless otherwise stipulated by a special rule, similar to the French Civil Code. Unlike in some jurisdictions, strict liability is exceptional in Japanese tort law. The liability system under the Space Activities Act has added one of such exceptions, combining the strict liability, channeling of liability and indemnification by the government.[36]

An entity that launches a satellite from the territory of Japan or a facility on board a vessel or aircraft of Japanese nationality is strictly liable for any launch vehicle fall-down damages.[37] Whether it is licensed or not does not matter. In this case, no other entity is liable for the damages.[38] Thus, the liability is channelled to the launching entity. The Products Liability Act is not applicable to launch vehicle fall-down damages.[39] It means that no service provider to the launch, manufacturer of components, or owner or operator of the satellite can be held liable to the launch vehicle fall-down damages. The launching entity may turn to the service provider or component manufacturer and demand recourse after compensating the victim, but such a recourse is limited to the case when the service provider or manufacturer has caused the damage with intent, unless otherwise agreed in writing.[40] Under this system, the Japanese space industry, other than the launching entity, is freed from the legal risk for incidents, while the launching entity will benefit from the preference of the customer (satellite operator) not to be involved in any legal disputes in case the launch fails.

When the launching entity compensates for the launch vehicle fall-down damages, it will make use of the liability insurance. The victims have no direct claim against the insurer but have a lien on

29 Art. 8, Space Activities Act.
30 Art. 9(1), Space Activities Act.
31 Art. 9(2), Space Activities Act.
32 Art. 9-2, Cabinet Office Order for the Space Activities Act.
33 CAO Public Notice no.121 (30 August 2021), Official Gazette (*Kampô*) 30 August 2021 no. 564, p. 4.
34 On the previous practice, see Masataka Ogasawara and Joel Greer (eds), *Japan in Space* (Eleven International Publishing 2021) 26.
35 Art. 2, no. 8, Space Activities Act.
36 Souichirou Kozuka, 'Strict liability and state indemnification under Japanese law', (2017) 43 ZJapanR 3.
37 Art. 35, Space Activities Act.
38 Art. 36(1), Space Activities Act.
39 Art. 36(2), Space Activities Act.
40 Art. 38, Space Activities Act.

the insurance proceeds and prevail over other claimants.[41] Still, as noted above, the amount to be insured is several billion yen and might be insufficient to make a full compensation. Furthermore, the contract of launch liability insurance usually has some exclusions, in which case no insurance proceeds are available. To address these problems, the Space Activities Act provides that the government may conclude an indemnification agreement with the licensed launching entity.[42] The maximum amount to be indemnified is 350 billion yen, including the amount to be covered by the liability insurance.[43] As the indemnification agreement by the government is not directly associated with the liability arising under the Space Activities Act, the indemnification may be made even if damages from the launch is incurred outside of the Japanese territory and the liability is determined by a foreign law (by way of the rules of private international law).

7.3.5 Licence for satellite operation

An entity that intends to operate a satellite from a facility located in the territory of Japan must be licensed by the Prime Minister.[44] The licence is issued if (i) the satellite is used for the purpose and in the manner conforming to the guiding principles under the Basic Space Act, without interference with the implementation of the relevant international treaties and public safety, (ii) the design of the launch vehicle prevents the dispersion of the components and parts, and does not give rise to harmful interference under Article IX of the Outer Space Treaty, (iii) the operation plan includes measures to avoid the collision with another satellite and prevent harmful contamination of the outer space, as well as the post-mission measures, and the applicant is capable of carrying out the plan, and (iv) the post-mission plan satisfies one of the listed measures.[45] The emphasis on the debris mitigation measures as in (ii), (iii), and (iv) is noteworthy.[46] As in the case of the launch licence, the requirements are supplemented in the Cabinet Office Order and further elaborated by the Guidelines and Manuals.

Curiously, the Space Activities Act has no provision on the registration of satellites. In practice, the government requires the operators of a satellite to register their satellite with the Secretariat within 30 days of launch and prepared a Manual for that purpose.[47] According to the Manual, the registration is required "on the basis of the Registration Convention and the General Assembly Resolution 62/101 on the practice of registering space objects".

7.3.6 Liability system caused by the operation of satellites

In parallel with the liability for surface damage from the launch, an entity that operates a satellite by using a control facility located in the territory of Japan is strictly liable for satellite fall-down damages arising in the course of the operation of the satellite. The "satellite fall-down damages" is a defined term under the Space Activities Act to refer to damages caused by a satellite that has

41 Art. 39(1), Space Activities Act.
42 Art. 40, Space Activities Act.
43 Art. 32-2, Cabinet Office Order for the Space Activities Act.
44 Art. 20, Space Activities Act.
45 Art. 22, Space Activities Act.
46 Hiroko Yotsumoto, Daiki Ishikawa and Tetsuji Odan, 'Japan', in: Joanne Wheeler (ed), *The Space Law Review* (third ed, Law business Research 2021) 107, 111.
47 The Manual for Registration of Space Objects.

been normally separated from the launch vehicle to the surface of the Earth.[48] If the satellite has not been normally separated from the launch vehicle, damages caused by such a satellite are "launch vehicle fall-down damages" and not "satellite fall-down damages".[49]

Differently from the case of launch vehicle fall-down damages, liability for satellite fall-down damages is not channelled to the operator. Therefore, the component manufacturer may be directly sued by the victim for its liability. Furthermore, the operator is not required to insure itself against the liability. Nor is the indemnification agreement by the government available to the operator of a satellite. When the Space Activities Act was enacted in 2016, Japanese satellites operated by private entities were either geostationary satellites or small satellites. Both were considered to have little risk of causing damages on the surface, hence the strict liability without any financial measures was introduced. It may need reconsideration before the on-orbit servicing is actually in operation.

No special provision is provided for damages incurred in the outer space. It means that the liability for an on-orbit accident is determined by the general tort law under the applicable law. The problem is that the private international law rules in the outer space have not been sufficiently examined.[50] If the Japanese law is applicable, then the fault-based liability under Art. 709 of the Civil Code applies.

7.3.7 Operation of remote sensing devices and distribution of remote sensing data

Remote sensing by satellite could give rise to concerns about national security. When the Space Activities Act was drafted, the concern was well understood. However, at that time there was no remote sensing satellite commercially owned and operated, while there was a case of a payload held by a Japanese company on a foreign satellite. There were also distributors of satellite data collected by a foreign operator. Against these backgrounds, the Remote Sensing Act was enacted to regulate the remote sensing payloads controlled from Japan, as well as the distribution of remote sensing data collected by such a payload.

The regulation of the use of a remote sensing device is applied in addition to the regulation of the satellite. Therefore, if a company operates a satellite with a remote sensing device on board, the company must be licensed both for the operation of the satellite (satellite bus) under the Space Activities Act and for the operation of the remote sensing device (payload) under the Remote Sensing Act.

The remote sensing device to be regulated is a device to make observation of the Earth, the resolution of which is capable of discerning the movement of vehicles, including automobiles, vessels, and airplanes. The specific threshold is to be determined by the Cabinet Office Order.[51] The current threshold is:

- for the optical remote sensor, two metres;
- for the synthetic radar aperture (SAR) sensor, three metres;

48 Art. 2, no. 11, Space Activities Act.

49 See the definition of "launch vehicle fall-down damages" in art. 2, no. 8, of the Space Activities Act.

50 See Souichirou Kozuka and Fumiko Masuda, 'Private International Law (Conflict of Law Rules) for Human Presence of Long Term in the Space', (2014) 57 *Proceedings of the International Institute of Space Law* 193.

51 Art. 2, no. 2, Remote Sensing Act.

- for the hyperspectral sensor, ten meters and detecting electromagnetic waves with wavelength bands of 49 or more in the ultraviolet, visible light, near infrared, and mid-wavelength infrared regions; and
- for the thermal infrared sensor, five metres.[52]

An entity that intends to use such a remote sensing device by controlling it from the facility located in the territory of Japan shall apply for a licence to be issued by the Prime Minister (CAO).[53] The licence is issued if (i) the design and capability of the device, the orbit of the satellite on which the device is carried, the location of the facilities for the uplink and downlink to the satellite, as well as the construction, capability, and the manner of operation of the satellite, satisfy the requirements to prevent other entities than the applicant from using the device and not interfering with the peace of the international society, (ii) measures against the divulgation, loss, and destruction of the remote sensing data are properly taken, (iii) the applicant is capable of carrying out the measures in (i) and (ii), and (iv) the use of the remote sensing device does not interfere with the peace of the international society.[54] As in the case of the Space Activities Act, the requirements are supplemented in the Cabinet Office Order and further elaborated by the Guidelines and Manuals.

As regards the regulation over the distribution of remote sensing data, the holder of the remote sensing data of a resolution above the threshold may distribute the data only to a certified handler of the data, licensed user of the remote sensing device concerning the remote sensing data at issue, or qualified handing entity, except when justified as the submission to the Diet or to the court or otherwise stipulated as meeting the emergency needs.[55] The threshold is specified in the Cabinet Ordinance by the level of object discrimination for the raw data and standard (processed) data, respectively, and by the length of time since collection for the raw data. The government may restrict distribution of the remote sensing data when there is a reason to find that the use of the remote sensing data interferes with the peace in the international society.[56] This provision introduces the system of so-called shutter control.

Under the regulation, the remote sensing data above the resolution of the threshold may be distributed only among the restricted circle of licensed user of the remote sensing device, qualified handing entities, and certified handlers. Qualified handling entities are central and local governments, as well as the agencies of such other states that have equivalent national law on remote sensing data (presently Canada, France, Germany, and the US).[57] An entity that intends to handle the remote sensing data may apply for certification by the government.[58] Certification is made if the purpose and manner of using the data, capability of analysing and processing the data, as well as the security measures to be taken concerning the data, satisfy the requirements not to interfere with the peace of the international society.[59] A foreign entity may apply also for certification.

52 Art. 2, Cabinet Office Order for the Remote Sensing Act.
53 Art. 4, Remote Sensing Act.
54 Art. 6, Remote Sensing Act.
55 Art. 18, Remote Sensing Act.
56 Art. 19, Remote Sensing Act.
57 Art. 2, no. 7, Remote Sensing Act, supplemented by Art. 2 of the Cabinet Ordinance implementing the Remote Sensing Act.
58 Art. 21(1), Remote Sensing Act.
59 Art. 21(3), Remote Sensing Act.

7.4 Legal framework for NewSpace activities

7.4.1 Space resources exploration and exploitation

7.4.1.1 Background for the enactment of the new law

In March 2018, when the Space Activities Act was fully in force, then Prime Minister Shinzo Abe announced the plan to invest 100 billion yen in the space sector during the next five years in partnership between the public and private sector.[60] The announcement signified the arrival of "NewSpace" to Japan. Start-ups with the non-traditional space project have emerged one after another.

One of such non-traditional projects is the space resources exploitation. Unfortunately, the initial challenge to the Google Lunar X Prize, whose mission was to land on the Moon and have the rover travel on the Moon to acquire data of its surface, failed due to the unavailability of the launch vehicle in 2018. However, the operator continued pursuing its business plan to explore water (reportedly existent as blocks of ice) and extract it from the Moon. At this point, the regulator faced the question whether such a project is permissible under the law.

As noted at 7.2.1 above, the term "satellite" in the Space Activities Act is broadly defined. A rover placed on the Moon for exploration of resources satisfies the definition and, therefore, its operation is regulated by the operation of a satellite under the Act. To clarify this point, the government amended the Cabinet Office Order implementing the Space Activities Act in 2019. The Appendix to the Cabinet Office Order included a form for application for a licence, which used to require the purpose of using the satellite to be described in free text. The form in the Appendix after the amendment prepares a multiple choice for the purpose of the use of the satellite: positioning, communication and broadcasting, remote sensing, space science, and space exploration (including the space resources exploration) or others.[61] The applicant intending to launch a rover to the Moon can tick the box for "exploration" and demand a licence from the government.

Nevertheless, the licensing scheme under the Space Activities Act seemed insufficient for issues involved in the space resources exploitation. The controversies over the subject since the enactment of the 2015 Space Resource Exploration and Utilization Act in the US were well-known in Japan. The criteria for issuing a licence, as discussed above at 7.2.5, do not deal with the international coordination and consultation that might become necessary in conducting the project. Whether the private entity that extracts the resource from the Moon has the legal title to it was an open question, which affected the availability of finance. After the government signed the Artemis Accords and committed to the exploration of the Moon and the resources on it under the multi-state framework, it has become apparent that a new law is needed to supplement the scheme under the Space Activities Act.

7.4.1.2 Regulation of space resources exploration and exploitation

The Space Resources Act was enacted in 2021. It requires an additional licence for the exploration and exploitation of space resources. An entity that intends exploration or exploitation of space resources by using a "satellite" (as having the same meaning as under the Space Activities Act)

60 The address of Prime Minister Shinzo Abe at the Awards Ceremony for the Third Space Exploitation Prize (20 March 2018).

61 Form 17, Cabinet Office Order for Space Activities Act as of September 2019. The "space resources exploration and exploitation" has become a separate choice after the entry into force of the Space Resources Act.

must apply for a licence for the space resources exploration and exploitation, which is a special case of a licence for the operation of the satellite under the Space Activities Act.[62] When applying for a licence of space resources exploration and exploitation, the applicant must state the purpose, site, manner, and other details of the project. The CAO examines whether the project conforms with the guiding principles of the Basic Space Act and does not interfere with the implementation of international treaties and public safety, and whether the applicant is capable of carrying out the project.[63] The Prime Minister (CAO) must make a consultation with the Minister for Economy, Trade and Industry (METI) before issuing a licence.[64] The first licence under the Space Resources Act was issued in November 2022.

The Space Resources Act, unlike the US Law, emphasises international coordination. When a licence is issued, the Prime Minister shall publish the applicant's name and its plan stated in the application,[65] which may enable other states to demand consultation under Art. IX of the Outer Space Treaty, if necessary. Furthermore, the Act demands the government to endeavor building an internationally coordinated scheme for the exploration and exploitation of space resources through engagement in the international framework.[66] It is explicitly declared that any provision of the Act does not unduly interfere with other states' interests in the exploration and use of the outer space, including the Moon and other celestial bodies.[67] It is also prescribed that the government shall pay due care not to interfere with the implementation of international agreements when implementing the Act.[68]

7.4.1.3 Ownership of extracted space resources

On the basis of such internationalism, the Space Resources Act affirms that an entity acquires ownership of the space resources that the entity extracts pursuant to the licensed project by possessing the space resources with the intention of owning them.[69] The text closely follows the provision in the Civil Code on the acquisition of ownership over a property without an owner.[70] However, it does not apply the Civil Code to the acquisition of space resources, as the Space Resources Act itself is the basis of the title. The drafters of the Act justify applying a Japanese statute for affirming title to the space resources extracted by the entity licensed by the Japanese government as the application of the law with the closest connection to the issue.[71]

7.4.2 On-orbit services

The second type of new space activities is the on-orbit servicing. Among the various kinds of on-orbit services, active debris removal has attracted the attention of the Japanese space sector. JAXA has launched the project of "commercial removal of debris demonstration" (CRD2) and called for a proposal of commercial service to remove a large piece of debris of Japanese origin.

62 Art. 3(1), Space Resources Act.
63 Art. 3(2), Space Resources Act.
64 Art. 3(3), Space Resources Act.
65 Art. 4, Space Resources Act.
66 Art. 7, Space Resources Act.
67 Art. 6(2), Space Resources Act.
68 Art. 6(1), Space Resources Act.
69 Art. 5, Space Resources Act.
70 Art. 239(1), Civil Code.
71 Takayuki Kobayashi and Keitaro Ôno, '宇宙資源法の背景・目的・内容', (2021) 1203 NBL 74, 78 (in Japanese).

On-orbit servicing is included in the operation of satellite under the Space Activities Act. The application for on-orbit servicing may require examination of specific issues, given its nature of making rendezvous and proximity operations towards another space object and affecting the latter's manoeuvres. The government published "Japan's rules commonly applicable to on-orbit servicing" (hereinafter "common rules") in 2021, recognising the need to ensure transparency vis-à-vis the international society. The specific guidelines on the application for a licence of on-orbit servicing was later published, based on the common rules.

The common rules discuss both legal and technical issues. The legal issue relates to the requirement for the licence of the operation of a satellite that "the satellite is used for the purpose and in the manner conforming to the guiding principles under the Basic Space Act, without interference with the implementation of the relevant international treaties and public safety" under the Space Activities Act. The common rules and the guidelines demand three conditions to satisfy this requirement.[72]

First, the service should not infringe on the rights of other parties. For this purpose, the consent to the service must be given by the right-holder of the client space object. Further, the service should not give rise to a situation in breach of the regulations of the state of registry of the client space object and the state having licensed the latter's operation. Thus, the common rules rightly care about both the interests of the private party and the relevant state.

Second, the intended outcome of the service shall not be contrary to the purpose of the Space Activities Act. While the on-orbit servicer must ensure that the client space object does not cause interference with space activities of others, it is not required that the standards of the Japanese Space Activities Act are literally satisfied with regards to the client space object. Otherwise, the service of moving an extremely dangerous debris to a less dangerous orbit could not be offered. Improving the risks of debris should be encouraged, even when the situation after the service still entails some risk.

Third, the provider of on-orbit service shall ensure transparency and contribute to space traffic management. To be specific, the common rules require that the service provider make disclosures about its plan in advance, as well as publish any accident encountered during its operation to the Japanese Government and those that could be affected.

The common rules and guidelines are helpful to the operators intending to provide on-orbit services. However, the liability rules have remained unchanged. As noted above, the operator of a satellite is strictly liable to satellite fall-down damages. While the provider of on-orbit service will probably be insured against its liability, the absence of the governmental compensation may still be a concern, both to the provider and the general public. Contrary to the operation of ordinary satellites, on-orbit service entails a higher risk of surface damages caused by the fall-down of the servicing or client satellites, or both. Furthermore, the risk of an on-orbit accident is also an actual problem. The issue was once discussed in 2018 but was found to be unmatured. The group having considered the common rules mentions that the time is ripe to reexamine the issue, given that the prospect for the commercial on-orbit service has become real.

72 Guidelines on a License to Operate a Spacecraft Performing On-Orbit Servicing, pp. 4–9.

7.5 Legal issues for human spaceflights

7.5.1 Lack of legal scheme for human spaceflights

Reflecting the absence of a national program on human spaceflight, as mentioned at 7.1.2 above, the current space law in Japan lacks a scheme for human spaceflights. The Space Activities Act does not cover them because it regulates the launch of a satellite. Unlike the Commercial Space Launch Act of the United States,[73] the rocket is not directly regulated but treated only as a vehicle for launching a satellite. As a result, launch of a rocket with a person on board is not regulated. One might argue that the absence of regulation means that the human spaceflight can freely be made. Such an argument is not convincing, however, as other space activities are regulated to conform with the international space law.

As a few start-ups have emerged with the aspiration of performing commercial human spaceflights, some people are making a case for a new law on human spaceflights. There are so many issues to be examined. In order to have a workable licence scheme, the regulator needs expertise on the safety of a spaceflight, regarding not only the design of the rocket, but the medical conditions required of the participants as well. Unfortunately, however, neither the government nor JAXA has sufficient expertise, as there has not been a national programme of its own. The liability of the operator in case an accident occurs is also a hard question. Some argue for a statutory approval of the validity of cross waiver agreements on condition that the participant makes an informed consent to the flight, inspired by the US law and practice.[74] Still, it is questionable whether such an arrangement is consistent with the public policy of limiting the validity of the exemption and limitation of liability in consumer contracts. With these difficulties remaining unresolved, the law-making process has not commenced yet.

7.5.2 Difficulties with suborbital flights

Further complexities are added by the fact that the commercial companies intending human spaceflights aim to start with suborbital flights. When the Space Activities Act was enacted, the launch of suborbital rockets was out of the scope of regulation. The aim was to keep JAXA's launch of sounding rockets unregulated as before. It is not clear whether a commercial entity may also launch a suborbital rocket freely, because a suborbital rocket could fall under the definition of "aircraft" under the Aviation Act.

The Aviation Act defines the "aircraft" as "airplane capable of being used for aviation with a person on board". Not only an airplane with a person actually on board, but a vehicle "capable of" flight with a person, given the size or weight of the airplane, is also included. If a suborbital rocket is large enough to have a person on board, even if it is not so designed, it could fall under the definition and be regulated as an "aircraft" under the Aviation Act. Then it must have its airworthiness certified before making a flight, which is extremely discouraging to the start-ups considering (unmanned) suborbital flights.

It is even more likely that a manned suborbital rocket would be treated as an "aircraft" and regulated by the Aviation Act. To facilitate commercial human spaceflight, the government has set up the Government-Industry Roundtable on Suborbital Flights, co-hosted by the CAO as regula-

73 See 51 USC § 50902 (11).

74 For example, the Japan Society for Aeronautical and Space Sciences, 'JSASS Space Vision 2050' (2019) 16.

tor of space activities and the Ministry of Land, Infrastructure, Transport and Tourism (MLIT) as regulator of aviation. However, no progress on the reform of regulation has been made yet.

7.6 Conclusions

During the first two decades of the 21st century, Japan has developed the system of space law to meet the transition of its space policy from one heavily reliant on the national programmes to one more commercially oriented. The primary statute, the Space Activities Act, appears to be simple, regulating only the launch of satellites and operation of satellites. It is, in fact, flexible enough to accommodate various types of new space activities that are emerging recently.

Three other statutes also play crucial roles in the Japanese system of space law. The Basic Space Act, preceding the Space Activities Act, sets the framework of Japan's space policy and prescribes the government organisations to advance the latter. The Remote Sensing Act introduces the additional regulation on the use of remote sensing device, as well as the regulatory scheme over distribution of remote sensing data, required due to the data's sensitivity. The Space Resources Act, most recently enacted, affirms the ownership to the space resources commercially extracted from the celestial body, while strongly committing to the internationalism concerning the subject.

The emphasis on international cooperation and transparency are features of the Japanese space law as a whole. It is one of the guiding principles under the Basic Space Act. Foreign entities are not excluded from the operative regulation. The Space Activities Act is ready to accept type certification of a launch vehicle manufactured by a foreign entity, while a foreign entity may apply for certification as a remote sensing data handler under the Remote Sensing Act. The title to space resources under the Space Resources Act is also open to a foreign entity, as long as the latter's exploration and exploitation is licensed under Japanese law. It may be added that the transparency is enhanced by the publication in English of the relevant statutes, ordinances, and other instruments, including the recent guidelines on on-orbit servicing, on the website of CAO.

There may be further developments in Japanese space law, as seen in the possible regulation of commercial human spaceflights, currently being discussed. It is hoped that the regulations to be introduced remain flexible and transparent, based on internationalism, as are the existing regulations. It shall be the way that the Japanese regulator can support development of the nation's commercial space sector.

8

REGULATING COMMERCIAL SPACE ACTIVITIES IN AUSTRALIA AND NEW ZEALAND

Joel A. Dennerley and Maria A. Pozza[1]

8.1 Overview of Australia's civil space sector

Australia's civil space sector is currently undergoing a period of growth and diversification. These trends are driven by factors such as the Australian Space Agency's (ASA) national coordination of growth initiatives designed to build domestic space capabilities; the ASA's brokering of strategic international partnerships with other space-faring nations; the Australian university sector's contributions to space research, development, and innovation and its close association with industry; a business ecosystem that supports space start-ups; space companies that leverage Australia's competitive advantages, such as the country's unique geography; as well as government, private, and foreign investment in the domestic space sector. The confluence of factors such as these means that the Australian commercial space market is poised for significant economic development during this decade.

Between 2018 and 2019, the Australian space sector generated revenues of roughly AUD$5 billion and employed a workforce of approximately 10,000.[2] These revenues represented a 13% increase from two years earlier and amounted to roughly one-quarter of a per cent of gross domestic product.[3] Over the next few years, the space sector's revenues are predicted to increase at an annual rate of about 8%.[4] In its *Civil Space Strategy*, the ASA has stated its longer-term goal of tripling the size of the civilian space sector so that by 2030, it generates approximately AUD$12 billion in revenue and employs 30,000 people.[5] Future growth will be stimulated by factors such as capital investment from the government, the private sector, and foreign investors. Over the ten

1 The views of the authors are the authors' alone and are intended to provide commentary and general information, and do not represent the views of any organisation. This chapter should not be relied upon as a substitute for professional legal advice or for any other purpose. Current as of 22 September 2022.
2 Australian Space Agency [ASA], 2019a, p. 3; AlphaBeta, 2021, p. 7.
3 ASA, 2020, p. 18; AlphaBeta, 2021, p. 7.
4 ASA, 2020, p. 18.
5 ASA, 2019a, p. 3.

DOI: 10.4324/9781003268475-12

years from 2018–2019 to 2027–2028, the estimated inflow of investment into the Australian space sector will be roughly AUD$2 billion, with a significant portion of this coming from the Australian Government.[6] Indeed, the importance of space from both a strategic and commercial point of view is a topic gaining much greater levels of awareness and respect within government. This has translated into tangible investments, initiatives, policies, strategies, and roadmaps designed to bolster the space sector's growth. For example, the previous Australian Government's *Modern Manufacturing Strategy* recognised space as a critical national manufacturing priority due to the fact that space industry technologies "enable [further] activity across the economy".[7] Plans for the Australian space sector, as an identified priority area, are further articulated in the *Space National Manufacturing Priority Road Map*. This document outlines an intention to develop "end-to-end" domestic manufacturing capabilities in a variety of space industry enterprises ranging from the production of satellite hardware to satellite launch.[8] Implementing roadmaps like this will be the responsibility of entities such as the ASA, which has been tasked with supporting the civilian space sector and integrating it with the broader Australian economy.

The ASA was formally established on 1 July 2018. Amongst its various responsibilities, the ASA sets the strategic and policy direction for the civil space sector and supports and coordinates the sector's development and linkages with other industry sectors.[9] Through its *Civil Space Strategy*, the ASA has identified seven "National Civil Space Priority Areas" which are those domains where Australia has distinct advantages over other space-faring nations and where Australia is set to make a significant investment and economic gains.[10] These seven priority areas include (1) the acquisition and use of position, navigation, and timing technologies and infrastructure, (2) undertaking Earth observation activities such as data collection and analysis, (3) developing communications technologies and services such as laser light communication, (4) acquiring space situational awareness capabilities and conducting space debris monitoring activities, (5) contributing to space sciences research and technology development, (6) developing robotics and automation technologies for both terrestrial and space environments, and (7) building a domestic launch capability.[11]

A variety of diverse Australian corporations and organisations are currently undertaking activities and operations that fall into the above priority areas, in addition to other space sector segments. There are roughly 550 corporations and organisations that conduct activities and operations in the Australian space sector.[12] A significant number of these firms would classify as start-ups or small to medium-sized companies. Indeed, the ASA's *Civil Space Strategy* acknowledges that Australia's space economy is "an emerging market" that will establish and develop its space capabilities, products, and services via the growing number of space businesses and start-ups.[13] Nevertheless, the ASA also notes that a variety of challenges exist for Australian space businesses or those seeking to undertake business in the Australian space sector.[14] One of these challenges includes navigating government regulation of space activities. Similar to other legal jurisdictions,

6 Department of Industry, Science and Resources [DISR], 2021, p. 3.
7 DISR, 2020, p. 17.
8 DISR, 2021, p. II.
9 DISR, n.d. a.
10 ASA, 2019a, p. 3.
11 ASA, 2019a, pp. 12–13.
12 AlphaBeta, 2021, p. 32.
13 ASA, 2019a, p. 7.
14 ASA, 2019a, p. 7.

undertaking space activities in Australia can involve a variety of governance, policy, and legal considerations. Depending on the activity, space corporations or organisations may be required to comply with various domestic laws, policies, duties, or standards. Of note is the fact that the Australian Government has recently amended its space legislation pertaining to the acquisition of licences, permits, or authorisations required to engage in certain space activities and has revised the insurance amounts relevant to such activities.

8.2 Australia's space law

An essential piece of legislation in Australia governing various space activities is the Space (Launches and Returns) Act 2018 (the SLR Act). The SLR Act entered into force on 31 August 2019, replacing an earlier piece of legislation entitled the Space Activities Act 1998. The SLR Act has been purpose-built to cover a number of different topics relevant to those parties undertaking, or planning to undertake, civil space activities "from Australia or by Australian nationals outside Australia".[15] From the Act's name, it is evident that the legislation pertains to the regulation of specific types of space activities, namely the requirement to obtain a licence, permit, authorisation, or certificate when undertaking space activities, such as the launch and/or return of a space object(s). Indeed, at its core, the SLR Act could be described as a licencing and permitting regime. The SLR Act outlines six major types of regulation. These include (1) a launch facility licence, (2) an Australian launch permit, (3) an Australian high power rocket permit, (4) an overseas payload permit, (5) a return authorisation, and (6) an authorisation certificate (see Figure 8.1).

A launch facility licence is required to operate a launch facility in Australia. An Australian launch permit is required to launch a space object from a launch facility in Australia or from an aircraft in flight. A high-power rocket permit is required to launch a high-power rocket from a launch facility in Australia. An overseas payload permit is required by an Australian national to launch a space object from a facility or location outside of Australia. A return authorisation is required to return a space object to Australia or required by an Australian national to return a space object to a location outside of Australia. Finally, an authorisation certificate authorises a party to undertake conduct that may not be covered by the legislation or that may have been prohibited by the legislation. Together, this regulation forms the legislative system in Australia for regulating space activities.

However, the SLR Act does more than just establish a regulatory system for the issuing and management of licences, permits, authorisations, and certificates. It aims to strike a balance between the need to control risk and ensure compliance with relevant safety standards and the need to remove "barriers to participation in space activities and [encourage] innovation and entrepreneurship in the space industry".[16] It does this in a number of ways, including simplifying the "application and assessment" process for those seeking to obtain approvals under the SLR Act, as well as reducing the insurance requirements incumbent on space actors seeking to obtain an Australian launch permit, high power rocket permit, or return authorisation.

The SLR Act (point 1 below) is a piece of primary legislation that is accompanied and supplemented by three other sets of Rules (points 2–4 below).[17] Indeed, these Rules support the SLR Act by elaborating upon the principles of law articulated in the SLR Act. In turn, the Rules refer to

15 Space (Launches and Returns) Act 2018 [SLR Act], s 3(a).
16 SLR Act, 2018, s 3(b)(i)–(ii).
17 DISR, n.d. b.

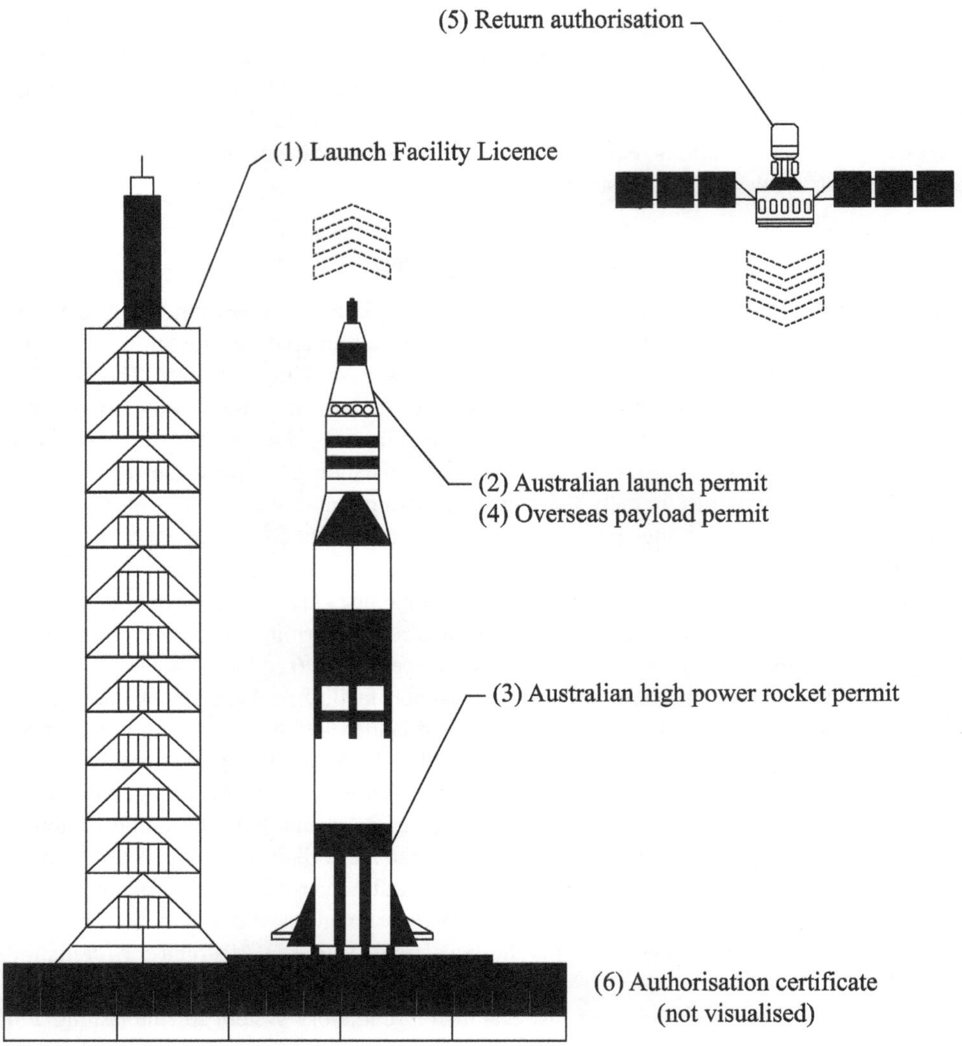

Figure 8.1 The six major types of regulation under the SLR Act

other documents (points 5–6 below) which taken together form the Australian legislative system regulating space activities. Figure 8.2 outlines the Australian legislative system for regulating space activities, which includes the:

1. Space (Launches and Returns) Act 2018;
2. Space (Launches and Returns) (General) Rules 2019;
3. Space (Launches and Returns) (High Power Rocket) Rules 2019;
4. Space (Launches and Returns) (Insurance) Rules 2019;
5. Flight Safety Code;
6. Maximum Probable Loss Methodology.

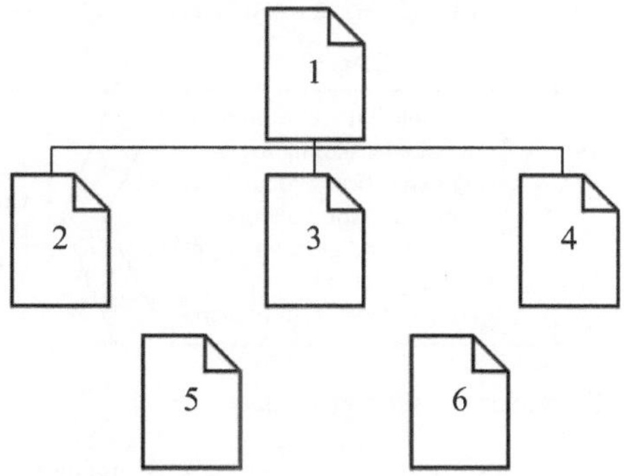

Figure 8.2 The Australian legislative system for regulating space activities

The following sections explain some essential considerations for those parties seeking to apply for and maintain one or more of the licences, permits, or authorisations under the SLR Act, including considerations of insurance. Please note that the following information does not constitute legal advice, nor is it a comprehensive description of all legal considerations that must be borne in mind. Instead, it is a legislative overview, and is intended to assist the reader in navigating the system of Australian space legislative instruments.

8.2.1 Launch facility licences

A launch facility is a location where launching occurs. Under the SLR Act, this includes both fixed and mobile launch facilities.[18] To construct and/or operate a launch facility within Australia, a party will need to apply to the ASA. The application will be assessed, and the responsible Minister will decide whether to grant the launch facility licence pursuant to s 18 of the SLR Act. Of note is the fact that s 18(f) of the SLR Act outlines that the applicant must satisfy the requirements outlined in the secondary legislation, namely the Space (Launches and Returns) (General) Rules 2019 (General Rules). Some important considerations to bear in mind when applying for a launch facility licence is that in line with s 5 of the General Rules, the Minister will consider what the purpose of the launch facility is and whether the "design and construction of the launch facility is as effective and safe as reasonably practicable".[19] There are numerous risks inherent in the act of launching objects into outer space, and the Minister will want to know how the applicant plans to minimise and manage these risks. This sort of information will likely be included as part of one or more of the required plans that the applicant must create and submit to the Minister. The application must include the following plans (1) a facility management plan, (2) an environmental plan, (3) a design and engineering plan(s), (4) an emergency plan, and (5) a technology security plan.[20] Pursuant to s 8 of the General Rules, these plans must be kept accurate, and if amended, they must

18 SLR Act, 2018, s 8 Definitions.
19 Space (Launches and Returns) (General) Rules 2019 [General Rules], s 5(2); Australian Government, 2019a, p. 6.
20 See General Rules, 2019, ss 15, 21, 19, 20, 22.

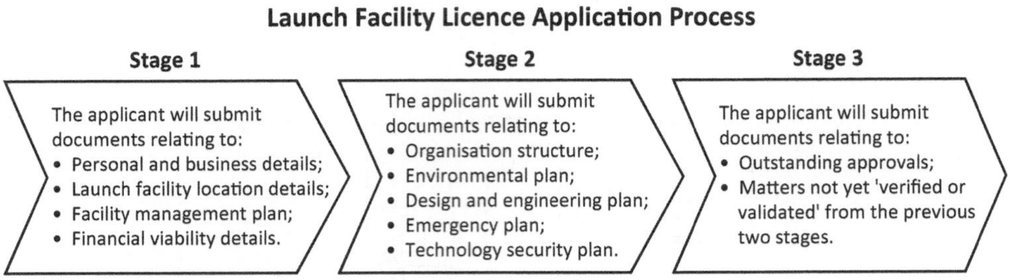

Figure 8.3 The launch facility licence application process

be re-issued to the Minister.[21] Taken together, these plans will describe how the launch facility will be constructed and/or operated.[22]

Applicants can expect the application process to occur in three stages (see Figure 8.3).[23] Stage one requires the applicant to submit documentation relating to (1) the personal and business details of the applicant, including details of those "persons or entities [possessing] ownership, control or direction [over] the applicant".[24] This information will be used to assess whether the planned launch facility goes against Australia's "security, defence or international relations"[25] posture, meaning a licence will not be issued if it runs contrary to these factors. Stage one also requires the applicant to submit (2) details regarding the launch facility location(s) itself, "including the frequency of launches and possible kinds of launch vehicles"[26] that are to be used. This information is required to build a picture of where launches will take place geographically, the physical characteristics of the facility, and the sorts of launching activities that will occur at the facility. Additionally, stage one will also require the lodgement of (3) a facility management plan that must include a range of information covering aspects such as approaches to operating the facility, for instance, the planned or in-place security protocols, as well as how the applicant will report on the facility's operation to the regulator.[27] Finally, stage one necessitates that the applicant proves it has (4) the financial resources needed to construct and/or operate the launch facility.[28]

Once the stage one documents have been submitted and assessed, the Minister will decide whether to progress the application to stage two. Stage two of the application requires the applicant to submit documentation that outlines (1) the applicant's organisation structure, including personnel roles and their associated responsibilities, as well as the personal details of individuals within the organisation.[29] Having suitably qualified persons operating the launch facility is essential, and the assessment will take into consideration aspects such as the "qualifications and experience"[30] of the individuals involved. Stage two also sees the applicant submitting a variety of other aforementioned plans, including (2) an environmental plan, (3) a design and engineering

21 Australian Government, 2019a, p. 7.
22 General Rules, 2019, s 8(2).
23 Australian Government, 2019a, pp. 8–14.
24 General Rules, 2019, s 13(e); Australian Government, 2019a, p. 9.
25 Australian Government, 2019a, p. 9.
26 See generally General Rules, 2019, s 14; see specifically General Rules, 2019, s 14(e).
27 General Rules, 2019, s 15.
28 General Rules, 2019, s 16.
29 General Rules, 2019, s 18.
30 General Rules, 2019, s 18(1)(b)(iii).

plan(s), (4) an emergency plan, and (5) a technology security plan.[31] These plans should provide a detailed view into how the applicant will govern and manage a variety of important operational aspects, such as how they will respond to "accidents and incidents"[32] through to the cybersecurity controls that have/will be put in place to prevent unauthorised access to the facility's networks.[33] Once stage two documentation has been lodged and assessed, the Minister will decide if it is necessary for the application to move to stage three. Stage three will only be necessary if the applicant must show that it has/will obtain other (1) "outstanding approvals"[34] that may be required under different Australian Commonwealth and/or State or Territory laws, as well as (2) those matters that have not yet been "verified or validated" from the previous two stages, and how the applicant will verify or validate these matters.[35]

The culmination of this application process is that the application for a launch facility licence will either be approved or rejected. If approved, a launch facility licence will be issued to the applicant. The licence will have specific terms[36] and conditions[37] attached to it, for instance, that the licence cannot be issued for a period longer than 20 years.[38] If rejected, the applicant has the right to request a review of the Minister's decision per s 61(a) of the SLR Act.[39]

8.2.2 Australian launch permits

Under the SLR Act, a space object is defined to mean:

(a) an object the whole or a part of which is to go into or come back from an area beyond the distance of 100 km above mean sea level; or
(b) any part of such an object, even if the part is to go only some of the way towards or back from an area beyond the distance of 100 km above mean sea level.[40]

An Australian launch permit is required when launching a space object(s) from an Australian launch facility or from an in-flight Australian aircraft or foreign aircraft in Australia's airspace. Such a launch permit may be granted to an applicant by the Minister pursuant to s 28 of the SLR Act. Section 28(3) sets out criteria that must be met by the applicant. Notably, s 28(3)(c) outlines that the applicant must satisfy the Minister that the probability of harm resulting from the launch(es) of the space object(s) is "as low as is reasonably practicable".[41] In determining this, applicants will use the Flight Safety Code, which is a document provided by the ASA that contains a methodology that should be used to ascertain whether space activities, such as launches and returns, are safe.[42]

31 See General Rules, 2019, ss 21, 19, 20, 22.
32 See General Rules, 2019, s 20(1).
33 General Rules, 2019, s 22; Australian Government, 2019a, pp. 12–13.
34 General Rules, 2019, s 24.
35 General Rules, 2019, s 25.
36 SLR Act, 2018, s 19.
37 SLR Act, 2018, s 20.
38 SLR Act, 2018, s 19(b).
39 This review will likely be undertaken by a government body that reviews administrative decisions.
40 SLR Act, 2018, s 8 Definitions.
41 SLR Act, 2018, s 28(3)(c).
42 ASA, 2019b, p. 5.

Additional criteria[43] to be met by an applicant are laid out in the General Rules. Examples of additional criteria include that the applicant must specify the date that the space object(s) will be launched, the "launch window" for that date, and show that the flight path followed by the space object(s) is "as safe as reasonably practicable".[44] Regarding the flight path, the applicant must identify any "critical assets" that lie under or near it.[45] The term "critical asset" is not defined in the SLR Act or General Rules. Indeed, the notion of a critical asset in the civil space context is not agreed upon. The term likely has within its extension different categories of critical assets that have relevance within different contexts. For instance, things such as transport networks, data centres, or power stations may be considered critical assets because they are infrastructure that is fundamental to the ongoing functioning of a country's society and economy. Nevertheless, in the absence of a legislative definition, the government will likely turn to the courts to decide what this means. However, in the event of a launch failure, there is a risk that a space object, or space debris created during the launch, may collide with, and damage a critical asset. This risk must be controlled and it is done so by requiring the applicant to submit details regarding how the launch vehicle to be used in the launch was manufactured. This includes how the manufacturer undertook quality assurance over the building of the launch vehicle and whether "recognised standards", tests, and inspections occurred and were followed during manufacturing.[46] This information is critical to an assessment of whether a launch permit should be granted.

Where a launch involves a payload(s), the applicant must submit a variety of information such as the payload(s) technical and manufacturing specifications, the payload(s) purpose and intended use, who the owner is and a commitment to report to the ASA if/when transmissions with the payload(s) are established or severed.[47] Other noteworthy requirements incumbent on the applicant include (1) the need to submit a flight safety plan for the launch,[48] (2) a debris mitigation strategy,[49] and (3) a technology security plan.[50]

8.2.3 Australian high power rocket permits

A permit is required to launch a high power rocket from an Australian launch facility. The Minister is authorised to issue this permit under s 38 of the SLR Act. Importantly, this type of permit only pertains to rockets that fall under the definition of "high power rocket" in s 8 of the SLR Act. The definition in the SLR Act, as primary legislation, points to the secondary legislation for a more detailed definitional description of high power rocket. Under s 5 of the Space (Launches and Returns) (High Power Rocket) Rules 2019 (Rocket Rules), a high power rocket is defined as:

(a) [...] a rocket propelled by a motor or motors with a combined total impulse greater than 889,600 Newton seconds; or

43 SLR Act, 2018, s 28(3)(f).
44 General Rules, 2019, ss 37(1), 35(3).
45 General Rules, 2019, s 47; Australian Government, 2019a, p. 23.
46 General Rules, 2019, s 48(1).
47 General Rules, 2019, s 50.
48 General Rules, 2019, s 53.
49 General Rules, 2019, s 54.
50 General Rules, 2019, s 56.

(b) [...] a rocket propelled by a motor or motors with a combined total impulse greater than 40,960 Newton seconds and is fitted with a system or systems that allow active control of its trajectory.[51]

A high power rocket is not defined by the location of its activity but rather by technical criteria related to impulse and rocket control. Nevertheless, the location of a rocket's activity will be significant because conducting a rocket launch will be regulated by both the ASA and the Civil Aviation Safety Authority (CASA). CASA is the Australian Government's aviation safety regulator. An applicant for an Australian high power rocket permit will likely also be required to apply to CASA for permission to launch a rocket from an "approved area".[52] There will be information about the area for the operation of the rocket that must be supplied to the ASA (and CASA), such as the intended flight path details, including the rocket's planned and "maximum altitude", its planned and potential range, as well as events likely to occur during its flight.[53]

Similar to other regulation, s 38(2)(e) of the SLR Act outlines that the Minister may grant a permit only if the applicant satisfies the criteria in the Rocket Rules. Standard requirements to comply with include that the applicant must (1) confirm the date that the rocket will be launched, as well as the "launch window" and its "planned trajectory",[54] (2) outline payload(s) details if applicable,[55] (3) describe the applicant's "organisational structure" and personnel's roles and responsibilities,[56] and (4) supply the rocket's manufacturing and technical specifications.[57] Importantly, all rocket activity must comply with the Flight Safety Code[58] and ensure that the rocket does not enter into a foreign jurisdiction(s) without permission.[59] Granting a high power rocket permit will be conditional on the documented description of the rocket's operation, as outlined in the following required plans, (1) a launch management plan, (2) a flight safety plan, (3) an emergency plan, (4) an environmental plan, and (5) a technology security plan.[60]

8.2.4 Overseas payload permits

Where an Australian national is engaged in (and is responsible for) the launch of a space object(s) from a location that is outside of Australia, they will require an overseas payload permit. Responsibility in this context is explained by the definition of "responsible party" found in the definition section of the SLR Act.[61] This includes that the person in question is an Australian national and is either the holder of the overseas payload permit or, if not, is the party that is undertaking the launching activity or owns all, or part, of a payload(s) connected to the launch.[62] The power to grant an overseas payload permit rests with the Minister pursuant to the required criteria being met

51 Space (Launches and Returns) (High Power Rocket) Rules 2019 [Rocket Rules], s 5.
52 See Subpart 101.H – Rockets in the Civil Aviation Safety Regulations 1998.
53 Rocket Rules, 2019, s 19.
54 Rocket Rules, 2019, s 8(1).
55 Rocket Rules, 2019, s 23; Australian Government, 2019b, p. 8.
56 Rocket Rules, 2019, s 17(1).
57 Rocket Rules, 2019, s 20.
58 Rocket Rules, 2019, s 10(1).
59 Rocket Rules, 2019, s 10(2).
60 Rocket Rules, 2019, ss 24, 26, 27, 28, 29.
61 SLR Act, 2018, s 8.
62 See the s. 8 definition section in the SLR Act 2018 for further clarification.

under 46B(2) of the SLR Act. Again, 46B(2)(d) explains that criteria set out in the General Rules must also be met for the granting of a permit.

Turning to the General Rules, one sees similar requirements to the other types of regulation incumbent on the applicant.[63] For instance, an applicant must (1) supply personal and business details, including details of those entities that have "ownership, control or direction" over the applicant,[64] (2) show that an appropriate organisational structure exists and is staffed with personnel capable of successfully building and operating the payload(s) to be launched,[65] and (3) supply copies of any contracts related to the launch, such as "use or lease of [launch] facilities", etc.[66] Similar to an Australian launch permit, the overseas payload permit will see the applicant provide detailed descriptive and technical information about the launch itself, the payload(s) to be launched, the country-specific safety measures that exist/are to be put in place, and the submission of a debris mitigation strategy.[67]

8.2.5 Return authorisations

Returning a space object from outer space to the Earth is a complex and risky activity. This sort of activity may see a space object return to a location within Australia, or an Australian national may be involved in returning a space object to a location outside Australia. Either way, a return authorisation will be required. The Minister may grant this authorisation pursuant to the SLR Act's s 46L(2) criteria being met. Turning to the General Rules,[68] a space object's return must be assessed against, and be consistent with, the risk hazard analysis methodology contained in the Flight Safety Code,[69] which identifies and quantifies risk(s) to the public or property that may unfold in the course of a space object's re-entry.[70] Section 98 of the General Rules specifies further risk hazard analysis requirements incumbent on the applicant. This includes the necessity that an analysis be undertaken by a ministerially approved, independent, and experienced assessor.[71] The analysis will examine things like the types of risks that the space object return poses to the public.[72] In addition, the applicant will also be required to create and submit a suite of plans related to the space object's return, such as (1) a return management plan, (2) a return safety plan, (3) an emergency plan, (4) an environmental plan, and (5) a technology security plan.[73]

8.2.6 Authorisation certificates

Sections 11, 12, 13, 14, 15, and 15A of the SLR Act outline conduct that is prohibited, and which constitutes an offence or civil penalty under the Act. Generally, this encompasses engaging in the space activities regulated by the Act without the required licence(s), permit(s), and/or

63 The ASA has made available an Overseas Payload Permit Application Guideline. For more information on this see ASA, 2022.

64 General Rules, 2019, s 74.

65 General Rules, 2019, s 75; Australian Government, 2019a, pp. 36–37.

66 General Rules, 2019, s 80.

67 General Rules, 2019, ss 76, 77, 78, 79.

68 See SLR Act, 2018, s 46L(2)(f).

69 General Rules, 2019, 91(4).

70 ASA, 2019b, p. 13.

71 General Rules, 2019, s 98(2)(a).

72 Australian Government, 2019a, p. 45.

73 General Rules, 2019, ss 97, 99, 100, 101, 102.

authorisation(s) or breaching a condition(s) of the regulation. An authorisation certificate may be granted to a space actor by the Minister which covers specific conduct that is either not addressed in the Act or which is prohibited by the aforesaid sections.[74]

8.2.7 Insurance

The space activities covered by the aforementioned regulation come with associated costs and expenses. Therefore, as part of the acquisition and maintenance of a licence, permit, or authorisation under the SLR Act, an applicant will need to prove a degree of financial viability. For instance, those applicants seeking to obtain an Australian launch permit, overseas payload permit, high power rocket permit, or return authorisation must supply evidence that they have appropriate financial resources and/or levels of insurance to manage or transfer the monetary risk(s) of harm or damage that may result from their intended space activity.[75] Insurance requirements are contained in the SLR Act, General Rules, and the Space (Launches and Returns) (Insurance) Rules 2019 (Insurance Rules). Section 48 of the SLR Act pertains to insurance, with s 48(4) specifying that the "minimum amount of insurance" required by an applicant will be the figure that is lowest, as determined by either an amount specified in the Insurance Rules or an alternative amount determined using another method. This other "method" that is referenced is specified in the Insurance Rules[76] and is entitled the Maximum Probable Loss Methodology (MPL Methodology). The MPL Methodology is contained in a separate document available from the ASA, which enables its user to determine the "maximum probable loss that might occur" in the course of undertaking specific space activities.[77] If an amount arrived at by using the MPL Methodology is lower than an amount specified in the Insurance Rules, then the former will be the total insurance required by the applicant.[78] Of note is the fact that no insurance amount will be higher than AUD$100 million.[79] The purchasing of insurance will be essential for many Australian space activities and is necessary to protect and develop Australia's civil space sector.

8.3 Overview of New Zealand's commercial space sector

Since the implementation of New Zealand's first national space law and its first launch in 2018, the country's commercial space sector has continued to grow rapidly. In a 2019 Ministry of Business, Innovation and Employment (MBIE) commissioned report (the Report), it was highlighted that New Zealand's space sector reportedly contributed NZD$1.69 billion to its national economy in 2018–2019 and employed an estimated workforce of 12,000 people (both direct and indirect full-time equivalent).[80] With more start-ups and small and medium-sized companies entering the commercial space sector, the Report identified high growth areas, such as the demand for space data, as being critical factors in driving increased commercialisation across the sector.[81] The Report identified that growth within New Zealand's space sector rested largely

74 See, SLR Act, 2018, Division 6A s 46U; General Rules, 2019, Part 6.

75 See General Rules, 2019, ss 57(a), 103(a); Rocket Rules, 2019, s 30(a).

76 Space (Launches and Returns) (Insurance) Rules 2019 [Insurance Rules], s 7.

77 ASA, 2019c, p. 5.

78 SLR Act, 2018, s 48(4); Insurance, Rules, 2019, s 6; ASA, 2019c, p. 5.

79 SLR Act, 2018, s 48(4)(a).

80 Deloitte Access Economics, 2019, p. 6.

81 Deloitte Access Economics, 2019, p. 10.

upon space manufacturing and identified other key growth areas such as research and development as well as ancillary services necessary to support the overall space sector.[82] Taken together, these trends indicate a diversification of services and capabilities within New Zealand's commercial space sector.

Established in April 2016, the New Zealand Space Agency (NZSA) is the country's national government agency responsible for the development of space law and policy as well as for supporting and growing the space sector.[83] In addition, it is tasked with promoting New Zealand as a potential region for launches and other space-based related activities.[84] As part of its mandate, the NZSA also plays a part in reviewing and approving applications for permits and licences related to space activities, with the Minister of MBIE reserving the ultimate decision-making power regarding such approvals. NZSA was established by the New Zealand Government after its recognition of the increasing commercial and strategic advantages associated with a presence in outer space. Specifically, this is related to the launching of rockets from New Zealand. The New Zealand Government found itself in a challenging position when Rocket Lab, an American space company with a New Zealand subsidiary, outlined its intention to begin launching rockets on the east coast of the country.[85] This situation required the New Zealand and American governments to enter into the Technology Safeguards Agreement (MBIE, 2016) in the absence of New Zealand having fit-for-purpose space law. This was one factor that led to the country developing its body of space regulations.

Of note, the rapid growth of New Zealand's commercial space sector must be considered in context. Unlike its neighbour, Australia, New Zealand's space sector has grown as a direct result of commercial and business interests, not military ones.[86] Unlike its Five Eyes (FVEY) counterparts, New Zealand's space sector is commercially driven and does not *per se* have a space history moulded nor informed by lessons learned from a Cold War era or Space Age context. This "fresh" approach to space regulation is best demonstrated by the wide and flexible nature of the country's primary piece of space legislation, entitled the Outer Space and High-Altitude Activities Act 2017 (OSHAA).[87]

8.4 New Zealand's space law

OSHAA legislates the licence and permit application process concerning space-related activities. The legislation is first-of-its-kind within New Zealand and was hastily created in response to the burgeoning commercial opportunities in space (as explained above). Importantly, OSHAA implements a framework that governs the application of, and regulation of, space-related activities and high-altitude activities conducted from New Zealand, as well as facility licences required to operate a space facility from New Zealand.[88] OSHAA's jurisdiction also reaches New Zealanders conducting space-related activities, in the form of launches of payloads, who are overseas.[89]

82 Deloitte Access Economics, 2019, pp. 14–16.

83 Ministry of Business, Innovation and Employment [MBIE], n.d. b.

84 MBIE, n.d. a.

85 MBIE, n.d. a; Office of the Minister for Economic Development Economic Growth and Infrastructure, 2016.

86 Pozza & Dennerley, 2022, p. 48.

87 Pozza & Dennerley, 2022, pp. 57–58.

88 *Outer Space and High-Altitude Activities Act 2017* [OSHAA Act], pt. 2.

89 OSHAA Act, 2017, pt. 2.

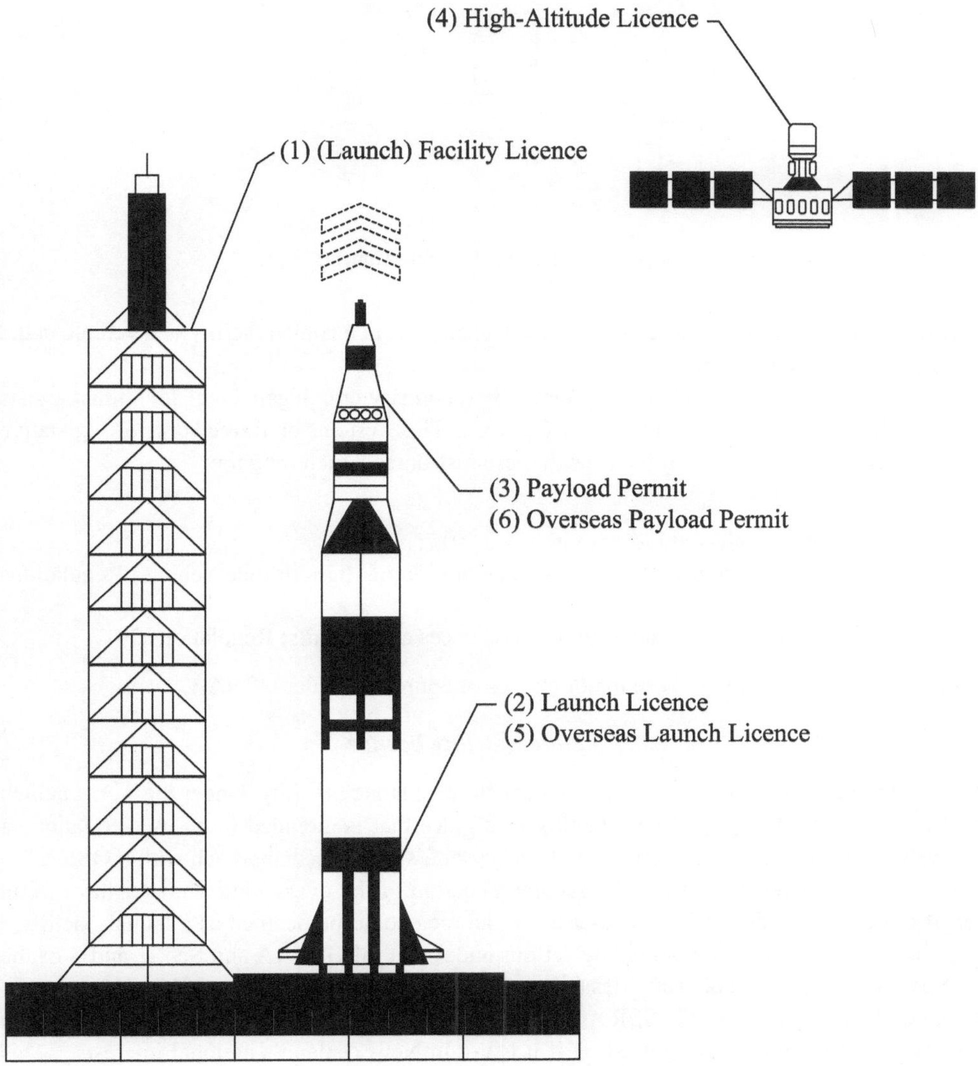

Figure 8.4 The six major classes of licences and permits under OSHAA

OSHAA outlines six major classes of licences and permit approvals. These include (1) a (launch) facility licence, (2) a launch licence, (3) a payload permit, (4) a high-altitude licence, (5) an overseas launch licence, and (6) an overseas payload permit (see Figure 8.4). A launch facility licence is required to operate a launch facility in New Zealand. A launch licence is required to launch a launch vehicle from a launch facility in New Zealand or from a vehicle in the air launched from New Zealand. A payload permit is required to launch a payload from a launch facility in New Zealand or a launch vehicle launched from a launch facility in New Zealand, or from a vehicle in the air launched from New Zealand. A high-altitude licence is required for the launch of a high-altitude vehicle from New Zealand or from a vehicle in the air launched from New Zealand (unless the activity is captured under a launch licence). An overseas launch licence is required by a New Zealand national to launch a launch vehicle from a launch facility or a vehicle in the air from outside of New Zealand. Finally, an overseas payload permit is required by a New Zealand national

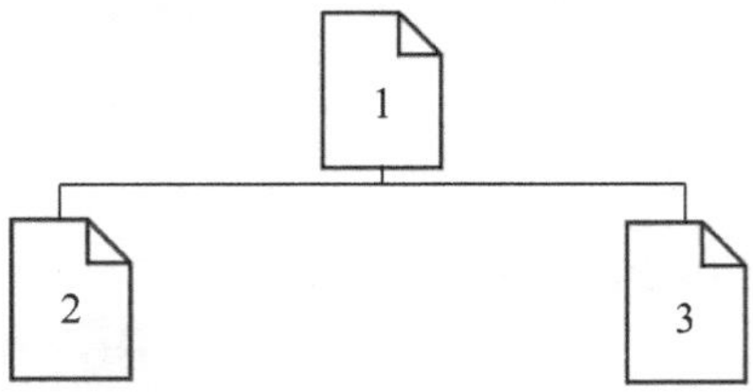

Figure 8.5 The framework of New Zealand's space legislative instruments

to launch a payload from either a launch vehicle launched from a launch facility or a vehicle in the air from outside of New Zealand.

As primary legislation, OSHAA is supported by secondary or delegated legislation that assists in further defining the requirements under OSHAA. This system, or framework, of legislative instruments is represented in Figure 8.5, with these instruments including the:

1. Outer Space and High-altitude Activities Act 2017;
2. Outer Space and High-altitude Activities (Definition of High-altitude Vehicle) Regulations 2017;
3. Outer Space and High-altitude Activities (Licences and Permits) Regulations 2017.

The following sections explain these major classes of approvals under OSHAA.

8.4.1 Launch facility licence

OSHAA is broad in its approach to what may constitute a launch facility. Under the Act, a launch facility can include a fixed or mobile facility or a place that is intended to be used to launch a launch vehicle.[90] Similarly, and pursuant to New Zealand's prescribed approach within OSHAA,[91] the New Zealand Governor-General, by recommendation of the overseeing Minister through an Order of Council, may determine whether or not an area could be deemed as a launch facility.[92] The application process is predominately set out under s 40 of OSHAA and Sch. 2 and 5 of the Outer Space and High-altitude Activities (Licences and Permits) Regulations 2017.

Importantly, and much like the SLR Act in Australia, s 40(2)(a) of OSHAA grants the Minister the ability to decline a facility application if it is not in New Zealand's national interests.[93] This power may, from time to time, cause problems for applicants because the timing at which an applicant applies for a facility licence may coincide with matters unfolding on the international stage, meaning that a licence may not be granted if there are aspects of New Zealand's international relations, or national concerns, important to the government that may see a licence rejected. Under s 40(3)(a) of OSHAA, New Zealand's national interests may include economic considerations, specifically benefits to New Zealand, associated with the licence. Further, other broader elements that form part of "national interests" include (but are not limited to) national security or public safety.[94]

90 OSHAA Act, 2017, s 4.
91 See generally chapter 3 in Pozza & Dennerley, 2022.
92 OSHAA Act, 2017, s 88(12).
93 OSHAA Act, 2017, s 40(2)(b).
94 OSHAA Act, 2017, s 40(3)(b).

The application process requires applicants to submit information about themselves[95] and the details about the launch facility.[96] Typically, this information is amalgamated and sent through to the NZSA at the same time for its consideration. This must also include safety requirements and evidence of the applicant's technical ability under the Schedule, as well as the applicant needing to satisfy the fit and proper person test as set out in s 52 of OSHAA.

Information concerning the applicant is set out predominately in Schedule 2 of the Outer Space and High-Altitude Activities (Licenses and Permits) Regulations 2017, which is applicable to all applications made under OSHAA. The information must include whether the applicant is an individual, a body corporate, or any other type of entity, as well as their name, contact details and nationality.[97] Where a body corporate (or another type of entity) is applying, information pertaining to the country of incorporation must be provided as well as a clear list of interests and ownership in the body corporate.[98] Information pertaining to the launch facility requires supplying details concerning the name and location of the launch facility or proposed launch facility, as well as confirmation as to whether or not the proposed launch will take place from within New Zealand or from a location overseas.[99] If the latter, then the application will need to include information about the foreign launch facility owner, which is largely a reflection of the same information required for a New Zealand launch facility licence, as discussed above.

However, the bulk of information required for a New Zealand launch facility licence application is contained within Schedule 5 of the Outer Space and High-altitude Activities (Licence and Permit) Regulation 2017. Here, it specifies that information supplied must include considerable details about the launch facility itself, for instance, the location, launch vehicles, and their frequencies of use at the facility.[100] Similarly, the application must include a site plan that illustrates the "launch site and the command and control centre".[101] Importantly, the application must also include whether or not there will be any protective security arrangements around the launch facility.[102] Specifically, applicants will need to include a safety case that details safety processes pursuant to safety critical systems,[103] safety risk assessments,[104] compliance with safety standards,[105] as well as the overarching safety of the launch facility[106] and emergency plans[107] to be used in the events of accidents.

Notwithstanding the Minister's power to reject an application despite meeting the application prerequisites under s 44 of OSHAA, if accepted, the facility licence may be issued with conditions imposed on it under s 41 of OSHAA. These are likely to relate to insurance and safety require-

95 *Outer Space and High-altitude Activities (Licences and Permits) Regulations 2017* [Licences and Permits Regulations], Sch. 2.
96 Licences and Permits Regulations, 2017, Sch. 3(6)(7) & Sc. 5.
97 Licences and Permits Regulations, 2017, Sch. 2(1).
98 Licences and Permits Regulations, 2017, Sch. 2(2) & (3).
99 Licences and Permits Regulations, 2017, Sch. 3(6).
100 Licences and Permits Regulations, 2017, Sch. 5(1).
101 Licences and Permits Regulations, 2017, Sch. 5(2).
102 Licences and Permits Regulations, 2017, Sch. 5(3).
103 Licences and Permits Regulations, 2017, Sch. 5(5)(a).
104 Licences and Permits Regulations, 2017, Sch. 5(5)(d).
105 Licences and Permits Regulations, 2017, Sch. 5(5)(e).
106 Licences and Permits Regulations, 2017, Sch. 5(5)(f).
107 Licences and Permits Regulations, 2017, Sch. 5(5)(h).

ments or conditions. A licence can be granted for up to five years[108] (and may be renewed) but will only apply to one single launch operator or one facility.[109]

8.4.2 Launch licences

Section 7 of OSHAA requires that any person wanting to launch a launch vehicle from New Zealand must have a launch licence to do so. The provision of the Act is specific and details that in most circumstances, a licence will only cover a specific launch, from a specific launch vehicle, from a specified launch facility. All details will need to be included within a launch licence application. Deviations from the specificities will likely require a variation or, in some cases, a new launch licence.[110]

The launch licence will necessarily apply to the proposed launch of a launch vehicle, which is defined under s 4 of OSHAA as:

a) a vehicle, the whole or any part of which—
    (i) reaches, or is intended to reach, outer space; or
    (iii) carries or supports the launch of, or is intended to carry or support the launch of, a payload; or
b) any component part of a vehicle described in paragraph (a).[111]

The application process will require the applicant to illustrate that they are technically capable of conducting a safe launch.[112] Further, the applicant will need to include in the application a plan concerning how any risk(s) to public safety will be mitigated[113] as well as how the applicant plans to mitigate the effects of space debris through an orbital space debris mitigation plan,[114] and any other prescribed requirements that the applicants may be subject to by the NZSA that forms part of the application.[115] Additional information to be supplied concerns the technical details of the proposed launch, which includes the launch date, location trajectory, and orbital parameters,[116] as well as evidence demonstrating that such technical information has been presented to the:

- Civil Aviation Authority;
- Airways Corporation of New Zealand Limited;
- Maritime New Zealand; and
- Land Information New Zealand.[117]

The most challenging part of the application process is likely the requirement incumbent on the applicant to demonstrate that "the proposed launch or launches under the licence are consistent

108 OSHAA Act, 2017, s 42(2).
109 MBIE, n.d. c.
110 See generally OSHAA Act, 2017, ss 7–14.
111 OSHAA Act, 2017, s 4 Interpretation.
112 OSHAA Act, 2017, s 9(1)(a).
113 OSHAA Act, 2017, s 9(1)(b).
114 OSHAA Act, 2017, s 9(1)(c).
115 OSHAA Act, 2017, s 9(1)(e).
116 OSHAA Act, 2017, s 9(1)(a).
117 OSHAA Act, 2017, ss 10(1)(d)(i)–(iv).

with New Zealand's international obligations".[118] This may require specific expert advice on both New Zealand's status and obligations under the five United Nations space treaties, as well as a thorough understanding of New Zealand's current international relations at the time the application is made. In most circumstances, it may be the case that a launch will not pose a challenge to the rules outlined in international space law, however, it is advisable that an applicant has a good understanding of the obligations New Zealand has, having ratified four of the five United Nations space treaties.

Like the other licences and permits discussed below, despite meeting all required prerequisites, the Minister may still decline an application based on two overarching policy considerations:

- New Zealand's national interests[119] which includes economic, national security, international relations, public safety, or other matters of national concern;[120]
- whether the applicant, or other person that is or may have control over the rights under the launch licence, is a fit and proper person.[121]

If a launch licence is granted, then the Minister of MBIE will seek consultation with the Minister(s) that oversees New Zealand's national security before a launch is undertaken.[122] Licences are usually awarded for up to five years[123] with the possibility of further five-year renewal.[124] However, it is important to note that the applicant's obligations associated with the launch licence continue "until all matters connected to the launch or launches under the launch licence have been completed".[125]

8.4.3 Payload permit

An applicant must hold a payload permit in order to launch a payload from a launch facility in New Zealand.[126] The same is also true of a payload that is launched from a launch vehicle that is launched from a launch facility within New Zealand, and similarly, if a payload is launched from a vehicle in the air that was launched from New Zealand.[127] A payload is defined under s 4 of OSHAA, where it details that payload:

a) means an object that is carried or placed, or is intended to be carried or placed, in outer space; and
b) includes components of a launch vehicle that are specifically designed or adapted for the object (but does not otherwise include a launch vehicle or any of its component parts); and
c) includes a load to be carried for testing purposes or otherwise on a non-profit basis.[128]

118 OSHAA Act, 2017, s 10(1)(a).
119 OSHAA Act, 2017, s 9(2)(a).
120 OSHAA Act, 2017, s 9(3).
121 OSHAA Act, 2017, ss 9(2)(b)–(c).
122 OSHAA Act, 2017, s 9(4).
123 OSHAA Act, 2017, s 11.
124 OSHAA Act, 2017, s 12.
125 OSHAA Act, 2017, s 13.
126 OSHAA Act, 2017, ss 15(a)–(b).
127 OSHAA Act, 2017, ss 15(a)–(b).
128 OSHAA Act, 2017, s 4.

When making an application for a payload permit, the applicant must include documentation addressing how the application will safely manage the operation of the payload[129] (including protective security arrangements),[130] as well as an orbital debris mitigation plan associated with the payload.[131] Whilst the Minister can prescribe further requirements or conditions[132] on the payload licence (i.e. insurance requirements),[133] the most difficult part of the application process will be the requirement by the applicant to show that the payload does not contravene New Zealand's national interests[134] or international obligations.[135] Much like the difficulties outlined in the launch licence section above, the Minister reserves the right to decline an application under these headings despite an applicant satisfying all other requirements. Therefore, understanding New Zealand's national interests, international relations, and international space law, including whether the proposed payload jeopardises or contravenes those interests, is a key consideration that the applicant will need to demonstrate confidently. This will ultimately require careful analysis of New Zealand's international legal obligations as well as its national laws when considering how certain elements of a payload might be problematic. For instance, this may relate to a spacecraft or payload that utilises nuclear power as its fuel source. In such a situation, the granting of a payload permit approval would likely be unsuccessful as a result of New Zealand's policy on nuclear power and weapons.[136]

The duration of a payload permit is open to further specification by the NZSA under section 19 of OSHAA. Thus, unlike the launch licence or facility launch licence, which is granted for an initial five-year period (and may be renewed thereafter), the payload permit is likely to be granted for the perceived lifetime of the payload. If this is the case, it must be borne in mind that the applicant's obligations under OSHAA may also be for the same period as the payload's lifetime.

Importantly, the applicant must provide accurate details pertaining to the payload as specified in Sch. 4 of the Outer Space and High-altitude Activities Regulations 2017. Specifically, this requires the applicant to provide information pertaining to:

- an overview of the mission and purpose associated with the payload;[137]
- a description of the system that the payload is intended to form a part of;[138]
- technical information concerning the payload's life span proposed launching date, details of the launch licence holder (if available), and intended orbital parameters;[139]
- where the payload was manufactured or assembled, including the manufacturer's or assembler's name;[140]

129 OSHAA Act, 2017, s 17(a).
130 Licences and Permits Regulations, 2017, Sch. 4(5).
131 OSHAA Act, 2017, s 17(b).
132 For instance, see OSHAA Act, 2017, s 18(2) which relates to the condition of a permit, requiring the payload permit holder to indemnify the Crown.
133 OSHAA Act, 2017, s 18(2)(b).
134 OSHAA Act, 2017, ss 17(2)–(3).
135 OSHAA Act, 2017, s 17(1)(c).
136 See generally, Ministry of Foreign Affairs and Trade, n.d.
137 Licences and Permits Regulations, 2017, Sch. 4(1).
138 Licences and Permits Regulations, 2017, Sch. 4(1).
139 Licences and Permits Regulations, 2017, Sch. 4(2).
140 Licences and Permits Regulations, 2017, Sch. 4(3).

- whether the payload integrator is the same or different from the applicant, and if different, the details of the integrator, including name, contact details, and entity status of the integrator, i.e., an individual or a registered entity;[141] and
- launch facility details.

Interestingly, the regulations also stipulate high-level technical requirements concerning the description of ground stations that will be used to control or transfer data from the payload.[142] This is further linked to the payload's remote-sensing capability and the recipients of that information, which must also be outlined within the application.[143]

8.4.4 High-altitude licences

Subpart 6 of OSHAA lays out the licensing framework for activities conducted at high-altitudes. High-altitude is defined under s 4 of OSHAA to mean:

> high altitude means an altitude above the higher of—
>
> a) flight level 600; and
> b) the highest upper limit of controlled airspace under the Civil Aviation Act 1990.[144]

A high-altitude vehicle is defined as an aircraft (or other vehicle) that travels, or is capable of travelling, at a high-altitude.[145] Much like a space payload, a high-altitude payload is defined under s 4 of OSHAA as:

a) an object that is carried or placed, or is intended to be carried or placed, at high altitude; and
b) includes components of a high-altitude vehicle that are specifically designed or adapted for the object (but does not otherwise include a high-altitude vehicle or any of its component parts); and
c) includes a load to be carried for testing purposes or otherwise on a non-profit basis.[146]

Considering these definitions, an applicant wishing to launch a high-altitude vehicle, or use a high-altitude payload, must have a high-altitude vehicle (HAV) licence. OSHAA is silent on the need for an applicant to hold a specific HAV licence, instead, the payload necessarily forms part of the HAV licence.

From a jurisdictional perspective, an HAV poses challenges when considering New Zealand's partial demarcation line higher than flight level 600, to which the definition of HAV applies. However, the demarcation as to when to apply for a launch licence and payload permit applicable to "outer space" continues to remain undefined. This will likely pose future problems for New Zealand and the NZSA, especially in light of increasing activities in areas like low earth orbit.[147]

141 Licences and Permits Regulations, 2017, Sch. 4(4).
142 Licences and Permits Regulations, 2017, Sch. 4(6).
143 Licences and Permits Regulations, 2017, Sch. 4(13)–(14).
144 OSHAA Act, 2017, s 4.
145 OSHAA Act, 2017, s 4.
146 OSHAA Act, 2017, s 4.
147 See MBIE, n.d. a, which outlines activities currently underway that are predominately in low-earth orbit. Note: when searching the NZSA's website, the search term "low earth orbit permitting decision" returns 49 results sug-

Application for the HAV licence incorporates measures required by the Civil Aviation Authority. Much like the space launch licences or payload permits, HAV licences require demonstration of technical ability[148] and evidence of the applicant's (or person in control of the rights of the HAV licence) fitness to hold an HAV licence,[149] safety plans,[150] how they intend to mitigate risk(s) to the public,[151] and how they will ensure compliance with New Zealand's international obligations.[152] The Minister will also require a confirmation from the Director of Civil Aviation that the applicant or operator and aircraft meet New Zealand legislative compliance requirements.[153] Similarly, the Minister reserves the right to decline an application despite an applicant fulfilling all specified criteria if the application would jeopardise New Zealand's national interests.[154]

Whilst applicants must furnish to the Minister information pertaining to the HAV's technical specifications, including its launch range, intended altitude, payload, communications controls,[155] and flight path/plan, it is important to note that technical requirements applicable to HAVs are contained within two parts of Sch. 6 of the Outer Space and High-altitude Activities (Licences and Permits) Regulations 2017. Part 1 relates to information required for each HAV and predominately concerns technical details concerning its launch,[156] payload,[157] remote-sensing capability,[158] and access to remote-sensing information.[159] On the other hand, Part 2 relates to the information required for each HAV that is not an aircraft, including safety management[160] and emergency planning.[161] However, both parts apply and must be addressed within an HAV application.

8.4.5 Overseas launch licences

A New Zealand national wanting to launch a launch vehicle overseas (including from a vehicle in the air that was not launched in New Zealand) must apply for an overseas launch licence under s 23 of OSHAA unless the "New Zealand national has an overseas launch licence for the launch of the launch vehicle".[162]

This licence has two facets: foreign applicants wishing to launch a launch vehicle or include a payload on a launch vehicle, and New Zealand national's wishing to launch a launch vehicle overseas or launch a payload on a launch vehicle overseas. For foreign applicants, all foreign licences or permits issued by foreign agencies to conduct a proposed launch or payload from New Zealand must form part of the application. New Zealand nationals equally must include

gesting that, at the time of writing, the NZSA has provided approximately 49 payload permits pertaining to low earth orbit activities. See MBIE, n.d. d.

148 OSHAA Act, 2017, s 47(1)(a)(i).

149 Licences and Permits Regulations, 2017, Sch. 6 pt. 1 s 5.

150 Licences and Permits Regulations, 2017, Sch. 6 pts. 1–2.

151 OSHAA Act, 2017, s 47(1)(a)(ii).

152 OSHAA Act, 2017, s 47(1)(a)(iii). The Minister may prescribe additional requirements per OSHAA Act, 2017, s 41(1)(a)(iv).

153 OSHAA Act, 2017, ss 47(1)(b)(i)–(ii).

154 OSHAA Act, 2017, s 48(1)(a)(i)–(ii).

155 OSHAA Act, 2017, s 48(1)(a)(i)–(ii).

156 Licences and Permits Regulations, 2017, Sch. 6 pt. 1.

157 Licences and Permits Regulations, 2017, Sch. 6 pt. 1(2).

158 Licences and Permits Regulations, 2017, Sch. 6 pt. 1(3).

159 Licences and Permits Regulations, 2017, Sch. 6 pt. 1(4).

160 Licences and Permits Regulations, 2017, Sch. 6 pts. 2(9)(a)–(g).

161 Licences and Permits Regulations, 2017, Sch. 6 pt. 2(9)(h).

162 OSHAA Act, 2017, s 23.

any foreign licences or permits within the application, but of note is the fact that the NZSA must deem that the licences or permits issued by foreign regulators (such as the United States Federal Aviation Administration or the European Space Agency) have close alignment to New Zealand requirements.[163] Overall, the same requirements pertaining to a New Zealand launch licence will also apply to an overseas launch licence.

8.4.6 Overseas payload permits

Overseas payload permits are governed by subpart 4 of OSHAA and emulate much of the same requirements as the New Zealand payload permit application discussed above. The applicant will also need to demonstrate the same level of detail as outlined above for payload permits required under Sch. 4 of the Outer Space and High-altitude Activities (Licences and Permits) Regulations 2017 concerning the technical operation of the payload. Importantly, this will also need to include the payload's remote-sensing specifications as well as a list of recipients of this information.[164]

Much like the SLR Act in Australia (Space (Launches and Returns) Act 2018), the Minister may refuse to grant an application if granting the permit will interfere with New Zealand's national interests.[165] The national interest requirement will be the same as that stipulated for launch licences, namely, considerations will be made to economic factors,[166] national security concerns,[167] issues of public safety,[168] and international relations.[169]

8.4.7 Insurance

Unlike s 48 of the SLR Act in Australia, OSHAA does not include a mandatory requirement for insurance. Instead, OSHAA contains provisions for the *allowance* of insurance if required by the Minister under each category of licence or permit.[170] If insurance is required, then the prescribed method and requirements that may be imposed are authorised and contained under Regulation 88 of OSHAA. Essentially, this means that when applying for a licence or permit under OSHAA, each application is assessed on a case-by-case basis and allows for the endorsement of a permit or licence in addition to specifying if insurance coverage must be obtained. This allows the NZSA to consider each type of space activity proposed and any relevant mitigation measures that insurance may provide, as opposed to a standard insurance requirement like that implemented under the Australian SLR Act. This has both beneficial and challenging consequences. For example, if commercial space actors do not have the requisite capital to pay high premiums on insurance products, then there is some flexibility built into the application to the NZSA where it may be determined that, for instance, two or more insurers might cover various layers of liability, or if the payload is small and meets both the NZSA's and international standards pertaining to space debris, then insurance may not be required.[171]

163 MBIE, n.d. c.
164 Licences and Permits Regulations, 2017, Sch. 4(13)–(14).
165 OSHAA Act, 2017, s 32(2).
166 OSHAA Act, 2017, s 33(3)(a).
167 OSHAA Act, 2017, s 33(3)(b).
168 OSHAA Act, 2017, s 33(3)(b).
169 OSHAA Act, 2017, s 33(3)(b).
170 See for example, OSHAA Act, 2017, ss 10, 18, 26, 34, 48.
171 New Zealand Space Agency [NZSA], n.d.

However, this situation also means that there is a lack of precedent to refer to when future applicants apply to the NZSA. The intent behind this flexible arrangement is to enable the NZSA and commercial operators to work collaboratively together to arrive at suitable measures that will apply to the unique risks associated with specific space activities.[172] Importantly, New Zealand has taken a position on how space insurance applies to space launches that involve a United States (US) commercial launch vehicle, whereby the maximum probable loss calculation is to be used to determine insurance amounts.[173] Similar to the Australian MPL Methodology outlined above at 8.2.7, in New Zealand, where launch vehicles involve the US, then New Zealand is required to be a co-beneficiary under the MPL insurance policy. Essentially, this requires "the benefits of the US indemnity for damage above that amount (MPL) to be passed on to New Zealand".[174]

8.5 Concluding remarks

For any space actor planning to undertake, or currently engaged in, commercial or civil space activities in Australia or New Zealand, there will be regulatory considerations that must be borne in mind. By assisting the reader to navigate the Australian and New Zealand space legal landscapes, this chapter has highlighted some of these considerations, and has broken down and described important components of each country's respective space legislation. However, this is no substitute for professional legal advice, which should be sought by space actors preparing to engage, and engaging in, space activities. Additionally, both the Australian Space Agency and New Zealand Space Agency should be the first and primary points of contact for such space actors, as these agencies actively encourage space actors to contact them in the early stages of planning their space activities. Overall, Australia and New Zealand are two jurisdictions that have robust yet flexible regulatory regimes for managing space activities and are well equipped to regulate commercial space activities now and into the future.

Bibliography

AlphaBeta Australia Part of Accenture. (2021). *The Economic Contribution of Australia's Space Sector in 2018–19*. Prepared for the Australian Space Agency. https://www.industry.gov.au/sites/default/files/2021-02/the-economic-contribution-of-australias-space-sector-in-2018-19.pdf

Australian Government. (2019a). *Explanatory Statement Issued by the Authority of the Minister for Industry, Science and Technology. Space (Launches and Returns) Act 2018, Space (Launches and Returns) (General Rules) 2019*. https://www.legislation.gov.au/Details/F2019L01118/Explanatory%20Statement/Text

Australian Government. (2019b). *Explanatory Statement Issued by the Authority of the Minister for Industry, Science and Technology. Space (Launches and Returns) Act 2018, Space (Launches and Returns) (High Power Rocket) Rules 2019*. https://www.legislation.gov.au/Details/F2019L01119/Explanatory%20Statement/Text

Australian Space Agency. (2019a). *Advancing Space Australian Civil Space Strategy 2019–2028*. https://publications.industry.gov.au/publications/advancing-space-australian-civil-space-strategy-2019-2028.pdf

Australian Space Agency. (2019b). *Flight Safety Code*. Canberra: Commonwealth of Australia, August; available at: space.gov.au

Australian Space Agency. (2019c). *Maximum Probable Loss Methodology*. Canberra: Commonwealth of Australia, August; available at: space.gov.au

172 NZSA, n.d.
173 NZSA, n.d., p. 4.
174 NZSA, n.d., p. 4.

Australian Space Agency. (2020). *State of Space Report: A Report by the Australian Government Space Coordination Committee. 1 July 2019–30 June 2020.* https://www.industry.gov.au/sites/default/files/2020-12/state-of-space-report-2019-20.pdf

Australian Space Agency. (2022). *Overseas Payload Permit Application Guidelines.* https://www.industry.gov.au/sites/default/files/2022-08/overseas_payload_permit_-_guidelines.pdf

Civil Aviation Safety Regulations 1998. https://www.legislation.gov.au/Details/F2021C01179

Deloitte Access Economics. (2019). *New Zealand Space Sector Its Value, Scope and Structure.* Prepared for the Ministry of Business, Innovation and Employment. https://www.mbie.govt.nz/assets/new-zealand-space-sector-its-value-scope-and-structure.pdf

Department of Industry, Science and Resources. (2020). *Make It Happen the Australian Government's Modern Manufacturing Strategy.* https://www.industry.gov.au/sites/default/files/October%202020/document/make-it-happen-modern-manufacturing-strategy.pdf

Department of Industry, Science and Resources. (2021). *Space National Manufacturing Priority Road Map.* https://www.industry.gov.au/sites/default/files/February%202021/document/space-national-manufacturing-priority-road-map.pdf

Department of Industry, Science and Resources. (n.d.a). *About the Australian Space Agency.* https://www.industry.gov.au/about-us/about-the-australian-space-agency

Department of Industry, Science and Resources. (n.d.b). *Regulating Australian Space Activities.* https://www.industry.gov.au/regulations-and-standards/regulating-australian-space-activities

Ministry of Business, Innovation and Employment. (2016). *Agreement between the Government of New Zealand and the Government of the United States of America on Technology Safeguards Associated with United States Participation in Space Launches from New Zealand.* https://www.mbie.govt.nz/assets/f8d81015b3/technology-safeguards-agreement-US.pdf

Ministry of Business, Innovation and Employment. (n.d.a). *About Us.* https://www.mbie.govt.nz/science-and-technology/space/about-us/

Ministry of Business, Innovation and Employment. (n.d.b). *New Zealand Space Agency.* https://www.mbie.govt.nz/science-and-technology/space/

Ministry of Business, Innovation and Employment. (n.d.c). *Permits and Licences for Space Activities.* https://www.mbie.govt.nz/science-and-technology/space/permits-and-licences-for-space-activities/

Ministry of Business, Innovation and Employment. (n.d.d). *Search Results.* https://www.mbie.govt.nz/search/SearchForm?Search=low+earth+orbit+permitting+decision

Ministry of Foreign Affairs and Trade. (n.d.). *Taking a Nuclear-Free Policy to the World.* https://www.mfat.govt.nz/en/about-us/mfat75/taking-a-nuclear-free-policy-to-the-world/

New Zealand Space Agency. (n.d.). *Operational Policy: Liability, Insurance and Indemnities.* https://www.mbie.govt.nz/assets/liability-indemnity-and-insurance-operational-policy.pdf

Office of the Minister for Economic Development Economic Growth and Infrastructure. (2016). *Contract between the New Zealand Government and Rocket Lab.* https://www.mbie.govt.nz/assets/a6f07cf6cf/cabinet-paper-contract-between-the-nz-government-and-rocket-lab.pdf

Outer Space and High-Altitude Activities Act 2017. https://www.legislation.govt.nz/act/public/2017/0029/latest/DLM6966275.html

Outer Space and High-Altitude Activities (Definition of High-Altitude Vehicle) Regulations 2017. https://www.legislation.govt.nz/regulation/public/2017/0251/10.0/DLM7416501.html

Outer Space and High-Altitude Activities (Licences and Permits) Regulations 2017. https://www.legislation.govt.nz/regulation/public/2017/0250/latest/DLM7364101.html

Pozza, M.A. & Dennerley, J.A. (2022). *Risk Management in Outer Space Activities: An Australian and New Zealand Perspective.* Springer. https://link.springer.com/book/10.1007/978-981-16-4756-7

Space (Launches and Returns) Act. (2018). https://www.legislation.gov.au/Details/C2021C00394

Space (Launches and Returns) (General) Rules. (2019). https://www.legislation.gov.au/Details/F2019L01118

Space (Launches and Returns) (High Power Rocket) Rules. (2019). https://www.legislation.gov.au/Details/F2019L01119

Space (Launches and Returns) (Insurance) Rules. (2019). https://www.legislation.gov.au/Details/F2019L01120

Space Activities Act 1998. https://www.legislation.gov.au/Details/C2016C01070

9

PRACTICAL EXPERIENCES WITH FINLAND'S NATIONAL SPACE LEGISLATION AND LESSONS LEARNED

Jenni Tapio[1]

9.1 Introduction

The space sector is undergoing an important transformation. More actors have become involved in space activities, and investment especially from the private sector has increased over the course of the last decade. In view of the growing privatisation of space activities (most notably "NewSpace") and the growing strategic importance of space activities to the functioning of the society, to national security, and to decision-making in different areas of government, the significance of space activities has become evident.[2] A strong and innovative space sector is growing also in Finland. In the period between 2014 to 2021, Finnish businesses had attracted the fourth-highest amount of private capital investments in Europe, totalling €160 million.[3] The robust evolution, especially in Finnish upstream space activities, has also had spill-over effects in the overall organisation and development of the Finnish space governance.

1 The research is current as of date it was submitted to the editors: 18.08.2022.

2 This chapter is partly based on previous works by the author on the topic of the Finnish national space law; Tapio, J. (2018). The Finnish Space Act: En Route to Promoting Sustainable Private Activities in Outer Space. *Air and Space Law*, 43 (Issue 4/5), pp. 387–409; Tapio, J. (2018). *Introduction: Finland* in Karl-Heinz Böckstiegel, Benkö M., and Hobe, S. (2019). Space law: basic legal documents. Utrecht: Eleven International Publishing. Tapio, J., Soucek, A. (2022). *The European Space Agency's Contribution to National Space Law*. In: Karjalainen, K., Tornberg, I., Pursiainen, A. (eds) International Actors and the Formation of Laws. Springer, Cham.; additionally the author has held various presentations in conferences and academic courses on this topic, most recently at the European Centre for Space Law (ECSL) and International Institute of Space Law (IISL) Symposium on "National Laws and Regulations to Ensure Space Sustainability" held in conjunction with the 61st session of the UNCOPUOS Legal Subcommittee in 2022.

3 ESPI Report 83 – Space Venture Europe 2021: Entrepreneurship and Investment in the European Space Sector, Full Report, ESPI, June 2022.

 DOI: 10.4324/9781003268475-13

The role of national space law is becoming more prominent in the governance of space activities. This is tied to the growing commercialisation of space operations and the diversification of space actors and activities. Authorisation and continuous supervision of space activities, including those carried out by non-governmental entities, fall under the traditional purview of national space law, as required by Art. VI of the Outer Space Treaty.[4] Accordingly, states have to take actions to ensure that domestic space activities, including those by private (non-governmental) organisations, are carried out in accordance with international law in order to promote safe, sustainable, and peaceful use of space.[5] Recently, many states are enacting national space legislation after becoming spacefaring[6] or revising their existing instruments to accommodate new types of national space activities.[7] This is also the context in which the Finnish Act on Space Activities was passed in 2018,[8] and is subject to amendment in 2023.

Capitalising on the example of Finland and its recent domestic space law, the aim of this chapter is to examine the ways in which national space legislation can support business activity while taking care of the international obligations of the state, and promoting norms for responsible space activities. Taking stock of the experience gathered over the four years since its inception, this chapter briefly outlines the main provisions of the Act on Space Activities and other important instruments such as the Finnish space strategy. Moreover, the overall organisation of the Finnish space governance is described. Last, the chapter highlights some of the recent activities in the implementation and further development of the Finnish national space law through two specific examples (a) implementation of norms in support of sustainable use of space, and (b) recently proposed amendment to the national space regulation dealing with earth observation and ground station activities.

9.2 The Finnish space governance

9.2.1 De-centralised space administration

Matters relating to space are by nature horizontal and crosscutting. The Finnish Space Committee, which is a committee set by the Government and working under the auspices of the Ministry of Economic Affairs and Employment, unites the viewpoints of several administrative branches

4 Treaty on Principles Governing the Activities of States in the Exploration and Use of Outer Space, including the Moon and other Celestial Bodies, 610 UNTS 205 (Outer Space Treaty).

5 This message to the spacefaring States has been highlighted in the UN General Assembly Resolution 'Recommendations on national legislation relevant to the peaceful exploration and use of outer space' (2013), calling for "appropriate action at national level" to organise authorisation and supervision of non-governmental entities. Most recently, the LTS Guidelines (2019) recognise the importance of national space laws in promoting sustainable use of outer space.

6 The most recent addition to European national space laws was Slovenia, see UN Doc. A/AC.105/C.1/2021/CRP.22, COPUOS, Application for membership of the Committee on the Peaceful Uses of Outer Space: Slovenia Note by the Secretariat, 19 April 2021.

7 Many European countries (such as Sweden, Norway, and the United Kingdom) are updating their current legislative bases to enable launch service provision in their territory.

8 Act on Space Activities (63/2018), English language translation from Finnish (legally binding only in Finnish and Swedish), Ministry of Economic Affairs and Employment of Finland, Finland Act on Space Activities, 2018. The explanatory note of the Act on Space Activities included in the Government's Proposal acts as an explanatory and supplementary guideline for the application and use of the Space Act (Explanatory Note), see: Government proposal to Parliament for the approval and implementation of the Convention on Registration of Objects Launched into Outer Space and for the Act on Space Activities and the Act on the Amendment of Section 2 of the Lost and Found Objects Act. Ministry of Economic Affairs and Employment of Finland.

and other stakeholder groups. The membership is comprised of various stakeholders within the Government, the research community (COSPAR national committee) as well as the private space sector through the involvement of the Finnish Defence and Aerospace Industries. The Space Committee has been convening since the 1990s but as part of the reorganisation of space governance, a Government Decree on the Finnish Space Committee (739/2019) was enacted.[9] The Act lays out the Committee's responsibilities and membership. At the time of writing this chapter, the Committee was starting its second triannual term.

The Finnish Space Committee has a secretariat appointed by the Ministry of Economic Affairs and Employment. The secretariat serves as the Committee's executive organ. Moreover, the Committee appoints divisions dedicated to further support the Committee's work. The current divisions are dedicated both to specific application areas (navigation, earth observation, and space situational awareness) as well as in horizontal matters (security, science and research, and commercialisation).

The Committee has an important function in the Finnish space administration. The Committee oversees the implementation of the national space strategy to ensure its efficiency. It strives to ensure a good operating environment for the space sector, and to support better coordination of the administrative branch. By taking active part in the programme selection and preparation for the Finnish participation in the European Space Agency ("ESA") activities, the Committee supports international cooperation and Finland's contribution to the space sector. In addition, the Committee is tasked to monitor the development of national and international regulations, practices, and trends in the industry, to draft proposals, release statements, and advocate for increased visibility and communication in the space industry.

The Ministry of Economic Affairs and Employment oversees matters pertaining to space regulation, but many players within the Government administration have varying levels of responsibility depending on the issue at hand.[10] For example, space matters concerning the European Union ("EU") Space Programme go through a multi-stakeholder coordination processes aiming to make sure that Finland is able to offer a coordinated position in keeping with Finland's overall EU policy on any topic being considered by the EU at any point in the deliberation process. This well established process is also applicable in relation to space matters, and has recently been applied with respect to the EU proposal for a Regulation on a space-based secure connectivity and the Joint Communication on the EU approach on Space Traffic Management ("STM").[11]

9 FINLEX – *Säädökset alkuperäisinä*: *Valtioneuvoston asetus avaruusasiainneuvottelukunnasta 739/2019* (in Finnish).

10 *Työ- ja elinkeinoministeriö*, National space legislation, Ministry of Economic Affairs and Employment of Finland [no date].

11 European Commission, Proposal for a Regulation establishing the Union Secure Connectivity Programme for the period 2023-2027, 2022; European Commission, Joint Communication: An EU Approach for Space Traffic Management – An EU contribution addressing a global challenge, 2022; Government notification to the on the Parliament on the Proposal for a Regulation establishing the Union Secure Connectivity Programme, U 42/2022 vp. (in Finnish), Parliament of Finland, 2022; Ministry of Economic Affairs and Employment notification to the Parliament on the Joint Communication: An EU Approach for Space Traffic Management, E 47/2022 vp. (in Finnish), Parliament of Finland, 2022.

9.2.2 Space strategy

The objective of the space strategy is to make Finland "the world's most attractive and agile space business environment that benefits all companies operating here, by 2025."[12]

Finland's national space strategy for years 2013–2020 was modified in the autumn of 2018 to take into account the significant changes occurring in the industry.[13] Small satellites and private launch services, which make space more accessible and affordable, as well as the new, globally scalable business models are helping to shape the so-called "New Space economy" bringing about changes the way that the space sector operates. The space strategy recognises that Finland has an opportunity to tap into the opportunities created by the disruption as it has competitive knowhow in fields such as telecommunications, artificial intelligence, quantum technology, and robotics, which are needed to fully benefit from space based infrastructure.

In the Finnish space strategy it was identified that to achieve this lofty goal the space administration and the wider public sector must work together with research organisations and companies *inter alia* to identify international business opportunities; provide ongoing funding; develop methods for creative public procurement; pass enabling legislation; actively promote Finnish space activities abroad; and to ensure ongoing contributions to foster Finnish expertise and know-how. Hence, in addition to reinforcing its space governance, Finland uses a variety of means to provide Finnish businesses with the assistance, finance, networks, and export services they need to grow their international reach. The establishment of Business Finland's NewSpace Economy programme, which supports access to new markets and draws foreign investment to the industry in Finland, is one of the essential measures to boost space economy.[14]

9.2.3 The Finnish Act on Space Activities (63/2018)

9.2.3.1 The international framework applicable to space activities

The main guiding principles for the use and exploration of space are outlined in the Outer Space Treaty, which also stipulates that states must authorise, continuously supervise, and ensure that all space activities, including those of non-governmental organisations, are conducted in accordance with international law. The Liability[15] and Registration[16] Conventions and the Rescue and Return Agreement[17] further develop the basic concepts established by the Outer Space Treaty regarding liability for damage caused by space objects as well as their registration. These United Nations

12 Finland 2025: The world's most attractive and agile business environment which benefits all companies operating here, Final Report of the Working Group, *Työ- ja elinkeinoministeriö*, The National Strategy for Finland's Space Activities, Ministry of Economic Affairs and Employment of Finland, 2022.

13 Ibid.

14 According to the 2021 Yearly Report by the Space Committee, "Business Finland funded piloting of enterprises in the space economy ecosystem (research and development projects, joint projects between companies and research organisations, and projects implemented in international cooperation) totalling €11.1 million. Piloting was promoted especially with regard to situational awareness solutions, satellite components, and small satellite technology. In 2021, Business Finland's grant authorisation was allocated to Finnish and international space activities in total €16.2 million" (translation from Finnish by author). See *Työ- ja elinkeinoministeriö, Avaruusasiain neuvottelukunta - Työ- ja elinkeinoministeriön verkkopalvelu*, Ministry of Economic Affairs and Employment of Finland, 2022; Kinnunen, L., *New Space Economy know-how from Finland*, BusinessFinland [no date].

15 Convention on International Liability for Damage Caused by Space Objects, 961 UNTS 187 (Liability Convention).

16 Convention on Registration of Objects Launched into Outer Space, 1023 UNTS 15 (Registration Convention).

17 Agreement on the Rescue of Astronauts, the Return of Astronauts, and the Return of Objects Launched into Outer Space, 672 UNTS 119 (Rescue and Return Agreement).

(UN) Space Treaties form the cornerstone of international space law, and the legal framework applicable to spacefaring States. Finland has ratified four of the UN Space Treaties, namely the Outer Space Treaty, the Liability Convention, and the Rescue and Return Agreement. Concomitantly with the Act on Space Activities, Finland acceded to the Registration Convention. According to the author's knowledge, Finland has presently no plans to ratify the Moon Agreement.[18]

In addition to living up to the obligations stemming from international law, one of the justifications in favour of enacting the Act on Space Activities was the existence of legal frameworks regulating national space activities in the majority of other Nordic nations, specifically in Norway, Sweden, and Denmark. Both Norway and Sweden have recently started a revision of their existing space laws. Due to the similar nature of the contemporary national space activities, the Danish Outer Space Act of in 2016 provided great inspiration to its Finnish counterpart. In general, Europe has seen a proliferation of national space laws during this decade. Currently, 12 Member States of the ESA have national space laws.[19]

The primary forum to deliberate on matters relating to the peaceful exploration and use of outer space is the UN Committee on the Peaceful Uses of Outer Space ("COPUOS"). Finland became a member of COPUOS in 2018. Since then, Finland has taken an active role in the Committee, currently comprising of 100 Member States.[20] Participation in COPUOS was seen as crucial, as the global norm-making has an important connection to national regulation of space activities. The Finnish space diplomacy has been evolving in recent years, and its positions on new questions have been guided, in addition to the space strategy, by the general national framework such as the Government's general programme, and its foreign and security policy. Finland has particularly advocated for the themes of sustainable use of outer space and sustainable growth of the space sector, in particular the NewSpace economy, which are the key priorities of the Finnish space policy. Two important organisations, EU and ESA, are both permanent observers to COPUOS. These institutional European space actors facilitate coordination and cooperation among their respective Member States *inter alia* in preparation for COPUOS meetings. The availability ESA's *intergovernmental mechanism* for its Member States to cooperate and exchange information on international and national space law[21] is recognised by ESA Council[22] and its International Relations Committee.[23] A recent example of such Member State coordination in the context of the International Relations Committee are the two proposals submitted to the Legal Subcommittee of COPUOS in relation to exploration, exploitation, and utilisation of space resources in 2021 and 2022, respectively. These papers aiming to facilitate the establishment and organisation of the

18 Agreement Governing the Activities of States on the Moon and Other Celestial Bodies, 1363 UNTS 3 (Moon Agreement).

19 Norway, Sweden, Finland, Denmark, the Netherlands, Belgium, Luxembourg, France, Austria, the United Kingdom, Portugal, and Greece. Recently, also Slovenia, an associate member of ESA announced the passing of its national space law.

20 Statements by Finland in 2021 and 2022 at the UNCOPUOS Main Committee meetings can be found at the UNOOSA website.

21 See Tapio, J., Soucek, A. (2022). The European Space Agency's Contribution to National Space Law. In: Karjalainen, K., Tornberg, I., Pursiainen, A. (eds) International Actors and the Formation of Laws. Springer, Cham.

22 ESA Council Resolution, 'Towards Space 4.0 for a United Space in Europe', 2016 and ESA Council Resolution on Space: The five dimensions of Space 4.0 (adopted on 28 November 2019) ESA/C-M/CCLXXXVI/Res.1 (Final).

23 On the occasion of its 100th meeting held on 4–5 November 2020, the International Relations Committee of the ESA Council unanimously adopted a Declaration entitled "Reaffirming the Importance of Multilateral International Cooperation in Space Activities", available at ESA website.

Working Group on Legal Aspects of Space Resources were initiated by Finland and Germany, and subsequently co-sponsored by number of European Member states of COPUOS.[24]

9.2.3.2 Main provisions of the Act on Space Activities

Finland is an epitome of a new spacefaring state in which the setting up of a regulatory framework was made in response to an innovative project by a somewhat non-traditional space actor – a university. The very first Finnish satellite was launched in summer 2017. At the time of writing this chapter, there are 18 space objects registered in the Finnish Registry of Space Objects, including the trailblazer satellite, Aalto-1.[25] Following suit, other Finnish non-governmental actors, including commercial companies, have become spacecraft operators. Today, there is no governmental space programme in Finland, nor does the government own or operate satellites. Hence, Aalto-1 and other small satellite missions for technological demonstration prompted the necessity to set up a national framework in Finland. The positive approach to non-governmental space activities continues to guide their implementation and further development.

The usual provisions found in most space laws, such as the scope of application, licensing procedure and its requirements, register for space objects, liability and insurance, as well as penalties for breach of licence are all covered by the Act on Space Activities.[26] The notion of "space activities" is rather broadly defined, accommodating licensing of new technology and missions. While not specifically mentioned, the definition could enable, at least in theory and subject to further legal analysis, licensing of space resource activities,[27] in-orbit servicing, and active space debris removal.[28]

In general, the Act on Space Activities covers actions in space carried out on Finnish territory as well as activities carried out abroad on a vessel or aircraft that is registered in Finland, as well as activities carried out by a Finnish national or a legal entity with a residence in Finland (Art. 1). In terms of the application's scope, Art. 4 of the Act on Space Activities stipulates that an "operator" is any natural or legal person who engages in, plans to engage in, or has actual control over space activity. Additionally, the Explanatory Note acknowledges that the concept includes responsibility for the operation and control of a space object as well as the launching of a space object or the procurement of a launch of a space object. As there are no launch services provided within

24 UN Doc. A/AC.105/C.2/2021/CRP.22, The Establishment of a Working Group on Potential Legal Models for Activities in Exploration, Exploitation and Utilization of Space Resources Proposal submitted by Austria, Belgium, Czech Republic, Finland, Germany, Greece, Poland, Portugal, Romania, Slovakia, and Spain; UN Doc. A/AC.105/C.2/2022/CRP.21*, Working paper on the endorsement of the Work Plan for the working group established under the Legal Subcommittee agenda entitled "General exchange of views on potential legal models for activities in the exploration, exploitation, and utilization of space resources" and proposals for a dedicated international conference on space resources under the auspices of the United Nations.

25 In fact, the very first satellite to be launched was Aalto-2 in May 2017 built by Aalto University, but this was not technically a Finnish satellite, as it formed part of the European QB50 mission as was registered by Belgium. See CORDIS, European Commission, 2022.

26 For detailed account of the provisions of the Finnish Act on Space Activities, see Tapio, J. (2018). *The Finnish Space Act: En Route to Promoting Sustainable Private Activities in Outer Space*, Air & Space Law, vol. 43 , no. 4/5, 387–409; Tapio, J. (2018). *Introduction: Finland in Space Law*: Basic Legal Documents, Eleven Publishing; Lönnqvist, M. (2019). *The Finnish Space Activities Act and Active Space Debris Removal* in Froehlich, A. (2019). Space security and legal aspects of active debris removal, ESPI, Springer, 2019.

27 UN Doc. A/AC105/C.2/2021/CRP.8, Responses to the set of questions provided by the Moderator and Vice-Moderator of the Scheduled Informal Consultations on Space Resources, 2021.

28 Lönnqvist, M. *The Finnish Space Activities Act and Active Space Debris Removal.*

the territory of Finland, the launch of the currently registered Finnish satellites has been procured abroad *inter alia* from India, the United States, and Russia.[29] Small satellites are often launched in a manner that is called "rideshare" meaning launching multiple payloads from multiple operators, possibly from all over the world, sharing the same launch vehicle. In addition, it may be that the private entities are procuring the launch from other states than their national state, either by themselves or using a launch service broker. Such cross-border situations involving actors of different nationalities, call for enhanced cooperation and information sharing among the prospective launching states.[30]

9.3 Legislation as an enabler for policy goals?

In face of the growing traffic and proliferation of space debris, the importance of having an operational space environment, including Earth orbits, is gaining more and more attention due to the steady increase of the number of space objects. This development can be attributed, at least in part, to the advent of "NewSpace", which has introduced novel space actors and innovative concepts for using and exploring space, such as plans for very large constellations of small satellites. The expectations for predictability and risk have changed as a result of these developments – protection of space infrastructure from risks, threats, and hazards has become ever more important. Although ecological or environmental concerns do not always come into play or always align well with the commercial, political, or other strategic interests of states or non-governmental organisations, it is now widely acknowledged that space debris poses a risk that needs to be taken seriously. The idea of "sustainable use of space" entails preserving the operational space environment for ongoing and future operations. Sustainability showcases how the interests of states and private actors might converge: it is the freedom of exploration and use which allows states, and in turn private actors, to carry out their activities in outer space today and for the benefits (referred to in Art. I of the Outer Space Treaty) to actually be derived.[31] Emphasising environmental and operational sustainability does not however have to mean that economic policy goals of supporting commercial space activities and fostering innovation could not materialise concomitantly.

9.3.1 Sustainability of space activities in the Space Activities Act

The constructive approach to environmental and space sustainability in the Finnish space legislation can be seen as progressive and acts to show how the public sector can work together with the industry supporting the growth of the space economy, while also driving important societal values such as sustainability. The Act on Space Activities specifically mentions reducing space debris and emphasizes the significance of environmental issues on Earth and in space. The Act on Space Activities and the supplementing Decree of the Ministry of Economic Affairs and Employment

29 *Työ- ja elinkeinoministeriö*, Registry of space objects, Ministry of Economic Affairs and Employment of Finland [no date].

30 New Zealand and the United States presented their cooperation in this respect at the 58th session of the Legal Subcommittee of COPUOS on 9 April 2019.

31 See J. Tapio. (2022, forthcoming) *Freedom of Exploration and Use of Outer Space*, in *Space Law Encyclopedia*. Thomas Leclerc (ed.) Wiley; IISL Space Law Knowledge Constellation: Anon, *Jenni Tapio on Large Constellations of Small Satellites*, April 2021, IISL Space Law Knowledge Constellation, 2022.

on Space Activities (74/2018)[32] include a requirement to mitigate space debris as a condition for a space activities license as well as a general legal obligation. According to Art. 10(2) of the Act on Space Activities, the operator shall seek to ensure that the space activities do not generate space debris. Article 3 of the Decree further emphasises that "the operator shall seek to ensure that, within 25 years from the end of the functional operating period of the space object, the space object moves or is moved into the atmosphere or is moved into an orbit where it is considered not to cause any danger or harm to other space objects or other space activities". Setting up requirements regarding space debris mitigation at national level can incentivise the development of the market for goods and services supporting the policy goal of sustainable use of outer space. What would be desirable is that this would be applied as widely as possible and ensure coherent approach to a global issue.

Furthermore, in order to promote sustainable use of space, Art. 10 of the Act on Space Activities expresses a general obligation to undertake space operations in an environmentally sustainable manner. A prior estimate of the environmental effects of the operator's space activities on both space and the Earth's atmosphere is specifically required. The operator is required to take any necessary steps to prevent or diminish any negative effects on the environment brought on by its space activities. According to the Explanatory Note, one requirement of Art. 10 is that the Ministry of Economic Affairs and Employment receives a yearly report on the actions performed and their effects.

Guidelines for the Long-Term Sustainability of Outer Space Activities ("LTS Guidelines") adopted by COPUOS in 2019 are also significant in this regard.[33] As the Act on Space Activities was passed before the adoption of the LTS Guidelines, it does not specifically mention the LTS Guidelines. However, as shown above, the Act on Space Activities promotes sustainable approach to space activities. To confirm its belief in sustainable, responsible and peaceful approach to space activities, Finland has in its statements in COPUOS recognised the importance of the LTS Guidelines, and announced that it has started to look into implementing the LTS Guidelines at national level.[34] One possible avenue for implementation is its existing space activities regulatory framework.

A process of national implementation is necessary for a "soft law" instrument such as the LTS Guidelines for it to produce the desired results.[35] A national authority wishing to "breathe life" into an instrument devised at international level can make those norms effective by including them in

32 Unofficial translation of the Decree of the Ministry of Economic Affairs and Employment on Space Activities (74/2018); see FINLEX data bank, 2018.

33 UN Doc. A/74/20, Guidelines for the long-term sustainability of outer space activities, Report by the Committee, Annex II, July 3, 2019. The LTS Guidelines were "welcomed with appreciation" by the UN General Assembly in the yearly "omnibus resolution" pertaining to international cooperation in the peaceful uses of outer space, see UNGA Res. 74/82, 13 December 2019.

34 See, e.g., Finland's Statement in the 59th session of the Technical and Scientific Subcommittee of the UNCOPUOS, February 2022, available at UNOOSA website.

35 See previous work by the author on the issue of non-legally binding instruments and national implementation: Soucek, A & Tapio, J: *Normative References to Non-Legally Binding Instruments in National Space Laws: A Risk-Benefit Analysis in The Context of Domestic and Public International Law*, Proceedings of the International Institute of Space Law, vol. 2018, no. 4, 553–580; Tapio, J & Soucek, A: *National Implementation of Non-Legally Binding Instruments: Managing Uncertainty in Space Law?*, (2019) Air & Space Law, 44(6), 565–582; Soucek, A & Tapio, J: *Does the End Justify the Means? A Legal Study on the Role and Consequences of Normative Pluralism in International Space Governance*, Proceedings of the International Institute of Space Law, vol. 2020, no. 6, 399–418; Palmroth, M., Tapio, J., Soucek, A et al.: *Toward Sustainable Use of Space: Economic, Technological, and Legal Perspectives*. Space Policy (2021), vol. 57; Tapio, J & Soucek, A: *Standardization As an Instrument of Cooperation:*

the national policy or legal instruments. While many national laws and commentaries prescribe the ways in which states implement their treaty obligations at national level, this does not hold true for non-legally binding instruments. Not only the implementation of "soft law" remains *voluntary*, but it also often escapes the traditional processes in which international obligations are transcended in the national framework. While a behavioural norm in a non-legally binding instrument should not be interpreted as creating a legal obligation for states stated in the LTS Guidelines ("nothing in the guidelines should constitute a revision, qualification or reinterpretation of the existing principles and norms of international law"),[36] such "soft law" instruments can arguably serve as a reflection of current international policy and, in doing so, foster some continuity in the development in the regulation of space activities at large.

To fulfil their goal of influencing community behaviour toward a more safe and sustainable use of space, these non-legally binding principles must be put into action on national level. Sharing of best practices on national implementation is important to enable common and coherent development of the regulation of space activities. Currently such information sharing is carried out in COPUOS in national statements under the various relating agenda items, by submitting working papers or adding information in "compendia" on the adoption of national policies or legislation. This is important as "[i]ndividual state behaviour cannot be isolated from the international context. If each state were to consider exclusively own interests and not the impacts of its legal and policy actions on others, the global governance of space activities would run the risk of becoming increasingly fragmented".[37]

9.3.2 The notion of "security" in the context of national space activities

The security and the strategic importance of space has increased globally. Space technology is dual or even multipurpose, making a strong interlinkage between space and security.

The private sector entities are increasingly participating in the space activities involving issues related to national and international security policy. Currently, a majority of the Finnish satellites now in orbit are for commercial use. A typical business case is to sell earth observation data products created by satellites operated by private companies. The customers comprise of public and private entities. The use of such remote sensing data and products may involve various foreign and security policy concerns, including imaging targets critical to national security, or relaying remote sensing images to a supplier who could use the information in violation of the interests of Finland, or of an allied country, or use the data for criminal purposes. In the above context, it was noted that these include areas that are not covered by the current legislation. Most importantly, it was identified that the areas in which legislation was needed included *inter alia* reception, use, and distribution of remote sensing data produced by Finnish satellites as well as the use of ground stations located in Finland for the reception and distribution of data.

A Silver Lining for Harvesting Common Benefits on The Way Back to The Moon? Proceedings of the International Institute of Space Law, vol. 2021, no. 7, Forthcoming 2022.

36 LTS Guidelines, Preamble, paras 14 and 15.

37 *See* Tapio, J., Soucek, A. (2022). The European Space Agency's Contribution to National Space Law, p. 117.

9.3.2.1 Proposal for a revision of the Finnish space legislation concerning remote sensing data and ground stations

Against this backdrop, in March 2021, the Ministry of Economic Affairs and Employment appointed a cross-administrative working group to prepare legislation on the distribution and use of satellite data. The Government Proposal[38] contains a proposal for a new Act on ground stations and certain radars as well as an amendment to the Act on Space Activities with respect to earth observation data. Moreover, simultaneously some of the provisions, e.g. relating to the reliability of the satellite operator, would be amended to match the new requirements imposed on the remote sensing operator. These requirements aim to strengthen and clarify the current process under the Act on Space Activities.

Concerning ground station operations, the Government Proposal proposes that an entity wishing to operate a ground station or certain type of radar in Finland needs a licence for that purpose. In accordance with the proposal, the licensing authority would be the Finnish Transport and Communications Agency (Traficom). Traficom is responsible for satellite frequency licensing in Finland, and currently handles the licensing of transmitting ground stations for radio frequency management purposes. While ground stations are closely interconnected to space activities, and form a critical part of satellite infrastructure, ground station operations are not considered as "national space activities" within the meaning of Art. VI of the Outer Space Treaty. Therefore, due to the differences in the normative base and rationale, it was seen important to separate ground station activities from remote sensing activities both at the level of legislation and licensing authority.

Concomitantly, the Act on Space Activities is proposed to be amended by adding provisions on the authorisation requirements for space-based earth observation. In accordance with the proposal, the licensing authority for remote sensing activity would be the Ministry of Economic Affairs and Employment, similarly to space activities licensing and supervision. In both cases, the requirement for a licence aims to ensure the fulfilment of national security and technical safety requirements.

The proposal for the new legislation package aims to take into account the rapid development of technology and the preconditions for business operations. In accordance with the Government Proposal, the starting point has been to recognise that remote sensing and ground stations offer many new business opportunities, therefore a balance between the public sector's security needs and the private sectors preconditions for financially sustainable business operations must be sought. Similarly, as with the Act on Space Activities, the aim is be to create a predictable and legally clear operating environment in order to promote effective supervision, competitiveness, and growth in the sector.

9.4 Concluding remarks

In the author's view, the goal set by the Finnish Space Strategy to legislation has been reached in many respects. The public sector has supplied finance and networks, and the Finnish space businesses have secured large private investments in their missions. This is not, of course, all due to the Act on Space Activities as encouraging entrepreneurship, innovation, growth, and private investment in space activities requires the involvement of the entire national space governance.

38 Government proposal on the law concerning ground stations and certain radars, as well as amendment to the Act on Space Activities and 1§ of the law on enforcement of fines (translation from Finnish by the author) of 25 August 2022, HE 113/2022 vp.

The Finnish Act on Space Activities has only been in force less than five years before its first revision. Rather than a shortcoming, this can be seen as a positive development. When the Act on Space Activities was passed in 2018 the law responded to the demand created by private actors, and in doing so, it took a forward-looking approach to space activities, which has enabled licensing of eighteen satellites with different mission profiles. Notwithstanding, already at the time of preparing the Government Proposal for the Act on Space Activities, the working group noted that due to the fast pace of technology development there might be need to supplement or amend the legislation in the future. This means that the administration can both anticipate, and respond also by legislative means to the changing operational and political landscape, and continue to provide to its subjects clear and predictable conditions in support of sustainable and profitable space business.

10

FRAMEWORK AND LICENSING REQUIREMENTS FOR SPACE ACTIVITIES IN RUSSIA, WITH A PARTICULAR FOCUS ON THE NEWSPACE SECTOR

Olga Volynskaya

10.1 Introduction

Private space business, as such, is not a new concept for Russia,[1] though NewSpace is still exotic in this country. The fundamental reform of the national rocket and space industry, which lead to the creation of the State Space Corporation "Roscosmos" instead of the former space agency, was aimed mainly at exploring – and exploiting – the commercial potential of the Russian space industry. The 2013 Space Policy Framework[2] put an emphasis on commercialisation of space activities, including those performed via public-private partnership, for the creation of a favourable investment climate for the development of the NewSpace sector. The Policy also set a task to transfer step by step the main space applications to the private domain.

These clearly formulated objectives required specific actions, including legislative ones. To date, the space industry in Russia is the monopoly of Roscosmos, a key regulatory authority in the area of space activities. Roscosmos is a unique entity in the sense that it formulates national space policy and implements it, acts simultaneously as contractor and customer, issues licences for space

1 In 1996–2003 the Russian Parliament considered a draft law entitled "On entrepreneurial activities in the area of exploration and use of outer space". The draft was vetoed by the President on the grounds of duplication of provisions set forth by the Law on Space Activities, as well as inconsistency with the said Law and other federal laws. For more information see State Duma. Legislative support system.

2 "Main provisions of the framework of state policy of the Russian Federation in the area of space activities for the period till 2030 and with a further perspective" (hereinafter "the 2013 Space Policy Framework"). Adopted by Presidential Decree N Pr-906 of 19 April 2013. The document was updated in 2020 by Presidential Decree N 64 dated 27 January 2020. The current version of the Space Policy Framework is not available to the general public. For more information see *"Роскосмос" поэтапно переходит с множества ФЦП на единую госпрограмму* [RUS "Roscosmos" is progressing from a multitude of federal target programs to a single state program], Russian Government, 7 April 2021; Annual report of the State Space Corporation "Roscosmos". 2020. P. 14.

DOI: 10.4324/9781003268475-14

activities, and directly manages the licensees. As a result, private businesses find it hard to fit into such a highly regulated and monopolised environment.

10.2 Regulatory framework

The Russian space legislation consists of over 900 acts of different levels,[3] either completely dedicated to space operations or containing particular provisions applicable to the field of exploration, exploitation, and use of outer space. The majority of such documents are decrees by the Government of the Russian Federation, regulatory acts of the ministries, agencies, and entities concerned, primarily those adopted by Roscosmos. The effective framework does not directly address NewSpace, although some regulation is implied by a number of legal acts.

10.2.1 Basic law on space activities

The 1993 Law on Space Activities[4] (hereinafter "Law on Space Activities") is the cornerstone of the legal foundation for every space activity performed under the jurisdiction of Russia. Besides the Law on Space Activities, the area of space activities is also regulated by the Constitution of the Russian Federation,[5] universally recognised principles and norms of international law, international agreements to which Russia is a party,[6] as well as applicable federal laws and other national regulatory acts.[7]

The Law on Space Activities determines the purposes, tasks, and principles of space activities, sets forth the organisational framework and economic conditions of space activities in Russia. The operation of spacecraft, management of space infrastructure, selection of cosmonauts, international cooperation, safety and insurance of space activities, responsibility, liability, etc., are also addressed by the Law on Space Activities.

Private space activities are not mentioned directly in the Law on Space Activities. However, the broad definition of space activities – "any activities connected with the direct conduct of operations on the exploration and use of outer space, including the Moon and other celestial bodies" (Art. 2 para. 1) – encompasses any current or future space activity performed either by a governmental or private actor.

Article 2 para. 1 of the Law on Space Activities also lists the following main directions of space activities:

1) space research;
2) use of spacecraft for communication, tele- and radio broadcasting;

3 Based on the data provided by the Russian legal database "Consultant Plus".

4 Law of the Russian Federation N 5663-I "On Space Activities". Adopted on 20 August 1993, last amended on 29 December 2022.

5 Constitution of the Russian Federation. Adopted on 12 December 1993, last amended on 1 July 2020. Article 71 para. (j) of the Constitution states that space activities fall within the competence of the Russian Federation (i.e. are regulated at the federal level).

6 The Constitution of the Russian Federation provides in its Art. 15 s 4 that "If an international treaty of the Russian Federation sets forth rules other than prescribed by national law, the rules of the international treaty shall apply". This provision is generally considered by the national legal doctrine and practice as confirmation of primacy of international law over domestic Russian law (except the Constitution itself which, according to its Art. 15 s 1, has the supreme legal force and direct effect within the whole territory of Russia).

7 Law on Space Activities, Art. 1.

3) remote sensing of the Earth from outer space, including state ecological monitoring (state environmental monitoring) and meteorology;
4) use of satellite navigation and geodetic survey systems;
5) manned spaceflight;
6) use of spacecraft, space materials, and space technologies in the interests of defence and security of the Russian Federation;
7) monitoring of objects and events in outer space;
8) testing of spacecraft in the outer space environment;
9) production of materials and other products in outer space;
10) other activities performed with the use of spacecraft.

The above list is non-exhaustive, which allows for the categorisation of any yet unknown types of activities on exploration and use of outer space, including private ones, as space activities.

Interestingly, the Law on Space Activities does not expressly mention space launch among the main directions of space activities, despite the fact that the launch of space rockets, including for commercial purposes, is one of the most important and resultative space activities performed by Roscosmos.[8]

In addition, the Law on Space Activities stipulates that space activities "comprise the creation (including the development, manufacturing and testing), use (exploitation) of spacecraft, space materials and space technologies and provision of other services connected with space activities, as well as the use of space activity results and international cooperation of the Russian Federation in the area of exploration and use of outer space".[9]

10.2.2 State responsibility for national space activities

The Law on Space Activities reiterates the obligation imposed on the Russian Federation by Art. VI of the Outer Space Treaty, stating that Russia bears international responsibility for the performed space activities.[10] This provision, listed among the main principles of space activities, does not specify the nature of the "performed space activities". In any case, participation of Russia in the Outer Space Treaty coupled with the constitutional principle of primacy of international law over domestic legislation[11] provide sufficient grounds to conclude that international responsibility of the Russian Federation extends to private space activities under its jurisdiction.

10.2.3 Jurisdiction

The Russian Federation exercises national, territorial, and in some cases[12] extraterritorial jurisdiction over space activities. According to Art. 27 of the Law on Space Activities, foreign organisations and citizens performing space activities under the jurisdiction of Russia are entitled to enjoy the legal regime set for Russian organisations and citizens, to the extent that this regime is

8 Annual report of the State Space Corporation "Roscosmos", 2020, p. 16.
9 Law on Space Activities, Art. 2 para. 2.
10 Ibid., Art. 4 para. 1.
11 See above footnote 6.
12 For instance, when Russian jurisdiction extends to space activities performed by foreign actors in outer space, i.e. outside the state territory of Russia.

provided to Russian organisations and citizens by the respective foreign state.[13] Russian legislation *inter alia* protects technologies and commercial secrets of foreign organisations and citizens carrying out space activities under the jurisdiction of Russia.[14]

National jurisdiction over crews of manned space objects registered in Russia remains unaffected during their stay on Earth, at any stage of a spaceflight or presence in space, on celestial bodies, including extra-vehicular activity, and on return to the Earth, till the completion of the flight programme, unless otherwise specified in international treaties of the Russian Federation.[15]

In addition, the Law on Space Activities establishes that Russia retains jurisdiction and control over space objects registered with it, while on the ground, as well as at any stage of spaceflight or presence in space, on celestial bodies, and also upon return to the Earth beyond jurisdiction of any state.[16] In case a space object is designed and manufactured by Russian organisations and citizens jointly with foreign states, foreign organisations and citizens, or with international organisations, the issues of registration of such an object, jurisdiction, and control over it are solved on the basis of applicable international treaties.[17]

Russian organisations are entitled to use (exploit) space infrastructure outside the jurisdiction of the state. In any case, such activities will still be governed by the Law on Space Activities and applicable international agreements to which Russia is a party.[18]

10.2.4 Public procurement

Public procurement in the area of space activities is led by the Russian Government, Ministry of Defense, and Roscosmos. The latter exercises public procurement for the development, production, and delivery of spacecraft and space infrastructure objects for scientific and social-economic purposes within the framework of the Federal State Program,[19] including works on international space projects of the Russian Federation.[20] Similar responsibilities with regard to dual-use spacecraft are assigned to the Ministry of Defense.[21]

The Government, in its turn, is in charge of the adoption of the Federal Space Program (including its financing), other long-term space programmes, public procurement procedures for the development, manufacturing, and delivery of spacecraft and space infrastructure objects,[22] as well

13 Law on Space Activities, Art. 27 para. 2.

14 Ibid.

15 Ibid., Art. 20 para. 4.

16 Ibid., Art. 17 para. 2.

17 Ibid., Art. 17 para. 4.

18 Ibid., Art. 18 para. 4.

19 Article 8 para. 1 of the Law on Space Activities states that "the Federal Space Program of Russia is a long-term planning document on the basis of which public procurement is exercised for the creation, manufacturing and use of spacecraft for scientific and social-economic purposes".

20 Ibid., Art. 6.

21 Ibid., Art. 7.

22 Since 2020 the Government has been drafting a decree on specific features of public procurement in the area of space activities. The document intends to prohibit the disclosure of information relating to the identification of contractors (suppliers) participating in most types of public procurement of the creation (development, production, and testing) of space materials and technologies, as well as creation modernisation, delivery, maintenance, exploitation, and disposal of spacecraft (para. 1 of the draft decree). According to the information of the Federal portal of draft laws and regulations, the draft was finalised, but there is no confirmation that it was adopted.

as public defence procurement procedures for the development, manufacturing, and delivery of space armament and military spacecraft.[23]

The Russian legislation does not prevent private enterprises (including foreign ones, except offshore companies)[24] from participating as contractors in public procurement in the field of space activities. According to the Law on Space Activities, organisations and citizens involved in the implementation of space projects may be granted state guarantees and privileges in conformity with the legislation of the Russian Federation.[25] This provision does not specify the type or form of ownership of such organisations, thus covering private actors. Foreign investment into space activities is also allowed by law.[26]

10.2.5 Ownership of space objects

Space objects of the Russian Federation are subject to registration in conformity with the rules and procedure established by Art. 17 of the Law on Space Activities and the Administrative regulation on registration of space objects adopted by Roscosmos in 2010.[27]

The Law on Space Activities specifies that spacecraft can be used by its owner or another authorised holder of rights therein on condition of public registration of these rights.[28] Decommissioned spacecraft may be transferred according to the established procedure to entities "whose main activities are aimed at the use of space activity results for educational, scientific and cultural purposes",[29] which assumedly includes private actors.[30]

The above provisions imply the possibility of transfer of ownership of space objects registered in Russia. However, the requirement to register rights in space objects with the public registry cannot be fulfilled because neither such a registry, nor the respective registration mechanism exist yet.

Article 1207 of the Russian Civil Code[31] states that the right of ownership and other proprietary rights in space objects subject to state registration are determined by the law of the state of registry of these objects. However, as mentioned above, the Russian law does not contain the necessary provisions yet. The registration data required by the Administrative regulation on registration of space objects includes information about the entity which exploits the space object in question (para. 1.1 and Annex I to the Administrative regulation), but there is no reference to proprietary rights. In 2014, Roscosmos submitted to the Russian Government a draft law entitled "On state

23 Ibid., Art. 5 para. 3.
24 Federal Law N 44-FZ, Art. 3 para. 1 subpara. 4.
25 Law on Space Activities, Art. 12 para. 3.
26 Ibid., Art. 12 para. 4.
27 Order of the Federal Space Agency N 44 "On the approval of the Administrative regulation of the Federal Space Agency on the performance of the public function to maintain the Registry of space objects launched by the Russian Federation into outer space". Adopted on 22 March 2010.
28 Law on Space Activities, Art. 15 para. 1.
29 Ibid., Art. 15 para. 2.
30 Space infrastructure objects can also be transferred from the federal (public) property to other organisations, including for the purposes of exploitation of such objects (Law on Space Activities, Art. 18 para. 2).
31 Civil Code of the Russian Federation. Part I adopted on 30 November 1994, Part II – on 26 January 1996, Part III – on 26 November 2001, and Part IV – on 18 December 2006 The Civil Code was last amended on 14 April 2023.

registration of rights in space objects and transactions with them",[32] but there has been no official information on further progress ever since.

The few general rules regarding the rights of ownership of space objects aligned with the UN space treaties are stipulated by the Law on Space Activities. According to its Art. 17 para. 3, the ownership of space objects remains unaffected while on the ground, as well as at any stage of spaceflight or presence in space, on celestial bodies and also upon return to the Earth, unless otherwise specified in international treaties of the Russian Federation. In case a space object is created by Russian entities together with foreign legal entities and individuals, or international organisations, the ownership is allocated based on applicable international agreements.[33]

The Law on Space Activities expressly states that jurisdiction, control, and ownership of space objects do not affect the legal status of the area (part) of outer space, surface, or subsoil of a celestial body occupied by the respective space object.[34] Despite that, the Law provides for the possibility to establish safety zones in direct proximity to Russian space objects to ensure safety of space operations. Interestingly, the Law on Space Activities obligates both Russian and foreign actors – even those performing space activities outside the Russian jurisdiction – to respect the special rules which may be imposed within such zones.[35]

10.2.6 Licensing

All space activities, either public or private, performed under the jurisdiction of Russia are subject to licensing.[36] General rules are established by the 2011 Law on the licensing of selected activities,[37] while specific regulation is provided by the 2022 Regulation on the licensing of space activities[38] (hereinafter "the 2022 Regulation").

According to the 2022 Regulation, licensing is mandatory for legal entities performing space activities in the territory of Russia or in other territories over which the Russian Federation exercises jurisdiction.[39]

Roscosmos is the licensing authority responsible for registration of the issued licenses for space activities, maintenance of the respective registry, and licensing control.[40]

The 2022 Regulation enumerates the works and services in the course of space activities that require a licence.

The licensed works are development, manufacturing, (serial) production, testing, maintenance and extension of the designated resource, and service period of rocket and space products. The

32 See Resolution of the Government of the Russian Federation N 2590-r "On the approval of the plan on lawmaking activity of the Government of the Russian Federation for 2014", 30 December 2013.

33 Law on Space Activities, Art. 17 para. 4.

34 Ibid., Art. 17 para. 5.

35 Ibid.

36 Ibid., Art. 19.

37 Federal Law N 99-FZ "On the licensing of selected activities". Adopted on 4 May 2011, last amended on 29 December 2022.

38 Decree of the Government of the Russian Federation N 168 "On the licensing of space activities". Adopted on 14 February 2022. The 2022 Regulation is for the most part identical to the previous Regulation on the licensing of space activities adopted by the Russian Government on 18 March 2020 (Decree N 298).

39 The 2022 Regulation, para. 1.

40 Ibid., para. 2; Art. 7 para. 11 of the Federal Law N 215-FZ "On the State Space Corporation 'Roscosmos'". Adopted on 13 July 2015, last amended on 1 April 2022 (hereinafter "Federal Law on Roscosmos").

development, manufacturing, and testing of prototypes (models) not intended for exploitation as part of space systems and complexes do not require a licence.[41]

As to the licensed services, their list is as follows:

1) preparation of space rockets for launch and of space objects for placement in orbit;
2) launch of space rockets and placement of space objects in orbit;
3) disposal of landers (capsules), component parts of space rockets, and/or spacecraft;
4) ecological survey of the territory of launch sites and impact areas;
5) search and rescue, emergency operations including evacuation of landers (capsules), and component parts of space rockets;
6) development, production, assembly, testing, putting into operation, exploitation, maintenance, improvement, and modernisation of ground-based space infrastructure objects, as well as equipment and systems for measuring, control, testing of rocketry at ground-based space infrastructure objects;
7) services of ground-based mission control centres;
8) receiving and initial processing of information obtained from remote sensing spacecraft (except the information used for educational purposes);
9) calculation of trajectories of launch vehicles and upper stages, as well as ballistic and navigational support of spacecraft;
10) ground-based experimental testing of spacecraft and its component parts;
11) training of spaceflight participants for a space mission.[42]

Compared to the previous licencing regime,[43] the current procedure provides for a shorter list of requirements and supporting documents to obtain a licence. Potential licensees are not obligated to have a contract for the planned works or services, or a program of research and experiments with the use of spacecraft. They no longer have to be assigned to a military office of the Russian Ministry of Defense.[44] Prior certification of products, works, and services is no longer mandatory; neither is the requirement to comply with international obligations of Russia in the area of protection and non-proliferation of missile and dual-use technologies.[45]

The new 2022 Regulation intends to simplify and clarify the licensing procedure, lower administrative barriers, and make space activities accessible to companies performing innovative space-related projects, as well as to small and medium-sized enterprises.[46]

10.2.7 Certification

The Law on Space Activities prescribes mandatory certification of spacecraft and space infrastructure objects created for scientific and social-economic purposes (both public and private) in

41 The 2022 Regulation, Annex, s I. The document contains a closed list of items which may qualify as rocket and space products, see footnote (asterisk) in the Annex to the 2022 Regulation.

42 Ibid., s II.

43 Decree of the Government of the Russian Federation N 160 "On the licensing of space activities". Adopted on 22 February 2012, lost force on 20 April 2020.

44 Ibid., para. 4 subparas. (c)–(e).

45 Ibid., para. 4 subparas. (i)–(j).

46 For more information see *Новое Положение о лицензировании космической деятельности* [RUS The new Regulation on the licensing of space activities], Roscosmos, 23 March 2020.

accordance with the effective Russian legislation on technical regulation.[47] The failure to comply with the rules of certification will entail liability in accordance with applicable law.[48]

10.2.8 Insurance

The effective Russian legislation provides for mandatory and voluntary insurance[49] in the area of space activities.

The life and health of cosmonauts, personnel of space infrastructure objects, as well as liability for damage to life, health, or property of third parties must be insured by the organisations and citizens using or responsible for the use of respective space objects.[50] Foreign organisations and citizens carrying out space activities under the jurisdiction of Russia are also obliged to insure spacecraft and risks connected with their space activity.[51]

According to the Law on Space Activities, mandatory insurance must comply with the procedure and conditions established by law. Alongside with the Civil Code,[52] general rules are set forth by the 1992 Law on insurance.[53]

Roscosmos attempted to propose special regulation on space insurance via a draft law entitled "On mandatory insurance in the area of space activities".[54] The draft, however, was not supported by the Russian Government.

10.2.9 Export control

The advancement of dual-use space technologies in Russia necessitates a clear and comprehensive export control mechanism. The legal regulation on export control is three-tiered:

1) international export control regimes;
2) export regulations of the Customs Union of Russia, Belarus and Kazakhstan;[55]
3) national legislation, primarily the Federal Law on Export Control.[56]

The Federal Service for Technical and Export Control[57] is the governmental body authorised to license foreign economic operations involving controlled goods and technologies, as well as to

47 Law on Space Activities, Article 10 paras. 1–2; Federal Law N 184-FZ "On technical regulation". Adopted on 27 December 2002, last amended on 2 July 2021.

48 Law on Space Activities, Art. 10 para. 3.

49 Voluntary insurance may take place regarding the risks of loss, shortage of, or damage to spacecraft (Law on Space Activities, Art. 25 para. 2).

50 Law on Space Activities, Art. 25 para. 1.

51 Ibid., Art. 27 para. 3.

52 Civil Code, Part II Chapter 48.

53 Law N 4015-I "On the organization of insurance business". Adopted on 27 November 1992, last amended on 29 December 2022.

54 For more information on the draft law see *Zhukov G.P., Volynskaya O.A.* International law aspects of third-party liability insurance in the area of space activities [RUS] // Moscow Journal of International Law, 2012 (2), pp. 105–116.

55 See *О Таможенном* союзе [RUS About the Customs Union], Eurasian Economic Commission.

56 Federal Law N 183-FZ "On Export Control". Adopted on 18 July 1999, last amended on 26 March 2022.

57 FSTEC of Russia.

control compliance with the respective requirements.[58] Roscosmos is the entity responsible for participation of Russia in international export control regimes[59] (see 10.3.2 *infra.*).

The lists of space-related equipment, materials and technologies subject to export control are adopted by the President of Russia[60] in accordance with Model Export Control Lists of the Customs Union.[61]

The export control regime does not differentiate between public or private space activities and is mandatory for all Russian participants of foreign economic activities.[62]

10.2.10 Prospects for NewSpace regulation

In 2021, the upper chamber of the Russian Parliament announced the drafting of laws on entrepreneurial space activities and on private activities in the area of remote sensing of the Earth from outer space. The mission of these documents is to create favourable conditions for private investment in the national space industry, increase competitiveness of private Russian companies in the world space market, and to develop Russian space technologies.[63] Both drafts have to undergo a complicated process of interagency review (which may take years). However, the previous law-making practice shows that the chances of adoption of such ambitious documents are questionable.

10.3 Practice

The private space sector in Russia is not very representative yet. One of the main reasons, according to space industry experts, is the absence of effective state support based on a clear regulatory framework.[64] In addition to that, the geopolitical upheavals of 2014 and 2022 have had a dramatic effect on the emerging NewSpace business in Russia and its ability to integrate in the global space market.

10.3.1 Attempts to develop NewSpace in Russia

One of the first Russian private space companies, *Dauria Aerospace*,[65] was established in 2012 to develop and manufacture new-generation small spacecraft and their component parts.[66] *Dauria Aerospace* successfully produced, and in 2014 procured the launch of five microsatellites, includ-

58 Federal Law on Export Control, Arts 7, 19–22.

59 Federal Law on Roscosmos, Art. 8.

60 Presidential Decree N 1005 "On approval of the List of equipment, materials and technologies which can be used for creation of rocket weapons and are subject to export control". Adopted on 8 August 2001, last amended on 26 December 2016.

61 Model List of equipment, materials and technologies which can be used for creation of rocket weapons and are subject to export control. Adopted by Decision of the EAEC Interstate Council N 190 of 21 September 2004.

62 Federal Law on Export Control, Art. 14.

63 See *В СФ разработали законопроект о предпринимательской деятельности в сфере изучения космоса* [RUS The Council of Federation drafts a law on entrepreneurial activities in the field of space exploration], TASS, 18 March 2021.

64 See *Частная российская компания инвестирует в разработку сверхлёгкой ракеты* [RUS A private Russian company is investing in the development of a superlight rocket], Vedomosti, 18 June 2020; *"Первым шагом упразднил бы монополию Роскосмоса"* [RUS "First of all I would eliminate the monopoly of Roscosmos"], Novaya Gazeta, 2 July 2020.

65 *Dauria Aerospace*, URL: http://eng.dauria.ru/ (last accessed 11 August 2022).

66 See *Dauria Aerospace, О компании* [RUS About the Company].

ing an experimental spacecraft *DX-1*[67] and two satellites of a *Perseus-M* series which were later sold to *Aquila Space* (USA).[68] In 2017, two remote sensing microsatellites, *MKA-N*, procured by Roscosmos were successfully launched but failed to communicate. Following litigation with Roscosmos, *Dauria Aerospace* declared bankruptcy.[69] According to the company's founder and former president Mikhail Kokorich, it was "a big mistake to create *Dauria* in Russia"[70] because such a start-up may exist only in two situations: if it is strongly supported by the government or has access to the open world market to exploit its country's advantages. The first option failed because of subjective factors, and the second ceased to exist after the Crimean crisis in 2014.[71]

The *Skolkovo Innovation Center*[72] via its Cluster of advanced industrial technologies, nuclear and space technologies aims at supporting Russian start-ups and promoting the participation of private business in space exploitation.[73] Some examples of such start-ups which have been residents of *Skolkovo* are:

1) *Avant Space* – launch into low Earth orbit of a group of microsatellites for projecting images from space;
2) *Azmerit* – serial production of low-cost star sensors for nano- and microsatellites;
3) *Alfasatcom* – creation of a complex for assessing the condition of satellite transponders;
4) *KosmoLab* – development of CubeSat deployers for launchers and cargo vehicles;
5) *Orbital Express* – creation of technologies for high-precision delivery of small satellites and payload into near-Earth or interplanetary orbits;
6) *Reusable Transport Space Systems* – creation of a reusable transport spacecraft Argo for delivery of payload to the ISS and return to Earth;
7) *Space Systems* – development of infrastructure for receiving data and controlling small spacecraft;
8) *SPUTNIX* – manufacturing of high-tech microsatellite components and technologies, provision of microsatellite-based services;
9) *Success Rockets* – development of superlight rockets for launching microsatellites;
10) *Tenzor Lab* – development of a service for calculation of an optimal orbital trajectory and maneuvering to prevent collisions, etc.[74]

At the same time, a number of promising Russian private space businesses have ceased to exist in the past few years mainly due to the excessive administrative burden and the lack of a clear, pre-

67 *DX-1*, URL: http://dauria.ru/on-orbit/dx1-sat (last accessed 11 August 2022).

68 See *Принято управление спутниками Perseus-M* [RUS *Perseus-M* satellites are operational]; *Perseus-M1*; *Perseus-M2*.

69 See *"Роскосмос" довел до банкротства российскую частную космическую ИКТ-компанию* [RUS Roscosmos has brought a private Russian ICT company to bankruptcy], CNews, 4 February 2020.

70 *"Стали шептать, что шпион": почему основатель первой в России частной космической компании уехал в США и как строит там водяные ракеты* [RUS "They began whispering that I was a spy": Why the founder of Russia's first private space company left for the USA and how he builds water rockets there], The Bell, 19 October 2018.

71 Ibid.

72 The *Skolkovo Innovation Center* was founded in 2010 with the aim to support research and commercialisation of research results by legal entities and individuals. See Art. 1 para. 1 of the Federal Law N 244-FZ "On the *Skolkovo Innovation Center*". Adopted on 28 September 2010, last amended on 28 December 2022.

73 *Promtech*. Skolkovo Resident.

74 See Members Search, *Skolkovo*.

dictable legal environment. In addition to *Dauria Aerospace*, a private space start-up, *KosmoKurs*, whose mission was to create the first private spaceport for suborbital tourism in Russia, was dissolved in 2021. According to the company's CEO Pavel Pushkin, *KosmoKurs* was unable to meet the normative requirements for the design of the spaceport and a suborbital launcher for tourist flights.[75] Other ambitious private space launch providers-to-be, including *S7 Space*[76] and the *National Space Company*,[77] are facing serious difficulties.

10.3.2 The role of Roscosmos

State Space Corporation "Roscosmos", which was established in 2015 in lieu of the Federal Space Agency, is a non-commercial legal entity authorised to govern the exploration, exploitation, and use of outer space on behalf of the Russian Federation, as well as to regulate the area of its competence.[78]

It is interesting to note that Roscosmos is entitled to act both as a government authority and a business entity.

Representing the state, Roscosmos develops national space policy (including scientific, technical, and investment policy)[79] and implements it through its subordinate organisations.[80] Public functions of the Corporation encompass a wide range of space activities, including the creation, production, and operation of spacecraft and infrastructure, organisation and performance of manned and automated space launches, development of *GLONASS*, licensing of space activities and state licensing control, registration of space objects, international cooperation, etc.[81]

As to business, Roscosmos has the right to participate in governmental and commercial hi-tech programmes and projects, invest in Russian and foreign organisations, enter into contracts (including commercial ones), and generate income by performing a multitude of activities prescribed by law.

These include, *inter alia*:

1) R&D;
2) licensing of space activities;
3) delivery of goods and services for public needs;
4) production and operation of spacecraft and space infrastructure (including launch sites and mission control objects, satellite navigation, remote sensing, communication, and geodetic survey systems);
5) training of cosmonauts;
6) export and import of space products, works and services, and others.[82]

75 See *Частная компания по развитию космического туризма "КосмоКурс" объявила о ликвидации* [RUS Private space tourism company KosmoKurs has announced its elimination], Kommersant, 6 April 2021.

76 The mission of S7 Space was to render space launch services on board of Ukrainian Zenith rockets from the Sea Launch offshore platform. See Space Launch, URL: https://www.s7space.ru/launch-sea/ (last accessed 11 August 2022); *"Роскосмос" предлагает компании S7 передать «Морской старт» государству* [RUS Roscosmos invites the S7 company to transfer Sea Launch to the government], 3Dnews, 19 June 2022.

77 See *Конкурент Илона Маска не вышел на орбиту* [RUS Elon Musk's rival fails to reach orbit], Kommersant, 16 May 2022.

78 Federal Law on Roscosmos, Art. 1 para. 2 and Art. 3 para. 1.

79 Ibid., Art. 7 paras. 1-2.

80 To date, Roscosmos is in charge of activities of 75 organisations forming the core of Russian rocket and space industry, see URL: https://www.roscosmos.ru/24028/ (last accessed 11 August 2022).

81 Federal Law on Roscosmos, Art. 7.

82 Ibid., Art. 14 para. 1.

The Corporation can carry out such economic activities directly or via its organisations. In the former case, it does not require a licence.[83]

In accordance with the 2013 Space Policy Framework, one of the principles of the national space policy of Russia is promotion of public-private partnership in the area of provision of services with the use of space activity results, gradual development of the capacity to create commercial space communication, broadcasting, navigation and remote sensing systems, as well as launchers and spacecraft for manned space missions.[84] The 2013 Space Policy Framework set the tasks to create favourable technological conditions and investment climate to promote the private space sector in Russia, step-by-step transfer of space applications to the area of responsibility of private business.[85]

In the previous years, Russian politicians and official representatives of Roscosmos regularly announced that the Corporation is determined to commercialise space activities, support the development of private space companies in Russia, including via public-private partnership.[86]

According to the 2020 Annual Report of Roscosmos, the Corporation supported the establishment by *NPO Energomash* (one of the leading companies of the Russian space industry) together with the Skolkovo Foundation of the first space business accelerator whose aim was to invite start-ups to cooperate in the creation of advanced space technologies. To invite external innovation projects for competition, Roscosmos launched an online service named "The Open Innovations Window".[87] Based on the results of the competition, Roscosmos intended to sign agreements with the top three business projects and promote their implementation.[88]

Much attention is given to the *Sfera*[89] project – the deployment of a multifunctional satellite system comprising several hundreds of Earth observation and communication satellites, including:

1) *Ekspress* series – communication and broadcasting;
2) *Skif* series – broadband internet;
3) *Marafon* series – internet of things;
4) *Yamal* series – communication;
5) *Smotr* series – remote sensing;
6) *Berkut-O, Berkut-VD* – optical observation;
7) *Berkut-X, L, P* – radar satellites.[90]

83 Ibid., para. 3.
84 The 2013 Space Policy Framework, clause 7(f).
85 Ibid., clause 17(d)–(f).
86 See, e.g., *В. Поповкин (Роскосмос): о роли частного бизнеса в развитии космической промышленности* [RUS V. Popovkin on the role of private business in the development of space industry], GIS Market Support Association, 9 April 2012; *Роскосмос: главные итоги и задачи на будущее* [RUS Roscosmos: Main results and tasks for the future], 2014, p. 195; *И. Морозов: Развитие механизмов ГЧП в космической сфере позволит реализовать наиболее амбиционные проекты* [RUS I. Morozov: The development of PPP mechanisms in the space area will enable the performance of the most ambitious projects], the Council of Federation, 31 March 2022.
87 See URL: https://www.roscosmos.ru/open-innovations/ (last accessed 11 August 2022).
88 Annual Report of the State Space Corporation "Roscosmos", 2020, pp. 46–47.
89 RUS sphere, domain; globe, orb.
90 *Правительство одобрило программу создания многоспутниковой группировки "Сфера"* [RUS The government approves the program to create a multisatellite constellation *Sfera*], TASS, 7 April 2022; *Роскосмос рассказал о статусе проекта «Сфера» на Международном навигационном форуме* [RUS Roscosmos outlined the status of the *Sfera* project at the International navigation forum], Roscosmos, 26 April 2022.

Sfera is viewed by Roscosmos as a foundation to develop the commercial space market in Russia.[91]

Further development of the Russian remote sensing satellite constellation is being considered by the government as a tool to implement the environmental policy of the country and ensure "green transition". Discussions are ongoing in the Parliament on how to ensure the efficiency of interaction between the state and business and make products of the national space industry globally competitive.[92] It is highlighted that a new law on remote sensing of the Earth from space is needed in this country, alongside relevant regulations on concession and insurance.[93]

The problems of safety of space operations, sustainability of space activities, space traffic management, protection against NEO hazards are also high on the national political agenda.

Roscosmos, jointly with the Ministry of Defense, other government bodies, Russian Academy of Sciences and other entities, is tasked to "strengthen the potential of Russia in the area of monitoring of objects and events in outer space, including a mechanism of international interaction in this domain".[94] To this end, Roscosmos relies on the Russian Automated Warning System on Hazardous Situations in Outer Space (*ASPOS OKP*).[95] The mission of *ASPOS OKP* is to ensure safety of space operations carried out by Russian spacecraft under conditions influenced by the human-made pollution of near-Earth space, issue warnings of hazardous situations in near-Earth space to users and support activities carried out to ensure the compliance of the Russian Federation with its international obligations in relation to space debris.[96]

In 2022, Roscosmos officially launched the *Mlechny Put*[97] initiative: creation of an information-analytical system to ensure safety of space activities in the near-Earth space for the period 2022–2025 and with a further perspective until 2035.[98] The strategic objectives of *Mlechny Put* are:

1) information support to ensure safety of space operations of Russia and other states in the light of the "growing congestion and anthropogenic pollution of the near-Earth space, change of the environment for the operation of orbital spacecraft, factors of deliberate threats (military threats excluded)";
2) detection, analysis, and assessment of risks associated with NEO hazards;
3) elimination of information dependency of Russia;
4) ensuring the leading role of Russia in coordinating international efforts to provide safety in the near-Earth space.[99]

91 See *Перспективы коммерциализации космической деятельности рассмотрели в Совете Федерации* [RUS Prospects for commercialization of space activities have been addressed by the Council of Federation], the Council of Federation, 2 July 2020.

92 *И. Морозов: Развитие механизмов ГЧП в космической сфере позволит реализовать наиболее амбиционные проекты*. See above footnote 87.

93 Ibid.

94 Federal Law on Roscosmos, Art. 7 para. 13.

95 ASPOS OKP is the transliteration of *АСПОС ОКП*, abbreviated Russian name of the system: *Автоматизированная система предупреждения об опасных ситуациях в околоземном космическом пространстве*.

96 See UN Doc. A/AC.105/C.1/2019/CRP.8, 8 February 2019, at 2.

97 RUS Milky Way.

98 The Concept of creation of an information-analytical system to ensure safety of space activities in the near-Earth space "*Mlechny Put*" for the period 2022–2025 and with a further perspective until 2035 (hereinafter "the 2022 Concept"). Adopted by Roscosmos on 12 January 2022.

99 Ibid., p. 10.

Mlechny Put is expected to globally promote Russian sci-tech innovations, space situational awareness (SSA) products and services, stimulate the growth of commercial space services rendered by Russian organisations,[100] as well as promote national standards and practices relevant to space safety at the international level.[101] In order to fulfil this mission, the *Mlechny Put* initiative includes harmonisation and development of national laws and regulations to create efficient economic and organisational mechanisms, including public-private partnership.[102]

10.4 Conclusion

Commercialisation of space activities in Russia is considered the prerogative of the state, more precisely – Roscosmos, which acts simultaneously as a governmental space agency and a business entity. When it comes to private business outside the "perimeter" of the national space industry (i.e. subordinate organisations of Roscosmos), its importance for the development of the domestic and global space markets is also acknowledged.[103] In recent years, the problem of supporting NewSpace in Russia has been widely discussed in political circles, by industry experts and scientists. The main emphasis is put on the need to create the regulatory environment to remove unnecessary barriers and facilitate private space activities. Some practical steps have already been taken in this regard, including liberalisation (to some extent) of the licensing regime of space activities. However, previous lawmaking practice shows that regulatory transparency and flexibility, on the one hand, and strong support of private space sector by the government, on the other, may not work out in the established state-centric space industry in Russia as long as Roscosmos is unwilling to give up its monopoly in space activities. In this light, the prospects for comprehensive and groundbreaking regulation of NewSpace remain uncertain.

100 The range of such products and services to be provided, including via an open information service as part of the *Mlechny Put* system, is listed in s 7 of the 2022 Concept, ibid. at pp. 35–36.

101 Ibid., para. 3.3.7, p. 19.

102 Ibid.

103 For instance, the State Policy Framework in the area of the use of space activity results in the interests of modernising the Russian economy and developing its regions for the period till 2030 (adopted by Presidential Decree N Pr-51 of 14 January 2014) sets the task to develop the internal market of space products and services *inter alia* by actively involving SMEs (including via PPP mechanisms) in the area of using space activity results, promoting access of Russian companies to the world space market to enhance global competitiveness of the country and strengthen its status as one of the leading spacefaring and hi-tech nations. See paras. 7(d), 8, 9(c), 12(e), 15(b), and 16(a) of the document.

11

HOW CHINA INCORPORATES AND FOSTERS COMMERCIAL SPACE ACTIVITIES BY ITS NATIONAL SPACE LAW INSTRUMENTS

Yun Zhao

11.1 Introduction

China has made remarkable achievements in space technologies and activities since the successful launch of its first satellite in 1970. China is now the third country to have grasped manned spaceflight technologies and has recently joined the club of the countries that brought back lunar soil to the Earth. In line with the ongoing trend of space commercialisation and privatisation, China has been on the steady move towards commercialising national space activities that were once monopolised by the state, including in the areas of satellite communications and broadcasting services, remote sensing, commercial application of satellites, and space technologies. At the moment, China has four launch sites: the Jiuquan Satellite Launch Centre in Gansu Province, the Taiyuan Satellite Launch Centre in Shanxi Province, the Xichang Satellite Launch Centre in Sichuan Province, and the Wenzhang Satellite Launch Centre in Hainan Province. China is planning to build a fifth space launch centre in Zhejiang Province to meet China's rising demands for commercial launches.[1]

China emphasises the importance of international cooperation in the space field, in particular the commercial aspect of international cooperation. Since 2016, China has signed 46 space cooperation agreements or memoranda of understanding with 19 countries and regions and four international organisations.[2] The cooperation in the space arena has been very impressive. For example, China and Russia jointly launched the international lunar research station project; for its Chang'e-4 lunar exploration mission, China cooperated with Russia and European Space Agency (ESA) on engineering technology, and with Sweden, Germany, the Netherlands, and Saudi Arabia

1 Across China: China to Build Commercial Launch Centre in Eastern Coastal Province, Xinhua Net, 15 April 2021.
2 White Paper on China's Space Activities, 2021 China's Aerospace, 28 January 2022.

DOI: 10.4324/9781003268475-15

on payloads; for its first Tianwen-1 Mars exploration mission, China cooperated with the ESA on engineering technology, and with Austria and France on payloads.[3]

Following a full membership of the United Nations Committee on the Peaceful Uses of Outer Space (UNCOPUOS) in 1980, China ratified the Outer Space Treaty in 1983 and the other three space law treaties (excluding the Moon Agreement) in 1988.

At the national level, China has been relatively slow in building a comprehensive legal framework for space activities, which is not conducive to the development of space activities at high speed.[4] However, the existing legal regime, comprising of several administrative regulations and rules dealing with specific aspects of space activities, serves as a solid basis for future national space legislation.

This chapter will examine the existing national policy and legal documents on facilitating the process of space commercialisation and privatisation in China. It will also look into possible ways of furthering this process in the future.

11.2 An overview of existing instruments for space commercialisation in China

China's aerospace industry started in the 1950s when the Fifth Research Institute of the Ministry of National Defence was tasked to develop missiles and launch vehicles. The Commission for Science, Technology and Industry for National Defence (COSTIND) was set up as a civilian ministry within the State Council in 1982 overseeing Chinese defence procurement and technology. It was later merged into the Ministry of Industry and Information Technology (MIIT) in 2008 and was renamed as State Administration for Science, Technology and Industry for National Defence (SASTIND). The China National Space Administration (CNSA) is the equivalent of the National Aeronautics and Space Administration in the United States (NASA), responsible for civil space administration and international space cooperation. It was assigned as an internal division of the former COSTIND in 1998 to represent the Chinese government in international exchanges and cooperation in the space field.

For a long time, China Aerospace Science and Technology Corporation (CASC) and China Aerospace Science and Industry Corporation (CASIC) have been the two major state-owned enterprises heavily involved in the development of space technologies and activities. CASC is responsible for the development of the launch vehicles and satellites;[5] CASIC designs, develops, and manufactures a range of spacecraft, launch vehicles, strategic and tactical missile systems, and ground equipment.[6] Since 2010s, truly commercial corporations (without state investments) have been incorporated in China for commercial space activities, including the following categories of private commercial companies:

(1) sixteen rocket and engine manufacturers: AA ENGINE (2018), Deep Blue Aerospace (2017), Dragon Drive (2012), Expace (2016), Galactic Energy (2018), i-space (2016), Jiuzhou Yunjian Space (2017), LandSpace (2015), LinkSpace (2014), Ningbo Space Engine Technology (2018), OneSpace (2015), S-Motor (2017), SN-AAPRI (2017), SpaceOne (2018), Spacetrek (2017), TSC (2007);

3 Id.
4 Yongliang Qi, A Study of Aerospace Legislation of China, 33(2) Journal of Space Law 406 (2007).
5 China Aerospace: Science and Technology Corporation (CASC).
6 CASIC, Company Profile.

(2) eleven satellite manufacturers: ADA space, AstroCruise, ATspace, MinoSpace, Qiansheng Exploration, Smart Satellite, Space TUBE, SpaceOK, SpaceTY, Xihua Technology, ZeroG Lab;
(3) twelve satellite operators: Changguang Satellite Technology, China Communication Technology, Commsat, Galaxy Space, Guo Dian Gao Ke, Hangsheng Satellite, HEAD Aerospace, LaserFleet, Orbita Aerospace, TATWAH Group, XingCloud, XINWEI;
(4) two ground service providers: Satelliteherd and Space Wisdom;
(5) one space resource developer: Origin Space;
(6) eleven satellite application service providers: Cissdata, DBLUESPACE, GAGO, GEOSPATIAL SMART, GEOVIS, JiaHe Info, PIESAT, RapiSense, Tianqibao, TIRAIN, XIN DE ZHI TU.[7]

China is still in the process of drafting its national space law. A practical reason why China is (and was) hesitant in formally adopting a basic law on commercial space activities is the prevalence of state ownership. As Li and Zhao correctly pointed out, "there is a *de facto* administrative hierarchical relationship between state organs and state enterprises, which is not formally dealt with by law".[8] As such, government regulations and rules appear to be a straightforward and cost-effective approach to govern space activities. A further practical reason is to avoid enactment (and updating) of laws dragging the feet of technological advancement. As a matter of fact, laws often lag behind technological development. In view of the fact that China was able to develop its space technologies rapidly without the existence of national space law in the last few decades, the urgency of enacting national space law is not widely acknowledged in the space expert community in China. This also accounts for the slow progress of national space legislation.

Consequently, Chinese space law at the current stage consists of the 2001 Measures for the Administration of Registration of Objects Launched into Outer Space (Registration Measures),[9] the 2002 Interim Measures on the Administration of Licensing the Projects of Launching Civil Space Objects (Licensing Measures),[10] and the 2015 Administrative Measures on Space Debris Mitigation and Management (Space Debris Measures).[11] Aside from the aforementioned binding legal instruments, the existing regulatory framework is supplemented by policy-oriented documents, including the White Papers on China's Space Activities. There are also various national instruments which are relevant but not specific to commercial space activities.

Legislative instruments previously played a weaker role in governing space activities. This is attributable to the division of powers between Chinese state organs, civil and military, in terms of controls over space activities. Due to their dual-use nature, it is rather difficult to differentiate civil space activities from military activities; moreover, different organs are involved in various stages of space activities, making the differentiation even more difficult and unrealistic.

7 Deep Blue Aerospace Selected into the Chinese Version of the New Space Power Map, 23 March 2019.
8 Bin Li & Haifeng Zhao, Governmental Regulations on Commercial Aspects of China's Space Activities, 3 Indian Journal of International Economic Law 28 (2010).
9 Order No. 6 of the Commission of Science, Technology, and Industry for National Defence of the People's Republic of China (dissolved) and the Ministry of Foreign Affairs.
10 Order No. 12 of the Commission of Science, Technology, and Industry for National Defence of the People's Republic of China (dissolved).
11 The Interim Measure was adopted in 2009 and then formalised in 2015 by the Commission of Science, Technology, and Industry for National Defence of the People's Republic of China (dissolved).

However, recent years have seen a change in attitude. The gradual commercialisation of space activities is notably reflected in the series of White Papers published in 2000, 2006, 2011, 2016, and 2021. With a national space law not yet in place, White Papers serve as an important tool in spelling out the principles and directions for space activities and space industry. It has been argued that the White Papers are "a kind of Chinese constitution" for space activities for each five-year period.[12]

The 2000 White Paper, the first ever White Paper on Space Activities released by the Chinese Government, touched upon China's achievements in the provision of commercial space launch services since the 1990s with China's Long-March launching vehicles.[13] Apart from encouraging further development of commercial launch services, the 2006 White Paper brought in satellite communications and broadcasting services, highlighting the two commercial contracts with Nigeria and Venezuela on the on-orbit transfer of communications satellites and relevant ground system services.[14] Building on the commercial space activities identified in the last two White Papers, the 2011 White Paper for the first time emphasised the efforts in promoting Chinese companies to participate in international commercial space activities.[15] It is noticeable in this version of the White Paper that a "diverse multi-channel space funding system" is called upon as a major policy guidance in funding space activities, indicating the support for possible involvement of private companies in space activities.[16]

The 2016 White Paper unprecedentedly acknowledged private investment and private companies in the realm of commercial space activities. The White Paper called upon the cooperation between private investors and the government to improve the diverse funding system. It specifically encouraged non-governmental capital and other social sectors "to participate in space-related activities, including scientific research and production, space infrastructure, space information products and services, and use of satellites to increase the level of commercialization of the space industry".[17] Apart from traditional telecommunications services, the White Paper mentioned another important area of space commercialisation by referring to the launch and services of a high-resolution remote sensing satellite, the Jilin-1, for commercial use; relevant to the remote sensing services, the White Paper reiterated the provision of business services concerning space information during 2011–2016.[18]

In line with the call for space commercialisation, the State Council released a White Paper on China's Beidou Navigation Satellite System (BDS) in June 2016.[19] This document also encourages the commercial and large-scale application of the BDS. With regard to a comprehensive service system of location data, China welcomes the introduction of commercial operations to help build the basic platform of location services based on its BDS augmentation systems, which will have extensive coverage of application fields and interconnections, and provide support services to different regions and industries and to the general public.

12 Olga Yeshchuk & Anna Vasina, Chinese Space Law: Problems and Areas of Reforming, 3 Advanced Space Law 142 (2019).
13 The State Council Information Office of the People's Republic of China, White Paper on China's Space Activities, November 2000, Beijing.
14 White Paper on China's Space Activities, October 2006.
15 White Paper on China's Space Activities, December 2011.
16 Irina Liu, et al., Evaluation of China's Commercial Space Sector, Institute for Defense Analyses, 2019, at 12.
17 White Paper on China's Space Activities, December 2016.
18 Id.
19 The State Council Information Office of the People's Republic of China, White Paper on China's Beidou Navigation Satellite System, 16 June 2016.

The 2021 White Paper includes one specific section on the encouragement of space commercialisation.[20] The paper reviews commercial space activities during the past years and puts forward further commercial development for the next five years, including building commercial launch pads and launch sites to meet various commercial launch needs, and promoting public and commercial application of China's satellites and space technologies through innovative commercial models. The scope of government procurement of space products and services will be expanded; major scientific research facilities and equipment will be open to commercial space enterprises.

It is also important to note that a "negative list", providing guidelines to both domestic and foreign investors for market access to space activities, will be established to ensure fair competition and orderly participation of commercial enterprises. China will optimise the role of the space industry in the national industrial chain, and encourage commercial space enterprises to engage in satellite application and the transfer and transformation of space technologies. China will support international cooperation in space commercialisation, including cooperation in launching services; technical cooperation on the production of whole satellites, sub-systems, spare parts, electronic satellite components, launch vehicles, ground facilities, and equipment.

11.3 Regulations of commercial space activities

11.3.1 Registration of space objects

China joined the 1975 Registration Convention in 1988 and undertook the obligation to set up a national registration system for space objects. The Registration Measures, the first national rules in the space field, were adopted for this purpose. This document provides clear rules on the contents for the registration of space objects, administrative body in charge of registration, procedures and requirements for the registration. China retains jurisdiction and control over such objects and any personnel thereof in accordance with Art. VIII of the Outer Space Treaty.

The Registration Convention defines the term "space object" simply as including "component parts of a space object as well as its launch vehicle and parts thereof".[21] The Registration Measures move one step further by detailing "space object" as "a human-made satellite, crewed spacecraft, space probe, space station, launch vehicle and parts thereof, and other human-made objects launched into outer space".[22] Sounding rockets and ballistic missiles that temporarily pass through outer space are excluded from the concept of "space object".[23] Registration is required for space objects launched from the territory of China as well as those jointly launched abroad by China and other states.[24] Accordingly, at the domestic level, all space objects, regardless of their ownership, once launched from the Chinese territory, shall be registered in the national registry.

While the Registration Convention provides the joint determination of the "State of registry" in case of two or more launching states,[25] the Registration Measures specify that the owner, or the main owner, of a space object shall register that object.[26] In any event, the state of registry of a space object should be the same in both national and international registries[27] since it is the duty of

20 White Paper on China's Space Activities, published on 28 January 2022.
21 The Registration Convention, Art. I(b).
22 The Registration Measures, Art. 2(1).
23 Id., Art. 2(2).
24 Id., Art. 4.
25 The Registration Convention, Art. II(2).
26 The Registration Measures, Art. 7.
27 Yan Ling, Comments on the Chinese Space Regulations, 7(3) Chinese Journal of International Law 688 (2018).

the state of registry to register the respective space objects in the International Register maintained by the Secretary-General of the United Nations in accordance with Art. III of the Registration Convention.[28]

The SASTIND is the administrative entity in charge of the national registry of space objects.[29] The SASTIND, via the Ministry of Foreign Affairs, shall register the respective space objects with the Secretary-General of the United Nations within 60 days after national registration.[30] The registrant shall modify relevant registration within 60 days after the occurrence of any significant changes, such as orbit change, inoperability, disintegration, cessation of functions, or reentry into the Earth's atmosphere of the space object.[31]

A distinctive feature of the Registration Measures is the provision of a clear timeframe for relevant action, i.e., 60 days, instead of the vague term "as soon as practicable" used in the Registration Convention. It is also to be noted that this document puts down more information that is required for national registration than that for international registration. Such information includes owner and launching enterprise of the space object, the status of the launching and orbiting of the space object.[32] However, the Registration Measures similarly fail to deal with the issue of on-orbit transfer of ownership of space objects, which happens frequently in this space commercialisation era.[33]

11.3.2 Space licensing

The Licensing Measures establish the licensing system for space launch activities for non-military purposes. The administrative rules were enacted to demonstrate China's efforts in complying with the requirements of authorisation and continuing supervision of private space activities under the Outer Space Treaty.[34] The Licensing Measures put down clear rules on the application and examination of permits, supervision and management, and liability, which lay a solid basis for commercial launch services provided by Chinese entities. Three points are worthy of mentioning as far as space commercialisation is concerned. First of all, they include the scenario of on-orbit transfer of ownership of satellites within the applicable scope of the administrative rules. As such, the term "the project of launching civil space objects" includes not only the launching of space objects from Chinese territory for non-military purposes, but also the launching from foreign territory of space objects with Chinese individuals or legal persons or other organisations as the owners before the launching or through on-orbit ownership transfer.[35]

Second, the element of sustainable development has been incorporated in the licensing process. The licence applicant, i.e., the project general contractor or the final owner of the space object, shall submit required application documents to the examination entity nine months before the prescheduled launch. The required application documents include, in particular, the materials evi-

28 The Registration Convention, Art. IV.
29 The Registration Measures, Art. 5.
30 Id., Art. 12.
31 Id., Art. 9.
32 Id., Art. 6.
33 Michael Chatzipanagiotis, Registration of Space Objects and Transfer of Ownership in Orbit, 56(2) German Journal of Air and Space Law 230 (2007).
34 The Outer Space Treaty, Art. VI.
35 The Licensing Measures, Art. 2.

dencing the project's compliance with environmental protection laws and supplemental materials on how to prevent/mitigate pollution and space debris.[36]

Third, the licence applicant shall include arranged insurance to cover possible damages arising from the launch project, including third-party liability.[37] Space insurance is particularly relevant to space commercialisation. While no specific laws on space insurance are in place, the Insurance Law[38] shall be applicable to all types of insurances. But further details on insurance rates and premiums shall be worked out in practice by taking into account the risks involved in the new space commercialisation industry.

The SASTIND, the entity responsible for reviewing and issuing licences for space launches, shall examine the application and make a decision on whether to grant the licence within 30 days after receiving the application.[39] For modification or cancellation of the licence, the licensee shall apply to the SASTIND within 90 days before the expiry of the licence.[40]

The licensee shall report the launching plan to the SASTIND, the supervising entity, six months before the prescheduled launch.[41] Within one month after the launch, the licensee shall report the completion of the launch to the supervising entity.[42] The Licensing Measures also put down possible liabilities for the licensee, unlicensed launching service provider, and the SASTIND.

The Licensing Measures function as the main instrument for China to carry out its commitment under the Outer Space Treaty. However, with the ongoing space commercialisation, several areas need to be further clarified. First, it is not clear whether the licensing applies to space activities after a successful launch. From the wording of the document, it appears that it applies only to the launch *per se*, and not any other activities afterwards. Since China has also the duty of continuing supervision, a broad interpretation of the respective document's wording that the licensing covers relevant activities by the space object after its launch into the orbit would be preferable and in line with the international obligations of the state. Similarly, this has something to do with the required insurance arrangement, which should ideally cover relevant on-orbit activities, instead of simply the launch. Second, with frequent launch of small satellites, it would be necessary to clarify whether there will be any differences in the required documents and arrangements (e.g., insurance) for such satellites. Third, while environmental protection has been briefly mentioned in the Licensing Measures further details should be worked out with regard to space debris mitigation, taking into account the latest legislative and practical development in the field at both national and international levels.

36 Id., Art. 6.

37 Id., Art. 19.

38 Insurance Law of the People's Republic of China, adopted at the 14th Meeting of the Standing Committee of the Eighth National People's Congress on 30 June 1995, promulgated by Order No. 51 of the President of the People's Republic of China, and amended in accordance with the Decision on Amending the Insurance Law of the People's Republic of China adopted at the 30th Meeting of the Standing Committee of the Ninth National People's Congress on 28 October 2002.

39 The Licensing Measures, Art. 7.

40 Id., Arts 13–14.

41 Id., Art. 20.

42 Id., Art. 22.

11.3.3 Export controls

Space technologies and products are essentially of dual-use nature. China has made extensive rules on export controls of space technologies and products. The Foreign Trade Law[43] provides general guidance and principles on export controls. More specific rules are drafted by the State Council and other relevant administrative entities. It is necessary to mention the Administrative Measures for the General Export Licensing of Dual-Use Goods and Technologies issued by the Ministry of Commerce in 2009.[44] The Ministry of Commerce is the administrative entity in charge of export licensing.

Another legally binding document of relevance is the Administrative Regulations on Export Control of Missiles and Missile-related Items and Technologies (Missiles Regulations) issued by the State Council in 2002.[45] This document sets down a licensing system for the export of rockets, unmanned aerial vehicles (UAVs), missiles (ballistic and cruise missiles), and missile-related items and technologies.[46] The administrative entity in charge of foreign trade and economic cooperation under the State Council, on some occasions jointly with other relevant departments of the State Council and the Central Ministry Commission, shall be in charge of examination and issuance of the respective export licence.[47] The accepting party of the exported missiles and missile-related items and technologies shall promise not to either use these items and technologies for purposes other than those originally declared, or transfer them to any third parties other than the end users as originally declared.[48] This arrangement is in line with the requirement of end-user certification under the Missile Technology Control Regime (MTCR).[49] The items put in the control list shall be presumed subject to denial of export, whose export is possible only if duly licensed. The competent authorities shall suspend or cancel the export license if the licensee fails to follow the conditions or restrictions, or if there is a risk of proliferation of the missiles and other carrier systems that could be used to carry weapons of mass destruction.[50]

11.3.4 Management of satellite data

Remote sensing data is highly valuable and plays increasingly important roles in all aspects of our daily lives. The SASTIND, together with the State Development & Reform Commission and the Ministry of Finance, issued the Interim Measures for the Management of Remote Sensing Data from China's Civilian Satellites on 29 December 2018.[51] The document applies to the management of remote sensing data supported by central fiscal funds in full or in part, or to relevant management of remote sensing data from commercial satellites operated independently within China,

43 Foreign Trade Law of the People's Republic of China, adopted at the 7th Meeting of the Standing Committee of the Eighth National People's Congress on 12 May 1994, revised at the 8th Meeting of the Standing Committee of the Tenth National People's Congress and promulgated by Order No. 15 of the President of the People's Republic of China on 6 April 2004.

44 Ministry of Commerce Order No. 8, 13 May 2009.

45 State Council Order No. 361, 22 August 2002.

46 The Missiles Regulations, Art. 2 and the Annex.

47 Id., Art. 10.

48 Id., Art. 6.

49 Yun Zhao, National Space Law in China: An Overview of the Current Situation and Outlook for the Future 165 (Leiden: Brill/Nijhoff, 2015).

50 Id., Art. 15.

51 SASTIND Division 1 [2018] No. 1866.

or to data from foreign satellites through commercial channels, or to space cooperation between governments or institutions.[52] These shall be governed *mutatis mutandis* by the document.

The three issuing entities mentioned above shall organise and coordinate major issues such as the operation and maintenance of the national civil satellite remote sensing system, its interconnection, sharing, and joint use, and be responsible for the overall coordination in military-civilian integration of remote sensing data and major emergency response. In the meantime, the China Earth Observation Satellite Data Centre, the National Satellite Meteorological Centre, and the National Satellite Ocean Application Services Centre shall be responsible for the acquisition, processing, archiving, and distribution of relevant remote sensing data. The CNSA Earth Observation System and Data Centre shall conduct effective mission planning and data management for high-resolution satellites.[53]

Depending on the means of observation and the main features of the observation objects, remote sensing data can be divided into optical data, microwave data, and geophysical field data. Data can also be divided into public data and confidential data depending on the publicity and differences in technical indicators. Data can be further divided into raw data, level 0 products, primary products, and advanced products depending on the processing degree.[54] Satellite data centres shall provide remote sensing data to main users in the agreed modes, and to other users through user authentication, requirement review, signing of an agreement.[55] In principle, only primary remote sensing data products will be provided.[56] The state departments shall have priority in adopting and purchasing domestically produced data and services.[57]

The CNSA is responsible for the overall coordination of the international exchange and cooperation in the area of remote sensing data and the conclusion of relevant data cooperation agreements between governments and institutions.[58] Remote sensing data with full support from central fiscal funds shall be owned by the state; anyone acquiring primary data products free of charge should not transfer them to any third party without prior approval.[59]

11.3.5 Development of commercial carrier rockets

While no major administrative documents have been adopted since the issuance of the Registration Measures and the Licensing Measures, China's efforts in space commercialisation continue. This is best exemplified by China's regular updates to the industrial catalogue[60] in encouraging foreign investors to invest in space-related industries.

The commercial carrier rocket market has been identified as one major area for development and regulation. The SASTIND and the Equipment Development Department of the Central Military Commission jointly released a departmental regulatory document entitled Notice on Promoting the Systematic and Orderly Development of Commercial Carrier Rockets in 2019 (2019 Notice).[61]

52 Id., Arts 2 and 27.
53 Id., Art. 4(1)–(2).
54 Id., Art. 6(1).
55 Id., Art. 8.
56 Id., Art. 12(1).
57 Id., Art. 14.
58 Id., Art. 16(1).
59 Id., Art. 23.
60 New Version of Catalogue of Industries for Encouraging Foreign Investment, Investment Policy Monitor, UNCTAD, 27 December 2020.
61 SASTIND, No. 647 [2019], 30 May 2019.

Bearing in mind the need to develop commercial space industry and speed up China's competitiveness in the relevant market, this document provides guidance on scientific research, production, testing, launching, safety, and technical control of commercial carrier rockets.

Commercial carrier rocket-related activities are defined to include scientific research, development, and production of carrier rockets and the launch of rockets into outer space for commercial profits, which are conducted by various enterprises through the use of their own funds, social capital, or joint venture capital in accordance with the market operation mechanism.[62] Such enterprises are required to obtain approval and licensing from the SASTIND. The Licensing Measures shall apply for the launch of rockets to outer space. However, the 2019 Notice moves further by requiring the enterprise to specify in the application materials such information as the registration and coordination of orbital frequency, space debris mitigation, safety measures adopted, third-party insurance, and relevant commercial insurance secured.[63] Relevant launching activities shall be conducted at a nationally recognised space launching site[64] which is defined as a basic resource in China.[65] The enterprises shall strictly comply with relevant rules on safety and export controls.[66]

The 2019 Notice carries with it important implications in the sense that it is the most elaborated instrument in specifying commercial space activities in China.[67] The comprehensive guidance on the involvement of relevant enterprises in the commercial carrier rockets market on each and every stage provides enterprises with clear procedures in entering the market, which is essential for these enterprises in assessing the market feasibility and viability, and for making relevant commercial decisions.

Different from earlier administrative documents, the 2019 Notice takes the form of "Notice", which does not intend to change the existing laws and rules in the field. The issuance of the document shows the urgent need for the promotion and regulation of commercial carrier rockets market by taking into account the current status of the market and the existing rules. With a national space law not yet in place, the 2019 Notice provides an interim solution for the regulation of commercial space industry.

11.3.6 Development of microsatellites and safety management

In light of rapid development of microsatellites and their potential collision risks in low-Earth orbit, the SASTIND released another notice in May 2021 to promote the orderly development of microsatellites and strengthen safety management.[68] Microsatellites are defined to be on-orbit spacecraft with a mass below 1,000 kilograms carrying out such specific missions as telecommunications, navigation, remote sensing, space science, and technological experiments.[69] The requirements listed in this document are highly relevant to space situational awareness and traffic management. Such requirements are to be satisfied in three different stages: scientific research and production; launch licensing; and on-orbit safety.

62 Id., para. 2.
63 Id., para. 8.
64 Id., para. 10.
65 Id., para. 17.
66 Id., paras 13–16.
67 Fabio Tronchetti, The Privatization of Chinese Space Activities: A Legal and Regulatory Perspective, 42(2) Journal of Space Law 586 (2020).
68 SASTIND Division No. 1, No. 466 [2021], 19 May 2021.
69 Id., para. 1.2.

In the first stage, microsatellites should possess a certain ability to avoid collision, ensure track control, and have mature and reliable de-orbiting capability to avoid long-term occupation of common orbits.[70] Microsatellites with orbital altitudes below 2,000 kilometres shall be de-orbited within 25 years of the end of the mission; those with orbital altitudes above 2,000 kilometres shall actively rise to graveyard or non-common orbits.[71] Furthermore, microsatellites shall take necessary technical measures to avoid the generation of separate fragments on orbit and disintegration of energy storage components.[72] In the second stage, a debris-mitigation plan, which includes theoretical analysis, technical measures to be taken and effect prediction shall be submitted when applying for a licence.[73]

With regard to the third stage, the owner of the microsatellite shall perform relevant registration procedures when the microsatellite is launched into orbit or changes its status in orbit.[74] Thirty days before the operations for orbit transfer, rendezvous and docking, debris removal and on-orbit maintenance, the owner shall notify relevant state departments; relevant operations shall be terminated or adjusted immediately in case of major security risks during the operation.[75] The owner of a microsatellite shall carry out active collision avoidance manoeuvres when discovering collision risks, and report to the state departments within one hour of such discovery. In case of collision, the owner shall report to the state departments within one hour of such an incident and obey the overall management of satellite resources in orbit by relevant state departments.[76] The state departments are responsible for daily monitoring and evaluation of the status of orbits and active de-orbiting activities of microsatellites. The owner shall promptly inform the state departments of any changes of microsatellites' orbit status.[77] Microsatellites for technical verification and scientific experiments have relatively short operation cycle and are encouraged to operate in orbits below 350 kilometres for quick de-orbiting by the end of the mission.[78]

The document further provides guidance on issues such as the management of satellite data and export controls, which are largely in compliance with the existing administrative regulations and rules.

11.4 Prospect and conclusions

Given that there is no single unified space law in China at the moment, the need for further legislative actions has been emphasised.[79] In particular, current legislation takes the form of "administrative regulations" and "administrative rules/measures" rather than "laws" in the hierarchy of the Chinese legal system. In the meantime, space commercialisation will continue to move ahead steadily, as confirmed in the 2016 White Paper.

In view of the Positioning, Navigation, and Timing (PNT) services to be provided by the BDS, China called upon the necessity of a regulatory regime for the BDS as early as 2016 in its 2016

70 Id., para. 2.7–2.8.
71 Id., para. 2.8.
72 Id.
73 Id., para. 3.11.
74 Id., para. 4.13.
75 Id., para. 4.14.
76 Id., para. 4.15–4.17.
77 Id., para. 4.18.
78 Id., para. 4.19.
79 Yun Zhao, National Space Legislation in Mainland China, 33(2) Journal of Space Law 434 (2007).

BDS White Paper. Another area that is worthy of notice is space resources utilisation.[80] Following the enactment of national laws in the United States and Luxembourg enabling private appropriation and utilisation of space resources, China, as the third country to collect samples of the lunar soil in 2021, needs to seriously consider its position on the issue of space mining. The conclusion of a Memorandum of Understanding (MOU) between the CNSA and the Ministry of Economy of Luxembourg in 2018,[81] with the areas for cooperation including legal and regulatory aspects of the utilisation of space resources, could signal an initial step in exploring a possible national/international regime for space resources utilisation.

Consequently, since the elaboration of national space legislation will still take some more years, China is taking a pragmatic and progressive approach in coming up with a regulatory regime for space activities. The administrative regulations and rules in the field of space registration, licensing, export control, to be combined with possible rules on dedicated legislation in the promotion of specific commercial space activities, could serve as an interim regime and provide a solid basis for future national space legislation.

80 Fabio Tronchetti, Space Law and China, in Peter Read (Ed.), Oxford Research Encyclopedia of Planetary Science 11 (Oxford: OUP, 2019).

81 Luxembourg Cooperates with China in the Exploration and Use of Outer Space for Peaceful Purpose, including in the Utilization of Space Resources, 16 January 2018.

12
INDIA
Recent developments in space business and regulation

Ranjana Kaul

Introduction

The "Space Reforms 2020"[1] is continuing across inter-connected and related sectors in India. The consolidation is aimed at accelerating satellite broadband connectivity, deeper digital transformation in the country, and expansion of technological capabilities. It is also intended to develop indigenous solutions to bridge socio-economic gaps and fault-lines identified during pandemic-led disruptions. The foundation for the present consolidation and expansion is rooted in the comprehensive economic reforms in 1990–1991,[2] when most sectors were partially de-regulated to allow private participation, and foreign direct investment permitted. These were the first steps that linked India to international markets and the global value chain. The focus in this paper is the recent reform process initiated by Prime Minister Modi on 24 June 2020 and extended in 2021 to reform space-enabled sectors including telecommunications, broadcasting, information technology and IT-enabled services, and geospatial data distribution policies.

This paper is presented in two parts. Part I is dedicated to India's space sector and impact of space reforms. Section 1 addresses traditional national space sector; and Section 2 addresses India's NewSpace, its emergence and development. Part II focuses on satellite-enabled services and prospects for commercial opportunities. Section 3 discusses commercial satellite telecommunication and broadcasting sectors. Section 4 is on information technology, IT-enabled service sector, data protection, and cyber security. Section 5 discusses reforms in the geospatial data access and distribution policy. The paper closes with brief concluding remarks.

1 For a detailed description of the "Space Reforms 2020", see Ranjana Kaul, Recent Space Reforms in India: Perspectives on Policy and Law 44 J. Space L. 450 (2020).

2 See *infra*, subsection 1.1. For more information, see, *e.g.*: Space India 2.0: Commerce, Policy, Security and Governance Perspectives. Rajeswari Pillai Rajagopalan, Narayan Prasad (Eds.) ORF 37, 54 (2017).

DOI: 10.4324/9781003268475-16

Part I – India's space sectors

12.1 India's civil space and commercial space sectors

12.1.1 Overview – geopolitical status and significance of space capabilities

India's national space programme is 50 years old in 2022.[3] India conceptualised the publicly funded, civil space programme for undertaking activities for the peaceful use of outer space, including the Moon and other celestial bodies, to develop and deploy space applications towards fulfilling national societal and developmental objectives. The Indian Space Research Organisation (ISRO), in compliance with the national space programme, remains dedicated to socio-economic, inclusive national development, to furthering bilateral, multilateral, and international cooperation and collaborations. Nevertheless, the Indian Government was convinced about the importance of space capability for a developing country, in preference to a military space programme.

In Dr. Vikram Sarabhai words,

> There are some who question the relevance of space activities in a developing nation. To us, there is no ambiguity of purpose. We do not have the fantasy of competing with the economically advanced nations in the exploration of the moon or the planets or manned space-flight. But we are convinced that if we are to play a meaningful role nationally, and in the community of nations, we must be second to none in the application of advanced technologies to the real problems of man and society.[4]

The 1990 reforms partially de-regulated the economy bringing in private sector participation, foreign direct investment, and regulatory reforms; accelerated innovations in technology and processes, and added new sub-sectors within traditional sectors of the economy. The introduction of commercial satellite telecommunications and broadcasting services in 2000, which opened the prospect, for the first time, to provide transponder capacity on commercial basis to commercial service providers. The "Space Reforms 2020" aims to permit private participation in outer space activities and a deeper engagement in ground segment activities. This has also coincided with reforms in satellite-enabled services.

12.1.2 National space programme

The focus in the early decades was on research in space sciences and on developing technology independence – for building launch vehicles, satellites, and ground stations. The aim was to develop end-to-end capability to build orbit-class launch vehicles[5] and satellites for the full range of space applications including satellite telecommunications, remote sensing, satellite navigation, deep space exploration, and scientific missions. India's traditional space programme pioneered and continues to nurture the ability and techniques to execute space missions successfully, deploying frugal engineering solutions within spartan budgets. Simultaneously, satellite applications for telecommunications and remote sensing were developed. During this early phase, international cooperation and collaborations played an important part.

In 1980 India successfully demonstrated space transportation capability when ISRO launched the *Rohini* satellite on the Satellite Launch Vehicle-3 (SLV-3). The satellite and launch vehicle were

3 See *infra*, subsection 12.1.4.

4 Vikram Sarabhai Space Centre, Dr. Vikram A Sarabhai.

5 Indian Space Research Organisation, Department of Space, Launch vehicles: SLV (1980), PSLV (1993); GSLV (2001).

both indigenously built. The success propelled India into the elite group of spacefaring nations. India has since developed capability across the space infrastructure constituents including satellite communications, remote sensing, meteorology, navigation, and the PSLV and GSLV launch vehicles. Year 2000 marks the time in which the Department of Space (DOS) started providing transponder capacity to Indian commercial satellite telecommunication and broadcasting services on a commercial basis. In 2005, DOS started supplying remote sensing data on a commercial basis and, in 2007, ISRO entered the international commercial space launch services market. The national space programme remains the exclusive remit of the government, with limited participation of the private sector through its public procurement policy.

12.1.2.1 Space programme funding

The national space programme of India continues to be supported by public funding. In February 2022, the Union of India Budget for 2022–2023 budgetary allocation for DOS[6] was increased. However, that may not be nearly enough, given the many challenges and critical missions of national importance, in addition to routine commercial and other launches. If it is India's hope to retain and gather momentum in national space activities, it must continually expand its signature techniques and ability to execute successful delivery of India's low-cost national space programme, and continually embrace new disruptive technologies and methodologies that private sector brings. To compete internationally would require big investments. Only the private sector can bring in investments and create new technological and innovative products and services, bring new dynamism, and accelerate avenues for employment generation. The "Space Reforms 2020" signalled a new phase in India's space journey.

12.1.3 Organisation and management

DOS, established in 1972, functions under the Prime Minister Office (PMO).[7] The Minister of State in PMO (Space) provides linkage between PMO and DOS. DOS represents the highest level in the space management structure and competent authority for matters related to national space activities. Consequently, DOS exercises jurisdiction over its downstream entities including, but not limited to:

(i) Space Commission of India, which is responsible for space policies;
(ii) ISRO;[8]
(iii) National Physical Research Laboratory (PRL);
(iv) National Atmospheric Research Laboratory (NARL);
(v) National Remote Sensing Centre (NRSC);[9] and
(vi) both public sector entities Antrix Corporation Limited (Antrix)[10] and NewSpace India Limited (NSIL).[11]

6 NDTV Budget 2022, Here's India's Space Budget Amid Preparations for First Human Spaceflight, Government of India, Union Budget 2022-2023 allocated INR 13,700 crores for Department of Space (US$ 18,32,137.993).
7 Department of Space and ISRO HQ.
8 Indian Space Research Organization, Department of Space.
9 National Remote Sensing Centre, Department of Space.
10 Antrix Corporation Limited (Antrix).
11 New Space India Company Limited.

Finally, the Indian National Space Promotion and Authorisation Centre (INSPACe) was constituted pursuant to the "Space Reforms 2020"[12] to promote and facilitate non-government private enterprises to participate in all aspects of space activities.

In September 2021, Dr. Pawan Goenka, an industry veteran, was appointed as Chairperson of INSPACe,[13] the sectoral regulator for private players. INSPACe has been proactively facilitating space start-ups to use ISRO facilities for undertaking technology validation experiments and tests and providing advisory support. In a first, two space start-ups – Dhruva Space and Digantara – were authorised to launch their technology payloads on board the PSLV on 30 June 2022[14] and have successfully validated their technology platforms.

12.1.4 Statutory basis for national space activities

DOS was constituted under provisions of the "Government of India Allocation of Business Rules 1961", related to the Department of Space, dated 18 July 1972[15] (AOBR) for undertaking activities in outer space and activities on ground required for undertaking space activities. In 2007 the AOBR para. 2 was amended to include commercial exploitation of space,[16] corresponding to the point in time when India entered the international commercial space launch market and Earth observation data commercialisation. On 7 February 2022,[17] the AOBR was again amended to allow use of satellite systems for providing 5G broadband communications in India.

12.1.4.1 International space treaties and state practice

The AOBR para. 4(a) deals with international relations in matters connected with space – including, *inter alia*, "international relations in matters connected with Space including matters relating to Space in the United Nations specialized agencies and in relation with other countries",[18] empowering DOS to undertake space activities in compliance with UN international space treaties, participate in UN specialised agencies and international collaborations relations. India has ratified the four principal UN treaties on outer space and is a signatory to the 1979 Moon Agreement. India has been undertaking national activities in outer space in conformity with the principles of the international space treaties since India launched the first indigenous satellite, *Aryabhatta,* in 1975.[19] This is the basis and foundation of India's state practice.

12 Indian Space Research Organization, Unlocking India's Space Potential in Space Sector Approved by Union Cabinet on 24 June, 2020.

13 Business Today, Ex M&M MS Pawan Goenka named chairperson of space regulator IN-SPACe, 12 September 2021.

14 Manish Pant, Indian start-ups take a giant leap into space, Business Today, 1 July 2022; 2 space start-ups authorised, marks beginning of private space sector launches in India, Economic Times, 28 June 2022.

15 Allocation of Business Rules, Government of India, DOS, S.O.498(E) 20/7/1972, 18 July 1972 (as amended on 7 February 2022), p. 176.

16 *Ibid.*

17 *Ibid.*

18 *Ibid.*

19 Encyclopedia Britannica, Aryabhata, first unmanned satellite built by India.

12.1.4.2 National outer space activities law

India does not have a national space activities law. In any event, the condition precedent to permitting private participation in outer space activities is necessarily a national space statute.

12.1.4.3 National procurement and management of commercial space business

Procurement contracts are subject to the Indian Contract Act, 1872,[20] applicable government regulations, and specific DOS sectoral requirements. Since 1972, DOS has successfully built an ecosystem of competent vendor base, consisting of about 250 private companies. At the core of this unique ecosystem are about 150 companies, which are highly skilled and competent vendors helping ISRO build rockets and satellites. Among these are some of India's iconic legacy companies, including Larsen & Tubro (L&T),[21] Godrej & Boyce,[22] Hindustan Aeronautics Limited (HAL),[23] Walchand and Industries,[24] and Tata Advanced Systems.[25] However, until recently, procurement contracts involved handholding entrepreneurs in technology transfer initiatives, and provided the safety net of buybacks to ensure business survivability.[26]

In 2018 for the first time, NSIL[27] awarded three-year contracts for development, assembly, integration, and testing of a total of 27 medium and small satellites, deliverable in July 2021.[28] Three contracts, each for nine satellites, were awarded to two private industry consortiums[29] and one to a public sector company.[30] In fact, the Earth Observation Satellite-04 (EOS-04), or Riasat-1A, for which the main payload was launched by NSIL on PSLV-C52 on 13 February 2022, was built by the consortium led by Alpha Design Technologies Pvt Ltd.

12.1.4.4 Impact of the "Space Reforms 2020"

An important step ahead for the "Space Reforms 2020" was the decision to allow transfer of technology developed by DOS (ISRO, Centers and Units), through NSIL to public and private sectors, academia as well as central and state governments (external entities). In 2021, NSIL invited Request for Proposals[31] for undertaking end-to-end manufacturing of three Polar Satellite Launch Vehicles (PSLVs), receiving bids from three industry consortia.[32] On 6 April 2022, NSIL awarded a contract for manufacturing five PSLVs to the winning consortium led by the HAL and L&T.[33]

20 Indian Contract Act, 1872.
21 Larsen & Tubro, Integrated Report.
22 Godrej & Boyce Manufacturing Limited.
23 Hindustan Aeronautics Limited.
24 Walchandnagar Industries.
25 Tata Advanced Systems Limited.
26 Narayan Prasad, Traditional Space and NewSpace Industry in India – Current Outlook and Perspectives for the Future.
27 New Space India Limited (NSIL).
28 The Hindu, ISRO ropes in three partners to assemble 27 satellites, 18 July 2018.
29 Alpha Design Technologies Pvt Ltd.
30 Bharat Electronics Limited (BEL), Government of India, Ministry of Defence.
31 The Hans India, NewSpace India to open price bids for industries making PSLV rocket next month, 22 March 2022.
32 The consortia are (i) HAL and L&T; (ii) BEL, Alpha Design Pvt. Ltd. and Bharat Earth Movers Limited (BEML).
33 Chethan Kumar, HAL-L&T win over Rs. 824 crores contract for making 5 polar space launch vehicles, Times of India, 9 April 2022.

The recent developments augur well as very early steps to allow for the establishment of a space industrial complex in India.

In a significant development in 2000, the government decided to progressively concede the canalised mechanism for providing transponder capacity to commercial satellite telecommunications and broadcasting sectors[34] in an effort to make up the shortfall in available INSAT capacity (Indian communications satellite systems). The new "On-Demand" supply chain mechanism involves building and launching communications satellite systems and leasing back 100% capacity to commercial users. The shift has been welcomed by the industry, as it will reduce operating costs for commercial service providers.

The first On-Demand contract was executed between NSIL and Tata Sky Limited (now known as Tata Play Limited)[35] for building and launching a dedicated four-tonne GSAT-24 communications satellite system – in Ku-Band for providing high-quality Direct-to-Home (DTH) broadcasting services over India. Developed by ISRO, the satellite was launched on board the Arian 5 launch vehicle by Arianespace from the Guiana Space Centre on 22 June 2022.

The NGP 2000 restatement[36] provides for a liberalised mechanism to facilitate provisioning of satellite broadband services in India. It includes prior consultation with DOS for grant of authorisation for use of a space-based system with foreign satellites for providing domestic satellite communication services, or for any other services over India. Proposals are considered:

(i) in an "end-to-end" perspective, and not be limited only to the frequency band of operation and equipment availability from vendor(s);
(ii) ensuring that no deliberate attempt is made to exclude Indian satellite systems, giving due consideration to other systems which have substantial Indian participation by way of equity or in kind contribution;
(iii) ensuring that the system is internationally coordinated for frequency and orbit; and
(iv) ensuring that security concerns have been fully addressed.

12.1.5 Remote sensing data distribution – National Remote Sensing Centre

Currently, India has 13 operational satellites in Sun-synchronous orbit: RESOURCESAT-1, 2, 2A; CARTOSAT-1, 2, 2A, 2B; RISAT-1 and 2; OCEANSAT-2; Megha-Tropiques; SARAL and SCATSAT-1. It also has four satellites in geostationary orbit: INSAT-3D, Kalpana, INSAT 3A and INSAT -3DR. The National Natural Resource Management System (NNRMS) is the national inter-agency system for integrated natural resource management. The NNRMS data portal[37] hosts catalogues for various sectors, including other details, and provides access to its data on NRSC geoportals[38] – *Bhoosampada*, *Bhuvan*, Disaster Management Support, and Biodiversity Information System.[39]

34 "Norms, Guidelines and Procedures for Satellite Communications 2000" (NGP) provided DOS statutory direction to support the newly permitted commercial satellite telecommunications and broadcasting services by providing required transponder capacity to commercial service providers on commercial basis.
35 Tata Sky Limited (now known as Tata Play Limited).
36 NGP 2000 Restatement.
37 National Portal of India, National Natural Resources Management System NNRMS.
38 *Bhuvan*, Indian Geo-Platform of ISRO.
39 Biodiversity Information System, India Institute of Remote Sensing.

Remote sensing data distribution regulated under the Remote Sensing Data Policy 2011 (RSPD 11)[40] subscribed to the institutional approach of restricted access to Indian non-government and commercial users, with tedious, time-consuming, expensive, and market-unfriendly procedures, and not consistent with international best practices. In effect, remote sensing data products remained almost out of reach for Indian citizens. The recent draft National Geospatial Policy 2021[41] has comprehensively reformed, liberalised, and democratised access to Earth observation data, and the policy is presently being implemented by concerned agencies (see *infra*. at 12.5).

12.1.6 International commercial space launch services 2007

In 2007, India successfully executed its first commercial space launch mission,[42] marking an entry in the highly competitive international commercial space launch market. The 2007 launch also established PSLV as a cost-effective and reliable "workhorse", capable of delivering – without compromising on quality and efficiency.[43]

NSIL is the national launch service provider for national and commercial missions. Commercial launch service is recognised as a "deemed export", thus attracts "Zero%" Goods & Services Tax liability under the applicable law. The same tax advantage has been made applicable to domestic companies procuring commercial launch services in India. In April 2022, OneWeb[44] entered into agreement with NSIL for the launch of its low-earth orbit satellites.

However, India's relative cost advantage of cheaper launch services has been under challenge by re-usable launch vehicles, which have brought down launch costs substantially. To address this issue, India designed the Small Launch Vehicle (SLV), now in experimental phase.

12.1.7 Private satellite systems (Indian satellite system) – authorisation and licensing

At present, the "Norms, Guidelines and Procedures for Satellite Communications 2000"[45] is the only document which provides information about authorisation for establishing and operating private satellite systems. However, the 2000 policy prescription remains un-operationalised. Pursuant to the "Space Reforms 2020", an appropriate statutory framework to regulate non-government commercial entities to undertake activities in outer space activities is awaited.

12.2 NewSpace India

12.2.1 Overview

The recent reports reveal that the US and the UK lead the way with high concentration of start-ups and scale-ups, followed by India and Europe.[46] The earliest buzz in India was when TeamIndus,[47]

40 Remote Sensing Data Policy 2011(RSPD 11) National Remote Sensing Centre.
41 Antrix, Remote Sensing Data and Services, Draft National Geospatial Policy 2021.
42 Stephen Clark, India Launches Italian Space Observatory, Space.com, 23 April 2007.
43 Launch History of PSLV, see Polar Satellite Launch, Wikiwant.com.
44 OneWeb is co-owned by the UK government and India's Bharti Group.
45 See footnote 34.
46 StartUp Insights Research Blog.
47 TeamIndus was registered as the Team Name for the Google X Lunar PRIZE Competition.

the only Indian team to participate in the Google Lunar X PRIZE competition (2007–2018), was adjudged one of the five finalists in 2011.

In 2012, Dhruva Space, India's first start-up, was incorporated.[48]

Presently, there are an estimated 80 space start-ups, developing new products and services to provide end-to-end solutions, with commercial potential across the domestic and global value chains. Several start-ups have established companies overseas, to explore and expand business, but also realistically accepting lessons from their experience with existing regulatory roadblocks, yet, remaining deeply committed to engaging with India.

12.2.2 Start-ups – government support schemes

NewSpace, like start-ups in other sectors, have benefitted from sector agnostic schemes initiated by government since 2016, including Start-up India,[49] India Seed,[50] Make in India,[51] and schemes to encourage manufacturing in the Medium, Small, Micro Enterprises (MSME) sector, including the space sector.[52] Furthermore, because ISRO procurement contracts do not prohibit its suppliers to undertake projects for other entities, NewSpace entities are able to leverage the readily available pool of expertise to support start up activities.

12.2.3 NewSpace funding

Typically, early start-ups were not able to draw angel and venture capital funds; however, we now see that companies are successfully raising funds. We are also seeing a trend for risk-taking, such that several local as well as international investors are actively exploring opportunities to invest in NewSpace ventures based in India. For example, Digantara, which is building active orbital surveillance platforms, raised part of its seed round with US$2.5 million in July 2021;[53] Pixxel, which is on a mission to build a health monitor for the planet through a constellation of 30 cutting-edge hyperspectral small satellites, closed its seed round with US$7.3 million also in March 2021[54] and has secured the launch of their constellation by closing a US$25 million Series-A funding round from Seraphim in 2022.[55] The satellite propulsion start-up, Bellatrix Aerospace, raised US$3 million for its pre-A round in 2019 from venture capital investors.[56] Women-led Astrom Technologies, a 5G wireless deep-tech start-up, has raised US$3.4 million in a funding round led by IAN Fund, Urania Ventures, Germany, and Cognizant founder Laxminarayanan. The Chennai-based aerospace manufacturing start-up Agnikul Cosmos, which aims to develop and launch its own small-lift launch vehicle, like the Agnibaan, capable of placing 100 kg payload into a 700 km orbit, has raised US$11 million in a Series-A funding round in May 2021.[57] Similarly, Skyroot Aerospace[58]

48 Dhruva Space Pvt Limited, Bangalore.

49 Ministry of Commerce and Industry, Department for Promotion of Industry and Internal Trade, Start Up India initiative launched in 2016.

50 *Ibid.* Guidelines for Start Up India Seed Capital Scheme, 1 April 2021.

51 India Brand Equity Foundation, Make in India, December 2021.

52 Ministry of Micro, Small and Medium Enterprises, Government of India, Udayam On-line Registration Services.

53 Digantara Research & Technologies Private Limited, Bangalore (Digantara).

54 Pixxel Space India Private Limited, Bangalore (Pixxel).

55 Seraphim Space Investment Trust,plc. United Kingdom.

56 Bellatrix Aerospace Private Limited, Bangalore (Bellatrix).

57 Agnikul Cosmos Private Limited, Chennai (Agnikul).

58 Skyroot Aerospace Private Limited, Hyderabad (Skyroot).

is building an indigenous rocket for commercial missions and has raised US$17 million to fund its upcoming launch of its Vikram-1 rocket powered by a solid propulsion engine, Kalam-5, which is slated for launch in 2022.

INSPACe is facilitating the new companies to avail themselves of ISRO facilities for undertaking technology experiments, and by providing guidance where required. However, a carefully structured national space policy, with clearly defined objectives to be achieved in a 30-year timeline, accompanied by a roadmap for implementation with milestones to be achieved, is awaited – so, too, the national space activities statute. Recently, Spaceport SARABHAI (S2), India's first independent, dedicated think tank on space matters launched its first Report, "Why do Indian Founders in the space industry start their start-ups abroad?" during the SIA-India Space Congress-22 at New Delhi on 26–28 October 2022.

Part II – Satellite-enabled services

12.3 Satellite telecommunications: broadcasting, internet information technology, IT-enabled services

12.3.1 Overview

In 2000, satellite telecommunication and broadcasting services, e.g., the internet, information technology, were introduced as new sub-sectors, and have witnessed boom growth in the past thirty years. Additionally, the information and technology (IT) communication revolution has driven IT business processes and IT-enabled services, software development, new technologies and innovations. Companies which have established global operations were India's first start-ups.[59]

12.3.2 Telecommunication and broadcasting services

12.3.2.1 Overview: satellite telecommunications and broadcasting services sectors

The satellite telecommunications and broadcasting sectors continue to attract global interest, particularly as India prepares to introduce satellite broadband services. Between the beginning of 2000 and April 2021, the telecommunications sector received foreign direct investment totalling US$37.97 billion,[60] and is recognised among the fastest-growing and among the top five employment generators in the country. In December 2021, India was the second largest telecommunications market worldwide, with a subscriber base of 1.18 billion (including wireless, wireline) and gross revenue at US$8.74 billion in the first quarter of fiscal year 2022.[61] Among the top commercial telecom operators in India are Reliance Jio,[62] Bharti Airtel Limited,[63] and Vodafone-Idea Limited.[64] Bharat Sanchar Nigam Limited[65] is the public-sector telecom services provider.

59 Tata Consulting Services Limited, Infosys Limited, Wipro Technology Services Limited, and Tech Mahindra Limited.

60 India Brand Equity Foundation, Telecom Industry in India, December 2021.

61 *Ibid.* Indian Telecom Industry Analysis, December 2021.

62 Jio Platforms Limited.

63 Bharti Airtel Limited.

64 Vodafone-India Limited.

65 Bharat Sanchar Nigam Limited.

The prospective markets for the ubiquitous 5G broadband-from-space services could be lucrative, particularly considering the substantially underserved and unserved land areas across India's geography. Indicative of the unmet potential are the projections for satellite broadband on the basis of market positions at the end of 2021. The overall tele-density was 86.90%, disaggregated to 36.51% urban tele-density at the end of November 2021 with 50.39% rural tele-density, static since October 2021. Similarly, of the total telephone subscribers as of the end of November 2021, 55.42% were urban, against 44.58% rural subscribers.[66] Among contenders for satellite broadband services are Bharti, led by OneWeb and represented by Oneweb India Communications Pvt Limited,[67] and Elon Musk's SpaceX,[68] represented by Starlink Satellite Communications Pvt. Limited.[69] Telecom Licensor has issued a Letter of Intent to OneWeb[70] for providing satellite broadband services under the Global Mobile Personal Communication Service (GMPCS) license category. Two existing telecom operators, Nelco Limited[71] in partnership with Telesat Canada,[72] and Reliance Jio[73] in partnership with SES Luxembourg,[74] also intend to provide satellite broadband-internet connectivity via geostationary orbit and medium earth orbit satellite systems.

Correspondingly, the Indian broadcasting and cable television market (terrestrial, cable, and satellite TV) was valued at US$11.62 billion[75] in 2020 and is projected to grow to US$19.6 billion by 2026. The digital media, already the second-largest segment in the Indian monitoring and evaluation (M&E) industry, has emerged as the fifth largest market in the world.[76] Led OTT ("over the top", referring to devices that go "over" a cable box to give the user access to TV content), gaming, animation, and visual effects[77] M&E is expected to reach US$100 billion by 2030 at 10–12% compound annual growth rate (CAGR), and expected to continue growing to a CAGR of 11% to touch US$30.9 billion by 2024. Recent reforms allow the media and broadcasting sectors further expansion.

In sum, the telecom and broadcasting and M&E sectors offer commercial opportunities to both established and new service operators, including in manufacturing.

12.3.2.2 Telecommunications: statutory basis for authorisation and functions

The AOBR provides the statutory basis to Department of Telecommunications (DOT) for undertaking specific activities including, *inter alia*, policy, applicable statutes, licensing, and coordina-

66 Telecom Regulatory Authority of India – Press Release No. 4/2022, 18 January 2022.

67 Oneweb India Communications Private Limited (OneWeb), is the wholly owned subsidiary of Nettle Infrastructures Limited which is 100% owned by Bharti Airtel Limited.

68 Business Standard, SpaceX sets up subsidiary in India, plans to apply for licence, 1 November 2021.

69 Starlink Satellite Communications Private Limited is the 100% wholly owned subsidiary of SpaceX.

70 Times of India, DOT issues LoI to Bharti's OneWeb for satellite communication service licence, 5 August 2021.

71 Nelco Limited is part of the US$116 billion Tata Group.

72 Gagandeep Kaur, Editor, Light Reading Newsletter, Telesat-Nelco to offer satellite services in India by 2024, 10 April 2021.

73 See footnote 62.

74 Sumit Arora, Current Affairs, Reliance Jio ties up with SES for satellite-based broadband service, 15 February 2022.

75 TechSci Research, Indian Broadcasting and Cable TV Market by Type (Terrestrial TV, Cable TV and Satellite) by Revenue Generation (Subscription, Advertising, Public Funds) by Region, Opportunities and Forecast by 2026, December 2020.

76 Statista, Digital Markets, Digital Media India, October 2021.

77 *Ibid.*

tion matters relating to telegraphs, telephones, wireless, data, facsimile, telematic services, and other similar forms of communications.

The statutory remit of DOT includes, *inter alia*:

(i) international organisations including ITU, Radio Regulation Board (RRB), Radio Communication Sector (ITU-R), Telecommunication Standardization Sector (ITU-T), and Development Sector (ITU-D). Consequently, the Wireless Planning & Coordination Wing (WP&C), being the national spectrum regulator, functions under the oversight of DOT;
(ii) Telecommunications Engineering Centre (TEC);[78]
(iii) Centre for Development of Telematics (C-DOT),[79] a vital constituent of the telecom ecosystem. For example, currently, C-DOT is developing indigenous Quantum Key Distribution solutions to address threats for data transportation/transfer, through existing communications networks.[80] C-DOT will provide a complete portfolio of indigenous Quantum Secure Telecom products and solutions to fulfil requirements of user segments. TEC and C-DOT work closely for developing new technologies specifically for domestic manufacturers;
(iv) licensing of terrestrial and satellite services, internet, and IT services;
(v) implementation of the National Digital Communications Policy 2018 (NDP 18);[81] and
(vi) administration of Telecom statutes including the Telegraph Act 1885,[82] Indian Wireless Telegraphy Act 1933,[83] and the Telegraph Wires (Unlawful Possession) Act 1950.[84] The statutes are under revision to be aligned with NDP 18.

The WP&C is the "Indian Administration" at ITU and RRB. It is spectrum licensor for all categories of telecom services and broadcasting services:[85] the Wireless Operating License is granted subject to the applicant having obtained a "service licence" from DOT, or a specific "broadcasting service license (television or radio)" from the Ministry of Information and Broadcasting (MIB).

12.3.2.3 NDP 18

"Digital India"[86] was initiated in 2015 to deploy innovative, inclusive public technologies for delivering online, citizen-centric public services. "Digital India" signaled a shift to digital communications. In 2018, the NDP 18 was announced. The NDP 18 is mandated, *inter alia*, to:

(i) develop digital communications infrastructure for providing broadband pan-India;
(ii) bridge the digital divide, rural-urban and rich-poor – this is a core objective;

78 Telecommunications Engineering Centre (TEC), Department of Telecommunications (DOT), Ministry of Communications, Government of India.
79 Centre for Development of Telematics (C-DOT), autonomous Telecom R&D centre.
80 The Economic Times, Telecom Secretary asks C-DOT to work on 6G, launches Quantum Communications Lab, 10 October 2021.
81 The National Portal of India, National Digital Communications Policy 2018 (NDP 18).
82 India Code (Digital Repository), Indian Telegraph Act 1885.
83 *Ibid.* Indian Wireless Telegraphy Act 1933.
84 *Ibid.* Telegraph Wires (Unlawful Possession) Act 1950.
85 Gagandeep Kaur, Light Reading Newsletter, 5G Spectrum Auction: Who has won what?, 8 February 2022.
86 Ministry of Electronics and Information Technology (MeitY), Digital India 2015.

(iii) enable investment, innovation, and intellectual property rights (IPR) in next-generation technologies and services, including 5G, Artificial Intelligence, Internet of Things (IoT), Cloud and Big Data, and Fourth Industrial Revolution technologies;
(iv) ensure sovereignty, safety, security of digital communications; and
(v) recognise data as a crucial economic resource.

12.3.2.4 Reforms in telecom licensing mechanisms

DOT has undertaken comprehensive reform to align the existing Unified License Regime with NDP 18. The licence reforms include new services, e.g.:

(i) In-Flight and Maritime Connectivity service providers with 100% foreign direct investment (FDI) permitted,[87] audioconferencing/audiotex, voicemail, and Virtual Network Operator (VNO) services;
(ii) permitting M2M and IoT services; and
(iii) permitting 100% FDI in VNO services.

DOT has rescinded the existing distinction between domestic and international services, rationalised Unified License Regime fees and charges by abolishing Network Operations and Control Centre levy regime payable to DOT,[88] and making satellite-based connectivity for low bit rate application-space-segment user charge henceforth payable to DOS.[89] Importantly, DOT has revised the definition of Adjusted Gross Revenue[90] (a step welcomed across the industry) and abolished the existing technical barriers inhibiting satellite service speeds, antenna sizes and usage of spectrum bands, thus facilitating optimal deployment of new satcom technologies, smaller antenna, and accelerating broadband in the country at lower operational costs without compromising quality.[91]

12.3.2.5 FDI in telecom services and IT[92]

100% FDI is permitted in all telecom services (including Telecom Infrastructure Providers Category-I and the Technology Sector),[93] specifically including basic, cellular, United Access Services, Unified License (Access Services), Unified License, National/International Long Distance, Commercial V-Sat, Public Mobile Radio Trunked Services, GMPCS, all types of ISP licences, Voice Mail/Audiotex/UMS, Resale of IPLC, Mobile Number Portability Services, Infrastructure Provider Category-I (providing dark fibre, right of way, duct space, tower) subject

87 Ministry of Communications, Department of Telecommunications (Access Service Division), Change in FDI Norms in Telecom-sector In-Flight and Maritime Connectivity Service Providers, 23 February 2022.
88 The Economic Times, ET Bureau, DOT scraps key levy on satcom players, 8 May 2022.
89 Department of Telecommunications (Satellite Licensing Division), File No. 60-SATCOM Plan/DOS/2020-SAT, Guidelines for establishing satellite-based communications network(s).
90 Department of Telecommunications, Amendment to Unified License Regime Agreement for Adjusted Gross Revenue, 25 October 2021.
91 Gagandeep Kaur, Light Reading Newsletter, India changes rules to advance satellite communications, 27 May 2021.
92 Ministry of Commerce and Industry, Department of Promotion of Industry and Internal Trade, Consolidated FDI Policy, 15 October 2020, pp. 46–47.
93 *Ibid.* para. 5.2.

to the condition that FDI above the threshold of 49% shall require prior permission from the Department for Promotion of Industry and Internal Trade.

With regard to other IT service providers, 100% FDI is permitted under the automatic route, i.e. without prior permission from government.

12.3.3 Broadcasting services: television and radio

12.3.3.1 Statutory basis: MIB

The AOBR authorises MIB[94] to undertake activities including, *inter alia*, licensing for radio and television broadcasting, and implementing policies and statutes related to national commercial radio and television broadcasting services.

12.3.3.2 TV and radio: applicable policies and statutes

TV Broadcasting Service Policies include:

(i) Guidelines for DTH;[95]
(ii) Headend-In-the-Sky (HITS);[96]
(iii) Internet Protocol TV Service;[97]
(iv) Television Rating Point agency;[98] and
(v) Broadcasting Content Code.

MIB also formulates Radio Broadcasting Services Policies for private FM radio networks; regulates private FM radio networks through the auction of FM channels; and ensures operationalising Community Radio Stations to provide radio services to communities in marginalised, rural, and remote areas.

The applicable sectoral statutes include the Cable Television Networks (Regulation) Act 1995[99] for regulating content broadcasting on private satellite channels, multi-system operators networks, and local cable operators, and the Sports Broadcasting Signals (Mandatory Sharing with *Prasar Bharati*) Act and Rules 2007.

12.3.4 Television and radio service licence regimes

Television Service Licenses are issued for up-linking-downlinking of TV channels, up-linking hub/teleport, uplink facility by a news agency and permission for use of SNG/DSNGs, and to *Prasar Bharati*,[100] the Public Service Broadcaster for providing free-to-air broadcasting services on *Doordarshan* national television channels.

94 See footnote 15, pp. 109–112.
95 Ministry of Information and Broadcasting (Min I&B), Guidelines (amended) for providing Direct-to-Home Services in India 2020.
96 *Ibid.* Guidelines (amended) for Providing HITS Services in India 2020.
97 *Ibid.* Policy Guidelines for providing IPTV services in India, 26 August 2020.
98 *Ibid.* I&B constitutes committee to review Guidelines for Television Rating Agencies in India, 4 November 2020.
99 India Code, The Cable Television Networks (Regulation) Act, 1995 Rules.
100 India Code, Prasar Bharati (Broadcasting Corporation of India) Act 1990.

Radio Broadcasting Service Licenses are issued for private FM radio broadcasting services[101] and *Prasar Bharati*, the National Radio Service Broadcaster, for providing *Aksahvani* services on AIR (All India Radio) channels.

12.3.4.1 FDI in television and radio broadcasting services

With regard to Television Services/Broadcasting Carriage services,[102] FDI of 100% is available for:

(i) teleports-setting up and up-linking;
(ii) DTH services;
(iii) cable network-multisystem operators (MSO) and for upgradation towards digitisation and addressability;
(iv) cable network (non-MSO);
(v) mobile TV;
(vi) HITS broadcasting services.

As to Broadcasting Content Services, FDI is permitted up to:

(i) 100% in up-linking and down-linking non-news and current affairs TV channels;
(ii) 49% for up-linking news and current affairs TV channels;
(iii) 26% for up-loading/streaming news and current affairs services through digital media.

FDI in Radio Broadcasting Services amounts to 49% for terrestrial broadcasting FM radio services.

12.3.5 FDI and telecom and broadcasting equipment manufacturing

FDI up to 100% under the automatic route was first permitted in 2000 for manufacturing telecom equipment and infrastructure, also electronics. With the deployment of 5G and wider coverage of existing technology, the market size of telecommunications equipment sector is set for a growth trajectory in the coming years.[103] The government has approved US$1.65 billion towards DOT production-linked incentive (PLI) scheme[104] for MSME, non-MSME, and global companies, for manufacturing telecom and networking products.

101 Pravin Jha, Mondaq, India: private FM Radio Stations: Govt of India Policy on Phase II FM Radio Broadcasting Services, 7 September 2005.

102 See footnote 92, pp. 36–37.

103 Shangliao Sun, Statista, Technology & Telecommunications, Telecommunication Equipment Market Size in India from financial year 2018 to 2020, 15 June 2022.

104 Department of Telecom (DOT), Guidelines for Performance Linked Incentive Scheme (PLI) for Promoting telecom and Networking Products Manufacturing in India, 3 June 2021.

12.4 Information technology and e-commerce services

12.4.1 Overview

The 1998 National Task Force on Information Technology and Software Development was set up to promote the Information and Communication Technologies (ICT) industry, and to lead India in developing into a global IT power.[105] According to the National Association of Software and Service Companies (NASSCOM),[106] the US$227-billion IT industry in India currently employs over five million professionals, contributes 9% relative to India's gross domestic product (including e-commerce), exports, has global visibility, and provides the highest employment in private sector.

India is among the biggest consumers of data worldwide. According to the Telecom Regulatory Authority of India, average wireless data usage per wireless data subscriber was 11 GB a month in fiscal year 2020.[107] It is expected that by 2025, India will need more than 22 million skilled workers in 5G-centric technologies such as IoT, AI, robotics, and cloud computing. Bengaluru, Gurgaon, Hyderabad, Pune, Delhi, and Chennai are among India's IT and Tech Cities.

Inevitably the runaway success of the sector, the rapid generation of datasets, which are expected to grow exponentially, and the demand for data localisation together pose critical cyber regulatory challenges in the absence of a national data protection law for personal and non-personal data. The present statute, the Information Technology Act 2000, is outdated, rendering the institutional cyber security regulator unable to effectively address current requirements. The absence of an appropriate regulatory and institutional framework is the weak link.

As Mr. Debjani Ghosh, president of NASSCOM, noted,

> India's sweet spot is its leadership in building inclusive public technologies. No other country has used and designed technology for the larger good of society as has India. India has attracted global attention for it. For example, Google, while proposing an inter-bank settlement system in the US, cited its extensive experience with India's Unified Payments Interface (UPI) and shared learnings that the West should emulate. So what sets India apart? Several factors, including India's focus on technology and service delivery, ease of doing business, world-class infrastructure, favourable demographics, a vibrant startup ecosystem, and a vast pool of digital talent, all allow India to strategically position itself as the innovation nerve center of the world. Indian tech companies have become an integral part of the global economy: according to a recent study by NASSCOM – S&P Global, Indian IT contributed not only $80 billion to the US gross domestic product in 2021 and employed over 600,000 people, but also strengthened the talent foundation with a strong focus on bridging the science, technology, engineering and math (STEM) gap.[108]

105 Shefali Rekhi, India Today, Taskforce for IT lays out plans to wire up India, propel it into the Information Age, 20 July 1998.

106 The National Association of Software and Service Companies (NASSCOM) a not-for-profit trade and advocacy group.

107 See footnotes 60 and 61.

108 Debjani Ghosh, NASSCOM, India could play the catalyst for tech innovation across the world, Mint, 9 August 2022.

12.4.2 Market readiness

IT companies have already adopted digital strategies, focusing on enhancing the scope of digital business streams in India's domestic market. There is no doubt that the pandemic shifted the way that technology is being adopted by businesses, and the cloud has now become a business strategy because it offers a scalable platform, allowing flexibility to scale up or down; it also allows businesses to collaborate with multiple industries. In a recent interview, the CEO of HCL Technologies suggested that the financial year 2022 will likely see a higher percentage of smaller deals in the overall pipeline, in addition to the mid-sized and large deals.[109] Telecom service providers are also focusing on digital business streams. Bharti Airtel has established its fourth technology hub in Pune, to support digital services in Western India across multiple experience and domains, e.g., Big Data, machine learning, Dev Ops, Tech ops – to support its digital strategy to pivot to a digital services company for satellite broadband services.[110]

India now is the largest technological hub, with US$227 billion in expected 2022 revenue. Not just technological services, the "software as a service" movement, emerging from India and built for the rest of the world, is expected to create US$1 trillion in value and almost a quarter of the industry's revenues by 2030

12.4.3 Statutory basis: information technology, IT-enabled service, e-governance and cyber

The Ministry of Electronics and Information Technology (MeitY) is mandated under the applicable Allocation of Business Rules of 16 July 2016[111] to undertake activities including, *inter alia:*

(i) policy matters relating to information technology, electronics, and internet (all matters other than licensing of internet service provider);
(ii) promotion of the internet, IT, and IT-enabled services;
(iii) digital transactions including digital payments;
(iv) cyber laws, Information Technology Act 2000;
(v) manufacturing semiconductor devices;
(vi) international agencies including Internet for Business Limited, Institute for Education in Information Society and International Code Council;
(vii) standardisation, testing, and quality in IT, IT application, and tasks;
(viii) electronics and computer software promotion;
(ix) National Informatics Centre; and
(x) Unique Identification Authority of India.

109 Ayushman Baruah, Interview with Mr. C. Vijaykumar, CEO & MD HCL Technologies Limited, "We see a higher percentage of smaller deals in the pipeline", Mint, 12 May 2022.

110 Bharti Airtel to set up digital technology hub in Pune, to hire 500 people by end of this fiscal, Economic Times, 16 May 2022.

111 See footnote 15, p. 56.

12.4.4 Digital India e-governance initiatives

12.4.4.1 Unique Identification Authority of India

The Unique Identification Authority of India is a statutory body established under the *Aadhaar* (Targeted Delivery of Financial and Other Subsidies, Benefits and Services) Act 2016[112] for providing a 12-digit unique identity number based on biometric information to residents in India, available on a voluntary basis. The *Aadhaar* ID card is accepted as proof of residence, of citizenship, or as proof of right of domicile in India. *Aadhaar* linked services are key tools for delivering reform initiatives particularly, *inter alia*, to promote financial inclusion of underprivileged and economically weaker sections. Especially during the pandemic lockdowns, for example, below-poverty-line families across the country were able to transact or make money transfers to merchants via the Unified Payment Interface by authorising the payment with their fingerprint by using the BHIM mobile app on their smart phones. Similarly, the Direct Benefit Transfer mechanism enabled the government to transfer subsidies or welfare amounts directly to the beneficiary *Aadhaar*-linked bank accounts.[113]

12.4.4.2 National Informatics Centre (NIC)[114]

The ICT infrastructure provider developed *Aadhaar*-linked platforms during the pandemic:

(i) *Aarogya Setu*[115] – digital service for "Covid-19 contact tracing, syndromic mapping and self-assessment", also made available on the internet and smartphone apps; and
(ii) Covid Vaccination Intelligence Network portal (CoWin) for users to register for vaccination, and status updates. CoWin is now linked to individual passport numbers to facilitate domestic and international travel.

NIC has developed *Meghraj*,[116] cloud computing platforms to support India's traditional market ecosystem of small and medium business entities across the country:

(i) Open Network for Digital Commerce platform (ONDC)[117] to promote and support digital transition of India's existing traditional market to e-commerce ecosystems; and
(ii) Electronic Solution for Augmenting Framers' Trade in Aquaculture (e-SANTA), an e-marketplace platform.[118]

112 Unique Identification Authority of India (Aadhaar Targeted Delivery of Financial and Other Subsidies, Benefits and Services) Act, 2016.
113 K. Deepalakshmi, The long List of Aadhar-Linked Schemes, The UID Number, popularly known as Aadhar, was envisaged to end fake or multiple identities, The Hindu, 24 March 2017.
114 National Informatics Centre, Government of India, (NIC).
115 *Aarogya Setu*, National Health App , by NIC and MeitY.
116 *Meghraj* (means "cloud"), National Cloud Computing Initiative by NIC.
117 NIC: Open Network for Digital Commerce e-marketplace (ONDC).
118 Electronic Solution for Augmenting Farmers' Trade in Aquaculture (e-SANTA).

12.4.5 Semiconductors

12.4.5.1 India semiconductors mission[119]

Pursuant to recent disruptions of supply chains, the Indian government has taken measures to become ready in electronics semiconductors across the ecosystem to development capability and capacity in design, manufacturing and skilling.[120] Key objectives include setting up greenfield semiconductor fabs and display fabs, developing R&D, with the goal to establish over 20 semiconductor design, component production, and display fabrication units, and providing performance linked incentives to encourage MSME. The objective is to build indigenous end-to-end capability in semiconductor chipset.[121]

12.4.5.2 Commercial potential

The Indian semiconductor market was at US$15 billion in 2020 and is estimated to reach US$63 billion by 2026. Recent initiatives have attracted participation by SPEL Semiconductor Ltd,[122] HCL Technologies,[123] Syrma Technology,[124] and Valenkani Electronics[125] in Semiconductor Packaging, and Ruttonsha International Rectifier Ltd[126] for compound semiconductors. Additionally, multinational companies – Vedanta Limited, India, Foxxcon, Taiwan joint venture, IGSS Ventures, Singapore, and ISMC have proposed setting up chip plants for 28 nm to 65 nm Semiconductor Fabs, with capacity of approximately 120,000 wafers per month, with a projected investment of US$13.6 billion.[127]

12.5 Geospatial data services sector

12.5.1 Overview

The 2015 Digital India Project[128] necessitated convergence of cartographic, thematic map and remote sensing data sets. Among the objectives of "Digital India" was to provide citizens online access to government services, possible only with extensive deployment of geospatial technologies. It was obvious that the success of "Digital India" location-based services depended on the Survey of India (SOI) and NRSC providing easy access to the geospatial data and information to other government departments involved with developing "Digital India" technology platforms.

119 Ministry for Electronics & Information Technology (MeitY): Scheme for Manufacturing Electronics Components and Semiconductors 2020.

120 *Ibid.* Industry Demand Linked Skilling in Electronic System Design and Manufacturing (ESDM) Sector.

121 *Ibid.* Semi-Conductor Laboratory, Mohali.

122 SPEL Semiconductor Limited, India.

123 HCL Technologies Limited (HCL).

124 Syrma SGS Technology Limited.

125 Velankani Electronics Private Limited.

126 Ruttonsha International Rectifier Limited.

127 Gulveen Aulakh, Mint, Construction of first chip factory likely to start by year-end, 14 May 2022.

128 See footnote 86, Digital India Project.

12.5.2 *Draft National Geospatial Policy 2021*[129] *(NGP 21)*

The draft NGP 21 has heralded balanced regulations to facilitate emergence of a robust geospatial technology ecosystem, facilitate commercialisation of data, spur further innovations, data products, and tools, and enable utilisation of public-funded national geospatial data for national and international cooperation projects. NGP 21 proposes implementation of earlier decisions, including the establishment of the National Spatial Data Infrastructure approved in 2006,[130] as well as implementation of the National Data Sharing and Accessibility Policy 2012[131] and NGP 16.

12.5.3 *Common regulatory framework*

The draft NGP 21 common regulatory framework replaces the existing frameworks to bring seamless synergy to Geospatial Data, Products, Services and Solutions (GDPSS) content constituents, which consist of:

(i) Mapping Infrastructure (Survey of India, DST);[132]
(ii) Earth Observation Infrastructure[133] (NRSC, DOS);
(iii) Sub-surface and Hydrographic Infrastructure[134] (DOS); and
(iv) Positioning, Navigation and Timing Infrastructure[135] (DOS).

12.5.3.1 Guidelines for Acquiring and Producing Geospatial Data and Geospatial Data services, including Maps, 2021 (NGP Guidelines)[136]

NGP Guidelines orient towards a B2B approach to GDPSS, and amplify terms, standards, and conditions for uniform compliance by government regulators, across all data repositories. It is significant that NGP Guidelines are mandated to be the single reference point on the subject, thereby superseding anything contrary which may be issued by way of Official Memoranda and Guidelines by the Ministry of Defense[137] and/or any other department of the government of India.[138] In terms of ease of doing business, the NGP Guidelines have liberalised maps and democratised data for enhanced commercialisation with Value Added Services, including a "self-certification" mechanism to indicate affirmation of adherence to the policy. A few important changes include:

(i) easing eligibility for accessing GDPSS;
(ii) granting ease of access for the first time Open Access GDPSS free of cost, without registration requirements;
(iii) liberalising threshold for Open Access;

129 Department of Science & Technology (DST), Draft National Geospatial Policy, 2021 (NGP 21).
130 *Ibid.* National Spatial Data Infrastructure.
131 *Ibid.* National Data Sharing and Accessibility Policy 2012.
132 See footnote 129, NGP 21, para. 5.3 Survey of India (SOI).
133 *Ibid.* para. 5.3, National Remote Sensing Centre (NSRC, Department of Space).
134 *Ibid.* para. 5.4, Department of Space.
135 *Ibid.* para. 5.5. See Draft Indian Navigation Satellite Policy 2021 (SATNAV Policy 21, Department of Space).
136 *Ibid.* Guidelines for Acquiring and Producing Geospatial Data and Geospatial Data Services (GDPSS) including Maps (DST F.No.SM/25/02/2020 (Part I), 15 February 2021.
137 Survey of India, National Map Policy 2005.
138 See footnote 40.

(iv) liberalising access conditions;
(v) providing clarity regarding:
   a. restrictions on user conditions;
   b. permitted user conditions; and
   c. access, user, and data sharing conditions.

12.5.3.2 Mapping infrastructure

Survey of India (SOI)[139] is licensor and repository of topographic data. Maps may be purchased online[140] at prices published on SOI website for the Open Series Maps.[141] SOI digital boundary data are approved standards are free for use, digital display, and printing. Vetting of publication of maps, atlases, textbooks for authentic international boundaries and coastlines is not required. Finally, publishers are to self-certify that the boundaries are as per the SOI standards.

A Digital Licence is required for internal business use of SOI digital products on payment of one time licence fee. A Publishing Licence permits publication of SOI mapping in books, pamphlets, CD-ROM, etc. subject to payment of one-time licence fee and additional fee per number of copies published. A Media Licence allows use of 1:1M and smaller-scale SOI mapping in compressed JPEG format in newspapers, magazine, television, and feature films, but does not allow use in advertisements, subject to annual licence fee. An Internet Licence allows hosting of 1:1M or smaller SOI mapping in compressed JPEG format on licensee's website, subject to annual licence fee.

12.5.3.3 National Atlas & Thematic Mapping Organization (NATMO)[142]

NATMO prepares atlases and thematic maps of the country including physiography, hydrology, climate, administrative, political, social, agricultural, industrial, cultural, economic, and spatio-temporal changes taking place in the country.

12.5.4 Earth observation infrastructure

12.5.4.1 Conditions for Earth observation data access[143]

The Satellite Imagery Data licensing mechanism has been aligned with the NGP 21, and the NRSC is providing Open Access Data up to Threshold level without registration or authorisation. Importantly, under the Registered Access mechanism, registered distributors are now accessing satellite imagery access up to 50 cm Ground Sampling Distance, without prior clearance. This an important development for space start-up companies which are establishing remote sensing satellite constellations and providing application solutions based on remote sensing/Earth observation data like the start-up Pixxel.

139 *Ibid.* New Guidelines on geospatial data and services.
140 *Ibid.*
141 *Ibid.* Price List for Open Series Maps.
142 National Atlas & Thematic Map Organisation (NATMO).
143 National Remote Sensing Centre (NSRC), Data Dissemination Policy.

12.5.4.2 Satellite navigation: positioning, navigation, and timing infrastructure

India's PNT infrastructure – consisting of GAGAN and the IRNSS-NavIC – is critical for the successful spherical implementation of NGP 21. Presently, the draft Indian Navigational Satellite Policy 2021 is pending finalisation.

12.5.4.3 GPS Aided GEO Augmented Navigation System (GAGAN)

GAGAN is a Space Based Augmentation System (SBAS) jointly developed by the Airports Authority of India and ISRO to provide navigational services over the Indian Flight Information Region (FIR) with capability of expanding services to neighbouring FIRs. GAGAN signals are being used for Communication, Navigation, and Surveillance/Air Traffic Management functions. It is the third SBAS to be certified for approach with vertical guidance (APV1) and the first to do so operating in the equatorial region. GAGAN satellites system and ground stations correct for GPS signal errors caused by ionospheric disturbances, timing and satellite orbit errors, provide vital information regarding the condition of each satellite, and provide better accuracy. GAGAN will provide services to intelligent transportation, maritime, highways, railways, surveying, geodesy, security agencies, telecom industry, personal users of position location applications, etc.

12.5.4.4 Indian Regional Navigation Satellite System (IRNSS)[144]

The Indian Regional Navigation Satellite System (IRNSS) – NavIC is India's independent regional navigation satellite system to provide accurate position information services to users in India, as well as the region extending up to 1,500 km from India's boundary. IRNSS is expected to provide a position accuracy of better than 20 m in the primary service area. Its applications include terrestrial, aerial, and marine navigation, disaster management, vehicle tracking and fleet management, integration with mobile phones, precise timing, mapping and geodetic data capture, terrestrial navigation aid for hikers and travelers, and visual and voice navigation for drivers. IRNSS-NavIC will provide two types of services: (i) Standard Positioning Service for all users; and (ii) Restricted Service which is an encrypted service only for authorised users.

12.5.5 Market expectations

The shift of government's approach to geospatial data as an exclusive strategic asset to include incentivisation of data-driven businesses through the draft reforms policies in 2021 was the fact that the lack of accurate data sets in the country was felt to be impeding the planning for infrastructure and other national development projects.[145]

The industry-defining "Geospatial Artha report"[146] suggests that India's geospatial economy is currently valued at 38,972 crore INR and has the potential to grow to 63,100 crore INR at 12.8%

144 ISRO, Indian Regional Navigation Satellite System – NaviC (IRNSS Programe), Signal-in-Space Interface Control Document (ICD Ver. 1.1) for Standard Positioning Service (SPS) is released to the public to provide the essential information on the IRNSS signal-in-space, to facilitate research & development and aid the commercial use of the IRNSS signals for navigation-based applications.

145 Esha Roy, Why is India Opening Up to the Geo-Spatial Sector? What Impact Will This Have?, The Indian Express, 22 February 2021.

146 GEOSPATIAL World: Geospatial Artha 2021, Indian Geospatial Market, Economy and Industrial Development Strategy.

by the end of 2025 if the government ensures timely implementation of the three geospatial policies by 2022. The Indian geospatial market is expected to grow to 23,200 INR by 2025 from its current size of 14,050 INR at CAGR of 13.36%. It is expected that the defence and the intelligence sector will be valued at 3,305 crore INR by 2025, while the water resources and irrigation sector will be worth 5,020 crore, urban development will account for 3,030 crore INR, and the utilities segment will touch 2,600 crore INR.

12.6 Conclusion

The chapter has outlined that 2020 and 2021 have brought extensive reforms across from the space sector to space-enabled services, including communications. Timely implementation of the policies is key to achieving predicted and projected benchmarks. It is national work in progress. Among the principle unfinished business is a national space policy, unambiguous, precisely articulated with clearly identified purpose and objectives in a 30-year timeline. The policy must necessarily be accompanied with a roadmap for implementation with realistically identified milestones, with frequent reviews and course corrections. The urgent need for a robust, balanced national data (personal and non-personal) protection law with appropriate balanced procedural and institutional mechanism to effectively address growing cyber threats cannot be emphasised enough. The gaps need further reiteration. Finally, it would be desirable for the Indian government to require comprehensive evaluation, aimed at facilitating evidence-based spherical assessment of the current status of space and space-enabled businesses, to determine the preparedness or otherwise, of existing applicable statutes, including anti-trust and competition laws, to effectively regulate India's digital economy.

D

Fostering innovation through competition and public procurement

13

THE EU AND ESA RULES ON PUBLIC PROCUREMENT

Oliver Heinrich and Jan Helge Mey[1]

13.1 Introduction – three elements of a successful tender

Success in a procurement process consists of three elements: first – awareness of the upcoming procurements in due time; second – knowing and – more importantly – understanding the procurement procedure and the applicable rules; third – putting it all together in a competitive and compliant tender for goods, services, or works. Each element turns out to be crucial for a successful offer, while each requires a different amount of effort.

13.2 First element: awareness of upcoming procurements

Competition is an essential element of public procurement. Contracting authorities employ systems addressing economic operators eligible for participation. ESA employs the esa-star publication system, and the EU uses Tenders Electronic Daily (TED). Both services offer content-sensitive keyword search, advanced searches, or the use of search profiles and alerts. There are also numerous free public and commercial offerings for search of current public procurements. Companies can achieve a timely overview of procurement projects of interest to their professional activities.

Under the ESA procurement regulations (ESA-PR),[2] registration in ESA's open, but mandatory, supplier list is a pre-requisite for acquiring the relevant procurement documents and participating in a procurement process. Any interested economic operator irrespective of location can register on the Doing Business with ESA portal. Full registration unlocks access to the ESA tender documents applicable for participation in open competitive procedures. The ESA Contracts Department manages the registration process. The registration process should be initiated before publication of procurement projects of interest. Procedural delays can otherwise prevent the participation.

1 The authors would like to thank Katharina Prall, Research Associate at BHO Legal, for her contribution to this chapter.

2 ESA/REG/001, rev. 5, Paris, 10 July 2019 (ESA-PR).

DOI: 10.4324/9781003268475-18

Economic operators may also be excluded from participation in ESA's projects due to industrial policy considerations.

In contrast, the EU procurement rules do not require economic operators to register in any supplier list. But with the increasing requirement to submit tenders electronically, it is nonetheless advisable to register on the TED eTendering portal and familiarise oneself with the submission processes early in the process. Furthermore, access to procurement documents, even if not classified, may be subject to additional confidentiality requirements such as the prior submission of a non-disclosure declaration.

Interested economic operators should clarify whether they can tender alone (single contractor) or need support from other companies. There are three forms of collaborative bidding: (1) the partners enter into a teaming agreement, forming a consortium for the submissions of joint tender, (2) one entity takes the lead as prime with the others acting as sub-contractors, and (3) a mixture of both – an industrial consortium and other companies as sub-contractors.

Small and medium-sized enterprises (SMEs) may want to look out for teaming opportunities and special provisions in the procurement for the benefit of SMEs. ESA provides for example an industrial matchmaking tool called "esa-match", operates incubator centres, and organises "mapping meetings" and "industry days". ESA may also impose on the prime contractor its "Best Practices for the Selection of subcontractors by Prime Contractors in the Frame of ESA Procurements" and tie the subcontracting to the review of the Industrial Policy Committee (IPC).[3] The EU Space Programme Regulation (EU-SPR) also expressly commands the encouragement of new entrants, SMEs, and start-ups by requesting the tenderer to sub-contract part of the contract by competitive tendering. For contracts above €10 million, the contracting authority shall aim to ensure that at least 30% of the value of the contract is opened to companies outside the group of the prime tenderer.[4]

As participation in procurement procedures may be a costly and time-consuming endeavour, economic operators weighing the pros and cons should be aware that both under EU and ESA procurement rules, the contracting authority may cancel the procurement procedure without the candidates or tenderers being entitled to claim any compensation.[5]

13.3 Second element: knowing and understanding the procurement process

Public procurement procedures follow specific rules laid down in the respective procurement regulations. This is no different for procurements in the space sector. As the EU and ESA are international organisations independent from each other, they operate under different procurement regimes. Before the beginning of this century, it was sufficient for economic operators in the space sector to achieve familiarity with the ESA procurement regime. This changed with the development of the European Space Policy (ESP). The ESP started to take more and more shape from 2003 onwards. Already with the flagship programmes Galileo/EGNOS and Copernicus (former GMES), the EU performed a number of complex procurement procedures. With the Commission's expanding competence into other areas of space activities, also the number of procurements continuously grew and became more complex and versatile. Programme components aside from Galileo/EGNOS and Copernicus now cover new areas like space situational awareness, space traffic management, GOVSATCOM, and the European Quantum Computing Initiative (EUQCI).

3 ESA-PR, Art. 17 and 43(3).

4 Regulation (EU) 2021/696 of 28 April 2021, OJ L 170, 12.5.2021, pp. 69 (EU-SPR), Art. 17.

5 Regulation (EU, Euratom) 2018/1046 of 18 July 2018, OJ L 193, 30.7.2018, pp. 1 (EU-FR), Art. 171; ESA-PR, Art. 32.

Since 2021, the different programme components are addressed in the European Space Programme under the responsibility of the European Union Agency for the Space Programme (EUSPA) which was established by the EU Space Programme Regulation (EU-SPR).[6] The complex topic of secure connectivity will be addressed in an additional regulation currently in the legislative process. It makes references to the EU-SPR but also introduces additional specific provisions. While ESA may be acting as procurement agent of the EU, nevertheless the EU procurement rules apply.[7]

13.3.1 EU procurement regime

13.3.1.1 Identifying the correct procurement regime

In order to understand the EU procurement procedures for the space sector, the first step is identifying the applicable rules. The EU rules are divided into two main sections depending on the legal entity acting as contracting authority.

All procurements performed by contracting authorities of the EU Member States are regulated by the "classic" Public Procurement Directive 2014/24/EU, Concession Directive 2014/23/EU, Public Utilities Directive 2014/25/EU, and Defence and Security Procurement Directive 2009/81/EC, as well as the Review Procedures Directives as amended by 2007/66/EC for legal remedies before the national administrative and/or judicial procurement review bodies. As directives, these rules require implementation into national law in order to have legally binding effect.

In contrast, all procurements performed by EU bodies follow the procurement rules of the EU Financial Regulation (EU-FR)[8] with legal recourse to the General Court in the first and the Court of Justice of the EU in the second instance. While this regulation makes frequent reference to the mentioned directives, it constitutes an independent set of rules, binding in its entirety and directly applicable throughout the Union. The EU Space Programme Regulation contains specific modifications for the implementation of the EU Space Programme which "may provide funding in any of the forms laid down in the EU-FR, in particular [...] procurement".[9] The programme shall be implemented under direct management (i.e. by the Commission) or under indirect management by entrusted bodies. Under direct management, the EU-FR is directly applicable. Under indirect management, it is up to the Commission and the entrusted entity to agree on the procurement rules applicable: either the EU-FR or the procurement rules of the entrusted entity, provided it offers an equivalent level of protection of the EU budget. Indirect management is of particular importance for implementation of the EU Space Programme by EUSPA, ESA, and EUMETSAT. In June 2021, the Commission, EUSPA, and ESA concluded the required Financial Framework Partnership Agreement (FFPA). The agreement is not publicly available, but Recital 29 EU-SPR mentions that "procurement contracts concluded under the Programme for activities financed by the Programme should comply with Union rules". The FFPA may declare ESA rules applicable for the implementation of the Copernicus budget by ESA, but only to the extent that they ensure a level of protection of the financial interests of the Union equivalent to the one that is provided for when the Commission implements the budget through direct management. Further procurement-related provisions can be found in the Regulation of the European Parliament and of the

6 EU-SPR, Art. 1 sentence 3 and Art. 3(1).

7 EU-SPR, recital (48), Arts 28(4) and 31(1)(c).

8 Regulation (EU, Euratom) 2018/1046 of 18 July 2018, OJ L 193, 30.7.2018, pp. 1 (EU-FR).

9 EU-SPR, Art. 13(2).

Council establishing the Union Secure Connectivity Programme for the period 2023–2027 (Secure Connectivity Regulation).[10]

13.3.1.2 Participation requirements

Once a procurement procedure is identified, the interested party needs to establish its eligibly for participation. Article 176 EU-FR stipulates eligibility requirements: access to a procurement process is only "open on equal terms to all natural and legal persons within the scope of the Treaties and to all natural and legal persons established in a third country which has a special agreement with the Union in the field of procurement under the conditions laid down in such an agreement". The number of special agreements with third countries is rather large but sometimes limited to specific areas. The tender documents regularly specify the eligibility requirements relieving interested entities from researching existing agreements themselves. More relevant are eligibility restrictions in relation to the protection of security interests of the Union programmes. The Commission may rely on Art. 24 EU-SPR on a case-by-case basis when deemed "necessary and appropriate to preserve the security, integrity and resilience of the operational Union systems, taking into account the objective to promote the Union's strategic autonomy, in particular in terms of technology across key technologies and value chains, while preserving an open economy". Participation may be restricted via three cumulative requirements of establishment, venue, and control: "(a) the eligible legal entity is established in a Member State and its executive management structures are established in that Member State, (b) the eligible legal entity commits to carry out all relevant activities in one or more Member States; and (c) the eligible legal entity is not to be subject to control by a third country or by a third country entity". By covering also "indirect" control including by "intermediate legal entities" also legal entities which are ultimately controlled from outside the European Union fail to comply with the eligibility requirement. This applies for prime contractors and sub-contractors alike, unless stipulated otherwise in the tender documents on a case-by-case basis. The requirements for the shareholding structure may pose a problem for stock-traded companies especially with substantive free-floating shares. The eligibility requirements have to be complied with during the entire term of a contract.

Even if an interested entity established its non-eligibility, it may still submit a tender together with a request for waiver of the participation requirements. While adequate protection of EU classified information (EUCI) is indispensable, a waiver should only be granted if (i) for specific technologies, goods, or services needed for the activities of the tender no substitutes are readily available in the Member States, and (ii) the entity is at least established in a country which is a member of the EEA or EFTA having concluded an international agreement with the Union, its executive management structures are established in that country, and the activities linked to the procurement are carried out in that country or in one or more such countries. This eases the "establishment" and the "venue" requirement. They may be completely waived for the benefit of any third-country established tenderer where the specific technologies, goods, or services are also not available in such EEA or EFTA states. Always provided that the tenderer itself is established in a Member State, the "control" requirement may be waived, if that entity provides guarantees that

10 Regulation (EU) 2023/588 of 15 March 2023, OJ L 79, 17.3.2023, pp. 1 et seq., cf. chapter IV.

> (a) control over the legal entity is not exercised in a manner that restrains or restricts its ability to (i) carry out the procurement [...]; and (ii) deliver results, in particular through reporting obligations; (b) the controlling third country or third country entity commits to refrain from exercising any controlling rights over or imposing reporting obligations on the legal entity in relation to the procurement [...]; and (c) the legal entity complies with Article 34(7) [ensuring compliance with the programme security requirements].

Assessment of the guarantees and measures for ensuring protection of EUCI lies with the Member State of establishment. Its findings are binding for the Commission.

The availability requirement is difficult to assess and predict for the individual tenderer, as it is put to the test in light of tenders received. This can be considered the viable market test and shows how the market responds to the request to tender. The merely theoretical availability of technology, goods, or services from entities established in Member States or an EEA or EFTA country with respective agreements but without actual tenders covering that aspect should not be sufficient to constitute a viable availability and should open the door for a complete waiver of this requirement. Alternatively, the contracting authority may abandon the procedure and relaunch with changed requirements for which it may hope to receive tenders from Member States, EEA, or EFTA established entities.

13.3.1.3 Understanding the general procurement principles

Public procurement under the EU rules is based on five general principles:

- equal treatment,
- non-discrimination,
- mutual recognition,
- proportionality, and
- transparency.[11]

These principles derive from the EU Treaty, and their understanding is fundamental for comprehending basic demands and the framework of public procurement procedures. It also helps to spot mistakes that may adversely affect an economic operator's position.

The principle of equal treatment is based on the idea that equal characteristics also have to be treated equally. The procurement regulations must be applied equally to all candidates/tenderers, especially in situations where the contracting authority offers clarifications, enters into negotiations, or assesses exclusion grounds.

The principle of non-discrimination goes one step further. It means that even when there are some aspects of differentiation between candidates or tenderers and tenders, these differences may not be taken into account but instead have to be disregarded in a procurement process.

The principle of mutual recognition guarantees free movement of goods and services without the need to harmonise EU Member States' national legislation. Goods that are lawfully produced in one Member State cannot be banned from sale on the territory of another Member State, even if they are produced according to different technical or quality specifications. The only exceptions allowed are those of overriding general interest such as health, consumer, or environmental

11 EU-FR, Art. 160.

protection. The same principle applies to services.[12] Transferred to a public procurement scenario, the contracting authority generally has to recognise requirements and standards for products and services established in one EU Member State as equivalent to those of another EU Member State. EU bodies may generally not require the fulfilment of standards of a specific EU Member State.

The principle of proportionality can be considered a result of the buyer power that contracting authorities regularly have and as a counterweight of the contracting authorities' right to define the subject matter and requirements. The principle forbids excessive requirements that curb fair competition and go beyond what is necessary in order to satisfy the particular procurement need.[13] The use of policy criteria for public procurement procedures in the space sector has to be handled cautiously. The geographic distribution system of ESA would not be compatible with EU law already for reasons of public procurement law. The EU resorts to "softer" measures to encourage "cross-border participation" and to offer "the widest possible geographical coverage" via imposing competitive tendering at various levels on the prime contractor. The EU may adopt multiple sourcing to avoid reliance on a single provider, ensure better overall control of the programme components, or to foster innovations.[14]

The principle of transparency requires the contracting authority to document the entire procurement process in real time and in an objectively conceivable manner, even before initiating the procurement vis-à-vis third parties. Defining the detailed procurement needs is essential for the preparation of the tender documents, from which the tenderer has to be able to ascertain all substantial conditions for submitting his proposal. The high demands are often underestimated by contracting authorities. This especially concerns documentation of contacts with tenderers, including keeping of minutes of negotiation meetings. Another common mistake is the insufficient disclosure of evaluation criteria. All aspects that factor into the evaluation of tenders have to be communicated either initially with the contract notice or with the tender documentations/specifications at the latest.[15] The evaluation method, such as a formula or scale, for ranking the tenders, does not need to be disclosed,[16] although this is still done in practice. A later change of the weighting of already communicated evaluation criteria or sub-criteria is permissible only under three cumulative conditions: first, that the ex-post determination does not alter the criteria for the award of the contract set out in the contract documents or the contract notice; second, it does not contain elements that, if they had been known at the time the tenders were prepared, could have affected that preparation; and, third, it was not adopted on the basis of matters likely to give rise to discrimination against one of the tenderers.[17]

13.3.1.4 Understanding the different procurement procedures

EU bodies in principle apply five different procurement procedures: the open, the restricted, the negotiated procedure, including without prior publication of a contract notice, the competitive procedure with negotiation, the competitive dialogue, and the innovation partnership.

Rules for conducting procurement under application of the open procedure are mainly found in Art. 164(2) and (5)(a) EU-FR. The contracting authority publishes a contract notice, and every interested economic operator may then request the tender conditions and the respective draft con-

12 COM(1999) 299 final of 16 June 1999, p. 4.

13 EU-FR, Annex I point 18.2 sentence 2; EU General Court, 2 March 2010, Case T-70/05 – *Evropaïki Dynamiki.*

14 EU-FR, Arts 14, para. 1 (b) and (c), 17, 20 para. 2 (c).

15 EU-FR, Annex I point 9.4 ; ECJ, 12 December 2002, Case C-470/99 – *Universale-Bau AG.*

16 ECJ, 14 July 2016, Case C-6/15 – *TNS Dimarso NV.*

17 ECJ, 24 January 2008, Case C-532/06 – *Emm. G. Lianakis AE.*

tract to be provided to it. Sometimes, these documents are already included in the contract notice or at least a link for download from the internet. Any economic operator may submit its offer, which then has to be evaluated by the contracting authority according to the published selection and evaluation criteria. The open procedure does not allow negotiations and is less suitable for complex procurement objects, which often can only be performed or delivered by a limited number of specialised economic operators.

Rules for the restricted procedure are located mainly in Art. 164(3) and (5)(a) and Annex I point 6.1 EU-FR. Calls for tenders may be restricted – hence the name – to a minimum of five economic operators which satisfy the pre-defined selection criteria published in the contract notice. Non-discriminating criteria are to be applied in order to achieve the announced reduction of tenderers, should more than the minimum number of five apply. The selected number of candidates then has to be invited simultaneously and in writing by the contracting authorities to submit their tenders. In case the minimum number of candidates is not participating, the contracting authority may still continue the procedure by inviting those candidates that applied and have the required capacities. This procedure is, together with the open procedure, the default procurement process to which contracting authorities have recourse. The possibility under the restricted procedure to reduce the number of candidates/tenderers down to five poses an advantage over the open procedure in situations where a high number of interested economic operators is likely to participate. Still no negotiations with the tenderers are permitted.

The negotiated procedure without prior publication of a contract notice and the competitive procedure with negotiations are regulated mainly in Art. 164(3), (4), (5)(e), and (f) and Annex I points 6, 11, and 12 EU-FR. In contrast to the open and the restricted procedures, the negotiated procedure without prior publication of a contract notice and the competitive procedure with negotiations may only be applied under enumerated conditions.[18] The contract notice for the competitive procedure with negotiations may set a maximum number of economic operators to be selected for participation as candidates, generally not less than three. The selection criteria have to be indicated in the procurement documents in accordance with the principle of transparency. Neither the requested nor any other selection criteria may be further regarded in the evaluation of the criteria for establishing the best value for money regarding the different tenders. It is an established judgment of the ECJ that the criteria for selection of economic operators and the criteria forming the basis for the award of the contract have to be clearly separated. Selection criteria may only be regarded in the selection process and award criteria may only regarded in the evaluation process.[19] The two groups of criteria can be differentiated in the following way: selection criteria typically concern the personal traits and characteristics of the economic operator important for its ability to perform the contract at all; award criteria are tender-related with regard to establishing the quality and price of the offered goods, service, or works necessary for determining the best value for money. In case the number of economic operators fulfilling the selection criteria exceeds the maximum number announced in the contract notice, the contracting authority ranks the candidates on the basis of objective, non-discriminatory selection criteria. The details of the procedure to shortlist the candidates must be indicated in the contract notice. One possibility commonly used in practice lies in grading the selection criteria and announcing in the contract notice that only, e.g., three, economic operators with the most points will be invited to the negotiations. The grading as outcome of the selection process must not be taken into account in the evaluation process.

18 EU-FR, Art. 164(3) sentence 3.

19 EU-FR, Annex I points 18 and 21; ECJ, 20 September 1988, Case C-31/87 – *Gebroeders Beentjes*; 25 March 2015, Case C-601/13 – *Ambisig*.

Following the selection of the economic operators in accordance to this procedure, the contracting authority invites the selected candidates to submit an initial tender as basis for negotiations. It may opt to award the contract on the basis of the initial tender only where it has expressly reserved the possibility to do so. Negotiations have to be conducted within the main cornerstones set by the contracting authority in the contract notice or the specification. These may not be changed as they motivated tenderers to apply for participation in the first place. The same is true for the evaluation criteria, which also have to be disclosed in their entirety, including any sub-criteria, previously in the tender documents. The contracting authority may choose to perform the negotiations in consecutive stages. Following each stage, economic operators may be eliminated from further participation by application of the award criteria published in the contract notice or the specifications. When making use of the possibility of reduction, genuine competition has nevertheless to be ensured, insofar as the number of appropriate solutions or candidates allows. The negotiation process is advantageous to the contracting authority as well as to the economic operators in complex projects. The possibility to directly negotiate provides better possibilities for the contracting authority to achieve the procurement objective that best satisfies its needs. The economic operators may better fine-tune their offer and present it in the most favourable way. However, as economic operators are frequently required during the procurement procedure to grant the contracting authority deep insights into the company (e.g., financial data, technical expertise, clients, and previous projects) and its product portfolio and innovative solutions (e.g., confidential technical data, new technology), the contracting authority must not disclose any of the information exchanged with one competitor to the other competitors. Accordingly, the economic operator should clearly mark documents with sensitive content as confidential.

Rules for the competitive dialogue procedure are laid down in Art. 164(3), (4), and (5)(e) and Annex I points 6.2, 10, and 12 EU-FR. The procedure may only be applied under enumerated conditions listed in Annex I point 12 EU-FR. Formally, the competitive procedure with negotiations and the competitive dialogue have become alternatives but generally, they are still tools for two different scenarios. In the competitive procedure with negotiations (and also the negotiated procedure without prior contract notice) the solution (the technical specifications) can be established, but not sufficiently clear for comparable offers, while in the competitive dialogue the solution has yet to be found, for instance with regard to technical specifications. This possibility of choice by the contracting authority to use either the competitive procedure with negotiations or the competitive dialogue procedure should not be underestimated for achieving a successful, timely, and cost-efficient procurement process. Especially the use of the competitive dialogue procedure should be considered with caution. Practical experiences with the competitive dialogue in the procurement of six lots for the European global satellite navigation project Galileo showed that the competitive dialogue procedure can be much more demanding on all participants than the competitive procedure with negotiations. The complexity is – at least for some part – due to the special nature of the dialogue procedure, which in essence is a mixture between first the competitive procedure with negotiations followed by a restricted procedure between the remaining candidates. Like the competitive procedure with negotiations, the competitive dialogue procedure may be structured in consecutive phases in which the candidates enter into a dialogue. Once the contracting authority decides that one or more of the proposed tender solutions could fulfil its procurement needs, it may request the candidates to submit their best and final offer (BAFO) for evaluation in accordance with the pre-defined criteria.[20] During the BAFO phase no further negotiations are allowed. There

20 EU-FR, Annex I point 10.3 sentences 1, 2, and 3.

is still the possibility to request clarifications; however, this must not change the pre-set parameters of the procurement process.[21] The competitive dialogue procedure shares the particular difficulties of the competitive procedure. In addition, the rules of the BAFO phase somewhat reduce the flexibility of negotiations and increase the demand to closely follow requirements of secrecy. The latter may collide with the necessity to draft specific conditions of tender for the BAFO phase which, on the one hand, have to adhere to the pre-set framework requirements of the initial contract notice and specifications, while taking into account the developments and insights achieved during the dialogue phase and, at the same time, safeguarding the secrecy of competition. With these particularities the involved economic operators have to be especially cautious to protect their economic interests and to safeguard against unwanted dissemination of their confidential information.

The innovation partnership is mainly regulated in Art. (5)(d) and Annex I point 7 EU-FR. The contracting authority may use the innovation partnership as a procurement procedure where research and development efforts are required to develop an innovative product, service, or innovative works and to subsequently purchase the developed results but only when the desired works, supplies, and services do not exist on the market or as a near-to-market development activity. This is ensured by conducting a preliminary market consultation before launching a procurement subject to this procedure. The EU can contract with multiple partners and give the early commitment to subsequently purchase the product, service, or innovative works from the partner who develops the most innovative solution. It is divided into two phases: firstly, the research and development phase and secondly, the acquisition phase. Prior publication of the contract notice and all tender documents is required, and a minimum of three candidates shall be invited. After negotiation rounds which may take place in successive stages, the candidates submit their final project plans and the contracting authority chooses the candidate(s) based solely on the best price-quality ratio. The innovation partnership places high demands on the contracting authority when drafting the underlying contract. It will have to serve all stages of the partnership and to also provide for termination scenarios. For the latter, specific rules for use of results and related background intellectual property rights (IPR) have to be put in place. The contracting authority usually has an interest in being able to use results for which it may also have already paid while the economic operator may likewise be interested in maintaining such rights for its business. This topic accordingly requires a likewise demanding payment scheme which ensures efficient use of resources and best value for money throughout the life of the partnership, including potential break off events. This complexity may on the other hand provide an advantage of the process, as it allows funded research and development with a potential anchor customer at the end. The legally binding early-commitment of the contracting authority to enter the acquisition phase, if and once the development targets are achieved, may be the mosaic stone necessary to attract private investment. An innovation partnership with multiple partners in parallel may also be a good way of allowing dual sourcing and establishing a more diverse market. But it may also substantially increase costs, which can however be justified with proper exploitation rights in place for the parties involved.

13.3.2 The ESA Procurement Regulations

The original procurement rules of ESA, implemented between 1978 and 1982, were extensively reformed in 2010.[22] The current revision of the Procurement Regulations and related Implementing

21 EU-FR, Annex I point 10.3 sentence 4.
22 ESA/C-M/CCVI/Res. 4 (Final) Page 5.

Instructions (ESA-PR) was adopted on 14 June 2019 during the 282nd Council Meeting and entered into force on 12 July 2019.[23]

13.3.2.1 Procurement principles

The ESA Procurement Regulations are based on the general principles laid down in Art. 10 ESA-PR. The ESA procurement rules as well as the placing of contracts shall always be interpreted so as to ensure transparency and fair and equitable treatment of all economic operators. These principles are however subject to interpretation in the light of the ESA Convention as well as the other principles and regulations of the ESA-PR. In particular Art. 10.1(d) ESA-PR ensures the prerogative of the industrial policy and implementation of the geographical return principle of Art. VII and Annex V of the ESA Convention.

Activities in the space sector are not restricted to private economic operators. Many public bodies, such as public research organisations or national space agencies, participate frequently as tenderers in ESA Projects. It is therefore noteworthy that ESA in Art. 10.1(b) ESA-PR has explicitly implemented the principle "that the participation of a Tendering Body does not cause any distortion of competition in relation to private economic operators". As the term "Tendering Body" – according to the regulation's list of definitions in Art. 2 ESA-PR – is understood as "a public body (including intergovernmental organizations) acting as potential contractor", the principle in Art. 10.1(b) ESA-PR requires the participation of such public bodies in ESA procurement projects to be restricted to cases in which competition in relation to private economic operators is not distorted. As this principle is clearly meant to protect the interests of private economic operators, it may be argued that any violation of this principle may give rise to a procurement review process under the ESA-PR.

13.3.2.2 Supplier lists and prequalification

The Agency maintains a supplier list through the esa-star Registration module.[24] Prior registration in the electronic supplier list remains a pre-condition for participation in any ESA procurement process, which in principle is open to all economic operators who are considered to belong to one of the Member States, Associate Member States, or Cooperating States of ESA with which the Agency may have made respective arrangements.

The question whether an economic operator belongs to one of the mentioned states may be determined by reference to Art. II.3 of Annex V of the ESA Convention. Most other requirements under Art. 18.1 ESA-PR concern an economic operator's general state of business and may be considered standard requirements for participation in public procurement procedures. The exclusion criteria under Art. 18.1(b) and 18.2 ESA-PR are problematic as general pre-qualification requirements (e.g., professional and technical qualifications, professional and technical competences, and the personnel to perform a contract, etc.) may vary from case to case.

Registered economic operators are obliged to update their entries at least once a year and in any case immediately should material changes occur. Failure to update the information results in the contract not being awarded. Any new application to the electronic register should be initiated well in advance before the actual procurement participation.

23 ESA/REG/001, rev. 5, Paris, 10 July 2019.

24 ESA-PR, Art. 18.3.

13.3.2.3 Procurement methods

The ESA Procurement Regulations in its Part II enumerates the procurement methods that are further detailed in Part IV: competitive tendering, non-competitive tendering, and two-stage tendering. Furthermore, the implementing instructions contained in the Annexes to the ESA-PR should be considered.

The term "competitive tendering" encompasses the so-called open competitive tender as well as the so-called restricted competitive tender, as further outlined in Annex III Part II. The open competitive tender "shall be the normal procedure for the placing of contracts" and any economic operator registered in the Agency's electronic tool dedicated to procurement (esa-star) should have the possibility to submit a tender.[25] This is however subject to the principles laid down in Art. 10 ESA-PR, most notably ESA's industrial policy, the overarching principle of geographic return and, possibly, restrictions of the participation of public bodies as tenderers in cases where this may lead to a distortion of competition toward the private economic operators. The restricted competitive tender is applied under the conditions enumerated under Art. 13.2 ESA-PR. The number of economic operators may be restricted to at least three. The reason for applying the restriction and the choice of the economic operators must be recorded in the contracts file.

Non-competitive tendering may be resorted to only in a limited number of cases provided in Art. 14.1(a)–(g) ESA-PR and is further outlined in Annex III Part III. As deduced from the non-application of Art. 42 ESA-PR in accordance with Art. 14.6 ESA-PR, negotiation in non-competitive tendering may be conducted without restriction. The non-competitive tendering is not ESA's pendant to the EU's competitive procedure with negotiations, as the latter requires the contracting authority to maintain a measure of competition. Instead, the non-competitive tendering under ESA-PR opens the possibility of direct procurement in the absence of any competition, more like the negotiated procedure without prior publication of a contract notice for cases with only one tenderer. ESA may invoke the waiver of competitive tendering in cases of urgency even if caused by the Agency itself.

The two-stage tendering is essentially a competitive dialogue procedure and ESA uses this term in the text further describing the process. Much like the competitive dialogue procedure under the EU procurement rules, two-stage tendering may be chosen in cases where ESA considers that it is not feasible to formulate detailed specifications for the supplies or where necessary inputs from economic operators are needed to detail these specifications.

The process of two-stage tendering provides for the possibility to enter into a dialogue with selected candidates and to thereby improve the tender specifications for which the selected candidates may then submit their offers. It also allows ESA a staggered approach during which the number of candidates may be consecutively reduced as the definition of the procurement object progresses through successive tendering rounds. This allows ESA to uphold competition far into the procurement procedure, which may be of particular interest for SMEs who may be provided with the opportunity to develop and present innovative solutions that otherwise would not have been taken into account.

A longer duration of the procurement procedure also binds resources of the bidding team of the economic operator. According to Art. 32 ESA-PR the ESA Directorate General may cancel an "Invitation to Tender" at any time. Such cancellation may not give rise to any claims by the economic operator. The Glossary of the ESA-PR defines the term "Invitation to Tender" as a formal

25 ESA-PR, Arts 13.1, 27.

communication to economic operators containing the conditions for the submission together with specifications and requirements and inviting them to submit tenders for a contract. It is questionable whether the waiver in Art. 32.2 ESA-PR may extend to costs incurred during stages of negotiations in a non-competitive tendering or to costs of the second stage of a two-stage tendering process as these costs may be regarded as incurred at stages following the initial "Invitation to Tender". It is also questionable whether such an extensive waiver would stand under applicable national law with regard to pre-contractual relations.

ESA requires itself to set out the particular needs and requirements in its solicitation documents. It provides interested parties with the necessary background information on whether the particular tender could be of interest for them. This allows a focused use of resources, provided that the particular needs and requirements are not substantially changed during the course of the procurement procedure. The possibility for such drastic changes is provided for in Art. 16.4 ESA-PR. ESA, at the beginning of the second stage of a two-stage tendering, may even change the previously announced evaluation criteria, in contrast to the rule of Art. 25.7 ESA-PR, which prohibits the change of once approved evaluation criteria. This may lead to discrimination of economic operators who should in turn be especially vigilant that the principle of fair and equitable treatment as laid down in Art. 10.1(a) ESA-PR is upheld.

13.4 Third element: writing a successful tender

Writing a successful tender often is demanding. The required resources for submitting the tender should be carefully considered before entering into the procurement process and in case the costs for the preparation of the tender are not properly calculated in the tender price, an already slim profit margin may melt to an unacceptable level.

13.4.1 Meticulous and systematic analysis – allocation of resources

The respective economic operator has to obtain and meticulously analyse all tender documents. This is preferably done by persons having much experience with public procurement procedures. Drawing on external expertise is generally advisable already in this early stage as the later rectification of a tender process gone wrong usually proves time consuming and demanding on the budget, if possible at all.

The applicable procurement procedure has to be identified and all relevant time periods and deadlines (e.g., for asking clarification questions, submission of application documents, proposals for negotiations, etc.) have to be put down in a diagram/timetable. All information and documents to be submitted, as well as the required manner of submission, must be identified and laid down in a table. It should be possible to already estimate some basic demands of the procurement at hand and to plan for adequate resources both with regard to personnel as well as budget. Regarding personnel, the team for preparation of the tender and subsequent negotiations has to be built up and made available when needed. This includes careful planning, also regarding vacations and – if necessary – mandating external advisors and experts sufficiently ahead of time. Also important, especially for larger procurements, is careful and efficient document management. It has proven beneficial for the preparation of a tender to implement an efficient document management system right from the beginning of the tender process, as this can greatly improve coordination and use of resources.

A careful analysis of the contract notice and specifications often identifies questions. It may prove risky to refrain from demanding clarifications and instead to try and solve suspected uncertainties with one's own interpretations. Questions may also be a potent tool for spinning ambiguities in a favourable direction and should be strategically relied upon. The same is generally true for suspected violations of the applicable public procurement rules. The contracting authority should be directly approached and asked to remedy the situation. Any undue delay on the side of the economic operator in this respect may block it from seeking effective legal remedy at a later stage.

13.4.2 Negotiations

The negotiations team has to be selected ahead of time and their availability for the meetings ensured. It should be composed of experienced members from all relevant disciplines which may become a topic in the respective negotiations. It is advisable to always have a person experienced in public procurement regulations, as well as contractual matters, participate in every negotiation meeting: this enables the economic operator to safeguard its interests, including the direct detection and reaction to violations of procurement rules. As already mentioned regarding the procurement procedures, the economic operator should always insist on the keeping of official minutes and, if possible, should keep minutes itself in order to provide a cross-reference in case of disputes.

13.4.3 Submission of the tender

When acting in an open or a restricted procedure, as well as in the competitive dialogue process, the submission of the tender always marks the point of no return. With the submission, the tender leaves the economic operator's sphere of influence and changes are no longer possible. This calls for an extra careful last check of all the tender documents.

The last but nonetheless crucial step is the timely submission of the tender to the designated address. Any false ambitions for savings in this respect can turn out to be catastrophic, as any delivery after the given deadline leads to the rejection of the tender, if the delay was caused in the tenderer's sphere of influence.

13.5 Defending the own interests

The complexity of public procurement holds a substantial risk that the rules may not be properly implemented by the contracting authority and that underlying procurement principles may be disregarded. Once the economic operator spots mistakes, it should be aware of the measures at its disposal to defend its interests. Depending on whether the procurement is implemented under the ESA or the EU procurement rules, these measures and the requirements for their use are quite different from each other.

13.5.1 Legal remedies in EU procurement procedures

The EU procurement law requires the Member States to establish effective legal remedy provisions for review of public procurement procedures. It is one of the very rare occasions that EU law prescribes procedural aspects for legal remedies on the national level in the Member States, but this was deemed necessary due to the peculiarities of procurement procedures. The core idea of the review system is to strike a balance between the interests of the contracting authority, the public, the successful bidder, and the frustrated bidder by ensuring that a review could be undertaken "as rapidly as possible" prior to the award of a contract.[26] Once the contract is awarded, its effectiveness should – in general – be upheld and the applicant may settle for compensation of any damages. Due to their legal nature as directives, these provisions are directly only binding for the Member States and therefore only applicable to procurement procedure of their respective national contracting authorities and to the national review tribunals. The legal remedies directive, however, is held by the ECJ to give specific expression to the general principle of EU law enshrining the right to an effective remedy in the particular field of public procurement. It must therefore be taken into consideration as regards the EU's own procurement procedures.[27]

Nonetheless, the review system for procurement by the EU has a different set-up than in the Member States. The participant of an EU procurement procedure has mainly three options: (1) to raise the violations of procurement rules with the contracting authority, (2) to file a complaint with the European Ombudsman, or (3) to initiate proceedings before the General Court of the EU.

In contrast to the review system established by the legal remedies directive for the Member States where frustrated may be precluded from raising an issue later on, there is currently no formal requirement to raise objections without undue delay for EU procurements. However, asking clarification questions, hinting at necessary changes to the tender documents, or raising objections against irregularities and violations of procurement rules as early as possible, are a practical approach to convince the contracting authority of amendments. The earlier in the procurement process, the easier it is for the contracting authority to rectify errors or cancel the procedure and re-start from scratch. Once the award decision is made, the forces of persistence are strong.

According to Art. 228 TFEU every Union citizen or legal person with registered offices in a Member State may file a complaint with the European Ombudsman concerning instances of maladministration. Such a complaint becomes time-barred only after two years of the date on which the facts came to the attention of the complainant.[28] So, there is plenty of time, the period usually starting with receipt of the information of the outcome of the tender procedures and the reasons for rejecting one's own tender. The European Ombudsman is empowered to make thorough inquiries and to report on maladministration to the EU institutions. While violations of procurement rules may be uncovered, and the authority concerned may draw the necessary consequences in the end, such as termination of a contract or lessons learned for the next procedure, the duration of the process is hardly suitable to achieve results with regards to the disputed procedure, in particular to secure the claimant's chance to overturn the award decision and to receive the contract instead.

Only the initiation of legal proceedings before the General Court of the EU offers the opportunity to suspend the procurement procedure and to halt the award of the contract to a competitor. Due to the lack of specific review provisions, economic operators have recourse to the general remedies against actions of EU bodies provided in the Treaty on the Functioning of the European Union (TFEU). Economic operators may initiate proceedings for annulment against decisions of the EU body responsible for the respective procurement. If the action is well founded, the act subject to the proceedings may be declared void. This offers the possibility for annulment of any award decision taken in breach of the EU procurement rules. Additionally or alternatively, a claim for compensation may be brought before the court for any damage caused by the EU's institutions or by its servants in the performance of their duties.

26 Directive 89/665/EEC as amended by Directive 2007/66/EC, Art. 1(1) subpara. 4.

27 ECJ, 23 April 2015, Case C-35/15 P(R) – *Vanbreda Risk & Benefits*.

28 Regulation (EU, Euratom) 2021/1163 of 24 June 2021, Art. 2(3).

These general remedies of the TFEU were not specifically designed for the needs of public procurement procedures. Most noteworthy is the fact that actions have no automatic suspending effect.[29] A procurement process may continue after an action is filed with the consequence that the contract subject to the contested action may have already been awarded before a judgment is passed. This can only be prevented by the Court which may order the suspension the contested procurement procedure, for example the signing of the contract.[30] Such an interim measure was only a theoretical possibility until 2015, when the ECJ eventually recognised that its jurisprudence lead to a Kafkaesque situation: for an interim measure on the one hand, it is necessary to establish that such an order is *prima facie* justified and that it is urgent in order to avoid serious and irreparable harm. On the other hand, settled case law held that actions in procurement matters are of a pecuniary nature. There was no irreparable harm because pecuniary compensation could restore the aggrieved person to the situation before suffering the damage.[31] Since then, the situation has somewhat improved. The lack of procedural provisions specific to procurement matters is remedied to a certain extent by Courts' increased sensitivity. Concerning the procurement of Galileo satellites by ESA in the name and on behalf of the EU, an aggrieved bidder brought an action for annulment and an application for interim measures before the signing of the contract. Within two days, the President of the General Court ordered the preliminary suspension at least as long as the Court needed to decide on the interim measures. The application for interim measures was rejected in the end and the contract could be awarded,[32] but the case shows that there is now a way to suspend the procurement procedure before a factual situation is created that leaves the frustrated bidder only with a claim for compensation.

13.5.2 Legal remedies and reviews in ESA procurement procedures

The ESA Procurement Regulations provided economic operators for the first time with the possibility to call for a review process for alleged breach of the procurement rules. Located in Part VI of the Procurement Regulations, the review is designed as a multi-step process.

13.5.2.1 Structure of the ESA review process

According to Article 51.1 ESA-PR, the Head of the Procurement Department acts as a first instance for any review process. In cases where a decision by the Head of the Procurement Department is challenged, the claim may be directly referred to the Industrial Ombudsman. In other cases of review, the Industrial Ombudsman may be contacted if the Head of the Procurement Department has not made a decision for a period of ten days after the claim has been brought before it. It is important to note that the Industrial Ombudsman does not act as a second instance but may only be requested to give recommendations for measures to be taken by the Head of the Procurement Department in the review process. This rule nevertheless substantially broadens the responsibility of the Industrial Ombudsman who formerly had no function regarding actions of ESA but acted only as a mediator for disputes between primes and subcontractors in ESA procurements.

29 TFEU, Art. 278.
30 TFEU, Arts 278 and 279.
31 ECJ, 23 April 2015, Case C-35/15 P(R) – *Vanbreda Risk & Benefits*.
32 EU General Court, 26 May 2021, Case T-54/21 R – *OHB System AG*.

Article 54 ESA-PR establishes the Procurement Review Board (PRB) as second instance. The PRB consists of six independent members external to ESA with proven legal and practical experience in the field of public procurement, with two members being selected by the ESA Director General, two members being selected by industry, and two members being selected by the Chairman of the Industrial Policy Committee (IPC). The Director General established detailed implementing instructions concerning the establishment and the proceedings of the PRB, included in Annex V to the ESA-PR. The decisions of the PRB are final and binding on the parties.

13.5.2.2 Personal right to review

The right to review under Art. 48 ESA-PR is open to any economic operator who is not merely acting as a sub-contractor, who can demonstrate a direct interest in the particular ESA procurement, and who claims a potential loss due to an alleged breach of the ESA-PR by ESA. It is up to the economic operator to be aware of the procedural aspects of and to make use of such right to review. ESA regularly fulfils its duty of transparency by making a reference to the review procedure in the tender documents.[33]

13.5.2.3 Exclusion of certain decisions from review

ESA also excludes a number of material decisions which may not be subject to review procedures, such as the choice of the applicable procurement procedure, the decision to suspend the procurement process, and generally any decisions of the IPC with regard to the award of the contract.[34]

By excluding the choice of the procurement process from review, ESA may increase its flexibility to structure the entire procurement process and influence the involvement of bidders and, therefore, the extent of competition in the procurement at hand. Further influence on the procurement process is gained with the dominant prerogative of the IPC's decisions regarding the award of contracts. Consequently, any policy decisions in the procurement process are excluded from review, allowing the IPC to virtually structure any procurement process in accordance with policy decisions. Furthermore, technical issues are excluded from the PRB's competence.[35]

13.5.2.4 Duration of a review process and deadlines

With speedy finalisation of public procurement projects in mind, ESA has taken measures to shorten the duration of review procedures. The result is extremely short time periods for reaction and filing against violations of the ESA procurement regulations.

According to Art. 50 ESA-PR, any alleged breach of ESA procurement rules that was apparent prior to the closing date and time stated in the invitation to tender (ITT) must be filed prior to that date and time, or, if the breach was not apparent before that time and date, no later than ten calendar days after the breach became apparent. Following the opening of the tender, another ten calendar days' deadline for claims based on an alleged breach of the procurement regulation is set in motion on the day the claimant knew or should have known the basis for the claim.[36]

33 ESA PRB Decision, Case 06/2022.
34 ESA-PR, Art. 49.2(a), (b), and (c); ESA PRB Decision, Case 03/2017.
35 ESA PRB Decision, Case 04/2017.
36 ESA PRB Decision, Case 06/2022.

The Head of the Procurement Department is given a period of ten calendar days after having received a claim to issue its decision. Following the decision of the Head of the Procurement Department the claimant has merely another five calendar days to decide whether to challenge it. The decision is then transferred to the Industrial Ombudsman who will offer a written recommendation within ten calendar days. Following that, the Head of the Procurement Department has another ten calendar days to issue a written decision to the claimant who may – again within five calendar days following its receipt – challenge this decision by submitting it to the PRB. If a claim to the PRB was submitted after the deadline due to circumstances beyond the claimant's control, the PRB may still admit it. The PRB may make a final decision within 15 to a maximum of 30 calendar days.

In sum a procurement review under the ESA-PR may take from 55 up to 70 calendar days to be concluded if all stages of the review process are involved.

13.5.2.5 Suspension of the contracts award

The initiation of a procurement review under the ESA-PR does not by itself suspend the contracts award process. Instead, the suspension has to be proposed on a case-by-case basis to the General Director by the Head of the Procurement Department, the Industrial Ombudsman, or the PRB.

For a suspension of the procurement process by the Director General, the claimant must demonstrate that it will suffer irreparable injury in the absence of a suspension, that it is probable that it will succeed, and that the granting of the suspension would not cause disproportionate harm to ESA.[37] As Art. 1 No. 4 of Annex V ESA-PR further clarifies, any decision by the Director General not to follow an interim measure recommended by the Board shall in no case constitute the basis for a further claim by the claimant, constituting the Director General's decision to reject a request for interim measures as final.

While the demands for suspension may be high and the claimant only has a single attempt to achieve its goal, any economic operator who has made the decision to file for review should seriously consider, at the same time, applying for the suspension of the procurement process in order to maintain the maximum effect of the review process.

13.5.2.6 Costs reimbursement and compensation

Costs incurred by ESA during a procurement review are regularly not levied on the claimant, unless the claimant was acting in bad faith. This is regardless of the outcome of the process.[38] In case the decision of ESA is upheld by the PRB, the claimant will not be reimbursed for his costs.[39]

There are, however, currently no particular rules available on how far ESA would compensate the costs of the claimant should it succeed – other than those provided in Art. 57 ESA-PR. This rule puts a cap of €100,000 on any compensation that the claimant may receive from ESA for the loss or injury suffered due to a procedural breach of the procurement regulation, including the costs for tender preparation and the costs incurred for the review procedure. Regarding such monetary damages, the cap of €100,000 applies to any compensation for loss or injury suffered due to the procedural breach of the procurement rules.

37 ESA-PR, Art. 56.2; ESA PRB, Case 02/2016.
38 ESA-PR, Art. 55.7.
39 ESA PRB Decision, Case 01/2012.

Considering that the costs for preparation of a tender alone may easily exceed the mentioned cap many times, this low limit for compensation may effectively discourage economic operators from initiating review procedures, which at the end only leave them with even greater costs. This, however, underlines the importance of a motion for suspension of the procurement process, by which the economic operator may not only prevent the award of the contract to its competitor, but ultimately preserve the chance that the contract is awarded to it.

13.6 Conclusion and outlook

The EU as well as ESA employ complex rules for their procurement efforts. However, the two organisations are acting on different backgrounds, with historically different policies.

ESA is very much driven by the industrial policy of its Member States and acting on the background of the geographical distribution principle. The EU operates on the background of the EU Treaties, is bound by the goal of creating and sustaining the functioning of the common market, most notably under the principle of fair and non-discriminatory competition. These different backgrounds influence the two organisations' procurement regulations. The ESA procurement regulations underline the prerogative of the Industrial Policy Committee, and its procurements may be influenced by policy decisions. The EU procurement rules are focused on competition and call for the adherence of strict rules in all stages of the procurement process.

A thorough understanding of the procurement rules of both organisations is not easily obtained, and the sheer complexity of the procurement regulations may be overwhelming. While both procurement regimes offer some measures of protection for the tenderers' interests through review procedures, none of these procedures is particularly effective. This underlines that any larger procurement project requires meticulous planning by both the contracting authorities and the candidates/tenderers in order to avoid mistakes from happening and allow an effective use of resources.

With the increase of space activities by the EU under the evolving European Space Policy, it can be expected that the EU's procurement actions in the space sector will steadily increase. It will be interesting to observe how the EU procurement regime evolves to deal with the specialities of this sector.

14

PROCUREMENT BY ESA IN TIMES OF PANDEMIC CRISES

Stefano M. Fiorilli

14.1 Introduction

Article VII of the Convention of the European Space Agency[1] (ESA, Agency) provides that "[t]he industrial policy which the Agency is to elaborate and apply [...] shall be designed in particular to: [...] improve the world-wide competitiveness of European industry by maintaining and developing space technology and by encouraging the rationalisation and development of an industrial structure appropriate to market requirements, making use in the first place of the existing industrial potential of all Member States".

This part of the fundamental mandate conferred to the Agency by its founders has often led to ESA's position as being depicted at the crossroads of political mandates and industrial realities.

As a matter of fact, the components of such crossroads and their intrinsic dynamics also command for ESA's implementing postures to evolve accordingly.

An example of such implementation has been ESA's rather unique regime regarding how intellectual property rights (IPR) generated under ESA contracts are dealt with: IPR vest in the economic operator who has generated them, and ESA, the Member States, and "persons and bodies" thereunder are entitled to a licence. The licence is free of charge when the IPR are used for the Agency's own requirements; it is granted on "favourable conditions" (i.e. it is charged, but taking into due account the initial funding by ESA) if the IPR are used for Member States' own national requirements; it is granted at market conditions for any other use. There are some exceptions (Operational IP, Open Source licensing, etc.). Background IPR, the choice of using them under an ESA contract being the operator's, are typically protected to the maximum extent, allowing the Agency's ultimate objectives to be achieved.

Another example has been the constant evolution of the ESA procurement process in a way that would secure a level playing field for all categories of economic operators (Large System Integrators, Midcaps, SMEs). In line with a continuously updated "taxonomy" of the European industry, procurement actions can be – and are – tailored through requirements (sometimes erected

1 Convention for the establishment of a European Space Agency (CSE/CS(73)19, rev.7), signed on 30 May 1975, entered into force on 30 October 1980.

DOI: 10.4324/9781003268475-19

at the level of "Key Acceptance Factors") that must be complied with by bidders in the preparation of their offers and the composition of their industrial consortium.

But that dynamism of the process must also stand for adapting to changing global or macro-economic contexts, and these last years have seen two emerging developments of that kind: the outbreak of the COVID-19 pandemic and the scarcity of electronic components/material, associated with increased inflation.

14.2 ESA and the COVID-19 pandemic

From the very first weeks of the pandemic and the lock-down decisions of various European authorities, ESA devised a specific plan, released on 23 March 2020, under the title "Measures to ensure business continuity in the European Space industry and in the implementation of ESA Programmes during the COVID-19 crisis".[2]

Its first objective was to ensure business continuity. In the new, challenging environment that COVID-19 posed, with people working from home and industry partially unable to operate, it became clear that some processes and procedures needed to be adapted or improved, and rather quickly. Procurement and finance matters were specifically called upon. As the entire industrial chain was affected, from the Large System Integrators (LSI) down to Small and Medium Enterprises (SMEs), it was paramount to execute on-going contracts and new procurements in a timely manner, also to provide more advance and partial payments. The continuity of cash flow towards industry and continuity in the initiation of new procurements were key.

In line with the objectives above, the Plan was structured around four main axes:

- Streamlining the tendering process and shortening the time-to-contract;
- Reducing time-to-payment;
- Facilitation of Partial Payments;
- Facilitation of new Advance Payments.

The following subsections present the content and the implementation of these four axes. They then describe the way the Agency's Executive clarified the application of "*Force Majeure*" throughout the first weeks of the crisis. They further elaborate on the Agency's Executive stance towards claims from industry based on "hardship" and/or that could be considered as "extra-contractual".

14.2.1 Tendering process and time-to-contract

The ESA-STAR system established to distribute Invitations to Tender/Requests for Quotations (ITTs/RFQs) and collect all offers received from industry, supports, by design, a dematerialised handling of the offer submission, opening, and dispatching to the Tender Evaluation Board participants.

The rules in place, allowing for Tender Evaluation Boards (TEB) to meet by tele/video conference, remained, and instruction was given to make use of them, ensuring continuity in the evaluation of the offers received.

2 Measures to ensure business continuity in the European Space industry and in the implementation of ESA Programmes during the COVID-19 crisis, published on EMITS News on 23 March 2020, extended to EU funded and co-funded programmes.

This allowed for full continuity of the Tendering process from the very first day of the crisis. In fact, with its total staff in tele-work, ESA's productivity rate in terms of release of ITTs/RFQs was higher than that measured for the same period in 2019.

14.2.2 Time-to-payment

From the early days of the crisis, the ESA Executive identified cash-flow as one of the central leverages in its resolution to stand by the entire industrial chain. Time-to-payment was the principal target acted on in that respect, derogating from the standard 30-day payment term and a systematic, exceptional action launched within the Executive to substantially reduce each of the steps involved in the handling of invoices up to the final disbursement payment, without compromising the necessary controls.

That action, involving all services concerned within the Executive, both at Programme and Administration levels, led to substantial improvements. The average time-to-payment for 2020 was more than halved, from an average of 26 calendar days at 21 March to around 12 calendar days during May.

14.2.3 Contract execution: partial payments

The exceptional measures put in place by the Executive foresaw an active financial support to the industry.

As a first instrument, and at the request of industry, ESA would, upon request, make partial payments against forthcoming milestones, in line with the level of technical progress reached at the date of the request. The conclusion of formal Contract Change Notices (CCNs) was not required under such requests, but evidence of technical progress had to be provided by industry to justify the amount of payment. Prime contractors were instructed to flow-down and implement the same throughout their entire consortium, to ensure all industrial partners shared the benefit.

14.2.4 Contract execution: advances

Under the measures, industry could also request additional advances in ongoing contracts, in particular when needed to accelerate payments to subcontractors. In line with standard procedures the new advances required a CCN to implement, which was implemented using electronic signature and submission by email between relevant parties.

Moreover, SMEs were offered the possibility to request, exceptionally, up to 50% advance of the contract value, rather than the nominal 35%.[3] The Agency indicated that it would consider such requests favourably, taking into account any advance already granted and the particular circumstances of the relevant contract. This would also be implemented via CCNs.

14.2.5 Contract execution: force majeure[4]

In general terms, *force majeure* occurs when the performance of a contract is made impossible due to unforeseeable events beyond the control of the Party(ies). *Force majeure* is thus a circumstance

3 Ibid., p. 3.

4 For a detailed analysis, see Lukas C. Jung, Lesley Jane Smith, *COVID-19 and Its Impact on Space Activities: Force Majeure and Further Legal Implications*, Air and Space Law, Volume 45, Special issue (2020) pp. 173–193.

that renders the fulfilment of (a) contractual obligation(s) impossible due to unforeseeable event, for instance epidemic. The General Clauses and Conditions for ESA Contracts (GCC) already foresee *force majeure* and explicitly mention *epidemic* as one of the circumstance constitutive thereof. A *force majeure* event relieves the affected party from liability for damages resulting from their breach of contract.

Neither the legal concept of *force majeure* nor the *force majeure* as laid down in the GCC link *force majeure* with a right of compensation for extra cost in Fixed Price and Firm Fixed Price contracts.

The ESA COVID Plan granted a first schedule and delivery remit/suspension, including penalties and incentives, for development contracts for the period of impact +1month.

In a refinement of that approach, the ESA Executive agreed, for the purpose of considering *force majeure* suspensions, to consider a nominal COVID-19 period, starting on 9 March 2020 (date corresponding to the first massive confinement measures adopted by national authorities in Europe) and ending on 15 May 2020 (date corresponding to the start of the de-confinement measures adopted in Europe).

That meant in practice that all delivery dates or milestones in ESA contracts (linked or not with payments, incentives, penalties, physical deliveries, etc.) could, at the request of industry, be postponed by three months and six days without negatively impacting on the industry.

14.2.6 Execution: hardship

As stated above, the right of a party to be exempted from its contractual obligations during the period of impact from a *force majeure* event is laid down in the GCC.

The Agency's regulatory framework does not define "hardship". This legal concept is addressed, in varying manners, in several national laws.

There may be legal provisions on hardship that could become relevant to an ESA contract through the application of the underlying national law. Although the legal concept varies between different legal orders, it does have a common denominator, that is, an occurrence beyond the control of the affected party that has made the performance of the contract excessively onerous and grossly disproportionate to the interest of its performance by the contractual counterpart (to an extent that insisting on performance could be seen as misuse of rights).

The hardship concept (or similar) is, as mentioned, not foreseen in all legal orders. Jurisprudence, as well as case law, shows a strict interpretation of the conditions. The concept of hardship intends to solve problems of such fundamentally altered circumstances by adapting the contract to the new situation. Hardship could potentially be called upon by the industry through the national law applicable to the contract. However, it would only be applicable in exceptional cases, where there is a proven dramatic financial impact on the contract, rendering its performance excessively onerous.

From the experiences reported by industry, it first appeared that the consequences of the pandemic such as the confinement measures and the tele-working arrangements, were very different across the industrial chain, depending not only on the geographical situation (even within the same country), but also on the type of activities conducted.

It was also reported that the only activities that have been entirely and irremediably affected by the COVID-19 pandemic, involving the consequences mentioned above, were manufacturing, assembly integration and testing, and production.

Since hardship is intended to cover cases in which unforeseen events occur that fundamentally alter the equilibrium of a contract, resulting in an excessive burden on one of the parties, the ESA Executive believed that cases meeting such conditions would be rather exceptional.

14.2.7 Extra-contractual claims

Besides exemption from the normal duty to fulfill contractual obligations under *force majeure*, benefitting from cash-oriented measures like partial and advance payments, hardship considerations apart, a number of economic operators had announced their intention to claim indemnification from ESA for the "general consequences" suffered in implementing their activities under an ESA Contract due to COVID-19.

Contrary to *force majeure* or hardship, these claims had no legal or contractual basis. They therefore had to be considered as "extra-contractual claims".

Extra-contractual claims have no basis in the contracts or in the GCC. There is no vested right of the industry to see these claims considered or accommodated by ESA. It was clear that the drastic measures imposed by states resulting from COVID-19 measures had impacted heavily on the productivity of industry in executing some ESA contracts. Since costs had not been reduced in proportion to the reduced productivity, this did affect the space industry's profitability.

The potential impact of COVID-19 on the productivity of industry depended upon several factors.

The four main factors were:

i. The country or region in which the facilities are located since the start/end date as well as severity of the COVID-19 measures taken by the applicable authorities were geographically dependent.
ii. The activity or nature of the contract (study, production, service).
iii. The organisation of the facilities, to the extent it would impact on the ability organise cleaning, shift work, etc.
iv. The delays due to supply chain/sub-contractors.

The magnitude of the economic consequences of the COVID-19 pandemic had provoked a substantial response from the public sector, manifested by various initiatives and measures taken at EU, national, regional, and even in some cases, local levels, to put in place structural and sectoral aids.

ESA acknowledged that additional costs might be directly generated by the reduced productivity due to COVID-19 conditions in ESA contracts and not covered by sectoral or structural measures (for example, partial unemployment benefits).

14.3 ESA and the scarcity of material and inflation

From the first half of 2021, the world-wide overall production and supply chain (e.g., in the automotive sector) became affected by a marked scarcity of electronic components.

During the second half of that year and the first quarter of 2022, that situation started to affect the space sector.

The period was also marked by the start of an inflationary trend that has brought us to the well-known situation prevailing at the time of writing.

With the outbreak of the crisis in Ukraine, the current Russian and Ukrainian role in space technology supply chains, raw materials supply, and space-related services in Europe give rise to critical situations.

Confronted with these circumstances, the industry started to approach the ESA Executive and Member States with questions and calls for assistance.

14.3.1 Inflation

The European space industry is concerned that, in the absence of assistance of the Agency and its Member States, this new situation may affect the economic operators' ability to meet their contractual commitments. Most European space companies see in particular their profitability and financial health significantly affected.

These concerns were clearly expressed to the Agency through the established dialogue channels (SME Forum, Midcaps Forum, Eurospace, LSI) as well as in the context of contractual relations for individual projects. This dialogue is on-going at the time of writing, and the most critical cases are handled by the Agency's Executive, with the appropriate priority for each relevant project.

ESA fully acknowledges the situation, but any possible assistance beyond current contractual obligations must be addressed with due consideration to specific consequences of such an evolution against related industrial commitments, as well as affordability and other constraints.

The following tools could be used for new procurements in response to the inflation concerns raised by industry:

- Adaptation of the industrial rates;
- Selection of Fixed Price with Variation (FPV)
  - either with a "classical" escalation formula based on dedicated Labour and Material Indices;
  - or with a "simplified" one based on the evolution of Harmonised Index of Consumer Prices (HICP);
- Maintaining the Firm Fixed price (FFP) approach but with
  - an adjustment clause based on the evolution of HICP and/or dedicated to material costs for contracts, where specific materials constitute a large share of the price;
  - eligibility of economic risk as part of the Management Reserve;
  - acknowledgement of exceptional hardship if the relevant conditions are demonstrated.

14.3.2 Scarcity of components/material

The scarcity of components was to be dealt with, as part of the risk register and of the Management Reserve with adequate mitigating measures (Long Lead Items anticipated procurement, schedule margin, combined orders, etc). This should be done for the whole supply chain (bottom-up) as far as possible.

The issue should also be well outlined in the tender conditions for new projects (similar to export control related requirements).

In view of the above, considering the variety of programmatic circumstances, it does not appear pertinent to pursue a general "one fits all" policy in handling these new economic challenges in the Agency's contractual relations with the industry. Instead, each contractual situation shall be considered on a case-by-case basis in their respective programmatic context, with due regard to the relevant project timeline, level of industrial commitment, affordability, level of flexibility of the programmatic framework, and level of influence that the particular circumstance has on the contractual commitment.

Clearly, that assessment will, depending on the case and the particular impact, base itself on the application of *force majeure*, or hardship, as mentioned above.

Finally, the events of the last three years have also triggered a reflection and analysis of the dependencies affecting the supply chains for the ESA Programmes.

To nurture that work and to ensure that it takes the reality of programmes duly into account, inputs have been collected around the following questions:

- Which are the current dependencies from European industry affecting the supply chains for the various programmes (launchers, best practices, lower-level equipment and components, raw materials, testing, calibration, etc.)?
- What is the analysis of said dependencies, including market assessment, alternative suppliers, capacities that might need to be developed, and potential cost of non-dependence?
- Which are the criteria that should be adopted/followed for selecting the dependencies to be further analysed?

14.4 Conclusion

As outlined in the introduction to this chapter, the very mandate conferred no ESA in its *Carta Magna*, its Convention in terms of industrial policy, and more particularly the improvement of the world-wide competitiveness of the European industry, places it in direct connection with industrial realities.[5]

This calls for the Agency's procurement process to evolve continuously, so as to not only tackle the challenges with which economic operators are confronted, but also innovate in line with the new forms that "industry competitiveness" takes.

The ESA procurement process has fundamentally evolved over the last ten years. A fully digital tendering system has been developed and implemented, which has probably saved the entire institutional industrial chain during the pandemic and the months of lock-down. Tailored procedures have been introduced, supporting time-to-contract, in line with support to innovation and commercialisation. Fit-to-size procurement approaches have been followed, guaranteeing a balanced level-playing field to all categories of economic operators.

The ultimate test of the performance of a procurement process lies in its capacity to react to changing global circumstances. The central role that ESA procurement played during the COVID-19 pandemic, that it is adapting in front of scarcity of components and inflation appears to be a model in that respect.

5 See. e.g., Communication on the "Measures to ensure business continuity in the European Space Industry and in the implementation of ESA Programmes during the COVID-19 crisis", published on 23 March 2020, last updated on 4 April 2022. The text is available at https://esastar-publication-ext.sso.esa.int/news/details/676.

15

NEWSPACE GROWTH THROUGH NASA'S CONTRACTUAL AND OTHER TRANSACTION AUTHORITIES

Julie Jiru and Allison Genco

15.1 Introduction

The current approach within the US is to foster and utilise commercial space capabilities. The regulatory schemes a country chooses, and the way it opts to develop, promote, and acquire space capabilities, greatly impacts its ability to do so – especially in the realm of commercial space. The United States' position regarding the use of space and commercial space is informed by several federal laws, regulations, as well as policy directives and declarations.[1]

NASA is successfully expanding on its history of effectuating the commercialisation of space through legal innovation and taking risks. This chapter will explore how such innovation accommodates the evolving goals of space commercialisation in the US while increasing the breadth, depth, and capabilities of new space companies within its borders.

15.2 NASA directorates and programmes

NASA has five operational directorates each with their own specialisation. These include two new directorates that were once under the Human Exploration and Operations Mission Directorate (HEOMD). One of these new directorates is the Exploration Systems Development Mission Directorate (ESDMD), which is responsible for planning, developing, and managing the Artemis Program. Notable programmes include the Human Landing System (HLS), Orion, Space Launch Systems (SLS), Gateway and Exploration Ground Systems, and Human Surface Mobility and Extravehicular Activity.[2] In mid-2022, the US Congress directed NASA to establish a Moon to

1 51 U.S. Code § 20102 Section C, Commercial Use of Space provides: Congress declares that the general welfare of the United States requires that the Administration seek and encourage, to the maximum extent possible, the fullest commercial use of space. See also, Space Policies – Office of Space Commerce, for a collection of Space Policy Directives, Executive Orders, and additional national policies.

2 Id.

 DOI: 10.4324/9781003268475-20

Mars programme within ESDMD to oversee these and any other programmes needed to meet Artemis missions and activities and to achieve the eventual goal of human exploration of Mars.[3] The other new directorate is the Space Operations Mission Directorate (SOMD), which is charged with "enabling sustained human exploration missions and operations in our solar system".[4] A key function of SOMD is overseeing NASA's current and future missions in Low Earth Orbit (LEO) and beyond, which include commercial transportation services to and from the International Space Station (ISS), as well as the orbital launch of payloads.[5] SOMD also manages NASA's communications and navigation services that support all of NASA's in-orbit space systems.[6] Notably, the Commercial Spaceflight Division (CSD) falls within this directorate.[7] The Science Mission Directorate (SMD) works in the areas of Astrophysics, Heliophysics Planetary Science, and Earth Science. The Aeronautics Research Mission Directorate (ARMD) is charged with increasing innovation in aircraft and airspace system. Finally, NASA's fifth directorate is the Space Technology Mission Directorate (STMD), which pioneers the new technical innovations and capabilities needed for current and future missions.[8]

15.3 Two primary acquisition strategies: other transaction authority and innovative FAR-based contracts

Broadly speaking, U.S. acquisition strategies take one of two paths – a Federal Acquisition Regulation (FAR)-based contract, or an agreement executed pursuant to an agency's "other transaction" authority (OTA).[9] NASA has successfully used both of these approaches to achieve US policies and goals related to commercial space. Below, we explore not only NASA's key legal vehicles that advance the commercial sector, but also how they fit into NASA's overarching goals in its various key programmes.

15.4 Other transaction authority – a critical backbone of commercial space progress

15.4.1 Genesis

Just as it forms the foundation of the US federal acquisition system, competition has played a critical role in the trajectory of US space exploration. On 4 October 1957, the Union of Soviet Socialist Republics (USSR) launched the world's first man-made satellite, Sputnik, stunning the world. With pressure mounting to demonstrate its own capabilities, the US accelerated work on its own man-made satellite, culminating in the launch of Explorer 1 on 31 January 1958.

But the US had no plans to rest on its laurels. Before 1958 came to a close, the US not only created the National Aeronautics and Space Administration (NASA), its first civilian space agency, but also simultaneously imbued NASA with authority to enter into a wide variety of legal agreements

3 NASA Authorization Act of 2022.

4 NASA, Space Operations Mission Directorate.

5 Id.

6 Id.

7 Id.

8 NASA, Small Spacecraft Virtual Institute, The Science Mission Directorate (SMD).

9 "OTA" can refer to either the other transitional legal authority possessed by an agency or to the legal agreement between two parties that is entered into based on that authority, in which case "OTA" is referring to an other transaction agreement. This chapter's use of OTA is referring to the latter of these.

"as may be necessary in the conduct of its work and on such terms as it may deem appropriate".[10] This aspect of the National Aeronautics and Space Act of 1958 (Space Act) conferred legal authority unto NASA that was, at that time, unprecedented.

After explicitly enumerating NASA's ability to enter into contracts, leases, and cooperative agreements, the Space Act contemplated a distinct category of instruments to which it simply referred as "other transactions".[11] For the federal procurement landscape, the groundbreaking nature of this Space Act language cannot be overstated. It would be 32 years before the US Congress would grant a component of the Department of Defense its own OTA authority, And while many procurement professionals today think of OTAs as a sort of secondary instrument, an alternative to the default of FAR-based contracts, it is notable that NSA's OTA authority predates the FAR by 26 years.

15.4.2 Scope of power

While the urgency of the situation that led to the creation of OTAs is clear, this history nonetheless raises the question of why OTAs were necessary at all; what was missing from other authorities such that Congress concluded that NASA needed this unique tool? As it turns out, existing instruments were not missing something so much as they were hamstrung, weighed down with the requirement to comply with a wide variety of federal procurement laws and regulations. Congress understood this and, with the high the stakes of the Space Race on its mind, sought to empower the newly formed NASA with "the necessary *freedom* to carry on research, development, and exploration ... to ensure the full development of these peaceful and defense uses without unnecessary delay" (emphasis added).[12]

Imbued with broad authority to enter into agreements unburdened by federal procurement laws and regulations, one might imagine that NASA has spent the last six and a half decades meetings its requirements exclusively through OTAs. But since the passage of the Space Act, Congress has clarified the circumstances in which it is appropriate for NASA to use an OTA. Specifically, NASA is required to use a FAR-based contract when the principal purpose of the instrument is to acquire, by purchase, lease, or barter, property or services "for the direct benefit or use of the United States Government".[13] NASA policy further provides that, when deciding between the use of an OTA or another available instrument, so-called "funded" OTAs (in which NASA makes payments to its OTA partner) may only be used when the agency cannot accomplish its objectives through the use of a procurement contract, grant, or cooperative agreement, and only after full and open competition.[14] These directives and the policies underpinning them are somewhat subject to interpretation, which has led to a spectrum of philosophies over the years within NASA as to when, and how much, NASA should be utilising its OTA authority. But as is discussed in the next section, while OTAs are a powerful tool, FAR-based contracts have their own benefits. After all, federal procurement laws and regulations exist to advance key US policies and, in theory, provide the US Government with optimal contract terms and conditions. This leads one to the conclusion

10 National Aeronautics and Space Act, Pub. L. 85-568, 72 Stat. 426 (1958), codified 51 U.S.C. §§ 20101–20164 (Supp. IV 2010).

11 Id. at section 20113(e).

12 U.S. Congress, House Committee of Conference, National Aeronautics and Space Act of 1958, Conference Report to accompany H.RE. 12575, 85th Cong., 2nd sess., July 15, 1968, Report No. 2166 (Washington: GPO, 1958), p. 16.

13 31 U.S.C. § 6303(1).

14 NASA Policy Directive 1050.7, Authority to Enter into Partnership Agreements.

that neither instrument is a perfect approach in isolation, but rather, other transaction authority nicely complements NASA's ability to enter into FAR-based contracts, grants, leases, cooperative and other transaction agreements. Together, this array of legal instruments empowers NASA to pursue its wide range of ambitious exploration projects and support the continued growth of the U.S. commercial space industry.

15.4.3 Differences and benefits of OTAs as compared to FAR-based contracting

OTAs live outside of the FAR, and in this legal chasm lay several key differences between OTAs and contracts.[15] In addition to not having to comply with the FAR, OTAs are also not beholden to comply with the Competition in Contracting Act (CICA),[16] agency-based FAR supplements, and related laws and regulations. This flexibility can be a benefit for both the Government customer and the commercial provider in that it allows the Government to tailor clauses and requirements that are mandatory in traditional procurements (e.g., intellectual property licences, termination clauses, limits on the duration of the period of performance), while reducing costly compliance and requirement burdens for the provider that are present in traditional Government contracts.

Another key difference between OTAs and FAR-based contracts is that the latter always involves payment by the Government to the contractor for goods or services, whereas Space Act Agreements establish a set of legally enforceable promises between NASA and the Partner to the SAA that simply requires a commitment of NASA resources.[17] These resources can take a variety of forms; while NASA's contribution to a Space Act Agreement can be monetary payment(s), it can also take the form of goods, services, expertise, facilities, or equipment.

Additionally, OTAs do not fall within the bid protest jurisdiction of either the Court of Federal Claims (COFC) or General Accountability Organization (GAO), and thus are generally not subject to bid protests.[18] Because a protest typically results in work stoppage for a minimum of 100 days on the awarded contract until the legal dispute is resolved, OTAs that are able to avoid this potentiality can be a significant benefit for both NASA and its commercial partners. In the rapidly flourishing state of space capabilities – both national and commercial – litigation-caused delays can be more impactful than in the past. Furthermore, actions an agency takes in its formation and administration of OTAs are also not subject to agency-level protests because procedures for such protests to Government agencies are promulgated by the FAR and FAR supplements (with which OTAs need not comply).

15 Despite these differences, OTA agreements are legally binding and should not be equated with nonbinding vehicles such as a Memorandum of Agreement (MOA) or Memorandum of Understanding (MOU).

16 41 U.S.C. §253.

17 NASA Space Act Agreements Guide.

18 In the matter of: *Rocketplane Kistler*, B-310741, at 3. The GAO noted: Under the Competition in Contracting Act of 1984 and our Bid Protest Regulations, we review protests concerning alleged violations of procurement statutes or regulations by federal agencies in the award or proposed award of contracts for procurement of goods and services, and solicitations leading to such awards. . . . We have found that Space Act Agreements, which are issued by NASA under its "other transactions" authority pursuant to [the NASA Act] . . . , are not procurement contracts, and therefore we generally do not review protests of the award, or solicitations for the award, of these agreements under our bid protest jurisdiction.

Additionally, the GAO stated it would generally only review a timely protest alleging that an agency is improperly using non-procurement instruments where a procurement contract is required. *See also* Exploration Partners-, LLC, B-298804.

In addition to differences in the terms and conditions of the agreements, the types of consideration the parties can offer, and the likelihood of an agreement being delayed by litigation, OTAs also empower the Government to use atypical agreement structures. Space Act Agreements, for example, can be executed between NASA and a wide variety of public entities, private entities, or foreign entities, not all of which are appropriate contracting partners under FAR-based contracts. But perhaps one of the most unusual features of a Space Act Agreement is that they can be structured to allow a partner to pay for work that NASA conducts for the partner's benefit, even in cases in which NASA also accrues a benefit.[19] Just as unusual is that they can also be structured such that each party assumes responsibility for its own costs. These flexibilities in defining the amount and form of value that each partner will bring to the agreement allow NASA and its Space Act Agreement partners to be creative in identifying mutually beneficial synergies and creating agreements that optimise the resources, capabilities, and goals of each partner.

15.4.4 Basic types and examples of OTAs

As will be shown below, NASA actively encourages entities to partner with NASA.[20]

15.4.5 Space Act Agreements[21]

Agreements formed under NASA's other transaction authority of the Space Act are typically called Space Act Agreements (SAA). Through these Agreements, NASA is able to provide "resources such as personnel, funding, services, equipment, information or facilities".[22] The different types of Space Act Agreements most commonly used for and by commercial space entities are discussed below.[23]

The purpose of a Space Act Agreement is to "establish a set of legally enforceable promises between NASA and the Partner to the SAA requiring a commitment of NASA resources (including personnel, funding, information, goods, services, facilities, or equipment) personnel, or funding to accomplish stated objectives".[24] The three key types of SAAs are: (1) Reimbursable SAAs – where NASA provides expertise, services, facilities, and the like to a partner at the partner's cost; (2) Non-reimbursable SAAs, where NASA and the partner assume their own costs; and (3) the Funded SAA, which provides full or partial payment to a partner – generally for or otherwise in line with a NASA goal.[25] As the Funded SAA is a key mechanism NASA is using more frequently to enable quicker commercial technical progress, this is explored in greater detail below.

19 NASA Space Act Agreements Guide, *supra.*

20 NASA, NASA Partnerships. Specifically, the activity type, partner type and legal mechanism for each type of partnership are provided in the NASA Partnership Guide, NASA Advisory Implementing Instruction NAII 1050-3B, last updated September 26, 2019 at page 43, Summary Table of Agreement Types/Legal Authorities Available for Partnerships.

21 NASA provides a running list of current Space Act Agreements, which are available publicly at NASA Partnerships, Current Space Act Agreements.

22 NASA, Jet Propulsion Laboratory, Commercial Technology Partnerships.

23 Publicly posted opportunities for OTAs and FAR-based contracts can be found on the U.S. Government's System for Award Management (SAM) website (https://sam.gov/content/home, last accessed May 7, 2022). Opportunities geared more toward scientific study than technological advancement are often found on the NASA Solicitation and Proposal Integrated Review and Evaluation System (NSPIRES) website.

24 NASA Advisory Implementing Instruction, NAII 1050-1D (effective date: 25 February 2013), at B-2.

25 See generally, The Space Act Agreement Guide (2017).

Reimbursable SAAs are the primary vehicle for a commercial entity to obtain services (such as specialised testing, training, and analysis); and use of NASA goods, facilities, and equipment. These agreements are set up with the NASA Center that provides the needed resources.

15.4.6 Key differences between terms under FAR contracts and Space Act Agreements

NASA maintains a Space Act Agreements Guide,[26] which explains in detail the different types and uses of SAAs, their formation and administration processes, as well as providing the general terms and conditions for SAAs. While each type of SAA generally uses similar types of clauses (e.g., intellectual property rights, insurance, termination, liability, risk of loss, waivers), the Guide recommends options for each type of clause.[27] Thus, the specific clauses that NASA and its partner will utilise within an SAA depend on several factors such as the type of activities, location of performance, types of consideration offered by each party, and amount of risk involved.

To the extent there is a "typical" SAA, it tends to have no more than a few dozen terms and conditions; this stands in contrast to typical FAR-based contracts in which it is not unusual for the agreement to contain over one hundred clauses. This is arguably the main reason SAAs are viewed by some as more efficient for NASA and the partner and can enable the parties to focus on making technical progress or otherwise achieving the goals of the SAA without being bogged down by unnecessary compliance provisions. And while the areas covered by SAA terms are similar to some of the terms and conditions in a FAR contract, they tend to differ, with the SAA terms often being more favourable to the partner.

An example of this are the intellectual property and data rights. It is still common in a NASA FAR contract for there to be two treatments of a contractor's data: Unlimited Rights, which provide no protection of the use and disclosure by NASA of the contractor's data; or Limited Rights, which generally prohibits NASA from disclosing or using the contractor's data outside of the US Government. Absent special contract language, to qualify as "Limited Rights Data", however, the data must be "data, other than computer software, that embody trade secrets or are commercial or financial and confidential or privileged, to the extent that such data pertain to items, components, or processes developed at private expense, including minor modifications".[28] If data does not meet this definition, it will typically be considered data under the contract that is delivered to NASA with the Unlimited Rights licence, which will apply to all other data first produced under a contract.

Technological and process innovation, and the intellectual property rights that accompany these innovations, are central to the competitiveness of commercial companies and comprise a significant portion of the company's overall value. In this way, traditional FAR-based contracts that require data to be delivered with, for example, the Unlimited Rights licence, can be a significant deterrent to private companies engaging in Government contracts. The theory and policy that are foundational to these standards FAR-based intellectual property licences are sound – Government contracts are funded with taxpayer dollars, and the utility and value of data created through the use of these funds should thus accrue to those taxpayers. But many contractors see the Unlimited Rights licence as an unnecessary overreach. Interestingly, the FAR supplements for some non-

26 Id. at xiii–xxii, last visited 24 April 2022.

27 The Space Act Agreement Guide at B-76.

28 Acquisition.gov, FAR, FAC Number: 2022-08, Effective Date: 28 October 2022, 52.227-14 Rights in Data-General.

NASA agencies have developed solutions in response to this issue. The most notable example is within the FAR supplement for the US Department of Defense (known as the DFARS), which explicitly creates a third, middle category of intellectual property licence known as "Government Purpose Rights". This licence permits the Government to use the data for Government purposes, including in subsequent Government contracts, but does not permit the Government to commercialise the data.[29] As the commercial space sector grows and competition for resources in space continues to increase, intellectual property rights may be a regulatory area for the US Government to revisit for space-related FAR-based contracts. Under SAAs, even Funded SAAs, it is common for data – even when it is first produced and paid for under the agreement – to be subject to an intellectual property rights scheme that is much more favourable to the commercial partner, including the ability to seek protection for data first produced by NASA under the SAA if certain criteria are met.[30]

Further, what also makes the FAR contract much more resource intensive over an SAA is the requirement that many FAR contracts require copious amounts of data deliverables. These Data Requirements Documents (DRDs) are commonly specified within a Contract Data Requirements List (CDRL) or a Data Procurement Document (DPD). Preparation and delivery of these required items can be time- and resource-intensive for a contractor, diverting energy away from performance of the work and towards creating paperwork. For these and other reasons, commercial companies tend to favour SAAs as their preferred legal instrument with the US Government.

15.4.7 Funded Space Act Agreements

Funded SAAs (FSAAs) are a flexible legal vehicle to fulfill one or many NASA goals while increasing the capabilities of the US commercial sector. While there are a variety of NASA goals, funded agreements are an effective and streamlined way to: (1) develop, evolve, and increase technology and capabilities NASA needs – often at a much lower cost than a FAR part 35 contract for Research and Development; and (2) enhance NASA's capabilities that might be needed for their various future missions and activities at an accelerated pace.[31]

Key differences between FSAAs and other SAAs include, but are not limited to, payment milestones, entrance and exit criteria, intellectual property rights, and termination clauses.

These types of agreements are initiated by NASA for the primary benefit of its commercial partners and advance a specific statutory objective. They are only available to domestic entities via competitive procedures and announced to the public through the System for Award Management (SAM) website. The announcements typically include:

- A description of the key purpose and goals of the FSAA;
- The information required to be provided in the proposal from the offeror, e.g.:
  - Information related to technical capabilities and approach;
  - Funding (always some from NASA and, if applicable, activities the partner will perform at its own costs);

29 See, generally, DFARS 252.227-7014, Rights in Noncommercial Computer Software and Noncommercial Computer Software Documentation.

30 The Space Act Agreement Guide at B-76.

31 The Space Act Agreement Guide, paragraph 1.8 Funded Agreement starting at B-16. For more information, see Alan Lindenmoyer's (former NASA Program Manager for Commercial Crew and Cargo) YouTube video titled "Structuring a Funded Space Act Agreement".

  - Proposed milestones, milestone criteria, and payments; and
  - Entity financial information;
- Due date for the proposals;
- How the proposals will be evaluated.[32]

Besides helping commercial entities develop technologies that benefit NASA and, increasingly, themselves, FSAAs are extremely streamlined and are not encumbered by resource demanding activities of a FAR-based contract such as copious amounts of large data deliverables, making facilities and information open to NASA insight – including personnel embedded in the entity's facility, required compliance with dozens of regulations all which take valuable resource away from the technical progress towards the goals of the agreement. This is a fundamental reason that developing and maturing commercial space technology is typically quicker under an FSAA as opposed to a FAR-based contract.

Additionally, encouraged by early success stories of commercial development, NASA is increasingly using FSAAs as a precursor to a follow-on FAR-based firm fixed price services contract. This started with NASA retiring the shuttle. The Agency needed to replace its capabilities to transport supplies, experiments, payloads, etc., and return the same, along with disposal items to and from the ISS. It also needed a shuttle replacement to transport astronauts to and from Station.[33] NASA could have taken a more typical approach of replacing the services with a cost-plus FAR-based contract – which places all the risk on the Government and provides no incentive for the company to reduce costs or perform efficiently. Instead, NASA took a brave approach to replacing the shuttle's capabilities – it started with FSAAs.

For cargo resupply, NASA understood that the capability did not currently exist in the US market. It also understood that to bring such capability into existence, it would need to provide a significant amount of funding and a business rationale for companies to undertake such a complex, difficult and expensive task. NASA also had the foresight to understand, even if companies put in valiant efforts, such development would be best performed in stages. Thus, NASA used a two-phased approach for cargo resupply. It started with the Commercial Orbital Transportation Services (COTS) FSAA to allow companies to initiate the design and development of the spacecraft capsule that would berth or dock to Station and include a test orbital mission and a test berthing/docking mission to prove out its capabilities.

As part of these Agreements, NASA also required each company to have "skin in the game" by providing a significant amount of self-funding as well. Therefore, at the end of the COTS SAA, NASA had two providers, Orbital Sciences Corporation (now Northrup Grumman) and Space Exploration Technologies Corp. (SpaceX) capable of filling the cargo transportation gap left by the shuttle's retirement.[34] COTS is also legally famous as NASA's first use of its SAA authority in a key and game-changing way.[35]

32 See generally, Announcement for Partnership Proposals (AFPP) to Advance Tipping Point Technologies, Amendment 8, 28 September 2022 Announcement Number: 80HQTR22SOA02 at pp. 16–76.

33 "Station" is another term for the International Space Station.

34 Alan Lindenmoyer, Program Manager, Commercial Orbital Transportation Services (COTS) Program Management, NASA,13 January 2015.

35 For an in-depth and interesting account of the use of the Funded SAA to initiate commercial spacecraft design, production, and test missions see Sumara Thompson-King Oral History. "We did develop an additional way of doing business. I say additional because we still conduct much of our business through contracts that we award, but when we started with COTS [Commercial Orbital Transportation Services], that's when NASA branched out into

NASA was then able to procure ISS resupply services from both companies under a firm fixed FAR-based commercial item contract under Commercial Resupply Services (CRS) 1 contracts. Both companies also went on to provide services under CRS 2 contracts. Finding this streamlined, lower cost method a valuable alternative to using a FAR-based contract (especially a cost-reimbursable one) to develop new commercial sector capabilities, NASA repeated this phased approach for astronaut (crew) transportation.

As a human rated spacecraft involves expanded technologies, NASA began early development of this capability also using FSAAs. Initial designs and development were started under the Commercial Crew Development (CCDev) 1 FSAAs, and greatly furthered by the CCDev 2 FSAAs and the Commercial Crew Integrated Capabilities (CCiCap) FSAAs.[36] These commercial crew funded agreements – which also required companies to partially fund the work – were then followed on by a firm fixed price non-commercial item contract, under which the two awardees would certify their human rated Crew Transportation Systems (an activity which included both a uncrewed test mission to and from the ISS and a crewed test mission to and from the ISS) before beginning regular post-certification missions to and from Station.

Thus, the FSAA provides funding to space companies to develop and enhance capabilities they cannot self-fund, while providing a market rationale for doing the FSAA work – NASA as a potential initial, then additional, customer for such capabilities. Additionally, as is occurring more frequently, the FSAAs are being aimed at creating new space technologies and/or services for which NASA is not intended to be the sole customer. This intention has been demonstrated through FSAAs such as the Commercial LEO Destination (CLD), and the Communication Services Project (CSP).[37] Such innovative use of a legal mechanism will likely play a vital factor in the provision of future commercial space capabilities by commercial companies.

For example, the Commercial Leo Destination is intended, in part, to serve as commercial version of the ISS where national astronauts can perform experiments, but with only a portion of the new space station devoted to such activities. The rest is open for other commercial endeavors such as research and/or tourism. However, unlike the earlier CRS and CCtCap programmes, CLD is intently focused on the creation and long-term viability of a station that is primarily for commercial use. Thus, part of the goal of the programme is to increase and expand a commercial market for the CLD and have a station that is fully commercially run, where NASA is one of many customers.[38] Thus, as part of the evaluation for proposals for these FSAAs, NASA required a section explaining the market and market research for a company's CLD. NASA is also expanding

a new direction, interpreting our 'other transactions' authority, or actually using it in a way we had not previously used it." This oral history provided by Sumara Thompson King (NASA General Counsel, retired December 2022) provides a wonderful in-depth discussion about the beginnings of NASA's SAA use, and specifically the formation of the COTS FSAA.

36 NASA Commercial Crew & Cargo.

37 NASA, Communications Services Project Subsonic Sigle Aft Engine (SUSAN) Electrofan (video). Upon announcing the awardees of the FSAA for this project, NASA noted "Private sector innovation in near-Earth space is accelerating quickly and dramatically. Tapping those advances will ensure NASA missions have the reliable, secure and continual space communications on which their long-term operations depend." NASA further explain benefits of increasing commercial sector abilities (here for satellite communication, but applicable to nearly all space sectors), "Adopting commercial SATCOM capabilities will empower missions to leverage private sector investment that far exceeds what government can do. Using commercial technology will provide NASA missions with cost-saving access to continual industry innovation, saving money that can be refocused on scientific work." *Id.*

38 NASA, Low-Earth Orbit Economy.

the commercial use of the ISS as explained at 15.4.1 above. In NASA's announcement of the CLD FSAA awardees, it explained:

> NASA seeks to maintain an uninterrupted U.S. presence in low-Earth orbit by transitioning from the International Space Station to other platforms. These awards will stimulate U.S. private sector development of commercial, independent space stations that will be available to both government and private-sector customers.
>
> "Building on our successful initiatives to partner with private industry to deliver cargo, and now our NASA astronauts, to the International Space Station, NASA is once again leading the way to commercialize space activities," said NASA Administrator Bill Nelson. "With commercial companies now providing transportation to low-Earth orbit in place, we are partnering with U.S. companies to develop the space destinations where people can visit, live, and work, enabling NASA to continue forging a path in space for the benefit of humanity while fostering commercial activity in space."[39]

In NASA's statement about the CSP, it explained how this project will use a three-phased approach with the first stage beginning "under Funded Space Act Agreements. Establishing mutually beneficial relationships will lead to increased public-private collaboration and will help encourage new industry innovations derived from the unique capabilities developed to support mission requirements".[40] Indeed, it is the goal for generally all new FSAA to foster the US commercial space industrial base while further enabling NASA to benefit from such advances while enabling greater focus of its resources on space exploration. The dual effect of this transaction authority tool is a powerful driver of the widespread growth of US space technology related companies and advancement of the Agency.

15.4.8 Nonreimbursable Space Act Agreements

While an agreement that does not provide funding may not sound valuable, these are in fact powerful vehicles towards enabling entities to increase the technological capabilities that they want and/or needs the most. Such Nonreimbursable Space Act Agreements (NSAAs) are generally for the benefit of both parties and further the interests of both. Under these agreements, each party is responsible for its own costs and there is no exchange of funds. Instead, NASA provides the partner with the "time and effort of personnel, support services, equipment, expertise, information, or facilities".[41] For these agreements, NASA requires each party's contribution be effectively equivalent.

Separate but related to NSAAs are a relatively recent type of instrument known as "unfunded" SAAs.[42] NSAAs are for collaborative, no-exchange-of-funds activities for the mutual benefit of both parties. They are typically non-exclusive and open to anyone. On the other hand, for unfunded SAAs, funds are not exchanged, and these instruments are for the primary benefit of the commercial partner. They are also typically exclusive arrangements, and NASA must compete them. The Collaborations for Commercial Space Capabilities is an example of an early unfunded SAA and the US's commitment to broadening and strengthening its domestic space industry. In 2014,

39 NASA Selects Companies to Develop Commercial Destinations in Space.

40 Id.

41 NAII 1050-1D, Space Act Agreements Guide at p. B-11.

42 See the NASA Partnerships Guide for more information.

after submission and evaluation of proposals, NASA selected four out of 18 participants with the objective to "advance private sector development of integrated space capabilities so that emerging products or services are commercially available to government and non-government customers within approximately the next five years".[43]

15.4.9 Reimbursable Space Act Agreements (RSAA)

What if your company only wants to obtain a specific NASA resource to advance its own interests? It might seek a RSAA. These can be requested at any time from any NASA Center, and they must (1) be consistent with NASA's mission and (2) the requested resources cannot be reasonably available on the commercial market. As long as the requested recourse(s) does not interfere with NASA's needs or its missions, the RSAA enables NASA to provide use of NASA's goods, facilities, training, analysis, testing, equipment, and expertise to an entity. Some examples of what can be obtained through these agreements include Micro Meteoroid Orbital Debris analysis, space communications, advanced optics, robotics, life support systems, crew training, space suits, as well as high-pressure oxygen systems, materials, and rocket propellant testing.[44]

An RSAA can be structured as either a single instrument or two or more instruments. The latter begins with an Umbrella Agreement (UA), which contains the purpose and scope of the agreement, as well as the specific terms and conditions.[45] This overarching document establishes the legal framework for the various tasks that will be accomplished through separate Annexes.[46] The second component, an Annex, is a smaller document meant to capture the work within the scope and purpose of the UA and will vary from task to task. An Annex outlines the parties' responsibilities, specific work and/or resources to be provided, the schedule, deliverables (if any), along with estimated price and payment terms.[47] Annexes provide an opportunity, where justified, to alter or tailor certain terms or conditions – such as liability – of the UA.[48] And while these agreements are called "reimbursable", the partner must pay the estimated costs in advance of NASA starting its work.

To initiate an RSAA, an individual/entity would first determine which NASA Center has the capabilities needed and contact the Point of Contact (POC) provided therein, asking to set up an RSAA.[49] The NASA POC should be able to provide the right Agreements Officer to get the SAA started. To establish the agreement, the initiator would provide a list of work to be provided by NASA and the activities the partner intends to do. The agreement will also include due dates and deliverables, if applicable.

15.4.10 Cooperative Research and Development Agreement (CRADA)

The US commitment to increasing the overall transfer of technology from the Government to use outside of it is also shown in the Utilization of Federal Technology – which provides in part as its policy:

43 Selection Statement Collaboration for Commercial Space Capabilities (Announcement Number NASA-CCSC-01) at p. 1.

44 NASA Partnerships, NASA Locations, Capabilities and Points of Contact.

45 See generally, NAII 1050-1D, Space Act Agreements Guide.

46 Id., at B-18.

47 Id.

48 Id.

49 NASA Partnerships, NASA Locations, Capabilities and Points of Contact.

> It is the continuing responsibility of the Federal Government to ensure the full use of the results of the Nation's Federal investment in research and development. To this end the Federal Government shall strive where appropriate to transfer federally owned or originated technology to State and local governments and to the private sector.[50]

Section 3710a provides the authority for a federal agency and all its government-operated federal labs to enter into CRADAs – providing access to and ability to work with US national labs.[51] The key benefit of CRADAs is that they aim to increase the application of commercial uses of technology which the Government has invested into research and development, hopefully spurring new products and services beyond the Government in a way that protects the intellectual property a partner contributes to the collaboration.[52]

15.4.11 Additional examples of NASA programmes/initiatives and use of OTAs

15.4.11.1 NASA Space Technology Mission Directorate (STMD)

This directorate greatly facilitates the commercial sector space technology capabilities for the US. It focuses on "advancing technologies and testing new capabilities at the Moon that will be critical for crewed missions to Mars".[53] In part to achieve this focus, the STMD engages in partnerships to advance current commercial space technologies aligned with its mission. Two key procurements related mechanisms to do this include (1) Tipping Point Agreements (and Contracts) and (2) Announcement of Collaboration Opportunity. Each of these is addressed below. Further, the STMD engages in grants. An example of this are the Space Technology Research Grants to accelerate development of future space sciences and exploration which call for a high risk/high payoff approach.[54]

At times, STMD uses a dual approach of allowing entities to propose a Funded Space Act Agreement or an Unfunded Space Act Agreement, enabling the entity to engage with NASA in the way best suited to it. For example, in 2022, the directorate announced two topics and two methods of partnering with NASA under a FSAA for technologies at Technology Readiness Level (TRL) of approximately four or higher.[55] The topics were (1) Cislunar/Lunar Surface Infrastructure and Capabilities and (2) In-Space Infrastructure and Capabilities. Under each topic, NASA provided potential areas of exploration such as for topic one: "Technologies that support global lunar utilization leading to commercial commodities and services for a robust lunar economy".[56] Topic two proposals were asked to address "Low Earth Orbit (LEO) to Geosynchronous Earth Orbit (GEO)

50 15 U.S. Code § 3710.

51 15 U.S. Code § 3710a.

52 NAII 1050-2, Cooperative Research and Development Agreement (CRADA) Program Information Package at p. 7.

53 Space Technology Mission Directorate.

54 Space Technology Mission Directorate, Programs. STMD covers several types of technology development programs, including but not limited to (1) Flight Opportunities, (2) Game Changing Development, (3) Lunar Surface Innovation Initiative, and (4) NASA Innovative Advances Concepts. Last visited 25 April 2022. Solicitations for STMD can be found at Space Technology Mission Directorate, STMD Solicitations and Opportunities.

55 Space Technology Mission Directorate, Tipping Point/ACO Industry Forum 02.28.22, Virtual Industry Forum at 7. The full solicitation is NASA Announcement for Partnership Proposals (AFPP) to Advance Tipping Point Technologies, Announcement Number 80HQTR22SOA02.

56 Space Technology Mission Directorate, Tipping Point/ACO Industry Forum 02.28.22, Virtual Industry Forum at 6, last accessed 1 May 2022.

technologies that support additional future services for a growing LEO/GEO economy".[57] In both focus areas, NASA made it clear that entities were not limited to the examples provided and were invited to offer technologies within the general topic scope.

This is a powerful driver for commercial innovation that is useful to the company proposing while simultaneously increasing NASA's capabilities. This, in turn allows for participation by a much broader range of commercial companies and particularly supports the support and growth of smaller and newer companies with niche specialties and other non-traditional Government contractors. Indeed, a stated policy of NASA's use of the FSAA here is specifically to "stimulate the commercial space industry while leveraging those same commercial capabilities through partnerships to deliver technologies and capabilities needed for future NASA, other government agency, and commercial missions".[58]

This approach also fuels innovation from the US commercial space base in a way typically not possible by traditional FAR contracting since such contracts fulfill specific Government needs to specific requirements – leaving entities limited discretion on the capabilities of the end product or service.

Additionally, the STMD often provides entities the ability to compete for a Tipping Point FSAA[59] or obtain a unfunded SAA. NASA uses the term "Tipping Point" where:

- The proposed technology system at a Technology Readiness Level (TRL) of approximately 4 or higher at time of submission of the Mini Proposal;
- An investment in a ground demonstration or flight demonstration will result in: a significant advancement of the technology's maturation to at least TRL of 6, and a significant improvement in the Lead Entity's ability to successfully bring the technology to market; and,
- The partner has a robust plan for commercialisation.[60]

Should the prospective partner not want to pursue the above funded opportunity, it is still able to benefit from NASA's expertise while helping the Agency meet strategic goals by proposing under the parallel Announcement of Collaboration Opportunity (ACO) for the award of unfunded SAAs. These unfunded SAAs differ from the Tipping Point FSAA in that these agreements will "focus on advancing commercially developed technologies (through use of NASA unique resources on a no-exchange-of-funds basis) that can benefit both the commercial and government use of space".[61] The primary beneficiary of an unfunded SAA is the commercial partner who is availing itself of NASA resources to advance the development of a commercial space technology. Under this arrangement, instead of funding, the partner can obtain hardware, software, test facilities, and technical expertise from any NASA Center in order to "accelerate the development and availability of these technologies and reduce costs associated with their implementation and use".[62] The unfunded SAAs under the ACOs are for the primary benefit of the partner than standard nonreimbursable SAAs. Opening the US space agency's knowledge base, facilities and other resources to

57 Id.

58 Id. at 6.

59 While NASA does not always use the FSAA for Tipping Point advancements, it is trending to much more expanded use of them. It is noted that even when a contract is used, they tend to be extremely streamlined compared to contracts for the procurement of goods and services.

60 Space Technology Mission Directorate, Tipping Point/ACO Industry Forum 02.28.22, Virtual Industry Forum at 10.

61 Id at 22.

62 Space Technology Mission Directorate, Tipping Point/ACO Industry Forum 02.28.22, Virtual Industry Forum at 22.

be leveraged by private entities greatly facilitates the rate and ability of the US industrial base to grow in a way that aligns with NASA's goals, as well as those of the partner. This flexibility is a key result of NASA's broad and deep use of its other transaction authority.

Finally, the grant programme Space Technologies Research Grants (STRG) Program under STMD is geared toward working with universities and students to conduct fundamental research and develop groundbreaking advances in technologies and increase the overall talent base and "to improve America's technological and economic competitiveness".[63]

15.4.11.2 Space Operations Mission Directorate (SOMD)

That NASA is expanding its use of the FSAA and the FSAA-to-future services-contract approach beyond just space transportation is shown in its recent SOMD solicitation under the Agency's Communication Services Project (CSP). As stated by Eli Naffah, CSP project manager,

> We are following the agency's proven approach developed through commercial cargo and commercial crew services. By using funded Space Act Agreements, we're able to stimulate industry to demonstrate end-to-end capability leading to operational service. The flight demonstrations are risk reduction activities that will develop multiple capabilities and will provide operational concepts, performance validation, and acquisition models needed to plan the future acquisition of commercial services for each class of NASA missions.[64]

Under this programme, NASA intends to decommission its long reigning Tracking and Data Relay System (TDRS) which provides critical communications between ground stations and assets such as the ISS, and Hubble Space Telescope.[65]

Under the first part of this programme, companies submitted proposals explaining their technical approach, along with their plans for end-to-end demonstration of the services, as well as how the service will be viable on the commercial market, with NASA being only one of many customers. As part of the proposals, each entity had to develop milestones showing progress – with NASA funding associated with the successful accomplishment of each. NASA awarded FSAAs to six companies for a total amount of US$278.5 million.[66] It is not hard to imagine how such a funding infusion can greatly incentivise commercial development of a capability that would, in the end, still be owned, maintained, and operated by the company but from which NASA could one day procure services.

After successful demonstrations of the commercial satellite communication (SATCOM) systems funded under this activity, NASA may procure SATCOM services from one or more providers under a FAR-based contract.

63 NewSpace Global Report: 2022 Cislunar Market Opportunities, NASA Research Announcement (NRA): Early Stage Innovations Appendix 80HQTR22NOA01-22ESI-B2).

64 Space Communications, Release 22-036, NASA, Industry to Collaborate on Space Communications by 2025.

65 Id.

66 Id.

15.5 Use of the Federal Acquisition Regulation to enable procurement and legal innovation for commercial space

The US Federal Acquisition Regulations (FAR) are often misunderstood and (perhaps unfairly) maligned. The purpose of the FAR and the agency-specific acquisition regulations that implement or supplement them (e.g., NASA FAR Supplement, (NFS)) is to codify a set of uniform acquisition policies and procedures for use by all executive agencies of the US Government.[67] While these regulations have room for improvement, they achieve their core goal of ensuring that the US expends public funds with integrity, fairness, and openness.[68]

Seen by some as inflexible and as a system that does not promote commercial interests, the FAR is anything but. The very first section of the FAR explicitly encourages US acquisition professionals to innovate, explaining that if a procurement approach is in the best interests of the Government but not specifically addressed by the FAR or prohibited by law, this absence of direction should be interpreted as permitting civil servants to develop business process innovations.[69]

NASA has been a leader in using such acquisition innovations to achieve another central mandate of the FAR – maximising the use of commercial products and services in meeting Government requirements.[70] In recent history, NASA's pivot to focusing on commercial solutions arguably began with NASA's Commercial Crew Program.[71]

In the wake of the Commercial Crew contract awards, NASA sought additional strategies to capitalise on the strengths of the commercial space sector. Although Space Act Agreements frequently come to mind when imagining fast and innovative procurement mechanisms, NASA sought ways to operate within the FAR while still innovating and improving its procurement processes. The constraint here is that NASA's OTA is not a procurement mechanism; this means that if NASA has known and immediate requirements, as opposed to overarching objectives and potential future needs, then pursuant to law and NASA policy, the agency must utilise a procurement contract to procure those requirements. With this in mind, in late 2014, NASA developed a powerful FAR-based contracting tool that would bear fruit for many years to come: the omnibus Broad Agency Announcement (BAA) known as Next Space Technologies for Exploration Partnerships, (NextSTEP).[72]

Before discussing NextSTEP specifically, and its even more impactful successor instrument, NextSTEP-2, it is necessary to understand the BAA instrument more generally. A BAA is a type of solicitation that is available to the Government when it is procuring basic research, applied research, and that part of development not related to the development of a specific system.[73] A broad agency announcement is defined in FAR 2.101 as "a general announcement of an agency's research interest including criteria for selecting proposals and soliciting the participation of all offerors capable of satisfying the Government's needs (see 6.102(d)(2))".

67 FAR 1.101
68 FAR 1.102-2(c)
69 FAR 1.102-2(b)(2) and 1.102-4(e)
70 FAR 1.102-2(a)(4) and 1.102(b)(1)(i)
71 NASA's Commercial Orbital Transportation Services (COTS) agreements were a critical precursor to the Commercial Crew Program. More information on COTS is available NASA, Commercial Space Economy, Commercial Orbital Transportation Services (COTS).
72 NASA, NextSTEP, NextSTEP Overview.
73 FAR 35.016(a).

Along with the aforementioned core goals of the FAR, discussed *supra*, perhaps its most fundamental goal is promoting and ensuring competition.[74] The basis for this is the Competition in Contracting Act (CICA)[75] as implemented at FAR Part 6. Subject to limited exceptions, CICA requires federal agencies obtain full and open competition for federal procurements through the use of the specific competitive procedures identified within FAR 6.102. These procedures include sealed bids; competitive proposals; a combination of competitive procedures; and what the FAR calls "other competitive procedures". BAAs are one of three such other competitive procedures enumerated in the FAR. Unlike sealed bidding or other competitive procurement methods, offerors who submit proposals in response to a BAA are not, by some measures, competing against each other.[76] Rather, they are attempting to demonstrate that their proposed research meets the agency's requirements.[77] This results in a situation in which offerors' proposals are generally not engaged in a head-to-head competition, but the agency is nonetheless considered to be acting in compliance with the competition mandates of CICA by competing the opportunity with interested vendors. This apparent curiosity is made possible by the FAR's explicit designation of a BAA as an "other competitive procedure". This designation allows agencies to use a BAA to fulfill certain types of requirements without using the competitive procedures at FAR Part 15, but while also not violating CICA's competition mandates. The NextSTEP BAA is an important example of just how powerful and innovative the use of BAA authority can be for federal agencies.

What is NextSTEP? NextSTEP is a BAA that was released by NASA at the end of 2014 for the purpose of soliciting proposals for concept studies or technology development projects that will be necessary to enable human pioneers to go to deep space destinations such as an asteroid and Mars.

Why a BAA? At the time NASA developed this tool, NASA was facing a challenge that is so common to federal agencies as to be practically axiomatic – ambitious goals coupled with funding insufficient to fulfill all of them. In addition, traditional procurements under FAR Part 15 were not always operating at the desired speeds, leading to dissatisfaction with the pace at which NASA could get to work with industry on advancing the state-of-the-art. Specifically, NASA sought a relatively streamlined acquisition approach that would enable NASA and industry partners to perform research, development, and sometimes demonstration of deep space human exploration capabilities in the cislunar proving ground and beyond. The three critical areas identified by NASA for technology maturation were Advanced Propulsion Systems, Habitation Systems, and Small Satellite Missions (EM-1 secondary payloads).

To meet these goals, NASA created a procurement vehicle, the NextSTEP BAA, which they hoped would rapidly enable public-private partnerships, thereby stimulating the US space industry while working to expand the frontiers of knowledge, capabilities, and opportunities in space.[78] This effort was spearheaded by Jason Crusan, the Director of NASA's Advanced Exploration Systems division within the Human Exploration and Operations Mission Directorate.[79]

74 See, for example, FAR *1.102(b)(1)(iii)*.

75 10 U.S.C. 3201(a)(1); 41 U.S.C. 3301(a)(1) for civilian, non-NASA agencies

76 FAR 35.016 (d) provides that proposals submitted in response to a BAA "need not be evaluated against each other since they are not submitted in accordance with a common work statement". Contrast this with federal procurements executed pursuant to the authority at FAR Part 15, which calls for the use of a "best-value tradeoff" procedure in which proposals are directly compared to one another in order for the Government to identify the proposal that represents the best value according to the solicitation's stated evaluation criteria.

77 Matter of: Tamper Proof Container Systems Corporation, B- 402191 (2010)

78 NASA, RELEASE 14-297, NASA Seeks Proposals to Develop Capabilities for Deep Space Exploration, Journey to Mars.

79 NASA Broad Agency Announcement Virtual Industry Forum, November 6, 2014, NextStep.

Key attributes of the NextSTEP BAA:

- Award fixed price, milestone-based contracts;
- Number of contract awards dependent on funds availability;
- Encourage the contribution of private corporate resources to the private-public partnership to achieve goals and objectives;
- Select partners with the technical capability to mature key technologies and demonstrate commitment toward potential commercial applications.

The NextSTEP BAA not only allowed for cost sharing between NASA and the commercial partner, the solicitation mandated it, resulting in the kind of cost savings to NASA that would support multiple contract awards to achieve a variety of critical technology maturation objectives. From among the proposals submitted in response to the NextSTEP BAA, NASA made a total of 12 contract awards – seven in the area of habitation, three in propulsion, and two in small satellites. This alone was a significant success story, but the timeline on which it occurred cemented the utility of BAAs and the NextSTEP BAA specifically; in a period of only about five months, NASA issued the NextSTEP solicitation, received dozens of proposals from industry, evaluated these proposals, and made an unusually high number of contract awards. As of March 2015, NASA had fully achieved proof of concept for the NextSTEP BAA procurement methodology.

Capitalising on this success, NASA maintained its momentum and issued the NextSTEP-2 BAA within the following year, releasing the first iteration in April of 2016. NextSTEP-2 constituted an important evolution from the original NextSTEP, keeping the attributes that had proven to be beneficial while also adding critical new features. Chief among the instrument's evolved capabilities was its classification as an "omnibus" BAA. The original NextSTEP was a standalone BAA that called for proposals in response to three enumerated areas of research. In contrast, NextSTEP-2 was meant to function as a sort of umbrella BAA off of which NASA would issue appendices. Each such appendix would then operate as its own standalone procurement.[80] This structure provided multiple benefits to both NASA and industry. Chief among these is that NextSTEP2 operated as a collection of readymade terms, conditions, eligibility requirements, and evaluation methodology. With these decisions already made and codified in its text, NASA programmes who desired to issue an appendix off of this omnibus were able to focus on defining their specific research objectives. This pre-determined BAA content allowed for the rapid issuance of appendices, operating as a sort of plug-and-play procurement instrument. Each time a programme desired to form a contractual partnership to advance research and development in a particular area, the NextSTEP-2 omnibus presented a standardised, tried and tested approach that was fast and enabled cost-sharing with industry. One can imagine why this technique quickly gained popularity within NASA, ultimately leading to the issuance of 14 distinct appendices to date. These appendices span a wide range of research and development efforts, including habitation systems, trash compaction and processing for deep space exploration, and perhaps the most well-known NextSTEP-2 appendices, those for development of crewed lunar landing systems, known as the Human Landing System (HLS).[81]

80 NASA, NextSTEP, NextSTEP Overview.

81 NASA's Artemis Plan, NASA's Lunar Exploration Program Overview, September 2020, at p. 21.

15.5.1 Commercial LEO programme – private astronaut missions as a case study

Private Astronaut Missions (PAMs) to the International Space Station (ISS) are part of NASA's strategy to develop a robust low-Earth orbit (LEO) economy. In 2019, NASA modified the existing ISS NASA Research Announcement (NRA) NNJ13ZBG001N to enable this.[82] An NRA is one of three BAA types specified within the NFS at part 1853. Focus Area 4 of the ISS NRA states:

- PAMs must use US transportation vehicles that meet NASA's ISS visiting vehicle requirements;
- A mission of four crew for up to 14 days has been determined to be feasible; proposals exceeding these constraints will be reviewed for feasibility but carry significant risk for execution;
- Scheduling availability is subject to overall opportunities, integrated requirements, and is subject to change;
- Where commercially available at a reasonable price, the PAM Provider should seek direct business-to-business arrangements for required services.

The NRA also instructs that the PAM Provider should coordinate with ISS International Partners (IPs) for use of any IP resources. NASA will continue to utilise existing CCP contracts with Space Exploration Technologies Corp. (SpaceX) and The Boeing Company to acquire transportation services for NASA astronauts. On 7 June 2019, NASA rolled out the agency's plan at that time for commercial development of low-Earth orbit at NASDAQ on Wall Street, opening the International Space Station (ISS) to expanded commercial activities.[83] The roll-out was precipitated by the NASA LEO Studies/Strategy (SIP & ASM) Feb–May 2019. This plan fulfills NASA Strategic Objective 2.1 that directs the Agency to "lay the foundation for America to maintain a constant human presence in low-Earth orbit (LEO) to be enabled by a commercial market".[84]

NASA's 5-Point Plan included the following activities:

- Establish ISS commercial use and pricing policy;
- Enable private astronaut missions to ISS;
- Initiate process for commercial development of LEO destinations;
- Seek out and pursue opportunities to stimulate sustainable demand;
- Quantify NASA's long-term needs for activities in LEO.[85]

NASA notes the following benefits of the Private Astronaut Missions:

- Allows commercial industry gain insight into the costs associated with owning and operating a future platform;
- Reduces market risk to LEO commercial destination developers by demonstrating market;
- Non-government human missions to LEO are a key market element for future commercial destinations;

82 Note that PAMs are also typically executed with the help of one or more Space Act Agreements in which the private mission owner reimburses NASA for support provided in executing those missions.

83 NASA, Explore Humans in Space, HEO NAC, Commercialization of Loew Earth Orbit at 8.

84 NASA Announces Intent to Procure a Future Short Duration Spaceflight Opportunity.

85 Id., at 4.

- Expands range of commercial activities that can be performed on ISS;
- New commercial use policy identifies activities that can be performed by private astronauts but not by NASA astronauts;
- Potential to increase flight rate and reduce costs for access to LEO;
- Potential to increase available crew time on orbit for NASA, commercial, and other R&D activities.[86]

15.6 NASA's future human spaceflight exploration endeavours

The HLS, *supra*, is a small part of NASA's overall exciting lunar plans of its Artemis programme – the goal of which is to methodically build the needed infrastructure and transportation needed to enable a habitable Artemis Base Camp, begin lunar surface development, and validate technologies needed to prepare for missions to Mars and increased deep space human exploration.[87] These plans include preparation by landing robots on the lunar surface to help determine prime spots for *in situ* resource extraction and use, as well as other validation of needed capabilities such as precision landing. The precursor unmanned lunar missions will also include delivering some of the larger elements of cargo to help support the later human missions.[88]

To provide for humankind's return to the Moon, NASA's plans call for an uncrewed mission to the Moon via Artemis I; a crewed test mission to and from the Moon via Artemis II; and culminate in landing the first woman and next man on the Moon under Artemis III.[89]

After these missions, work on Artemis Base camp will be begin in earnest.[90]

These lunar exploration activities executed through Artemis missions and under the management of NASA's forthcoming Moon to Mars Program Office will help NASA and the commercial space industry to develop the technologies and capabilities necessary for humankind's next major space exploration endeavor: landing a human on Mars.[91]

15.7 Conclusion

While laws and regulations are often seen as barriers to innovation, especially in the commercial space realm, NASA has defied this expectation and developed unique strategies and instruments to quickly and affordably meet its needs and those of its commercial space partners, all without sacrificing safety for its astronauts and value to the taxpayers. NASA's creative policies and agreement vehicles provide the framework for a multitude of flexible methods to achieve the Agency's goals, while also beneficially impacting and supporting the continued growth of the US commercial space sector.

86 Id., at 14

87 NASA, Artemis Plan, NASA's Lunar Exploration Program Overview September 2020 at 2.

88 Id., at 10.

89 Id., at 15.

90 Id., at 20.

91 For a helpful visual showing the components of the NASA's Artemis plan and pre-Mars activities, see NASA's Artemis Plan, NASA's Lunar Exploration Program Overview, September 2020, at p. 64.

16

PUBLIC-PRIVATE PARTNERSHIP TO PROMOTE NEW ENTRANTS TO SPACE R&D ACTIVITIES IN JAPAN

Mizuki Tani-Hatakenaka

Introduction

In March 2020, Japan Aerospace Exploration Agency (JAXA) concluded a new partnership-type contract for active debris removal (Commercial Removal of Debris Demonstration, CRD2) with a start-up, Astroscale Japan Inc., which was working in on-orbit services as a partner, including in active debris removal (ADR).[1] CRD2 consists of two phases. The aim of Phase I is to demonstrate key technologies for rendezvous and proximity operations (RPO) relative to non-cooperative targets and the acquisition of images showing the attitude motion and surface damage of space debris. The aim of Phase II is to demonstrate the technologies to remove large space debris. The partner was selected for Phase I. The contract was concluded as the first public-private partnership (PPP) of the research and development (R&D) spacecraft in the Japanese space sector. As a new framework to acquire the private sector's technical capability and to implement ADR as a business, the idea is for the partner company to develop a spacecraft and demonstrate the technologies by itself based on its own business plan. In this framework, JAXA supports the partner company technically in order to achieve the results. The framework was made based on policies and JAXA's experiences from its procurement.

In the past, there had been discussion that fostering an existing launch or satellite manufacturer is more important than promoting new entrants, in order to work within tight government budgets. However, innovation cannot occur in such an oligopolistic market, and it is essential to stimulate start-ups, as actors, in the so-called NewSpace and companies in non-space fields.

This chapter discusses the public procurement in Japan's space sector from the perspective of promoting new entrants with innovative ideas. The first section gives an overview of traditional public procurement in the space field by referring to the national R&D of H-IIA launch vehicle. In the second section, after discussing issues around promoting new entrants like start-ups, the focus turns to procurement for H3 launch vehicle (Japan's new flagship rocket) and CRD2 as examples

1 Japan Aerospace Exploration Agency (JAXA), 'JAXA Concludes Partnership-Type Contract for Phase I of Its Commercial Removal of Debris Demonstration (CRD2)' (Japan Aerospace Exploration Agency, 23 March 2020).

DOI: 10.4324/9781003268475-21

of how to solve the issues. The final section sets out additional challenges to promote new entrants through public procurement for future R&D in the space sector.

16.1 Traditional public procurement for R&D in Japan's space sector

Before discussing specific public procurement in the Japanese space sector, general public procurement is addressed. General public procurement, which is not customised for R&D, is designed based on procuring commercial off-the-shelf products and generic services in an environment where multiple companies compete in a large market. For this reason, fair competition, such as competitive bidding, is the primary method many governmental offices use. In competitive bidding, the ordering party determines the requirements and specifications and selects the company that can achieve them at the lowest price. In addition, once the bid is opened and the contractor is selected, the ordering party cannot change the requirements in principle to ensure fairness among the companies participating in the bidding process.

In contrast, in the space R&D sector, it is difficult for a national agency to define by itself what kind of specifications can be achieved because it is necessary to integrate the technologies owned by the government agency and manufacturing technologies owned by private companies to conduct large-scale and long-term development. Therefore, instead of general competitive bidding, in which changes in requirements are not permitted after contractor selection, the Request for Proposal (RFP) has been adopted.[2] The RFP's central feature is that the parties can adjust the details of the requirements, specifications, schedule, the initial scope of the contract, the contract amount, and so on, based on the company's proposal, even after selection of the contractor, until the contract is concluded. Also, the RFP usually involves a competitive dialogue prior to contractor selection in order to exchange views efficiently to avoid misunderstanding the contents of the RFP by the ordering party and the proposal by the firms.

In addition, traditional procurement for R&D in the space sector was designed in line with Phased Project Planning for waterfall development, a method in which design, implementation, and each process are carried out step by step to meet the strictly predetermined requirements faithfully, to mitigate uncertain risks in large-scale and long-term R&D projects. After a series of significant failures in launch vehicles and satellites in the early 2000s, JAXA made improvements to its project management.[3] Phased Project Planning divides the entire project into several phases: concept studies, concept development, project formulation, basic design, detailed design, production, testing, and operation. In each phase, detailed work packages are created. The results of each phase are then reviewed, and a decision is made on whether to proceed to the next phase. The contract is amended as and when requirements and specifications are added as the project progresses. A framework based on waterfall development, in which specifications are clearly determined before a contract is signed, makes it easier for both parties to predict risks in the contract and to reduce the cost of risk included in the contract amount. Such reduction of the risk cost is important because private insurers often are not able to underwrite insurance in a large R&D project, or the insurance premiums are incredibly high due to a lack of precedent.

2 JAXA, Procurement Department, 'Art. 62 of Keiyaku Jimu Jissi Yoryo [Contract Administration Procedures]' (Japan Aerospace Exploration Agency).

3 JAXA, Chief Engineer Office, 'Shisutemuzu Enjiniaringu no Kihonteki Kangaekata [Basic Concept on Systems Engineering]' (BDB-06007, 2007). Masashi Okada, Shizuo Yamamoto and Toshifumi Mukai, 'Systems Engineering Enhancement Initiative in JAXA' (2009) 7 Transactions of the Japan Society for Aeronautical and Space Sciences 1.

Furthermore, a market price does not often exist in the small space R&D sector. Accordingly, a cost accounting method[4] is used to calculate the contract amount in which all costs involved in performing any process, project, or developing a product are noted and analysed. That makes the contract amount closer to the actual cost, thus permitting the ordering party to be accountable for its appropriateness. It also has the advantage that private companies can expect a guaranteed minimum cost and participate in a project with high difficulty levels. To ensure the appropriateness of this cost accounting method, every few years JAXA conducts a system survey to examine the accounting systems of contractors and a cost rate survey to determine the cost rate to be used in contracts with major manufacturers.[5]

Concerning the method of determining the contract amount, in the days of the National Space Development Agency of Japan (NASDA), one of JAXA's predecessors, the cost-reimbursement contract was the predominant method, whereby the contract was signed for an estimated amount at the time of contracting, and the actual costs and profit percentage as agreed before were paid after completion of the contract performance, with confirmation by an audit of the actual costs. A cost reimbursable contract is used when the scope of the work to be performed cannot be properly defined at the time of contract award, or when the risks associated with the works are high. This is a high-risk contract for the space agency because the final cost to pay is not clear when the contract is entered into. Therefore, the space agency sets out a ceiling in the cost-reimbursement contract. As a result, if the actual cost exceeded the ceiling, the space agency was not required to pay the excess amount, but the contractor was even required to return the extra amount to the space agency because the contractor is entitled to actual cost and profit percentage as agreed before. However, this result was deemed to be unfair and not to provide incentives for companies to reduce costs in a case in 1999 in which companies overcharged by posting fees up to the maximum limit to make up for deficits in the national space project.[6] After that, JAXA admitted the flaw in the method and shifted to a fixed-price contract in principle. A contract amount close to the actual cost was achieved, using both a fixed-price contract and a cost accounting method, and by making a series of contract amendments in response to changing requirements.

In terms of contract conditions, procurement for space activities needs terms and conditions that are in line with international space law and the domestic regulatory framework, as detailed in the "Contract Practice in the European Space Sector",[7] for example, third-party liability and compulsory insurance for damages.

The development and operation contract of H-IIA launch vehicle, which has been Japan's core rocket for more than 30 years, can be taken as an example. First, the contractors were selected separately for development and operation. The development contract was concluded with one manufacturer in charge of system integration and seven manufacturers in charge of the development of each key technology. Furthermore, each contract was divided into a development phase, and the contract was amended dozens of times in accordance with the clear requirements and specifications that arose as the project progressed. The contract amounts were calculated based on the cost accounting method and concluded at an amount as close to the actual cost as possible. After H-IIA No. 13, the launch programme was transferred to the selected private launch operator, and JAXA

4 JAXA, 'Investigation Report on Overcharges by Mitsubishi Electric Corporation' (21 December 2012) 6.

5 Ibid. 40.

6 National Space Development Agency (NASA), 'Results of Additional Investigation into Overbilling by NEC and Request for Restitution Based on the Results of the Investigation' (11 August 2000).

7 Lesley Jane Smith and Ingo Baumann (eds), *Contracting for Space: Contract Practice in the European Space Sector* (Ashgate 2011).

took on the responsibility for ensuring flight safety and ground safety during launch and so on. The launch service agreement provided by the private sector includes terms and conditions such as third-party liability in the event of the launch vehicle being in an accident and compulsory insurance. That is to implement obligations and conditions resulting out of the space treaties, including the Outer Space Treaty[8] and the Liability Convention[9] since domestic legislation other than the Act on Japan Aerospace Exploration Agency (Act No. 161 of 2002, JAXA Act)[10] was absent prior to enactment of the Act on Launching Artificial Satellites and Managing Satellites (Act No. 76 of 2016, hereinafter the Space Activity Act) in 2016.

16.2 Towards public procurement to promote NewSpace

16.2.1 Basic idea to promote NewSpace

The traditional procurement method described in the previous section is still necessary to use for a large, long-term, and high-risk project. However, the method is complex for accountability purposes and can be a barrier to new entrants. Three major problems with this conventional approach can be identified in promoting NewSpace.

The first is the cost accounting method. In conventional procurement, the contract amount is usually calculated by adding the accumulating costs and multiplying them by a certain profit margin due to the absence of the market price. Moreover, a contract amount is decided within a narrow scope where specifications are fixed but added dozens of times as the project progresses to avoid an excess burden on the manufacturer and prevent the risk cost in the contract amount from becoming excessive.

However, there are three important sub-issues in the cost accounting method. First, cost data is confidential information that contains a list of suppliers and know-how. Thus, new entrants are usually disinclined to disclose their cost data as traditional manufacturers do. The second sub-issue is that the cost is multiplied by a fixed profit rate. This results in a small total profit amount in a small-scale project like a small satellite, and even in a reduction of total profit if a cost reduction is realized. On this point, JAXA basically adopted a fixed price contract in which the payment amount is fixed when concluding a contract so that it serves as an incentive for the company to reduce the cost after the contract is signed. However, a contract is concluded after confirming the detailed work package in line with Phased Project Planning, and the contract amount is reduced by amendment if the work is found no longer necessary as the project progresses. The mechanism is effective in that it lets a company to charge necessary expenses and guarantees a certain amount of profit but makes it difficult for companies to make profits. The Ministry of Defense adds a profit of about 7% to the cost price in its procurement and so does JAXA, but the rate is still low compared

8 Treaty on Principles Governing the Activities of States in the Exploration and Use of Outer Space, including the Moon and Other Celestial Bodies (adopted 27 January 1967, entered into force 10 October 1967) 610 UNTS 205.

9 Convention on International Liability for Damage Caused by Space Objects (entered into force September 1972) 961 UNTS 187.

10 For further details, see Mizuki Tani-Hatakenaka, 'The Proposed Public Procurement for Projects to Enhance Industrial Capabilities through Japanese Lessons Learned' in PJ Blount and others, *Proceedings of the International Institute of Space Law 2018* (International Astronautical Federation 2019). See also Seiko Morikawa, 'Comparative Analysis on the Legal Framework of the Privatization of Space Transportation' (2012) 10(28) Transactions of the Japan Society for Aeronautical and Space Sciences 7.

to the US, where it is said to exceed 10%.[11] Profits are recognised in the US as an important factor to stimulate efficient contract performance and to maintain a viable industrial base,[12] and such low profitability hinders the virtuous cycle from profit to investment[13] and leads to the withdrawal from a business. In the example of a large company, following the Renault–Nissan alliance, its aerospace division was sold to IHI in 2000. That sale was said to have been made to concentrate on core business[14] and to avoid outflow of solid launch vehicle technology overseas. It was also said that the aerospace division was sold because it was not in a position to achieve the 7% profit margin target set by former President Ghosn.[15] Third, in the private sector, contract amounts are often determined by evaluating total costs rather than by accumulating costs. When entering a new business or starting up a company, resources are limited, and it is not easy to build a system dedicated solely to the public procurement of space.

The second public procurement challenge to facilitate the entry of NewSpace is the delivery of spacecraft in accordance with the national space agency's stringent quality and reliability standards and inspections. Since spacecraft are generally difficult to repair once launched, the agency has developed reliability assurance, quality assurance, system safety, and configuration. However, private companies are more sensitive to cost-effectiveness, and have to set up and achieve a competitive development process, struggling between the pressure to reduce costs and the pressure to improve quality and reliability with sales to customers outside the government. For example, NASA's Commercial Orbital Transportation Services (COTS) team was aware that the large volume of detailed technical requirements typically levied on NASA contractors could stifle innovation. In lieu of strict requirements, COTS provided a set of straightforward guidelines to allow companies to provide the necessary services to the International Space Station (ISS) in the manner that best fits their unique potential.[16] It is also possible to change the responsibilities so that the existing strict standards do not apply. For example, when the national agency sets not spacecraft development but the final outcomes, it can leave the development processes to the private sector's discretion. Such a framework leads the private sector to apply its own approach to quality and reliability, making it easier for new entrants to be inventive. This concept also appeared in NASA's COTS as "Buy a Ticket, Not a Vehicle".[17] This generates room for ingenuity and innovation for a new entrant as it can apply its own quality and reliability ideas instead of existing standards.

The third point is bulk procurement. The national space agency often procures only the necessary amount as R&D progresses, and bulk purchasing to support the industry is not recognized as an appropriate act for an R&D agency. In this regard, the Cabinet Office of Japan has emphasised the importance of continuous R&D that responds to market needs, such as developing a series of spacecraft, and has announced a government plan for the next five years in the Basic Plan for Space since 2008 when the Basic Act on Space (Act No. 43 of 2008) was enacted. The inten-

11 Ministry of Finance, Fiscal System Council, Fiscal Reform Subcommittee, Expenditure Reform Subcommittee, 'Document 3 "Boei" [Defense]' (20 April 2022) 26.

12 48 C.F.R. § 15.404-4(a)(2) (1998).

13 Cabinet Office, Committee on National Space Policy, 'Uchu Sangyo Bijon 2030 [Space Industry Vision 2030]' (29 May 2017) 20. See also, Committee on National Space Policy, Space Industry Promotion Subcommittee, 'Document 5 "Chotatsu Seido no Arikata no Kento ni tsuite" [Examination of Procurement System]' (10 March 2017) 5.

14 Nissan Motor Corporation, 'Sale of Nissan's Aerospace Division' (14 February 2000).

15 Shinya Matsuura, 'Naze Kokusan Roketto ha Ochiru no ka [Why do domestic rockets crash?]' (Nikkei BP, 2004) 212.

16 NASA, Johnson Space Center History Office, 'Commercial Orbital Transportation Services: A New Era in Spaceflight' (NASA/SP-2014-617, May 2014) 22.

17 Ibid. 12.

tion is to enable the private sector to forecast demand and to make business plans. However, the announcement is not a legally binding obligation. From the start-up's standpoint, obtaining stable sales through certain public contracts can be an indication that the company will not go bankrupt, which can lead to more favourable investment from venture capitalists.

The Space Industry Vision 2030,[18] which was formulated in 2017, also stipulates that the public sector should consider a start-up-friendly system of procurement, such as seeking outcomes rather than approaches and evaluating total contract amount rather than the cost accounting method. These ideas were taken into account when launching CRD2.

16.2.2 Cases

16.2.2.1 H3 launch vehicle

H3 is Japan's next-generation heavy-lift launch vehicle as the successor to H-IIA. H3 is designed to attract commercial satellite users by achieving high flexibility, high reliability, and high cost-performance, i.e., a target launch cost that is half the previous one.[19] This procurement is a transitional case in terms of the second issue above because the development and launch operations of H3 launch vehicle were designed to enhance its competitiveness by leveraging private-sector ingenuity rather than promoting NewSpace. For example, the prime contractor to develop H3 and its launch provider were selected collectively so that the prime contractor could develop it with its operation in mind. Moreover, in contrast to H-IIA, where JAXA defined the entire development plan, the specifications, and the development cost of the launch vehicle, the prime contractor for H3 determined them at its discretion. It is also noteworthy that the procurement methods of H3 and Ariane 6 have much in common.[20]

On the other hand, some key technologies such as engines and ground facilities remain under development by JAXA. After delivery and inspection of H3 launch vehicle by JAXA, JAXA conducts a test flight as a comprehensive test including JAXA's key technology and ground equipment. Hence, H3 launch vehicle is inspected as a deliverable based on JAXA's quality and reliability standards. As for the cost amount, the cost accounting method is applied as before. Finally, regarding collective purchasing after development, as in the past, the government's launch plan is only indicated in the Basic Plan on Space without any legal obligation.

16.2.2.2 CRD2

The CRD2 procurement was planned to pave the way for new entrants to implement ADR as a business. The intention behind it was to commercialise space debris removal and open up new markets for private business through the world's first technology demonstration to remove large-scale debris in orbit. The on-orbit environment is said to be improved by two services: End-of-Life (EOL), which is primarily for commercial satellite operators and involves the installation of docking plates on satellites prior to launch to remove the failed satellite from operational orbit; and ADR, which is mainly for the public sector and aims to eliminate existing non-cooperative

18 Cabinet Office (n 13).

19 JAXA, 'Shingata-Kikan-Rokketo no Kaihatsu-Jokyo ni tsuite, [Development Status of the New Flagship Rocket]' (16 June 2014). See also, Shigeru Mori and others, 'H3 Launch Vehicle Development Concept of Operations' (SpaceOps 2016 Conference, May 2016) 1.

20 Tani-Hatakenaka (n 10).

massive debris.[21] While the European Space Agency (ESA) signed an agreement with a European industrial consortium led by Swiss start-up, ClearSpace SA, to develop debris removal services, as a technical demonstration equivalent to so-called EOL,[22] JAXA selected Astroscale as its partner in the narrowly defined ADR demonstration, which targets massive existing debris of approximately three to nine tons with a high collision probability. During the procurement review, JAXA consulted with external business experts and investors, and experts have participated in the project reviews.[23]

The responsibilities of JAXA and the partner company differ considerably from those in previous procurement agreements. In Phase I, JAXA set out only the service requirements and the safety requirements and procured the demonstration service and the image data obtained by approaching and imaging the target debris. A satellite was recognised as a byproduct of the service process and was not subject to delivery to JAXA. Thus, the spacecraft system specifications were left to the discretion of the private sector. In addition, JAXA is in a position to provide technical support to the partner company, including licensing its intellectual properties on request.[24]

Through this framework, JAXA aims to enable a company to acquire the capability to develop its technology and operate its own satellites using its own business plans. CRD2's website announces that the only JAXA standards applicable to CRD2 Phase I are the Safety Standard for On-orbit Servicing Missions (JERG-2-026) and the Space Debris Mitigation Standard (JMR-003). Accordingly, the partner company will obtain a competitive development process at its own discretion, balancing cost reduction and improvement of reliability and quality. Since the responsibility of launching the satellite is allocated to the company, the company procures a launch service from the global market by itself, contrasting with governmental satellites which have often been launched by domestic rockets. This enabled Astroscale to reach an agreement with Rocket Lab Inc. in 2021 to launch its satellite from New Zealand in 2023.[25] Also, the partner company can apply a different development process than the waterfall development. However, JAXA still conducts its review such as a Preliminary Design Review (PDR), Critical Design Review (CDR), Post Qualification Review (PQR), and so on at each milestone.[26] Lastly, since satellite ownership remains with the company, it can plan and conduct its own technology demonstration missions. For example, in addition to JAXA's service requirement for rendezvous performance, fixed-point observation, fly-around observation, and mission termination, Astroscale plans target inspection and diagnosis, a close approach to target, and extra mission as its own mission.[27]

Since the partner company performs the satellite specifications, manufacturing, testing, and operations, intellectual property related to the satellite system, including RPO technology, is

21 Brian Weeden and others, 'Development of Global Policy for Active Debris Removal Services' (First International Orbital Debris Conference, December 2019) 2.

22 European Space Agency (ESA), 'Clearspace-1 SOR' (CS-ESA-SOR-TD-005). See also, JAXA, 'CRD2 Fezu I ni tsuite [About Commercial Removal of Debris Demonstration (CRD2) Phase I]' (Council for Science and Technology, Research Planning and Evaluation Subcommittee, Space Utilization Subcommittee, Document 63-1, 13 December 2021).

23 JAXA, Research and Development Directorate, 'Overview of CRD2 Phase I Project'.

24 Toru Yamamoto and others, 'Pave the Way for Active Debris Removal Realization: JAXA Commercial Removal of Debris Demonstration (CRD2)' in T Flohrer, S Lemmens and F Schmitz (eds), *Proceedings of the 8th European Conference on Space Debris* (ESA Space Debris Office 2021).

25 Astroscale Japan, 'Astroscale Selects Rocket Lab to Launch Phase I of JAXA's Debris Removal Demonstration Project' (21 September 2021).

26 JAXA (n 23).

27 Yamamoto and others (n 24).

granted to the partner company in general. JAXA provides technical advice, including licensing JAXA's intellectual property, only when the partner needs them. In this way, the partner company increases the project's feasibility to realise ADR, which no one else in the world has yet accomplished. JAXA may also improve its own technology by receiving feedback from the partner company. The intellectual property created by the contractor is generally granted to the contractor in principle, but the CRD2 procurement is structured such that JAXA can enhance its own R&D through this project if the partner uses JAXA's intellectual property.

In terms of the development cost, JAXA shares it with the partner because it benefits in business terms by being involved in the CRD2 project.[28] The shared cost amount has not been disclosed.[29] In addition, a firm-fixed price was selected as JAXA's service requirement of acquiring debris image data will not change in principle.[30] In other words, the additional costs in CRD2 will be borne by the partner, unlike in conventional procurement where JAXA often has to bear them. Thus, the cost sharing and the firm-fixed price encourage the private sector to meet the costs within the schedule specified in the contract. Payment is also made in steps, after each milestone is reviewed and approved, instead of in a lump-sum payment after services are completed. That lowers the barrier to entry for a company that does not have a large amount of capital.

16.3 Additional challenges for future procurement

16.3.1 Lessons learned using a comparative approach between CRD2 and NASA's COTS

As mentioned above, the CRD2 procurement process intends to encourage the partner to achieve its business goals. CRD2 Phase I is ongoing, and new challenges may still arise. This section identifies five lessons learned, compared them to NASA's COTS, which is one of the most successful PPPs in the space sector and credited with boosting SpaceX.

Firstly, NASA's COTS applied the funded Space Act Agreement in which appropriated funds are transferred to a domestic partner to accomplish a goal consistent with NASA's mission.[31] In contrast, CRD2 was a bilateral contract in which one party's promise serves as consideration for the promise of the other, not unilateral funding. This was because JAXA was not supposed to support the private sector without reasonable consideration under the JAXA Act prior to 2020.[32] JAXA, therefore, set out two deliverables: image data and R&D results report. In addition, JAXA may place too much emphasis on its identity as an R&D organization. CRD2 has established a mechanism in which JAXA, as an R&D organisation, improves its technologies through JAXA's technical advice and licence. However, for projects such as NASA's COTS, where the space agency already has the technology, it is unlikely to result in the accumulation of many new technologies on the part of the space agency. In such a case, a mechanism such as CRD2 is not applicable. If JAXA realises that it is not just an R&D organisation but also a core implementing agency that supports the government-wide utilisation of space development with technology, as stipulated in the July 2012 enactment of the Act for Partial Amendment of the Act for Establishment of the

28 JAXA (n 23).

29 Caleb Henry, 'Astroscale Wins First Half of JAXA Debris-Removal Mission' (Space News, 12 February 2020).

30 Yamamoto and others (n 24).

31 NASA, Office of the General Counsel, 'Space Act Agreements Guide' (NASA Advisory Implementing Instruction, NAII 1050-1C, 11 August 2014) 17.

32 Act on Japan Aerospace Exploration Agency (Act No 161 of 13 December 2002) Art. 18.1.

Cabinet Office, it may be possible to create a project that genuinely stimulates the market like COTS.

The situation surrounding JAXA is expected to change following the amended Art. 34 of the Act on Activation of the Creation of Science and Technology Innovation (Act No. 63 of 2020) that introduces the investment function to JAXA entering into force in April 2021. In response to the amendment, JAXA solicited ideas to utilise its investment function for two consecutive years beginning in 2021.[33] The investment function will allow JAXA to facilitate the entry of NewSpace with more flexibility.

The second point is that JAXA eventually selected only one partner for CRD2, while NASA's COTS selected two partners. NASA's COTS was concerned with space transportation, which ensures autonomous access to space, and it is necessary to hedge the risk by selecting multiple suppliers. Furthermore, NASA was in the process of developing its own space transportation system. Even if all of the selected contractors failed, the risk of losing the US space transportation was hedged. Unlike space transportation, ADR failures would not immediately affect national autonomy. Thus, in the case of CRD2, a compromise could be made to limit the number of partners to one. However, if the budget allows, obtaining multiple partners creates competition and leads the ordering party to hedge the risk of failure. It is noteworthy that as of August 2022 two contractors had been selected for the front-loading technical study to implement Phase I.[34]

Third, CRD2 distinguished between Phase I and Phase II and selected the partner for each. That made it easier for private firms to decide whether to also participate in Phase II or withdraw. It helped to open the door for new entrants. However, if a different company is selected for Phase II, JAXA may have to undertake additional work. To prevent that, it might be possible to stipulate terms and conditions that require the entity implementing Phase I to disclose its Phase I results to the entity implementing Phase II. However, it would not be practical to transfer the know-how from the Phase I partner to the Phase II partner.

The fourth point concerns bulk purchases. NASA employed a two-phase acquisition strategy for cargo to ISS. COTS was a demonstration of partners' capability. Then Commercial Resupply Services (CRS) was an independent purchase of a fully-developed service.[35] CRS employed Indefinite Delivery Indefinite Quantity (IDIQ) procurement.[36] IDIQ is used when the government cannot predetermine the exact quantity or supplies or services needed during the contract period.[37] In IDIQ, maximum and minimum quantities or prices are stated, and the government bears an obligation to order the minimum.[38] In contrast, CRD2 has no post-development/technical demonstration phase. If a lump-sum procurement phase had been announced, CRD2 would have been more attractive to venture firms and investors as Development Bank of Japan reported concerning H3.[39] In Japan, Art. 14-2 of the Public Finance Act (Act No. 34 of 1947) stipulates a five-year term for the national debt, but if the Act on Promotion of Private Finance Initiative (Act No. 117 of 1999)

33 JAXA, Business Development and Industrial Relations Department, 'Investment' (Japan Aerospace Exploration Agency).

34 JAXA, Procurement Department, 'Public Notice of the Results of the Selection of the Contracting Party' (22TK00209GKCI, 8 August 2022).

35 National Aeronautics and Space Administration (n 16) 81.

36 48 C.F.R. § 16.504 (1998).

37 Ibid. § 16.504(b).

38 Ibid. § 16.504(a)(1).

39 Development Bank of Japan, 'Nihon ni okeru Uchu Sangyo no Kyosoryoku Kyoka [Enhancement of the Competitiveness of the Space Industry in Japan]' (11 May 2017) 138.

is applied, debt is to be paid off within 30 years from the relevant fiscal year if the government incurs the debt arising from a selected project according to Art. 68 of the Act. While the use of the Private Finance Initiative (PFI) method is expanding in the field of public procurement, it has only been applied in the space sector to three practical satellites: the X-band communications satellite (Ministry of Defense), the earth observation satellite (Japan Meteorological Agency), and the QZSS satellite (Cabinet Office). It would be worth exploring the applicability of procurement for R&D satellites through the PFI method if the government determines to become an anchor tenant.

The fifth point relates to the cost accounting method used as the basis for calculating the contract amount. Because the partner firm was bearing some of the costs of CRD2, JAXA should be able to carry out the project with a smaller budget than originally planned. Thus, it appeared that JAXA could account for the reasonable contract amount and efficient budget execution without resorting to the cost accounting method. However, there is no indication that the cost accounting method was not applied. In fact, it is not sufficient simply to state that JAXA was able to execute the project with a smaller budget because of the cost burden on the corporate side; as a prerequisite, it is necessary to show that the entire cost quotation with no cost sharing is accurate.

On this matter, JAXA usually assesses the contractor's quotation and uses it as the basis for the contract amount. However, especially when everything is initially contracted at a firm-fixed price, as in the case of CRD2, the contractor finds it challenging to make an accurate quotation for the entire project because the project has not fully developed and the work has not been finalised. Thus, it would be effective that the ordering agency develops the ability to estimate the cost by itself by establishing a cost database like NASA or ESA. When JAXA was overcharged by the major satellite manufacturer in 2012, JAXA decided to accumulate actual costs to provide more accurate estimates for new developments.[40] However, there are many challenges in building a cost database. Chief among these are:

1. Costs are treated as confidential information, and companies do not disclose them unless they have an incentive like a contract award.
2. It is difficult for both current projects and companies to obtain incentives to accumulate cost data unless a system automatically accumulates cost data.
3. Applying the data may no longer be meaningful when the market environment has already changed.

The accumulation of cost data has long-term benefits because it facilitates estimating similar projects in the future. However, it faces a problematic task because the number of spacecraft is small and the accumulated cost data may not be utilised.

16.3.2 Challenges using a comparative approach between CRD2 and future projects

This section attempts to identify issues that were not necessarily addressed in CRD2, assuming a framework that new entrants may desire. The challenges are enumerated with the planning phase, contracting phase, and project implementation phase in mind.

One of the challenges in the planning phase is open innovation. The vision, concept, and service requirements of CRD2 were defined by JAXA. However, there will be an increasing number of

40 JAXA (n 4) 36–37.

cases where JAXA and the private sector will collaborate on more upstream visions and concepts. Therefore, JAXA has launched J-SPARC[41] as an open innovation initiative in which private companies and JAXA can bring together their human and financial resources to co-create business concepts from the planning stage in an early cycle with the aim of early commercialisation or project realisation at JAXA.

To attract new entrants, it is not enough for the government to simply post on government portals; it is necessary to push the opportunity through private channels such as TechCrunch, Wired, and TheFunded.[42] In this respect, J-SPARC is notable for its media exposure. The issue, however, is how to select partners after launching a project from J-SPARC. In other words, if a project is launched with an idea based on a J-SPARC partnership and multiple candidate companies may participate, it remains unclear whether direct negotiation with the J-SPARC partner is possible or whether competitive bidding with the possibility of selecting other companies is required. If another company were to win the bid, the companies involved in the initial J-SPARC partnership would be demotivated. Public procurement needs to have a mechanism that ensures fair opportunities and does not discourage firms.

For example, instead of limiting the partner to a single firm from the beginning, a down-selection method would be effective in which multiple companies are selected as contract partners at an earlier stage and the number of contractors is narrowed down later. An earlier selection means that this will be made at a stage when technical feasibility is uncertain. In order to reduce risk about the feasibility of project and to create a competitive environment in the future, multiple firms need to be selected as contractors. CRD2 also selected two companies to implement front-loading technical studies in Phase II. The number of contractors will then need to be narrowed down at a later stage, when a larger budget is required.

One of the challenges in the contracting phase is the need to simplify not only the technical standards, but also the security, green purchasing, and various forms required for contracts, as many of these standards have been elaborated based on lessons learned in the past. It is not practical for new entrants to participate in a bidding process with a full understanding of these standards. Such simplified standards must be transparent as a matter of course.[43]

A challenge during the implementation phase of the project would be agile development, a method of iterative development in small increments. Currently, start-ups, such as Planet Lab PBC and Spire Global, Inc., tend to develop small satellites and launch vehicles with an agile rather than a waterfall methodology, and public procurement needs to accommodate these development methods. CRD2 allows the partner company to adopt non-waterfall development methods by shifting responsibility for satellite development to the corporate side. However, when JAXA conducts its review with waterfall development in mind, this may not be consistent with agile development by the partner. While it is significant for JAXA itself to gain experience in agile development, it will also be necessary to specifically consider how to handle the procurement aspect if the partner company adopts agile development.

Conventional waterfall development is a method in which design, implementation, and each process are carried out step by step to meet the strictly predetermined requirements faithfully. The method has advantages in that the obligation is clear and budget and personnel management is less

41 Japan Aerospace Exploration Agency, 'J-SPARC' (Japan Aerospace Exploration Agency).

42 Geoff Orazem and others, 'Why Startups Don't Bid on Government Contracts' (August 2017).

43 Keisuke Shimizu, 'The Procurement System of the Japanese Space Agency: A Comparative Assessment' (2014) 44(1) Public Contract Law Journal 31, 77.

ambiguous because of the precise work scope. However, there are disadvantages, such as the difficulty in modifying requirements and the considerable additional work when the process moves downstream. Waterfall development assumes that all requirements can be accurately collected at the beginning of the project, but this assumption may not always be reasonable.

In contrast, agile development is a method of iterative development in small increments and over a short period incorporating a collaborative process with the client, as stated in the 2001 Manifesto for Agile Software Development.[44] Agile methodology is widely recognised in software development. NASA applied an iterative approach to the STS-1's flight software system from 1997 to 1980 because the size, complexity, and evolutionary nature of the programme precluded strict application of a waterfall method.[45] Agile development is suitable for products whose requirements rapidly change in a changing environment, or for projects that are unpredictable in the planning stage and are increasingly examined as they proceed.

For instance, in public procurement of software development, the Obama Administration in the US took a proactive stance toward adopting agile development to achieve shorter delivery times for IT systems. In June 2012, the White House Office of Management and Budget (OMB) issued Contracting Guidance to Support Modular Development (OMB Directive), and the Government Accountability Office (GAO) issued a report[46] noting the importance of sharing best practices for agile development and related documents across government agencies. In August 2014, OMB released the Digital Service Play Book and the TechFAR Handbook for Procuring Digital Services Using Agile Processes.

One of the challenges of public procurement in agile development is that partner selection needs to be done at the vision establishment stage, which is much earlier than the definition of requirements since these are not defined in detail in agile development.[47] In this regard, the Request for Partner is offered as an alternative solution to the RFP. The Request for Partner is a term coined by researchers at the University of Tennessee to describe a highly collaborative competitive bidding process for strategic and complex sourcing initiatives.[48] The method of soliciting partners with visions and concepts further upstream than requirements definition is also advocated in the telecommunications field.[49] As noted above, since selecting one partner at an early stage can result in selection at a technically uncertain stage or unduly restrict the competitive environment, it will be effective to select multiple partners or to implement a down-selection.

Second, since a contract for agile development is reached before the requirements and the deliverables are defined in detail, the contract is not usually a fixed-price contract that commits to completion of the deliverables but rather a time and materials or labor-hour contract in which consideration is paid for the work.

44 Kent Beck and others, 'Manifesto for Agile Software Development' (Agile Manifesto).

45 William A Madden and Kyle Y Rone, 'Design, Development, Integration: Space Shuttle Primary Flight Software System' (1984) 27(9) Communications of the ACM 917.

46 Government Accountability Office, 'Report to the Subcommittee on Federal Financial Management, Government Information, Federal Services, and International Security, Committee on Homeland Security and Governmental Affairs United States Senate: Effective Practices and Federal Challenges in Applying Agile Methods' (GAO-12-681, July 2012).

47 Office of Management and Budget, 'TechFAR Handbook for Procuring Digital Services Using Agile Processes' (August 2014) 3.

48 Kate Vitasek and others, 'Unpacking Collaborative Bidding: Harnessing the Potential of Supplier Collaboration While Still Using a Competitive Bid Process' (Haslam College of Business, 28 April 2017) 13.

49 Mark Newman, 'Time to Kill the RFP? Reinventing it Procurement for the 2020s: Volumes 1 & 2' (tmforum, 14 May 2019).

Third, the ambiguity of the scope at the time of the contract award makes it difficult to establish an accurate estimate, which affects competitive bidding based on price considerations. In this respect, it is proposed, for example, that price competition be based on the total estimated cost, which is the team's weekly unit price multiplied by the vendor's proposed number of weeks.[50] Also, the ordering party should anticipate fluctuations in the number of weeks quoted after the contract is concluded.

In relation to the second and third points, it has been pointed out that agile development is incompatible with outsourcing, especially public procurement, due to the high uncertainty. However, the US Department of Defense has already been working on the issues, and Japan Digital Agency established in 2021 has begun to study. In the space public sector, JAXA has set an agile development and demonstration programme for small satellites as a mid- to long-term goal.[51] It will be necessary to build a public procurement methodology suitable for agile development that NewSpace adopted.

16.3.3 Future on-orbit servicing from the perspective of international space law

Lastly, an issue specific to on-orbit servicing, especially RPO missions including ADR potentially causing damage to another space object during orbital docking, will be addressed from the perspective of space law. Much legal research on ADR has addressed issues from military use regarding its dual-use nature, ownership, prior permission, liability, payment, security to insurance.[52] As such, the main points will be concisely pointed out in this section from a practical perspective.

First, a launching state is internationally liable for damage to another state in a collision in outer space during an on-orbit service including ADR under Art. VII of the Outer Space Treaty. In such a case, fault liability is applied according to Art. III of the Liability Convention, but it can be problematic to determine which state is at fault under the ambiguous definition of launching state, the lack of definition of fault, and the unclear burden of proving fault. Furthermore, existing space debris mitigation norms are not legally binding, and Space Traffic Management continues to be hotly debated. Therefore, insurance is necessary to solve at least the financial problem that legal uncertainty may generate in that case.[53] Since the Space Activity Act is also silent regarding in-orbit damage, the insurance policy for in-orbit damage has to be designed with no legal basis.

In 2018, the Committee on National Space Policy addressed the issue of government compensation for third-party damage to satellites in orbit. After five meetings, the Committee suspended discussions due to concerns over the effect of insurance and tens of thousands of dollars per year in

50 Pradeep Krishnanath, Kevin White and Jeff Myers, 'Agile Acquisition & Contracting in Government' (REI Systems, 14 May 2021).

51 JAXA, 'JAXA's Mid- and Long-term Objectives' (Japan Aerospace Exploration Agency, 1 March 2018).

52 Tanja Masson-Zwaan and Mahulena Hofmann, *Introduction to Space Law* (Kluwer Law International 2019) 8.5 Debris Remediation; Brian Weeden, 'Overview of the Legal and Policy Challenges of Orbital Debris Removal' (2011) 27(1) Space Policy 38; Jinyuan Su, 'Active Debris Removal: Potential Legal Barriers and Possible Ways Forward' (2016) 9(2) Journal of East Asia and International Law 403; Anne-Sophie Martin and Steven Freeland, 'Exploring the Legal Challenges of Future on-Orbit Servicing Missions and Proximity Operations' (2019) 43(2) Journal of Space Law 196.

53 Neta Palkovitz, 'Dealing with the Regulatory Vacuum in LEO: New Insurance Solutions for Small Satellites Constellations' in *Proceedings of the 59th Colloquium on the Law of Outer Space 2016* (IISL 2017) 419.

premiums for low probability losses.[54] In 2021, the Ministerial Meeting of the Task Force on Space Debris resumed considerations and stated that government compensation and related third-party indemnity insurance should be applied on a voluntary basis, depending on the risk and profitability of each project.[55]

In addition, to implement State responsibility and State liability for non-governmental activities under Arts VI and VII of the Outer Space Treaty, JAXA set out a RPO safety standard and applied it to CRD2 in 2019, and the 2021 Guideline on a License to Operate a Spacecraft Performing On-Orbit Servicing released by the Cabinet Office will be applied to obtain a satellite operation licence. Where debris is caused by a collision accident in on-orbit services like ADR, the launching state is not liable for the event unless an affected state exists. However, it needs to avoid harmful contamination with a high standard of care and due diligence as set out in Art. IX of the Treaty, and other relevant non-legal guidelines, including UN Space Debris Mitigation Guidelines,[56] IADC Space Debris Mitigation Guidelines,[57] Long-Term Sustainability Guidelines,[58] and so forth.

Ownership and control of the space object to be removed is another well-known issue. In Phase II of CRD2, the space object to be removed is a Japanese rocket's upper stage. Therefore, there is no particular problem related to ownership and control under Art. VIII, consultation under Art. IX of the Outer Space Treaty, etc. However, where there is an owner, states must have affirmative consent from that owner to remove.[59] If the states are compliant with RPO safety standards such as ISO 24330:2022 collaborated by an industrial consortium, the Consortium for Execution of Rendezvous and Servicing Operations (CONFERS),[60] establishing a mechanism to agree on comprehensive mutual debris removal is possible. The best practices of those states would act as the basis of the international framework. In terms of comprehensive consent, security concerns also must be eliminated due to dual-use technologies in RPO missions. For example, even observing other space objects before removing requires consultation with the owners of the objects to determine whether the acquired imagery raises security concerns such as export control.[61] A more systematic method is required for commercial removal.

Conclusion

The public sector tends to invest in only one private partner due to its limited budget. However, innovation never occurs in such an environment. To foster innovation, a competitive market and

54 Cabinet Office, Committee on National Space Policy, Subcommittee on Space Legislation, 'Jinko Eisei no Kidojo deno Daisansha Songai nitaisuru Seifu Hosho no Arikata (Chukan Seiri) [Government Compensation for Satellite In-orbit Damage to Third Parties (Interim Arrangement)]' (20 December 2018).

55 Cabinet Office, Task Force on Space Debris, 'Fifth Meeting, Reference 3-2' (27 May 2021).

56 UNGA Space Debris Mitigation Guidelines of the Scientific and Technical Subcommittee of the Committee on the Peaceful uses of Outer Space, UNGA Res 62/20 (6 March 2007).

57 Inter-Agency Space Debris Coordination Committee, 'IADC Space Debris Mitigation Guidelines' (IADC-02-01, September 2007 and revision 2, March 2020).

58 United Nations Office for Outer Space Affairs, 'Guidelines for the Long-term Sustainability of Outer Space Activities of the Committee on the Peaceful Uses of Outer Space' (ST/SPACE/79, 7 June 2021).

59 Martin and Freeland (n 54) 210.

60 CONFERS, 'Guiding Principles for Commercial Rendezvous and Proximity Operations (RPO) and On-Orbit Servicing (OOS)' (November 2018).

CONFERS, 'Recommended Design and Operational Practices' (October 2019).

61 Spacewatch, 'Astroscale Works with Mitsubishi on Space Debris Removal' (Spacewatch, 27 July 2021). The news reported that initial efforts would include discussions and development of debris removal methods for the upper stages.

the promotion of new entrants is essential. If the public sector can attract a newcomer, including in NewSpace and Non-Space by changing its procurement system, then innovative products and services may be brought to the space sector. There may be risks in partnering with an unknown entity, but many space start-ups have ideas to meet the market's needs and focus on what services they can offer through spacecraft as a means, not an end.

In order to take advantage of such innovative ideas, the procurement that focuses on outcomes and leaves spacecraft development to private-sector discretion should be considered as one of the options. For example, the H3 procurement is an outcome-oriented transitional project, and the CRD2 procurement emphasises private-sector discretion. Also, committing bulk purchases after the development phase as PFI and not applying the cost accounting method will play a significant role in the partnership with NewSpace. In the future, JAXA's shareholdings and investments will further promote industrial development. Moreover, it is necessary to establish public procurement methods suitable for open innovation and agile development rather than waterfall development, such as the Request for Partner and methods that are changed more flexibly even after the contract is awarded, whilst ensuring fair bidding. Public procurement should be enhanced to bring innovation to the space industry through constant constructive dialogue between space agencies and all the stakeholders, including start-ups, entrepreneurs, investors, accountants, and lawyers.

PART II

Specific markets

A

Commercial space solutions for earth observation data and space applications

17

LEGAL CONSIDERATIONS FOR NEWSPACE COMPANIES WHEN SELLING DATA (AND ASSOCIATED PRODUCTS AND SERVICES) TO THE US GOVERNMENT

Kevin Pomfret[1]

Introduction

Some predict the space industry will reach US$1 trillion by 2040.[2] NewSpace companies are expected to play a significant role in this growth by offering a wide range of products and services, including launch, communications, hardware, and space tourism. One of the largest sectors of the NewSpace industry is expected to be selling data – and associated products and services – from space-based sensors (collectively referred to in this chapter as "Space-derived Information"), particularly to the US Government (USG). In the near-term, Space-derived Information is likely to represent a significant portion of the NewSpace market. For example, there are a number of companies that are launching – or plan to launch – satellites for Earth observation. Many of these satellites are small satellites placed in low earth orbit (LEO) and collecting data from a wide variety of sensors. This data can be sold (licensed) directly to customers, or aggregated with data from other government and commercial sources to create valuable products and services. Technological improvements, such as lower launch costs, lower cost production of small sats, improved on-board processing capabilities, cloud computing, 5G, and application programme interfaces (APIs), make a variety new of business models more viable.[3]

1 Catherine Ryan, a law student at The George Washington University Law School in Washington, DC provided assistance in the research and substantiation of this chapter.

2 *The space industry is on its way to reach $1 trillion in revenue by 2040, Citi says.* (2022). CNBC. Retrieved on 16 July 2022, from https://www.cnbc.com/2022/05/21/space-industry-is-on-its-way-to-1-trillion-in-revenue-by-2040-citi.html.

3 *To cheaply go: How falling launch costs fueled a thriving economy in orbit.* (2022). NBC. Retrieved on 23 July 2022, from https://www.nbcnews.com/science/space/space-launch-costs-growing-business-industry-rcna23488.

DOI: 10.4324/9781003268475-24

While the US$1 trillion figure represents revenue from both the private (i.e. industry) sector and public (i.e. governments) sector, in the near term the public sector is likely to be a major customer for such products and services. Historically, the USG has been one of the largest consumers in the world of Space-derived Information. For example, the Department of Defense (DoD) (e.g., the National Geospatial Intelligence Agency (NGA), the National Reconnaissance Office (NRO) and the combatant commands) both generate and acquire significant amounts of Space-derived Information. Civil agencies such as the National Aeronautics and Space Administration (NASA), the National Oceanic and Atmospheric Administration (NOAA), and the Department of Interior are also significant consumers.

One of the most common uses by the USG for Space-derived Information is Earth observation and other types of remote sensing. There are a number of government applications for this data including: (i) transportation, (ii) defence and intelligence, (iii) disaster response, (iv) climate change, (v) weather, and (vi) mapping. However, NewSpace also is developing Space-derived Information for new applications to be used in the space domain. These include (i) tracking other satellites to avoid collisions, (ii) satellite inspection, (iii) space weather, and (iv) tracking orbital debris.

Given the increased recognition within the US of the importance of space from an economic, geopolitical, and national security standpoint, the USG is expected to continue to require significant amounts of Space-derived Information in the future. Moreover, there is a growing push both in Congress[4] and the White House for government agencies to acquire Space-derived Information from the commercial sector, particularly from small and medium companies (SMEs) and non-traditional government contractors.[5] As a result, a number of New Space companies see an opportunity to sell their Space-derived Information to the USG. This chapter focuses on those requirements and challenges facing companies wishing to sell to the USG.

17.1 Selling products and services to the US Government (USG)

While the business opportunity exists, as this chapter will discuss, there are a number of challenges associated with selling Space-derived Information to the USG. Some of these are due to the differences between federal procurement and commercial transactions. For example, most contracts with the USG include clauses from the Federal Acquisition Regulation (FAR), as well as agency specific FAR supplements, that are very different from standard commercial terms. This is particularly true for issues of importance to NewSpace companies, such as intellectual property rights.

Other challenges are associated with difficulties the USG faces in acquiring any new technologies. As a result, it has developed several programs to address acquiring these technologies to make it easier for both the private sector and the government agencies. However, these programmes are also governed by US laws and policies. Consequently, it still takes a deep knowledge about how these programmes work in order for a NewSpace company to realise the intended benefits.

A third set of issues is related to concerns over US national security and economic competitiveness. Space is an increasingly important domain from a geopolitical, economic, and national security standpoint. As a result, there are laws and regulations in place to protect US employees

4 See, e.g., *Palantir USG, Inc. v. United States*, 904 F.3d 980 (Fed. Cir. 2018).

5 Executive Order 13,881: Maximizing Use of American-Made Goods, Products, and Materials. (2019, July 15). [Order]. Retrieved on 31 July 2022, from https://govinfo.gov/content/pkg/DCPD-201900473/pdf/DCPD-201900473.pdf.

and technology from foreign competitors and threats. This legal framework is evolving to address the threats associated with new technologies. NewSpace companies will need to understand this environment in order to compete in the US market.

Finally, there are traditional space law considerations that may apply. The US has a number of laws, regulations, and policies regarding the full range of space activities. Some of these may also be applicable to NewSpace companies selling Space-derived Information to the USG. These challenges are addressed below.

17.1.1 Standard types of government contracts

There are several different contract types that US government agencies use to procure products and services.[6] Each has its own benefits and risks for a company selling products to the USG. The most common types are:

- Fixed-Price – Under a fixed-price contract, a company agrees to complete the agreed upon work for a fixed price.
- Cost-Plus Reimbursement – Under a cost-plus reimbursement contract, a company is paid for all of its allowed expenses, plus an additional amount for profit.
- Indefinite Delivery & Quantity (IDIQ) – An IDIQ contract provides for the delivery of an indefinite quantity of products or services over a fixed period of time.
- Time and Materials (T&M) – Under a T&M contract, a company charges separate, specified fixed hourly rates (to include wages, overhead, general and administrative expenses) and a profit for each category of labor.
- Incentive – An incentive contract is a cost-reimbursement contract or fixed-price contract in which a company receives incentives as a reward based upon agreed-upon specifications.

Negotiating these contracts with a government agency can be time intensive and complex, particularly when, as will be described below, taking into account the FAR and other unique aspects of government contracts. As a result, the USG created a more streamlined process for government agencies to procure products and services. The General Services Administration (GSA) Schedule is a long-term, government-wide contract with commercial companies that provides government agencies access to commercial products and services at competitive prices. The Schedules are broken into categories, sub-categories, and Special Item Numbers, based upon the product or service being offered. Companies can apply to the GSA to be added to the appropriate GSA Schedule.

17.1.2 GSA Schedule – Special Item Number 541370GEO

In 2016, in order to address changes to the Earth observation market and the federal government's growing need to acquire Space-derived Information, Special Item Number 541370GEO was added to the Information Technology Schedule (generally known as GSA Schedule 70). Special Item Number 541370GEO is a blank purchase order for all Earth observation products, services, and solutions. The stated goals in creating this new category were (i) increased visibility and rapid access to commercially available imagery, data, services and capabilities, and (ii) flexibility to

6 See 48 C.F.R. Ch. 1, Subch. C, Pt. 16.

adapt to changing market needs and participation by new and innovative vendors. Special Item Number 541370GEO includes:

- Advanced data analytics;
- Change detection;
- Crowdsourcing;
- Delivery to ground and mobile ground terminals;
- Direct access service to cell phones, ships, aircraft;
- Geospatial products and services;
- Imagery;
- Machine learning;
- Mosaics;
- Predictive analytics;
- Remote sensing and analytical software products;
- Sensor data includes;
  - Electro-optical;
  - Synthetic aperture radar (SAR);
  - Hyperspectral;
  - Geomagnetic field, gravity field;
  - Thermal;
  - Sonar;
  - Other current and emerging technologies; and
  - Other products and services relevant to Earth Observation Solutions.

A NewSpace company must meet certain eligibility standards in order to sell Space-derived Information on this schedule. In addition, it will need to satisfy country of origin requirements[7] and agree to pricing that is "fair and reasonable".[8]

17.1.2.1 Set-aside programmes

There are also a number of programmes in the US to encourage new market entrants, such as NewSpace companies, to compete for US government contracts. These programmes require that certain contracts, or portions thereof, be "set aside" for designated categories of companies. The key programmes are:

- 8(a) Business Development programme[9] – for small businesses that are at least fifty-one percent (51%) owned and controlled by U.S. citizens who are socially and economically disadvantaged.
- HUBZone programme[10] – for small businesses that are at least fifty-one percent (51%) owned and controlled by U.S. citizens, and at least thirty-five percent (35%) of its employees reside in a designated HUBZone.

7 19 U.S.C. § 2501, *et seq.*
8 FAR 8.404 (Use of Federal Supply Schedules).
9 13 C.F.R. 124.
10 13 C.F.R. 126.

- Women-Owned Small Business programme[11] – for small businesses that are at least fifty-one percent (51%) owned and controlled by women who are U.S. citizens.
- Service-Disabled Veteran-Owned Small Business programme[12] – for small businesses that are at least fifty-one percent (51%) owned and controlled by one or more service-disabled veterans.

The scope of set-aside contracts for small businesses will vary based upon several factors, including the value and quantity of the goods or services the government wants to purchase. Depending upon the size of the contract, it may automatically be awarded to small business, or there may be requirements in larger contracts for a certain portion of the contract to be subcontracted to small businesses. It is important to note however, that these set-aside programmes may not be suitable for many NewSpace companies that are interested in raising significant amounts of capital, as the minimum ownership requirements can make it difficult to raise outside investment.[13]

17.1.3 Federal Acquisition Regulation

As mentioned above, US government contracting is subject to different laws and regulations than commercial contracts. These differences can raise challenges for NewSpace companies. For example, most contracts with the federal government are subject to the FAR. The FAR contains a number of provisions that differ from standard commercial contractual arrangements. These include:

- Cost Accounting/Pricing – If the transaction is considered noncommercial, the contractor may be subject to a number of pricing and accounting requirements. These requirements include: (i) any cost charged to the government, must be (x) allowable, (y) reasonable, and (z) allocable,[14] (ii) maintenance of a particular type of accounting system that can properly account for certain types of costs,[15] and (iii) submitting certain cost or pricing data so that the contracting officer may make a price reasonableness determination.[16]
- Indemnity – In many commercial transactions, there is often a provision that one party must indemnify the other party for certain legal claims that may arise. However, the USG generally is precluded from contractual indemnification of a commercial entity due to the Anti-Deficiency Act.[17]
- Liability – The False Claim Act (FCA)[18] applies to contracts with the federal government. A violation of the FCA occurs when there has been a false statement or fraudulent course of conduct that was: (1) made or carried out with knowledge of the falsity; (2) material; and (3) involved a claim (i.e. a request or demand for money or property from the United States). A violation of the FCA can result in significant penalties to a company.

11 13 C.F.R. 127.
12 13 C.F.R. 125.
13 *Types of Contracts*. (2022). Small Business Administration. Retrieved on 23 July 2022, from https://www.sba.gov/federal-contracting/contracting-guide/types-contracts.
14 48 C.F.R. § 16.306 (Lexis Advance through the 20 July 2022 issue of the Federal Register).
15 Id.
16 48 C.F.R. § 16.505 (Lexis Advance through the 20 July 2022 issue of the Federal Register).
17 31 U.S.C. § 1341.
18 31 U.S.C. § 3729.

- Choice of Law – The USG is generally precluded from agreeing to be subject to laws other than federal laws of the US.
- Disputes – There is a specific process that must be followed if there is a dispute with how a contract was awarded or if a company feels the government has failed to perform according to the terms of a contract. For example, disputes between the parties many only be heard in designated administrative bodies or the US Court of Federal Claims.
- Intellectual Property – Since intellectual property (in both data and software) is a key asset of many NewSpace companies selling Space-derived Information, it is also critical to understand the USG's approach to intellectual property rights. Under the FAR, computer software is defined as executable code, source code, code listings, design details, processes, flow charts, and related material that would enable the software to be reproduced, recreated, or recompiled, but excludes computer databases or computer software documentation.[19] Technical data is defined as "any recorded information of a scientific or technical nature (e.g., product design or maintenance data, computer databases, and computer software documentation)".[20] Generally, for both non-commercial software and data, the USG's rights are dependent upon the role of government funding in its creation:
  - Solely Government Funds – If the software or technical data is created exclusively from government funds, the USG receives unlimited rights. "Unlimited rights" means that the USG can use, modify, reproduce, release, or disclose technical data or computer software in whole or in part, in any manner, and for any purpose whatsoever, and to have or authorise others to do so.[21]
  - Mixed Funding – If the software or technical data is created using a combination of private funds and government funds, the FAR provides that the government receives "government purpose rights". Government purpose rights is defined as the right to "use, modify, reproduce, release or disclose the technical data or computer software within the Government without restriction and outside the Government for a Government purpose".[22] "Government purpose" includes any activity in which the USG is a party, including cooperative agreements with international or multi-national defence organisations or sales or transfers by the USG to foreign governments or international organisations. Government purposes include competitive procurements, but do not include use for commercial purposes.[23] Unless the parties negotiate otherwise, a government purpose licence remains in effect for five (5) years, after which the Government receives "unlimited rights".[24]
  - Solely Private Funds – If only private funds are used in the creation, then the FAR provides that government receives restricted rights – for software – and limited rights for data. "Restricted rights" means the government's rights to use a computer programme with one computer at one time; transfer a computer programme to another government agency without permission of the contractor if the transferor destroys all copies of the programme and related computer documentation; make the minimum number of copies of computer software required for safekeeping (archive), backup, or modification pur-

19 See FAR 52.227-14 (Rights in technical data); DFARS 252.227-7013 (Rights in technical data – Noncommercial items), and DFARS 252.227-7014.
20 Id.
21 Id.
22 Id.
23 Id.
24 Id.

poses; modify computer software; and permit contractors or subcontractors performing services in support of a contract to use computer software for correcting deficiencies.[25] "Limited rights" means the right to use, modify, reproduce, release, perform, display, or disclose technical data, in whole or in part, within the government.[26]

When submitting Space-derived Information to the USG, it is critical to properly designate which intellectual property rights apply, as failure to do so may give the government unlimited rights in the software or data.

With respect to patents, a NewSpace company that develops a "subject invention" using USG funding must comply with a number of legal requirements in order to protect its intellectual property rights. A subject invention is defined as "any invention of the contractor conceived or first actually reduced to practice in the performance of work under a funding agreement".[27] These requirements, as prescribed by statute, include timely:

- Disclosure of the invention to the funding agency;
- Written election to retain title of the invention; and
- Filing an initial patent application on the invention.[28]

Failure to comply can result in the USG taking ownership of the patent.[29]

The FAR also covers USG rights in commercial software and data.[30] If permitted under a contract, a NewSpace company can license its Space-Derived Information to the USG under a commercial licence. However, it is important to note that there are challenges in applying commercial licences in federal contracts. For example:

- Many of the FAR requirements set forth above will apply – for example the choice of law and indemnification requirements.
- The USG has an Open Data Policy that strongly encourages government agencies to obtain data with broad reuse and redistribution rights.[31] This can make it a challenge for NewSpace companies that wish to limit reuse and distributions of the information so they can sell to other government agencies rather than have the government freely distribute it.
- The adoption of different business models can blur the line between purely commercial and government supported creation of Space-derived Information. For example, when the commercial entity offers a commercial platform, but the government contract supports the development for improvements to that platform for defence or intelligence purposes.

25 Id.

26 Id.

27 48 C.F.R. § 252.

28 35 USC. § 202.

29 See, e.g., *Campbell Plastics Engineering & Mfg., Inc. v. Brownlee*, 389 F.3d 1243 (Fed. Cir. 2004).

30 See FAR 12.211 (Technical Data) and FAR 12.212 (Computer Software).

31 Open Licenses. (2022). Federal Enterprise Data Resources. Retrieved on 23 July 2022, from https://resources.data.gov/open-licenses/.

17.1.3.1 FAR supplements

Several government agencies have issued supplements to the FAR. These supplements should be read in conjunction with the FAR and can impose additional requirements. Most notable of those for purposes of NewSpace companies are the supplements published by the DoD[32] and NASA.[33]

17.1.4 Special programmes

Recognising that the government procurement is time-consuming and complicated, and therefore often limited to traditional defence contractors that may not provide the innovation, flexibility and agility needed to face today's challenges, Congress and government agencies have tried to develop other means for non-traditional contractors to participate. As stated in a 2014 report jointly issued by the Office of Science and Technology (OSTP) and the Office of Management and Budget (OMB):

> Over the years, much progress has been made to help Federal agencies gain greater access to the innovation and synergies generated by the commercial marketplace. Despite this progress, the standard procurement processes that agencies rely on to meet most of their needs may remain highly complex and enigmatic for companies that are not traditional government contractors. Many of these companies can offer Federal agencies valuable new ways of solving long-standing problems and cost effective alternatives for meeting everyday needs. As budgetary constraints continue to reduce available resources, there is a heightened need to grow new innovative contracting models that can help agencies reach these entrepreneurs, and can reduce the complexity and cost of doing business with the government. Such tools allow Federal agencies to pay contractors for results, not just best efforts.[34]

17.1.4.1 Other transactions (OTs)

Of particular interest to NewSpace companies should be those government agencies with the authority to conduct "other transactions" (OTs). OTs are contracts that are not subject to many of the FAR provisions and therefore are much more flexible. Often, they are tailored to particular projects and programmes. However, an agency must have been given statutory authority by Congress to use an OT as a contracting vehicle.

Congress has authorised a number of federal agencies to use OTs. NASA was the first agency to receive this authority and it has used this authority on a number of occasions to partner with NewSpace companies through Space Act Agreements.[35] Subsequently, agencies within the DoD were given this authority, and by 2015 Congress codified the DoD's authority to issue OTs.[36] According to the DoD's Other Transaction Guide:

32 48 C.F.R.Ch. 2.

33 48 C.F.R. Ch. 18.

34 *Innovative Contracting Case Studies.* (2014). Retrieved on 31 July 2022, from https://techfarhub.cio.gov/assets/files/innovative-contracting-case-studies-2014.pdf.

35 NASA. (n.d.). Space Act Agreement Guide. Retrieved on 31 July 2022, from https://www.nasa.gov/sites/default/files/files/NAII_1050-1C_NASA_Advisory_Implementing_Instruction_Space_Act_Agreements_Guide_Tagged.pdf.

36 10 U.S.C. § 4022

> [T]he OT authorities were created to give DoD the flexibility necessary to adopt and incorporate business practices that reflect commercial industry standards and best practices into its award instruments. When leveraged appropriately, OTs provide the Government with access to state-of-the-art technology solutions from traditional and non-traditional defense contractors (NDCs) through a multitude of potential teaming arrangements tailored to the particular project and the needs of the participants. [37]

Benefits of OTs of particular applicability to NewSpace companies include:

- Fostering new relationships and practices involving non-traditional defence contractors;
- Supporting dual-use (i.e. both commercial and defence applications) projects;
- Encouraging flexible, quicker, and cheaper project design and execution; and
- Leveraging commercial industry investment in technology development and partnering with industry to ensure DoD requirements are incorporated into future technologies and products.[38]

DoD's OTs can be structured in a variety of ways:

1. Research OTs – authorised for basic, applied, and advanced research projects.[39]
2. Prototype OTs – authorised to acquire prototype capabilities and allow for those prototypes to transition into Production OTs.[40] Successful Prototype OTs can be a streamlined method for transitioning into follow-on production without competition.
3. Production OTs – authorised as noncompetitive, follow-ons to a Prototype OT that was competitively awarded and successfully completed.[41]

17.1.4.2 The Small Business Innovation Research and Small Business Technology Transfer programmes[42]

The Small Business Innovation Research (SBIR) and Small Business Technology Transfer (STTR) programmes are designed to encourage domestic small businesses to engage in research and development with the potential for commercialisation. The programmes allow small businesses to explore the potential applications of their technology as well the profit opportunities from commercialisation. A number of government agencies, including the US Air Force, Space Force, and NASA have SBIR/STTR programmes for NewSpace companies.[43]

The SBIR Program is structured in three phases:[44]

37 Other Transactions (OT) Guide. (2017, January). Retrieved on July 30, 2022, from https://aaf.dau.edu/aaf/ot-guide/.
38 Id.
39 10 U.S.C. § 2371.
40 10 U.S.C. § 2371b.
41 10 U.S.C. § 2371b(f).
42 15 U.S.C. § 638.
43 See, e.g., SBIR Ignite. (2022). NASA. Retrieved on July 23, 2022, from https://sbir.nasa.gov/ignite.
44 See, e.g., Small Business Administration. (2020, October). Small Business Innovation Research (SBIR) and Small Business Technology Transfer (STTR) Program.

- Phase I – The objective of Phase I is to establish the technical merit, feasibility, and commercial potential of the proposed R/R&D efforts and to determine the quality of the company's performance prior to providing further Phase II support. SBIR/STTR Phase I awards are generally between US$50,000 and US$250,000 and last for six months (SBIR) or one year (STTR).
- Phase II – The objective of Phase II is to continue the research and development efforts initiated in Phase I. Funding is based on (i) the results achieved in Phase I and (ii) the merits and potential of the proposed Phase II project proposed. Typically, only Phase I awardees are eligible for a Phase II award. SBIR/STTR Phase II awards are generally for two years and US$750,000.
- Phase III – When appropriate, a Phase III award allows the small business to pursue commercialisation objectives resulting from previous awards. However, the SBIR/STTR programmes do not fund Phase III; funding must come from federal agencies, often from research and development or production contracts intended for use by the USG.

Another benefit of the SBIR/STTR programme for NewSpace companies is that awardees retain greater rights in the intellectual property that they create than they would have under a traditional FAR-based contract. Specifically, the government receives a limited nonexclusive licence to use the technology, but is prohibited from disclosing it for a period of 20 years. This gives the company a significant competitive advantage over other companies.

However, in order to qualify for an SBIR/STTR Program a NewSpace company must satisfy a number of requirements, including:

- be a US small business;[45]
- be more than fifty percent (50%) owned and controlled by one or more individuals who are citizens or permanent resident aliens of the United States, or by other small business concerns that are each more than fifty percent (50%) owned and controlled by one or more individuals who are citizens or permanent resident aliens of the United States; and
- have no more than 500 employees (including those of affiliates).[46]

One of the benefits of the SBIR/STTR program for NewSpace companies that wish to raise capital is that in some instances[47] government agencies can award a contract to a company owned and controlled by more than one venture capital, private equity, or hedge fund, provided one such firm does not own a majority of the company's stock.[48]

17.1.4.3 Grants and cooperative agreements

The Federal Grant and Cooperative Agreement Act (FGCA)[49] gives government agencies the authority to establish grants and to enter into cooperative agreements if the purpose of the activity

45 13 C.F.R. § 121.702.

46 For STTR, the partnering nonprofit research institution must also be (i) located in the US and must be either a nonprofit college or university, a domestic nonprofit research organisation or a federally funded R&D centre (FFRDC).

47 15 USC. § 638(dd)(1).

48 However, it is important to note that while this chapter was being written Congress was considering limiting funding of the SBIR Program.

49 31 USC Ch. 63.

is to support or stimulate activities that are not for the direct benefit or use of the federal government. The principal difference between a grant and cooperative agreement is that a cooperative agreement requires substantial involvement by the government agency. (If the government agency is not expected to be involved, a grant can be awarded.)

Cooperative Research and Development Agreements (CRADAs) are between one (or more) federal agencies and commercial companies. The federal agency may not provide funding to the company, but can provide for personnel, facilities, equipment, or other resources.

17.1.5 Other government contracting considerations

Given the size and scope of the USG space market, many NewSpace companies located outside the US would like to sell their products and services to the USG. However, there is a growing push in Washington DC to "Buy American". This effort manifests itself in several ways that could impact NewSpace companies.

17.1.5.1 Buy American Act[50]

The Buy American Act (BAA) grants a price preference in certain federal contracts to US companies over foreign companies. The price preference can vary, depending upon the size of the foreign business purchase. One of the considerations is what qualifies as a domestic or US made product. Under the BAA, a manufactured product qualifies as a domestic end product if:

- it is manufactured in the US; and
- the cost of its components, produced or manufactured in the US, exceeds fifty percent (50%) of the cost of all of its components.[51]

There are a several exceptions that should be of particular interest to NewSpace companies. For example, the BAA does not apply if the product is considered as "commercial off-the-shelf" (COTS). A COTS is exempt from the BAA's component cost test described above if it is:

(i) sold in substantial quantities in the commercial marketplace; and
(ii) offered to the federal government, under a contract or subcontract in the same form in which it is sold in the commercial marketplace.[52]

The other important exception to BAA is that NewSpace companies from a country that has entered into a multilateral or bilateral trade treaty with the US may be exempt from the Act.

17.1.5.2 USG policy on purchases of commercial imagery[53]

For a number of years, the USG has stated its preference to support the US commercial remote sensing industry. For example, the US Commercial Remote Sensing Policy stated that the US

50 41 U.S.C. § 8301
51 48 C.F.R. § 25.101(a).
52 48 C.F.R. § 25.103.
53 86 Fed. Reg. 6,180 (Jan. 19, 2021). Available at: https://www.govinfo.gov/content/pkg/FR-2021-01-19/pdf/2021-00710.pdf.

should "rely to the maximum practical extent on U.S. commercial sensing space capabilities for filling imagery and geospatial needs for military, intelligence, foreign policy, homeland security, and civil users".[54] Similarly, the 2020 US National Space Policy stated that "[t]he Secretary of Commerce shall license and regulate private remote sensing systems consistent with the recognition that long-term United States national security and foreign policy interests are best served by ensuring that United States industry continues to lead the rapidly maturing and highly competitive commercial space-based remote sensing market".[55] In light of this, the USG has begun to take affirmative steps to favour US companies in certain government procurements of satellite imagery. For example, in a recent solicitation for electro-optical imagery it limited the opportunity to US companies.[56]

17.2 National security considerations

While NewSpace companies emphasise the commercial opportunities associated with space, there are still a number of national security concerns associated with space operations. As a result, there are several national security-related laws and regulations that NewSpace companies need to consider when doing business in the US.

17.2.1 Export restrictions

The US has a number of laws that restrict the export of technologies. Of particular applicability to NewSpace companies are:

- International Traffic in Arms Regulations (ITAR) – ITAR, administered by the Directorate of Defense Trade Controls (DDTC) in the Department of State, restricts access to certain defence articles or defence services. These defence products and services are listed in the United States Munitions List (USML).[57] Export of these products and services requires State Department authorisation, such as a Technical Assistance Agreement (TAA).
- Export Administration Regulations (EAR) – EAR, administered by the Commerce Department's Bureau of Industry and Security (BIS), controls items and technologies considered to be "dual use", meaning applicable to both commercial and military use. These items are detailed in the EAR under the Commerce Control List (CCL).[58]

While these programmes are applicable to any company doing business in the United States, there are some unique aspects that are of particular importance to NewSpace companies. First, given the international nature of NewSpace companies, compliance can be much more difficult. For example, it is important to note that an export is not simply the actual shipment or transmission of

54 *US Commercial Remote Sensing Policy*. (2003, April). National Security Presidential Directives. Retrieved on 31 July 2022, from https://irp.fas.org/offdocs/nspd/remsens.html.

55 US National Space Policy (2020). Retrieved on 30 July 2022, from https://trumpwhitehouse.archives.gov/wp-content/uploads/2020/12/National-Space-Policy.pdf.

56 NRO Erects Buy American Barriers Against Allied Satellite Data. (2021). Breaking Defense. Retrieved on 23 July 2022, from https://breakingdefense.com/2021/07/exclusive-nro-erects-buy-american-barriers-against-allied-satellite-data/.

57 Those most relevant to the space industry are Category IV and Category XV.

58 68 USC. § 1324b(a)(3).

an export-controlled product out of the United States. Under US law it also includes a "deemed export", such as releasing or otherwise transferring technical data to a foreign person in the United States.[59]

Second, there have been some recent changes to the law that could have a profound impact on Space-derived Information. The Export Control Reform Act of 2018 directed the Commerce Department to adopt new export controls on "emerging and foundational technologies".[60] Subsequently, on January 6, 2020, BIS adopted export licensing requirements on certain artificial intelligence software used to automate the analysis of geospatial imaging.[61]

17.2.2 Facility clearance

The USG procures much Space-derived Information under contracts that require a company have access to classified information. As a result, an important consideration for NewSpace companies is a Facility Clearance (FCL). An FCL and approved safeguarding of classified information is required for firms bidding on a contract in which they will be provided with classified information. A company must be sponsored for an FCL either by the USG or by another cleared company that wants to utilise the company as a subcontractor on a classified contract.[62] A company must work with the Defense Counterintelligence and Security Agency (DCSA) and comply with the requirements of the National Industrial Security Program (NISP) in order to obtain an FCL.[63]

17.2.3 FOCI mitigation

A foreign company cannot be issued an FCL.[64] However, a foreign-owned US subsidiary can be issued an FCL, pending mitigation of any foreign ownership, control, or influence (FOCI) that a foreign entity may exercise over the US subsidiary. There are several measures that DCSA may require a company subject to foreign influence to take in order to mitigate risk.[65] These include the US subsidiary, the foreign parent, and DCSA entering into one of several types of agreements outlining each party's respective responsibilities:

- Security Control Agreement (SCA) – SCA is used when a foreign party has representation in a company, but the company is not controlled by the foreign party.
- Special Security Agreement (SSA) – An SSA is used when a foreign person effectively owns or controls a company. DCSA will generally require that there are a majority of outside directors on the company's board of directors that are independent from the foreign entity and have clearances. The US entity must operate independently, and the parent must have no access to or control of classified information.

59 22 C.F.R. § 120.17.

60 85 Fed. Reg. 71,012 (Nov. 6, 2020). Available at: https://www.bis.doc.gov/index.php/documents/regulations-docs/federal-register-notices/federal-register-2020/2658-85-fr-71012-commerce-control-list-proposed-controls-on-software-for-the-operation-of-certain-automated-nucleic-acid-assemblers-and-synthesizers-request-for-comments/file.

61 15 C.F.R. § 774.

62 *Facility Security Clearance (FCL) FAQ*. (2022). State.Gov. Retrieved on 23 July 2022, from https://www.state.gov/facility-security-clearances-faq/.

63 Id.

64 Id.

65 *FOCI Mitigation Agreements*. (2022). Defense Counterintelligence and Security Agency. Retrieved on 23 July 2022, from https://www.dcsa.mil/mc/isd/foci/mitigation/.

- Voting Trust Agreement/Proxy Agreement – Voting Trust and Proxy Agreements are the most restrictive mitigation measures. Essentially, the parent company must give up control, other than for some fundamental matters, such as sale of substantially all the US company's assets, the filing for bankruptcy, or dissolution.

The US company will also be required to create a permanent committee of the board of directors, to be known as the Government Security Committee (GSC). The GSC ensures that the US entity maintains policies and procedures to safeguard classified information and controlled unclassified information and to ensure that company complies with the NISP, relevant contract provisions, and export control laws. These policies and procedures generally include:

- Electronic Control Plan to ensure effective oversight of electronic communications and networks between the US company and its affiliates;
- Technology Control Plan outlining how the US company will provide physical protection to classified and export-controlled information;
- Affiliated Operations Plan detailing operations with affiliates such that national security concerns are addressed.

17.2.4 Committee on Foreign Investment in the United States (CFIUS)

CFIUS is an inter-agency committee within the Executive Branch with substantial authority to review certain transactions involving foreign investments in the US. In 2018, its role was further strengthened by the Foreign Investment Risk Review Modernization Act of 2018.[66] CFIUS now has the authority to review the following transactions which could impact NewSpace companies:[67]

1. Transactions in which a foreign person would obtain control – through a majority ownership or the ability to control important matters – of a US business ("Covered Transactions");
2. Investments in which a foreign person receives a non-controlling interest – generally (i) access to material non-public technological information or (ii) membership on or observer rights of the company's board of directors – in a US business that operates within the following three sectors:
   - Critical Technology;[68]
   - Critical Infrastructure including (i) those subject to ITAR, (ii) certain dual use technologies subject to EAR, and (iii) Emerging and Foundational Technologies;[69] and
   - Collecting or maintaining sensitive personal information of US citizens.[70]

Parties to a proposed transaction may decide to seek prior approval from CFIUS and receive safe harbor protection. Alternatively, CFIUS may initiate its own review. CFIUS may prohibit a

66 Foreign Investment Risk Review Modernization Act, H.R. 5841, 115th Congress, 2018. Available at: https://www.congress.gov/115/bills/hr5841/BILLS-115hr5841eh.pdf.

67 See, e.g., *Momentus founders to divest shares after Defense Department concerns*. Space News (March 9, 2021). Retrieved on 31 July 2022, from https://spacenews.com/momentus-founders-to-divest-shares-after-defense-department-concerns/.

68 31 CFR § 801.204.

69 50 U.S.C. § 4817.

70 31 C.F.R. § 5800.241.

transaction or require the companies to take certain steps to mitigate the potential risks, such as (i) divesting of certain assets or business operations, (ii) creating a proxy board, or (iii) forfeiting contracts.

17.3 Space law considerations

This chapter is not intended to address all potential space law issues associated with the launch and operation of satellites in space; those are being addressed in this book. However, if the sale of Space-derived Information to the USG involves the launch or operation of satellites for a federal agency, it will be important to note which laws and policies apply to the agency being contracted with, as they can differ for a number of critical issues such as frequency allocation, information security, and orbital debris mitigation. For example, the process for obtaining approval for frequency allocation differs between civil and defence agencies.[71] There are also significant differences on the requirements associated with protecting against cybersecurity incidents.

17.3.1 Commercial Satellite Imagery Regulations

Another key consideration for NewSpace companies is NOAA's commercial remote sensing regulation, published in May 2020. The regulation is meant to improve the licensing process and to make US commercial remote sensing companies more competitive globally. The new regulation creates three tiers of licensing:[72]

- Tier 1 systems are those whose capabilities to collect unenhanced data are substantially the same as those of systems not licensed by NOAA;
- Tier 2 systems are those which US commercial providers subject to NOAA's jurisdiction have similar capabilities to collect unenhanced data, but not foreign commercial operators;
- Tier 3 systems are those offering capabilities to collect unenhanced data that are not available from either foreign or US commercial providers.

NOAA's authority to regulate Tier 1 and Tier 2 companies is limited. Tier 2 licensees can be required to (i) obtain the consent of the owner of any satellite orbiting Earth before imaging it, and (ii) to notify the Secretary of Commerce five days before conducting such an imaging operation. In addition, a Tier 2 licensee must comply with NOAA directives to limit operations due to national security concerns (often referred to as "shutter control").

NOAA, however, has much broader authority to regulate Tier 3 companies. In addition to Tier 2 restrictions, NOAA can impose temporary licence conditions on Tier 3 companies. These restrictions can include restricting or limiting the frequency of collection over a certain area and limitation of the spectral bands used for collection.

One of the challenges frequently faced by NewSpace companies that operate remote sensing systems based outside the United States is at what point do their operations in the US subject them to NOAA licence requirements. For example, does tasking by a US citizen of a foreign owned

71 See, e.g., *Policy Compliance Roadmap for Small Satellites*. The Aerospace Corporation 2021.

72 85 Fed. Reg. 30,790 (May 20, 2020). Retrieved on 31 July 2022, from https://www.nesdis.noaa.gov/s3/2021-08/15%20CFR%20Part%20960%20Regs%202020.pdf.

and operated company subject the operator to NOAA licensing requirements? NOAA guidance on these issues shows that the answer is very fact-specific.[73]

17.4 Closing comments: next steps/lessons learned

The USG will continue to be a large market for Space-derived Information as the importance of the space domain is likely to grow and the push for it to acquire these products from commercial providers will likely persist. However, despite numerous calls for the USG to streamline its procurement process, particularly for emerging technologies and capabilities, the traditional procurement rules likely will remain in place for the foreseeable future. (In fact, these difficulties are likely to increase as new technologies – such as machine learning and artificial intelligences – and new data types from space – such as thermal and hyperspectral – become more common.) Therefore, NewSpace companies looking to sell Space-derived Information to the USG will need to learn to deal with – and adapt – to a complicated procurement process.

Understanding these rules will be particularly important for non-US companies as, given both economic competitiveness and national security concerns, there are likely to be increased laws and policies for such companies to navigate.

73 *Determining whether a license is required based on mixed US and foreign involvement in a private remote-sensing space system.* (2022, March). Commercial Remote Sensing Regulatory Affairs. Retrieved on 31 July 2022, from https://www.nesdis.noaa.gov/s3/2022-03/Policy%20Guidance%20Example%202_%20US%20Person_Operating.pdf.

18

REGULATION OF COMMERCIAL EARTH OBSERVATION SYSTEMS AND DATA

Ingo Baumann and Erik Pellander[1]

18.1 Introduction[1]

"Earth observation is the gathering of information about planet Earth's physical, chemical, and biological systems via remote sensing technologies."[2] With the development of remote sensing satellites, drones, and ground-based "*in situ*" instruments, Earth observation has become more and more sophisticated. Satellite remote sensing can be defined as "sensing of the Earth's surface from space by making use of the properties of electromagnetic waves emitted, reflected or diffracted by the sensed objects".[3] As with any other uses of outer space, satellite remote sensing was confined to state actors for decades. Early missions such as the meteorological satellite Tiros-1 in 1960 and the land remote sensing satellite ERTS-1 (subsequently re-named Landsat-1) in 1972 were governmental missions. There was no need to establish any special legislation for the implementation of such governmental missions. In the early days of satellite remote sensing, legal issues were rather concerned with the question of whether and to what extent states are entitled to sense the territory of another state and whether and under which conditions data should be shared with other countries. This led to the adoption of the UN Remote Sensing Principles in 1986.[4]

With the advent of a commercial satellite remote sensing industry, states were faced with the issue of how to ensure that data generated by commercial systems do not affect national security, defence, and foreign policy. For commercial systems and data, governmental oversight needs to be established through an appropriate legal framework at national level.

Legislative initiatives are driven by the development of a commercial satellite remote sensing industry, and the development of a commercial satellite remote sensing industry is in turn driven

1 The authors would like to thank Katharina Prall, Research Associate at BHO Legal, for her contribution to this chapter.

2 European Commission, Joint Research Centre, Earth Observation.

3 UN General Assembly Resolution 41/65, Principles Relating to Remote Sensing of Earth from Outer Space, 3 December 1986.

4 Id.

DOI: 10.4324/9781003268475-25

by an appropriate legislative framework. According to recent market reports, the global commercial satellite imaging market size was estimated at US$2,964.12 million in 2021, US$3,327.47 million in 2022, and is projected to grow at a compound annual growth rate of 12.43% to reach US$5,988.40 million by 2027.[5]

National law makers are faced with the dichotomy to protect national security while ensuring competitiveness and growth of the national industry in view of global competition. The more technology advances, the more security concerns may arise. However, the more commercial satellite remote sensing becomes a global market, the more there is a risk of causing competitive disadvantages by setting regulatory requirements more restrictive than in other countries. Such disadvantages may namely arise when data with certain characteristics (e.g. a certain level of resolution) are offered on the global market by competitors subject to less stringent regulatory regimes.

Through which frameworks countries have dealt with this dichotomy is addressed in the following.

18.2 Comparative review

While many states have governmental Earth observation systems operated by their military or intelligence services, a relatively small number of countries used to have a commercial satellite remote sensing industry. Accordingly, there was and still is a relatively small number of countries that has adopted special legislation on commercial satellite remote sensing. This concerns:

- the US, which was the first country that established a national framework on commercial satellite remote sensing in 1984;
- Canada, which adopted a special law on commercial satellite remote sensing in 2005, in response to an Earth Observation system developed under a public-private partnership (PPP);
- Germany, which adopted a special law on high-grade Earth remote sensing systems in 2007 in response to a PPP in this area;
- France, which adopted certain rules on satellite remote sensing as part of its national space legislation;
- Japan, which adopted a dedicated national framework on the handling of remote sensing data in 2016; and
- Finland, which is currently in the process of developing a dedicated framework on satellite remote sensing in response to NewSpace endeavours.

However, it can be anticipated that the number of nations with commercial remote sensing activities will increase in the coming years. In the light of rapid technology and market developments, countries with regulatory frameworks will have to run regular review and amendment processes.

5 Global Information, Commercial Satellite Imaging Market Research Report by Technology (Optical and Radar), End Use, Application, Region (Americas, Asia-Pacific, and Europe, Middle East & Africa) – Global Forecast to 2027 – Cumulative Impact of COVID-1, 18 July 2022.

18.2.1 The US

The US has a very mature policy and regulatory foundation for commercial satellite remote sensing. Already in 1978, President Carter signed a directive, noting the economic benefits of commercial satellite remote sensing. The directive underlined that exploitation of such benefits "will require United States Government authorization and supervision or regulation".[6] The 1981 National Space Policy issued by President Reagan provided that "[t]he United States encourages domestic commercial exploration of space capabilities, technology, and systems for national benefit". At the same time, it acknowledged that "[t]hese activities must be consistent with national security concerns, treaties, and international agreements".[7] In order to comply with such policies, the US adopted the first ever regulatory framework – the Land Remote Sensing Commercialization Act of 1984. It provided a licensing authority – the Secretary of Commerce – the mandate to grant, suspend, modify, or revoke licences for private remote sensing space systems, and to set forth conditions for the operation of such systems. However, under the Land Remote Sensing Commercialization Act of 1984, only two licences were issued – one for Landsat and the second for the Large Format Camera, which flew aboard the Space Shuttle. Though commercial satellite remote sensing capabilities emerged in the 1980s, the development of private systems failed. This was, according to policy assessments, primarily owed to the fact that the legislation was too restrictive.[8] Under the Land Remote Sensing Commercialization Act of 1984 and its accompanying regulations, government and private remote sensing systems were treated as if they were the same. Commercial operators were obliged to sell their data at the same prices, terms and conditions to all potential customers.[9] Thereby, competitive pricing was barred, and companies were prevented from attracting capital via exclusivity clauses.

It took until the adoption of the Land Remote Sensing Policy Act of 1992 to develop the new commercial industry. The Act generally allowed commercial operators to sell data to whomever they wish at market terms and conditions. Quickly after the implementation of the act, applications from commercial operators such as WorldView Imaging Corporation, Lockheed Corporation, and Orbital Sciences Corporation were filed with the Department of Commerce. In a 1994 hearing before the US Congress, an expert argued that he is "convinced that these companies would not have come forward if the Congress had not supported changes to the Commerce Department's licensing process".[10]

At this time, it was anticipated that within few years the image quality offered on the commercial market would reach a 1-metre resolution, raising security concerns. The Clinton Administration addressed these security concerns in Presidential Decision Directive (PDD) 23 on the US Policy on Foreign Access to Remote Sensing Space Capabilities in 1994.[11] The policy goals of PDD 23 pretty much highlight the dilemma lawmakers are facing when regulating commercial satellite remote sensing, i.e. "to support and to enhance US industrial competitiveness in the field of remote

6 The White House, National Space Policy, Presidential Directive / NSC-37, 11 May 1978.

7 The White House, National Security Decision Directive Number 42, 4 July 1982.

8 James A. Vedda, Updating National Policy on Commercial Remote Sensing, March 2017.

9 Id.

10 The Regulation of Commercial Remote Sensing, Testimony of Dr. Scott Pace before the Committee on Science, Space, and Technology and the Permanent Select Committee on Intelligence, United States House of Representatives, 9 February 1994.

11 The White House, US Policy on Foreign Access to Remote Sensing Space Capabilities Presidential Decision Directive/NSC-23, 9 March 1994.

sensing space capabilities while at the same time protecting US national security and foreign policy interests".

The policy has been superseded by various subsequent policies, but it still highlights the general US approach for dealing with security concerns when licensing commercial satellite remote sensing. The policy was based on the assumption that satellite remote sensing technology would always be a moving target. Accordingly, the policy did not set (and the US still does not set) a particular resolution limit, but rather stipulated that "license requests by US firms to operate private remote sensing space systems will be reviewed on a case-by-case basis". When undertaking such case-by-case review, according to the policy, "there is a presumption that remote sensing space systems whose performance capabilities and imagery quality characteristics are available, or are planned for availability in the world marketplace, will be favourably considered". In line with this approach, US licences for commercial space remote sensing have traditionally set thresholds for the level of resolution based on the best resolution available or expected to become available from foreign competitors. Some commentators argue that "[t]his holds back U.S. companies until foreign competitors advance their capabilities, creating what is effectively a perpetual second-mover disadvantage".[12] Others claim that "[i]n practice, licenses have been issued that keep U.S. operators ahead of their foreign competition, at least for optical imaging systems".[13]

Unlike other jurisdictions, the US does not set any resolution limits for the general licensing requirement. According to Section 202 of the Land Remote Sensing Policy Act of 1992, any person who is subject to jurisdiction or control of the US requires a licence for the direct or indirect operation of a private remote sensing space system. This general licensing requirement applies to all types of systems, irrespective of their capabilities and the security concerns implied by their operations. The underlying conditions for a licence set in in Title 15 of the Code of Federal Regulations (CFR) in part 960 also used to be the same for all types of systems. The US did overcome this practice through a reform of the licensing framework which became effective on 20 July 2020. Under this new licensing framework, not only the level of resolution allowed by US commercial satellites, but also the conditions for operations are determined by availability of data from other sources than the licensed system.

The reform was based on the findings of the National Space Council "that long-term U.S. national security and foreign policy interests are best served by ensuring that U.S. industry continues to lead the rapidly maturing and highly competitive private space-based remote sensing market".[14] The US aimed "to establish a regulatory approach that ensures the United States remains the 'flag of choice' for operators of private remote sensing space systems".[15] Accordingly, in May 2018, President Trump signed Space Policy Directive-2, Streamlining Regulations on Commercial Use of Space (SPD-2). The directive required the Secretary of Commerce to review private remote sensing licensing regulations in light of SPD-2's stated policy, i.e. "promote economic growth; minimize uncertainty for taxpayers, investors, and private industry; protect national security, public-safety, and foreign policy interests; and encourage American leadership in space commerce", and rescind or revise them accordingly. The 2020 licensing framework was the outcome of this process.

12 Center for Strategic & International Studies, Commercial Space Remote Sensing and Its Role in National Security, 2 February 2022.

13 James A. Vedda (note 7).

14 National Oceanic and Atmospheric Administration, Licensing of Private Remote Sensing Space Systems, Final Rule, 85 FR 30790, 20 May 2020.

15 Id.

Under this framework, 15 CFR 960.6 requests the licensing authority – the NOAA Commercial Remote Sensing Regulatory Affairs (CRSRA) office – to categorise each private remote sensing space system "it licenses based on an analysis of whether the system produces or is capable of producing unenhanced data already available from other entities".[16] The categories are, according to 15 CFR 960.6, defined as follows:

- "a system with the capability to collect unenhanced data substantially the same as unenhanced data already available from entities or individuals not licensed under this part, such as foreign entities", is categorised as Tier 1;
- "a system with the capability to collect unenhanced data substantially the same as unenhanced data already available, but only from entities or individuals licensed under this part", is categorised as Tier 2;
- "a system with the capability to collect unenhanced data not substantially the same as unenhanced data already available from any domestic or foreign entity or individual", is categorised as Tier 3.

Among others, the factors for determining whether unenhanced data are substantially the same as other data, include spatial resolution, spectral bandwidth, number of imaging bands, temporal resolution, persistence of imaging, local time of imaging, ..., and geographic ... or other restrictions imposed by foreign governments.[17]

According to 15 CFR 960.6, a "system shall remain in the tier assigned to until such time as the [licensing authority] determines, after consultation with the Secretaries of Defense and State as appropriate, that the system belongs in a lower-numbered tier due to the advancement of non-U.S. commercial remote sensing capabilities or due to other facts, or until the [licensing authority] grants the licensee's request for a license modification".

The standard licensing conditions for all tiers are set forth in 15 CFR 960.8. They require operators to comply with the Land Remote-Sensing Policy Act of 1992, the regulation on the licensing of Private Land Remote Sensing Space Systems, applicable domestic legal obligations, and the international obligations of the US, and to operate systems in such manner as to preserve the national security of the US and to observe international obligations and policies.

Tier 1 systems, i.e. systems having "the capability collect unenhanced data substantially the same as unenhanced data already available from entities or individuals not licensed" in the US, are not subject to any additional licensing conditions. They are in particular not subject to limited-operations directives that require licensees to temporarily limit data collection and/or dissemination (colloquially known as shutter control). According to the Department of Commerce, "[t]his is because where the same capability exists outside the United States, a limited-operations directive would be less effective: even if all U.S. licensees complied fully with a directive restricting certain data, some foreign systems (lying beyond U.S. licensing jurisdiction) would be able to continue to generate such data without restriction".[18]

For Tier 2 systems, i.e. "system[s] with the capability to collect unenhanced data substantially the same as unenhanced data already available" from US licensed entities or individuals, additional standard licence conditions set down in 15 CFR 960.9 apply. Such systems shall, among others:

16 National Oceanic and Atmospheric Administration, Remote Sensing License Tiering, Q2 2022.

17 Id.

18 Id.

- [c]omply with limited-operations directives [...] that require licensees to temporarily limit data collection and/or dissemination during periods of increased concerns for national security and where necessary to meet international obligation or foreign policy interests [shutter control]; and
  - [b]e able to comply with limited-operations directives at all times [...];
  - [p]rovide and continually update the Secretary with a point of contact and an alternate point of contact for limited-operations directives; and
  - [d]uring any such limited-operations directive, permit the [licensing authority] to immediately access any component of the system for the purpose of ensuring compliance with the limited-operations directive, the [Land Remote Sensing Policy] Act [of 1992], 15 CFR 960, and the license.
- Conduct resolved imaging[19] of other artificial resident space objects (ARSO) orbiting the Earth only with the written consent of the registered owner of the ARSO to be imaged and with notification to the [licensing authority] at least five days prior to imaging.

Tier 3 systems, i.e. "system[s] with the capability to collect unenhanced data not substantially the same as unenhanced data already available from any domestic or foreign entity or individual", are, according to 15 CFR 960.10(a), subject to the same additional standard licence conditions as Tier 2 systems. In addition, they may be subject to temporary licensing conditions developed in accordance with the procedures set forth in 15 CFR 960.10(b) and (c). Under these procedures, among others

- [t]he Secretaries of Defense and State shall upon notification of the licensing authority determine whether any temporary licensing conditions are necessary to meet national security concerns or international obligations and policies of the US;
- [t]he Secretary of Defense or State shall notify the licensing authority of any such conditions and the lengths of time such conditions remain in place (which shall not exceed one year, unless the lengths of such conditions is extended);
- [t]he licensing authority shall review such notification from the Secretary of Defense or State and aim to craft the least restrictive temporary license condition(s) possible.

At the time of writing, Tier 3 licences were granted up to a resolution limit of 10 cm per pixel.[20]

For all types of systems, according to the Kyl–Bingaman Amendment which entered into force with the Defense Authorization Act of 1997,[21] no licences shall be granted for satellite imagery of Israel if such imagery is more detailed or precise than satellite imagery that is already available from commercial sources. Under this law, the Department of Commerce shall make findings as to the level of detail or precision of satellite imagery of Israel available from commercial sources. In July 2020, "[t]he Department has found that satellite imagery of Israel is readily and consistently available from non-U.S. commercial sources at a resolution of 0.4 meters Ground Sample Distance

19 According to 15 CFR 960.9 (b), "resolved imaging" means the imaging of another ARSO that results in data depicting the ARSO with a resolution of 3 x 3 pixels or greater.

20 Debra Werner, Albedo wins license to sell 10-centimeter imagery, SpaceNews, 14 December 2021.

21 Section 1064, Public Law 104-201.

(m GSD). The Department has therefore changed the existing resolution limit of 2.0 m GSD to 0.4 m GSD".[22]

18.2.2 Canada

In Canada, the operation of a remote sensing space system

- from Canada, or
- the operation of such systems outside Canada by
  - permanent residents,
  - corporations that are incorporated or continued under the laws of Canada or a province, and
  - members of any prescribed class of persons having a substantial connection to Canada related to remote sensing space systems

is governed by the Remote Sensing Space Systems Act (RSSSA)[23] and the Remote Sensing Space Systems Regulations (RSSSR).[24] The RSSSA was adopted in 2005 and entered into force together with the RSSSR in 2007.

The adoption of this framework was driven by the development of Radarsat-1 and Radarsat-2 – a series of world-leading Canadian Synthetic Aperture Radar (SAR) satellites.[25] These systems had capabilities of military and national security value. As Radarsat-2 eventually became a fully commercial system, Canada could, in the absence of an appropriate legal framework, have been left without means to exercise governmental oversight over the generation and dissemination of data from that and other systems.

According to a press release issued by Foreign Affairs and International Trade Canada when the bill was first tabled in the House of Commons, the RSSSA aims to protect "Canada's national security, national defence and foreign policy interests while supporting [Canada's] continued leadership in the provision of satellite remote sensing data and services to government and private clients".[26] Though this statement acknowledges the desire to support Canada's leadership in the provision of satellite remote sensing data, the primary focus of the RSSSA and the RSSSR is on protecting Canada's national security, national defence, and foreign policy interests.

Operators (whether government, military, or civil) require a licence from the Minister of Foreign Affairs who consults with the Department of National Defense, Public Safety Canada, Industry Canada and the Canadian Space Agency.[27] As the term "operate" is not defined by law, every activity that is directly or indirectly connected to the operation of remote sensing systems could be covered by the RSSSA. Like in the US, the licensing requirement applies to systems regardless of specific resolutions or the content of the generated information.

22 National Oceanic and Atmospheric Administration, Notice of Findings Regarding Commercial Availability of Non-U.S. Satellite Imagery with Respect to Israel, 85 FR 44059, 21 July 2020.

23 S.C. 2005, c. 45.

24 SOR/2007-66.

25 Space Strategies Consulting Ltd., 2022 Independent Review of the Remote Sensing Space Systems Act (RSSSA), 21 March 2022.

26 Id.

27 RSSSA (note22), s 5.

The RSSSA defines standard licensing conditions which include, for instance, that licensees keep control of the licensed system as well as raw data until disposal and provide raw data about the territory of other countries in accordance with the UN Remote Sensing Principles.[28] Licensees must provide and regularly evaluate a plan designed to protect the commands given to a remote sensing satellite and the sales orders (command protection plan) as well as one to protect the raw data and the products produced from it (data protection plan).[29] The Minister of Foreign Affairs can prescribe additional conditions in the licence.[30] After a licence has been issued, the Minister of Foreign Affairs and the Minister of National Defence have the authority to make an order requiring a licensee to interrupt or restrict any operation under the conditions of Section 14 of the RSSSA. The Minister of Foreign Affairs, the Minister of National Defence, and the Minister of Public Safety and Emergency Preparedness can order priority access to some services.[31]

In 2017, an independent review of the RSSSA found that the Act and the associated licensing conditions were helpful in facilitating compliance with Canada's international agreements and treaties and may have had a positive impact on the development of technology (for example in data handling), but it had a lack of clarity on scope and it leaned more in favour of protecting national security interests at the expense of commercial interests and technological development.[32] The review found ... "[t]hat although the Act was appropriate and useful at the time of its enactment in 2005, the players, activities, technology and internationalization of remote sensing activities have since changed significantly and outgrown the confines of the Act".[33] One of the issues identified by the review, i.e. that the "office in charge of implementing the Act is underfunded and under-staffed",[34] materialised in the licensing procedure for five ground station dishes operated by US-based Planet Labs Inc. at the Canadian Satellite Ground Station Inuvik. The office at Global Affairs Canada (GAC) responsible for issuing licenses under the Act is supposed to complete a review of license applications within 180 days. However, it took almost three years until a provisional licence to operate the ground station was issued on 11 February 2019.[35] Planet Labs Inc. even threatened to pull its ground station assets out of Inuvik due to the delays in the licensing procedure.[36]

In 2019, the Canadian Minister of Innovation, Science and Economic Development declared in the national space strategy the aim to create a simpler, clearer, and more modern regulatory system for space-related activities.[37] In the same year, an Ad-Hoc Review Advisory Committee, comprised of experts from industry, academia, and the government, was formed for providing information, advice, and recommendations on the RSSSA, its regulations and the implementation in line with emerging trends and developments in the industry.[38] In a meeting of the committee in

28 Id., s 5 (4).
29 RSSSR (note 23), Schedule 1 ss 14 to 29.
30 RSSSA (note 22), s 5(5), (6) and (7).
31 Id., s 15 (1), (2) and (3).
32 Ram S. Jakhu and Aram D. Kerkonian, Independent Review of the Remote Sensing Space Systems Act, 17 February 2017, p. iv.
33 Id., p. 3.
34 Id.
35 Marc Boucher, Global Affairs Canada Approves Provisional License for Planet Ground Station in Inuvik, SpaceQ, 4 March 2019.
36 Marc Boucher, Planet and KSAT Threaten to Pull Ground Station Assets out of Canada, SpaceQ, 22 February 2018.
37 Minister of Innovation, Science and Economic Development, Canada, A New Space Strategy for Canada, 2019, ST99-60/2019, p. 16.
38 Government of Canada, Space Policy and the Remote Sensing Space Systems Act (RSSSA), available online.

2021 it was brought forward that "some potential international clients decided not to conduct business within Canada due to the heavy Canadian regulations".[39]

In 2022, an independent review of the RSSSA came to the conclusion that "[t]he regulatory regime created by the Act allowed for the successful licensing and oversight of Radarsat-2 and other remote sensing space systems in a manner consistent with Canada's security and foreign policy needs".[40] However, the review found that "[t]he original problem the RSSSA addressed – managing security risks from a small number of unique and sophisticated Canadian remote sensing space systems – has been replaced by a new reality".[41] Currently, "large numbers of very capable imaging satellites from many countries are producing a flood of high-quality Earth observation data".[42] In the light of this new reality, the reviewers brought forward that "using the RSSSA to control some data from the very small Canadian portion of this international flood of data provides little, if any, [security or foreign] policy benefit for Canada". Relaxing the current framework is, in the view of the reviewers, required for the following reasons:

- Implementing the requirements of the RSSSA creates incremental costs and complexity for the Canadian space industry and R&D organizations.
- Such incremental costs and complexity inhibit innovation and disadvantage Canadian businesses with respect to international competitors.
- Canada risks falling behind other international jurisdictions that either have no restrictive space remote sensing regulations, or, like the United States, are liberalizing their RSSSA-equivalent regulations to promote their remote sensing space industries and prioritize innovation and commercialization of space remote sensing information.

18.2.3 Japan

In Japan, the legal instruments governing the use of satellite remote sensing instruments, as well as the handling of data generated thereby are the Space Basic Act (2008),[43] the Act on Ensuring Appropriate Handling of Satellite Remote Sensing Data (2016),[44] the Regulation for Enforcement of the Act on Ensuring Appropriate Handling of Satellite Remote Sensing Data (2017),[45] and the Order for Enforcement of the Act on Ensuring Appropriate Handling of Satellite Remote Sensing Data (2017).[46]

The Act and its underlying regulatory instruments aim to strike a balance between promoting data distribution and services, ensuring international peace and security, as well as protecting the national security of Japan. Under this framework, a person wishing to operate satellite remote sensing instruments with the capability of acquiring high-resolution data through ground stations for command and control located in Japan is required to obtain a licence from the Cabinet Office.

39 "Follow-up" to the RSSSA Ad-Hoc Advisory Meeting – May 2021 Secretarial Summary Notes.
40 Space Strategies Consulting Ltd. (note 24), p. 17.
41 Id., p. 18.
42 Id.
43 Space Basic Act, Law No. 43 of 2008, Cabinet Office, Japan.
44 Act on Ensuring Appropriate Handling of Satellite Remote Sensing Data, Act No. 77 of 16 November 2016.
45 Regulation for Enforcement of the Act on Ensuring Appropriate Handling of Satellite Remote Sensing Data, Cabinet Office Order No. 41 of 9 August 2017.
46 Order for Enforcement of the Act on Ensuring Appropriate Handling of Satellite Remote Sensing Data, Cabinet Order No. 282 of 15 November 2017.

Unlike the US and Canada, this general licensing requirement is limited to the use of remote sensing instruments with certain capabilities, namely sensors "capable of discerning the movement of vehicles, ships, aircraft and other moving facilities".[47] The thresholds for determining whether a sensor is capable of discerning the movement of vehicles, ships, aircraft, and other moving facilities are set forth in Art. 2 of the Regulation for Enforcement of the Act on Ensuring Appropriate Handling of Satellite Remote Sensing Data as follows:

- An optical sensor with a Distinguishing Accuracy of Target not exceeding two metres.
- A SAR sensor with Distinguishing Accuracy of Target not exceeding three metres.
- A hyperspectral sensor with Distinguishing Accuracy of Target not exceeding ten metres and with the number of wavelength bands exceeding 49.
- A thermal infrared sensor with Distinguishing Accuracy of Target not exceeding five metres.

The licensing requirements for the use of satellite remote sensing instruments include measures to prevent persons other than the applicant from the use of the satellite remote sensing instrument; measures for the prevention of divulgence, loss or damage of satellite remote sensing data; and a requirement to ensure that the use of the satellite remote sensing instrument does not cause adverse effects on ensuring peace in the international community.[48]

The so-called specified user organisations, which are exempted from the licensing requirement for the use of satellite remote sensing instruments, are determined in the Order for Enforcement of the Act on Ensuring Appropriate Handling of Satellite Remote Sensing Data.[49] According to the Order, the Cabinet Secretariat is exempted from the licensing requirement for the use of satellite remote sensing instruments.[50]

The Act on Ensuring Appropriate Handling of Satellite Remote Sensing Data, furthermore, limits the dissemination of data "where the use of such information is likely to cause adverse effect on ensuring the peace and security of the international community and the national security of Japan".[51] Limitations apply to raw data up to five years after the recording which are

- recorded by an optical sensor with Distinguishing Accuracy of Target not exceeding two metres,
- recorded by a SAR sensor with Distinguishing Accuracy of Target not exceeding three metres,
- recorded by a hyperspectral sensor with Distinguishing Accuracy of Target not exceeding ten metres and detectable wavelength bands exceeding 49,
- recorded by a thermal infrared sensor with Distinguishing Accuracy of Target not exceeding 5 metres.

For data which has been processed by radiometric or geometric correction ("standard data"), limitations apply to

47 Act on Ensuring Appropriate Handling of Satellite Remote Sensing Data (note 43), Article 2 (ii).
48 Id, Article 6.
49 Id, Article 2 (v) and Article 4 (1).
50 Order for Enforcement of the Act on Ensuring Appropriate Handling of Satellite Remote Sensing Data (note 45), Article 1.
51 Act on Ensuring Appropriate Handling of Satellite Remote Sensing Data (note 43), Article 2.

- data recorded by an optical sensor with Distinguishing Accuracy of Target less than 25 centimetres,
- data recorded by a SAR sensor with Distinguishing Accuracy of Target less than 24 centimetres,
- data recorded by a hyperspectral sensor with Distinguishing Accuracy of Target not exceeding five metres and detectable wavelength bands exceeding 49,
- data recorded by a thermal infrared sensor with Distinguishing Accuracy of Target not exceeding five metres.

Under the Act on Ensuring Appropriate Handling of Satellite Remote Sensing Data, a person possessing such data shall not disseminate the data, except when

- data are disseminated to persons holding a certificate for the handling of satellite remote sensing data in accordance with the procedures set forth in the Act;
- data are disseminated to a person holding a licence to use the instruments through which the data are produced in accordance with the procedures set forth in the Act;
- data are disseminated to a specified data handling organisation (which is exempted from the certification requirement) in accordance with the procedures set forth in the Act;
- data dissemination is undertaken for special purposes determined in the Act on Ensuring Appropriate Handling of Satellite Remote Sensing Data and the Order for Enforcement of the Act on Ensuring Appropriate Handling of Satellite Remote Sensing Data such as public interest or an urgent situation when measures must be taken to rescue human life, for disaster relief, or for other emergencies.[52]

The so-called specified data handling organisations, which are exempted from the certification requirement for the handling of data, are listed in the Order for Enforcement of the Act on Ensuring Appropriate Handling of Satellite Remote Sensing Data. This list numbers over 32 organisations including, among others, the Public Prosecutor's Office, the Supreme Court and the Ministry of Justice, applications users in the Ministry of Agriculture, Forestry and Fisheries, as well as the government organisations in Canada, France, Germany, and the USA (incidentally or not the countries which also have adopted national laws on satellite remotes sensing).

The Prime Minister may, moreover, limit the dissemination of data with the characteristics prescribed above by issuing an order to a person possessing such data which prohibits data provision, to the extent and for the period specified in the order.[53]

The development of the above-mentioned national framework on satellite remote sensing has raised concerns amongst Japanese Earth observation companies. Lawmakers claimed that this framework will provide legal clarity for companies conducting commercial activities related to satellite data. However, several companies expressed concerns that this framework may have negative impacts on their business. Companies requested that restrictions should be placed only on the operations of Earth observation satellites, whilst the dissemination of data should be left at the

52 Id., Article 18 (3); Order for Enforcement of the Act on Ensuring Appropriate Handling of Satellite Remote Sensing Data (note 45), Article 4.

53 Act on Ensuring Appropriate Handling of Satellite Remote Sensing Data (note 43), Article 19.

discretion of the companies.[54] Companies were also concerned about additional costs for meeting restrictions on sensor types, resolution, and delivery times.

18.2.4 Germany

Germany has so far not adopted any overall national space legislation, but it does have specific laws concerning satellite Earth observation data. The applicable laws in Germany are the Satellite Data Security Act (SatDSiG) of 2007[55] and the Satellite Data Security Ordinance (SatDSiV) of 2008.[56] The SatDSiG sets the higher-level conditions, while the SatDSiV further specifies the scope[57] and includes the technical characteristics that are used to review a customer request for Earth observation data as being either sensitive or non-sensitive.[58] The competent authority for the SatDSiG and the SatDSiV is the Federal Ministry for Economic Affairs and Climate Action (BMWK), while the operational administration is performed by the Federal Office for Economic Affairs and Export Control (BAFA).[59] The German Foreign Office (AA), the Ministry of Defence (BMVg), and the Ministry of the Interior (BMI) are closely involved for policy issues, while the Federal Office for Information Security (BSI) is involved in cybersecurity checks during the licensing procedure.

The focus of the SatDSiG and SatDSiV is on the operation of (non-military) "high grade" Earth remote sensing systems from within the German territory and the first level of dissemination of data generated by such systems from within the German territory.[60] Accordingly, the SatDSiG pertains to the operator and/or primary data distributor, but not to re-sellers, value-adding companies, service providers, or further downstream companies. The SatDSiG does also not pertain to the dissemination of data generated by foreign systems that are not operated from within the German territory. Both the operation of systems falling under the scope of the Act as well as the dissemination of data generated thereby are subject to a licensing requirement.[61]

The definition of "high grade" is concerned with the ability of payload sensors to generate data with very high information content due to their geometric resolution, spectral coverage, number of spectral channels, spectral resolution, radiometric resolution, temporal resolution, polarisation characteristics (for microwave sensors or radar sensors), and phase history (for microwave sensors or radar sensors).[62]

The concern with a law on high grade data grew out of the German initiatives for high spatial resolution radar systems, implemented as a PPP between the German Aerospace Centre (DLR)

54 EU-Japan Centre for Industrial Cooperation, Japan-Space/Earth Observation News: 2 New Bills on Satellite Observation and Space Activities to be Discussed in the Next Parliamentary Session in August.

55 Act to Safeguard the Security Interests of the Federal Republic of Germany from Endangerment by the Distribution of High-Grade Earth Remote Sensing Data, 23 November 2007 (BGBl. I S. 2590) as amended by Art. 5 of the Law of 19 April 2021 (BGBl. I S. 771).

56 Statutory Ordinance to give Protection against the Security Risk to the Federal Republic of Germany by the Dissemination of High Grade Earth Remote Sensing Data, 26 March 2008 (BGBl. I S. 508) as amended by Art. 1 of the Ordinance of 30 July 2014 (BGBl. I S. 1314).

57 SatDSiV (note 55), s 1.

58 Id., s 2 together with its Annexes.

59 SatDSiG (note 54), s 24.

60 Id., s 1.

61 Id., ss 3 and 11.

62 Id., s 2(1) Nr. 4, (2); SatDSiV (note 55), s 1.

and Astrium (today Airbus). Germany launched the TerraSAR-X satellite[63] in June 2007, followed by the almost identical TanDEM-X satellite in June 2010. These missions are "high grade" which has stimulated concern for whether the data produced could be sensitive and potentially misused.

Under the SatDSiG, there is a detailed procedure to check whether a request for the dissemination of data is sensitive. These checks are to be undertaken by the data provider. The procedure is an algorithmic one based on a defined set of rules. The sensitivity check is performed based on metadata, not the data sets themselves. That is to say that the images are not checked for content, but the sensitivity check concerns the overall characteristics of the data set.

A request from the Federal Republic of Germany under Section 21 of the Satellite Data Security Act or from a German military or intelligence agency is not sensitive.

The main characteristics of the sensitivity check are as follows:

1. Information content of the individual data product as specified by the operation mode of the sensor and the processing level: at different stages of the evaluation, the spatial resolution limit is first 2.5 m and then later 1.2 m depending on other criteria. This part of the evaluation also includes whether the data are hyper-spectral or whether radar phase information is supplied,
2. Ground segments to which the data are to be transmitted, as defined by a list of sensitive ground segments,
3. The target area surveyed by the data is assessed as to whether the area belongs to a defined list of sensitive target areas,
4. The time period between data generation and supply to the customer: the time period criterion is five days.

The sensitivity checks are performed automatically against these criteria. If the result of the check is "non-sensitive" then the data supplier is free to supply the data. If the result of the check is "sensitive" then a permit by the Office for Economic Affairs and Export Control (BAFA) is required. BAFA has the right to prohibit dissemination of the data or permit dissemination with certain conditions attached or permit dissemination with no conditions attached.

The technical thresholds for the scope of the SatDSiG, as well as the details on the sensitivity assessment of a request provided in the SatDSiV shall be regularly reviewed regarding:

- whether technical thresholds/details on the sensitivity assessment need to be adapted, for example, due to the fact that data with certain technical criteria are otherwise available on the market,
- threats to national security remain to be the same (as regards ground segments to which the data are transmitted or as regards target areas surveyed by the data) or whether there are any new threats to be considered.

The German approach has been described as clear, efficient, and very responsive to industry needs.[64] However, the German industry raised concerns that the sensitivity check procedure may cause competitive disadvantages vis-a-vis foreign competitors who can provide data much faster.

63 Michael Eineder / Achim Roth / Alberto Moreira (eds) (2019) Ten Years of TerraSAR-X – Scientific Results, Remote Sensing 11, 364.

64 Space Strategies Consulting Ltd. (note 24), p. 46.

Furthermore, in view of industry, the technical thresholds for the scope of the SatDSiG, as well as the criteria of the sensitivity check procedure need to be updated and relaxed, namely in view of the most recent US regulatory practice. The SatDSiG theoretically requires regular reviews against technological progress and market development. However, besides minor adjustment of the SatDSiV in 2014, no amendments have been made since the original adoption 15 years ago.

18.2.5 France

In France, satellite remote sensing is governed by the Space Operations Act of 2008 (SOA),[65] Decree 2009-640 of June 2009,[66] and an Order of September 2013.[67] The development of the framework was driven by the privatisation of the initially government-controlled operator SPOT Image. The entire framework is currently under review in light of technological advancement and market developments. This review is implemented through a step-by-step reform process. By Ordonnance n° 2022-232, several provisions regarding national defence interests have already been amended, including provisions on the use of a payload for the collection of Earth observation data and their subsequent dissemination.[68] At the time of writing, the underlying legal instruments have not yet been amended in the course of the ongoing reform process.

Unlike other jurisdictions, France does not foresee a licensing procedure for collecting and disseminating Earth observation data *per se*. Whilst the launch and operations of Earth observation satellites are subject to a fully-fledged licensing procedure under the French Space Operations Act, the use of a payload for the collection of Earth observation data and their subsequent dissemination are only subject to a prior declaration.

Under Art. 23 of the Space Operations Act, any primary space-based data operator undertaking in France an activity having certain technical characteristics defined in a decree passed at the Council of State must make a declaration to the competent administrative authority which is the Secretary-General for Defence and National Security. The assessment by the Secretary-General for Defence and National Security determines whether the activity harms the fundamental interests of France, particularly defence matters, foreign policy, and international commitments. The declaration is not subject to a formal statement of approval. However, the competent authority is entitled to provide individual notification of any reservations during a two-month period before the activity begins. The absence of a response from the competent authority does not mean that the activity is prohibited. On the contrary, it means that the operator is entitled to undertake the activities notified to the competent authority without any reservations.

According to Art. 23 of the Space Operations Act, the technical characteristics setting the scope of the declaratory procedure are related to the nature of the data acquired, their origin and their precision. This wording has been amended by the recent regulatory reform to the extent that the nature of the data acquired and their origin was added, whilst the technical characteristics described in the

65 République Française, Loi n° 2008-518 du 3 juin 2008 relative aux opérations spatiales, amended by Ordonnance n°2022-232 du 23 février 2022 – art. 2.

66 République Française, Décret n° 2009-640 du 9 juin 2009 portant application des dispositions prévues au titre VII de la loi n° 2008-518 du 3 juin 2008 relative aux opérations spatiales, amended by Décret n°2022-233 du 24 février 2022 – art. 1.

67 République Française, Arrêté du 4 septembre 2013 relatif à la déclaration préalable d'activité effectuée par les exploitants primaires de données d'origine spatiale.

68 Ordonnance n° 2022-232 du 23 février 2022 relative à la protection des intérêts de la défense nationale dans la conduite des opérations spatiales et l'exploitation des données d'origine spatiale.

previous version have been replaced by the general term "precision". Thereby, French lawmakers acknowledged that other parameters than the precision of the data are to be taken into account when assessing security concerns raised by the generation and dissemination of Earth observation data. The more general wording "precision" offers flexibility when determining the technical characteristics for the scope of the declaratory procedure. At the time of writing, however, the underlying decree has not yet been amended.

Implementing Decree 2009-640 of 9 June 2009, as amended by Decree 2013-653 of July 2013, currently defines the following key technical characteristics of space data that are subject to a prior declaration:

- data from panchromatic optical sensors with a spatial resolution less than or equal to two metres;
- data from multispectral optical sensors with a spatial resolution less than or equal to eight metres and with the number of spectral bands greater than or equal to ten;
- data from stereoscopic optical sensors with a spatial resolution less than or equal to ten metres or with altimeter accuracy less than or equal to ten metres in relative value (15 metres in absolute value);
- data from thermal infrared sensors with a spatial resolution less than or equal to five metres;
- data from radar sensors with a spatial resolution less than three metres;
- data with an intrinsic location accuracy less than ten metres (circle of error at 90%).

That these types of data fall under the scope of the declaratory procedure under the Space Operations Act, does not mean that the acquisition and/or dissemination of the data is prohibited and/or might be restricted. It only implies that these data are subject to the declaratory procedure, under which restrictions might be imposed. In turn, the threshold definitions listed above imply that data produced from systems that do not meet these technical characteristics are not subject to the declaratory procedure and are not subject to any restrictions.

According to Art. 1 (7) of the Space Operations Act, the term "space-based data primary operator" means any natural or juridical person ensuring the programming of an Earth observation satellite system or the reception of Earth observation data from outer space. In other words, the entity that is subject to the declaratory procedure under Title VII is the entity that controls the programming of the satellite payload through control of sensor activation and parameter adjustment or the entity that directly receives the data from the satellite at its installations on the ground surface. The primary operator under the terms of the Space Operations Act is not necessarily the same entity as the entity applying for the (prior) authorization to proceed with the launch and the (prior) authorisation to command the satellite in outer space. Any entities other than the primary operator (namely those in the upstream and downstream sectors) are not subject to the declaratory procedure. As provided in Art. 26(f) of the Space Operations Act, the declaratory procedure is also not applicable to activities undertaken by the Ministry of Defence and to public missions assigned to CNES.

Under Art. 24 of the Space Operations Act, together with Art. 5 of Decree 2009-640 of 9 June 2009 and Art 3 .of Decree 2013-654 of July 2013, the Secretary-General for Defence and National Security may at any time prescribe restrictive measures to the use of an instrument for high-resolution observation, the reception of data, the production of images and to the dissemination of data in order protect fundamental interests of France. Under Art. 5 of the Decree 2009-640 of 9 June 2009, restrictive measures on the use of an instrument, the reception of data and the production of images may consist of the immediate, total, or partial suspension of satellite programming or data reception for a renewable temporary period; the obligation to postpone satellite programming, data reception, or the production of images for a renewable temporary period; a permanent ban on programming or data reception; the limitation of the technical quality of the data; and/or the geographical limitation of coverage areas. According to Art. 3 of Decree 2013-654 of July 2013, restrictive measures to the dissemination of data may consist of the immediate, total, or partial suspension of the supply of data concerning specific geographic areas for a renewable temporary period; the obligation to postpone delivery of data relating to specific geographic areas for a renewable temporary period; the limitation of the technical quality of the data relating to specific geographic areas for a renewable temporary period; and/or the permanent limitation of the technical quality of the data concerning certain areas of the French territory.

18.2.6 Finland

Finland regulated the licensing and supervision of satellite operations by the Ministry of Economic Affairs and Employment in the Act on Space Activities of 2018.[69] More detailed provisions on the authorisation, registration, and operation are laid down in the Decree on Space Activities.[70] However, the reception, processing, and dissemination of data generated by Finnish Earth observation satellites as well as the use of ground stations in Finland for data reception and distribution were not yet regulated in detail. In March 2022, there were 18 Finnish satellites in orbit, 13 of them for commercial Earth observation. The Finnish company ICEYE operates Earth observation satellites and provides related data and services. As Earth observation activities can raise concerns regarding security interests, Finnish lawmakers acknowledged the need for a dedicated framework for balancing security interests with the interest in competitiveness and growth of the Finnish space sector.

In March 2021, the Ministry of Economic Affairs and Employment set up a working group which elaborated a draft law on ground stations and certain radars and proposed amendments to the Act on Space Activities by adding special provisions on Earth observation activities. These provisions would introduce a separate licensing regime for Earth observation, also under the authority of the Ministry of Economic Affairs and Employment. The draft includes thresholds regarding the licensing requirement, for instance on resolution, positional accuracy, and return rate. The draft licensing conditions include the absence of risks for national security and compliance with technical safety requirements. The draft prescribes consultations with the safety authorities before issuing a license. The operator would be obliged to ensure that certain safety requirements are met and to report on its activities, including its customers, to the Ministry of Economic Affairs and Employment. It should be noted that the satellite carrying the payload used for Earth observation is still subject to the licensing requirement under s 5 of the Act on Space Activities.[71] For the dissemination of the generated data, Section 11(d) of the draft includes limitations with regard to the customers, for instance that the operator shall provide data only to identified and known customers; more detailed provisions on restrictions should be laid down in an additional decree. For certain emergency situations, the draft foresees priority access to the data by Finnish authorities.

69 Act on Space Activities (63/2018).

70 Decree of the Ministry of Economic Affairs and Employment on Space Activities (74/2018).

71 If an operator is operating both, the satellite that carries the payload used for Earth observation as well as the respective payload, the draft envisages the possibility of a joint application for both licences at the same time, upon which the authority would decide together.

The draft law on ground stations and certain radars includes a licensing requirement applicable to the establishment and operation of ground stations and radars on Finnish territory or on a vehicle or vessel registered in Finland. The authority responsible for authorisation and supervision would be the Transport and Communications Agency. During the licensing process, special attention would be paid on data security. After issuing the licence, the Transport and Communications Agency would possess far-reaching enforcement powers, including immediate suspension of operations. The law was adopted by the parliament on 19 January 2023.

18.3 Conclusion and outlook

States employ different approaches for regulating commercial satellite remote sensing. Two out of six jurisdictions reviewed – the US and Canada – require a licence for the operation of a satellite remote sensing system irrespective of the security concerns raised thereby. One of these jurisdictions – the US – has developed relaxed licensing procedures for systems that do not cause security concerns, whilst the other – Canada – generally applies the same procedures to all systems, regardless of related security concerns. The US, furthermore, traditionally sets limitations on the level of resolution allowed for satellite remote sensing systems operated under US jurisdiction based on availability of data from other sources, and more recently refers to availability of data from other sources when determining licensing conditions. Four out of six jurisdictions reviewed – Japan, Germany, France, and Finland – require a licence (or a declaration) only for systems with certain technical characteristics. Two out of these four jurisdictions – Japan and Germany – set additional thresholds upon which dissemination of data can be restricted.

Besides the differences in approach and details, all national frameworks target a balance: protecting national security, defence, and foreign policy interests whilst at the same time supporting the development of a commercial satellite remote sensing industry and its global competitiveness.

The existing national frameworks are aligned to each other, and the competent authorities regularly exchange informally on application and reviews. Those states that have set a threshold for determining the scope of their licensing regime have set nearly the same thresholds for the different types of sensors covered. The same is true when it comes to thresholds for potential restrictions of data dissemination or for applying more robust licensing requirements, respectively. Alignment of national frameworks is required, as national security, defence, and foreign policy interests cannot be adequately protected through licensing requirements and/or restrictions under national law, when similar types of data are available in the global market from other sources.

National regulatory frameworks and their application must be constantly reviewed and as necessary adapted against political, technological, and market developments. In view of the speed and impact of such developments, rebalancing must occur at ever shorter intervals and under increasingly complex circumstances. Commercialisation is now also taking hold of sensor types that were previously reserved for military or scientific missions – this mainly concerns thermal infrared and hyperspectral sensors. There are commercial plans for continuous video-streaming via satellites, for commercial weather satellites or for space object tracking and space surveillance. Constellations of observation satellites allow a high revisit rate and thus a much faster servicing of user requests. On-board data processing, the use of artificial intelligence in data analysis, and the enhanced data fusion capabilities provided by powerful cloud computing platforms influence sensitivity assessments. Downloading data via laser links to geostationary satellites or directly to the ground significantly reduces the time between data generation and servicing user requests. As high-quality commercial data with new characteristics enters the international market, other countries will be forced to review and adapt their own regulations.

To the extent that competitiveness of national industry becomes the primary focus, the will for international coordination of regulatory approaches may diminish. As more countries develop commercial Earth observation systems, efforts for international coordination will also increase. This causes the risk of a race to the bottom in regulatory frameworks, thereby threatening international peace and security. To overcome such issues, a coordinated approach – at least among allies – is highly desirable. The US Space Priorities Framework released by the Biden administration in December 2021 pretty much outlines such desire by setting the priority to foster a "regulatory environment that enables a competitive and burgeoning U.S. commercial space sector" while working "with allies and partners to update and harmonize space policies, regulations, export controls, and other measures that govern commercial activities worldwide".[72]

72 The White House, United States Space Priorities Framework, December 2021.

B

Large constellations: Frequencies, registration, and interference

19

A SATELLITE OPERATOR'S PRACTICAL EXPERIENCES WITH LICENSING AND MARKET BARRIERS FOR GLOBAL SATELLITE CONSTELLATIONS

The case of OneWeb

Ruth Pritchard-Kelly

19.1 What is OneWeb, and why is that "NewSpace"?

OneWeb, a London-based telecommunications company, is building a new kind of global communications network that will deliver low latency, high-speed broadband through a "low Earth orbit" (LEO) constellation of satellites – what is known colloquially as a "large constellation".[1] The first generation of OneWeb's constellation ("Gen1") will operate approximately 650 satellites which began launching in 2019 and began services in much of the world in 2022, and will be able to serve the whole globe by the end of 2023.

Traditionally, communications satellites have used an orbit much further away (35,800 km) in which the satellites orbit the Earth at the same speed as the Earth's rotation, making the satellites appear stationary when viewed from Earth. This "geostationary" orbit (GEO) has been used by most of the world's legacy communications satellites, making the new LEOs unusual and exciting, and part of the "new space" revolution that includes revolutions in manufacturing and launching that led to lowered production costs at just the same time that revolutions in the internet and in personal mobile devices led to higher demand for space-based delivery of broadband.

OneWeb's satellites use spectrum allocated to Fixed Satellite Services (FSS) in the Ku and Ka bands.[2] Unlike traditional GEO satellites, OneWeb's LEO satellites (which are orbiting Earth

1 Other operators around the globe are also launching LEOs, among them Amazon's "Kuiper", SpaceX's "Starlink", Telesat's "LightSpeed", and China's "StarNet".

2 Specifically 10.7–12.7 GHz and 14.0–14.5 GHz for user terminals, and 17.8–18.6 GHz and 18.8–19.3 GHz for gateway Earth stations.

DOI: 10.4324/9781003268475-27

at 1,200 km in a pattern that covers the whole globe) provide a broadband link with under 75ms latency, a significant improvement over the 250ms delay via GEO that makes real-time, two-way applications such as audio or video calls difficult. The quality of the connection equates to 4G services offered by terrestrial mobile networks.

LEOs require more than one gateway earth stations spaced around the world, so as to be able to communicate with any user anywhere (including in the air or out at sea). OneWeb's architecture will require roughly 45 gateways.[3]

OneWeb will start by offering wholesale services to existing mobile network operators or large enterprises, and will expand into aero, maritime, and land mobile services as those user terminals come to market. Only a large LEO constellation can provide connectivity to every spot on the globe, including in the air and at sea.

19.2 Why do countries benefit from "new space" technologies?

"Connecting the Unconnected" is a phrase heard everywhere, but this is the goal for every country, no matter its government or economy: connectivity itself is the prize. More recently the International Telecommunication Union (ITU) has begun campaigning for "meaningful connectivity".[4] If a community is connected, the people have access to jobs, education, government information and programmes, healthcare, and each other. Connectivity brings not just jobs in the immediate community, but the ability to perform myriad jobs based all over the world while staying in one's own community. No longer will people leave for education or jobs and not return; no longer must a government worry about how to reach its people with information and services. And the only technology in the world that can reach literally everyone, whether at sea, in the air, or anywhere on land is a satellite. So, while much of the land in our world can be connected with wires or terrestrial-based wireless technologies (such as mobile phones), there are still great swaths of land that will never get a terrestrial-based technology, whether because of geographic difficulties or business-case realities, and for those communities and markets there are now the new LEOs, offering connections as fast and as clear as a fiber connection anywhere in the world.

19.3 How do "new space" technologies like LEOs get authorised to provide services in every nation in the world?

One of the challenges of a technology that intrinsically covers the entire globe is getting authorised to provide services over the entire globe. As "the globe" doesn't grant authorisations (and neither does the ITU), the LEO industry needs to apply for authorisation in every single nation in which it wishes to offer services. Unfortunately, almost every nation handles this sort of licensing slightly differently, making provision of a global service sometimes quite difficult. Market access, service, and equipment licensing can take years, and this usually needs to happen before the operator is receiving income or revenue from customers, which is one of the reasons that a global constellation is such an expensive prospect.

3 Other LEOs may require many more (such as Starlink) or fewer (such as Telesat) depending on the size and altitude of the constellation. Traditional GEO satellites need no particular "gateway" as any Earth station (either the operator's or the user's) may act as the gateway to connect to the traditional phone network or the internet.

4 ITU, New UN targets chart path to universal meaningful connectivity, Press Release (19 April 2022).

The first set of licences comes from a satellite's "home administration", which is the nation that is authorising the satellite to operate in outer space. That nation must also have filed paperwork at the ITU regarding the spectrum and orbits to be used.

Once that set of licences is granted, the satellite operator needs to get permission from every single country in which it wishes to offer service. Every nation in the world has regulations regarding access to their market, which often include spectrum licensing, service licensing, and equipment licensing. Some nations also require local entities or local partners.

19.4 How do satellites get the rights to use spectrum all over the globe?

19.4.1 The ITU and globally harmonised allocations

As with market access, the use of spectrum around the globe is complicated by the multiple nations involved. Fortunately, every nation in the world belongs to the ITU which allocates frequency bands to the different services that need wireless spectrum.

However, even with global (or sometimes regional) allocations to particular services, each Member State of the ITU retains the sovereign right to allocate spectrum within its own territory, and often nations believe they have reason to mete out spectrum rights in a slightly different way than the region or neighboring states might be doing. This means a satellite constellation, whose technology perforce extends beyond the political borders of any single state, might have to contend with differing allocations around the globe.

The more that allocations can be harmonised around the world – or at least within a region – the easier it is for any space-based technology to provide services quickly and efficiently to that region.

19.4.2 The ITU regulations protect each nation's need for connectivity

The ITU recently updated its rules in two ways in response to concerns that large constellations might block access to spectrum and orbits for other services.

- First, it changed the way it charges its administrative "cost recovery" fee to account for the complexity of these filings, and the concomitant increase in resources (whether hardware, software, or human) needed to assess the filings.[5]
- Second, it instigated build-out milestones to ensure that the systems holding rights to the spectrum come to fruition, and if not, that the spectrum can be used by another constellation or technology. Constellations will have to deploy 10% of their constellation within two years after the end of their "regulatory period" for "bringing into use" ("BIU" – most systems have seven years to BIU), and then build 50% within five years and complete the deployment within seven years.
- If a system fails to build 10% of what it filed for by the milestone, its system will be adjusted down in size, such that the number of satellites it *does* have at the milestone will now define 10% of the full constellation size. The same will be true for the other milestones.[6]

5 ITU, International Telecommunications Union, Decision 482 (modified 2020).

6 Note that in the United States, the FCC developed its own milestone regime which is slightly different and considerably more restrictive. In the US, a constellation has only six years from grant of its US licence in which to launch and operate 50% of its system; if the constellation has not done that, the entire system is capped at whatever has been

The ITU's Radio Regulations provide what is one of the world's most successful examples of international comity and coordination. All satellite systems and networks must work out the use of the spectrum with all other users of that spectrum. This "coordination" takes years, and among the most important rules is that, should there be interference caused by a system that has not yet completed its coordination with other systems, the system that *submitted its filing to the ITU first* is considered to have "priority" in the use of the spectrum, and the later-filed system must modify its operations to alleviate the interference. Although the word "priority" is not used in the Regulations, this is the practical effect, and the guiding principle between operators as they work out their coordination with each other.

19.4.3 Priority of filings

Note that a satellite operator does not apply to the ITU directly for spectrum rights: an operator must request its government to file the paperwork at the ITU, and legally any spectrum rights adhere to the nation, not the operator. Thus, operators try to have good relationships with their home administrations, since the operator is dependent upon its "admin" to protect those spectrum rights vis-à-vis other nations and other operators.

Sometimes an operator will submit filings to the ITU via several different admins, which can be advantageous both because of the additional political support the operator gains by having multiple nations interested in its spectrum rights, but also because commercial alliances such as joint ventures make it useful to have filings from related nations.

19.4.4 OneWeb's ITU filings

OneWeb has so far chosen to file for spectrum rights via the UK, France, Canada, and Mexico. New filings can be made either through the same or other nations. For example, current shareholders include companies from the United Kingdom, France, Republic of Korea, India, and Japan, which makes those countries attractive as possible "ITU admins". However, newer filings are required to accommodate earlier-filed systems when working out coordination, so an operator will try to use its earliest filing for coordination negotiations. In OneWeb's case, a UK filing offers the best priority for the Ku band, and a French filing has the best priority for Ka band. Future generations of satellites can use the same filings as the first generation, assuming the parameters of the system are compatible with those listed in the filing. Otherwise, either a modification to that filing will be needed, or perhaps a whole new filing.

19.4.5 National licensing

Individual licensing will always remain for infrastructure that is based in a particular territory (such as Earth stations and points of presence (PoPs)). Many nations also require authorisation to use spectrum in their territory, or to provide a service via that spectrum. Some nations also require "market access" licences, sometimes known as "landing rights" when describing market access for satellites whose ITU filing was handled by a different nation. These landing rights are con-

launched – no further satellites may be used to offer service to the USA. The licensee then has three more years (for a total of nine) in which to launch the full constellation. See *In the Matter of Updates to Parts 2 and 25 Concerning Non-Geostationary, Fixed-Satellite Service Systems and Related Matters*, Second Report and Order, FCC 20-119, adopted 26 August 2020, and released 28 August 2020.

troversial. Nations that impose them consider the process to be one of equity: have those foreign satellites been regulated effectively in their home nation and are those satellites subject to the same obligations as the domestic operators would be? Or have their home nations been somehow more relaxed in the licensing requirements than the nation requiring landing rights? On the other hand, satellite operators often perceive "landing rights" as simply a way to keep out competition that might threaten domestic operators.

The harmonisation of spectrum allocations is vital for a technology that spans entire regions if not the entire globe. If there were different spectrum allocations in every nation, it would likely preclude the provision of space-based services, as no one satellite could be sure to have all the possible frequencies included. (Among other issues is simply the weight of the equipment: it is vital to have specific frequencies so as to have specific equipment so as to minimise extraneous weight on the spacecraft.) Harmonisation of international and regional spectrum allocations creates economies of scale and allows roaming and interoperability, which is vital for technologies that are not containable within a single national border, such as satellites and other space-based technologies.

19.5 Why is operating in outer space expensive?

19.5.1 Expensive for the operator

Satellites must be almost fully funded before they ever see a cent of income (let alone profit) – there will be no customer payments until services start, and before services can start there are years of design, manufacturing, and launch. And if the satellite or launch has an anomaly, there will not be any customer payments for even longer. Generally speaking, individual geostationary satellites cost close to half a billion dollars, and the LEO constellations will cost more like US$6–10 billion.[7] If a satellite fails, it must be de-orbited and a replacement must be launched – at this time, there is no fixing or refueling possible in space, although both concepts are being explored.[8]

19.5.2 Expensive for the licensing nation

Nations typically pass-through much of their liability for putting objects in outer space (imposed via the Liability Convention[9]) by requiring insurance of their licensees.

One way in which the launching states try both to lessen their liability and increase the chances that the object being launched is well-tested and unlikely to cause damage to others is to impose two types of insurance on the would-be operator:

- "Indemnification" is often required from the operator, which prevents the operator from turning to the state for funds if the operator is sued by a "third party" and can be used by the nation to off-set its own unlimited liability in the case of a lawsuit; and

7 Caleb Henry, Geostationary satellite orders bouncing back, SpaceNews (21 February 2020). See also Mark Holmes, Credit Suisse Report Says LEO Constellations Will be Challenged by Increasing Data Use, Via Satellite (31 January 2022).

8 See for example, Sarah Scoles, There Are No Real Rules for Repairing Satellites in Space – Yet, Wired (18 December 2020).

9 United Nations Office for Outer Space Affairs, Convention on International Liability for Damage Caused by Space Objects.

- "Third-party liability insurance" must be carried by the operator, usually for a specified minimum amount.[10]

Another way states control their exposure to liability is by requiring licences for any objects being launched, as the state can then set criteria to protect its international obligations under the Outer Space Treaty[11] and the Registration Convention. [12]

The licensing process is usually long and involves multiple feasibility assessments, including financial, technical, and business case.

Once an object is in outer space, the nation that launched it is supposed to register the object with the United Nations Office for Outer Space Affairs.[13] Occasionally this registration does not happen as quickly as might be expected, for example when it is not entirely clear which nation ought to register the object. This confusion might stem from the fact that the launch vehicle might be owned by a company from one nation but operated or launched from a second or third nation, while the object being launched might be operated by a company from a fourth nation. (Not to mention the situation where a country declines to register an object for political reasons.)

If a satellite is not registered, and is not licensed by some nation, it is hard to gain market access to other nations to provide services. This may be of little concern to a satellite being used by a government itself for its own services; however, for a commercial communications satellite it is imperative to be licensed by a nation and registered at the UN. Note that OneWeb is registered at the UN by the United Kingdom for its first generation of satellites (roughly 650 satellites).

For large constellations such as OneWeb, whose "footprint" will cover every nation in the world, it is not enough for a single nation to use the constellation's service; the constellation must have customers across the globe, and thus must have market access in as many nations as possible.

19.6 Which policies hinder or support the growth of LEO constellations?

LEOs have the potential to truly bridge the digital divide literally everywhere. These orbits, combined with powerful satellites that provide broadband at high speeds, will give users at least a 4G-quality experience *no matter where they are*. Nations should view this technology as a tool to be used by their nationally licensed telcos and mobile network operators (MNOs) as a way to fulfill universal service mandates, and by the government itself to deliver e-health, e-education, and other e-services.

However, most nations view access to their market as something to control, so as to promote and sustain domestic industry while also avoiding any potential damage to their economy or to humans from unproven technology.

10 It is worth noting that as of the date of this writing, no lawsuit has ever been brought by a third party for damage caused by an object launched into outer space. Yes, there have been damages caused, but the injuries were addressed outside of a court room.

11 United Nations Office for Outer Space Affairs, Treaty on Principles Governing the Activities of States in the Exploration and Use of Outer Space, including the Moon and Other Celestial Bodies, Art. VI.

12 United Nations Office for Outer Space Affairs, Convention on Registration of Objects Launched into Outer Space.

13 United Nations Office for Outer Space Affairs, Convention on Registration of Objects Launched into Outer Space, Art. II.

19.6.1 Move beyond the old model of jobs and taxes, and capitalise on connectivity itself

Traditionally, nations have looked to jobs and taxes as the way to measure the value a new technology or company brings. But it is unsustainable for a space-based technology like LEO satellites – that will automatically cover all nations simply by virtue of the constellation's – design to provide jobs (or pay taxes) in all nations, so other models need to be examined.

Nations should reposition their thinking to see "connectivity" itself as the desirable investment in their nation: with connectivity comes jobs (and thus taxes). With connectivity comes a way to address every single one of the UN's "Sustainable Development Goals" (SDGs).[14]

Sometimes nations see telecom licences as a way to raise money for the general treasury, which is unfortunate, as such fees or auctions can be prohibitive to the development of satellite connectivity in that nation. Fees or taxes on telecoms should only exist to cover the administrative costs of running the independent regulatory bodies in that nation.

Interestingly, there has long been a concept known as "universal service" that is based on the idea that every citizen should have at least a "life-line" connection in case of emergency. Nations have long required build-out of infrastructure to connect the most remote citizens, and have funded such "universal service" by taxing telecom providers in that nation. If the economics were balanced, the telecom providers would be encouraged to build the needed infrastructure and thus also receive funding/subsidies from the fund equal to or exceeding that which they paid. However, the economics of building terrestrial-based infrastructure have meant that it was still more cost-effective for a telecom provider to pay the universal service tax and not attempt to build infrastructure to cover the remote communities. It is only with the advent of the LEO satellites that the infrastructure building is cost-effective (and in fact, exists whether used by that community or not), and thus universal service will develop globally.

High fees imposed by one nation on multi-national technology (such as satellites) usually mean that the nation simply does not get served by the new technology – that nation is overlooked, as the satellites can more affordably serve the surrounding nations that do not impose unreasonable fees.

This is also the argument against auctioning satellite licences: satellite tech (regardless of the orbit) covers multiple countries, if not entire regions and the globe, and for any one nation to try to auction their market access means (at the simplest level) that the one nation will be omitted from the satellite operator's services, and if the surrounding nations all attempt to impose auctions, perhaps thinking to even the playing field, what results is that the region has now priced itself out of the services entirely, as such a high cost of entry to the market is prohibitive.

19.6.2 Classify satellites as "critical infrastructure" to exploit the use of the technology for the nation itself

"Critical infrastructure" are those assets whose destruction or incapacitation would have a debilitating effect on a nation's security or public safety. Most nations have identified communications networks as critical, not only for the first responders to an emergency, but for the affected population as well.

14 United Nations, Department of Economic and Social Affairs, Sustainable Development, The 17 Goals.

Many emergencies and disasters wipe out infrastructure that is terrestrial-based, making the resilience of space-based technology such as satellites vital.

Even if satellites are not the everyday technology used for communications in a particular area, satellites have always been able to be used as back-up capability during disasters. Now that large constellations of satellites can offer the lower latency, higher throughput, and higher user count than previous satellites could, the use of these constellations is becoming required insurance against both known threats (seasonal weather disasters, for example) and unknown ones (e.g., vandalism or terrorism).

19.6.3 Treat access to broadband as a human right

In 2016 the UN pronounced that access to the internet had become a human right, necessary to facilitate education, and as a driving force in accelerating development in its various forms, including in achieving the Sustainable Development Goals.[15] As mentioned above, in 2022, the UN began aspiring to "meaningful connectivity" to ensure that everyone in the world would have access to fast, affordable, broadband connections.[16]

It is vital that nations realise that connectivity itself is the prize.

"Digital poverty" is a better name for what we have been calling the "digital divide" because it helps us focus on the calamitous effect of not having internet connectivity. Without access to high-quality internet, people around the world suffer from a lack of resources, information, education, and jobs, without which those people and their nations cannot find the basic necessities, let alone the better jobs that lead to higher national GDPs (gross domestic products).

National reputation and pride have always been strong reasons for a nation to invest in space-faring technology, and in the last few decades of the 20th century, notably to launch its own domestic satellites. These are still strong drivers, but in the era of global constellations that cost upwards of US$6 billion each just to build, launch, and start operations, it is not just impractical but likely impossible for every nation in the world to launch an entire constellation. Thus, the goal is to find a way for each nation still to find pride and a sense of ownership (if not actual ownership) in a technology that will revolutionise access to education, jobs, and a government's own most-needed services.

19.6.4 "Best practices" need to be "best" for both the nation and the operator

"Best practices" protect existing licensees if they are providing good service, and allow the introduction of new providers and new services – moreover, they encourage it. "Best practices" also protect the government, and ensure that concerns over national security, data privacy, and policies such as universal service are addressed.

Practices that governments and regulators can take to improve their nation's overall connectivity, service quality, and affordability include:

- *Allowing new technologies and operators to enter the market.* Governments sometimes believe they must protect the incumbent because it is the current operator (and disruption to

15 United Nations General Assembly, Oral Revisions of 3 June [2016], Human Rights Council. Note that calls for such a designation had been ongoing for many years before that.

16 ITU, New UN targets chart path to universal meaningful connectivity, press release (19 April 2022).

its services or customer base could disrupt the nation's services), or because it paid for the licence, or because it is an arm of the government itself. However, much evidence exists to show that services improve and GDP rises if there is fair competition in a market.[17] Some level of competition is necessary to improve the entire nation's wealth. Thus the emphasis on allowing new technologies and operators to enter a market.

- *Promulgating outcome-based regulations*. Regulators can encourage the entry of new technology and services by writing regulations that are focused on outcomes, such as service quality or population coverage, rather than defining the specific technology.
- *Maintaining technology-neutral goals and policies* (such as supporting the development of "broadband services" without specifying the technology (e.g., talking about international mobile telecommunication (IMT), when satellite or another technology might also be able to provide broadband).
- *Encouraging competition both within the country (domestic) and across borders* (such as to allow foreign companies to hold licences and provide services). New operators also need not be local or even originally from within that nation: best practices will allow foreign operators to provide services, assuming they can protect the national security and other legal interests of the government.
- *Being transparent in licensing and using "public consultations"* to gather facts and information are paramount for any nation hoping to encourage the growth of new technology. The Regulator's internet site should have lists of all licensees; links to the rules and regulations which apply to each technology or service; clear guidance for applying for a licence; and of course, a way to contact the regulator directly.
- *Supporting blanket licensing for services and equipment*, and supporting exemptions from licensing and the free-circulation of equipment that has been certified and licensed in other jurisdictions.
- *Encouraging the deployment of innovative technologies and service models.*
- *Promulgating overt policies to close the digital divide and have universal service.*
- *Publicising policies to promote the social inclusion of all peoples.*
- *Inviting the public to participate in consultations* and holding consultations in advance of any rule changes.
- *Facilitating service rollouts and fair coexistence* (so that both new and incumbent operators are encouraged to provide better services at lower prices).
- *Creating licensing timelines and processes which will provide certainty for operators* (thus encouraging them to offer new and better services) and certainty for users (who will trust the regulator to provide new and better services). Some suggested processes include online application portals; digital signatures; known timeframes for application review; default approval process; and licence exemptions.

19.6.5 National investment can speed introduction of a service, but should not be used to limit competition in that market

As satellites are usually considered "critical infrastructure", it is often considered to be in the national interest to own that infrastructure, or at least to have legal control over its operations.

17 "Factsheet on how competition policy affects macro-economic outcomes", Organization for Economic Cooperation and Development (OECD), 2014.

However, it can be difficult to attract competitors if any one infrastructure provider is seen as a monopoly, *de jure* or just *de facto*.

Competition, of course, is valued in most countries as the most effective way to introduce new services while keep pricing low. Competition is also a proven way to increase a nation's GDP.[18]

It can also be difficult for that nationally supported company to get market access in other countries, especially those that have political differences with the host nation, or whose own national companies are in competition with a nationally supported provider of services.

19.6.6 Licensing should not be viewed as a way to raise money for the general treasury, and auctions are not economic for space-based spectrum

Fees for licences should only cover the administrative cost of handling the processing or analysis of that application.[19] Fees and annual charges should not be viewed as a way to support the entire budget of the regulator, nor, as is sometimes the case, as a way for a government to raise money for other purposes. Too often the auction of spectrum has been used to raise money, not to find the highest economic use of that spectrum.

With a space-spaced technology such as satellites, auctions are an impossible barrier to entry. As the technology covers multiple countries (and in the case of large constellations, every single country in the world), if any one country auctions the rights to use the spectrum in its country, a constellation will seriously consider not offering service to that country, if it is more affordable to offer the service to neighboring countries. So, rather than making money for a country's treasury, the auction denies the country both of the income and the services. Furthermore, if multiple countries auction the spectrum rights, the barrier to entry will be insurmountable for these space-based technologies, and they will likely never come to fruition.

19.7 Sustainability and responsible behaviour in outer space

There is an opportunity for forward-looking regulators to show leadership by adopting requirements for responsible design and operational practices. The current situation drives the necessity for national administrations to have a global impact. Nevertheless, the call for stronger rules is far from uniform. OneWeb has committed to being a leader in the field of responsible space. Regulators are encouraged to view "outer space" as an environment to protect, just as they protect environments in their territory. Like any environment, with proper husbandry, the resources within that environment will thrive and nations can continue to reap the rewards of that careful stewardship for decades to come. Many nations have already adopted debris mitigation guidelines and regulations, some based on the guidelines of the Inter-Agency Space Debris Coordination Committee (IADC) which comprises the space agencies of numerous space-faring nations, or on the guidelines of the United Nations Office for Outer Space Affairs.[20]

18 *Id.*, and more recently "The role of competition policy in promoting economic recovery", Organization for Economic Cooperation and Development (OECD), 2020.

19 ITU, Guidelines for the Review of Spectrum Pricing Methodologies and the Presentation of Spectrum Fee Schedules, Report (2016).

20 Inter-Agency Space Debris Coordination Committee (IADC) Guidelines; UN Office of Outer Space Affairs (UNOOSA), Scientific & Technical Subcommittee, Space Debris Mitigation Guidelines.

19.7.1 Regulators should think of outer space as a global natural resource

For the global space economy to flourish, all nations and operators must preserve a safe operating environment. Keeping space sustainable is only possible if users of that environment adopt responsible designs, responsible operation, and effect responsible demise (de-orbiting). Nations that launch objects into this environment should consider how to incentivise responsible behaviour, and how to discourage unsustainable practices.

Widespread adoption of progressive debris mitigation measures will necessitate government engagement and international coordination in order for national regulatory administrations to establish consistent licensing rules and create a level playing field for industry.

19.7.2 Forward-looking regulatory frameworks support forward progress in the space sector

19.7.2.1 Responsible behaviour in outer space is required to sustain the environment for all users

The most urgent space safety imperative is the adoption of responsible design and operational practices. Principal safety themes include:

- *Reliability*: Satellites should be subjected to rigorous ground qualification programs, particularly when developing large satellite systems.
  - Operators should demonstrate a minimum reliability figure before launch and have it vetted by an independent authority (e.g. National Space Agencies), as satellites with undemonstrated or low reliability levels can become uncontrollable.
  - Operators should demonstrate limited risk from accidental explosions and associated orbital debris throughout the mission phases with the adoption of standards for calculating the probability of accidental explosions on an aggregate basis (such as the metric in the US Orbital Debris Mitigation Standard Practices (ODMSP).
- *Control*: Operators should be responsible for being able to identify their assets, know where they are, and control their trajectories.
- *Coordination*: Operators should share orbit information and manoeuvring plans with other operators and coordinate to avoid collisions.
- *Disposal*: Upon decommissioning LEO operators should promptly, reliably, and safely deorbit their hardware. The Post Mission Disposal (PMD) requirement should be reduced from 25 years to five years. The satellite should be designed so that, once it has completed its operational phase, it should be decommissioned with a controlled deorbit. Operators should disclose if they plan to release deployment devices to lower the orbit at end of life.
- *Safety-by-Design*:
  - Orbits and constellations should be designed to minimise the number of satellites in orbit.
  - The satellite should be designed so that it can be passivated before losing contact with the satellite:
    - all the on-board energy reserves should be permanently depleted or placed in such a condition that they entail no risk of generating debris, and
    - all the means for producing energy on-board should be permanently deactivated.

19.7.2.2 Space Situational Awareness (SSA) and Space Traffic Management (STM) are crucial to sustainability

The key to effective SSA and STM remains the open and transparent cooperation between operators and SSA systems. Transparent coordination should include publication of satellite Two Line Elements (TLEs), sharing ephemeris and covariance data with space controllers (e.g., the US's Joint Space Operations Center (JSpOC) or its 18th Space Control Squadron (18th SPCS)) as well as publicly accessible platforms, such as CelesTrack. Note that OneWeb publicly shares TLE on its website and on CelesTrack.

Operators should also hold coordination/awareness briefings with each other to confirm the actions each will take in the event of a possible conjunction. Regulators should incentivise coordination among operators and satellites' owners.

Operators should be incentivised to launch fewer satellites, and to design for smaller constellations. Larger constellations should be disincentivised. Regulators should prevent orbit altitude overlap for constellations greater than ten satellites.

19.7.2.3 Collision avoidance

Transparency and openness are effective tools for collision avoidance as well. Operators should disclose the extent of manoeuvrability of planned satellites, including the description of the expected manoeuvring methods and capabilities, as well as propulsive technologies. Regulators should require comprehensive collision avoidance capabilities through responsive, reliable, and robust onboard resources. If an operator uses on-board autonomy for collision avoidance manoeuvres, they should publish the details so other operators understand how their satellites will move and what the decision timeline is. The autonomous feature should be able to be disabled if necessary. Operators should establish a collision risk calculation with large objects on an aggregate basis.

19.7.2.4 Assisted disposal and removal (ADR)

Satellite operators must work together with regulators and service providers to develop the legislative and technical ecosystem to remove debris from outer space. Diverse technical solutions and new commercial business models are being developed to address both large debris (such as inoperable satellites) and smaller pieces.

The term "ADR" has traditionally meant "active debris removal"; it might be more accurate to think of it as meaning "assisted disposal and removal" since not all objects are "debris" and some of the new technologies might be more passive than active. But whatever the term used, ADR is a growing commercial industry that governments should support, as it may be vital to keeping the space environment usable for future generations.

While satellite *reliability* and *safety-by-design* remain the foundation of the behaviour of any responsible operator, several ADR mission demonstrations are advancing the technical developments required to deorbit an uncontrollable satellite. To this end, satellites operating in high-LEO orbits (that is, orbits above the point where atmospheric drag will affect their deorbit) should be designed with features that will facilitate the docking from In-Orbit Servicers to facilitate post-mission disposal for defunct or uncontrollable satellites.

OneWeb is actively engaged in the development of an ADR mission with Astroscale as part of the European Space Agency's Sunrise programme, and is also in discussions with several other ADR companies.

19.7.2.5 Radio astronomy

Responsible operators should commit to finding ways to coexist with radio astronomy observatories, protecting radio astronomy sites and going forward working together to find mutually acceptable, creative solutions regarding dynamic coordination.

OneWeb has held coordination meetings with both US and international astronomy communities such as the National Science Foundation (NSF) and the International Astronomical Union (IAU).

19.7.2.6 Optical astronomy

Responsible operators must acknowledge that satellites and large constellations can potentially affect large field of view observatories. Operators should strive to mitigate the brightness of the satellites as seen from the ground minimising the impact on night sky observers. Providing access to high accuracy public data on predicted locations of individual satellites (or ephemerides) is key. This will enable the real-time use of high-accuracy public data on satellite locations to adjust observational strategies and minimise the disruption on the observations. Operators shall develop brightness prediction models of their satellites and share their orbital position.

OneWeb has conducted observations in partnership with professional astronomers, among them the team at the GAL Hassin Observatory in Sicily, targeted at measuring the brightness of the constellation in the night skies. The data is being used to generate a model that will guide the design choices of the next generation of OneWeb satellites.

19.7.2.7 Carbon footprint

The space industry must commit to play an active role in the reduction of the carbon footprint across the supply chain. More specifically, responsible operators should establish appropriate systems for the collection, aggregation, and analysis of quantitative data for determination of Greenhouse Gas (GHG) emissions for the stated period and boundaries and engage with institutions like the École Polytechnique Fédérale de Lausanne (EPFL) and the World Economic Forum (WEF) on the definition and adoption of Space Sustainability Rating (SSR).

OneWeb engaged Carbon Footprint Ltd to verify its carbon footprint assessment and supporting evidence for the period 1 January 2020 to 31 December 2020 with a Carbon Footprint Verification Report for OneWeb Issued in July 2021. As a demonstration of its commitment, OneWeb also included the Carbon Footprint Guidelines in the design request for its next generation satellites (Gen2).

19.7.2.8 Green launchers

Although there are many factors involved in choosing a launch vehicle, satellite operators must no longer ignore the environmental effects of the fuel expelled into the atmosphere or the rocket stages that drop into the oceans or burn up in the atmosphere (or stay in orbit). Satellite operators should evaluate launch providers on their ability to mitigate the effects on these environments. For example, upper stages and dispensers can often be de-orbited after payload separation with a controlled procedure, and operators should choose launchers with this capability. Regulators can incentivise "green" launchers by requiring less insurance for them, and perhaps providing tax or fee breaks for the re-use of first stages.

19.8 Conclusion

LEOs will revolutionise civilization. No longer will being remote mean being disconnected. People can stay in their village and get advanced education, work at jobs, find e-health and government services. There will be less need to emigrate, less disruption to governments and families. Thus, governments should find it in their interest not only to allow this technology, but to actively encourage its adoption, and to find ways to use it to better the lives of the people in their nation.

20

REGISTRATION REQUIREMENTS FOR SATELLITES AND THE REALITY OF LARGE CONSTELLATIONS

Ensuring a symbiosis of international law requirements and practicability

Bernhard Schmidt-Tedd

Introduction

From its very beginning, registration of space objects is one of the basic principles of space law to allocate "jurisdiction and control" over space objects in this international area free of territorial sovereignty and, if applicable, over any personnel thereof. It is a key factor for responsibility and transparency and most relevant for actors in space operations. This relevance is also recognised by the recent "Guidelines for the Long-term Sustainability of Outer Space Activities of the Committee on the Peaceful Uses of Outer Space" (LTS-Guidelines). With a growing number of large constellations and increasingly complex multi-cluster launches, the present registration system is challenged. In view of the new realities, this chapter examines the current registration practice and highlights necessary adjustments. It proposes the practical steps necessary for prospective operators and national registrars. It includes examples of national practice and recommendations for the implementation on the side of project management.

20.1 Applicable international legal framework

The international legal framework derives from the first space-related UN General Assembly (GA) Resolution 1721 B (XVI) of 20 December 1961,[1] followed by UN GA Resolution 1962 (XVIII) of 13 December 1963.[2] The basic rule of registration of space objects is contained in Art. VIII Outer

1 'International co-operation in the peaceful uses of outer space'.

2 'Declaration of Legal Principles Governing the Activities of States in the Exploration and Use of Outer Space'.

DOI: 10.4324/9781003268475-28

Space Treaty (OST) of 1967:[3] "A State Party to the Treaty on whose registry an object launched into outer space is carried shall retain jurisdiction and control over such object, and over any personnel thereof, while in outer space or on a celestial body". The Registration Convention (REG) of 1975[4] specifies rules and procedures.[5]

The Registration Practice Resolution of 2007[6] formulates "Recommendations on enhancing the practice of States and international intergovernmental organizations in registering space objects".[7] This UN GA Resolution is the foundation for the first major adjustment of registration practices to the framework of registration of space objects, necessitated by practical needs and developments. The cause was the increasing number of non-registered space objects during a period of privatisation of international organisations of satellite operators. In a wider context, the recent "Guidelines for the Long-term Sustainability of Outer Space Activities of the Committee on the Peaceful Uses of Outer Space" (LTS-Guidelines)[8] should be mentioned, as they contain some specific guidelines on registration practice.[9]

UN GA Resolutions form part of the so-called "soft-law"[10] instruments, in contrast to international treaty law. They are nevertheless an important part of the international legal framework for space activities and a more flexible instrument to influence application practice.

20.2 The basic principles of registration[11]

An adjustment and further development of registration practice has to keep in mind, and to safeguard the basic principles of, the registration system and the specific function and purpose of registration under space law. More specifically, Art. VIII OST (registration of space objects) is part of three essential, interrelated legal articles: state responsibility (Art. VI OST), liability (Art. VII OST), and registration. Article VII OST has a wide-ranging definition of launching states as connecting point for liability. Article VIII OST reduces the focus from a number of launching states (of a specific launch event) to one single registering state of a space object to which "jurisdiction and control" is allocated. This form of responsibility is indivisible and comparable to the status of a flag state in air or maritime law. The international responsibility of states for national space activities comprises the correct registration of space objects, including those of "non-governmental" space objects, respective private space actors. Non-governmental activities under Art.

3 Treaty on Principles Governing the Activities of States in the Exploration and Use of Outer Space, including the Moon and Other Celestial Bodies, done 27 January 1967, entered into force 10 October 1967, 610 UNTS 205.

4 Convention on Registration of Objects Launched into Outer Space, adopted by UN GA 12 November 1974, entered into force 15 September 1976, 1023 UNTS 15.

5 About that: Hobe, Stephan/Schmidt-Tedd, Bernhard/ Schrogl, Kai-Uwe (Eds.), Cologne Commentary on Space Law, Vol. I (Art. VIII) and Vol. II (Registration Convention), Cologne 2009/2013.

6 Resolution on Recommendations on enhancing the practice of States and international intergovernmental organizations in registering space objects (Registration Practice Resolution), adopted 17 December 2007, UNGA Res. 62/101.

7 About that: Hobe, Stephan/Schmidt-Tedd, Bernhard/Schrogl, Kai-Uwe (Eds.), Cologne Commentary on Space Law, Vol. I (Art. VIII) and Vol. III (Registration Practice Resolution), Cologne 2015.

8 Adopted by the Committee on the Peaceful Uses of Outer Space (COPUOS) in June 2019 (A74/20, para. 163 and Annex II).

9 See Guideline A.5 Enhance the practice of registering space objects.

10 Marboe, Irmgard (Ed.), Soft Law in Outer Space, The Function of Non-binding Norms in International Space Law, Wien 2012.

11 For further explanation see Schmidt-Tedd, Bernhard/Soucek, Alexander, Registration of Space Objects, Oxford Research Encyclopedias, online 30 June 2020.

VI OST are all space activities, which are not under the directive and hierarchy of governmental structures, which means activities of *inter alia* private entities, independent public entities, and self-determined universities.

The identification of all launching states of a specific launch event is the first step of a registration procedure. In the case of "non-governmental entities"/private actors, the relevant launching state behind those actors has to be identified. In the case of there being more than one launching state, a joint determination of the state of registry is the necessary second step in accordance with Art. II, para. 2 REG.

Registration is restricted to the launching states of a launch event. This limitation is also valid in case of any transfer of operation. A transfer of registration to a state responsible for the new operator is only possible in the exceptional case that this state was already (one of) the launching states for this space object. Otherwise, the launching state originally registering the space object remains state of registry and the state of the new operator is under international law (only) responsible according to Art. VI OST for the (new) national space activity of its operator, which exists in parallel to the (remaining) responsibility of the original launching state under Art. VIII OST (following the *dictum* "once a launching state – always a launching state"). Nevertheless, the two states, namely the one behind the original operator and the one behind the new operator, are free to set up a bilateral arrangement concerning an adequate responsibility and liability scheme, taking into account the new realities of operation for the space object. For the state parties involved, this is highly recommendable and some national licensing procedures explicitly take into account the possibility of a transfer of operations in orbit.[12]

Registration of space objects is an act of public administration and the notification to the UN Register is transmitted via diplomatic channels. In most cases, since the responsibility of the UN Secretary-General has been delegated to the UN Office for Outer Space Affairs (UNOOSA) seated in Vienna, Austria, it will be the permanent mission in Vienna for states submitting information to UNOOSA. Regarding space objects of non-governmental entities, cooperation and information by those entities to their state(s) of jurisdiction is necessary, but "non-governmental entities", or private actors, cannot execute the registration at both the national and international levels by themselves.

20.3 A two-fold organisational scheme/national implementation

Originally, in 1961, a central UN registry[13] was envisaged. But since the Outer Space Treaty of 1967, the registration system of space objects is two-fold: one at the national level and one at the UN level. Member States insisted on their respective decentralised registries. Article VIII OST implies such a national registry and Art. II (1) REG formulates (under defined conditions) a binding obligation to establish a national registry for state parties to REG. The UN register[14] is a collection of Member States' notifications of their nationally registered space objects. However, the national registration of a space object is the relevant legal act, which brings forth the legal effects of registration (allocation of "jurisdiction and control"). The UN register is an international publicity tool, which allows for transparent access to registered space objects world-wide.

12 Art. 2 French Space Operation Act (SOA), which was adopted by the French Senate on 22 May 2008, signed and dated on 3 June and published 4 June 2008 (Journal Officiel); Loi no. 2008-518 du 3 juin 2008 relative aux operations spatiales.

13 Original wording.

14 Present wording: UN register and national registry/registries.

The UN register consists in strict legal terms only of the collection of national registration notifications. In practice, UNOOSA has structured the registration information into a comprehensive data bank and information system with different search parameters, the "Online Index of Objects Launched into Outer Space". It has to be underlined that the information about orbit positions in the registration system is indicative in order to identify the space object. This information is not suitable for real-time tracking. A space tracking system in the context of space traffic management would need a distinct, separate tool.

The effectiveness of the UN registration system relies on an effective, timely, and up-to-date national registration system and the timely notification to the UN. With the growing number of commercial space activities, the interface between those non-governmental space activities and the national registrar as part of an administrative, state-owned registration system becomes more and more relevant. Such regulations should be addressed in national space legislation.

20.4 Management of the registration procedure in complex launch situations

In the past, launch campaigns have been relatively simple and transparent. A launch service provider (governmental or non-governmental) launched its own or a foreign payload (space object). In some cases, more than one satellite was deployed, either in the same category or divided into primary and secondary payloads.

20.4.1 Legal aspects of complex launch situations

The situation became increasingly complex with (a) multi-cluster launch events, where a multitude of participants of different countries[15] is involved and (b) the launch of constellations, where the set-up is broken up into a sequence of different launch events. The registration procedure must reflect these actualities.

The LTS-Guideline[16] A 5.1. states: "States […] should ensure the development and/or implementation of effective and comprehensive registration practices, as proper registration of space objects is a key factor in the safety and the long-term sustainability of space activities. Inadequate registration practices may have negative implications for ensuring the safety of space operations". The implementation of adequate registration procedures is primarily a duty of the appropriate state party to the Space Treaties. Nevertheless, the non-governmental entities involved, such as private launch service providers, payload customers, and operators have a corresponding interest in handling registration information in a proactive and transparent manner.

Private actors are acting under the international responsibility of the appropriate state party for that "national activity" (Art. VI OST). Under the special regime of space law, with state responsibility for non-governmental national activities, it is necessary to identify the state behind the private actor. The connecting factor for legal persons is the registered office or branch. State

15 An early example is the Kanopus-V-IK mission, launched 14 July 2017 from Baikonur. Besides the primary Russian payload 72 further satellites had been launched to different orbits, 48 Cube Sat's of Planet's EO fleet and others from Canada, Ecuador, Germany, Japan, and Norway. See www.spaceflightinsider.com.

16 Adopted by the Committee on the Peaceful Uses of Outer Space (COPUOS) in June 2019 (A74/20, para.163 and Annex II).

responsibility under space law goes beyond the limits of state responsibility under general public international law.[17]

In the past, a launch event of one or two space objects involved only a limited number of launching states under the definition of Art. I, *lit.*(a) REG, e.g., the state of the launch territory and the state behind the payload customer, meaning the state that procures the launch. Those situations were unequivocal, and it was obvious between which state parties an arrangement about registration had to be agreed (Art. II (2) REG). However, with respect to complex launch events as are taking place today, involving a multitude of participants from different countries,[18] it is indispensable to organise a procedure to identify – as part of the project management – the state parties behind the different actors. The three main reasons are: (1) The state parties of a specific launch event form a risk community vis-à-vis third parties. According to the Liability Convention,[19] they are jointly and severally liable in case of damage (Arts IV and V LIAB). Third parties have a right to know all potential debtors. Internally, the actors have a natural interest to know with whom and how to organise the debtor recourse. (2) Governments behind the different private actors have to clarify their potential role as launching state in view of relevant licensing procedures and registration decisions. (3) Since the adoption of the Registration Practice Resolution of 2007, it is foreseen that "in case of joint launches of space objects, each space object should be registered separately".[20]

Those rights and duties of state parties, as described under (1) to (3) above, can have direct influence on the position of the private actors involved, if the national space legislation of those states foresees a right of recourse against the private actor in case of damage caused by or attributed to the private actor. A key question for the launch service provider is "who is my contract partner under aspects of launching state". Basically, there are two constellations in the case of multi-cluster launches: (1) either the launch service provider has one contractual point of contact with one company for an adapter unit, able to accommodate a multitude of "passengers" (standardized small satellites) or (2) the launch service provider has a contractual relationship directly with a multitude of "co-passengers". A company acting as a broker, without any hardware to be launched, does not make the state of its residence a launching state. The situation is different when a company provides an adapter unit, re-selling the launch capacity to different customers with or without accommodation service. In this constellation, the company launching the adapter unit makes its state a launching state (after successful launch) and the same is applicable for each co-flying passenger.

20.4.2 Aspects of project management and timeline

Under aspects of (contractual) project management, the launch service provider must be aware of all launching states, even if it has only a contractual relationship with the reseller of payload capac-

17 Compare Draft Articles on Responsibility of States for Internationally Wrongful Acts, text adopted at its 53rd session in 2001 (Commission Report in UN General Assembly Doc. A/56/10). State responsibility: Chapter II Attribution of conduct to a State; see Art. 4 Conduct of organs of a State, Art. 5 Conduct of persons or entities exercising elements of governmental authority and Art. 8 Conduct directed or controlled by a State.

18 See, e.g., the Spaceflight rideshare mission FSSO A of December 2018 aboard a Space X Falcon 9, launched from Vandenberg in California; website: spaceflight.com.

19 Convention on International Liability for Damage Caused by Space Objects (LIAB), adopted by UN GA 29 November 1971, entered into force 1 September 1972, 961 UNTS 187.

20 Registration Practice Resolution para. 3 (c).

ities in a rideshare mission. The information exchange is a "must" for the contract. With regard to rights and duties under space law it is not acceptable that the intermediary covers a client in view of the launch service provider or offers a black box to be launched. The launch manifest must be complete and transparent in view of the required registration information. Private companies are not directly bound by the space treaties (under public international law), but the national space legislation should ensure that the state can fulfill its international obligations. In case of national space legislation being absent, it would nevertheless be expected that the private sector acts in compliance with the basic legal framework of outer space activities.

The identification of launching states follows the logic of the definition under Art. I (a) REG. The qualification is either national territory-related (the state from whose territory or facility) or action-related (the state which launches or procures the launching). The private launch service provider makes the state of domicile in any case a launching state. The payload customer will be affected by the criteria "procures the launching".

It is furthermore relevant to consider which actions of persons involved will not result in a launching state qualification. Producers of hardware, service providers, contract agents, and brokers are irrelevant in this regard. Support services for the launch campaign and transfer flights for an air launch[21] are irrelevant as well. The crucial point for "procures the launching" is the self-interest of the customer to have this space object be placed in space. With regard to new developments, it is also important to mention that the concept of "launching state" means a launch from Earth to space. If an object is launched from Earth to, e.g., a space station, and in a second step deployed to an independent orbit, this second action does not constitute a relevant launch campaign in the sense of the registration system and does not result in additional launching states.

There are important aspects regarding the timeline. Especially in complex launch constellations, it is necessary to clarify and distribute the obligations of registration (respectively, initiation of registration by the appropriate state) and information exchange well in advance, as part of the contract management. For the public administration side, registration obligations start only after launch and possible deadlines for licensing decisions after a completed application. For the private launch service provider, it is important to have a proactive contract management and therefore already a full picture at the beginning of a project or a campaign of the envisaged responsibility scheme. The launch service provider needs the certainty that its customer has or will get the necessary authorisation by the appropriate state (Art. VI OST) and that it cooperates for the registration procedure. If the customer fails to get the authorisation until launch, a clause about the contractual consequences is required.[22]

According to the LTS-Guidelines, launch service providers should conduct pre-launch conjunction assessments. "States [...] are encouraged to advice launch service providers under their jurisdiction and control to seek support, as necessary".[23] Communication, information exchange, and a proactive assessment is demanded from the governmental as well as from the private actor

21 Schmidt-Tedd, B./Khalimova, G./Teselkin, S., The legal problems of providing the space activity of space objects launching by aerospace launch systems with the participation of several States (Polyot Air Launch Project as an example), in: IISL, Proceedings of the International Institute of Space Law 2011, Eleven International Publishing, The Hague 2012, p. 500, 506.

22 In the 'Space News' of 23 August 2019 Jeff Foust describes the rideshare mission SSO-A organised by Spaceflight Inc. in December 2018. Part of the article is an interview with Jeffrey Roberts who describes an interesting detail of the launch manifest: "One customer, he said, had its cubesat locked in its dispenser, remaining attached to the payload adapter. 'They were unable to get the appropriate licensing,' he said".

23 Guideline B.5 Develop practical approaches for pre-launch conjunction, para. 2.

side. For the conjunction assessment during all phases of controlled flights, the focus is on the spacecraft operator.[24] A key point for the responsibility scheme ("entities under their respective jurisdiction and control") is a correct and complete registration. Those Guidelines concerning safety of space operations underline the need of an early clarification of potential launching states.

20.5 Registration practice of mega-constellations

20.5.1 Registration and an interacting entity of objects

The classic space object is an individually hand-built satellite with a specific function. The new development of satellite constellations changed this paradigm, whereby a large number of modular designed satellites form a network that produces a specific function as an interacting entity of objects. Large telecommunication satellites of the geostationary orbit are replaced by a network of hundreds or thousands of small satellites in low Earth orbit. Instead of one operator behind one satellite, we now have an operator behind a dynamic fleet of a multitude of satellites, launched at different launch campaigns and with a regular replacement of single objects from time to time.

With this development, there is a certain discrepancy between the multitude of objects forming one functional entity[25] and the basic approach of a registration system focusing on objects placed in space, launch event by launch event. The inherent logic of this approach – registering space object launch event by launch event – is fundamental, since each launch event may result in a different constellation of launching states. The territory of a follow-up launch may change and the launch campaign may include space objects not forming part of a satellite constellation under construction. Therefore, in order to reflect the particularities of a satellite constellation in the registration system, it is necessary to concentrate on possible adjustments in the registration practice, without changing the system.

20.5.2 Registration practice of OneWeb and Starlink satellites

Widely known are the mega-constellations of OneWeb,[26] a British company, and Starlink,[27] operated by SpaceX (US), but there are a number of other important constellations planned or being realised.[28]

The OneWeb satellite constellation started with six satellites launched with the Soyuz launcher from Kourou (French Guiana) on 27 February 2019.[29] On 6 February 2020, the first bloc of 34 satellites was launched with Soyuz from Baikonur (Kazakhstan),[30] followed by similar launches with 34 up to 36 satellites, launched each in one bloc. In December 2020, the location of the launch

24 Guideline B.4 Perform conjunction assessment during all phases of controlled flight.

25 Under law as to real property and rights *in rem*: the entirety of objects/satellites are connected by a common economic purpose and the economic value depend on the totality of objects.

26 OneWeb planned a constellation of 648 satellites for 2022. The deployment started in February 2019. See UN Registration: ST/SG/SER.E/935, 3 April 2020 (Note verbale by UK in conformity with the Registration Convention).

27 A satellite internet constellation of 1,700 satellites in 2021, with an ITU filing of 12,000 satellites and a supplement of further 30,000 satellites. The deployment started with a bloc of 60 satellites in May 2019.

28 Table of constellations in: Benkö, M./Schrogl, K.-U. (Ed.), Outer Space future for humankind, The Hague 2021, p. 271 f.

29 UN Registration: ST/SG/SER.E/897, 16 July 2019 (Note verbale by UK in conformity with the Registration Convention).

30 UN Registration: ST/SG/SER.E/935, 3 April 2020 (Note verbale by UK in conformity with the Registration Convention).

switched to Vostochny (Russian Federation).[31] Already this example shows the changing constellation of launching states from one launch event to the next in case of the same constellation. The constellation planned for more than 600 satellites reached a status of 218 spacecrafts in May 2021. Financial difficulties delayed the set-up of the constellation. After bankruptcy of OneWeb in March 2020, the company was taken over and stabilised by Bharti Global and the Government of the UK. Fresh funding came also from Eutelsat (France).[32] This demonstrates that even the national link of the operator can change in an early stage. Concerning the registration practice, it can be noted that the first fleet of OneWeb satellites was registered in the UN system in a complete and timely manner.[33]

For the Starlink constellation, the situation is more complex. In 2021, the constellation reached a dimension of 1,700 satellites. The deployment started with two prototypes in February 2018, followed by the first 60 operational satellite bloc, deployed in May 2019.[34] Looking at the UN Register it can be noticed that a large number of the Starlink satellites are not yet registered and that a large number of registration notifications are being processed by UNOOSA.[35] The UN Register is not able to handle this magnitude of registrations within the limitations of the existing financial resources in a timely manner. The limited staff capacity results from a period of only a hundred classical launch events per year.

Looking through the different notifications concerning the Starlink constellation, it is interesting to note some remarks of third countries concerning close proximity events and necessary manoeuvres of preventive collision avoidance.[36] Well known is the collision avoidance manoeuvre by ESA in September 2019 with regard to ESA-Aeolus and Starlink-44.[37] An essential problem in this case was the unorganized communication structure and the difficulty to reach a responsible point of contact for Starlink. Looking at the registration and operational practice of this first real mega-constellation, it is obvious that there is a need for action.

31 UN Registration: ST/SG/SER.E/965, 18 January 2021 (Note verbale by UK in conformity with the Registration Convention).

32 See Wikipedia, OneWeb satellite constellation, History.

33 For the registration of the OneWeb (OWLID) satellites in the UN register see: ST/SG/SER.E/1026 (V2108161) (UK); ST/SG/SER.E/1020 (V2107691) (UK); ST/SG/SER.E/1025 (V2108308) (Russian Federation), 34 OneWeb satellites; ST/SG/SER.E/1021 (V2107667) (Russian Federation), 34 OneWeb satellites; ST/SG/SER.E/1008 (V2105794) (UK), 36 OneWeb satellites; ST/SG/SER.E/1000 (V2104964) (UK), 36 OneWeb satellites;

ST/SG/SER.E/991 (V2104502) (UK), 36 OneWeb satellites; ST/SG/SER.E/969 (V2108267) (Russian Federation), 36 OneWeb satellites; ST/SG/SER.E/985 (V2103738) (UK), 36 OneWeb satellites; ST/SG/SER.E/965 (V2100336) (UK), 36 OneWeb satellites; ST/SG/SER.E/968 (V2101941) (Russian Federation), 36 OneWeb satellites; ST/SG/SER.E/937 (V2002288) (UK), 34 OneWeb satellites; ST/SG/SER.E/938 (V2002659) (Russian Federation), 34 OneWeb satellites; ST/SG/SER.E/941 (V2003229) (Russian Federation), 34 OneWeb satellites; ST/SG/SER.E/935 (V2002103) (UK), 34 OneWeb satellites; ST/SG/SER.E/897 (V1907090) (UK), 6 OneWeb satellites.

34 UN Registration: ST/SG/SER.E/924, Annex VII, 8 October 2020 (Note verbale USA of 8 January 2020).

35 ST/SG/SER.E/1024 (annexed as V2108395) for Starlinks 3003-3005; ST/SG/SER.E/1010 (V2107956 with numerous Starlink satellites (partially de-orbited); ST/SG/SER.E/1004 (V2107909); ST/SG/SER.E/995 (V2104851); ST/SG/SER.E/983 (V2103552); ST/SG/SER.E/977 (V2101977); ST/SG/SER.E/967 (V2100470); ST/SG/SER.E/964 (V2100342); ST/SG/SER.E/956 (V2007692; ST/SG/SER.E/954 (V2006336); ST/SG/SER.E/951 (V2005079); ST/SG/SER.E/945 (V2005742); ST/SG/SER.E/942 (V2006583); ST/SG/SER.E/928 (V2005748); ST/SG/SER.E/924 (V2005736).

36 See, e.g., China in A/AC.105/1262 (event of 1 July2021 with Starlink-1095 and 21 October 2021 with Starlink-2305) in www.unoosa.org/oosa/index.html; Andrew Jones, China's space station manoeuvred to avoid Starlink satellites, in Space News 28 December 2021

37 J. Foust, ESA spacecraft dodges potential collision with Starlink satellite, 2 September 2019.

20.6 Adjustment of registration practice

The Registration Practice Resolution of 2007 was a first step to enhance the registration practice. The "State from whose territory or facility a space object has been launched should, in the absence of prior agreement, contact States or international intergovernmental organizations that could qualify as 'launching States' to jointly determine which State or entity should register the space object; (c) In cases of joint launches of space objects, each space object should be registered separately".[38] This was a reaction to deficits on the side of contractual management to clarify the registration arrangements. In consequence, the state from whose territory or facility a space object was launched was assigned additional duties to handle the situation. This can be mirrored for the non-governmental side, the (private) launch service provider: "States should encourage launch service providers under their jurisdiction to advice the owner and/or operator of the space object to address the appropriate States on the registration of that space object".[39]

The LTS-Guidelines of 2019 picked up the topic again.[40] Proper registration is described as "a key factor in the safety and the long-term sustainability of space activities".[41] The Guidelines affirmed the need of a pre-launch communication to determine how to proceed with the registration (Guideline A.5, para. 3.). The specific role of the launch service provider is emphasised. States "should request all necessary information from the launch service providers and users under their jurisdiction and/or control to meet all registration requirements" (A.5, para. 6.). As a result, for launch service providers and operators, pre-launch agreements on registration matters are indispensable tools to fulfill those obligations. On the public side of the registrar, it is necessary to identify all launching states of a launch event and to make those co-launching states visible in the UNOOSA registration template[42] and correspondingly in the national registry.

For satellite constellations an additional information approach seems to be unavoidable in order not to lose the publicity function of the UN register under a mass of single notifications. A registration of the constellation as such would be in contradiction to all basic principles of the registration system. The way out can only be a connectivity in the information system. As long as there is no adjustment of the UNOOSA registration template, this information can be delivered under Part D (Additional voluntary information).

As a first step, the first registration of a space object (satellite) of a constellation under construction should indicate the envisaged constellation, its operator and a clear point of contact for all questions of emergency and collision avoidance. All follow-up registrations should refer to this first basic information, which might be updated, if necessary. With this additional information, the functional connectivity of the multitude of objects (and corresponding registrations) of a constellation would become transparent.

A further aspect is the sheer mass of information for the registrar, timely processing issues, and the specific responsibility of the operator and of the appropriate state behind. The operator and investor will have an up-to-date full picture of all satellites of a constellation already launched, non-functional objects, and decayed satellites. It would not be too much to ask to deliver and link this information with the registration system. This up-to-date information tool could be an

38 Registration Practice Resolution 3(b) and (c).

39 Registration Practice Resolution 3(d).

40 Guideline A.5 Enhance the practice of registering space objects.

41 Guideline A.5 Enhance the practice of registering space objects, para. 1.

42 United Nations Register of Objects Launched Into Outer Space, Registration Information Submission Form by UNOOSA (Part A: Other launching States).

"additional information" under Part D of the template, linked to the first registration of an object of the constellation. This living document would not overrule the formal registration under the UN system but fill the time gap between the reality in space and the unavoidable processing time.

This approach of additional information was discussed in the Working Group on the "Status and Application of the Five United Nation Treaties on Outer Space" at the 61st session of the Legal Subcommittee in 2022, based on a working paper, prepared by the Chair.[43]

As an outcome of the session, it was agreed to further discuss the following points at the sixty-second session of the subcommittee,[44] with a view of reaching an agreement on recommendations to be addressed to the states of registry that could support the enhancement of registration practices:

(a) The state of registry could inform the Office, as part of the registration process, whether the object being registered formed part of a constellation;
(b) The state of registry could inform the Office, as part of in the registration process, about the operator and owner of a constellation;
(c) The state of registry could identify, in the information contained in the registration document, the point of contact responsible for queries on space objects in the constellation. That focal point could be a governmental entity or an authorised private entity with delegated responsibilities, such as the operator;
(d) In view of the multitude of space object registrations related to a constellation, the state of registry could use the first space object registration of a constellation to provide basic information on the constellation, the point of contact and the operator authorised to provide up-to-date information on the status of the constellation;
(e) The operator of a constellation would have the best overview of the objects in orbit, the objects intended to be launched, the objects already decayed, and any general information about the constellation. Therefore, the state of registry could consider how to link the information available to the operator with the formal registration of the objects of the constellation, without affecting the official registration information submitted by states.

20.7 The way forward

The "Space2030" Agenda[45] and implementation plan is a forward-looking strategy, prepared by UNCOPUOS and adopted by the General Assembly, addressing long-term sustainable development concerns and matters of global governance of outer space activities.[46] In that regard, issues arising from new technologies and commercial activities in outer space are addressed. The Member States are committed to ensure "that the Committee, and its subcommittees, supported by the Office for Outer Space Affairs, continue, as appropriate, to respond to such changes, in their

43 LSC 61. session (28 March–8 April 2022), Discussion paper by the Chair of the Working Group on the Status and Application of the Five United Nations Treaties on Outer Space on the topic of registration of large constellations and megaconstellations, Paper submitted by the Chair of the Working Group, A/AC.105/C.2/2022/CRP.20 of 30 March 2022.

44 LSC 61. session (28 March–8 April 2022), Draft report, Annex I, Report of the Chair on the Working Group on Status and Application of the Five United Nation Treaties on Outer Space, para. 14, /AC.105/C.2/2022/TRE/L.1 of 5 April 2022.

45 The "Space2030" Agenda: space as a driver of sustainable development (A/RES/76/3) of UNCOPUOS.

46 See "Space 2030" Agenda Part A., I. Introduction, para.6.

role as unique platforms for international cooperation in the peaceful uses of outer space".[47] Under aspects of "global governance of outer space activities", the enhancement of registration practice is explicitly mentioned: "[e]nhance existing registration practices and information exchange and acknowledge the role of the Office for Outer Space Affaires in maintaining the United Nations Register of Objects Launched into Outer Space to increase transparency and improve the efficiency of registration mechanism and the timeliness and consistency of the registration of objects, including by providing technical assistance to Member States in this regard".[48] In this context it is emphasised to implement the LTS-Guidelines, to promote cooperation and exchange of information and best practices on the supervision of space activities of non-governmental entities, and to discuss the prediction and prevention of potential collisions.[49] The implementation of the objectives of the "Space2030" Agenda depends nevertheless on a corresponding engagement and cooperation by COPUOS Member States.

Capacity-building and technical assistance for the national implementation of the international legal regime is an important topic of the UNISPACE+50 process and part of the "Space2030" Agenda. One outcome of the efforts under thematic priority 2, "Legal regime of outer space and global governance: current and future perspective"', is a guidance document especially for new space actors, named "Bringing the benefits of space to all countries: a guidance document on the legal framework for space activities".[50] Dedicated chapters are focused on the registration regime and jurisdiction and control as well as to the registration practice.

Summary remarks

Registration of space objects is one of the fundamental principles of space law and global space governance, formulated and continuously adjusted from 1961 onwards. It is a legal approach to allocate "jurisdiction and control" in an area free of national appropriation, not a traffic management mechanism. The registration system is two-fold: the national registration is the first essential legal step, followed by the international registration in the UN space object register as an act of international publicity. National registries and the UN register depend on each other. An information exchange is crucial between Member States and UNOOSA, as well as a constructive interaction with the non-governmental entities involved.

However, a first challenge in this context is the complexity of multi-cluster launch events, with a large number of space objects of different countries, integrated in one launch manifest. All participants involved are required to contribute to the necessary identification of all launching states as the basis of a proper registration.

The registration system of space objects considers single objects of a specific launch event. All related legal consequences depend on this approach. The new realities of constellations challenge this approach, since constellations are based on a multitude of space objects, launched in different batches, but resulting in a functional unity with a constant renewal of disused objects. An adjustment of registration practice can be realised by additional, complementary information tools, which do not affect the registration system as such.

47 See "Space 2030" Agenda Part A., II. Strategic vision, para. 13.

48 See "Space 2030" Agenda Part A., III. Objectives, para. 19, 4.4.

49 See "Space 2030" Agenda Part A., III. Objectives, para. 19, 4.5–4.8.

50 A/AC.105/C.2/117 of 26 January 2022.

New space law and policy documents, such as the LTS-Guidelines and the "Space2030" Agenda are important landmarks for public and private space actors in order to keep the registration system up-to-date and efficient, and to reflect new technological developments. Furthermore, the international community of states should be future-oriented in leading a discussion of these issues, which involve working towards a solution applicable to all, thereby supporting the continuing benefit to be had from the UN register of space objects.

C

New launchers, small launchers, space ports, and space tourism

21

HOW CAN THE INSURANCE MARKET PROVIDE NEW AND EFFECTIVE SOLUTIONS TO NEWSPACE TECHNOLOGIES AND SERVICES?

Cécile Gaubert

21.1 Introduction

What has been named, for some years now, "NewSpace" is a concept that encompasses activities of a very different nature. What they have in common is the intention to develop access to space and satellite services at a lower cost than that practiced today by traditional institutions and companies, but also to develop new activities compared to traditional telecommunications, positioning, or observation. These activities, without being exhaustive, include the deployment of nano-satellites, constellations of small satellites, such as SpaceX's Starlink project,[1] but also access to space including in suborbital areas for tourism or transport purposes, such as Virgin Galactic or Blue Origin's suborbital flight projects.[2] In-orbit services provided by satellites furnishing assistance to other satellites in outer space are also part of NewSpace. This type of service satellite can be compared to a kind of space service station. It would have the ability to reposition satellites to their initial orbits when they move away from them, to move them into a graveyard orbit, to re-enter the satellites into the atmosphere with the aim of their almost total destruction, or to provide them with power refueling services. The crucial question of "Space Traffic Management" is important in view of these expanding activities, in order to be able to supervise the movements in space in a safe way.

The core of international space law is formed by five international treaties.[3] The purpose of this regulatory regime was to regulate the space activities of states and not private entities. However,

1 C. GOYA, "SpaceX now holds the largest constellation of telecommunications satellites in orbit", *Business Insider France* 12 November 2019.

2 A. KNAPP, "With Virgin Galatic's Latest Flight, Has Space Tourism Finally Arrived?", *Forbes*, 14 December 2018.

3 Treaty on Principles Governing the Activities of States in the Exploration and Use of Outer Space, including the Moon and Other Celestial Bodies (OST) 27 January 1967.

DOI: 10.4324/9781003268475-30

the rise of private activities since the 1980s has led states to legislate specifically on space activities of their national companies. NewSpace, for its part, leads us to question the legal and contractual framework of these new activities.

Currently, the question of whether international regulation is appropriate for in-orbit service activities does not really arise. Indeed, the treaties cover all space activities regardless of their purpose.[4] States signatories to treaties will therefore be subject to their provisions, in particular with regard to obligations of control, jurisdiction, and will also bear responsibility under Art. VI, and liability under Art. VII OST as a launching state[5] in the event of damage caused by a space object to a third state or its nationals.

It should be noted here that in-orbit service activities must not be performed in contradiction of the space law fundamental principle of freedom of access, use, or non-appropriation.

Some states have decided to legislate and bring into force national provisions dedicated to certain activities, but not specifically to in-orbit services. In our view, the main reason is that national space laws have a sufficiently broad scope to include in-orbit service activities. It will therefore be up to the operator wishing to carry out such a service mission to obtain the authorisation or licence from the supervisory authority and to meet the requirements laid down by the regulations.

When addressing NewSpace, the issue that arises is the one of managing the risks, as new risks are associated with these activities. Those new risks need to be assessed in order to identify the various possibilities of having them insured. The insurance market has been active in the space sector since the 1980s and provides for insurance solutions that are tailored to traditional space activities. Therefore, we have to question the adaptation of the current insurance scheme to NewSpace and more particularly to in-orbit services.

Before detailing the risk management process for in-orbit services and related insurance solutions (see 21.3, *infra.*), a review of the contractual mechanisms that can be set up and how to apply them to potential risk transfer to the insurance market is necessary (see 21.2, *infra.*).

21.2 In-orbit mission requirements for adjustment of contractual liability and space insurance contracts

We will see in this section to what extent commercial contracts, on the one hand (see 21.2.1, *infra.*), and insurance contracts on the other hand (see 21.2.2, *infra.*) have to be the subject of special adjustments in order to take into account the activities of in-orbit services.

Agreement on the Rescue of Astronauts, the Return of Astronauts and the Return of Objects Launched into Outer Space 22 April 1968.

Convention on International Liability for Damage Caused by Space Objects 29 March 1972.

Convention on Registration of Objects Launched into Outer Space 14 January 1975.

Agreement Governing the Activities of States on the Moon and Other Celestial Bodies 18 December 1979.

4 Article XIII of the Outer Space Treaty: "The provisions of this Treaty shall apply to the activities of States Parties to the Treaty in the exploration and use of outer space, including the moon and other celestial bodies, whether such activities are carried on by a single State Party to the Treaty or jointly with other States, including cases where they are carried on within the framework of international intergovernmental organizations".

5 Convention on International Liability for Damage Caused by Space Objects, Article I: "For the purposes of this Convention: (a) 'Damage' means the loss of or damage to human life, bodily injury or other injury to health, or loss of, property of, States or of persons, whether natural or legal, or of property of international intergovernmental organizations; (b) The term 'launch' also includes the attempted launch; (c) 'Launching State' means: (i) A State that launches or causes to be launched a space object; (ii) A State whose territory or facilities are used for the launch of a space object'.

21.2.1 Commercial contracts

Space contracts have borrowed their structure and many of their clauses from conventional non-specific contracts. These contracts are relatively similar, with for each of them[6] specificities related to the mission, technical characteristics, and other features. In the following subsection, we will focus on contractual liability arrangements that have an impact on the exposure of the parties to a contract and their insurers, if any.

21.2.2 Contractual adjustment of liability

The contractual liability regime will have to be interpreted in light of the applicable space law and also according to the law applicable to the contract for services in orbit. The choice of the law applicable to the contract is crucial, since it is in particular with regard to this law that the validity of the liability clauses will be analysed.

In their contract, the parties may waive in advance, in whole or in part, their rights of recourse against the other party, by way of using "waiver of recourse" and/or "hold harmless" clauses. By means of these clauses, the contracting parties avoid any recourse between them and allocate in advance the responsibilities for damages caused to third parties. These reciprocal waiver of recourse and hold harmless clauses are generally completed by a "flow down" obligation towards sub-contractors, under which sub-contractors shall be bound by such allocation of liability.

Some national space laws have specifically rendered mandatory the above-mentioned clauses, such as the French Law on Space Operations (LOS)[7] which establishes the legal framework for space activities carried out by natural or legal persons falling within its application. The LOS makes waivers of recourse between contracting parties involved in space operations mandatory and sets up a guarantee pact system. By applying the provisions of its Arts 19[8] and 20,[9] the LOS has thus specifically validated the current practice of launch service contracts, including a waiver of recourse and "non-liability" clause between participants in a space operation.

However, it should be recalled here that, with regard to the contractual satellite chain, the practice of "waiver of recourse" is not systematic and provisions on the liability of satellite manufacturers or sub-contractors can be found in supply contracts or sub-contracts. This is also what the LOS takes up since it specifies that in the contracts of the contractual chain of monitoring satellite

6 L. RAVILLON, "Typology of Contracts in the Space Sector in Contracting for Space", *Contract Practice in the European Space Sector edited by Lesley J. SMITH and I. BAUMANN*, 2011.

7 Law No. 2008-518 of 3 June 2008 on Space Operations – available online.

8 Law No. 2008-518 of 3 June 2008 on space operations, Article 19: "When the insurance or financial guarantee mentioned in Article 6 as well as, if necessary, the governmental guarantee have been laid out to indemnify a third party, one of the persons having taken part in the space operation or in the production of the space object which caused the damage cannot be held liable by another of these persons, except in case of a wilful misconduct" (cited from unofficial translation of France's "LOI no 2008-518 du 3 juin 2008 relative aux opérations spatiales" by Philippe Clerc and Julien Mariez 34 *Journal of Space Law* at 465).

9 Ibid., Art. 20: "In the case of a damage caused by a space operator or the production of a space object to a person taking part in this operation or in that production, any other person taking part in the space operation or in the production of the space object having caused the damage and bound to the previous one by a contract cannot be held liable because of that damage, unless otherwise expressly stipulated regarding the damage caused during the production phase of a space object which is to be commanded in outer space or during its commanding in orbit, or in case of a wilful misconduct" (cited from unofficial translation of France's "LOI no 2008-518 du 3 juin 2008 relative aux opérations spatiales" by Philippe Clerc and Julien Mariez 34 *Journal of Space Law* at 465).

in orbit, the parties can expressly provide for recourse clauses and therefore defeat the principle of renunciation of cross-recourse between or among the participants in a space operation.

Another interesting national space regulation is the US Commercial Space Launch Act (CSLA)[10] which is the first national space regulation having imposed an obligation of reciprocal waiver of claims among the participants to the launch or re-entry operation, including the customer or the launch provider. This reciprocal waiver of claims is coupled with a waiver afforded by the Secretary of Transportation, in case of any damage sustained by the US Government or executive agency resulting from an activity that was carried out by the licensee.

In the specific case of in-orbit services, the parties to a service contract, i.e. the service satellite operator and the customer satellite operator, may therefore validly provide for clauses of full and complete liability of each party or limited liability, or even no liability to the other party, subject to the applicable space legislation. To enable the development of these missions, it would be advisable to provide for waivers of recourse between the parties, if not full and complete, at least limited to the most technically risky phases, such as the docking phase of the service satellite to the customer's satellite.

Some considerations regarding the contractual sharing of responsibilities among the co-contractors in the event of damage caused to third parties shall be made. It will be a question here of highlighting the possibilities of contractually regulating these risks. Damage to third parties may be caused at different periods and raises the question of assessing the liability between the operator of the service satellite and the customer operator. Thus, when the service satellite is not yet docked to the customer's satellite, or after the execution of the mission, the service satellite operator may be held liable to third parties in accordance with the provisions of the law applicable to the activity and it will be difficult to envisage transferring it to the customer of the service satellite. There is the same rationale for the liability of the customer's satellite operator.

On the other hand, it is possible that damages to third parties are caused when the service satellite is docked to the customer's satellite for an in-orbit positioning or for a refueling mission. In this case, it may be contractually provided for a sharing of responsibility between the operator of the service satellite and the customer operator. If the customer's satellite is fully controlled by the service satellite, it will be highly likely that the service satellite's operator will be held liable for any damage caused to third parties, not only under applicable space law, but also contractually.

It is understood that liability to third parties must be analysed in the light of applicable international space law, principles of state responsibility, national space law, national law, or common liability law that may be applied by the third-party victim of damage. Obviously, this liability vis-à-vis third parties cannot be limited contractually, but an allocation between both operators may be envisaged. This allocation of liability between the parties to a contract, which cannot be enforced against third parties, may be done by means of a clause of exemption, sharing, or allocation of liability. Pursuant to this clause, both parties agree to hold one of them liable for damage caused to third parties.

Particular attention will therefore have to be paid to the allocation of responsibilities, and its validity will have to be analysed in the light of the law applicable not only to the contract but also to the space operation envisaged.

10 Commercial Space Launch Act, Public Law 98-575, 98th Congress, H.R. 3942, 30 October 1984; 98 Stat. 3055; Space Law – Basic Legal Documents, E.III.3; now codified as Subtitle VII, 51. U.S.C.

21.2.3 Contractual arrangements in the event of non-performance or poor performance of the in-orbit service

There are several ways to determine in advance the contractual consequences of non-execution or improper execution of the mission of the service satellite. The parties may decide in advance on the partial or total non-payment of the contract price or provide for a penalty clause or "liquidated damages" to fix in advance in the contract the amount of damages or compensation for damages in order to avoid court litigation to evaluate the compensation for damage.

By using a penalty clause, the parties determine in advance contractually and independently a fixed amount without regard to any possible loss that will be due by the defaulting party in the event of non-performance of a contractual obligation. Thus, by application of that clause, a debtor undertakes to pay the creditor a sum of money in an amount fixed in advance if he fails to fulfil his obligation or performs it beyond the time limits laid down in the contract.

The mechanism of a "liquidated damages" clause is different from a penalty clause in the sense that it entails the payment of a sum of money or at least the promise of the performance of an obligation. The purpose of this stipulation is to establish a pre-estimate of the loss that must be paid if a party fails to perform its obligation in whole or in part. Certain conditions are prerequisites for the validity of these clauses:

(1) the harm must be "uncertain" or "difficult to quantify";
(2) the amount is reasonable and takes into account the actual or anticipated harm caused by the breach of contract, the difficulty of proving the loss, and the difficulty of finding an appropriate alternative remedy; and
(3) the damages are structured as damages and not as a penalty.

If these criteria are not met, a liquidated damages clause will be unenforceable.[11]

Other clauses such as performance clauses or "incentives" may also be included. Satellite manufacturing contracts sometimes provide that the buyer pays the manufacturer amounts based on orbital performance at the end of a certain specified period after the in-orbit tests, the amount being adjusted according to the performance of the satellite.

There may also be provisions for the reimbursement of all or part of the sums already paid, if the satellite is not operating at the contractual levels, depending on proof that the non-performance may be attributable to the satellite manufacturer. Such provisions on orbital performance shall form an integral part of the overall economic transaction of the contract.

These penalties, liquidated damages, or incentive performance clauses, are commonly found in satellite manufacturing contracts and could be duplicated to in-orbit service contracts and adapted according to the technical characteristics of the service mission (for example, if power refueling cannot be carried out or if the customer satellite cannot be moved). Thus, to limit the contractual liability of the service satellite operator, contracts could contain disclaimers in the event of defective service. For instance, the service satellite operator would not be liable for damages suffered by its customer as a result of a delay in service, or in the event of a service interruption or degradation. The service satellite operator therefore offers no guarantee as to the satellite's ability to provide the service, but only price reductions would apply.

11 Uniform Commercial Code, §2-718. Liquidation or Limitation of Damages, Deposits.

Finally, it will be necessary to be vigilant on the inclusion of clauses according to which, under no circumstances, each of the parties will be obliged to compensate for indirect, incidental, consequential, special, or punitive damages, loss of turnover, profits, or other financial or economic losses of any kind, that would be due to the fault or negligence of this party, regardless of that party's performance obligation, or its failure to perform an obligation under the contract, and even if that party has been advised of the possibility of such damages or losses.

There are therefore several ways to regulate the contractual relations between the parties to an in-orbit service contract. These contracts will have to be negotiated and drafted taking into account not only the technical specificities and purpose of each mission, but also the legal framework of the contract (including any applicable space law and contract law).

Even with proper contractual liability mitigation in place, insurance might be necessary to cover the interests or the liability of the in-orbit service operator or its customers.

21.2.4 Insurance contracts

Insurance contracts for space risks are well known and monitored. They aim to cover damage or loss to insured space assets, but also the liability of an insured in case of damage caused to third parties. We will detail in this subsection the existing space insurance schemes and their specificities, in order to understand their mechanisms and to better assess their applicability to in-orbit service missions (see 21.3, *infra.*).

21.2.4.1 Damage insurance during launch and operation in orbit

The launch insurance coverage phase starts at the time the launch is considered irreversible, i.e. it cannot be interrupted as defined in the applicable launch services agreement. Such a definition differs from one launcher to another and will depend on its technical context: it can be at the intentional ignition or when the clamps open to release the launcher.[12]

Typically, the launch insurance policy ends one year after launch, which means that the launched satellite can be covered during its first year in orbit via launch insurance. Practically, the duration of the launch insurance policy varies from "launch plus a few days" to "launch plus one year". Today, the majority of space insurers offers launch insurance policies for a period of one year after launch, which can then be renewed in the form of in-orbit life insurance. Some insurers also offer multi-year policies with adapted premiums, which include the period of operation in orbit after the launch of an insured satellite and up to the end of the satellite's operational life.

During the launch phase and during the operation in orbit, only satellites are covered by the insurance policy. Non-reusable launchers are not directly insured in the event of loss or damage because, because on one hand, the launcher is destroyed once it has performed its launch service and its value is included in the launch services fee and, on the other hand, launch service agreements generally provide that the launch service is deemed to be performed at launch of the launcher.

The types of insured damages are as follows:

12 Example of definition from SpaceX Launch Services Agreement referenced EX-10.2 2 d468141dex102.htm EX-10.2: "Launch means Intentional Ignition, for the purpose of Satellite Batch carriage, followed by either (i) Lift-Off or (ii) the loss or destruction of the Satellite Batch and/or the Launch Vehicle".

i. total loss

The "total loss"[13] of the satellite is generally defined as the destruction of the satellite, the loss of the satellite (meaning that the satellite cannot be controlled by ground stations), or when the satellite cannot reach its orbital position within a certain period predefined in the insurance policy. In the event of a total loss of a satellite, insurers will compensate the insured for the full value of the insurance amount.

ii. constructive total loss

The "constructive total loss"[14] corresponds to a reduction in the life or operational capacity of the insured satellite below a threshold, traditionally between 70% and 90%. This threshold is called the "quantum of loss" and is defined as the actual capacity in relation to the nominal (contractual) capacity of the satellite. This capability is evaluated according to the technical specifications of the satellite. If the actual capacity is less than the nominal capacity, the percentage of the capacity lost by the satellite will be calculated. If the percentage of loss falls between two identified percentages (generally between 70% and 90% depending on the provisions of the insurance contract), the satellite will then be declared a "constructive total loss", in which case it will be fully compensated by the insurers, as if the satellite had indeed been totally lost.

iii. partial loss

The "partial loss"[15] of the satellite is a partial reduction in the life or operational capability of the satellite below the threshold used to determine the "constructive total loss". In this case, the amount of compensation will correspond to the actual loss of capacity or lifespan suffered by the satellite. To calculate compensation for a partial loss, the same concept of "quantum of loss" as for "constructive total loss" will be used. If the percentage of loss is below the threshold defined in the policy, then the satellite will be declared a "partial loss" and insurers will only compensate the amount of insurance corresponding to the percentage of loss.

As we discuss below, the in-orbit service providers, or the customer wishing to call upon the service of a servicing satellite, may wish to insure themselves in case of failure or loss of their satellite(s). In this respect, the insurance community will base their insurance offer on the above detailed basis.

The satellite property damage insurance policy is systematically offered on the basis of "all risks" coverage. This means that the insurance covers any loss or damage to the satellite, regardless of the cause, with the exception of causes specifically excluded from the policy. This notion is

13 Total loss as commonly defined in space insurance contract: (a) the complete loss, destruction or failure of the Satellite; or (b) the Partial Loss Quantum (PLQ) equals 0 during the Coverage Period; or (c) the Satellite cannot be separated from the Launch Vehicle; or (d) the Satellite cannot reach within 180 days after Launch or maintain its specified Sun Synchronous orbit in accordance with the Contract on a permanent or permanently intermittent basis.

14 Constructive total loss as commonly defined in space insurance contract: "Constructive Total Loss" means that the Loss Amount or the cumulative Loss Amount for all Partial Losses is equal to, or greater than [TBA] % of the Amount of Insurance, and that following Insurers agreement to the Constructive Total Loss, the Satellite is not used for its intended mission purpose.

15 Partial loss as commonly defined in space insurance contract: "Partial Loss" shall mean any loss that does not result in a Total Loss or Constructive Total Loss.

opposed to the notion of a policy based on "named perils", whereby insurers will only cover loss or damage specifically listed in the policy.

The importance of the distinction between these two concepts lies in knowing on which party (insured or insurer) the burden of proof rests. Under an "all risks" policy, the insurer will have to prove that an exclusion is applicable to refuse coverage. On the other hand, under a "named perils" policy, the insured will have to prove that a risk covered by his insurance policy has occurred. In addition, the scope of coverage of an "all risks" policy is broader (covering essentially all causes) than a "named perils" policy (covering only specific listed causes). It is therefore clearly in the interest of the insured that his insurance damage to satellite property is taken out on the basis of an "all risks" formulation. Applying this cover basis to in-orbit service insurance cover would ease the indemnification process and would give some comfort to the insured in the responsiveness of the insurance.

21.2.4.2 Space liability insurance

Spacecraft liability insurance covers the financial consequences of an insured's liability for damage caused to a third party as a result of a space activity. These guarantees are available, in the current state of the market, up to $500 million and even $750 million in some cases, and are generally underwritten for an insurance amount from $50 million to $500 million, depending mainly on the existing legal insurance obligations, for example as per French LOS[16] or US CSLA.[17] Moreover, the duration of these guarantees also varies, ranging from a few days to a maximum of one year after launch for the launch phase and for the in-orbit life of a few days (if the insurance is taken out for specific activities) to a maximum of one year after the insurance policy came into effect (multi-year guarantees were available a few years ago, but are no longer available today, in the current state of the insurance market). Generally, the entities subscribing said insurance are the launch agencies for the launch phase and the satellite operators for the in-orbit life phase, knowing that, traditionally, the launching states are named "additional insureds", meaning that they will benefit from the coverage (in the amount, conditions and exclusions of the guarantee) in the event

16 The French Law on Space Operations as stated in a Loi de finances (Art. 119, Loi n° 2008-1443 du 30 décembre 2008 de finances rectificative pour 2008) stipulates an amount of insurance between €50,000,000 and €70,000,000.

17 The US Commercial Space Launch Act provides for the required amount of mandatory insurance in Title 51 – 51 USC Ch. 509: "§50914. Liability insurance and financial responsibility requirements

(a) General Requirements.—(1) When a launch or reentry license is issued or transferred under this chapter, the licensee or transferee shall obtain liability insurance or demonstrate financial responsibility in amounts to compensate for the maximum probable loss from claims by—

(A) a third party for death, bodily injury, or property damage or loss resulting from an activity carried out under the license; and

(B) the United States Government against a person for damage or loss to Government property resulting from an activity carried out under the license.

(2) The Secretary of Transportation shall determine the amounts required under paragraph (1)(A) and (B) of this subsection, after consulting with the Administrator of the National Aeronautics and Space Administration, the Secretary of the Air Force, and the heads of other appropriate executive agencies.

(3) For the total claims related to one launch or reentry, a licensee or transferee is not required to obtain insurance or demonstrate financial responsibility of more than—

(A)(i) $500,000,000 under paragraph (1)(A) of this subsection; or

(ii) $100,000,000 under paragraph (1)(B) of this subsection; or

(B) the maximum liability insurance available on the world market at reasonable cost if the amount is less than the applicable amount in clause (A)(i) or (ii) of this paragraph."

that their liability is called upon. Furthermore, all participants in the launch operation are also generally covered under said insurance policies (in particular, the manufacturers of the launcher and the satellite or satellites, and all their respective subcontractors and suppliers at any level). The same is often true for in-orbit liability policies. The intent of such broad additional-insured provisions is to focus the indemnification for damage caused to a third party on the appropriate insurance coverage and to avoid multiple litigations that would render very difficult dispute resolutions.

Based on the applicable national space legislation, the in-orbit service providers might need to subscribe such an insurance.

21.2.4.3 Waiver of subrogation

As a principle, and under most national insurance laws, further to indemnification of an insured or indemnification of a third party, the insurers have a right of subrogation. As a consequence, the insurers will have the benefit of the rights of recourse of their insured against the entity responsible of the loss. If the insured has waived its rights of recourse, then depending on the applicable law, the insurers may decide not to indemnify the loss at all or offer a reduced indemnification due to the absence of right of recourse.

In respect of space insurance policies covering property damage caused to satellites (during the launch or in-orbit phases) or in the case of space liability insurances, those insurances traditionally include a waiver of subrogation rights from the insurer in favour of the participants to the launch/satellite contractual chain. It means that the insurers contractually agree not to use their right of recourse against the party responsible for the damage to the insured satellite, after having indemnified the insured for its loss or after having indemnified a third party, except in case of gross negligence or wilful misconduct of the responsible party. It has to be noted that, usually, the insurers agrees to waive their rights of subrogation if the insured has also waived its rights of recourse before subscription of the insurance contract.

This is an important concept to be applied also to in-orbit services, as it leads to focus the indemnification of a loss or a damage on the insurance market and protects the operator's and subcontractor's liability. The application of waiver of subrogation from the insurers would protect the operators affording in-orbit service by forbidding recourse from the insurers further to payment of an indemnification. As of today, there is no reason to have a different scheme applicable to in-orbit service.

21.2.4.4 Insurance market

With respect to property damage insurance, for the last ten years, except 2018 and 2019, the insurance market has been profitable and, despite some losses, the premium earned has been higher than paid losses.

We notice that the insurance capacity remains on a high level with a theoretical capacity of less than $1 billion in 2021 (Figure 21.2) which is well above the capacity that is really needed. Furthermore, the insurers do not give their full theoretical capacity on an insured risk, but a much smaller line. Therefore, the insurance market has a capacity that could be used to support in-orbit service missions, if they have some appetite for it and some confidence in insuring such missions.

The insurance market is a very volatile market and we also notice high competition for attractive risks, leading to lowering premium rates for such risks. However, for NewSpace risks, the insurers today have less appetite due mainly to the new technology used and to the specificities of the in-orbit missions. But, with time and growing confidence, the insurers may be more present on this sector of activity.

As for third party liability insurance, in the absence of loss for decades, there is no real evolution of the capacity, which is roughly at US$500 million, nor on premium rates, which are still quite low, being roughly 0.1% of the sum insured.

Having detailed the current space market and insurance schemes, the question is how the insurance market can insure and support the development of in-orbit service missions.

21.3 How can the insurance market support the development of in-orbit services?

We will see in this section to what extent existing insurances are applicable to in-orbit service missions and require amendments in order to best meet the risk management needs of NewSpace operators.

21.3.1 New missions, new risks

There is no doubt that, taken separately, the servicing satellite and the satellite subject of the service might be insured under a property damage insurance by their respective operators, with the subjectivity of having adapted terms, conditions, and premium rates.

However, there are some new risks compared to traditional space missions that arise from in-orbit service[18] and that will need to be taken into account by the insurance market to tailor adapted insurance contracts.

The most obvious one is where the in-orbit service requires the docking between two satellites. This docking will concern two satellites, one performing the required service, i.e. refueling or repositioning or other, and the other one being the subject of the service. It therefore implicates physical contact between the satellites. In this event, the servicing satellite may cause physical damages to the satellite being the object of the service. In this case, the operator of the satellite on which the service is performed, and that is damaged due to the service, may wish to claim compensation from the operator of the servicing satellite for its damage. The issue is whether the insurance market would be inclined to cover docked satellites. In our view, this could be achieved if the insured and the insurers can provide comprehensive loss formulas to assess the quantum of the loss and the basis of the loss. However, due to the technical risks associated with a docking procedure, the insurers may impose specific conditions to reduce their exposure.

Another new risk is the one of non-performance or improper performance of the service. In this situation, the question is what would be the insurance that would respond to damages caused to the satellite subject of the service, or in case of failure to perform the service. In this case, the customer may wish to claim compensation for defective service under the ground of breach of an obligation under its contract with the operator performing the service. The operator receiving the in-orbit service may claim for additional costs incurred due to the default, for loss of revenue, for loss of contracts, or damage to its satellite. The issue that arises here is to know whether a space insurance may provide for a cover for the above detailed cases. The space property damage insurance is able to cover damages to the insured satellite, but also the situation where the satellite fails to perform nominally compared to its nominal operational capacity or cannot be used for its

18 Assurance through insurance and on-orbit servicing. Rebecca Reesman. The Aerospace Corporation February 2018.

intended purposes.[19] In such a case, if the property damage insurance is subscribed by the operator performing the service, a cover might be in place if the execution of the service is defective, based on the applicable loss formulas as included in the relevant insurance policy: in which event, said operator will be indemnified by the insurance under the terms and conditions of the insurance. But this means that the insurance proceeds will be paid to the operator having subscribed the insurance and not the operator of the satellite being the subject of the service. This indemnification will aim to cover the prejudice sustained by the operator of the servicing satellite, but not the prejudice sustained by the operator of the serviced satellite.

The space liability insurances and more particularly the products liability insurance shall be discussed here. First, space third party liability will not provide for any cover as it only covers damages caused to third parties, and in the case of in-orbit services, the customer's operator is not a third party. Furthermore, such cover does not extend to non-execution or improper performance during the execution of the mission. Therefore, the insurance cannot provide any cover. Second, as for the space products liability, it only provides for a cover in case of material damage, bodily injury, or consequential damages[20] after performance of the service and due to a defect in the mission. Then, the sole non-performance of the service cannot be covered under such an insurance as a damage or bodily injury shall occur and the service must have been rendered. Furthermore, such type of insurance is currently available to manufacturers and not to satellite operators. Therefore, at this stage, discussions are needed with the space insurance market to know to what extent such insurance could be extended to cover also non-performance of the service.

As for the satellite being the subject of the service, the question is whether it can be insured under a property damage insurance while the service is being performed. If the operator has its satellite insured under a property damage insurance based on an "all risk" concept, then it is likely that any damage caused by the satellite performing the service might be covered, unless a specific exclusion is provided for in the insurance contract. However, it might also be likely that the insurers would tailor the insurance policy based on the contractual provisions between the operator of the servicing satellite and the operator requesting the service.

Another issue relates to the difficulty to calculate the damage suffered by the operator, which is particularly complicated in case the satellite has reached the end of its life and no longer has a commercial value. In the event that the satellite on which the service is operated still has a value, damage insurance could be available with perhaps the exclusion of damage caused by the service satellite, in which case we could consider some kind of combined policy taken out by the operator of the service satellite and including damage to the satellite object of the service.

These insurances will have to be analysed in the light of the possibilities of recourse contractually provided for by the parties to the contract for services in orbit.

In the event of damage caused to third parties, the space third party liability insurances subscribed by the satellite operator providing the service, or even the one subscribed by the customer, are intended to cover the financial consequences of liability claims in the event of property damage, bodily injury, and consequential damage caused to third parties. The traditional space liability insurance affords a cover for in-orbit missions, but there is a crucial issue that will need to be solved not only via the insurance provisions, but also via regulation. Indeed, the question is whether a liable operator can be identified and to be able to assess the fault, if the damage

19 See ibid. at 16.

20 In insurance, consequential damage corresponds to damage resulting from a right lost by a natural or legal person over a good, a thing, a service, a deprivation of a movable or immovable asset or a deprivation of a right.

occurs in outer space. If applicable, under the 1972 Liability Convention, the servicing satellite operator's launching state would be liable. But this convention does not take into account the case where two or more satellites are docked; we may therefore assume that several launching states would be liable and would apply their national space regulation that may impose space liability insurance obligations. Therefore, the space liability insurances will have to take into account the risks related to the mission and in particular any difficulties concerning the determination of the operator responsible for the damage caused to third parties, even in case where both satellites are docked. In this case, it could be envisaged that the insurance would operate without seeking the liability of one or the other of the operators, in particular by applying the additional insurance clauses, well known in space liability insurance. We have to bear in mind that a third party victim can claim compensation for its prejudice on the ground of international regulation, national space law, or even tort law.

Insurance solutions are therefore currently available for this type of risk. The question is whether the insurance is sufficiently innovative to cover risks associated to in-orbit services missions.[21]

21.3.2 Application of insurance known-concepts to in-orbit services

In this subsection, we will discuss ways for the insurers to support in-orbit services by using existing insurance provisions that could be adapted to new projects.

21.3.2.1 Corrective measures

The corrective measures provision is usually included in space property damage insurance. Such provision allows the insured to take specific measures to mitigate or reduce a loss. In case an insured satellite suffers a total loss, partial loss, or constructive loss, and if some corrective measures are identified, then the insurers will pay for their implementation. If these measures are not effective, the insurers will then indemnify the following loss.

There are some conditions attached to this provision, which is usually worded as follows:

> If a Loss may be satisfactorily corrected or compensated for within a reasonable period of time of the Loss by additional ground installations, procedural changes, software development or any other reasonable corrective measures ("Corrective Measures"), the Insurers, after consultation with the Named Insured, must at their choice either:
>
> - pay the Loss Payee in accordance with Insuring Agreement; or
> - indemnify the Named Insured for the costs required to implement the Corrective Measures.
>
> If the Corrective Measures do not achieve satisfactory correction of or compensation for the Loss, the Insurers must then proceed with Insuring Agreement in addition to bearing the cost of implementing the Corrective Measures.

21 Katarzyna Malinowska, In-orbit services and Insurance, a marriage of convenience? Room: Space Journal of Asgardia, room.eu.com.

The issue is whether such a provision could be used by the operators to use an in-orbit service satellite as a corrective measure in case an already in-orbit satellite is suffering a loss and is also insured under a property damage insurance, and such insurance includes a corrective measures provision.

There are several questions attached to the application of this provision in such a case.

The corrective measures should be performed within a reasonable period of time. Can we really think that the use of an in-orbit satellite as a corrective measure can be done within a period of time that would be reasonable, knowing that using a servicing satellite might take some time to position it in the right orbit?

The quoted provision is drafted broadly, as it refers to corrective measures as being "ground installations, procedural changes, software development or any reasonable corrective measures". What are the reasonable measures foreseen under this provision? Can we assess that using a servicing satellite is a reasonable measure as per the insurer's assessment? We have serious doubts about it.

As per the quoted provision, the corrective measure shall also provide for a "satisfactory correction", bringing the question of what is a satisfactory correction and to whom is it satisfactory, i.e. the insured or the insurers? One important issue is that the decision to pay the costs of corrective measures relies only on the insurers. It is not the insured's decision to implement or not those measures and it will only be consulted on the effectivity of the measures. Therefore, we might assume that such measures shall be satisfactory to the insurers, but they may have contradictory interests to the insureds.

Another issue to be discussed is the application of this provision in conjunction with the "due diligence" concept. The space insurance policy includes a due diligence provision under which the insured has to act as if uninsured and must take all reasonable actions to avoid or diminish a loss.[22] Once again, there is the notion of "reasonable" used here and for which we might question whether using in-orbit services would be a "reasonable" measure. This being said, the issue remains where to draw the line between the corrective measures that the insured and the insurers may implement and the due diligence obligation of the insured. In our view, the use of in-orbit service to reduce or avoid a loss might fall under the corrective measures provision, but we could, on the other hand, also argue that the insured should use in-orbit services to act as if not insured under its due diligence obligation. The answer to the question is not of a simple matter and should be reviewed carefully between the insured and the insurers, who will have to draw a clear and non-contestable line between both provisions.

Concerning this corrective measure provision, we have some doubts about its efficiency and its practical applicability, due to the questions raised above.

21.3.2.2 Salvage provision

Generally, a salvage provision is attached to the loss trigger in an insurance policy. Under this provision, in case an insured satellite, declared a total loss, partial loss, or constructive total loss, is indemnified by the insurers, but said satellite can still generate revenues, then under the insurance policy, such satellite can be saved. It means that if the indemnified satellite can generate revenue after having been indemnified, the insurers are entitled to receive proceeds from the salvage.

22 Due diligence provision: "The Named Insured must use due diligence and do all things reasonably practicable to avoid or diminish any Loss under this insurance and must act at all times as if uninsured".

Salvage undertakes different forms: it can be the selling of the indemnified satellite, the sharing of the revenues still generated by the satellite, or even transfer of the property of the satellite to the insurers.[23] This salvage provision is not automatic and is subject to an additional premium that was included in the total premium.

23 A common example of salvage clause would read:

"At the request of the Insurers, the Named Insured must make itself available to meet with the Insurers after the submission of the Proof of Loss to decide upon the disposition of a Satellite and to negotiate the financial arrangements to effect that disposition. Salvage after Constructive Total Loss or Total Loss:

After a Claim Payment has been made for a Constructive Total Loss or a Total Loss, the Insurers have the sole right to the maximum benefit of salvage, subject to any contractual restrictions that apply to the Named Insured.

The Insurers must notify the Named Insured in writing by the date of the Claim Payment whether or not they intend to take title to the Satellite.

(a) If the Insurers intend to take title to the Satellite and intend to sell the Satellite, the Named Insured must, for a period of two months from the date when Insurers notify the Named Insured in writing that they plan to sell the Satellite, be granted the exclusive first right to purchase the Satellite. In the event that the Named Insured and Insurers fail to agree on a purchase price or other provision of sale by the end of the abovementioned period, the Insurers have the right to offer the Satellite for sale to any party. If the Satellite is sold to any third party, the Named Insured must, subject to Condition 14 (Government Export Control):

(1) provide the Insurers with the documentation required to operate the Satellite; and

(2) provide the Insurers with all information necessary to enable the Insurers to sell the Satellite to a third party, subject to the Insurers obtaining the required confidentiality undertakings from any potential third party purchaser of the Satellite and the Named Insured obtaining the necessary government approvals.

The Insurers must decide whether to take title to the Satellite and inform the Named Insured within 15 days after the information outlined in (a)(1) and (a)(2) of this condition is received by the Insurers. When the Insurers take title, they assume sole responsibility for maintaining, monitoring or operating the Satellite.

The Named Insured is not required to take any other action or grant any other right, including without limitation assigning the Specified Orbit to the Insurers and is not precluded from replacing the Satellite at the Specified Orbit. The Insurers agree to remove the Satellite from the Specified Orbit promptly upon taking title to the Satellite.

The Insurers must reimburse the Named Insured for the costs reasonably incurred by the Named Insured in maintaining, monitoring or operating the Satellite from the date of the Claim Payment, except for those costs incurred during the period from the date of Claim Payment until the date the Named Insured confirms to Insurers that they do not wish to purchase the Satellite. The Insurers must also reimburse the Named Insured for all pre-agreed costs incurred by the Named Insured in obtaining salvage for the Insurers.

(b) If the Insurers decline to take title to the Satellite and the Named Insured continues to own, use or operate the Satellite for revenue generating purposes, the Insurers agree to meet with the Named Insured to negotiate any associated financial arrangements relating to the Named Insured's continued ownership, use or operation, or other participation with respect to the Satellite.

(c) If Insurers decline to take title to the Satellite and choose not to seek salvage, the Named Insured may use the Satellite for scientific, testing and demonstration purposes, or may otherwise dispose of the Satellite by ejecting it from its orbital position.

Except if the Insurers take title to the Satellite, the net salvage recoveries of the Insurers are limited to the amount of any Claim Payments.

Any requirements imposed on the Named Insured by any regulatory body or under any law applicable to the Satellite or the Named Insured, supersede any obligations the Named Insured has under this insurance.

Salvage after Partial Loss:

After the Claim Payment has been made for a Partial Loss, the Named Insured agrees to do all things reasonably practicable to maximize salvage opportunities for the affected part of the Satellite, subject to any contractual restrictions that apply to the Named Insured. The net salvage recoveries of the Insurers are limited to the amount of any Claim Payments made.

However, salvage is not required to the extent that it conflicts with the Named Insured's ability to meet contractual obligations to its customers, with respect to the equipment associated with the Partial Loss, which existed immediately before the event giving rise to the Partial Loss."

This concept does not relate to the fact that the damaged satellite can effectively be "saved", but rather presents conditions of sharing, between the insurers who have paid a loss and the insured, of the profits that an indemnified satellite can still procure. With this mechanism, the insurers and the insured will agree on a fair share of the revenues, to permit the insured to keep enough revenue to carry on operating the satellite and to compensate the insurers for the indemnification paid under the property insurance contract, with the limit that the salvage for the insurers shall not exceed the total amount of insurance paid as indemnification under the insurance policy.

This provision has been triggered in the past, where the insured and the insurers agreed on sharing the revenues generated by the damaged satellite.

With respect to in-orbit service, this concept of salvage could be useful, in the sense that using the services of a service satellite in orbit would reduce the rate of loss of a damaged satellite and the insurers and the insured could agree upstream if the damaged satellite can generate profits; then these profits will be shared between them on the basis of a pre-determined sharing upstream in the insurance contract. In this situation, the insurers would be motivated to use the services of an in-orbit service satellite to maximise the revenues generated by a lost satellite, as they will receive a share of the proceeds of the damaged satellite. But in this situation, there is still the question of who is going to pay for the use of an in-orbit service satellite.

This path could be discussed with the space insurers to support space operators in using servicing satellite to save their damaged satellites, after having been indemnified for their loss.

21.3.2.3 Loss payee provisions

The "loss payee" concept is discussed at this stage. The loss payee clause is often used in space property insurance to secure the rights of lenders under a space projects. In this respect, and when a loss payee provision is in place, the loss payee is entitled to receive the portion of the indemnification relating to its interests under the project. Depending on the interests, such portion can be full indemnification or partial indemnification. As we have seen earlier, the property damage insurance subscribed by the operator of the service satellite, to cover its satellite, can provide for a cover in case the satellite performing the service executes an improper service. This indemnification will therefore be calculated based on the service that should have been performed and the actual service executed. As the indemnification will be paid to the insured, i.e. the operator of the servicing satellite, we could imagine that the insurance contract includes a provision under which the operator receiving the indemnification would be the operator receiving the service. This scheme permits, on one hand, that the operator executing the service can be insured in case of non-performance or improper performance of its satellite, and on the other hand, allows for an indemnification directly to the operator receiving the service. The insurers have a long experience of using this provision, especially with respect to finance contracts where there is often an obligation to name the lenders as loss payee.

21.4 Conclusion

To conclude, the development of in-orbit service activities will lead lawyers to question the content of commercial contracts in the very near future, either by adapting existing contractual mechanisms, or by creating new contractual frameworks, specifically adapted to these missions. On the insurance side, the insurance market could design specific and full insurance programmes including property damage, third party liability, and even loss of revenues cover in one single policy. This could facilitate the subscription of the insurance, having one policy instead of three for the same mission, and it could cover all parties to the in-orbit mission. It will also ease the indemnification process.

What will need to be assessed is which operator should subscribe the relevant property damage insurance. We could imagine an amended insurance policy for damage caused to satellites (the servicing one and the one using the service) where damages to both satellites can be covered in one single policy. This policy could be subscribed by one operator who will pass on, totally or partially, the costs of the insurance to the other operator through the commercial contract. Having a single programme would ease the subscription of the insurance cover for both operators.

As for third party liability insurance, a guarantee from authorising states would help to support the development of in-orbit service missions, by reducing the exposure of the operators as well as their insurers. But, in any case, the liability insurance will have to be affordable for every mission, customised to each mission, and the premium must be assessed based on the service and not the size of the satellite at stake.[24]

To permit the insurance market to propose adapted insurance solutions, the important key is the confidence the insurers may have in an operator and its missions (from a technical point of view, but not only). Therefore, it is crucial for in-orbit service operators to liaise as early as possible with the insurance market to give a full and comprehensive understanding of their operations to insurers, in order to instill as much as confidence as possible allowing for the insurers to then offer insurance solutions.

24 On Orbit Servicing as Space Resource – Liability Challenges. Dr. Cristiana Santos, Researcher at Chaire SIRIUS Ms. Maria Rhimbassen, PhD Candidate at Chaire SIRIUS.

22

LEGISLATING FOR SPACEPORTS, COMMERCIAL SPACE MARKETS, AND SPACE TOURISM

Lesley Jane Smith, Ruairidh J.M. Leishman, and Alan Thompson

22.1 Introduction

As the terrestrial element of space transportation, spaceports have been in existence for as long as space transportation itself, first emerging in the United States (US) in the 1940s.[1] Despite this, their regulation is not specifically addressed by the core international space law treaties.[2] The treaties were negotiated and ratified in the 1960s and 70s, when space was principally the domain of states rather than private companies. As recently as 2016, the regulatory framework was still in its infancy because spaceports were being operated exclusively by, or in cooperation with, states as the major shareholders of projects.[3] Those days are behind us.

Nevertheless, the treaties are not completely silent about spaceports, placing obligations on the launching states providing the spaceport facilities. In turn, these obligations are foisted onto operators as the performers of those activities.[4]

Many states previously relied on bespoke national contractual measures between the major parties involved in space operations. These were amended on an ad hoc basis as opposed to having, or updating, their own national space legislation.[5] The best European example of this was the "French paradox": until it passed national legislation in 2008 (in force from 2010), an increasing number of (private) space activities were taking place from French territory without being subject to specific

1 Diane Howard, 'The emergence of an effective national and international spaceport regime of law' (McGill University 2014) 12.

2 Michael Gerhard and Isabelle Reutzel, 'Law Related to Space Transportation and Spaceports' in Ram S Jakhu and Paul Stephen Dempsey (eds), *Routledge Handbook of Space Law* (Routledge 2016) 286.

3 Ibid. 285.

4 Howard (n 1) 21; Erik Seedhouse, *Spaceports Around the World, A Global Growth Industry* (Springer International Publishing 2017) 34.

5 Annette Froehlich and Vincent Seffinga (eds), *National Space Legislation: A Comparative and Evaluative Analysis*, vol 15 (Springer International Publishing 2018).

DOI: 10.4324/9781003268475-31

legislation.[6] Like France, many states have now enacted national legislation or updated existing legislation. The different approaches taken, however, are fuelled by the specific rationale underlying the legislation's enactment,[7] and depend upon the type of space activity that the state wants or can promote. With the UK, for example, the regulations focus on spaceports and commercial small satellite launch because the national and regional governments are encouraging that activity.[8]

The treaties impose binding obligations on states for both governmental and non-governmental space activities, so there can never truly be a purely private space endeavour.[9] With the construction of commercial spaceports now completed or underway around the world,[10] the growing participation of private spaceport operators in the sector has led to an enhanced need to regulate spaceports and space transportation.[11] Many states have taken the step of regulating spaceports and the space activities taking place there.[12] The rationale behind the increase in regulation is clear: "commercial agitation" in favour of a developing launch market, followed by a governmental response in the form of licensing requirements.[13] Introducing regulation is understandable because launch is the moment of highest risk,[14] and the launching state bears that risk.[15]

22.2 Regulation

The decrease in the operational role of the state correlates with the increase in its regulatory role. International space law imposes obligations not only on all space-faring nations that are parties to the treaties, but arguably on all space-faring states.[16] The cornerstone of the need for states to regulate the activities of their nationals is the requirement to authorise and supervise those space activities.[17] This reality is universal regardless of the status of the state as a "space-power". Although each state's regulatory framework is different, most rely on a combination of legislation, subordinate legislation, strategy documents, and guidance material.[18] Each state will make use of these instruments differently depending on its internal legal structures, the context of its space activities, and its priorities. Therefore, no two space regulatory frameworks are identical.[19]

6 Gerhard and Reutzel (n 2) 274; Bruno Lazare and Jean-Pierre Trinchero, 'Chapter 15 – Regulations and Licensing at the European Spaceport' in Joseph N Pelton and Ram S Jakhu (eds), *Space Safety Regulations and Standards* (Butterworth-Heinemann 2010).

7 Froehlich and Seffinga (n 5) 188.

8 Ibid; HM Government, 'National Space Strategy' 41; AstroAgency, 'A Strategy for Space in Scotland 2021' 3.

9 Howard (n 1) 14.

10 Seedhouse (n 4) chapter 2; Howard (n 1) 12.

11 Gerhard and Reutzel (n 2) 285.

12 Ibid 287.

13 Melissa de Zwart and Joel Lisk, 'Development of the New Zealand and Australian Space Industries: Regulation for a Sustainable Future' [2017] RUMLAE Research Paper No.17-11 3.

14 E.g. NASA operated the Space Shuttle missions based on a 1-in-65 risk of loss of mission and crew – Diane Howard, 'The Elephant in the Room: Informed Consent from the Spaceport Operator's Perspective' (2012) 25 The Air and Space Lawyer 9; Gerhard and Reutzel (n 2) 287.

15 Maria A Pozza and Joel A Dennerley (eds), *Risk Management in Outer Space Activities: An Australian and New Zealand Perspective* (Springer 2022) chapter 1.

16 Ekta Rathore and Biswanath Gupta, 'Emergence of Jus Cogens Principles in Outer Space Law' (2020) 18 Astropolitics 1.

17 Art. VI, Treaty on Principles Governing the Activities of States in the Exploration and Use of Outer Space, including the Moon and other celestial bodies, entry into force on 10 October 1967, 610 UNTS 206 1967.

18 Aram Daniel Kerkonian, *Space Regulation in Canada: Past, Present and Potential: The Case for a Comprehensive Canadian Space Law*, vol 12 (1st edn, Springer International Publishing 2021) 1.

19 Ibid.

Having an agile regulatory framework can be advantageous to swiftly respond to technological progress. As emerging space activities transition from the hypothetical to feasible, commercial operators will need, and demand, regulatory support; this will require states to invest in their regulatory roles to enable their domestic space industry to compete in an ever-increasing international marketplace.[20] Certainty over the legality of an activity is also an essential component for (potential) investors to manage risk.[21]

Launching facilities and operations require a pertinent regulatory framework to support activities at national level[22] to ensure compliance with various aspects, be this the environmental impact, or stemming from commitments that attach to launching states and those undertaking space activities under international space law.[23] States that accommodate spaceports on their territory are absolutely liable, as the launching state, for damage caused to third states by the space object on the surface of the Earth or to aircraft in flight.[24]

The impetus behind much of the national regulation is clear. To address their own liability, many states impose comprehensive insurance and indemnification requirements on spaceport operators.[25] Some states have answered the call by entrepreneurs for clarity in the law;[26] others have regulated to protect people, property, and the environment, and to ensure technical competence and financial adequacy.[27]

The existence of a spaceport is not only one of the key driving forces behind the continued growth of the space economy but is a necessary pre-condition.[28] States, and their self-governing regions, have long seen their existence as a strong pull for a space company, competing to provide the most desirable facilities and environment for companies and operators.[29] The space industry is no exception to the general rule of tax incentives spurring industry growth, with these types of incentives known in the US as "Zero G, Zero Tax bills".[30] Operators and businesses within the UK's Green Freeport zones benefit by not being subject to normal tax and customs rules.[31]

22.2.1 Licensing and development

By 2016, only a handful of states had enacted legislation specifically regulating the building and operation of spaceports.[32] The focus was on domestic concerns rather than compliance with international obligations. Those that license spaceports usually address all aspects of their operation,

20 Ibid. 54–55.

21 Mahulena Hofmann and PJ Blount, 'Emerging Commercial Uses of Space: Regulation Reducing Risks' (2018) 19 The Journal of World Investment & Trade 1001, 1002.

22 Lesley Jane Smith and Ruairidh JM Leishman, 'Up, up and Away: An Update on the UK's Latest Plans for Space Activities' (2019) 44 Air and Space Law 2.

23 Ibid.

24 Art. I and II, Convention on International Liability for Damage Caused by Space Objects (LIAB) 1972.

25 Jack Wright Nelson, 'Securing Europe's Spaceports: A Legal Perspective' in Annette Froehlich (ed), *Spaceports in Europe* (Springer International Publishing 2021) 5.

26 Hofmann and Blount (n 21) 1010.

27 Gerhard and Reutzel (n 2) 285.

28 Kerkonian (n 18) 28.

29 PJ Blount, 'If You Legislate It, They Will Come: Using Incentive-Based Legislation to Attract the Commercial Space Industry' (2009) 22 The Air and Space Lawyer 20.

30 Ibid.; Michael Mineiro, 'Chapter 14 – Regulation and Licensing of US Commercial Spaceports' in Joseph N Pelton and Ram S Jakhu (eds), *Space Safety Regulations and Standards* (Butterworth-Heinemann 2010) 172.

31 Viktoria Urban, 'Spaceport in Discussions to Become Green Freeport Subzone' [2022] *SpaceWatch.Global.*

32 Gerhard and Reutzel (n 2) 282.

including protecting people and property on and around the spaceport; protecting the environment; coordination with air traffic control; maritime agencies; occupational health; and protection of national security.[33] States also impose distinct requirements depending on the type of launch (i.e., horizontal or vertical) and narrate any preconditions the operator must meet.

Spaceport operators must usually engage with several regulators to obtain a licence, because their operation extends across a broad range of domestically regulated sectors. While it is beyond the scope of this chapter to discuss all of these, this section addresses some commonalities.

22.2.1.1 Assessment of environmental effect and permits

Spaceflight activities present a dilemma for states because of their environmental impact. Downstream activities are often used for earth observation and communication to assist in our understanding of, and combatting, climate change. However, commercial spaceflight, launching from national spaceports, has an international impact on the Earth's climate.[34] Spaceports are the gatekeepers to outer space (another environment). This presents an opportunity to encourage responsible and sustainable use by launchers through "soft" guidance about sustainability.[35]

The UK tries to balance the harm caused with the social, economic, and environmental objectives.[36] The regulator must not grant a licence unless the applicant has submitted an assessment of the environmental effects (AEE).[37] In Italy, the operator is obliged to notify the regulator immediately of, *inter alia*, events that may endanger the environment within and around the spaceport.[38] US operators find themselves at a potential commercial disadvantage because of inflexibility by the regulator as far as permits for single sites within the same spaceport, or for the same vehicle with the same impact on multiple sites are concerned. Repeat assessments on existing permitted sites is costly and time-consuming.

22.2.1.2 Local (regional) planning agency application

An AEE is akin to the final dossier of environmental information that accompanies a licence application to the regulator.[39] The assessment of the spaceport's impact on the environment begins at the planning permission stage, with a comprehensive environmental impact assessment (EIA) that acts as the underlying methodology for the subsequent licence application.[40] While there is some harmonisation, it is understood that the EIA won't determine the outcome of a licence application based on the AEE.

33 Ibid. 284–285.

34 Nancy Riordan, 'UK Spaceports and Launch Services: An Overview of the Assessment of Environmental Effects and Environmental Impact Assessment' in Annette Froehlich (ed), *Spaceports in Europe*, vol 34 (Springer International Publishing 2021) 89.

35 'Guidelines for the Long-Term Sustainability of Outer Space Activities' (COPUOS 2019) A/74/20, Annex II.

36 Riordan (n 34) 89.

37 Ibid.

38 Maura Zara, 'Spaceport: The Bridge Between Aviation Law and Space Law. The Grottaglie Sample' in Annette Froehlich (ed), *Spaceports in Europe*, vol 34 (Springer International Publishing 2021) 124.

39 Riordan (n 34) 93.

40 Ibid.

Operators should be alert to the cost and delay that can be caused when *prima facie* reasonable planning objections are made by the public or other regulatory bodies.[41] In Scotland, planning permission for a spaceport was challenged by an adjacent landowner in the courts over environmental concerns. Ultimately, the court determined that the challenge was not well founded, but the case led to delay, commercial uncertainty, and significant additional expense.[42]

22.2.1.3 Public consultation

Effective public communication can lead to the local community supporting the spaceport's development and is fundamental to the project demonstrating that the proposed activity can be undertaken in harmony with the environment. The "Consultation on criteria to determine the location of a UK spaceport" neither gathered local communities' nor stakeholders' preferences[43] and one spaceport subsequently received 223 objections from 229 public comments.[44]

Even when the public is supportive, it is not always perpetual. In 2015, officials in Camden County, Georgia pitched a commercial spaceport. Environmental concerns expressed about the proposal to launch rockets along a protected seashore were deemed to have been addressed by the Federal Aviation Authority (FAA) including measures to minimise risks in its EIA.[45]

Promotional materials heralded the project as "Georgia's gateway to commercial space", with the county's administrator referring to their efforts to create a "Silicon Marsh".[46] Yet, seven years later, having spent nearly 20% of its annual budget on the initiative, Camden County finally has a licence but not a single part of the spaceport has been built.[47] This should be a salient lesson to communities, regulators, investors, and other stakeholders of a spaceport project – the economic case must be sound. Across the US, 14 spaceports have been licensed but more than half of them have yet to host a single launch.[48]

22.2.1.4 Light pollution

Public uproar over light pollution in space is not a new phenomenon. In 1993, a US corporation proposed to orbit a one-mile-wide display satellite at an altitude of 180 miles that would be "legible to the naked eye". Public opposition lead the US to prohibit licensees from launching payloads to be used for "obtrusive space advertising". As a result, advertising in outer space has been limited to corporate sponsorship logos and product placement.[49]

Pollution in outer space is to the fore once again with a challenge being made to the US Federal Communications Commission's (FCC) decision to authorise the deployment of 2,800 satellites without requiring an EIA, most notably of the (alleged) light and radio frequency pollution being reflected or emitted. The FCC allegedly took a "narrow, terrestrial-focussed view of the 'human

41 Frankie Adkins, 'The Battle over space emissions in Cornwall', Aljazeera.com (23 October 2022) ; Jonathan Amos, 'Shetland Spaceport Gains Planning Approval' *BBC News* (28 February 2022).

42 'Petition of Wildland Limited for Judicial Review' [2021] CSOH 87.

43 Riordan (n 34) 85.

44 Comhairle nan Eilean Siar, 'Spaceport1 Planning Application'. (June 2019) 19/00311/PPD.

45 Denise Chow, 'Failure to Launch', NBCnews.com (2 September 2022).

46 Ibid.

47 Ibid.

48 Ibid.

49 Mineiro (n 30) 168.

environment'", determining an EIA was not required.[50] The disruption light pollution causes to the practice of astronomy by indigenous peoples – integral to their way of life – is also being studied.[51]

This has prompted spaceport operators to review their role and responsibilities as space transportation providers. While a US court case, public awareness of these matters compels spaceport and launch vehicle operators to align themselves with a fast-evolving area of soft regulation,[52] to demonstrate not only compliance, but also to take responsibility for future launch activity, and reduce any negative impact. From a compliance standpoint, this increases complexity, not just demonstration of NetZero compliance but also being aware of the possible extra-terrestrial application of national environmental laws.

22.2.2 Spaceflight regulation

22.2.2.1 Range control and safety

Range control and safety are possibly two of the most contentious issues when considering the steps leading to launch. These are quite possibly the defining elements, and the way societies dictate that operators should relate to these two items, determine the volume and detail of regulations in place to regulate the spaceflight activity.

"Safety" is far more widely applied and understood than "range". Attempts to place finite measurement on safety, to determine what is safe, are most successful in controlled regimes or environments. That is, in controlled environments where human activity is limited or nil, the risk to life is minimal, suggesting that this environment is "safe". Such logic leans towards the activity of launch being undertaken in a controlled environment or regime (range) where risks can be managed to a degree that could be called safe. However, the current trend in spaceflight is seeing a greater ubiquity of commercial projects. The civil status of spaceports and locations calls on regulators to be seen to ensure a greater requirement to determine what is safe.

The UK adopted a health and safety inspired approach, using the basic risk determination model as the fundamental rule to evaluate an acceptable level of risk by reducing all risks to "As Low As Reasonably Practicable" (ALARP),[53] which is also applied in Australia.[54] This means that operators must demonstrate that they have identified all reasonable and relevant risks that need to be mitigated, what the investment or "sacrifice" is required to minimise that risk, and compare the two. The guidance iterates that "these steps should be proportionate to the nature of the hazard, the extent of the risk and the control measures to be adopted".[55]

Thus, the applicant must prove that the measures deployed to manage the risk are optimal, and that any further cost or resource investment would not proportionately reduce the level of risk. This approach allows for inexperience of both regulator and applicant, which as the UK argues

50 *Amicus Curiae Brief in Support of Viasat, Inc v FCC* US Court of Appeals, District of Columbia Circuit USCA Case #21-1123 10.

51 Ciara Finnegan, 'Indigenous Interests in Outer Space: Addressing the Conflict of Increasing Satellite Numbers with Indigenous Astronomy Practices' (2022) 11 Laws 26.

52 N.B. on 3 November 2022, a reorganisation of the FCC was announced to meet the needs of the growing satellite industry, promote long-term technical capacity at the FCC, and navigate 21st century global communications policy – 'Chairwoman Rosenworcel Proposes Space Bureau' (3 November 2022).

53 'Assessing ALARP and Acceptable Risk' (UK Civil Aviation Authority 2021) CAP 2220.

54 Pozza and Dennerley (n 15) 69.

55 'Assessing ALARP and Acceptable Risk' (n 53) 6.

will enable this activity to be undertaken for the first time within its proposed regulatory framework.

The US's definition of "Range" specifically identifies the actor as the military in designated areas of land, sea or airspace, with specific procedures prescribed by the FAA.[56] Such a concept of "Range" is perceived by the sector – particularly in the US – as cumbersome, outdated, and the most restrictive aspect of compliance for launch vehicle operators. This may be why the UK did not insist upon including military actors when legislating, perhaps reflecting the lack of clarity over what role the Ministry of Defence would play in spaceflight,[57] and a clear aspiration that commercial companies would be able to undertake these activities without much intervention from government.[58] Within the concept of Range Control services, the UK does not overtly stipulate the necessary geographic limitation of the range, but it does have a necessary connection to "infrastructure relating to ground control, transport, power".

Regulating to enable spaceflight to take place, while the means of control or management of Range, and indeed the fundamental understanding of what Range is being determined in a NewSpace context, is a complicated task. This became apparent during the industry consultation for the UK's then proposed regulations. Industry pointed to relevant solutions for range control that would disrupt the existing limited understanding of range and range control services represented mostly by military contractors. These included the provision for airborne monitoring systems, or even space-based capability, dispensing with the need for ground-based assets, and thus making the creation of range more flexible and agile, adapting to where the vehicle launched from. Solutions such as NASA's own Tracking and Data Relay Satellite form the basis of a space-based solution, which have now been further elaborated by commercial legal entities.

In the UK and Australia, the ALARP principle acts as the basis from which innovative solutions can arise. Implementing any innovative or disruptive changes could necessitate a complete review of the existing framework.

22.2.2.2 Licensing spaceflight

Safety remains the foremost issue for all aspects of spaceflight, whether approval and licensing of the spaceport; the launch and accompanying payloads (including review); and orbital operator licences. Each operation is subject to a specific national regulatory requirement of certification and approval, involving various regulators.[59] Beside their national statutory provisions, launching states have catalogued the technical requirements to be demonstrated when applying for a licence. The US, with the most annual launches,[60] has the most accessible and widely known agencies and licensing provisions, as does France[61] and now the UK.[62] It is not possible to do justice to the provisions applicable to spaceflight licensing in the other major launch jurisdictions, notably

56 10 USC § 101(e)(1).

57 'Defence Space Strategy: Operationalising the Space Domain' (Ministry of Defence 2022).

58 UK Space Industry Act 2018 s 5.

59 'Guidance on Duties for All Licensees under The Space Industry Act 2018' (UK Civil Aviation Authority 2021) CAP 2214.

60 Global Orbital Rocket Launch Statistics, RocketLaunch.Live (2022).

61 LOI n° 2008-518 du 3 juin 2008 relative aux opérations spatiales (1) (FSOA) 2008 (2008-518).

62 UK Space Industry Act 2018.

China, Russia, and India.[63] Kourou continues to provide core government launch services. Recent developments, however, exposed the need for uninterrupted and independent access to space. The French Space Agency, CNES, recently concluded an agreement with a newer European micro-launcher company for launch from 2024.[64]

Different national spaceflight regulations have common denominators in their requirements, with their own distinct terminology. Firstly, the various government agencies assuming authority over the approval process range from civil aviation, to environment, telecommunications (radio communication for orbital operations under ITU R-REGS), and not least, the ongoing oversight of regional authorities. In the US, the Office of Space Transportation (AST), newly re-organised within the FAA, and no longer part of Department of Defence, is responsible for all commercial spaceflight.[65] The Civil Aviation Authority (CAA) is the UK regulator.[66] In France, authorisation is divided between the licensing authority (Ministry for Higher Education and Research) and CNES.[67] There are no specific provisions for manned spaceflight, as this is deemed to fall under the agreement with NASA as regards collaboration on the ISS.[68] The national statutes empower the respective agencies to inspect, authorise (licence), interrupt and cease all flight operations in specific circumstances, and include powers to investigate accidents. Breach of the statutory provisions and licence conditions leads to penalties and can lead to licence termination.[69] The provisions reflect the relevance of safety considering these ultra-hazardous activities. Non-compliance is a formal public or criminal law offence.[70] The nationality of natural and legal persons imposes another supervisory licensing requirement at national level, by virtue of international obligations on the state and particularly where the activity takes place from a foreign spaceport.[71] Controlling interests of companies are, therefore, also subject to scrutiny in the context of licensing.

Details of operator licence requirements are contained in secondary legislation, largely technical, including detailed issues such as responsibility for command and communication.[72] The UK, for example, provides guidance about how to apply for a licence.[73] The authorisation process has various stages, the first being fulfilling conditions of financial eligibility as vehicle and orbital operator, and insurance provision.[74] Thereafter, the licence types and conditions depend on the

63 See the chapters by Olga Volynskaya (Russia), Yun Zhao (China), and Ranjana Kaul (India) in this volume for further details.

64 ISAR Aerospace, Munich is a new space microlauncher, established in 2018 and fully privately funded.

65 14 CFR Part 420 1; 14 CFR Part 450.

66 UK Space Industry Act 2018, s 2; The Space Industry Regulations 2021, Part 2, para. 3.

67 'Authorisation for a French Launch Operator', in Philippe Clerc, *Space law in the European context: national architecture, legislation and policy in France* (Eleven International Publishing 2018) pp.196–199.

68 Ibid. p. 183.

69 The Space Industry Regulations 2021.

70 This extends to failure to have a radio communications license for satellite operators, see the case of the US Swarmbees satellites, refused a US licence by FCC in 2018 but subsequently launched without FCC authorisation out of India. Here, the FCC issued a so-called Enforcement Advisory, a notice reminding of the duties to be licensed by the state of nationality of the company or individual in question; 'Guidance On Obtaining Licenses For Small Satellites' (Federal Communications Commission 2015) 28 FCC Rcd 2555 (3).

71 This arises by virtue of jurisdiction over nationals under international law, as well as Art. VI, OTS formulation of "appropriate state".

72 E.g. U.S. Commercial Space Launch Competitiveness Act, 51 USC 10101 2015; The Space Industry Regulations 2021; 14 CFR Part 450.

73 'Regulator's Licensing Rules' (UK Civil Aviation Authority 2021) CAP 2221.

74 E.g. UK Space Industry Act 2018, s 42; 14 CFR Part 420.

specific operation. This covers the full chain of operational activities, from operator licence, which covers launch operator, return operator, or orbital operator licence.[75]

Applications are formal administrative acts and subject to procedural rules, including time limits for responses to communications. The US, France, and the UK all provide for some form of review or appeal in the event a refusal.

22.3 Transition in technology: small launchers and business growth in expanding LEO markets

The space sector is currently undergoing a major industry transition, often described as "NewSpace" or "Space 4.0", and promising radical technological innovation, especially through cheapening hardware and miniaturisation, wider access to satellite data, and sectoral growth in previously peripheral geographies.[76]

New spaceports are springing up across the world with the list constantly in flux.[77] The European Space Agency's christening of the *Centre Spatial Guyanais* as "Europe's Spaceport" will soon sound anachronistic,[78] particularly because of the potential for new spaceports to turn the continent into a global launch hub.[79] Equally, senior orbital management of Andoya Space, Norway and the chief operating officer of the UK's dedicated space business accelerator, have emphasised customers' desire for more dedicated launches, as opposed to "piggybacking as a slave to a larger payload"; a quicker path to launch and reach orbit; and "agility of access".[80] This is to satisfy the demand for launch services, access to space over the next decade, and to ensure there is sufficient capacity to meet it.[81]

Different types of rockets serve different orbital markets and require different types of spaceports: some require large scale steel structures while others only need a small pad of concrete.[82] Likewise, different types of satellites require different types of rockets: larger satellites are launched differently from a group of satellites that will form a cluster, each of which can be individually replaced or reconfigured to expand the cluster's lifecycle while in orbit.[83] Indeed, the concept of a mobile spaceport has been propagated by nascent launch firms that are developing the "spaceport in a box" – a mobile launch system that can be packed into shipping containers and transported worldwide.[84]

What these different spaceports and operators have in common is that they need to be regulated by the state from where they operate,[85] because of the ultimate international responsibility the

75 The Space Industry Regulations 2021.

76 Matjaz Vidmar, 'New Space and Innovation Policy: Scotland's Emerging "Space Glen"' (2020) 8 New Space 31, 2.

77 Thomas G Roberts, 'Spaceports of the World' (*CIS Aerospace Security*).

78 European Space Agency, 'Europe's Spaceport'; Nelson (n 25) 1.

79 Jeffrey Hill, Podcaster, 'Can Europe's Newest Spaceports Turn the Continent into a Global Launch Hub? – Via Satellite'.

80 Ibid.

81 Ibid.

82 Seedhouse (n 4).

83 E.g. 'OneWeb Is a Global Communications Network Powered by a Constellation of 648 Low Earth Orbit (LEO) Satellites', available online at *OneWeb*.

84 Ben Spencer, '"Spaceport in a Box" to Launch UK's First Rocket from Home Turf' *The Sunday Times* (21 August 2022) 10, discussing Skyrora's concept.

85 Art. VI, OST.

treaties impose upon the state.[86] Launching states are liable in perpetuity and a state becomes a launching state if, *inter alia*, the launch is from its facility,[87] namely the spaceport.[88]

22.3.1 Competition on price market and geo-political considerations

To have meaningful access to space, and to meet the burgeoning demand for launch services, it is claimed that the world needs more spaceports.[89] But transporting a payload far from the place of manufacture adds to the overall cost of the launch. While that may appear advantageous for some smaller launchers and the operators of the spaceports who hope to attract them to use their facilities, there are advantages to economies of scale. Adolescent company entrants to the launch market will not necessarily be able to compete at cost-price level with larger incumbents such as the US launcher, SpaceX.[90]

Despite this, the understanding is that newer launch companies will offer a bespoke service that will deliver the payload to a specific orbit and altitude.[91] This will allow smaller launchers to compete commercially with larger operators.

As events in Ukraine demonstrate, commercial operators should consider geo-political factors, as well as cost, when selecting a spaceport. At the time of writing, launching from Russia, or even engaging with Russian-owned organisations, is unlikely to be an option for many commercial operators because of sanctions imposed by the West.[92]

The consequences of the changing political situation for those companies that had already chosen to launch from the Russian-controlled Baikonur Cosmodrome, Kazakhstan are already being felt. The Ukrainian conflict resulted in an effective *force majeure* situation, requiring satellite operators to terminate their Soyuz launch contract, and make alternative arrangements in third countries.[93] This led to a serious financial impact for one operator, which could not repatriate or access its satellites already at Baikonur, leading to an impairment charge of $229.2 million in its annual report and accounts.[94]

22.3.2 Brief comment on selected spaceport locations and markets they serve

22.3.2.1 New Mexico, US

Self-proclaimed as the "world's first purpose built commercial spaceport", Spaceport America, New Mexico is still categorised as a suborbital range. Boasting an arrangement with Sierra Space to be the landing site for the "Dream Catcher", Spaceport America covers a small area but can support larger launches due to its partnership with White Sands Military base.

86 Art. I and II, LIAB.

87 OST: the definition of "launching state" under Art. VII is the same under all three relevant treaties: OST, LIAB and REG.

88 Howard (n 1) 14.

89 Hill (n 79).

90 Spencer (n 84), quoting Skyrora's COO: "it is going to be very difficult to compete with SpaceX on cost because SpaceX's huge rockets can take around 100 satellites on a single launch".

91 Ibid.: "a kind of Uber service [providing] a specific orbit to the specific altitude, with very specific parameters for how the vehicle is delivered".

92 Hill (n 79).

93 'OneWeb Holdings Limited, Annual Report & Accounts' (2022) 13.

94 Ibid. 21.

Spaceport America is looking to position itself as a partner for both horizontal and vertical launch but has full permission for suborbital flight only at present. Any vehicle looking to launch over an amateur level requires FAA clearance. Within the context of its current operations, Spaceport America plays host to the Spaceport America Cup, in collaboration with the experimental sounding rocket association.

22.3.2.2 Portugal (Azores)

In March 2018, Portugal adopted its "Space Strategy 2030" and in 2019 enacted national legislation, but specifically decided not to include the licensing of spaceports beyond requirements such as certifying the operator's technical competence and financial capacity.[95] This is believed to be because the spaceport will be in the autonomous Azores region, which required a specific regional legislative decree.[96]

The geographical limitations are such that the Azores can only fit a suborbital range, so the regulator and regional government initiated the Atlantic International Satellite Launch Programme to provide a spaceport for small-to-medium launch vehicles.

22.3.2.3 Italy

The Italian government is promoting the sustainable development of suborbital commercial flight and autonomous access to space.[97] Airport Marcello Arlotta of Grottaglie, Taranto, was officially designated the first Italian spaceport on 9 May 2018.[98] In October 2020, the Italian Civil Aviation Authority (ENAC) approved the domestic regulation enabling Grottaglie to operate as a spaceport.[99]

Italy clearly considers there is a strong relationship, and continuity, between air and space law, with the regulation referring to domestic, as well as European, air navigation, and safety legislation.[100] They are to be understood with the necessary modifications made – e.g., "aircraft" is to be understood as "suborbital vehicle".[101]

Given that launch will be from an airport and the close connection to air law, the regulation defines "spaceport" as a facility that allows for "horizontal launch/take-off, re-entry/landing and ground/flight operation of a single-stage or multistage reusable sub-orbital vehicle".[102] Therefore, spaceports offering vertical launch are presently prohibited, but may be permitted in the future.[103]

Although no such limitation is provided for in the regulations, the explanatory notes confirm that the Italian government views commercial suborbital flights as operating around 100km above the Earth.[104]

95 Regulation on access to and exercise of space activities 2019 (Regulation no 697/2019).

96 Kerkonian (n 18) 282; Approving the Regulation for licensing space activities in the Azores Autonomous Region 2020 (Regional Regulatory Decree No 6/2020/A).

97 'Explanatory Report – Regulation on Construction and Operations of Spaceports' 1.

98 Ibid.; Occasionally erroneously referred to as the first country in Europe to enable a spaceport on its territory – e.g. Zara (n 38) 120. However, French Guyana is as much a part of France as Paris.

99 Regulation on Construction and Operations of Spaceports 2020; Zara (n 38) 119.

100 Zara (n 38) 122.

101 Definitions, Regulation on Construction and Operations of Spaceports 1.

102 Ibid. 7.

103 Ibid. 2.

104 'Explanatory Report – Regulation on Construction and Operations of Spaceports' (n 97) 1.

22.3.2.4 Brazil

Brazilian space activities have been developed in accordance with a comprehensive and ambitious space programme, first envisaged in the early 1960s.[105] The Alcantara Launching Centre ("Centro de Lançamento de Alcântara", CLA) was established in 1983 as the prime launch facility in Brazil.[106] Strategically located near the Equator, more than two hundred sounding rockets have been launched from CLA. Owing to its location, rockets benefit from the Earth's rotation to achieve greater speed, allowing for greater fuel efficiency and increased payload capacity.[107] Space objects can be launched from CLA into equatorial and polar orbits, without passing over inhabited regions, because of its proximity to the Atlantic Ocean.[108]

Despite its impressive pedigree, Brazil awaits the enactment of a comprehensive national space law,[109] with the current framework composed of myriad regulations and edicts forming a fragmented body of rules that are under constant review.[110]

Of particular relevance to the commercial launch market is the 2019 Technology Safeguards Agreement (TSA) executed by Brazil and the US.[111] It establishes the safeguards for US-licensed technology to support the launch of satellites or space launch vehicles from the CLA and opens new opportunities for commercial space cooperation and investment.[112] For Brazil, it allows the CLA to enter the global commercial launching market, and for the US it is a prerequisite to permit launches of US-licensed satellites or launch vehicles from CLA.[113]

In 2021, the Brazilian Space Agency (AEB) updated rules regarding licensing and authorisation for commercial launching activities from Brazil.[114] The AEB also introduced the Brazilian Space Regulation, which is composed of the procedures and requirements applicable to a private operator's licence for space launches from Brazilian territory; and the procedures for authorising launch.[115] Authorisation is required for launching activities carried out from Brazilian territory and all licensees must have third party liability insurance, the level of which is determined by the AEB.[116] Therefore, commercial operators must be aware that while Brazil acknowledges that the state is ultimately liable in terms of international space law, this liability is passed on, and is not to be transferred to public bodies by means of any private agreements, leaving the management of risk to applicable insurance requirements.[117]

Following the execution of the TSA and the recent regulatory framework for licensing launches, several foreign space companies announced that they will conduct launches from CLA, including

105 Olavo de O Bittencourt Neto and Daniel Freire e Almeida, 'Space Security in Brazil' in Kai-Uwe Schrogl (ed), *Handbook of Space Security* (Springer International Publishing 2020) 657.

106 Olavo de O Bittencourt, 'Brazilian Space Law: Launching Regulation' (University of Luxembourg, May 2022).

107 Bittencourt Neto and Freire e Almeida (n 105) 658.

108 Ibid.

109 Ibid. 660.

110 Bittencourt (n 106).

111 Taciana Moury, 'Brazil and US Sign Agreement on Use of Alcântara Launch Center' (*Diálogo Américas*, 17 January 2020); U.S. Mission, Brazil, 'Fact Sheet: U.S.-Brazil Space Cooperation' (*U.S. Embassy & Consulates in Brazil*, 19 August 2021).

112 US Mission, Brazil (n 111).

113 Ibid.

114 Bittencourt (n 106).

115 Ibid.

116 Ibid.

117 Ibid.

one which announced its intention to construct a new launch area and expand existing infrastructure as part of an agreement with Brazil's Air Force.[118]

22.3.2.5 Canada

Successive Canadian governments showed foresight in recognising the need to develop a domestic space industry, and in recognising that there is a distinction between science and technology: the former is "open" and easily shared within the scientific community regardless of national borders; and the latter is "closed" and comprehensible only through experience and experimentation.[119] Despite this, Canada has not historically had an indigenous launch capability, consistently postponing the establishment of a significant long-term launch program and preferring to rely on allies for its launch needs.[120] Canada's 1974 space policy provided, *inter alia*, that its space industry was to rely on foreign launch providers.[121] While there was one attempt at constructing a spaceport in Canada in the 1990s, it proved unsuccessful.[122]

In August 2022, however, Maritime Launch Services (MLS) received approval to begin construction of Spaceport Nova Scotia within the framework of an Environmental Assessment approved in 2019.[123] MLS is targeting the small-to-medium class launch market and has gathered 14 letters of intent from different providers, including satellite operators with large constellations.[124] MLS will use the Ukrainian Cyclone-4M rocket for now, but given that several domestic companies are in the development stage of building rockets, MLS may pivot to them in the longer-term.[125] Spaceport Nova Scotia may also support non-traditional launches from balloons that lift rockets into the stratosphere from where the rocket will ignite and deliver small-sat payloads into orbit.[126]

Canada has not enacted a comprehensive national space law that applies to all space activities, instead, enacting five specific laws that apply to single space activities; therefore, any space activity that does not fall within the scope of these laws cannot be regulated or licensed.[127] Canada's current regulatory framework does not address spaceports.[128] It prohibits any significant rocket

118 Ryan Duffy, 'Innospace Will Conduct Suborbital Launch from Brazil's Alcântara Spaceport' (*Payload*, 5 May 2022) <https://payloadspace.com/innospace-will-conduct-suborbital-launch-from-brazils-alcantara-spaceport/>; Marc Boucher, 'C6 Launch Systems Subsidiary to Build New Launch Area at Brazil's Alcantara Space Center' (*SpaceQ*, 30 August 2022) <https://spaceq.ca/c6-launch-systems-subsidiary-to-build-new-launch-area-at-brazils-alcantara-space-center/>; TBR Newsroom, 'Virgin Orbit Gets License for Space Launches in Brazil' (*The Brazilian Report*, 28 June 2022).

119 Kerkonian (n 18) 90.

120 Ibid. 544.

121 Andrew B Godefroy, *The Canadian Space Program: From Black Brant to the International Space Station* (1st ed. 2017, Springer International Publishing : Imprint: Springer 2017) 119.

122 Kerkonian (n 18) 28–29.

123 Nathan Barker and Chris Gebhardt, 'Maritime Launch Services Breaks Ground on Canada's First Orbital Launch Site' (*NASASpaceFlight.com*, 9 September 2022).

124 Ibid.

125 C6 Launch Systems Inc., 'C6 Launch' (*C6 Launch Systems Inc.*) <http://www.c6launch.com/>; Reaction Dynamics, 'Reaction Dynamics' <https://www.reactiondynamics.space/> accessed 24 October 2022.

126 Marc Boucher, 'SpaceRyde Releases Video of First Test Flight' (*SpaceQ*, 8 July 2019).

127 Kerkonian (n 18) 128 and 323.

128 Ibid. 550–551.

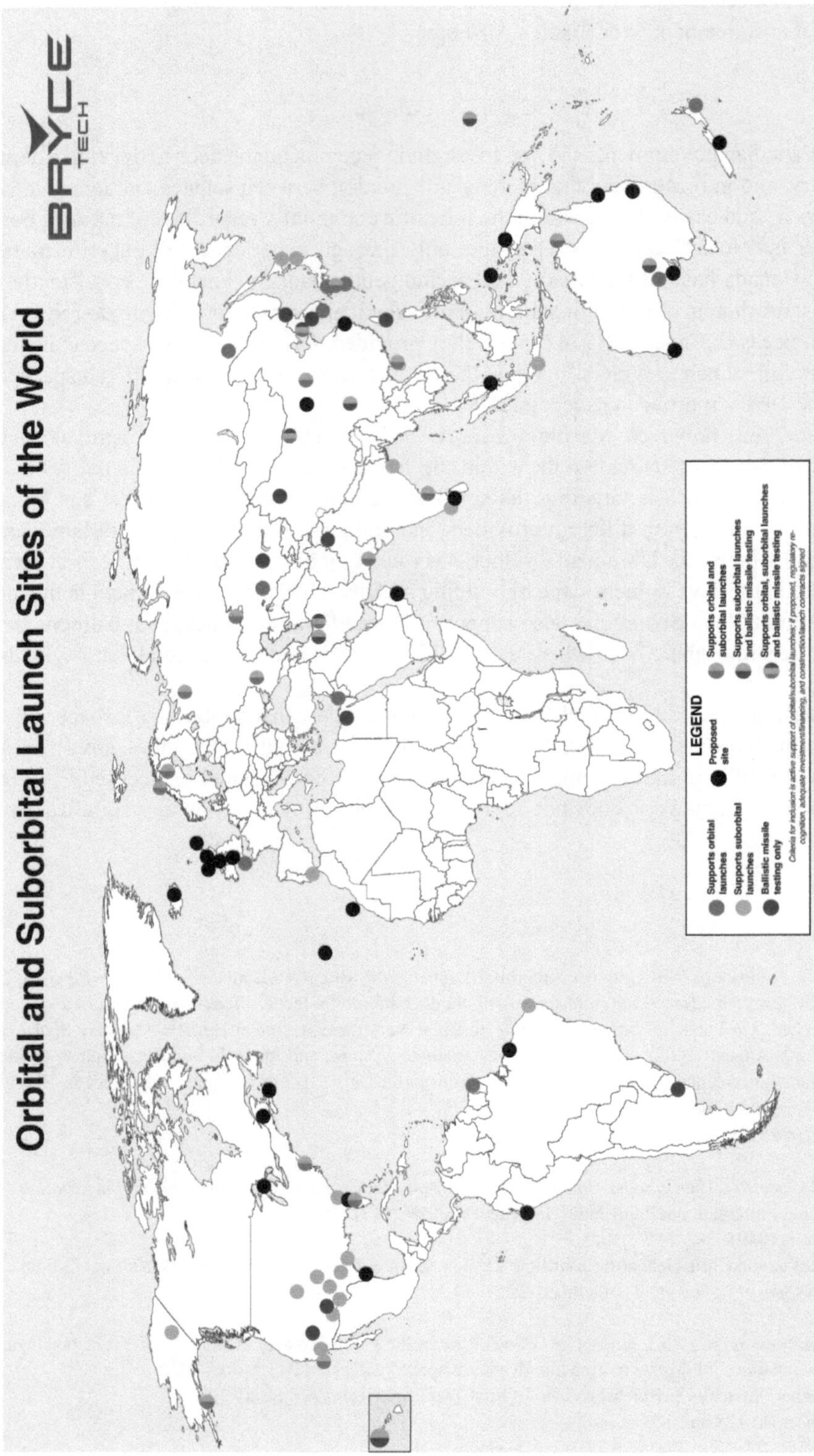

Figure 22.1 Orbital and suborbital sites of the world as of 3 January 2022. Courtesy of BryceTech https://bryctech.com/reports/.

activity without a licence and no licensing procedure exists.[129] Therefore, while MLS has signed letters of intent with customers, it will not be able to host launch activities under the current regulatory framework.[130]

22.3.2.6 United Kingdom

In July 2018, the UK announced that out of 26 proposals, three entities were being funded to effect vertical launch – Lockheed Martin, Orbex, and Space Hub Sutherland; and three horizontal projects would also receive funding – Spaceports Cornwall, Prestwick, and Snowdonia. At the same time, there was a commitment to the conclusion of a TSA between the US and UK enabling US Space Launch vehicles to operate from UK launch sites – realised in June 2020.[131]

The other two vertical spaceport projects that did not receive funding, but that are at a similar stage of development to Space Hub Sutherland, are the (rebranded) SaxaVord Spaceport, and Spaceport1.

By 2021, the UK Space Agency had produced a brochure marketing seven national spaceports.[132] All three of the vertical spaceport projects are geographically remote. This brochure was produced before the regulations entered into force that provide the licensing procedure for all actors seeking to launch from the UK.[133] However, at the time of writing, the regulations have not been evaluated or been put to test in the context of any actual launch activity.

The competition for the provision of vertical launch services is already in an active phase. This includes a significant airspace change process which each spaceport is required to conclude prior to having airspace designated for space-related activities and provisioning. In November 2022, Orbex signed a 50-year lease to develop and operate Space Hub Sutherland, making it the first European launcher to also manage a dedicated spaceport.[134]

Spaceport Cornwall saw its first orbital launch in early 2023, unfortunately ending in failure.[135] Following this, the CAA is investigating the robustness of the UK regulations As for the remaining three horizontal projects, all are seeking to pursue other forms of horizontal launch. Prestwick has an agreement with Astraius for an airborne launch solution, launching from 2024. The other two spaceports are pursuing diverse opportunities, including the opportunity for human spaceflight or space tourism.

129 Ibid. 546; 1336–1337: 'The upper limit…is 40,960 newton-seconds of thrust, significantly less than the thrust needed by even a smallsat launcher'.

130 Ibid. 323; e.g. 'Maritime Launch and Skyrora Partner to Launch Skyrora XL from Spaceport Nova Scotia' (*Maritime Launch*).

131 UK-US Technology Safeguards Agreement (TSA) for Spaceflight Activities 2020.

132 UK Government, 'Brochure: A Guide to the UK's Commercial Spaceports'.

133 The Space Industry Regulations 2021.

134 Tereza Pultarova, 'Rocket Startup Orbex Signs Lease to Build UK's First Vertical Spaceport' (*Space.com*, 1 November 2022).

135 'Spaceport Cornwall Receives First-Ever UK Spaceport Licence' *Civil Aviation Authority* (16 November 2022). Jonathan Amos, 'UK space launch: Historic Cornwall launch ends in failure', *BBC News* (10 January 2023).

22.4 Space tourism

22.4.1 Current status

Out of the 263 individuals that have visited the International Space Station (ISS), 13 are considered space flight participants (SFP), the flights all having had a commercial background.[136] The first space tourist to the ISS was the American entrepreneur Dennis Tito, in 2001 and the first female, Anousheh Ansari, CEO of the X Prize Foundation, flew in 2006.[137] These flights were based, *inter alia*, on a deal between US-based Space Adventures Ltd. and Russia, launched to the ISS on Soyuz rockets, for reportedly US$20 million per trip.[138] The requirement that these SFP undergo extensive training prior to travelling to the ISS was a challenge to the notion of "space tourists".[139] In April 2022, the Axiom Mission 1 launched from Kennedy Space Center to the ISS, the first privately funded and operated crewed mission to the ISS.[140] The crew of SpaceX's Crew Dragon consisted of one trained astronaut hired by Axiom, and three passengers who were trained and allocated positions as pilot and mission specialists.[141]

In the field of suborbital space tourism, the first all-private flights to the height of 90km and 107km in July 2021 were, respectively, Virgin Galactic's VSS Unity,[142] and Blue Origin's New Shepard,[143] each carrying four passengers. The tickets for Virgin Galactic's flight were reportedly around US$250,000, with a horizontal launch from Spaceport America, New Mexico. A ticket for a seat on Blue Origin's New Shepard, which launched vertically from Corn Ranch, Texas, was reportedly bought in an auction for US$28 million.[144] With Inspiration4, SpaceX operated the first orbital spaceflight with only private citizens on behalf of an American entrepreneur, Jared Isaacman, in September 2021.[145]

22.4.2 Terminology and definitions

The framework within which space tourists participate in manned spaceflight, and the differences between professional astronauts and private space travellers, call for further reflection. The foregoing overview of millennial tourist flights serves to demonstrate that the space tourist, as currently known, does not formally correspond with the format and legacy of human spaceflight, as envisaged in the space treaties and lived by astronauts in their early voyages of space exploration as

136 Mark Garcia, 'Visitors to the Station by Country' (*NASA*, 10 May 2016).

137 Heather Maher, 'Reaching Out To The Stars' *Radio Free Europe/Radio Liberty* (15 September 2006).

138 BBC, 'Profile: Tito the Spaceman' (28 April 2001).

139 European Space Agency, '"I Am NOT a Tourist"'.

140 'Ax-1 Crew Returns Safely to Earth, Successfully Completing First All-Private Astronaut Mission to ISS' (*Axiom Space*) 1.

141 Milton 'Skip' Smith, 'Op-Ed | Representing the Private Astronaut Is a New Step for Human Spaceflight – and for Space Lawyers' [2021] *SpaceNews*; the astronaut was Michael López-Alegría, the other crew members were Larry Connor of the United States, Mark Pathy of Canada, and Eytan Stibbe of Israel.

142 Tariq Malik, 'Virgin Galactic's SpaceShipTwo Unity 22 Launch with Richard Branson', Space.com (11 July 2011).

143 Eric Berger, 'Blue Origin Successfully Completes Its First Human Launch [Updated]' (*Ars Technica*, 20 July 2021).

144 Meredith Deliso, '$28M Is Winning Bid for Seat Aboard Blue Origin's 1st Human Space Flight' (*ABC News*).

145 'Ax-1 Crew Returns Safely to Earth, Successfully Completing First All-Private Astronaut Mission to ISS' (n 140).

"*envoys of mankind*".[146] Indeed, Dennis Tito was called a space tourist by the media, the Russians called him a "guest cosmonaut", and the Americans called him an "amateur astronaut".[147]

The term *astronaut* is used without an accompanying definition in international space law.[148] The Moon Agreement, ratified by 18 states, provides that "any person on the Moon shall be regarded as an astronaut" within the meaning of Art. V OST and as part of "personnel of spacecraft" within Art. 1 of the Rescue and Return Agreement (ARRA).[149] It can be assumed that the term "personnel of spacecraft" is to be interpreted and applied in the context of the treaty provisions for traditional astronauts, involved in space exploration and discovery and bearing an international flag of recognition. The term "personnel", in contrast, points to a pre-existing professional relationship.[150] This definition excludes those considered informally as "space tourists", where travelling to space is an experience with a commercial operator.

The status of space travellers, whether SFP, personnel, or tourists, has profound significance as regards passenger – and operator – rights and duties. It is directly relevant in the context of commercial space tourism because of the special benefits and protection accorded under international space law to astronauts. Were space tourists to be considered astronauts, states would have to "render … all possible assistance in the event of accident, distress, or emergency landing on the territory of another State Party or on the high seas".[151] ARRA applies these same duties to rescue and assist to the "personnel of spacecraft".[152] There is also authority in support of the position that only those exercising particular operational functions can be seen as personnel.[153] SFP outside of these categories would not enjoy these special rights under international space treaty law. This is particularly relevant for the future of human space travel, as well as in the context of suborbital flights, duties of care, management, insurance, and more. Dennis Tito was rated as cargo on his inaugural space flight – i.e., as a satellite for insurance purposes.[154]

Space tourism was defined early on as "any commercial activity offering customers the direct or indirect experience with space travel", and as a service offered by commercial operators.[155] The activities of space tourists have specific characteristics, namely, the length of stay (in orbit) and the heights flown.[156] As a generic term, "*space tourism*" includes "visits" to the ISS, as well as suborbital or even parabolic flights, for the passengers seeking the experience of shorter periods of weightlessness.[157] It may also become a concept applicable to point-to-point orbital transporta-

146 Agreement on the Rescue of Astronauts, the Return of Astronauts and the Return of Objects Launched into Outer Space, entry into force on 3 December 1968, 672 UNTS 1218 1968.

147 Ruwantissa Abeyratne, *Regulation of Commercial Space Transport: The Astrocizing of ICAO* (1st ed. 2015, Springer International Publishing: Imprint: Springer 2015) 54.

148 ARRA; OST.

149 Status of International Agreements relating to activities in outer space as at 1 January 2022 (A/AC105/C2/2022/CRP10); Art. 10, Agreement Governing the Activities of States on the Moon and Other Celestial Bodies, entry into force on 11 July 1984, 1363 UNTS 3 1979.

150 Colin McIntosh (ed), 'Personnel' Cambridge Dictionary, "people who are employed in a company, organisation or one of the armed forces".

151 Art. V, OST.

152 Art. I, ARRA.

153 Stephan Hobe, 'Legal Aspects of Space Tourism' (2007) 86 Nebraska Law Review 21, 456.

154 Darcy Beamer-Downie, 'Some Legal and Insurance Issues for Discussion', *Symposium on the Regulation of Sub-Orbital Flights in the European Context* (2010).

155 Stephan Hobe and Jurgen Cloppenberg, 'Towards a New Aerospace Convention? Selected Legal Issues of "Space Tourism"' [2004] Proceedings of the 47th Colloquium on the Law of Outer Space 377.

156 Ibid.

157 Hobe (n 153) 439.

tion, should the predicted developments in air travel technologies and altitudes enable faster, post supersonic forms of travel, where fast flight and not weightlessness is the core feature.[158]

The more recent growth towards serving commercial space markets sees some spacefaring states currently preparing for a return to the Moon, with the Gateway planned as successor platform habitat to the ISS.[159] The notion of travelling to outer space must be looked at from two distinct perspectives: the dynamic development of aerospace transport, where point-to-point travel stands to become reality in the not-so-distant future; and the continued fascination and interest of humankind in moving off-Earth and possibly even visiting other planets.[160]

22.4.3 Spaceflight participants under the ISS Intergovernmental Agreement

The four space agencies participating in the ISS reached agreement on the principles regarding ISS crewmembers in 2002.[161] While neither binding nor directly applicable to other forms of space tourism, the agreement defines and distinguishes between professional astronauts and SFP on board the ISS. According to the agreement, a professional astronaut is an individual "who has completed the official selection and has been qualified as such at the space agency of one of the ISS partners and is employed on the staff of the crew office of that agency". SFP are defined as "individuals (e.g. commercial, scientific and other programs; crewmembers of non-partner space agencies, engineers, scientists, teachers, journalists, filmmakers or tourists) sponsored by one or more partners. Normally, this is a temporary assignment that is covered under a short-term contract".[162] This definition requires the sponsorship of a partner, but also mentions tourists as possible SFP.

22.4.4 Demarcation, liability regimes, and informed consent

Suborbital spaceflights take place at an altitude higher than 100km, above the *von Kármán* line. Although not formally defined in international space law, the *von Kármán* line was proposed in the 1960s to try to define the boundary between air space and outer space.[163] Suborbital spaceflights achieve three to six minutes of microgravity before the vehicle falls back into the Earth's atmosphere. Technical concepts for suborbital flights include horizontal launches, sometimes from an aircraft, or vertical launches.

Whether air or space law applies, depends on where the activities take place; in some situations, both regimes could be applicable, independently. The legal regimes are mutually exclusive. This can already be seen in the principle of sovereignty, relevant for airspace, whereas the freedom

158 Ankit Kumar Padhy, 'Legal Conundrums of Space Tourism' (2021) 184 Acta Astronautica 269, 269.

159 'Everyone's Going to the Moon' [2022] *The Economist* 58; The Artemis Accords: Principles of Cooperation in the Civil Exploration and use of the Moon, Mars, Comets, and Asteroids for Peaceful Purposes 2020.

160 On life off-Earth, see the final chapter in this volume, Adriana Marais, 'Mission Off-World: A Technology-Enabled Vision for Reimagining Our Society on Earth and Beyond'.

161 Space Station Agreement Between the United States of America and Other Governments 1998; ISS Multilateral Crew Operations Panel, 'Principles Regarding Processes and Criteria for Selection, Assignment, Training and Certification of ISS (Expedition and Visiting) Crewmembers'.

162 ISS Multilateral Crew Operations Panel (n 161).

163 Fédération Aéronautique Internationale, '100km Altitude Boundary for Astronautics' (21 June 2004); to define the boundaries between regimes, the UK chose 'craft capable of operating above the stratosphere' as the delineation between air and space: 'Guidance on Applications to Launch a Large Rocket under the Air Navigation Order' (UK Civil Aviation Authority 2021) CAP 2194, paragraphs 1.6 - 1.7.

of use principle is enshrined in space law.[164] Suborbital spaceflight does not take place in orbit, indicating that air law is the relevant regime. The absence of a legal definition as to where the distinction is drawn between the end of airspace and the start of outer space, means the issue is somewhat fluid; the physical boundaries are reported as approximate.[165] This has led various states to provide for a formal demarcation between airspace and outer space in their national statutes; establishing legal certainty.[166] Even if a strict distinction between air and space law were desirable, the reality of technological development brings its own complications that combine against providing for a definitive demarcation between the systems. Virgin Galactic's Spaceship 2, for example, is a hybrid version, comprising both aircraft and spacecraft. In practice, the aircraft delivers the aerospace vehicle to a certain height in airspace before the spacecraft is ignited and launched into space. The question surrounding space tourism activities, suborbital or orbital, is which legal regime should apply; indeed, whether air law should apply to the airspace part of the journey, while space law at some point thereafter. It is moot whether the situation would differ for horizontal, as opposed to vertical launches.

National commercial operations ultimately see operators apply contractual solutions to provide some clarification as to how the risks are to be allocated. The US was the forerunner of the statutory introduction of an "informed consent" disclaimer for the private SFP in the CLSA.[167] "Informed consent" is the waiver writ large to prevent commercial operators from massive damage claims for losses arising out of personal injury to the SFP. Under the CSLA, the operator is required to inform "any individual serving as crew in writing [...] that the United States Government has not certified the launch vehicle as safe for carrying crew or space flight participants" to be able to launch or re-enter crew.[168] This requirement is also found in the Human Spaceflight Requirements, under which a SFP has to be informed by the operator of the risks of launch and re-entry before agreeing to fly.[169] The information must include the safety record of all launch or re-entry vehicles by both the US Government and private sector vehicles.[170] The UK is now relying on the equivalent statutory form. The operator must not allow an individual to take part in spaceflight activities unless the consent to accept risks involved in the activities has been signified in writing (consent form) and specified criteria concerning training, qualifications, and medical fitness are fulfilled.[171]

It seems impracticable to have two regimes apply to the same activity. One option is to follow the functional goal of the activity and apply space law to space tourism.[172] Under international and national space law there are still open issues regarding (commercial) space tourism. These relate to authorisation, scope and any incumbent liabilities. The registration (including authorisation) of space tourism activities depends on their scope. Under air law, the aircraft must be registered

164 Padhy (n 158) 270.

165 Fédération Aéronautique Internationale (n 163).

166 E.g. The Danish Outer Space Act 2016, s 4(4) defines space as an altitude of 100km above sea level.

167 Federal Aviation Administration, 'Guidance on Informing Crew and Space Flight Participants of Risk, Version 1.1' (2017); National and Commercial Space Programs, 51 U.S. Code §50905(b)(4)(B); 14 CFR §460.45.

168 Federal Aviation Administration (n 167); National and Commercial Space Programs, 51 U.S. Code §50905(b)(4)(B); 14 CFR §460.45.

169 14 CFR §460.45, (a)(b).

170 Ibid., (c).

171 UK Space Industry Act 2018, c.5, ss 17–18.

172 See Thomas Gangale, *How High the Sky? The Definition and Delimitation of Outer Space and Territorial Airspace in International Law* (Brill Nijhoff 2018) chapters 11–14.

according to the nationality of the state of registry.[173] Under space law, the launching state must register the object in its domestic, as well as in the UN register.[174] However, space law calls for registration when the flight is to Earth's orbit or beyond, therefore not necessarily applying to suborbital spaceflights.[175] In addition to safety standards applicable to the design and construction of space tourism vehicles, a suitable system should be in place dealing with incumbent liabilities. A space tourist or passenger who suffers damage could claim for compensation under national, but not international law.[176] The private, commercial nature of space tourism activities leads to the development of contractual exclusions and cross waivers of liability that could be invoked.[177] Challenges to standard waiver agreements are not inconceivable, if space tourism is to continue. Both for future space tourism activities and the parallel development of an insurance market, a new international system of liability connecting private operators conducting those activities, also addressing third party liability, should be put in place.[178]

Although the experience gained through the private astronaut Axiom Crew flight stands as a prototype model that could lend itself to other such operations, those on board were delivering to the ISS, and already to be seen as "personnel" if not SFP.

22.4.5 Future space traveller markets?

In 2016, it was claimed that there had not been any credible market studies that specifically addressed the use of spaceports in support of point-to-point transportation.[179] The authors are unaware of any having been carried out since then. Although there may be some hype around the idea of flying from London to Sydney in three hours, just because point-to-point transport may be technically feasible does not mean that it will happen. A significant issue to overcome is the inconvenience factor.[180] As discussed *supra*, spaceports tend to be geographically remote. If individuals are wealthy enough to afford a parabolic point-to-point flight, they will likely be wealthy enough to pay for a private jet – a form of transport that does not entail lengthy training, security checks, specific schedules and that can land at a geographically convenient location, i.e. a conventional airport.[181]

Whether the market ever becomes accessible to those beyond the very affluent, is moot. The global space tourism market was valued at around $598 million in 2021 with an expected annual growth rate of 37% from 2022 to 2030,[182] justifying the first projects for commercial, habitable structures in outer space that were previously marketed.[183] Targeting potential alternative living scenarios apart from Earth and their affordability, depend on the lowering of entry barriers and

173 Art. 17, Convention on International Civil Aviation, 'Chicago Convention', entry into force 4 April 1947, 15 UNTS 295 1947.

174 Art. II, Convention on Registration of Objects Launched into Outer Space, entered into force on 15 September 1976.

175 Ibid.

176 Padhy (n 158) 271.

177 E.g. 'Space Business and Insurance Issues in the United States', in Andrea Harrington, *Space Insurance and the Law* (Edward Elgar Publishing 2021).

178 Padhy (n 158) 271–272.

179 Seedhouse (n 4) 99.

180 Ibid. 100.

181 Ibid.

182 ResearchFDI, 'We Have Liftoff: Space Tourism and the Space Economy' (*ResearchFDI*, 26 July 2022).

183 'Orbital Assembly Corporation'.

costs, growth of competition, and the general evolvement of the sector in the coming decades.[184] The Gateway programme under the Artemis Accords will deliver the first tangible indicators. That programme is supplying and provisioning the return to the Moon, and preparation for trips beyond to Mars. The Artemis Accords capture the provisions of existing treaties, emphasising the need for transparency, sustainability, international collaboration, and adherence to the rule of law in all space operations. They are a nonbinding policies to be implemented through bilateral agreements between NASA and those (currently twenty-one) participating agencies.[185] The technical side of what is planned for these missions will enhance the level to which space tourism can be extended to encompass mission off earth and habitation.[186]

22.5 Conclusion and future developments

Currently, there is no overarching authority administrating the regulation of spaceports. Instead, governance falls within states' domestic law,[187] but it has been persuasively argued that one is needed.[188] Yet, whether states will agree international coordination of spaceports in a similar vein to that of international aviation, through legally binding treaties or otherwise, remains to be seen.[189]

Regulatory challenges have existed for some time and continue to do so. Launching from the high seas, for example, will have impacts not only environmentally, but from a regulatory perspective. Since national regulations often reflect the international space law treaties, domestic application of the treaties will not always help to bridge any regulatory gap.[190] For example, the launches from a sea platform demonstrate that the applicability of the treaties to sea launches has been uncertain for some time.[191] These regulatory gaps are neither fully addressed by the international law of the sea nor international space law, and states need to adopt transparent and workable regulations for sea launches.[192]

The space sector remains a high-risk industry in terms of safety, operations, and investment. If states are serious about promoting launch capabilities from domestic spaceports to support the growth of their own national industry, then it is vital that they recognise there is value in supporting new space services prior to the maturation of a commercial market for them.[193] As the Canadian government recognised in 1981:

> "the leading-edge nature of space technology means that applications are innovative, sometimes offering the capability to provide new services in advance of the recognition of a commercial market for these services".[194]

184 Marais (n 160).

185 Fabio Tronchetti and Hao Liu, 'Australia's Signing of the Artemis Accords: A Positive Development or a Controversial Choice?' (2021) 75 Australian Journal of International Affairs 243, 244.

186 See Marais (n 160).

187 Howard (n 1) 1.

188 Abeyratne (n 147).

189 Gerhard and Reutzel (n 2) 285.

190 Ibid.

191 Ibid.

192 Alla Pozdnakova, 'Oceans as Spaceports: State Jurisdiction and Responsibility for Space Launch Projects at Sea' (2020) 26 Journal of International Maritime Law 267, 289.

193 Kerkonian (n 18) 101.

194 *The Canadian Space Program Plan for 1981/82-1983/84* (Minister of State, Science and Technology Canada 1981) 3.

As a result, sometimes the front-end costs of a healthy space programme need to be borne by the government and ought to be seen as an investment not a financial burden.[195] Getting a domestic spaceport initiative off the ground is no different.

195 Ibid. 3–4; Kerkonian (n 18) 101.

D

Space mining

23

NATIONAL AND INTERNATIONAL NORMS TOWARDS THE GOVERNANCE OF COMMERCIAL SPACE RESOURCE ACTIVITY

Tanja Masson-Zwaan and Mark J. Sundahl

23.1 Introduction

The emergence of the space resources industry has been one of the great innovations of the current wave of private space activity. Current governmental programmes, most notably the US Artemis Program with its Chinese and Russian counterpart, the programme to establish the International Lunar Research Station, will require the use of local natural resources on the Moon to support a permanent human presence. Transporting all the required resources to sustain life and construct facilities from Earth is economically infeasible, and so it will be necessary to utilise local resources, primarily water ice (a source of water, oxygen, and hydrogen fuel), as well as regolith as a construction material. Private industry is already mobilising to fill this need by offering to locate, extract, process, and deliver the needed product. Due to NASA's policy of purchasing private services, when possible, a market for space resources will soon spring into existence with NASA as the largest (but hopefully not the only) customer.

With the business case closing and the industry emerging, attention has turned to legal questions, such as how resource extraction interfaces with existing space law. There is also the question of whether additional laws or regulations are needed to regulate the new industry. This chapter begins in Section 23.2 with an analysis of existing international law related to space resource activity followed in Section 23.3 by a description of current national legislation regarding the industry that has been enacted by a growing number of states, led by the United States and Luxembourg. Section 23.4 examines the actions of the United Nations Committee on the Peaceful Uses of Outer Space (UNCOPUOS) as it takes up the issue of space resources with the creation of a new working group. Section 23.5 then turns to the effect of NASA's Artemis Accords on the development of international law. In Section 23.6, the legal reform initiatives undertaken by non-governmental organisations (NGOs) are described, such as the Building Blocks developed by the

DOI: 10.4324/9781003268475-33

Hague International Space Resource Governance Working Group. The chapter concludes with final observations about the road that lies ahead for the governance of space resource activity.[1]

23.2 Existing international law regarding space resource activity

To determine the legality of commercial space resource activities under international norms, the 1967 Outer Space Treaty[2] and the 1979 Moon Agreement[3] are the most important of the five United Nations treaties on outer space, but there are also instruments of soft law that are relevant in the context of space resource activities.

23.2.1 Hard law

The Outer Space Treaty provides in Art. I that the exploration and use of the Moon and other celestial bodies "shall be carried out for the benefit and in the interests of all countries, irrespective of their degree of economic or scientific development", and shall be "the province of all mankind". Whenever the treaty refers to the Moon, this includes all other celestial bodies, although it does not define that term. States Parties are free to explore and use outer space, as long as the activities are in line with the provisions of the treaty. This means for instance that celestial bodies must be used "exclusively for peaceful purposes" (Art. IV), and that activities by private entities must be authorised and supervised by the "appropriate State" (Art. VI). Furthermore, launching states are internationally liable for damage caused by their objects to another State Party (Art. VII), and states have jurisdiction and control over their registered space objects and personnel thereof (Art. VIII).

Article II forbids the "appropriation" of outer space, including the moon and other celestial bodies but does not specify whether extracting and commercialising their resources is in line with this provision.[4] It is unclear whether resources are covered by the non-appropriation principle.[5]

Article IX provides that states must explore outer space in a manner that avoids its harmful contamination or adverse changes in the environment of the Earth resulting from the introduction of extra-terrestrial matter. States Parties are also obliged to enter into consultations when harmful interference with the peaceful activities of another State Party may result from its activities. This

1 This article is based, in part, on a previously published article which examined the laws applicable to lunar activity in general. T. Masson-Zwaan and M. Sundahl, *The Lunar Legal Landscape: Challenges and Opportunities*, Air and Space Law 46, no. 1 (2021), pp. 29–56.

2 Treaty on Principles Governing the Activities of States in the Exploration and Use of Outer Space, including the Moon and Other Celestial Bodies (referred to as Outer Space Treaty or OST), opened for signature on 27 Jan. 1967, entered into force on 10 Oct. 1967, UNTS, vol. 610, No. 8843. The OST currently has 112 States Parties.

3 Agreement Governing the Activities of States on the Moon and Other Celestial Bodies (referred to as Moon Agreement or MA), opened for signature on 18 December 1979, entered into force on 11 July 1984, UNTS vol. 1363, No. 23002.

4 See IISL Position Paper on Space Mining (20 Dec. 2015, s. II.1.b), https://iisl.space/iisl-position-paper-on-space-resource-mining; see also T. Masson-Zwaan & M. Hofmann, Introduction to Space Law, ch. 7, (Kluwer 2019) and T. Masson-Zwaan & N. Palkovitz, Regulation of space resource rights: Meeting the needs of States and private parties, 35 QIL, Zoom-in 5-18 (2017).

5 See for various views on this matter, e.g., F. Lyall & P. Larsen, *Space Law: A Treatise* 163–188 (2nd. ed., Routledge 2018); F. Tronchetti, *Legal Aspects of Space Resource Utilization*, in *Handbook of Space Law* 769–813 (F. von der Dunk & F. Tronchetti eds, Elgar 2015); R. Jakhu & S. Freeland, *Article II*, in *Cologne Commentary on Space Law*, Vol. I, 44–63 (S. Hobe, B. Schmidt-Tedd, K.U. Schrogl eds, Heymanns 2009); M. Hofmann & F. Bergamasco, *Mining in Outer Space: Legal Aspects*, Eur. Y. B. Int'l Econ L. 313-336 (2018); G. Oduntan, *Who owns space? US asteroid-mining act is dangerous and potentially illegal*, The Conversation (25 Nov. 2015). See also 23.4 below, giving an overview of discussions in UNCOPUOS on this matter.

obligation to consult in the event of potential harmful interference, particularly when coupled with the Art. IX duty to exercise "due regard to the corresponding interests of all other States Parties to the Treaty", which should include the interests of their respective private operators, serves as the cornerstone of legal protection for those engaged in resource extraction activities by deterring other parties from interfering with existing activity. For those states that accept the legality of properly authorised and supervised private mining missions, this protection can then be supplemented by domestic laws that can prevent interference through license conditions when authorising mining missions, as discussed in greater detail below.

The Outer Space Treaty, which codifies these principles, has been ratified by over 110 countries including all the major space powers and emerging spacefaring nations alike. No state has ever withdrawn, nor has any amendment been proposed.

The Moon Agreement reiterates and reinforces many of the principles of the Outer Space Treaty, but also differs, e.g., by providing in Art. 11(1) that celestial bodies and their natural resources are "the common heritage of mankind" (CHM). This principle finds its expression in particular in Art. 11(5), which mandates States Parties "to establish an international regime, including appropriate procedures, to govern the exploitation of the natural resources of the moon as such exploitation is about to become feasible".[6] Article 11(3) further specifies that until such international regime is established "neither the surface nor the subsurface of the moon, nor any part thereof or natural resources in place, shall become property of any State, international intergovernmental or non-governmental organization, national organization or non-governmental entity or of any natural person". Although the States Parties to the Moon Agreement have thus committed to reach an international agreement to govern commercial mining activities, it is unclear whether this means that no commercial activity can take place before such an agreement is in place. A Joint Statement was issued by the States Parties in 2008, proclaiming that the "common heritage of mankind" principle as embodied in the treaty does not constitute an obstacle to space mining initiatives.[7] The first steps toward an international understanding of these issues now has begun in the Legal Subcommittee of the UN COPUOS under the auspices of the new Working Group on Legal Aspects of Space Resource Activities.[8]

The Moon Agreement so far has just 18 States Parties, which include none of the major space powers, although it was adopted by consensus in the UNCOPUOS. Much remains to be done to agree on the details of a multilateral framework to govern space resource activities. However, the creation of a Working Group on the Legal Aspects of Space Resource Activity by the UNCOPUOS Legal Subcommittee has been a strong step forward in the process, as described in greater detail below.

6 The proper meaning of the CHM concept must be determined in the context of its use and for the purpose of the future applicable regulatory regime. States Parties must make good faith efforts to reach an agreement, but the result of such negotiations could be a rejection of the concept or giving it a new scope, as has also happened in the field of the law of the sea. See *Cologne Commentary on Space Law* vol. II, 395 (S. Hobe, B. Schmidt-Tedd & K.U. Schrogl, eds, Heymanns 2013).

7 Joint Statement on the benefits of adherence to the Agreement Governing the Activities of States on the Moon and Other Celestial Bodies of 1979 by States Parties to that Agreement, UN Doc. A/AC.105/C.2/2008/CRP.11 (2 Apr. 2008).

8 See 23.4. below.

23.2.2 Soft law

There are also "soft law" instruments that directly or indirectly apply to activity on the Moon (as well as applying to activity on other celestial bodies and/or in space in general, as the case may be). Although these instruments are not legally binding, they may evolve into customary international law with sufficient state practice and *opinio juris*, and thus become binding on states.[9] Their adoption by consensus by all UN Member States further reinforces their validity. Moreover, national space legislation often includes an obligation for private entities to comply with such instruments, making them binding under national law. The most pertinent soft law instruments are examined in the following sections.

23.2.2.1 The Space Benefits Declaration

The 1996 Declaration on International Cooperation in the Exploration and Use of Outer Space for the Benefit and in the Interests of All States, taking into Particular Account the Needs of Developing Countries[10] (Space Benefits Declaration) is based on Art. I of the Outer Space Treaty. Besides reflecting the concerns of the developing countries and stressing the need to take their interests into special account in para. 1, it further provides that "States are free to determine all aspects of their participation in international cooperation in the exploration and use of outer space on an equitable and mutually acceptable basis" (para. 2), and that "contractual terms in such cooperative ventures" should be "fair and reasonable" and in "full compliance with the legitimate rights and interests of the parties concerned"; intellectual property rights are explicitly mentioned in this context. This resolution is mentioned here as it is the only international space law instrument that refers explicitly to contracts and IPR, though its focus lies on the need to ensure equitable sharing of the benefits of lunar exploration and space resource utilisation.

23.2.2.2 The UN Space Debris Mitigation Guidelines

The Inter-Agency Debris Coordination Committee (IADC), which includes space agencies from around the world, adopted debris mitigation guidelines in 2002.[11] These served as the basis for the discussions in UNCOPUOS, leading in 2007 to the UN General Assembly endorsement of the Space Debris Mitigation Guidelines previously adopted by UNCOPUOS.[12]

The UN guidelines use the same definition of space debris as the IADC guidelines: "space debris is defined as all man-made objects, including fragments and elements thereof, in Earth orbit or re-entering the atmosphere, that are non-functional". This seems to exclude debris on celestial bodies. It may be advisable to address the characteristics of debris located on a celestial body, as opposed to in orbit; this waste will not eventually re-enter the earth's atmosphere, meaning that debris disposal methods will have to be reassessed.[13]

9 See Statute of the International Court of Justice, Art. 38.

10 UN Res. 51/122 (13 Dec. 1996).

11 IADC Space Debris Mitigation Guidelines, IADC-02-01 rev. 3, June 2021.

12 UN Res. 62/217, International cooperation in the peaceful uses of outer space, UN Doc. A/RES/62/217 (22 Dec. 2007).

13 See in this context A. Salmeri *e.a.*, *Waste Management for Lunar Resources Activities: Towards a Circular Lunar Economy*, 71st International Astronautical Congress, IAC-20-D4.5.16 (2020).

23.2.2.3 The UN Guidelines for the Long-Term Sustainability of Space Activities

After nearly ten years of debate marked by political tensions, UNCOPUOS adopted twenty-one guidelines on the *Long-term Sustainability of Space Activities* (LTSSA) in 2019.[14] The long-term sustainability of outer space activities is defined as:

> the ability to maintain the conduct of space activities indefinitely into the future in a manner that realizes the objectives of equitable access to the benefits of the exploration and use of outer space for peaceful purposes, in order to meet the needs of the present generations while preserving the outer space environment for future generations.[15]

The 21 non-binding, voluntary guidelines address the policy, regulatory, operational, safety, scientific, technical, international cooperation, and capacity-building aspects of space activities. They do not explicitly mention celestial bodies but these will of course have to be taken into account when developing a system for the governance of space resource activities. The LTSSA guidelines will be periodically reviewed, revised, or added to, so that they may continue to ensure the long-term sustainability of outer space activities.[16] In 2019, a new working group on LTS was established under the Scientific and Technical Subcommittee of UNCOPUOS.[17]

23.3 Current national legislation and policies regarding space resource activity

Article VI of the Outer Space Treaty requires the "authorization and continuing supervision" of any private space activity by the "appropriate State".[18] This obligation is tied to the imputation of responsibility to a state for the actions of its nationals as well as liability for any damage caused by the space objects of a private entity that were launched by, from, or for such state. The duty to authorise and supervise private activity is typically fulfilled by the enactment of domestic statutes and accompanying regulations that institute a licensing mechanism for authorising and overseeing private space missions.[19] Since private space resource missions are a new development, the enactment of domestic laws addressing space resource activity has only recently begun and only in a small number of states that have (or hope to have) such missions undertaken by their nationals. This list of states at the time of writing includes the United States, Luxembourg, Japan, and the United Arab Emirates. The laws enacted by each of these will be described in the following sections. Before delving into these domestic laws on space resources, it should be kept in mind that space resource missions will be subject to the existing legal framework of the responsible state that regulates the launching of space objects, payload review, radio spectrum utilisation, or other

14 Report of the Committee on the Peaceful Uses of Outer Space, UN Doc. A/74/20, para 163 and Annex II (3 July 2019). For an overview of the work of UNCOPUOS on the Long-Term Sustainability of Space Activities. Consensus could not be reached on seven remaining guidelines, they can be found in UN Doc. A/AC.105/2018/CRP.21 (27 June 2018).

15 Report of the Committee on the Peaceful Uses of Outer Space, UN Doc. A/74/20, Annex II.I.5 (3 July 2019).

16 See P. Martinez, UN COPUOS Guidelines for the Long-Term Sustainability of Outer Space Activities: Early Implementation Experiences and Next Steps in COPUOS, 71st International Astronautical Congress, IAC-20-E.3.4.1 (2020).

17 *See* UN Doc. A/74/20, para. 165.

18 The text of Art. VI reads: "The activities of non-governmental entities in outer space, including the Moon and other celestial bodies, shall require authorization and continuing supervision by the appropriate State Party to the Treaty."

19 OST Arts. VI and VII; Liability Convention Arts. II, III, *et passim*.

activities that are part and parcel of a space resource mission. An analysis of these more general domestic laws is beyond the scope of this chapter which will focus only on those regulations that apply specifically to space resource activity.

The domestic laws relating to space resource activity have in common the shared purposes of (1) clarifying the legality of resource extraction on celestial bodies, (2) establishing the right of ownership by operators over any resources extracted, and (3) collecting information from operators regarding their plans to engage in resource extraction. There are many other issues related to space mining that will demand additional legislative attention in due course (such as priority rights, environmental protection, technical standards, and the fair allocation of limited resources), but these three issues relating to legality, ownership, and information-sharing are of primary importance to enable the new industry to take root. Without assurance that a company's plan to mine resources on the Moon, Mars, or an asteroid is legal and that the company will have the right to own and sell the minerals it extracts, investors would have good reason to withhold funding. Moreover, the sharing of information regarding a mining mission is necessary to allow states to properly oversee the activity as required by Art. VI of the OST, as well as to assist other space actors in avoiding the possibility of harmful interference with the mining operation, which would trigger mandatory consultations under Art. IX of the OST.[20]

23.3.1 United States

The United States was the first country to enact legislation specifically addressing space resource activities. As part of Title IV of the 2015 US Commercial Space Launch Competitiveness Act (CSLCA) Congress enacted a new s 51303 of the United States Code, which both implicitly recognises the legality of space resource activity under international law and allows for operators to assert ownership rights over extracted "space resources", which are defined as "abiotic resource[s] *in situ* in outer space … includ[ing] water and minerals":[21]

A United States citizen engaged in commercial recovery of an asteroid resource or a space resource under this chapter shall be entitled to any asteroid resource[22] or space resource obtained, including to possess, own, transport, use, and sell the asteroid resource or space resource obtained in accordance with applicable law, including the international obligations of the United States.

Although this legislation was a bold and unprecedented step forward, the law has its limitations that may reduce its ability to deliver on its promise to promote and facilitate this new industry. First of all, the law only recognises the right of a "United States citizen" to own space resources, which narrows the reach of the law and leaves uncertainty as to the rights of foreign entities who may come before a US court or administrative agency claiming ownership rights in space resources.[23] An obvious remedy for this shortcoming is for a non-US company to operate through a US

20 Article XI of the OST states that "[i]f a State Party to the Treaty has reason to believe that an activity or experiment planned by it or its nationals in outer space … would cause potentially harmful interference with activities of other States Parties … it shall undertake appropriate international consultations before proceeding with any such activity or experiment". See also *supra.*, s 2.1

21 51 USC §§ 51301 & 51303.

22 For a reason that is unclear from the reading of the statute (and is likely a relic of an earlier draft), Congress makes a distinction between "asteroid resources" and "space resources", the former being defined as "a space resource found on or within a single asteroid." *Id.* §51301.

23 The phrase "United States citizen" is defined as including, in addition to an individual with US citizenship, any company organised in the United States, or a company organised in another country that is controlled by a US company or citizen. *Id.* §50902.

subsidiary, however, this may cause a problem if other states (such as Luxembourg) also limit its protections to companies organised it their jurisdictions. This would seem to force operators to choose between the protections of one jurisdiction over another.

Another shortcoming of the US law is that it provides no clear process or mechanism for resolving one of the primary concerns of space mining pioneers: how will companies be protected from other operators (both domestic or foreign) who interfere with their planned or ongoing mining activity (i.e., "claim jumping")? An earlier draft of the law did address this issue directly by creating a new civil action precisely for the resolution of conflicting claims.[24] Moreover, that earlier version of the law instructed the judge presiding over such an action to issue judgment in favour of the party that was "first in time to conduct the activity" – provided that the activity was "reasonable for the exploration and utilization of [space] resources". In effect, this would have created a "first in time" system of establishing priority rights to space resources.

That said, the wording of this draft bill presented its own problems, including the difficulty of determining what point a company's activity would lock in the company's priority rights. For example, would the remote identification of future mining sites have qualified as an activity that was "reasonable for the exploration and utilization of [space] resources", thus giving the company priority rights to the identified site?[25] Although this approach was ultimately not adopted by Congress, the authors discuss it here because it is an important part of the evolution of the law and still stands as a potential model for future legislation.

Although Congress decided not to create a new cause of action to protect mining claims, Title IV of the CSLCA does instruct the President, through federal licensing agencies, to "promote the right of United States citizens to engage in commercial exploration for and commercial recovery of space resources free from harmful interference, in accordance with the international obligations of the United States and subject to authorization and continuing supervision by the Federal Government".[26]

In short, rather than creating a civil court action, Congress left it to federal agencies to ensure non-interference through its existing licensing processes. One way in which this could be done is by making all licences conditional on the licensee not interfering with the existing space resource activities of former licensees. But will the licensing agency also prohibit the licensee from operating at a site that has been publicly identified as a future mining site by another company (thus allowing companies to, in effect, stake a claim)? If so, how would the agency decide which future sites should be given such protection? Without further regulatory guidance, the agency would have to make an *ad hoc* determination regarding which mining claims deserve protection and which do not. But this leads to an even more fundamental question: which US agency will make these determinations and enforce these conditions?

Congress has not yet given any agency in the US government authority to license space resource activity or, for that matter, any other private activity on the Moon. The likely candidates for receiving such authority are the Federal Aviation Administration Office of Commercial Space Transportation (FAA-AST), which currently issues launch and re-entry licences in addition to licensing spaceports, and the Office of Space Commerce in the Department of Commerce, which

24 Space Resource Exploration and Utilization Act of 2015, H.R. 1508, 114th Congress (2015).

25 It has also been argued that the US missed an opportunity to create a broader solution to the problem of potential disputes over space resources by failing to provide for the mutual recognition of mining authorisations granted to commercial entities by foreign states as had been done for deep seabed mining. See Th. E. Simmons, *The Unfortunate Provincialism of the Space Resources Act*, The Space Review (25 Jan. 2016).

26 51 USC §51302. What type and how much activity would have been needed to trigger this protection was unclear.

currently licenses remote sensing activity, enforces export controls, and oversees space traffic management. Although, practically speaking, it would appear easier to give the FAA such authority as part of the existing launch licensing process, another view has emerged that suggests that the FAA (which is part of the Department of Transportation) is not the appropriate agency because mining is not related to transportation and therefore falls outside the mission of the agency. In the meantime, until a delegation of this authority is made, the *de facto* authority will be the FAA-AST which will have the ability to include protective conditions in launch licences (in consultation with the Department of Commerce).

On 6 April 2020, the White House issued an Executive Order on Encouraging International Support for the Recovery and Use of Space Resources.[27] This was a bold statement that removed any doubt regarding the US position on space resources (and on outer space in general) and was crystallised in the following excerpt: "Outer space is a legally and physically unique domain of human activity, and the United States does not view it as a global commons. Accordingly, it shall be the policy of the United States to encourage international support for the public and private recovery and use of resources in outer space, consistent with applicable law".

In another part of the order, the administration also clarified it stance on the legal effect of the Moon Agreement: "[T]he Secretary of State shall object to any attempt by any other state or international organization to treat the Moon Agreement as reflecting or otherwise expressing customary international law".

Although this Executive Order has no direct legal effect, it did make an impact on the international community and received pushback from expected places, but also from places that are typically supportive of US space policy. The Russian State Space Corporation "Roscosmos" responded with claims of colonialism and warned that "attempts to expropriate outer space and aggressive plans to actually seize territories of other planets hardly set the countries (on course for) fruitful cooperation".[28]

23.3.2 Luxembourg

Two years after Title IV of the CSLCA took force in the United States, Luxembourg enacted the Law of July 20th 2017 on the Exploration and Use of Space Resources in order to provide regulatory clarity to the nascent space mining industry and, by virtue of being the first European state to legislate on the topic of space resources, to establish the Grand Duchy as an industry hub (an aspiration that has begun to materialise in the interceding years).[29]

Like the US law, the core of the Luxembourg legislation is the recognition in Art. 1 that "[s] pace resources are capable of being owned". In contrast to the US law, this ability to own space resources is not limited to citizens.[30] Beyond this recognition of ownership, the Luxembourg law states that "no person can explore or use space resources without holding a written mission authorisation from the minister or ministers in charge of the economy and space activities".[31] In order to apply for an authorisation, the applicant must either incorporate in Luxembourg or take the form of a *société européenne* with a registered office in Luxembourg. This does not prevent foreign com-

27 Executive Order on Encouraging International Support for the Recovery and Use of Space Resources (6 April 2020).

28 Russia Compares Trump's Space Mining Order to Colonialism, Moscow Times (7 April 2020).

29 Law of July 20th 2017 on the Exploration and Use of Space Resources. Although the English version will be quoted in this article, the French version is authoritative.

30 *Id.* Art. 1.

31 *Id.* Art. 2(1).

panies from seeking the protections of Luxembourg law – the entity need only form a subsidiary or open a registered office in Luxembourg.

The remainder of the law sets out the requirements and procedures for acquiring authorisation. An authorization will only be granted if, and is made conditional on, the applicant showing (i) financial means, (ii) robust internal governance and auditing systems, (iii) the requisite skill, knowledge, and experience, and (iv) the "good repute" of its shareholders.[32] Once an authorisation is issued, the law requires that it be worked.[33] The authorisation will be withdrawn if the operator "does not make use" of the authorisation within 36 months of issuance. Likewise, the authorisation will be withdrawn if work ceases for six months or more at any time. The requirements to use the authorisations, along with the requirements of financial means and skill, are critical for ensuring that celestial mines will actually be worked and to avoid a problem analogous to the "paper filing" phenomenon that threatened to prevent the full and efficient use of geosynchronous orbits due to the issuance of orbital slot allocations by the International Telecommunication Union to operators that did not subsequently use the orbits.

Unlike the US law, there is no mention in the Luxembourg law of the need to avoid harmful interference with the activity of other operators. However, the law does provide for the operator's responsibility for damage caused by its activities, in addition to imposing steep fines and even prison time, for conducting space resource activity in contravention of any condition of an authorisation.[34]

As under the US law, the question arises how Luxembourg will protect the interests of companies engaged in space resource activities and, in particular, protect against harmful interference by another operator. Perhaps the Minister will require as a condition of its authorisations that the authorised party not interfere with another party's existing operations on the Moon. Compliance with any such conditions is required under Art. 2 of the law, but whether the Minister uses these conditions as a method of protecting its operators from interfering with one another is yet to be seen.[35] A related question is how *future* mining sites will be protected from being poached by another company. In other words, would the Minister condition authorisation on the licensee not operating in an area to which another company lays claim? It would theoretically be possible for the Minister to attach such conditions to an authorisation, but only if the ministry were aware of such planned operations and if the government felt compelled to protect them.[36]

23.3.3 United Arab Emirates

In 2019, the UAE enacted its Federal Law No. (12) of 2019 on the Regulation of the Space Sector, an omnibus national space law that contains an Art. 18 on "Exploration, Exploitation and Use of Space Resources".[37] Article 18 grants clear authority to the Council of Ministers to regulate space resource activity. More specifically, the law gives the Council the authority to issue permits "for the exploration, exploitation and use of Space Resources, including their acquisition, purchase,

32 *Id.* Arts 7–11.

33 *Id.* Art. 14.

34 *Id.* Art. 16.

35 In the English version of the statute, Art. 2(3) states that an "operator may only carry out [space] activity … in accordance with the conditions of the authorization" *Id.* Art. 2(3).

36 Unlike the US law, the Luxembourg statute makes clear which government agency will have the responsibility, namely, the Ministry of the Economy and the Luxembourg Space Agency. *Id.* Art. 2(1).

37 UAE Federal Law No. (12) of 2019 on the Regulation of the Space Sector.

sale, trade, transportation, storage and any Space Activities aimed at providing logistical services in this regard". The legal effect of this article is perhaps greater than it first appears. Although the article appears to be merely a grant of regulatory authority, it contains within it two critical presuppositions: first, that the extraction of space resources is permissible under the UAE's interpretation of international law and, second, that extracted resources can be privately owned and traded. The UAE law is distinguished by the breadth of its language regarding the type of activity that is to be authorised (and facilitated). In addition to the core business of extracting natural resources, the law recognises that the industry will be comprised of an array of logistical services, such as transportation, storage, and delivery of the processed resources.

23.3.4 Japan

On 23 December 2021, Japan's new Act on Promotion of Business Activities Related to the Exploration and Development of Space Resources entered into force.[38] The Act defines "space resources" as water, minerals, and other natural resources in space and on celestial bodies.[39] Under the Act, a person needs to obtain a permit to conduct space resources extraction activities. As to process, the application for the permit will be sought in connection with the request for a launch permit. In addition to information required to acquire a launch permit, an applicant for a space resource activity permit must provide a business plan to show the feasibility of the planned activity. The activity plan must include the purpose of the proposed space resources activity in addition to the time and duration, location, method, and other details of the activity. As is true under the laws of the United States and Luxembourg, the Space Resources Act provides that the permittee will own the resources extracted in accordance with the permit.[40] Upon the grant of a permit, the name of the applicant and the business plan will be made public.[41] This public notice puts the world (and, most importantly, other operators) on notice regarding the permittee's intent to mine a particular area on the Moon so that interference can be avoided.

As is true under the laws of the UAE and Luxembourg, Japanese law is silent on issues relating to priority rights and protections against harmful interference with space resource activity. That said, the Japanese authorities could conceivably include a prohibition against harmful interference with the activity of others as a condition of a permit.

23.4 Developments in UNCOPUOS

In 2016, shortly after the adoption by the US of Title IV of the Commercial Space Launch Competitiveness Act of 2015, the Legal Subcommittee (LSC) of UNCOPUOS adopted an agenda item titled "General Exchange of views on potential legal models for activities in exploration, exploitation and utilization of space resources". This item was addressed during sessions of the

38 Act on Promotion of Business Activities Related to the Exploration and Development of Space Resources (Act No. 83 of 2021) art. 1, Official Gazette (Japan) (June 23, 2021); see also S. Umeda, *Japan: Space Resources Act Enacted*, Library of Congress (2021). Prior to enacting the Space Resources Act, Japan made changes to their administrative process to accommodate space resource activity. Specifically, in the application form for a licence to operate a satellite (Form 17), the question regarding "the purposes and methods of using the spacecraft" had been changed so that applicants now select from a number of choices, one of which is "Space Science and Exploration (including space resources exploration)".

39 *Id.* Art. 2.

40 *Id.* Art. 5.

41 *Id.* Art. 4.

LSC since 2017, except in 2020, when the session was cancelled due to the COVID-19 pandemic for the first time in the history of COPUOS; for the same reason, the sessions of 2021 and 2022 were arranged in hybrid mode.[42]

Initially, some states were quite critical about commercial space resources utilisation.[43] It was suggested that a broad debate should take place within the Legal Subcommittee as the appropriate forum, involving especially developing countries. There were states which felt that national laws in this field could lead to the development of multiple incompatible national frameworks, which would pose a risk of conflicts among states and potentially impact the sustainability of outer space. Some delegations suggested that all stakeholders, including both government and private actors, should closely cooperate, so that future activities would be developed in a proper and practical manner as well as in accordance with international law, and that it would be appropriate for such discussions to take place in the Legal Subcommittee.

In 2018 and again in 2019, a proposal was made to create a working group with the mandate to develop and propose to the Legal Subcommittee alternative legal solutions capable of providing the legal certainty necessary for acts of exploration, exploitation, and utilisation of outer space resources, but the proposals were not adopted.[44] Gradually the discussion no longer centred so much on the legality of using or owning resources, but focused on its modalities and governance. Principles of sustainable use, avoidance of harmful contamination, and efficiency were brought up as possible elements of such a framework, and the need for appropriate international safety standards as well as for international coordination to avoid competing interests and conflicts.

The LSC hosted eight rounds of "scheduled informal consultations" during its session in May–June 2021, with the aim "to have a broad and inclusive exchange of views on the future deliberations concerning the exploration, exploitation and utilization of space resources, including the possible establishment of a working group under the relevant agenda item, taking into account possible future coordination with the Scientific and Technical Subcommittee, as appropriate".[45] The consultations were informed by a number of working papers, conference room papers, and statements, and it became clear that although there was widespread support for the establishment of a five-year Working Group, views differed on the details and no agreement could be reached on the exact mandate, terms of reference, workplan, and methods of work.[46]

The Working Group held four meetings during the COPUOS session in August–September 2021, and decided on its mandate, terms of reference, and workplan and methods of work.[47] It was

42 See the consecutive reports of the Committee on the Peaceful Uses of Outer Space and of the Legal Subcommittee. For 2017: UN Doc. A/72/20 and UN Doc. A/AC.105/1122, paras. 221-250. For 2018, UN Doc. A/73/20 and UN Doc. A/AC.105/1177, paras. 229–265. For 2019, UN Doc. A/74/20 and UN Doc. A/AC.105/1203, paras. 239–267. For 2021, UN Doc. A/76/20 and UN Doc. A/AC.105/1243, paras. 233-258. For 2022, at the time of writing only the draft report of the Legal Subcommittee was available, see specifically UN Doc. A/AC.105/C.2/L.321/Add.1, paras 14–35.

43 See, e.g., UN Doc. A/AC.105/C.2/2017/CRP.19. Some of the early reactions at UNCOPUOS were summarised by O. Bittencourt Neto & Th. Cheney at the *Symposium on Legal Aspects of Space Resource Utilization* held in Leiden on 17 Apr. 2016.

44 See, e.g., UN Doc. A/AC.105/C.2/L.311, Working paper by Belgium and Greece.

45 As agreed during the 2019 session of the Legal Subcommittee, see UN Doc. A/AC.105/1203, para. 279.

46 See for a good overview of the various views and themes discussed, V. Oosterveld and A. Campbell, *Space Resource Discussions in the UN Committee on the Peaceful Uses of Outer Space*, Opinion Juris, 11 July 2021.

47 See Report of the Committee on the Peaceful Uses of Outer Space, Sixty-fourth session (25 August–3 September 2021), UN Doc. A/76/20, Annex III; see also A. Salmeri, *#SpacewatchGL Interviews: Ambassador Misztal and Professor Freeland on COPUOS Working Group on Space Resources*, SpaceWatchGlobal, 20 Sept. 2021.

agreed that besides legal and governance considerations, technical, economic, political, cultural, scientific, and other factors should also be taken into account.

At the 2022 Legal Subcommittee meeting, the Working Group adopted a new name, "Working Group on Legal Aspects of Space Resource Activities" and held nine meetings to adopt its detailed workplan and methods of work. It agreed to use the intersessional period to collect information from states, including on potential topics and issues to be addressed through one or more dedicated international UN conferences open to governments as well as invited academics and other stakeholders. The chair and vice-chair would prepare a summary of the information received for discussion at the 2023 session of the Legal Subcommittee.[48] The ultimate goal is to adopt, by 2027, a set of "initial recommended principles" for space resource activities for possible adoption by the UN General Assembly as a dedicated resolution or other action.[49]

23.5 The Artemis Accords' effect on space resource activity

The Artemis Accords form the legal foundation for NASA's Artemis Program, an international partnership of space agencies dedicated to returning humans to the Moon by 2025 (according to the most recent projections).[50] The underlying purpose of the Accords is "to increase the safety of operations, reduce uncertainty, and promote the sustainable and beneficial use of space for all humankind".[51] Any party that joins the American effort must sign on to the Accords (although any state's space agency is welcome to sign the Accords even if not participating in the program). At the time of writing, the number of Artemis Accord signatories had risen to 20.[52] Although the mission to the Moon is the primary objective at this point in time, the Accords are also intended to govern future missions on "Mars, comets, and asteroids, including their surfaces and sub-surfaces, as well as in orbit of the Moon or Mars, in the Lagrangian points for the Earth-Moon system, and in transit between these celestial bodies and locations".[53]

The Artemis Accords ensure that, whatever the specific nature of NASA's cooperation with a particular space agency, all Artemis-related activity will comply with the fundamental principles of international law, such as the duty of due regard and the duty to consult in the event of potential harmful interference.[54] All obligations under the Accords will then flow down to any agencies or other parties acting on behalf of the signatories (including any private companies that play a role in the program).[55]

In addition to reinforcing general existing legal principles, s 10 of the Accords addresses space resource activity specifically. The section makes four fundamental points:

48 See Report of the Chair and Vice-Chair of the working group established under the Legal Subcommittee agenda item entitled "General exchange of views on potential legal models for activities in the exploration, exploitation and utilization of space resources", UN Doc. A/AC.105/C.2/2022/SRA/L.1, 5 April 2022.

49 See Co-Chairs' Proposed Five Year Workplan as of 5 April 2022.

50 The text of the Artemis Accords is available online.

51 *Id.* s 1.

52 The 20 signatories of the Artemis Accords are the US, the UK, the UAE, Japan, Italy, Canada, Australia, Luxembourg, later joined by South Korea, New Zealand, Brazil, Ukraine, Israel, Poland, Mexico, Romania, Bahrain, Singapore, Colombia, and France.

53 Artemis Accords s 1.

54 The more detailed terms of NASA's cooperation with particular space agencies will be captured in separate bilateral agreements, which will incorporate the terms of the Accords by reference *Id.* s 2.1.

55 *Id.* s 2.1(d).

- Resource extraction promises to be beneficial to humankind;
- The extraction of space resources does not violate the ban on national appropriation under Art. II of the Outer Space Treaty;
- States will inform the UN of their space resource extraction activities as required under the OST; and
- States will engage in multilateral initiatives on the legal aspects of resource extraction, including any UN initiatives.

Most importantly, this section of the Accords confirms the legality of space resource activity under the Outer Space Treaty and confirms that such activity can be commercial in nature. Section 10's encouragement of information-sharing is also critical to the sustainability of space resource activity since an operator can only benefit from the protection provided by the OST Art. IX duty to operate with due regard if the operator shares information about the nature and location of its activities. In the absence of this information, other operators will not be able to exercise due regard or avoid harmful interference with the space resource activity.

Perhaps the most significant innovation of the Artemis Accords is the concept of "safety zones" that signatories are encouraged to declare around their operations. The definition of "safety zones" in s 11 of the Accords clarifies that these zones have no legal effect, but are merely informational in nature (to enable others to exercise due regard and avoid harmful interference).[56] Safety zones will benefit commercial mining operations on the Moon by putting other actors on notice regarding planned or existing activity so that special caution can be taken to maintain safety and avoid interference when operating within or near a safety zone. A variety of factors might influence the size of a safety zone. For example, the size of a safety zone could be significantly influenced by the nature of the activity. The safety zone for a mining operation that utilised explosives would require a relatively large zone, in contrast to an operation that merely scrapes ice off the surface of the Moon. The Accords provide the following principles to determine the appropriate dimensions of a safety zone:[57]

- "A safety zone should be the area in which nominal operations of a relevant activity or an anomalous event could reasonably cause harmful interference."
- "The size and scope of the safety zone … should reflect the nature of the operations being conducted and the environment that such operations are conducted in …"
- "The size and scope of the safety zone should be determined in a reasonable manner leveraging commonly accepted scientific and engineering principles."

Finally, the Accords promote taking a multilateral approach in the future "to further develop international practices, criteria, and rules applicable to the definition and determination of safety zones and harmful interference".[58]

Some commentators have expressed concern that the United States intends to treat safety zones as "exclusion zones" in contravention of the Outer Space Treaty.[59] Such concerns should be put to rest by the language of s 11(10) where it is made clear that there is no prohibition against operating

56 *Id.* s 11.7.
57 *Id.*
58 *Id.* s 11.6.
59 See e.g., A. Boley & M. Byers, *U.S. Policy Puts the Safe Development of Space at Risk*, Science 174 (9 Oct. 2020).

within a safety zone, but only a duty to give notice and coordinate.[60] The principle of universal free access is emphasised again in s 11(1):

The Signatories commit to respect the principle of free access to all areas of celestial bodies and all other provisions of the Outer Space Treaty in their use of safety zones.

Although the UNCOPUOS Legal Subcommittee has taken up its work on space resource activity (as described above), the product of the Working Group will take at least five years to complete and even then, the product is intended to take the form of a non-binding resolution. In the meantime, NASA has moved forward with setting some ground rules for its team of international partners through the Artemis Accords.

In March 2021, the Chinese and Russian space agencies signed a Memorandum of Understanding (MoU) for the creation of an International Lunar Research Station (ILRS), to be established in three phases, concurrently but separate from the Artemis programme. As in the Artemis programme, Russia and China have invited other countries to join the ILRS programme as partners. These partnership opportunities are described in a jointly published *International Lunar Research Station (ILRS) Guide for Partnership*.[61] However, the guide does not discuss any norms of behavior expected of its partners except for a statement in the introduction in which Russia and China commit themselves to the principles of "equality, openness and integrity".

23.6 Initiatives by non-governmental organisations

Several non-governmental organisations (NGOs) have used their platforms to engage experts and the public in initiatives regarding space resource activity. These organisations all share the fact that they are not a legislative body and their products are therefore not legal instruments, but instead take the form of non-binding principles, best practices, guidelines, and other similar hortatory documents. The work product created by these groups will ideally feed into the UNCOPUOS proceedings as reference material brought to the Committee's attention by one or more delegations. The remainder of this section provides a brief overview of several legal reform efforts, although one initiative is by far the most prominent: the Hague International Space Resources Governance Working Group (the Hague Working Group).

23.6.1 The Hague International Space Resources Governance Working Group

The multi-stakeholder Hague Working Group was created in 2016 as the outcome of a Roundtable on the Governance of Space Resources which had been convened in December 2014 by The Hague Institute for Global Justice. The Working Group concluded its work at the end of 2019 with the adoption of 20 "Building Blocks for the Development of an International Framework on Space Resources Governance".[62] The Building Blocks aim to lay the groundwork for potential future negotiations on a framework to govern space resource activities. The Building Blocks are based on the concept of "adaptive governance", meaning that they do not try to address all issues in detail

60 *Id.* s 11.10.

61 International Lunar Research Station (ILRS) Guide for Partnership; see also A. Jones, China, Russia reveal roadmap for international moon base, Space News, 16 June 2021.

62 The Working Group was hosted by the International Institute of Air and Space Law at Leiden University. Five papers with annual updates were published between 2017 and 2020, the last of these was T. Masson-Zwaan et al., *The Hague International Space Resources Governance Working Group: Conclusion and Way Forward*, 71st International Astronautical Congress, IAC-20-D4.5.1 (2020).

from the start, but are instead intended to serve as basic principles that will underly an evolving system of law as the industry matures.

The Building Blocks include technical, legal, scientific, industrial, business, and social perspectives, thus reflecting the multifaceted character of space resource utilisation. The Building Blocks include provisions regarding (1) the basic right to free access to celestial bodies, (2) the recognition of an operator's rights over extracted space resources, (3) safety measures related to space resource activities, (4) prevention and mitigation of potential harm, and (5) the sharing of benefits from space resource activities. Among the more innovative provisions of the Building Blocks is Building Block 7 regarding priority rights. This provision recommends that operators be able to, in effect, stake a claim (termed by the Building Blocks as acquiring "priority rights") over a particular area of the moon or another celestial body where resources have been discovered.

To receive such priority rights, an operator would register them in an International Registry. The duration of the priority rights and the size of the area subject to the operator's rights would be determined on an *ad hoc* basis depending on the nature of the space resource activity. In addition to these rights to the mining area, operators can (under Building Block 11.3) establish so-called "safety zones" to help "assure safety and to avoid any harmful interference with that space resource activity".[63] This concept of safety zones was later adopted in NASA's Artemis Accords (see above, 23.5).

23.6.2 Other non-governmental initiatives

In addition to the Hague Working Group, several other nongovernmental entities have undertaken initiatives of various types in an effort to influence the governance of space resource activity. These groups include the Moon Village Association, the Article XI Project, the Outer Space Institute, the Open Lunar Foundation, and the Breaking Ground Trust.

The Moon Village Association (MVA) was created in 2017 with the goal of implementing the "moon village" concept which contemplates an international collection of efforts (some in partnership, others independently) that involve both governmental and private entities operating in a spirit of cooperation and mutual assistance.[64] Among the many legal, technical, and ethical issues that have been the focus of MVA projects, two merit mention with respect to the governance of space resource activity: the Best Practices for Sustainable Lunar Activity (published in 2020) and the Global Expert Group on Sustainable Lunar Activities (GEGSLA).

The purpose the 2020 MVA Best Practices was the development of a set of voluntary standards of behavior and principles that will support the long-term sustainability of lunar activities.[65] The section on space resource activity is reproduced here in its entirety:

> **Space Resources**
>
> Space actors are encouraged to conduct all space resource extraction and utilization activities in compliance with Article II of the Outer Space Treaty with the understanding that space resource activity does not inherently constitute national appropriation of celestial bodies. Space actors should also support the development of both hard and soft laws that provide guidance and legal certainty regarding safety standards, priority rights, and non-

63 *Id.* Building Block 11.3.

64 Further information about the Moon Village Association can be found online.

65 Best Practices for Sustainable Lunar Activity, Moon Village Association.

interference, among other issues, to actors involved in space resource activity. In time, it may be beneficial to create a process to limit space resource activity as to location and duration in order to ensure equitable and responsible use of limited resources.

Following the publication of the Best Practices, the MVA launched a new initiative with the same broad scope of the Best Practices, but with a far more elaborate process and more ambitious goals: the Global Expert Group on Sustainable Lunar Activities (GEGSLA).[66] The GEGSLA membership is comprised of major stakeholders in lunar activities including representatives from space agencies/government, industry, international organisations, academia, and civil society. The final product of the GEGSLA, the Recommended Framework and Key Elements for Peaceful, and Sustainable Lunar Activities, will be complete in 2023. Although the GEGSLA has traditionally deferred to the recommendations of the Hague Working Group with respect to space resource activity, the GEGSLA has elaborated upon some of the issues addressed in the Building Blocks, such as the creation of safety zones.

The Article XI Project is another NGO initiative that is focused narrowly on the need for a universal approach to information-sharing as governments and private industry return to the Moon. The Project is a joint venture of the Global Space Law Center (GSLC) at Cleveland State University and the E.A.G.L.E. Team of the Space Generation Advisory Council (SGAC). The core recommendation of the Project is for all states to use the existing Index of Submissions by States under Art. XI of the Outer Space Treaty maintained by the United Nations Office for Outer Space Affairs (UNOOSA) to share information on their lunar activity.[67] This information-sharing project could be beneficial for the space mining industry if the Index is used to provide notice to other operators of ongoing (or even planned) activity with the goal of peaceful coordination among operators. To assist states in making submissions to the Art. XI Index, the Art. XI Project has developed a template specifically designed for the notification of modern space activities, including space resource activity.

In March 2020, the Outer Space Institute in Vancouver organised a multi-disciplinary roundtable with participants from a wide range of countries and backgrounds, including government, industry, and academia. The discussions at this meeting led to the adoption of the "Vancouver Recommendations on Space Mining".[68] They "are intended to support other recommendations and guidelines, most notably the 'Building Blocks' adopted by the Hague International Space Resources Governance Working Group in November 2019". The recommendations focus on an international regime for space mining and provide that negotiations to that effect should be open to all states and seek input from science, industry, and other non-governmental stakeholders.

The recommendations consist of seven points, the last of which contains 25 items that states should consider during such negotiations. These are in some instances similar to what is contained in the Hague Building Blocks but place a stronger focus on environmental and scientific aspects. For instance, the Vancouver Recommendations not only recommend compliance with the COSPAR planetary protection policy,[69] but also the elaboration of further planetary protection standards specific to space mining. They also mention avoidance of potentially hazardous orbital changes to celestial bodies; securing samples in a manner that is compatible for eventual return for scientific research prior to extraction; and minimising the lifting and transport of lunar dust. In respect of benefit sharing,

66 The Global Expert Group for Sustainable Lunar Activities, Moon Village Association.

67 Available at www.unoosa.org/.

68 Vancouver Recommendations on Space Mining.

69 COSPAR Panel on Planetary Protection.

the Vancouver Recommendations go further than the Hague Building Blocks, as they encourage the establishment of a mandatory benefit-sharing mechanism, including the sharing of monetary benefits.

The Open Lunar Foundation, based in San Francisco, has provided a popular online platform for the discussion of a wide range of topics related to the settlement of the Moon, which has included webinars regarding space resource activity. Open Lunar has also issued reports and recommendations on the governance of space resource activity and has launched the Res Lunae Project which is described as "an initiative articulating options for tangible governance of natural resources on the Moon".[70]

23.6.3 Three useful analogs: ITU frequency allocation, deep sea mining, and the CIIME

Looking at other industries and areas of law, there are three models for allocating limited resources (or for allocating assets in the case of one analog). At some point, the international community will likely need to create a system of governance that establishes a supervisory authority to oversee the implementation of rules and procedures put into place by a multilateral treaty. A full analysis of these analogs and their potential for guiding space resource governance is beyond the scope of this article, so a brief overview must suffice.

The first example is the ITU's mechanism for allocating radio frequencies and orbits under the ITU Constitutions and the ITU Convention (as implemented by the World Radio Regulations).[71] The ITU's use of a Master International Frequency Registry to coordinate the use of signals and to avoid interference among users could be translated into a new system for the registration of mining interests.

Another potential model for governing space resource activity is found in the regulation of deep seabed mining under the UN Convention on the Law of the Sea (UNCLOS) and the 1994 Agreement relating to the Implementation of Part XI (with regard to deep sea mining).[72] The regulations and procedures implementing the 1994 Agreement will be developed in a "Mining Code" to be issued by the International Seabed Authority for the prospection, exploration, and exploitation of deep seabed resources.[73] Although these rules are still under development, one lesson that seems clear is that it is dangerous to rush regulations.[74] The risk is that without sufficient time, there cannot be a careful consideration of all interests and stakeholders, including the environmental interests, business interests, and the interests of today's society – as well as the societies of the future. The approach of adaptive governance seen in the Hague Building Blocks as well as in the approach of the UN working group suggests that this lesson has been learned and that regulations in the coming years will grow, as appropriate, in step with the expansion of space resource activity in space.

A third international system for allocating property and resolving disputes among competing claimants is the International Registry that has been instituted under the Convention on

70 Open Lunar Foundation, The Res Luna Project: Resource Systems and Governance Approaches.

71 Constitution and Convention of the International Telecommunication Union (with annexes and optional protocol), 1825 & 1826 UNTS, Concluded at Geneva on 22 December 1992.

72 United Nations Convention on the Law of the Sea (UNCLOS), Montego Bay, 10 Dec. 1982, 1833 UNTS 3; Agreement relating to the Implementation of Part XI of the United Nations Convention on the Law of the Sea of 10 December 1982 (Implementation Agreement), New York, 1994, 1836 UNTS 3; ISA Mining Code.

73 For a concise explanation of the evolution of the UNCLOS, an examination of the political dynamics affecting deep sea mining, and examples of the challenges that face the industry see A. Zalik, *World-making and the Deep Seabed: mining the area beyond national jurisdiction*, in Routledge Handbook of Critical Resource Geography 35 (2021).

74 See J. Watts, Race to the Bottom: the disastrous, blindfolded rush to mine the deep sea, THE GUARDIAN, 27. Sept. 2021.

International Interests in Mobile Equipment (CIIME).[75] The CIIME creates an international legal regime to govern "international interests" (which are primarily security interests) in high-value mobile equipment, including aircraft, rolling stock, space assets, and mining, agricultural, and construction (MAC) equipment.[76] The secured party ensures the priority of its interest by filing its interest in an online public registry. The simplicity of the system is its beauty: the first to file is assured priority among competing claimants. A similar "first to file" system could be adapted to mining rights.

23.7 Conclusion: a road towards a governance system and a potential model in deep sea-bed mining

It seems likely that international and national law governing space resource activities will continue to evolve in parallel for the near future. The Outer Space Treaty provides general principles and does not, as most would agree, prohibit commercial use of space resources; the Moon Agreement is more detailed but of limited relevance because of the low number of ratifications. International soft law fills in some of the details, especially in terms of sustainability, but leaves other issues open. Since the first years of discussions on this topic in the UNCOPUOS Legal Subcommittee, a shift has occurred from questioning the legality of space resources utilisation towards a gradual conviction that this activity will be happening and should be regulated internationally.

The development of national laws has so far been limited to a few cases, but they are more or less consistent in scope and nature and recognise that all activity must be conducted in accordance with international law. Moreover, these domestic regulations are necessary for states where space resources activities are expected to occur, as State Parties to the Outer Space Treaty are under the obligation to authorise and supervise such space activities pursuant to Art. VI. It is however not desirable that many more states revert to unilateral lawmaking, as that might lead to fragmentation.

The preferred solution is the creation of a multilateral regime for space resource activities developed under the auspices of UNCOPUOS. Reaching agreement on a universal approach to resource activity will be a complex and lengthy process, but is not impossible and the first steps have already been taken in the creation of the new UN working group. Hopefully the considerable work of non-governmental organisations such as the Hague Working Group's Building Blocks and the MVA Best Practices will be considered as the Working Group moves forward.

Since the adoption of a new treaty is not likely in the current geopolitical climate, the eventual result of the discussions in UNCOPUOS will likely take the form of a General Assembly resolution providing guidelines for equitable and sustainable lunar activity by governmental as well as non-governmental actors, accompanied perhaps by recommendations to states wishing to adopt national legislation in this field. Nevertheless, peering further into the future, as the need for governance grows, we will likely eventually see the creation of an international system of governance for space resource activity of the type seen in the ITU, UNCLOS, or CIIME examples.

75 Convention on International Interests in Mobile Equipment, Nov. 16, 2001, S. Treaty Doc. No. 108-10 [hereinafter CIIME].

76 For further reading see the official commentaries written by the chief drafter of the CIIME and its protocols, Sir Roy Goode. R. Goode, *Convention on International Interests in Mobile Equipment and Protocol Thereto on Matters Specific to Space Assets: Official Commentary* (2013) (reprinted with corrections 2014). Regarding the Space Assets Protocol see also M. Sundahl, *The Cape Town Convention: Its Operation and Relation to the Law of Outer Space* (2010).

E

Specific aspects of smart contracts and blockchain technology

24

BLOCKCHAIN AND SMART CONTRACTS IN SPACE OPERATIONS

P. J. Blount and Giulia De Rossi

24.1 Introduction

Blockchain technology is a method for creating a common, unchangeable register to record transactions or to verify assets. Blockchain technology emerged in the public conscience with the advent of Bitcoin and other cryptocurrencies. Though cryptocurrencies had long been contemplated, for instance in popular works such as Neil Stephenson's *Cryptonomicon*, blockchain served as an enabling technology that could be used to ensure that these assets were not duplicated like other digital files.[1] The seeming success of cryptocurrency applications turned blockchain into an innovation buzzword, and scads of new applications have been floated as ways to best leverage this technology. The space industry has not been immune to this phenomenon and numerous companies have made pitches for how blockchain technology could be used in space applications and operations.[2] To some extent this is a technology still in search of an application. Though the discourse on blockchain has been dominated by cryptocurrencies, the extension of blockchain into other applications is inevitable and may result in more profitable and useful applications. At the same time, as the volatile cryptocurrency market suggests, there is still much to be learned about the opportunities and risks of incorporating blockchain into a given activity.

This chapter will explore blockchain technologies, including non-fungible tokens (NFTs) and smart contracts, as applicable to space operations and investigate the legal ramifications of these technologies. Specifically, this chapter will seek to explain how these technologies work and how they interface with a variety of space operations including authorisations, intellectual property, and financial attributes. At the moment, there is thin legislation regarding blockchain, but these technologies have significant legal ramifications, nonetheless.

This chapter will first address the technical aspects of blockchain and explain how it is deployed to solve a variety of technical problems. This paper will then illustrate the potential applications

1 Neal Stephenson, *Cryptonomicon* (New York: Avon Books, 1999).

2 *See* Debra Werner, "Sure, There's Hype. But Blockchain Has Concrete Space Applications," *SpaceNews* (15 November 2021).

DOI: 10.4324/9781003268475-35

of this emerging technology to be used to enhance space activities through concrete use cases. Specifically, the following section will address how distributed ledger and smart contracts can improve the inefficiencies of today's industries' mechanisms, especially the aerospace one. Finally, this chapter will turn to the legal issues surrounding these technologies and discuss salient points of which a lawyer in this field should be aware and the gaps that may exist in the law.

24.2 Blockchain and smart contracts

This section will seek to give a brief introduction to blockchain technology. This will, of course, not be a full technical assessment of the technology, but will, rather, give the basic characteristics of the technology in order to enable a legal analysis of its applications in the space domain.

The idea of a decentralised ledger where digital economic resources could flow among different parties involved in the network establishing the ledger was an idea that was already present in the research work of Nick Szabo in 1998.[3] However, it was on 1 November 2008, when "Bitcoin: A peer-to-peer Electronic Cash System" was released on the internet, by the pseudonymous Satoshi Nakamoto, that blockchain became a global phenomenon.[4] This document would go on to create waves in cryptography, finance, and information technology through the introduction of blockchain technology as an enabler for a digital currency system. The intent of the creator of Bitcoin was to provide a payment system that is able to guarantee a secure exchange of money among actors who may lack trust in each other. These actors can rely on the security, traceability, and immutability of the distributed ledger, or blockchain, underlying the cryptocurrency system. Such a structure is independent from the centralised control exerted by authorities, such as banks and governments, and it relies on the transparency of an open and public ledger on which all transactions are recorded, but not necessarily the identities of the individuals or entities engaging in the transactions.

At the core of this technology structure is a ledger of all transactions that is distributed among the different nodes on the blockchain rather than being stored on a central server, which means that all nodes share duplicate copies of all the transactions. Nodes represent users on the blockchain.[5] The duplication of the ledger across nodes increases the trustworthiness of the transaction for the parties involved and ensures that the transactions that are registered and executed as the transaction is confirmed on the blockchain without the need of an intermediary.[6] Importantly, this system creates greater security in the data surrounding the transactions and protects against cyber-attacks through the duplication of the ledger.

In short, a blockchain system is a "way of creating a shared database that can record and track transactions and assets".[7] The name "Blockchain" itself indicates how this system works. It is a chain with different blocks distributed in a "shared, immutable ledger".[8] This means that every transaction that is executed between two or more parties is registered automatically in all the nodes of the system through a specific cryptographic process. Each new transaction is included in the

3 Nick Szabo, "Bit Gold," Satoshi Nakamoto Institute (29 December 2005).

4 Satoshi Nakamoto, "Bitcoin: A peer-to-peer Electronic Cash System," (November 2008).

5 Nathan Fulmer, "Exploring the Legal Issues of Blockchain Applications," *Akron Law Review* 52, no. 1 (2019): 167.

6 Eliza Mik, "Smart Contracts: Terminology, Technical Limitations and Real World Complexity," *Law, Innovation and Technology* 9, no. 2 (July 3, 2017): 277–278.

7 Miriam Stankovich, "Is Intellectual Property Ready for Blockchain?," *Digital@DAI* (blog), 2 September 2021.

8 IBM, "What is Blockcahin Technology?" (n.d.; accessed 9 September 2022) https://www.ibm.com/topics/what-is-blockchain.

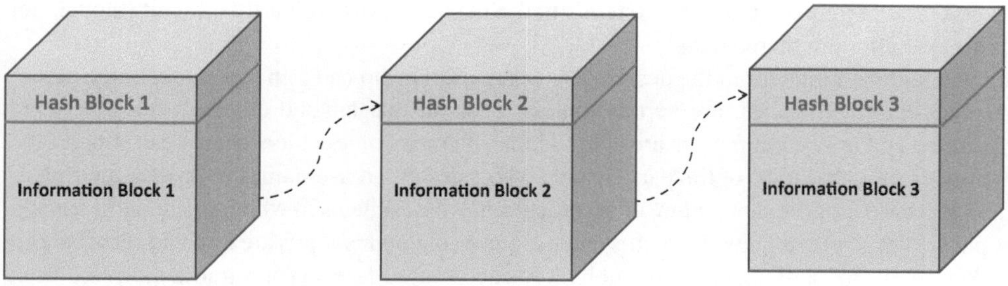

Figure 24.1 Block chain illustration

public ledger as a new block using a hash that is built from the previous block (see Figure 24.1). As a result, "[e]ach block contains a list of all prior transactions", and these "blocks are mathematically chained together and guarantee that a transaction cannot be modified without modifying the block that records it and all following blocks".[9] This creates resilience in the integrity of the ledger as all the blocks are connected and cannot be altered without changing other transactions in the ledger – resulting in "distributed consensus".[10]

In the case of cryptocurrencies, these transactions are pseudo-monetary in nature, but transactions are not limited to monetary exchanges and can essentially represent any change in the data. Blockchain is a "generic technology" that can be tailored to the particular needs of the participants and the shared database they seek to create and are sometimes referred to as "distributed ledger technologies".[11] In simple terms, when a transaction occurs, the nodes in the blockchain calculate the value of the new block associated with that transaction based on the value of the transaction and the value of the previous block. "Value" here refers not to the economic worth of the transaction, but to the cryptographic hash or representation of the transaction. The calculation is done through a hashing algorithm, which creates a unique outcome that creates the new block on the chain. In cryptocurrencies this process is called mining,[12] which indicates that each user that is part of the system competes against others to calculate the hash for new blocks with the reward of this computation being a specific amount of the cryptocurrency.[13] The new block is distributed across the public ledger. If a previous block is tampered with it will be evident because it will affect the value of future blocks, which are known throughout the ledger, making the chain of transaction resilient to interference.[14] This, of course, does not protect future transactions; so, for instance, if a cryptocurrency wallet is breached and the funds are transferred to another wallet.

Depending on the purpose of the blockchain, the information contained in the blocks can vary from cryptocurrencies to electronic votes, demonstrating the versatility of this technology. One of the essential aspects to consider is the intrinsic security guaranteed by a specific code that identifies the sequence of registered blocks. The chronological storage of all the transactions in multiple

9 Eliza Mik, "Smart Contracts," 276.
10 *Id.* at 277.
11 *Id.* at 274–275.
12 *See* Mik, "Smart Contracts," 276; Mark Giancaspro, "Is a 'Smart Contract' Really a Smart Idea? Insights from a Legal Perspective," *Computer Law & Security Review* 33 (2017): 826
13 Fulmer, "Exploring the Legal Issues of Blockchain Applications," 168-169 and Jack Gilcrest and Arthur Carvalho, "Smart Contracts: Legal Considerations," in *2018 IEEE International Conference on Big Data (Big Data)* (IEEE, 2018), 3278.
14 Fulmer, "Exploring the Legal Issues of Blockchain Applications," 170.

bonded blocks distributed across the system's nodes makes it extraordinarily difficult (though not impossible) to alter the shared data.[15]

Another significant factor in the design of blockchains is who can join as a node. Some blockchains, like cryptocurrencies, are permissionless meaning that anyone can join, but others are permissioned and only certain users are able to join.[16] Permissionless blockchains can support the anonymity or pseudonymity of the participants, who can rely on usernames to protect their identity. This has been a significant feature of cryptocurrency blockchains in which participants usually adopt public-key cryptography. In such systems, a user maintains a private key and distributes a public key to all the participants. The public key can be used to encrypt a transaction to a user, but it can then only be decrypted by using the private key held by the user.[17] While anonymity is important in some applications, it is not necessarily a specific feature of all blockchains, and applications that require non-anonymous transactions exist.

The advantages of a database based on the blockchain's principles are numerous including "relatively low maintenance cost, increased transparency, reduced administrative burden, and resilience to fraud".[18] The nature of the shared ledger increases the integrity of the data through transparency. If a centralised authority, such as a bank, suffers a breach of its data, then that data may be completely compromised and the resulting compromised data will then spread to all the entities that are dependent on the central source of the data. This is because the nodes in a centralised system treat the central database as true and correct. Blockchain on the other hand distributes its transaction record among all participants to ensure that everyone involved in the system can verify in real time what happens in the network. This distributed security is directly related to the transparency of the system, and all nodes have a claim to the ledger they store to be correct and verifiable.[19] Since all the data are chained to each other, it is implicit that any data alteration is visible and tracked meaning falsified blocks cannot be injected, and a node with incorrect data will be exposed as it will not match the data held by the rest of the network. In order to compromise the blockchain, an attacker would have to be able to alter the data held on more than 50% of the nodes, which becomes increasingly difficult as a network grows in size.

Though the predominant application of this technology has been cryptocurrencies, blockchain has served as a platform for innovation and numerous other applications have been developed.[20] Some of these applications replicate existing models in a wholly autonomous and digitised version. This is the case of so-called smart contracts, which are agreements that are made in a digital format and are designed to self-execute when the conditions of the agreement are met. Though smart contracts do not necessarily need to be within a blockchain environment,[21] blockchain is viewed as an enabling technology without which "smart contracts could not feasibly operate".[22] It has been suggested that connecting these instruments to the blockchain reduces the risk of a powerful actor manipulating a centralised infrastructure and compromising the automated performance of the

15 John Salmon and Gordon Myers, "Blockchain and Associated Legal Issues for Emerging Markets," *EM Compass,* Note 63 (January 2019): 1.

16 Mik, "Smart Contracts," 275; Gilcrest and Carvalho, "Smart Contracts," 3280.

17 Fulmer, "Exploring the Legal Issues of Blockchain Applications," 167 and Salmon and Myers, "Blockchain and Associated Legal Issues for Emerging Markets," 4.

18 Stankovich, "Is Intellectual Property Ready for Blockchain?"

19 Giancaspro, "Is a 'Smart Contract' Really a Smart Idea?," 826.

20 Fulmer, "Exploring the Legal Issues of Blockchain Applications," 171–172.

21 Mik, "Smart Contracts," 274.

22 Giancaspro, "Is a 'Smart Contract' Really a Smart Idea?" 827. *See also* Gilcrest and Carvalho, "Smart Contracts," 3278.

contract.[23] Blockchain implementation serves to make the automated transactions "trackable and irreversible" and also enables contracts to be executed between and among anonymous parties.[24]

Essentially, smart contracts are contracts or parts of contracts "where the terms of the agreement are written as lines of computer code that can automatically monitor, execute, and enforce performance of the agreed terms".[25] These can come in a variety of forms from natural language contracts with code elements to contracts completely written in code.[26] These can increase efficiency by exploiting distributed ledger technology to automate performance under the terms of the contract, thereby eliminating the need for intervention by third parties, removing time delays, and alleviating the bureaucratic impact.[27] At the same time, a significant trade-off is that once the contract has been entered into the blockchain it becomes immutable and cannot be changed or amended.[28] As a simple example, a small business could finance the purchase of a piece of equipment by selling tokens on the blockchain to investors. The token in this case represents the investor's share in the financed equipment. A smart contract could be implemented to pay investors back, for instance when the small business hits a certain threshold of funds in a digital account the tokens could be automatically redeemed repaying investors at a predefined rate of interest. The "if … else" condition in code allows application of this technology to many fields that range from crowdfunding opportunities, intellectual property rights protection, and supply chain monitoring, among others.[29]

Both blockchain and smart contracts are often surrounded by rhetoric of increased trust among actors and "reflect a surprising lack of trust in humans in general".[30] Indeed, these technologies are "inextricably tied to the elimination of human judgement, the reduction of dependence on financial intermediaries and, in many instances, a detachment from the legal system".[31] Cryptocurrency, in particular, is often discussed in terms of wresting power over monetary transactions from the state, and the rhetoric of decentralisation "has … often been associated with the abandonment of traditional legal institutions".[32] This elimination of the human element for an automated system, of course, has risks and benefits. At the same time, though, it should be remembered that as a technological implementation the human element is never completely eliminated from these instrumentalities. As a result, it must be accepted that blockchain and associated technologies do present opportunities for innovations that can benefit society, but at the same time there can be significant risk that results from the usage of these technologies. As one commentator has observed "it is … difficult to evaluate many claims concerning their [smart contracts] actual capabilities and real potential to change (speak: revolutionise) the commercial and legal landscape".[33]

23 Giancaspro, "Is a 'Smart Contract' Really a Smart Idea?" 826.

24 James Lewis and Bhavul Haria, "Smart Contracts – How Smart Are They?," *Fieldfisher* (blog), (December 13, 2021) and Giancaspro, "Is a 'Smart Contract' Really a Smart Idea?" 827.

25 Lewis and Haria, "Smart Contracts." *See also* Giancaspro, "Is a 'Smart Contract' Really a Smart Idea?" 826; Mik, "Smart Contracts," 272-74; and Gilcrest and Carvalho, "Smart Contracts," 3277.

26 Law Commission, *Smart Legal Contract: Advice to Government* (November 2021) Para. 1.4; Lewis and Haria, "Smart Contracts"; and Mik, "Smart Contracts," 287.

27 Giancaspro, "Is a 'Smart Contract' Really a Smart Idea?" 827.

28 *Id.* at 826.

29 Salmon and Myers, "Blockchain and Associated Legal Issues for Emerging Markets," 5.

30 Mik, "Smart Contracts," 270.

31 *Id.*

32 *Id.* at 284.

33 *Id.* at 270.

24.3 Blockchain in the space industry

As blockchain has emerged as a platform for innovation, new applications have been sought, including in the space industry. Generally, blockchain is most applicable to activities that need high reliability of data or a traceability of transactions, and this trend will likely hold true in the space industry as well. Herein we address three applications – space finance, space data, and space resources – but we note that this is certainly not a comprehensive assessment of the potential applications of this technology.[34] Rather this selection gives a flavour of how blockchain may be applied in the space domain, which will be used to then discuss the potential legal issues that result from these applications. It should be emphasised at the outset that we reserve judgment as to whether these applications will, or would, prove useful and viable business cases. Often an assumption is made "that because a particular technology is innovative or revolutionary, it is also commercially useful or capable of solving actual legal problems".[35] With regards to this technology as applied to the space industry, it should be acknowledged that there are potential applications, but at the same time there is still a great deal of uncertainty as to which (if any) will bring benefits to the space sector.

24.3.1 Space finance

The space industry has undergone profound changes in the last few decades, leading private enterprises seeking economic gain to drive the technological development and innovation that lies within this environment. This industry was estimated to be worth US$370 billion in 2021[36] and projected to become a trillion-dollar industry by 2040.[37] Space technologies are a key enabler to the digital transformation that characterises contemporary society, and there has been increased human's reliance on these services. Satellite networks have increased the amount of data exchanged around the globe, and the information acquired from satellites creates value for those who own them. Start-ups represent the motor of this economy and are supported by huge investments fund that are distributed in both the upstream and downstream sector, worth US$37 billion and US$300 billion, respectively.[38]

The rise in start-ups has led some of these companies to use blockchain technologies to achieve funding goals. Though not unique to the space industry, the use of Initial Coin Offering (ICO) has emerged as a new digitised way to access crowdfunding through communities distributed geographically worldwide. Essentially, this method allows companies to sell shares or stakes in their company as tokens on a blockchain. This is similar to an initial public offering (IPO) of stock, but it does not require the company to be listed on a stock exchange nor does it give the purchaser an

34 Other applications include, using satellites as nodes in crypto currency blockchains (Shaochi Cheng et al., "Blockchain Application in Space Information Network Security," in *International Conference on Space Information Network* (Springer, 2018), 4–5); using blockchain to increase security in satellite communications (*Id.* at 5–7); sync and management in tracking and data relay satellite systems (Mohamed Torky, Tarek Gaber, and Aboul Ella Hassanien, "Blockchain in Space Industry: Challenges and Solutions," *ArXiv Preprint ArXiv:2002.12878* (2020): 6); launch logistics (*Id.* at 7); and supply chain management (Karen L. Jones, "Blockchain in the Space Sector," Aerospace Corporation (March 2020): 8–10), among others

35 Mik, "Smart Contracts," 270.

36 Euroconsult, "Euroconsult estimates that the global space economy totaled $370 billion in 2021" 11 January 2022).

37 Morgan Stanley, "Space: Investing in the Final Frontier," (24 July 2020).

38 Euroconsult, *Space Economy Report 2021: An outlook of the key trends in the global space Market* (2022).

equity stake in the company.[39] If the company is successful, it is assumed that the tokens will rise in value. The success of ICOs can be seen by the funds raised through this method: as of 2018 that amounted to over US$22 billion.[40] The popularity of this alternative crowdfunding lies in speed and access. As a result, this may be an attractive process to fund space exploration missions, especially in the age of NewSpace. Monetising data from outer space exploration missions, in particular from missions to asteroids, the Moon, and Mars.[41] The use of ICO's could "break barriers of entry in the space industry, which has been known to be capital intensive and highly risky".[42] An example of this is Space Decentral, a business that represents itself as "a decentralized autonomous space agency, that will utilize blockchain technology to enable collaborative, transparent and self-directed action toward building the future of space exploration".[43] This example illustrates the hope of numerous start-ups that blockchain can be used to "overcome geographic, political and economic barriers".[44]

24.3.2 Space data

The collection and dissemination of data from and about space is one of the most significant space activities. In this subsection we address how blockchain might be used in two different types of space data, namely remote sensing data and space situational awareness data.

24.3.2.1 Remote sensing

Remote sensing, as used herein, is the sensing of the Earth by a satellite from space.[45] This sensing could be as simple as an optical camera pointed at the Earth or it could use complex active sensing means such as radar. Furthermore, such data does not need to be "imagery" as there is an emerging market for systems that sense radio-frequency emissions from the surface of the Earth. Blockchain could serve a number of roles with regards to remote sensing data, but is most likely to be connected to situations where such data needs to be highly verifiable or in cases in which it is being licensed for use.

An example of when such data may need high verifiability is the use case of remote sensing data as evidence in a judicial proceeding or indeed in any type of situation wherein the data is being relied on. Issues connected to the verifiability of remote sensing data are not new and have been discussed in the literature.[46] The core issue is that such data is often collected for use by a

39 Luigi Scatteia and Aravind Ravichandran, "Blockchain, what are the applications for the space industry?," PricewaterhouseCooper (February 2019): 1.

40 *Id.* at 2.

41 *Id.*

42 *Id.* at 3.

43 Space Decentral, "Space Decentral: A Decentralized Autonomous Space Agency," White Paper Community Draft Version 0.9.2 (n.d.): 4.

44 Jones, "Blockchain in the Space Sector," 7.

45 *See generally*, Shaida Johnston, "Technical Introduction to Satellite EO," in *Evidence from Earth Observation Satellites: Emerging Legal Issues*, ed. Ray Purdy and Denise Leung (Leiden ; Boston: Martinus Nijhoff, 2013), 11–42.

46 *See* Ronald J. Rychlak, Joanne Irene Gabrynowicz, and Rick Crowsey, "Legal Certification of Digital Data: The Earth Resources Observation and Science Data Center Project," *J. Space L.* 33 (2007): 195-219 and Willibad Croi, Frederic-Michael Foeteler, and Harold Linke, "Introducing Digital Signatures and Time-Stamps in the EO Data Processing Chain," in *Evidence from Earth Observation Satellites: Emerging Legal Issues*, ed. Ray Purdy and Denise Leung (Leiden ; Boston: Martinus Nijhoff, 2013), 379–398.

party in such a proceeding and then processed by that party to be used as evidence. In such cases, when the evidence is introduced into the proceeding a foundation must be laid for it to be authenticated, and for processed data this means that the processing itself needs to be shown to flow from the original imagery and should be replicable by the other party. In the past, this has been accomplished with a digital certification or signature so that the data is traceable to an original image.[47] It is not outside the realm of possibility that a blockchain could be used to track the original data through processing so that all parties have a verifiable record of the origin of the data through to its final, processed form.[48]

As the use of geographical information systems and databases has become more significant, so too have licensing issues surrounding the intellectual property (IP) in these databases and the remote sensing data that they leverage. A second example of how blockchain could be leveraged with regards to remote sensing is implementations that use the blockchain "as a technology-based IP registry where IP owners can keep hashed digital certificates of their IP and use the platform to get royalties from those who use their creations and inventions using smart contracts".[49] In such a system, a smart contract could be entered into by the vendor and the customer governing the license for use of the data.[50] This contract could be used to automate the paying of royalty fees between these entities based on usage of the intellectual property. This could have a number of benefits, for example it could trace the usage of data through the supply chain to better enable the owner to gather royalties related to the use of that data by clarifying ownership of IP that has been integrated into other products.[51] Indeed, it could be used to follow licensing through the supply chain even when fees are not being collected. For instance, Copernicus data is licensed under a Creative Commons licence and blockchain could be leveraged to ensure that use of the data is compliant with this licence.[52]

24.3.2.2 Space situational awareness data

Space situational awareness (SSA) and the related concept of space traffic management (STM) are significant issues in the current era of space usage. This is because there is currently a proliferation of satellites and debris on orbit. The advent of very-large constellations has led to a significant increase of on-orbit space objects, and the number of objects considered to be space debris has steadily risen over the years. This has led to a need for better data about the space environment and has created an environment where there are increasing calls for some sort of STM system that can coordinate actors and reduce potential interference. Any functional STM programme will be highly dependent on reliable SSA data.[53]

The need to provide reliable data is significant and problematic. In particular, SSA data has strong military and national security linkages for states, and as a result there can be suspicion and distrust among actors as to the veracity of the data that is being disseminated. At the same

47 Croi et al. "Introducing Digital Signatures," 380.

48 European Space Agency, "Blockchain and Earth Observation" (April 2019): 10–11.

49 Miriam Stankovich, "Is Intellectual Property Ready for Blockchain?"

50 Jones, "Blockchain in the Space Sector," 12.

51 Stankovich, "Is Intellectual Property Ready for Blockchain?"

52 Marco Trovatello, "Copernicus Sentinel Satellite Imagery Under Open Licence," European Space Agency (4 May 2017) https://open.esa.int/copernicus-sentinel-satellite-imagery-under-open-licence/

53 *See* P. J. Blount, "Space Traffic Management: Standardizing on-Orbit Behavior," *American Journal of International Law* 113 (2019): 120–124.

time, all operators need to have an understanding of the space environment to properly plan their activities, coordinate with other operators, and avoid interference with other actors. To this end, the United States has adopted a policy that endorses the development of an "open architecture" data repository that would distribute this information on an open access basis to operators.[54] Such a repository could be strengthened through the use of blockchain as a way to maintain the security and verifiability in the data. While a blockchain implementation might not prevent the entry of false data into the repository, it could still increase trust in the data by ensuring that once entered the data has not been tampered.

It has also been suggested that a blockchain could be used to facilitate the distribution of data among actors that may lack trust in each other and, in particular, state actors.[55] The actors that would enter into such a blockchain could share SSA data directly within the chain allowing for comparisons strengthening the overall understanding of the space environment. In such an implementation, the blockchain would be used to enhance trust among the actors by creating verifiable and secure data products that increase transparency among these actors. This could also enhance coordinative practices among all orbital operators.[56]

Finally, if properly implemented, this technology could be linked to licensing and authorisation, as smart contracts, between the licensor and the licensee.[57] States have a duty to authorise the space activities of their non-governmental actors and most choose to do this through licences.[58] Connecting such an authorisation to an SSA blockchain could automate functions such as conjunction data messages (CDM), which are used to inform an operator of a potential conjunction between its space object and another on orbit object, or even to trigger provisions in a space traffic management regime that require the operator to engage in avoidance maneuvers.

24.3.3 Space resources and exploration

Another potential application of blockchain is to space resource activities. In the 2010s a significant shift in the discussion over space resources took place. The discourse changed from one about whether space resource activities were legal under Art. II of the Outer Space Treaty to one of how such activities can be managed so as to reduce potential conflicts among actors. This shift was occasioned by a number of states adopting space resource activities laws,[59] the introduction of the

54 White House, "Space Policy Directive-3, National Space Traffic Management Policy," 18 June 2018.

55 *See generally* Harvey Reed et al., "Blockchain Enabled Space Traffic Awareness (BESTA): Automated Comparison of SSA to Agreed Behavior for Discovery of Anomalous Behavior," (2020): 2.

56 Swapnil Anil Surdi, "Space Situational Awareness through Blockchain Technology," *Journal of Space Safety Engineering* 7, no. 3 (2020): 295–301.

57 *See generally* Ronghua Xu et al., "Exploration of Blockchain-Enabled Decentralized Capability-Based Access Control Strategy for Space Situation Awareness," *Optical Engineering* 58, no. 4 (2019): 041609.

58 *See generally* Irmgard Marboe and Florian Hafner, "Brief Overview over National Authorization Mechanisms in Implementation of the UN International Space Treaties," in *National Space Legislation in Europe: Issues of Authorisation of Private Space Activities in the Light of Developments in European Space Cooperation*, ed. Frans G. von der Dunk (Leiden ; Boston: Martinus Nijhoff, 2011), 29–71.

59 *See generally*, P. J. Blount, "Outer Space and International Geography: Article II and the Shape of Global Order," *New Eng. L. Rev.* 52 (2017): 95.

Artemis Accords,[60] and the establishment of a Working Group on the topic at the UN Committee on the Peaceful Uses of Outer Space.[61]

One of the core issues related to interference reducing management of space resources is developing a way for actors to manage claims to areas for exploitation.[62] To this end, some have suggested that the tokenisation of potential resource areas through blockchain could be a potential way to accomplish such a task. As an example, the Lunar surface could be divided into plots each of which is associated with a token, the token then is a commodity that can be subject to transactions within the blockchain.[63] Such a system could take advantage of NFT technology since each token would represent a unique portion of the Lunar surface. As an example of the potential for such an application, there has been significant discussion of using the blockchain for managing terrestrial real property records with at least one US jurisdiction, Cook County Illinois, experimenting with the technology.[64]

While such a system would enable a market in claims for space resource activities, it is unclear as to why this might be better suited than a traditional notice and register system as used by the International Telecommunication Union for claims to the orbit-spectrum resource.[65] One possible answer to this would be to avoid centralised control of the system and to better distribute power. Another issue with such a system is that these claims may be difficult to assert due to the difficult access to these areas and extraordinary technology development costs for carrying out these activities. Thus, a terrestrial actor could own a token representing a particular area for resource activities, but be powerless to stop (or even ignorant of) another actor's exploitation of that resource.

24.4 Legal issues

This section of this chapter charts the legal issues connected to blockchain across two dimensions. First, this section addresses the legal issues that result from the implementation of blockchain and smart contracts in a general, in a non-space-specific sense, and then this section explores how blockchain could contribute to the extant space law paradigm.

24.4.1 Blockchain – legal issues

The use of blockchain in space does not necessarily raise significantly different issues than the use of blockchain in other applications. As a technology for creating a secure ledger of transactions, the use in space technologies does not impact many of the underlying legal questions surrounding blockchain implementation, thus novel legal issues connected to space are difficult to identify. This subsection will address legal issues general to blockchain technology and those specific to smart contracts.

60 The Artemis Accords: Principles for Cooperation in the Civil Exploration and Use of the Moon, Mars, Comets, and Asteroids for Peaceful Purposes (13 October 2020).

61 UNOOSA, "Working Group on Legal Aspects of Space Resource Activities" (n.d., accessed 9 September 2022) https://www.unoosa.org/oosa/en/ourwork/copuos/lsc/space-resources/index.html.

62 Vidvuds Beldavs, "Blockchains and the Emerging Space Economy," *The Space Review* (10 October 2016) and Brian R. Israel, "Space Resources in the Evolutionary Course of Space Lawmaking," *American Journal of International Law: Unbound* 113 (2019): 118.

63 Scatteia and Ravichandran, "Blockchain," 4.

64 Fulmer, "Exploring the Legal Issues of Blockchain Applications," 177–178.

65 *See generally*, Tanja Masson-Zwaan, "Orbits and Frequencies: The Legal Context," in *Dispute Settlement in the Area of Space Communication*, ed. Mahulena Hofmann (Baden-Baden, Germany: Nomos, 2015), 59–68.

Due to the fact that blockchain is a generic technology, it is difficult to identify the full array of legal issues connected with its various implementations. There are, however, some generalisable legal issues that can be readily identified. The first is the question of jurisdiction. Blockchains, and particularly permissionless ones, can have nodes spread around the world, meaning that "it is often difficult to establish which jurisdictions' laws and regulations apply to a given application".[66] This can create significant issues, especially as more regulators are pursuing rulemaking with regards to blockchain assets and markets.[67] Further, organisations that want to leverage blockchain, for instance, to raise capital will need to find ways to ensure that investors buying these tokens are from jurisdictions that do not create legal issues under their domestic law. For instance, some states have sanctions in place that prohibit their nationals from doing business with certain entities or classes of entities. Anonymity on blockchains could create potential for these rules to be violated unintentionally.

A second legal consideration is that of privacy and data protection, which is again a larger issue in permissionless blockchains.[68] The transparent nature of these systems means that all nodes have access to the publicly available ledger, which may contain personally identifiable information. This could run counter to laws such as the EU General Data Protection Regulation (GDPR), which gives data subjects enhanced control over their data.[69] As a salient example, under GDPR data subjects have a right to be forgotten through the deletion of their data from a database, but as already seen, this is an impossibility due to the immutability of the blockchain. Though in blockchains like Bitcoin, data protection authorities will have a difficult time identifying a controller, organisations that implement blockchains could be held accountable for GDPR violations as the controller of the data within that ledger.[70] A third legal issue is the classification of blockchain assets for the purposes of regulation and taxation.[71] There is debate as to whether these assets should be considered as currency or securities, and further how to assert a valuation on these assets for taxation purposes.[72] The classification adopted by a local regulator will have a significant impact on the legal obligations connected to crypto-assets.

Smart contracts have been recognised as valid instruments for executing contractual agreements. For instance, the United Kingdom's Law Commission has adopted a report that states that "[c]urrent legal principles can apply to smart legal contracts in much the same way as they do to traditional contracts".[73] At the same time, there may be unique issues related to smart contracts in cases of disputes especially as these instruments are sometimes characterised as self-enforceable so as to "eliminat[e] … the need to seek judicial assistance".[74] For example, Gilcrest and Carvalho suggest that traditional enforcement mechanisms "can be fully automated using smart contracts since, as soon as a breach is automatically detected, actions can then be automatically taken".[75] This, however, may be a misnomer. Smart contracts self-execute by automating the associated

66 Salmon and Myers, "Blockchain and Associated Legal Issues for Emerging Markets," 2.

67 *Id. at* 2–3.

68 *Id.* at 3.

69 EU Regulation 2016/679, General Data Protection Regulation (2016) and Riccardo De Caria, "The Legal Meaning of Smart Contracts," *European Review of Private Law* 26, no. 6 (2018): 749–750.

70 Salmon and Myers, "Blockchain and Associated Legal Issues for Emerging Markets," 3–4.

71 Fulmer, "Exploring the Legal Issues of Blockchain Applications," 173–174.

72 *Id.*

73 Law Commission, *Smart Legal Contract,* para. 1.26.

74 Mik, "Smart Contracts," 280.

75 Gilcrest and Carvalho, "Smart Contracts," 3278. It is notable that the language that Gilcrest and Carvalho use to describe the traditional enforcement process aligns more with criminal procedures than with civil procedures.

performance, but enforcement "[i]n a legal context ... is associated with the state-sanctioned protection of the parties' economic interest in the performance of the contract".[76] Enforceability is connected to the intent of the parties to enter into a contract through the traditional mechanisms of offer, acceptance, and consideration.[77] As such, enforceability is a legal, rather than a technical decision. Such legal decision making though can be hampered or challenged by technical self-execution, which may hamper an adjudicator's ability to resolve a dispute with a "justiciable solution".[78] At least one commentator has suggested that "smart contracts are technically not legally binding, they are a tool to execute agreements".[79]

Other legal issues flow from the enforceability-execution problem. For instance, the act of interpretation in dispute settlement that seeks to determine the intent of the parties could be hampered when the intent is written in computer code, in particular because it is unlikely that the parties were both fluent in computer code.[80] Indeed, smart contract implementation likely requires a third party to write the code to be executed, which means that coders must translate the intent of the parties into machine readable code.[81] Such translation requires the implementation of contract clauses as a set of objective verifiable actions, but this is problematic when it comes to subjective terms such as the implied obligation of "good faith effort" in performance.[82]

In addition to interpretive problems, this raises questions about who bears the risk for mistakes in the code.[83] Further, because the transactions become nonreversible, as they are logged in the blockchain ledger, this could create issues when disputes over performance occur.[84] A prominent example of these risks is a smart contract that due to a coding error and its own immutability has locked approximately $34 million worth of cryptocurrency in a wallet. In this case, the coding error made performance under the contract an impossibility.[85] Numerous other issues can be identified, such as, determining the capacity to enter into a contract by the parties when anonymity is used;[86] problems of contracting by mistake when a party has represented themselves as someone they are not;[87] and issues related to the timing of contract formation.[88] Most of these issues will be dealt with on a case-by-case basis in the dispute resolution system agreed upon, or turned, to by the parties, but actors will need to be aware of how, in particular, courts address these issues and take them into account when devising future instruments. Legal advisor's will need to seek innovative methods to deal with the particularities of smart contracts and properly manage risk

Specifically, they argue that this requires "enforcement agencies to ensure that a punishment is followed". *Id.* This highlights the distance between the technical literature on smart contracts and the legal literature.

76 Mik, "Smart Contracts," 280.

77 *Id.* at 285 and Fulmer, "Exploring the Legal Issues of Blockchain Applications," 176.

78 Fulmer, "Exploring the Legal Issues of Blockchain Applications," 176.

79 *Id.* at 175. See also De Caria, "The Legal Meaning of Smart Contracts," 746 and Reggie O'Shields, "Smart Contracts: Legal Agreements for the Blockchain," NC Banking Inst. 21 (2017): 185.

80 Giancaspro, "Is a 'Smart Contract' Really a Smart Idea?" 831–833.

81 Mik, "Smart Contracts," 290.

82 Gilcrest and Carvalho, "Smart Contracts," 3279.

83 Lewis and Haria, "Smart Contracts." *See also* Mik, "Smart Contracts," 281–283 and De Caria, "The Legal Meaning of Smart Contracts," 747.

84 Giancaspro, "Is a 'Smart Contract' Really a Smart Idea?" 832.

85 "Aku's Nightmare: $34M Locked Forever as Flaw Highlights Danger of Smart Contracts," *pymnts.com* (25 April 2022).

86 Giancaspro, "Is a 'Smart Contract' Really a Smart Idea? 828.

87 *Id.*

88 *Id.* at 829.

for their clients. Though in the right contexts smart contracts can be powerful tools, "they are not omnipotent, and are unlikely to ever be able to automatically resolve every dispute or conflict".[89]

24.4.2 Blockchain and space law

While space may not create novel legal issues for blockchain and smart contracts generally, these technologies could have effects on the nature of space law. As noted in the space applications section on this above, these technologies have the potential to be deployed in a variety of ways that could impact space operations. These technologies will not change the core substance of principles found in space law, but could be transformational in its application.

A salient example can be found in the authorisation process. If a state were to implement smart contract technology within the framework of its obligation to authorise and continually supervise, it could potentially streamline the oversight of the authorised entity. An operator's authorisation could be linked to the blockchain, and oversight actions could be executed on the same. This could give both parties a full view of the status of the mission and the fulfillment of obligations connected to the authorisation, and allow a state to more fully comply with its obligation to "continually supervise" the operator.[90] At the international level, blockchain could be a significant tool in data sharing among states and operators, for instance, in the field of SSA data. Such data exchanges could help to build trust among actors in the veracity of the data and lead to more effective cooperative practices in pursuing space sustainability. In particular, the Long Term Sustainability Guidelines seek to have states better share data regarding the orbital environment and enhance its accuracy.[91] Similarly, blockchain could be used within the auspices of the Registration Convention[92] or through industry groups to build a shared ledger of space operations and allow operators to better fulfill their obligations under the treaty.

At the same time, blockchain technologies are wrapped in narratives of decentralisation and separating transactions from the state.[93] This is highly problematic within the context of space law, which envisages centralised control over operators through the auspices of the state. Space actors attempting end-run state regulation using blockchain may have a difficult time. States are required to supervise their non-governmental actors' space activities, and are incentivised to do so through legal[94] and national security incentives.[95] Further, space activities are not easily hidden from the state due to the transparent nature of the space environment. As a result, any transformation of space law effectuated by blockchain technology will not likely be the usurpation of the state as the central regulator of space activities, but blockchain does present opportunities to enhance overall governance functions in the space domain. Blockchain will not solve all ambiguities in the space domain, but as a tool to better practices it should not be ignored. Specifically, where there is a need

89 Gilcrest and Carvalho, "Smart Contracts," 3279.

90 Treaty on Principles Governing the Activities of States in the Exploration and Use of Outer Space, Including the Moon and Other Celestial Bodies (1967) Art. VI [hereinafter Outer Space Treaty].

91 See, specifically guidelines B.1, B.2, and B.3. Guidelines for the Long-term Sustainability of Outer Space Activities, U.N. Doc. A/AC.105/2018/CRP.20 (27 June 2018).

92 Convention on the Registration of Objects Launched into Outer Space (1976).

93 Primavera De Filippi and Andrea Leiter, "Blockchain in Outer Space," *American Journal of International Law* 115 (2021): 413–418.

94 Outer Space Treaty (1967) Arts VI-VIII.

95 *See generally*, James Clay Moltz, *The Politics of Space Security: Strategic Restraint and the Pursuit of National Interests* (Stanford, CA: Stanford Security Studies, 2008).

for secure trackable sharing of data or a need to create coordination among actors in their operations, blockchain has potential as a tool to enhance the application of space law principles.

24.5 Conclusion

It is yet to be seen how blockchain technologies and smart contracts will change the space industry, but it is fair to say that as long as these technologies remain prominent that space actors will seek to leverage them to enhance their operations. To that end, legal advisors in this industry need to be aware of blockchain architecture and the legal issues connected to it. In particular, when operators seek to use blockchain to find decentralised solutions and avoid the hand of the state, the lawyers will need to carefully evaluate these cases to ensure that they do not run afoul of the law. This is particularly salient in the space domain where the state maintains a unique role that flows from international space law. As with any enterprise, technology presents a variety of opportunities and risks within a given legal paradigm, and as blockchain evolves these risks and opportunities for space will become more clear.

25

AGILE CONTRACTS FOR SPACE PROJECTS

Gerhard Deiters

25.1 Background: "Traditional" and "agile" approaches in space projects and contract design

Agility is considered the counterpart to the "traditional" approach, the prototype of which is the so-called "waterfall model". While "traditional" approaches are "linear", agile approaches are characterised by "iterative" procedures. In order to recognise the challenges for contract design, one has to be aware of the differences, but also the similarities of the two approaches. For the space sector in particular, it is important to look at how space projects traditionally proceed and where agile approaches are already in use today.

25.1.1 The traditional space project: lots of hardware and a little software

The prototype of the space project is the development of satellites and other space objects, their placement in orbit and subsequent operations. Satellite systems for communications, Earth observation, meteorology and other applications are circulating the Earth in different orbits. The focus of space and ground segment development and commissioning is mainly on hardware. Traditionally, software elements were limited and often underestimated.

Traditional space projects are divided into phases. During phase 0, the mission definition and feasibility are examined, concluding with the Mission Definition Review. After the requirements definition phase, the design phase begins. The Preliminary Design Review (PDR) is followed by the Critical Design Review (CDR). With the achievement of CDR, a design freeze occurs, i.e. later changes are only possible to a limited extent. On the basis of the CDR, the overall system is developed, manufactured, and delivered. After successful acceptance (on ground or in space), the system is put into operation. Often, all phases are covered in one contract, whereby the contractor may be either responsible also for operations or only provides support (e.g., in case of anomalies). The phases run according to a clearly established, linear project plan. If changes occur, especially after CDR, these are introduced by way of contract amendments. They regularly imply impacts on cost and schedule. System acceptance by the client depends on compliance with the initially defined requirements. While requirements are evolving during the first phase until CDR, this does

DOI: 10.4324/9781003268475-36

not make the overall project an agile project; however, agile approaches are certainly conceivable during the early project phases, but also later.

Software elements in the space and ground segment are defined, developed, and accepted according to same traditional phasing. They are subject to dedicated work packages and the development is part of the milestone plan. Acceptance of software can either take place individually or as part of the overall system acceptance events.

In Europe, the traditional approach is defined in the ECSS (European Cooperation for Space Standardization) standards and reflected in the standard contract clauses of the European Space Agency (ESA).[1] Remuneration can be based on several price models; in most cases, a firm fixed price is applied.

25.1.2 "Newer" space projects: increased focus on the software and data driven downstream market

Latest space projects continue to require infrastructure with ground and space segments. However, modern systems are much more driven by and dependent on software and software development correspondingly gains importance in the overall works. Satellites are increasingly flying computers onto which new software versions can be uploaded. Other new developments concern the data generated by satellite systems. Massive amounts of data are delivered, e.g., through the Sentinel satellites of the EU Copernicus programme and made available as "open data".[2] So-called downstream companies use such data and transform them into enhanced, value-added data and services. On-board processing, data download through geostationary laser links, storage, and accessibility through cloud computing platforms and the use of artificial intelligence (AI) for data analytics by means of data links are employed to improve data availability, quality, and information output. Software is a key element in all relevant steps.

As software is omnipresent in space and ground segments, data centres, and on the user side, agile approaches are gaining relevance. However, the standard contracts used by space agencies (and other customers) are not tailored towards agile procedures. In practice, contracts continue to adhere to the "traditional" approach, but they are "lived" according to the agile approach. Some contracts may refer to agile approaches, but regularly only with few and generic sentences. If problems occur, it may be questionable what exactly is owed by the contractor according to the contract concluded.

25.1.3 Basics of the "waterfall model" in the client-contractor relationship

25.1.3.1 Practical basics

The "waterfall model" is a linear model from traditional project management. The project is divided into successive phases. The result of one phase is the basis for the subsequent phase.

In the waterfall model in its pure form, a comprehensive catalogue of requirements (requirements specification) is drawn up, which ideally already contains all the requirements for the product to be procured at a generic level. On the basis of the requirements specification, more detailed specifications are created and ultimately describe the subsequent object of acceptance. If a client accepts the detailed specification together with milestones and acceptance criteria (these can also

1 Current version ESA/REG/002, rev. 3 of 5 July 2019.

2 Copernicus, Copernicus Open Access Hub.

be contained in the statement of work or in the contract itself), the development of the product by the contractor begins on the basis of the detailed specification. Adjustments of the specifications require contract changes, usually implying cost increases and schedule delays. A clear disadvantage of development under the waterfall model is that the client cannot regularly check the development status. Checks are limited to the formal reviews along the milestone plan. Regarding software, much of the development takes place in a "black box" and client feedback comes late in the development cycle. Corrections at such late stage are often time-consuming and costly.

To put it bluntly, with this model, the client receives the product at the end of a development according to requirements formulated at the beginning, but which may no longer be up to date. Changes in requirements lead to cost increases and schedule overruns, and sometimes even to the failure of the overall project.

25.1.3.2 Contractual basis

From a contractual point of view, product development according to the waterfall model is relatively easy to present. For the definition of the subject matter of the contract and the works to be developed by the contractor, reference is made to the specifications, which in turn also describe the object of acceptance. Remuneration is based on firm fixed price, sometimes on time and material or on mixed types. In legal systems, where contract types such as the works or services contracts are defined by law and provisions on acceptance, warranty, liability, etc. are standardised, e.g. German Civil Code, there is theoretically no need for expansive contractual provisions. In practice, of course, the contract will include detailed provisions on milestone achievement, acceptance, contractual penalties, rights of intellectual property (IP) use, and other matters.

25.1.4 Basics of agile approaches

25.1.4.1 General principles of agile approaches

Agile procedures are characterised by an iterative approach. They are based on the idea that the requirements for a product (namely software) are constantly changed, expanded or eliminated in the course of the project. A complete set of requirements and specifications at the beginning of a development is therefore generally considered neither necessary nor adequate; rather, it is assumed that the extensive preliminary work in the waterfall model leads to a later start of development and regularly only represents the illusion of a complete catalogue of requirements already at the beginning. Furthermore, it is assumed that only regular delivery and testing of usable development stages of a product (e.g., an executable software) at the shortest possible intervals, the so-called "Increment", together with a continuous exchange of ideas between client and contractor, enable product development really tailored to the client's needs. The agile manifesto,[3] written in 2001, is considered the basis of agile methods in software development and reads:

> We are uncovering better ways of developing
> software by doing it and helping others do it.
> Through this work we have come to value:
> Individuals and interactions over processes and tools
> Working software over comprehensive documentation

3 Manifesto for Agile Software Development.

Customer collaboration over contract negotiation
Responding to change over following a plan
That is, while there is value in the items on
the right, we value the items on the left more.

Twelve principles for agile (software) development were formulated in the agile manifesto.[4] These are aimed at software developers based on development experience, they are not a comprehensive description of agile project management. Nevertheless, in its brevity and conciseness, the manifesto remains a valuable guideline for agile projects.

If agile procedures are applied to a project, the considerable effort required for writing requirements and specifications is generally omitted. However, there are exceptions, especially in public funded projects. Under public procurement (but also in procurements carried out by private companies), budgets are typically not released without a justification of need and at least a rough catalogue of requirements. However, the extensive planning phase at the beginning of a development in the waterfall model is at least partially omitted in the agile approach, and the development phase can start earlier. However, planning is by no means omitted in total, but it is conducted throughout the entire project. Requirements are constantly re-evaluated and as necessary reformulated. The client is presented with Increments to be tested at short intervals. This implies a higher effort and involvement of the client compared the waterfall model. If agile approaches are chosen on the assumption that the client efforts on defining requirements and specifications can be reduced during tender preparation, this is counterproductive and regularly leads to the client being hopelessly overwhelmed during project implementation. Therefore, agile approaches should only be chosen if the client can ensure availability of the required resources and where such approaches provide added value for the project.

25.1.4.2 Basics of Scrum

The most popular agile approach at present, at least in software development, is Scrum. Scrum is originally a term from rugby and means sticking the heads together. The term is meant to symbolise the close cooperation of all parties involved in the project.

Scrum is a simple framework for the development of a product with specific roles, meetings, and artefacts. Therefore, it does not specify any techniques or project management methods to be used. These are to be determined individually.

The development work is done in iterations, the so-called "Sprints". The roles in Scrum are the "Product Owner", the "Scrum Master", and the "Scrum Team". The Scrum Master is responsible for fostering an environment in which (1) the Product Owner orders the work for a complex problem into a Product Backlog, (2) the Scrum Team turns a selection of the work into an Increment of value during a Sprint, (3) the Scrum Team and the stakeholders in the project inspect the results and adjust for the next Sprint, and (4) a permanent repetition of these processes takes place. In most cases, the client provides the Product Owner and the contractor provides the Scrum Master and the Scrum Team. However, this is not specified by Scrum itself since Scrum can also be used within an organisation without commissioning a service provider or for cooperative projects where several entities come together for joint development.

4 Id.

In Scrum, the development of a product takes place within the framework of Sprints. The planning of the Sprint takes place in the "Sprint Planning Meeting". In the Sprint Planning Meeting, those requirements are taken over into the Sprint that are prioritised highest in the Product Backlog and that can realistically be implemented during the Sprint. These requirements then go into the so-called "Sprint Backlog". This ensures that planning always takes place on the most urgent requirements, so that a higher proximity is created compared to the waterfall model, where requirements that are only implemented late in the course of the project are also defined at the beginning. In theory, only the requirements that are taken over into the Sprint need to be ordered in the Product Backlog. In practice, it is not desirable to take the risk of entering a Sprint with "unfinished" requirements. Further requirements are therefore formulated in the course of maintaining the Product Backlog (e.g., in the course of a so-called "Backlog Refinement Meeting"). The Scrum Team meets daily in the Daily Scrum and discusses the progress of the previous day and the planned activities for the current day. In the Sprint Review, the Increment with the implemented requirements tested by the Scrum Team is presented. Requirements that have not been implemented and/or tested according to agreed criteria may not be presented. During the Sprint Review Meeting, it is decided which requirements have been implemented to the satisfaction of the client and what still needs to be improved. The latter requirements are considered not implemented. In the subsequent Sprint Retrospective, it is examined what went well and what went badly in the past sprint and how improvements can be implemented for the upcoming Sprints. The Sprint Retrospective concludes the Sprint, after which the next Sprint begins.

One of the reasons why Scrum is so popular in software development is that it is a simple, comprehensible framework that can be individually adapted by the parties, e.g., by defining the sprint length and the staffing of roles.

25.1.4.3 Contractual basis

In some respects, contracts for agile approaches do not differ from traditional contracts. Provisions on granting rights to the development result, as example, are typically identical. Standard clauses on data protection, information security, confidentiality, or applicable law also do not require adaptations.

However, there are features of agile approaches that are not reflected in standard contracts and can only be implemented with considerable redesign. For example, the subject matter of the contract is not firmly defined from the beginning, but is only contained in a more or less detailed product vision. In contrast to the waterfall model, the agile approach and cooperation throughout the entire development do not have a purely formal character, but are the "master plan" for development. Since agile approaches such as Scrum only establish basic rules, the concrete processes must be defined in the contract (or an annex); this – together with clauses on remuneration – is often the most time-consuming part of contract drafting and negotiations. The subject matter of (partial and final) acceptance only emerges in the course of the project. Since the subject matter of the contract is not conclusively determined at contract signature, agreement on the remuneration is a challenge. Remuneration based on time and material is not desired by the client, while a firm fixed price is in turn rarely accepted by the contractor. Unlike in the waterfall model, changing requirements is part of the process in the agile approach. They are therefore only subject to contract amendments if they affect the content, scope or milestones of the development.

25.1.5 When are agile approaches suitable in space projects?

When one thinks of agile approaches, one thinks primarily of software development. Therefore, agile approaches are particularly suitable for all software elements of space systems and for software involved in downstream applications. If certain functions with specific requirements can already be fixed at the beginning, while further functions can only be added later and requirements are still volatile, a "hybrid" approach can be chosen, in which parts are developed according to the waterfall model and other parts according to the agile approach. The already fixed requirements can also be "embedded" in the agile approach and marked as fixed, thus not being subject to (re) definition. It is also possible, of course, that requirements that were originally considered fixed are adapted in the course of development. This is more the rule than the exception in an agile approach.

The advantage of the agile approach is that, at the end of the development, the software meets the then latest requirements. Considering that space projects often take years of implementation, during which external and internal factors may significantly change, agile approaches appear especially appealing.

However, agile approaches should not be restricted to software development alone. Especially in the early space project phases, agile approaches can lead to the development of "better" requirements due to the close interaction between the different parties and roles involved. Early consideration and focus on end user requirements may be specifically supported by agile approaches.

In large system projects, agile approaches are not only suitable for the development of software (e.g., for satellite control or the processing of transmitted data), but also for the development of requirements for a space mission or even in the context of the development of ground and space segments. In a complex space mission, however, they will practically always be used together with classical procedures in hybrid models. The special features of agile approaches (subject matter of the contract, type of contract, procedure, acceptance, remuneration, etc.) must be taken into account in the corresponding contract, as well as in the project management plan.

25.2 Contract design in an agile approach, part 1: the specifics of an "agile" contract

As already outlined above, it is not sufficient to simply add a new sentence to a contract stating that a product will be developed using an agile approach. In the following, some essential points to be considered when drafting the contract are addressed. Depending on the individual project, further points may of course become relevant.

25.2.1 The "legal nature" of the contract

When applying agile approaches, the appropriate contract type must be identified. In the space industry, the typical contract is a contract for works. Here, the contractor owes the creation of a work according to predefined criteria. After completion, an acceptance takes place and the remuneration for the work is only earned if the work is in condition for such acceptance.

In agile approaches, however, use of a contract for work is sometimes questioned, as the volatility of the product to be developed could argue against its classification as work. In fact, it is often argued that development contracts using agile approaches are to be qualified as pure service contracts. The argument sounds reasonable at first glance but does not meet the legal core of the underlying question. Whether a contract is a contract for work or a contract for services does not depend on whether the specifications for a product are already fixed at the beginning of a development, but on whether the contractor owes the development and delivery of a product under his own responsibility. The point in time at which the applicable specifications are formulated is not decisive in this respect. Even with the traditional approach, requirements can change fundamentally through contract changes during the project. Acceptance is then conducted according to the latest agreed criteria.

For the determination of the type of contract, it is decisive what is contractually owed. If the contractor develops a product in a mixed team together with the client (and potentially with third parties employed by the client), a contract for work can only be considered if the individual contributions can be distinguished from each other in such a way that the contractor can take responsibility for the success of its contribution. If this is not possible, a contract for services must be assumed; performance monitoring must then be conducted via mechanisms other than acceptance. If a process is contractually agreed which gives the client sovereignty over the definition of the requirements and the contractor sovereignty over their implementation, one can regularly assume a contract for work. This does however not apply if successful implementation of the requirements is uncertain so that the contractor only owes best efforts. This can be the case for very innovative or new types of products, where achievement of specific results cannot be guaranteed. In this respect, the agile approach does not differ from the traditional approach.

If the contractor owes a work, it makes sense to define the boundaries of the development in addition to the process for defining the respective work. This should relieve the contractor from the concern that the client will impose requirements during the agile process that are outside the originally intended scope and the contractor's competences or capabilities.

25.2.2 Determination of the subject matter of the contract

In traditional space projects, the subject matter of the contract can be conclusively described when the contract is concluded. The relevant provision will then make reference to the applicable requirements laid down in contract annexes. When using agile approaches, there is no final definition of the applicable requirements at contract signature, but the subject matter of the contract must nevertheless of course be described. To this end, the product to be created must be described thematically together with an objective (Product Vision). At the same time, it must be stipulated that the requirements for the product will be continuously reviewed, changed and prioritised. One can thus speak of an evolving subject matter of the contract. In addition to the Product Vision, it is a good idea to roughly describe the planned product and to describe the already defined requirements in more detail. Here, one can rely on terminologies such as "Themes", "Epics", and "User Stories", which are explained in the list of definitions at the beginning of a contract or respective annexes. To avoid disputes, at least a rudimentary catalogue of requirements (e.g., a Product Backlog) should exist at the beginning of the contract and should be referred to therein.

A formulation of the subject matter of the contract could look as follows (based on Scrum terminologies):

> The subject of the contract is the development by the contractor of software for optimising satellite control. The software is defined in Annex 1. Annex 1 contains the objective of the development (Product Vision), the Themes, Epics and User Stories envisaged by the client, in the form of the Product Backlog existing at the time of conclusion of the contract. The Product Backlog shall be continuously adjusted during the development in accordance with the processes set out in this contract, with a constant re-evaluation of the prioritisations contained therein and a specification of the Themes, Epics and User Stories.

25.2.3 Collaboration and processes for requirements definition

In traditional space projects, close monitoring of project progress is conducted through project meetings, formal reviews and reporting obligations. However, the implementation of the work as such follows the requirements specified at the time of contract conclusion. Implementation can thus progress, even if project meetings are cancelled, e.g., due to holiday periods. This is not easily possible with agile approaches, as the requirements are not conclusively determined and continuous cooperation is essential to ensure the success of the project. In the following, some related aspects are examined in more detail.

25.2.3.1 Minimum requirement for processes to be agreed by contract

Since in agile approaches the requirements are defined during ongoing development, the processes for defining requirements are crucial and to be stipulated in the contract or its annexes (e.g. in an annex "Roles and Processes"). In particular, the following must be specified:

- duration of the iterations within the development;
- project meetings;
- roles, with related competences;
- escalation processes for conflicts that cannot be resolved at working level.

25.2.3.2 Processes for defining requirements to be implemented

Since the client's objective is to meet a given need, the processes must be designed in such a way that the client ultimately decides which requirements are to be implemented. However, it makes sense to also define processes that come into play if the parties cannot agree on the details of individual requirements at working level.

A related contractual process description could look as follows:

> The Product Owner, supported by the Scrum Team and the Scrum Master, specifies the User Stories in the Product Backlog, at least to the extent of the expected delivery of the next two Sprints. The decision on the content of the User Stories and the prioritisation for the subsequent Sprints is made by the Product Owner.
>
> Before development begins in a Sprint, the Scrum Team, together with the Product owner, estimates the effort required for the individual User Stories. The estimate also includes the effort for project meetings, Sprint Planning Meetings, Sprint Review Meetings and other meetings, the creation or updating of documentation and other organisational activities of the contractor. A procedure should be chosen that allows for an estimate of effort that is as uninfluenced as possible.
>
> The contractor is obliged to choose the most favourable solution for the client in compliance with the technical requirements and to propose more favourable solutions in terms of effort, provided that these are suitable for implementing the User Story.
>
> In cases where the contractor anticipates difficulties in implementation that would lead to disproportionate effort, it shall submit an alternative proposal to the client. If the client decides in favour of an alternative solution proposal submitted by the contractor, the corresponding User Story shall be adjusted. If the contractor wishes to deviate from previously made effort estimates, it must justify this to the Product Owner. Any disagreements

that cannot be resolved within the scope of the estimate shall be submitted to the Steering Committee for a decision; this shall not affect the implementation of the respective Sprint.

In the above example, the contractor is not a mere recipient of requirements decided by the client. The contractor participates in the requirement definition at least to a certain extent. Since agile procedures in space projects are likely to constitute only sub-elements of the overall project and there are dependencies with other areas, the contractor should have extensive duties regarding the assessment of the impact of new or changed requirements to such other areas. Of course, the challenge also arises in classic procedures, but not to the same extent as in agile procedures, since new and changed requirements are an inherent part of the process and must therefore constantly be checked for effects on other areas.

The first paragraph of the above example contains a self-commitment on the part of the client. It does not have to be contractually stipulated but is nevertheless necessary to ensure the progress of the project. As described at 25.1.4 above, an essential aspect of agile procedures is that requirements are bindingly defined as close to implementation as possible. This can imply a risk that fewer requirements are defined for an iteration (see 25.2.3.2 below) than development resources are available. In deviation from the above example, the contractor could be required to inform the client if there are not enough requirements for the next iteration. Alternatively or cumulatively, a project meeting can be scheduled in the middle of an iteration (e.g., Backlog Refinement Meeting), in which the contents of the requirements catalogue (e.g., Product Backlog) are prepared in such a way that they are suitable for implementation in the subsequent iteration. In such a meeting, dependencies on other areas can also be discussed.

25.2.3.3 Defining iterations

Since the development and review of the development results takes place in short iterations compared to classic projects, the contract must specify how these iterations are to proceed. The focus is on which requirements are to be implemented by the contractor, in which order and when the implementation is to be presented to the client. A provision for determining which requirements are to be implemented within an iteration could read as follows:

During the four-week Sprints, the Scrum Team develops the elements of the solution planned for the respective Sprint. For this purpose, the Scrum Team transfers the number of User Stories from the Product Backlog into the Sprint Backlog that corresponds to resources planned for the Sprint. The Scrum Team is bound by the prioritisation of the User Stories in the Product Backlog. User Stories that are not implemented, not implemented completely or implemented incorrectly in a Sprint are either taken back into the Product Backlog by the Product Owner and scheduled in one of the next Sprints, or removed from the Sprint Backlog and the Product Backlog as User Stories that no longer need to be implemented, while the User Stories that were implemented completely and without errors are marked as implemented in the Product Backlog.

Since project progress can only be measured based on implemented requirements, it should be contractually stipulated under which conditions the contractor may present implementations at the end of an iteration. The following example shows the minimum requirements, which of course need to be specified in much more detail depending on the project and possible integration into an overall project:

Implementations of User Stories are only presented by the Scrum Team in the Sprint Review together with the Increment if the following requirements are fulfilled:

- all acceptance criteria were fulfilled and the documentation according to the provisions of this contract was carried out;
- implementation tests were created and carried out according to the specifications of the statement of work without critical errors, for example module test (unit test), system test, integration test, front-end test, regression test;
- user tests have been carried out by the contractor, i.e. the implementation has been tested, integration tests have been carried out and acceptance tests of the User Stories have been carried out successfully and essentially without errors.

> Exceptions to the above requirements may be mutually agreed by the parties at the relevant Sprint Planning Meeting.

In space projects, testing in real environment is usually not possible. However, there are no special features compared to the traditional procedure, so that proven processes for testing can be used.

25.2.3.4 Provisions for the approval of implementations at the end of an iteration

In an agile approach, the completion of an iteration is regularly not due to the implementation of a certain number of requirements. Only the "delivered" functions of the Increment can be tested. Theoretically, it is possible to make each individual iteration a "mini contract for work". This however not only breaks with the principles of agile development, but also brings unnecessary time delays if, for example, the results of a Sprint must first be improved before the next Sprint can begin. In addition, losses in velocity can be expected, as a contractor would, in case of doubt, take on fewer requirements for implementation in the iteration. Another problem is that the contractor's focus in such case is purely on the acceptance of the iteration, instead of overall progress and customer satisfaction. It is therefore recommended not to carry out "partial acceptance" at the end of an iteration, but to carry out a test of the Increment with the "delivered" functions.

A provision for the approval of implementations at the end of an iteration could read as follows:

> The client will approve the User Stories contained in the Increment and implemented in the Sprint if the respective User Stories have been implemented without defects and the Increment as a whole is functional. The client will also approve implemented User Stories if they only have minor defects that can be corrected by the contractor without major effort (maximum 0.5 person days) and whose function could otherwise be fully checked in the Sprint Review Meeting.

It should be noted that regular underperformance, in the sense that the delivery of implementations is continuously below expectations, should not happen. This is especially important where the agile development is only part of an overall project. Therefore, contractual mechanisms, such as an obligation for the contractor to ramp up resources, should be foreseen if delivery according to the project plan cannot otherwise be ensured.

25.2.4 Acceptance provisions (only for contracts for work)

The definition of the object of acceptance is essential. In qualitative terms, there are no special features compared to the traditional procedures. However, the object of acceptance with all related requirements is not fixed from the beginning. Therefore, a mechanism must be found that determines which (functional) scope is ultimately owed by the contractor. The client can choose from a number of different options when drafting the contract. If the contractor is to implement all requirements formulated by the client, final acceptance can be made against the complete catalogue of requirements available at this stage. The counterpart to this is acceptance based on the functions implemented by the contractor at the given point in time. It is also possible to provide a mechanism for evaluating efforts on individual requirements combined with a "total effort" that must be implemented at a given point in time. Finally, it can be considered to define minimum requirements that must be implemented in any case. Which option is chosen depends largely on the individual project circumstances.

The last iteration of a development plays a special role regarding final acceptance, since during individual iterations no fixed delivery is owed by the contractor (see 25.2.3.3). If a certain scope of delivery owed by the contractor is desired with the last iteration, it makes sense to make such last iteration "atypical" in a way that all requirements adopted for this iteration must be implemented and that this iteration is therefore not fixed in time like the other iterations. In this case, the contractor owes a predefined scope (e.g. the functionalities required for satellite control) with the completion of the last iteration. In addition, it can be foreseen that after the implementation of the last owed requirement, the remaining time of an iteration and, if necessary, another iteration is used to "stabilise" the product to bring the developed work to acceptance maturity.

A short provision for final acceptance could be as follows:

> The object of the final acceptance is the software with the accepted functions and the functions for the implementation of the User Stories that were transferred to the Sprint Backlog of the last Sprint.

25.2.5 Remuneration

The traditional space project is regularly remunerated with a firm fixed price (whereby the fixed price can relate to a phase or to the entire project), although a cost reimbursement price with a ceiling is also applied in some contracts. Both remuneration models have the supposed advantage of budget certainty, but this becomes obsolete in the moment of change requests with price impact.

25.2.5.1 Options for remuneration in an agile approach

In the agile approach, the fundamental question is how the contractor should be remunerated for the development of a product that exists only as a more or less "finished" vision. In principle, the traditional remuneration models are also conceivable for agile approaches. A firm fixed price is however usually not accepted by the contractor as he does not yet know all requirements of the product to be developed. On the other hand, invoicing based on time and material is regularly rejected by clients as a "bottomless pit". Therefore, it is necessary to adjust the remuneration models to the agile approach. In this respect, one must free oneself from the idea that a contract for work leads to a firm fixed price, while a contract for services leads to remuneration according to time and material. The contract type itself has no relation to the type of remuneration but determines whether the contractor owes a success or merely best efforts. A firm fixed price is definitively conceivable for service contracts.

25.2.5.2 "Pay per Sprint"

The "Pay per Sprint" method is often used as a relatively simple way of remuneration. As the name suggests, the individual Sprint is remunerated, irrespective of whether a specific delivery is made at the end of the Sprint. The contract specifies which resources the contractor has to provide in a Sprint. With this type of remuneration, it is often specified that the client must either explicitly commission the subsequent sprint or has a short-term exit option. A short-term exit option is quite appropriate whenever a proof of concept is to be created with an existing budget, or if the development itself has no particular criticality and can be terminated by the client at any time without significant disadvantages. In a project in which the client is dependent on a specific result at a given point in time, this type of remuneration is less suitable. The latter should be the case in most type of space projects.

25.2.5.3 Remuneration according to time and material

Remuneration according to time and material is also conceivable. However, it will only make sense if the client is given exit options without having to pay "residual compensation". Similar to "Pay per Sprint", time-and-material remuneration should only be considered if the client can terminate a project at short notice without significant disadvantages. If this is not the case, mechanisms must be included in the contract to ensure that the contractor does not receive full payment in case of delayed or poor performance. Remuneration according to time and material on the basis of effort estimates (see 25.2.5.4) or the "agile fixed price" (see 25.2.5.5) are discussed in the following.

25.2.5.4 Remuneration according to time and material on the basis of effort estimates

Typically, a contractor will estimate efforts when submitting a fixed price offer. However, the estimate can contain a high degree of inaccuracy if implementation of requirements is "far away". Estimates that are close to implementation, as they are inherent in the agile approach, are much more accurate because they consider the experiences of the previous development and the cooperation between the parties. If, for example, the parties have discovered during the update of a software used for satellite control that the dependencies on the satellite itself cause considerable efforts not previously foreseeable, these can be included in the estimate. If the effort is already determined at contract signature, such experiences and circumstances cannot be considered and the initial assumptions may later prove to be incorrect.

For the purpose of remuneration (and schedule planning), it is conceivable to make a joint estimate of effort during the Sprint Planning (at the latest), which is then taken into account in the

Table 25.1 Underperformance

User Story	*Estimated effort*	*Actual efforts*	*Accepted*	*Estimate included in the remuneration*	*Relevant for the settlement*
U1	1 day	2 days	Yes	1 day	2 days
U2	2 days	1 day	Yes	2 days	1 day
U3	1.5 days	2 days	Yes	1.5 days	2 days
U4	2 days	3 days	Yes	2 days	3 days
U5	1 day	0.5 days	No	~~1 day~~	~~0.5 days~~
Total	**7.5 days**	**8.5 days**		**6.5 days**	**8 days**
Result	6.5 days paid in full, remaining 1.5 days paid with deduction of X %, U5 carried over to next Sprint.				

Table 25.2 Overperformance

User Story	*Estimated effort*	*Actual efforts*	*Accepted*	*Estimate included in the remuneration*	*Relevant for the settlement*
U1	1 day	1 day	Yes	1 day	1 day
U2	2 days	1 day	Yes	2 days	1 day
U3	1.5 days	1 day	Yes	1.5 days	1 day
U4	2 days	3 days	Yes	2 days	3 days
U5	1 day	0.5 days	Yes	1 day	0.5 days
Total	**7.5 days**	**6.5 days**		**7.5 days**	**6.5 days**
Result	6.5 days are paid in full, 1 "bonus day" is carried over to the next Sprint.				

Table 25.3 Transfer of a "bonus" from a previous Sprint

User Story	*Estimated effort*	*Actual efforts*	*Accepted*	*Estimate included in the remuneration*	*Relevant for the settlement*
"Bonus"	1 day	"0" days	N/A	1 day	"0" days
U2	2 days	3 days	Yes	2 days	3 days
U3	1.5 days	1 day	Yes	1.5 days	1 day
U4	2 days	3 days	Yes	2 days	3 days
U5	1 day	0.5 days	Yes	1 day	0.5 days
Total	**7.5 days**	**7.5 days**		**7.5 days**	**7.5 days**
Result	The "bonus day" from the previous Sprint compensates for the "underperformance" in the current Sprint. The contractor is compensated for all efforts in the Sprint.				

settlement of the Sprint. This can be done, for example, by comparing the cumulative estimated efforts of accepted implementations of requirements with the actual efforts. If the actual efforts exceed the estimated efforts, the excess efforts can be remunerated with reduced rates and, after a certain point, be capped in absolute terms (e.g., 30% deduction up to 25% additional effort, then no more remuneration). Incomplete implementations can then be carried over to the next Sprint at the estimated and actual efforts incurred to date. In addition, further "corrective measures" can be provided for. If, for example, the client waives requirements whose implementation has already begun but has not yet been completed, the contractor is paid for the actual effort, possibly limited by the estimated effort. If the contractor falls short of his estimate, it can carry over the shortfall as a "bonus" into the next Sprint to compensate for a possible underperformance there. Estimates of reference requirements could be developed during contract negotiations and used as benchmark.

A contractual description of remuneration according to time and material on the basis of effort estimates can look as follows:

> Implementations of User Stories approved by the client in the Sprint Review Meeting shall be remunerated according to actual effort. If the effort according to the preceding sentence exceeds the sum of the estimated efforts for the approved implementations, the remuneration for the effort exceeding the estimate shall be reduced by 25 percent. However, additional expenditure shall only be remunerated up to a maximum of 20 per cent of the expenditure exceeding the estimate.

> Actual efforts for the implementation of User Stories not approved by the client in the Sprint Review Meeting will only be remunerated if the client expressly waives further implementation, but only up to the estimated effort for the corresponding User Story. This also applies accordingly to User Stories whose implementation has already been started but which were not presented for approval with the executable Increment in the Sprint Review Meeting.
>
> The limitation of the remuneration according to the above provisions shall not apply insofar as the contractor proves that the client is responsible for the corresponding additional efforts.
>
> With regard to the remuneration of User Stories that have not been implemented or User Stories whose implementation has not been approved by the client and whose implementation has not been waived by the client, both the estimated and the actual efforts incurred to date shall be carried over into the subsequent Sprint; in this case, a new effort estimate shall not be made. In the event of approval of the corresponding implementation by the client in the corresponding Sprint Review Meeting, the provision in paragraph 1 shall apply.

This type of remuneration requires a high degree of effort and budget control, but this is not unusual in space projects and should therefore not be a particular challenge. Tables 25.1, 25.2, and 25.3 illustrate the practical application.

25.2.5.5 Remuneration according to "agile fixed price"

If, for example, Storypoints (a measurement unit to describe the size of a requirement especially in agile approaches) are used to estimate effort, an agile fixed price can be determined by assigning a value to a Storypoint (e.g., "1 Storypoint = 1,000 EUR"). This agile fixed price can then be set as a "real" calculated fixed price or as maximum ceiling price with billing according to time and material. In the case of remuneration on time and material basis, bonuses can be agreed for earlier or cheaper completion, or penalties can be agreed for delays and cost overruns. The agile fixed price has the advantage that requirements can be changed, added or removed in a transparent way without the need for contract changes.

A contractual provision for an "agile fixed price" could look as follows:

> The contractor's efforts shall be invoiced monthly in arrears according to actual efforts. The total amount is limited to an amount equal to the agile fixed price. Any remuneration in excess of this is not owed by the client. The agile fixed price is calculated as follows:
>
> [TOTAL NUMBER OF AGREED STORYPOINTS] * [AMOUNT PER STORYPOINT]

In such an approach, it is important to realise that Storypoints were not originally used to estimate effort, but to assess the complexity of requirements. Even complex requirements can be implemented with little effort. Therefore, if Storypoints are used to determine an agile fixed price, it must be clear to all parties that the Storypoints in this case are effort estimates instead of estimates of complexity.

25.2.5.6 Summary on remuneration in an agile project

Remuneration in agile projects must be adapted to the specifics of the individual project. Methods such as "agile fixed price" and "estimate-based remuneration" can offer solutions that meet the interests of both parties, but they are associated with considerable effort. If a short-term exit from the project is possible, remuneration according to time and material or "Pay per Sprint" can make more sense. Remuneration according to a firm fixed price will only very rarely be considered.

25.3 Contract design in an agile approach, part 2: internal arrangements

If an organisation decides to carry out a project according to the agile approach, attention should be paid to internal organisation and related arrangements. This is especially relevant if the organisation does not yet have extensive experience with agile approaches. Internal arrangements are also needed if several organisations are involved on the client side (e.g., European Commission, EUSPA, and ESA within the EU Programme).

25.3.1 Risks of agile approaches in the absence of internal organisation

If there is a lack of internal arrangements with regard to the agile approach, this can lead to considerable risks in implementation. If a software is developed according to Scrum with two-week sprints, this means that the project managers and users on the client side must not only be available for the Sprint Planning and the Sprint Review Meeting, but they must also define the requirements for the contractor in this cycle. Otherwise, the contractor may provide the contractually owed resources, but the Product Backlog does not contain enough requirements to carry out a Sprint. In such case, the question arises whether the contractor shall receive the applicable remuneration although it has not provided corresponding development services. Similar problems can arise when the client's project manager is not empowered to make decisions in terms of defining requirements or prioritising them. If the project manager has to assess for each new or changed requirement whether it is still in line with the overall objectives or if he requires higher-level authorisations, this can lead to considerable delays.

25.3.2 Contents of internal arrangements

The internal arrangements should bindingly clarify the stakeholders involved in the project, their roles and responsibilities. In addition to the project manager and his team, the IT department, the IT security department, and the end users should be included as additional stakeholders. The end user involvement is especially relevant in requirements definition, but also in the testing of the implemented functionalities at the end of an iteration. If an agile development is only a part of an overall project, the dependencies on other parts of the project must be taken into account when determining the internal organisation.

At an early stage, the project manager (in Scrum, for example, the Product Owner) must be selected and its competences must be clarified. It should be determined in which cases the project manager requires higher-level authorisations (e.g. decision on a Sprint termination or disputes that cannot be resolved at the working level). In contrast to the traditional approach, the tight pace of development in individual iterations makes very short-term decisions necessary. Complex internal decision-making structures may lead to delays or standstill.

25.4 Summary

Agile approaches are widely recognised and used for software development. While space projects still follow classical approaches, agile elements are already included in the early phase of requirements definition. As space systems become ever more software-dependent and as space-related data applications grow, agile approaches may become more important.

In large and long-term space projects, agile procedures can help to incorporate changes of requirements and feedback from users into the further development stages. This can avoid that products or functionalities developed are effectively useless at time of delivery. This applies in particular to software but can potentially be applied for the overall space project up to the design freeze or possibly even beyond. Since the specific works to be provided by the contractor are not yet conclusively determined at the beginning, contractual mechanisms must be foreseen for requirements definition, how implementation is checked and how the contractor is remunerated. Since the client's involvement is required to a considerable extent, internal arrangements regarding involved stakeholders, the project manager, decision-making authority, availability and participation of key persons and other aspects are of special importance.

PART III

Cross-cutting items and challenges

A

International standards and export control

26

EXPORT CONTROL AND NEWSPACE

Reciprocal challenges

Matthias Creydt and Lisa Gräfin von der Schulenburg

26.1 Introduction

Regardless of the geographic starting, there is an international consensus when it comes to the need for export controls. This can be seen through the numerous countries which make up the list of international participants in the various multilateral export control regimes. Despite this consensus, there are variations in how each country implements and applies these controls because of differing national security and foreign policy goals. Contributing to the differing views of necessity and application is the challenge posed by the changing environment of emerging technologies, and sectors like the commercial space industry. The overall challenge presented by NewSpace and the related emerging technologies is not new, however it is unique. Originally the space industry was only accessible through government funded and regulated projects. But advancements in technology and private interests in funding innovative projects have led to the commercial space industry that evolves on a different tract than the one originally set out by government bureaucracy. Taking the commercial space industry one step further is NewSpace. Even though this new space industry draws its stakeholders from a combination of government, large companies, and start-up companies, it is the start-up companies that are revolutionising this sector of commercial space.

While there is an excitement surrounding advancements in technology and its benefits, there is also risk and uncertainty surrounding emerging technologies, such as space technology; information communications technology (ICT); artificial intelligence (AI), particularly in terms of machine learning and robotics; nanotechnology; biotechnology; and quantum computing. The common risk posed by each of these technologies is the potential for misuse or the potential negative impact on society. These key concerns factor into how space technologies and related emerging technologies should be regulated by export controls.

What makes NewSpace start-ups, as both a concept and an industry, extremely challenging is the rapid pace at which technology is advancing and being developed and the resulting products. As new technology is developed, and new standards are set, the current export control system has to adapt. What also sets these companies apart from the government funded projects is that they are focused on technology and innovation, possibly profit, and that their focus is not national secu-

DOI: 10.4324/9781003268475-39

rity or foreign politics. International teams work on international projects, possibly even working together on the same projects but coming from different countries.

This chapter will first show the impact and challenges posed by the commercial space industry, specifically NewSpace, on the current export control regimes of the EU and US. It will then look at how, although export control laws and regulations are evolving to adapt, they are not always able keep pace with the advancements in technology. However, it will also show that despite the developments from the NewSpace industry, the existing export control laws and regulations do not need to be changed as a whole because, to a certain extent, they are able to cope with the challenges from NewSpace. Principally, it will be necessary to amend the lists of export-controlled goods and authorities will need to adopt their way of handling such export control matters in order to keep up with the pace of NewSpace industry.

26.2 What is export control?

Export control is one measure which governments employ to meet foreign policy and national security goals. Export controls are laws and regulations that regulate and restrict the release of critical technologies, information, and services to foreign nationals, and foreign countries, primarily through customs and licensing. Exporters must apply for and obtain a licence to export, if they or their goods or services fall within these categories.

The two main categories that are controlled are military goods, dual-use items (goods, software, and technology that can be used for both civilian and military applications). To be effective, export controls must be easy to implement and sustainable.[1] This is a challenge for policy and lawmakers, especially in current times as the geopolitical landscape of different countries undergoes changes.

Countries implement these laws and regulations to protect national security, foreign policy, to combat terrorism, and to further the non-proliferation of weapons of mass destruction. At the same time, these national security and foreign policy goals must be balanced against countries' needs to remain economically competitive and allow for innovation and advancement in technology. Maintaining this balance remains an ongoing task for policy and lawmakers; companies affected by these laws and regulations must constantly remain informed.

While there is a consensus among most countries to prevent the unauthorised transfer of certain goods and information, the way different countries implement and regulate export control varies. The variations in which a country implements export controls is ultimately determined by its individual foreign policy and national security goals. It is the environment and the current status of each country that determines the implementation and regulation. While these factors are not constant, they contribute to an ever-changing environment, which in turn presents policy and lawmakers with the challenge of adapting to these new circumstances.

When it comes to regulating the transfer of technology, export control laws and regulations – which are mainly list driven and based on technical standards, are faced with the challenge of categorising, and defining technology parallel to development before the final product has been realised.

Finally, non-compliance with export laws and regulations may also have an additional economic impact on companies as it could expose them to fines for these violations. Especially for start-up companies in space, this means that they must deal with export controls and respective

1 Brockmann K., "Drafting, Implementing and Complying with Export Controls: The Challenge Presented by Emerging Technologies." *Strategic Trade Review*, no. 4 (2018): 5–28.

export compliance programs from the very beginning of their activities, at a time where newly founded companies normally focus on other matters.

26.2.1 Defining emerging technology

The way a country's continuously changing geopolitical landscape impacts the overall regulatory framework of export control can be seen in the attempts to define the technology that it is trying to control. The challenge that arises here is that while countries may agree conceptually on what they want to control, the terms they use to defining these "items" may vary due to their numerous different application possibilities and the lack of technical standards in their development. This becomes even more evident in attempts to define and regulate emerging technologies, which are often used for newly developed products in the NewSpace industry.

The challenge here for policy and lawmakers is that, traditionally, export control laws and regulations employ lists that capture commodities, software, and technology that are subject to controls. However, in order to place an item on such a list, existing list entries must be amended, or there even might be a need to create a whole new category. The latter of course would make the system of item-based controls even more challenging to master.

Especially in the NewSpace sector, there is a great use of emerging technologies. Further the space industry itself, due to many new developments and inventions, may also generically be seen as an emerging industry. Emerging technologies currently in the context of export controls therefore generally include the following: space technology, ICT, AI – particularly in terms of machine learning and robotics, nanotechnology, biotechnology, and quantum computing.[2]

When it comes to regulating these "emerging" technologies, capturing them on lists that are definition-based is difficult. The absence of a set of technical standards may require a new approach to categorise these technologies. Shifting the focus away from "what" is being controlled and more to the potential "use", and why the technology should be controlled, would enable export control laws and regulations to account for technology in a more accurate way.

One definition presented by Rotolo, Hicks, and Martin analyses commonalities of existing definitions of "emerging technologies" and identifies five main attributes: "(i) radical novelty, (ii) relatively fast growth, (iii) coherence, (iv) prominent impact, and (v) uncertainty and ambiguity".[3] While this definition has identified five main attributes, applying this definition further relies on a common interpretation of each of these attributes.

That which presents a particular challenge is the attribute of "uncertainty" when it comes to emerging technologies, because of the uncertainty of the risk associated with the unknown potential uses.

26.2.2 The dual-use character of emerging technologies used in NewSpace

The reason for regulating emerging technologies is that they are often of a dual-use nature. They are products normally used for civilian purpose however they may also have military application. Most space technologies are dual-use by nature, due to their technical characteristics and unique

2 Kavanagh C., "New Tech, New Threats, and New Governance Challenges: An Opportunity to Craft Smarter Responses?" Carnegie Endowment for International Peace (2019).

3 Rotolo D., Hicks D., Martin B. R., "*What is an Emerging Technology*?", Research Policy, Volume 44, Issue 10 (2015): 1827-1843, ISSN 0048-7333.

possibility of applications.[4] Often the individual components used in space technology are classified as dual-use. What sets emerging technologies used in the NewSpace industry apart is that as a typical NewSpace feature, systems are often tried to be developed and assembled with industrial norm components rather than "traditional" dual-use components. Industrial norm components last longer in space since they are radiation-hardened, which also makes them subject to export controls. The result may be that, while the application of the technology may have dual-use potential, the components are not classified as dual-use.

This wavering dual-use aspect poses a challenge for implementing export controls for the NewSpace industry and the emerging technologies used, as they must fit into a predefined category even when these technologies themselves have not yet been clearly defined, there are no technical standards, and the potential for misuse remains unknown. On the other hand, the government has a policy interest in not restricting such technologies too much, in order to promote and support new technical developments and innovative ideas.

26.3 Defining the NewSpace dilemma

NewSpace has evolved out of the commercial space sector and is an ongoing revolution within the commercial space industry. NewSpace companies are young, innovative, and have private funding. For the large part, and like any start-up, they may be inexperienced when it comes to export control compliance and dealing with government agencies. They do not work on structured projects with set outcomes. That which also sets NewSpace apart from "Old Space" is the application and possible accessibility of their technology, as NewSpace sees new opportunities for the application of space data and a new futuristic model for space tourism.[5] What has not changed with NewSpace is that day-to-day activities in the NewSpace industry may be subject to export licensing requirements.

In contrast to start-up companies in most other industries, even for a small space start-up, compliance with export control laws and regulations becomes important, to ensure that the transfer of software and technical data export control is compliant and consistent with foreign defence policy and international obligations. Therefore, for NewSpace companies export controls and export compliance play an important role, even at a very early stage.

For NewSpace companies outside the US, even the hiring of US citizens or green card holders may subject them to US export control laws and regulations. On the other end, US companies in the space industry may be subject to their national export controls, when employing non-US citizens. This often contravenes the aim to have a diverse workforce.

The movement away from "Old Space", where government space agencies worked together with large companies, has taken place as an increased interest in space arose from smaller companies and commercial investors. While this movement away from "Old Space" has contributed to rapid innovation and advances in technology, it has also left a regulatory gap.[6]

Under the traditional space industry model, there was in most cases continuous communication between government regulators and the large space companies. Government agencies had more insight into the technology that was being developed and its functions and uses, which in turn ena-

4 Goergen P., "Space Technologies' Compliance with Export Control Regimes." Cross Borders & Respect Us, Luxembourg (August 2019).

5 Aglietti G. S., "Current Challenges and Opportunities for Space Technologies." *Frontiers in Space Technologies* 1 (2020).

6 Ibid.

bled them to more accurately capture these developments in their regulations and anticipate them. Because NewSpace companies operate differently and most times without government actors, this very important channel of communication is missing. The challenge that arises here is that government agencies attempt to regulate technology on which they have not been fully informed. On the one hand, this challenge could be met by a requirement that would improve communication between NewSpace companies and government agencies. If NewSpace companies had the opportunity to effectively communicate with government agencies on all the potential applications of the technology they are developing, then the agencies would gain insight into this new industry. On the other hand, the challenge for NewSpace companies is that due to their inexperience in dealing with government agencies they may not know how to go about interacting with these government agencies. Further, reaching out to improve communication with government agencies would be for NewSpace companies to communicate effectively to government agencies all the potential applications of the technology they are developing. This would not result in a constructive outcome for NewSpace companies, if the companies themselves do not know how to classify their technology, or if their intended use of the technology is not within the scope of an existing dual-use function. Another challenge arising from the lack of information or understanding could result in ambiguity in interpreting the application of the export regulations and potentially increase the time in obtaining a licence if one is necessary.

Even for a small NewSpace start-up, compliance with export control laws and regulations is essential to ensure that they are able to develop their business cases in line with existing export controls. Respective licences may already be required at an early stage, if technology or software is developed in with an international team, perhaps from different locations. Implementing appropriate export control compliance measures can be challenging for a NewSpace start-up. However, it also has to be stated that what sets the NewSpace industry apart from others is its level of awareness on export controls. Many companies even in their start-up phase are already aware of the challenges that may affect their work because of the international nature of the criticality of their products. Beyond this awareness they are also motivated to address these challenges from day one so that their compliance measures can grow as their business grows and gains complexity.

The rapid speed of development that characterises technology in the NewSpace industry also contributes to this regulatory gap. Frequent communication with government agencies as technology is being developed would have a positive effect on both the NewSpace industry and the government regulators. Therefore, both the government agencies and the NewSpace companies should take an interest in each other's work and intentions. Providing regulating government authorities with input and technical expertise on their technologies in order to clarify the often-hyped technical capabilities of emerging technologies would provide transparency to government agencies and enable them to create better applicable and more reasonable export control regulations.[7]

Currently, there are no industry specific export control laws or regulations in place to regulate NewSpace and the laws and regulations which are in place are not yet able to capture all of the new technology as it is developed. This challenges both the NewSpace industry and government agencies. One reason this continues is because key conversations needed to fill this regulatory gap between the government and small space companies are not taking place as often as they should. For the future, it might even reveal that NewSpace warrants a new category for export controlled items rather than amending or adapting the existing categories. The challenge with regard

7 *Supra*. note 3.

to NewSpace is finding a balance between a space companies' commercial goal and maintaining the governments' interest in national security and non-proliferation.

26.4 Export control regulations meet NewSpace

The challenges to the regulatory framework of export control presented by NewSpace are not new. However, they do present a unique set of challenges which in a changing environment can only be resolved by applying a new approach. Due to the changing geopolitical landscape of individual countries, different approaches are currently being used to address this issue. These different approaches can be seen through engagement in multilateral agreements and in the way the export control laws and regulations are being changed on a national level to account for the changing environment created by the NewSpace industry. Both the EU and the US have adapted their export control laws to keep up with changes in technology. Despite this, their methods of doing so, and overall approach, must also change in order to keep up with the rapidly changing environment of NewSpace.

26.4.1 Multilateral export controls

Internationally, export control regulations have been aligned with several major multilateral control regimes to which each member country is committed. The four major international regimes today are the Wassenaar Arrangement on Export Controls for Conventional Arms and Dual-Use Goods and Technologies (Wassenaar Arrangement, WA), the Australia Group (AG), the Nuclear Suppliers Group (NSG), and the Missile Technology Control Regime (MTCR).[8] Each of these regimes maintains one or multiple control lists that specify the goods and technologies that should be subject to licensing requirements in their areas of concern.[9]

Of particular interest to commercial and NewSpace companies are MTCR, which controls items needed for missile development, production and operation, and WA, which is charged with promoting a common approach to international standards and harmonised control lists on dual-use goods and technologies.[10]

While these multilateral agreements provide member countries with lists of goods and technology that they have agreed should be regulated, these organisations are not able to properly consider the emerging NewSpace industry, or the emerging technologies used within this industry, at the pace at which it they are being developed. Further, while there may have been a common ground or consensus at the time these agreements were initiated, this may no longer be the case. For example, Russia is a member to both of these agreements, however it is uncertain how long they will honor these commitments considering changing events.

Also, considering this geopolitical tension, countries may not want to disclose their technology as this may conflict with their own national security interests. China for example is a country where there may be uncertainty from both sides about the benefits or interest of participation of the multilateral regimes. With that in mind, balancing the disclosure of technology against national security interest is risky and becomes moot as soon as the technology is disclosed by someone else. Alternatively, even if all countries were to come forward and disclose their technology develop-

8 Bureau of Industry and Security, U.S. Department of Commerce, Multilateral Export Control Regimes.

9 *Supra.* note 3.

10 Department of Commerce and Federal Aviation Administration, Introduction for U.S. Export Controls for the Commercial Space Industry. (2017).

ments, the process of updating or amending these existing lists would likely progress at a slower pace than the technology that is being developed, due to a longer process and procedure.

26.4.2 The European Union

The EU has been active in policy making to manage advanced technologies, most of them important for the NewSpace industry. On 9 September 2021, the EU effected several amendments to its export control regime via the implementation of Regulation (EU) No 2021/821 (referred to as the Recast Dual-Use Regulation), replacing Regulation (EU) No 428/2009 as the key legislative instrument governing EU exports of "dual-use" items.[11]

The new legislation aims to modernise and enhance the EU's controls on exports of "dual-use" items, to address the emergence of new technologies, to enhance compliance with the restrictions, and to improve coordination between EU Member States and the EU Commission, as well as between the EU and international partners. The core list of "dual-use" items subject to EU export controls, now contained in Annex I of the Recast Dual-Use Regulation, remains broadly unchanged as a result of the new legislation.[12]

The EU dual-use regulation, the main policy tool the EU uses to implement controls under the multilateral export control regimes, does not include any similar temporary controls or a common approach to emerging technologies within the EU system. In addition to implementing this regulation into their national laws, some EU Member States also maintain further national lists of purely national listed dual-use items, in order to capture additional commodities and technologies for space. Under the EU dual-use regulation, catch-all controls for non-listed items may apply if an exporter or the authorities of the state where it is situated are aware that the end-use of the good is in chemical, biological or nuclear weapons, or their delivery systems. The last one is of special importance for many NewSpace related developments. The EU applies a similar catch-all provision to goods that may be used in connection with a military end-use in an embargoed country. In addition, beyond these catch-all provisions (and another one with regard to items for cyber surveillance), Art. 8 of the dual-use regulation allows for additional controls on non-listed goods for reasons of public security or human rights considerations.[13]

The benefit for catch-all controls is that they allow for a balance between the security-driven need for controls by states and the trade-facilitation imperatives that seek to limit the administrative and economic burden on companies. They may even function to reduce the volume of licensing applications that might result from more list-based approaches. However, from an industry perspective catch-all controls increase the burden on companies by placing more emphasis on due diligence procedures and creating uncertainties over when controls may apply, therefore affecting operations planning.[14]

For the NewSpace industry, these catch-all controls are an additional administrative burden not only because they take time away from their core focus of innovation and development, but also because these young companies are not versed in dealing with government agencies and such compliance checks when doing business. While the majority of NewSpace companies would agree that compliance with export control regulations is important, they also agree that the controls that

11 EUR-Lex, document 32021R0821.

12 Forrest J., Barker C., Ekblom R., DLA Piper, Publications, Export controls: the EU's dual-use regime.

13 *Supra*. Note 3; EUR-Lex, document 32021R0821.

14 *Supra*. note 3.

are put in place should consider the ease of implementation and rules and possible licensing procedures reasonable for the industry they are trying to regulate. The EU approach, again, emphasises that the approach to regulating NewSpace companies needs to change and that the best way to do this is though bridging the communication gap through continuous input from stakeholders in the NewSpace industries.

26.4.3 Germany

Germany is an example of one of the EU Member States that maintains an additional national list of further dual-use items (including items for space). While these lists provide an additional level of compliance and security for government agencies and companies, they also provide an additional administrative burden on NewSpace companies acting out of Germany. To increase the effectiveness of the implemented export controls and to alleviate the administrative burden on NewSpace companies, optimised and faster licensing processes within the authorities, along with an increasing frequency and quality of communication between the government licensing agencies and the applicant companies, are needed. [15]

An open and continuous dialogue between the government authorities and companies would be a basis for this.

26.4.4 The United States

The US has two main legal frameworks for controlling exports: the Export Administration Regulations (EAR) and the International Traffic in Arms Regulations (ITAR). Under the EAR, the Bureau of Industry and Security (BIS) regulates exports of "dual-use and less sensitive military items" by placing them on its Commerce Control List (CCL). In contrast, the ITAR restricts those articles and services with explicit defense purposes on the United States Munitions List (USML). However, the latest export control reform, which was under the Obama administration, resulted in many items being moved from the USML to the CCL in order to expedite their approval processes.[16] Especially with regard to items and systems relevant in the space industry.

Additionally, the US export control system is supplemented with a variety of additional governance mechanisms, for example, controls on deemed exports and re-exports, as well as legislation to control foreign direct investment into companies that are deemed as being of strategic importance to US national security.[17]

In recent years, the US export control laws and regulations have undergone significant change in order to adapt to the changing environment presented by technological advancements of the commercial space industry. One way this has been evident over the years is when tracing the regulatory path of the commercial satellite which has changed categories over the years, and which presented unique challenges in 1996 during the Export Control Reform.

In 1996, commercial communications satellites were transferred from the USML to the CCL in an effort to reduce burden on industry. However, a catastrophic launch failure involving a Chinese

15 For more information on Germany see: Federal Office for Economic Affairs and Export Control, Foreign Trade.

16 European Parliament Research Service, "United States: Export Control Reform Act ECRA", 2019, European Parliament, United States: Export Control Reform Act (ECRA) (Briefing).

17 *Supra.* note 1 at 5–28.

rocket carrying a US-built Intelsat satellite drew attention onto these regulations.[18] After the launch failure, a review group consisting of Loral and Hughes Space & Communications and Chinese engineers identified the potential failure points of the Chinese launch vehicle.[19]

In reviewing the investigation, the US Department of Defense concluded that the entire investigative process had been a risk by providing China with too much insight into launch vehicle technology. US Congress then in turn reviewed technology transfers to China which culminated in the Cox Report.[20] In it they concluded that "Loral and Hughes committed a serious export control violation by virtue of having performed a defense service without a license".[21] As a result of this incident, commercial communication satellites and related equipment were transferred back to the ITAR.[22]

It was not until years later, in 2012, as part of the Export Control Reform Initiative, that USML was once again under review. As it had been in 1996, the aim was again to move items from the USML the CCL, in an attempt at reducing the regulatory burden on the industry. Because the commercial communications satellites had been transferred back to the USML by an act of congress, the US president now needed special authorisation to revise the USML Category XV regulations. During this next round of review of Category XV (Spacecraft and Related Articles) items were only kept on USML if they were:

- inherently military and otherwise warrant control on the USML; or
- common to non-military space applications, possessing parameters or characteristics that provide a critical military or intelligence advantage to the United States, and that are almost exclusively available from the United States. [23]

All items that did not meet this criterion were moved off the USML. This was the beginning of the new "500 series" of Export Control Classification Numbers (ECCNs) on the EAR.

Commercial satellites are a good example of how lawmakers are able to see the need for change in policy, react, and adapt the export control laws and regulations to a changing environment. The situation with the commercial communication satellites also shows the balance which lawmakers are trying to maintain with policy, on the one hand seeking to lessen the administrative burden on the space industry while, on the other hand, protecting national security interests that might be at risk by disclosing technology to a foreign country. The movement of the commercial communication satellites back and forth between the USML and the CCL also shows that the US Department of Defense first had to consider what it was trying to regulate and then define the terms for regulating.

The example of the commercial satellites also shows that while the export control laws and regulations can be adapted to a changing environment, the process of doing so takes many years.

18 US Department of Commerce, Department of Industry and Security, Office of Technology Evaluation, US Space Industry "Deep Dive" Assessment: Impact of US Export Controls on the Space Industrial Base (2014). DOI:10.13140/RG.2.2.16632.47368.

19 Ibid.

20 For more information on the Cox Report see: Stanford, Center for International Security and Cooperation, Cos Committee Report, The: An Assessment.

21 Ibid.

22 For more information see the Strom Thurmond Defense Authorization Act, once again placing the commercial communication satellites under the jurisdiction of the US Department of State, see H.R.3616 – 105th Congress (1997–1998): Strom Thurmond National Defense Authorization Act for Fiscal Year 1999, H.R.3616, 105th Cong. (1998).

23 *Supra*. note 18.

Ultimately the commercial satellite industry and many NewSpace companies benefited from the changes, but the bureaucratic process took a long time. Considering the current pace at which the NewSpace industry and emerging technologies used within this industry advance, a time frame of years to adopt or make change to a regulation could greatly impact the overall economic success of these companies.

26.4.4.1 Continuing the definitional debate: The US: Export Control Reform Act

In August 2018, the US enacted the Export Control Reform Act (ECRA). The ECRA enables increased controls on "emerging and foundational technologies [that are] essential to the national security of the United States". It does this by limiting (controlling) the release of technology to end uses and destinations of concern. Within the context of the ECRA, "control" refers to "export, re-export, or transfer". Export is defined as "the shipment or transmission of the item out of the US, including the sending or taking of the item out of the US, in any manner; and the release or transfer of technology or source code relating to the item to a foreign person in the US (deemed export)".[24] Also re-exports of US items by non-US companies are generally subject to US export regulations, including "deemed" re-exports.

ECRA differs from other laws on dual-use items in that it targets new digital technologies whose transfer is not subject to customs checks at physical borders, and that would therefore evade enforcement of existing regulations.[25] This is significant as the digital nature of emerging technologies posed a challenge for the traditional customs controls which were only enforceable on the physical transfer of a good across a border. Further the ECRA goes beyond the emerging technologies that may have a wide range of functions beyond traditional dual-use. This omni use, or "omnipresence", can be seen as these technologies are embedded throughout various sectors of society, such as infrastructure and military. Most of these sectors are also connected to NewSpace.[26]

Almost two years after the enactment of the ECRA, on 5 October 2020, the BIS published long-awaited controls on six categories of "emerging technologies". These new controls will affect technology sectors such as biotechnology, artificial intelligence, and advanced materials and will almost always require BIS authorisation in order to provide certain items to most jurisdictions outside the US, or even to import technical knowledge about these items with foreign national employees (under the deemed export rules).[27]

The act of balancing the economic interests (of both the companies and the government) and the country's foreign policy goals become difficult in a changing environment. While the US government agencies recognise the need to adapt export control laws, the process and pace of doing so is disproportionate for the rapid pace of the NewSpace industry for which these regulations are being adapted. In addition, the challenges presented by defining the technology all contribute to an increased administrative burden when it comes to licence applications from the NewSpace companies.

24 *Supra*. 16.

25 Dekker B. and Okanjo-Heijamns M., "The U.S.-China Trade-Tech Stand-off and the Need for EU Action on Export Control", Clingendale (2019).

26 Ibid.

27 Lee, Judith A. et al., Gibson Dunn, New Controls on Emerging Technologies Released, While U.S. Commerce Department Comes Under Fire for Delay. (October 2020).

26.5 Conclusion: a new approach for export control for NewSpace

Advances in technology have always been a challenge for the regulatory framework of the export control system. While the challenge of having to adapt to technological advances in a changing environment is not new, the NewSpace industry challenges export control laws in a new and unique way. NewSpace by virtue of its characteristics of rapid innovation, development, risk, and uncertainty, challenges the ability of an existing regulatory framework to adapt at an equally rapid pace when the methods in place to change this framework lack flexibility and information.

It is evident through the actions of policy and lawmakers that they are aware of the need for change. Attempts to continuously adapt the export control system can be seen on both a multilateral level and a national level. However, on both levels, policy and lawmakers are still trying to understand and fit NewSpace technology into the existing export control lists. They face a definitional dilemma and one of divergent technical standards. This uncertainty is an additional factor that challenges policy and lawmakers in their ability to implement new export control laws that balance both the economic interest of the NewSpace companies and maintain foreign policies and national security goals.

As the NewSpace industry continues to advance at a rapid pace, policy and lawmakers should consider a flexible approach that mirrors that of the industry it is trying to regulate. Policy and lawmakers should look beyond their current methods of dealing with export control lists and the time-consuming traditional approaches. They may have to go beyond amending current export control categories in existing lists and may perhaps create a new category that could protect and encourage technological advances in the NewSpace industry. In order to do this, they must increase communication with stakeholders and get an understanding of how NewSpace works to be able to gain insight into the technology, understand the potential use of technology, and to know what controls could be reasonably implemented. This communication would aid in the advancement of the interests of both the NewSpace industry and the policy and lawmakers.

Finally, there must also be awareness, sufficient knowledge, and a respective focus within NewSpace companies that deal with export control laws and regulations and to implement internal export compliance programs (ICP) to be able to conduct their business in a compliant manner.

B

Active debris removal, on-orbit servicing, and space traffic management

27

TOWARDS SPACE TRAFFIC MANAGEMENT

Holger Krag and Lesley Jane Smith

27.1 Introduction

27.1.1 Achieving stability of the outer space environment

The implementation of space debris mitigation requirements designed to preserve the long-term stability of the environment implies that space objects should be tracked effectively on the basis of internationally binding principles.[1] The tracking must cover the operational phase, and include the mandate to request immediate disposal and passivation action, should the reliability of the associated functional chain have degraded. This means that future space systems will have to follow more demanding technical standards to ensure the safety of spaceflight. Improving orbital data precision and accuracy have become pressing goals, and the availability of technology to improve trackability and identification of small objects enables greater precision in undertaking the requisite collision avoidance manoeuvres.[2] This chapter explains how new and affordable technical solutions can stimulate more ambitious steps in international regulation, and how the international regulation required to encompass these solutions could be formulated.

Today, space-faring nations recognise the need for better information on the orbital position of space objects, a task denoted as space surveillance.[3] Here, the accuracy of the information has

1 United Nations, Committee on the Peaceful uses of Outer Space, *Space Debris Mitigation Guidelines of the Committee on the Peaceful Uses of Outer Space*, A/62/20, 2007, Resolution adopted by the General Assembly on 22 December 2007, U.N. Doc A/RES/62/217, 1 February 2008; United Nations, General Assembly, *Guidelines for the Long-term Sustainability of Outer Space Activities of the Committee on the Peaceful Uses of Outer Space*, in: Report of the Committee on the Peaceful Uses of Outer Space, Sixty-second session, 12–21 June 2019, U.N. Doc A/74/20 (3 July 2019), Annex II.

2 See for example, the proposals for collision risk assessment in: D. Saez, N. Marick, E. Arias, et al, *Modern Methods for Collision Risk Assessment*, Paper, IAC-22,A6,9,x72919, 73rd International Astronautical Congress (IAC), Paris, France, 18–22 September 2022.

3 For a fuller description of the objectives and technical capabilities involved in space surveillance operations, as well as the categories of Space Situational Awareness (SSA), Space Domain Awareness (SDA), Space Surveillance and Tracking (SST), see D. Oltrogge, M. Strah, M. Skinner, et al, *Recommendations of the IAF Space Traffic Management Terminology Working Group*, Report, International Astronautical Federation 2019; see *infra*. 27.4.1.

DOI: 10.4324/9781003268475-41

a significant influence on the alert rate and the associated avoidance efforts of the operators.[4] A global data share on the level of "tracklets" can increase accuracy and trust in the data. However, additional dedicated instrumentation is also required, for which ground-based laser tracking enters into the focus. A more systematic deployment of this technology could raise the accuracy of space traffic data, and limit the number of collision avoidance alerts dramatically. This chapter also explains how an evolution in laser technology could even transfer a small momentum to the object, leading to a minimal change of its orbit, just large enough to avoid collisions between two uncontrolled objects.[5] This would open the door for the management of uncontrolled objects, which will otherwise continue to remain responsible for the majority of environment-contaminating collisions.

The development of the European Space Agency's Clearspace-1 mission, designed to undertake the first removal of space debris, is an important milestone for space traffic management.[6] Equivalent test missions such as Astroscale Japan's CRD2, one of the world's first technology demonstrations of removing large-scale debris from orbit,[7] will contribute to a better understanding of the debris environment, reduction and tracking, as well as contributing to its sustainability. Governments, notably Japan, already incorporate commitments towards the development of STM and congruent with the UN Guidelines for the Long-term Sustainability of Outer Space Activities (Long-term Sustainability Guidelines, LTSG) in their licensing rules.[8] Regulators will expect to be shown that an active removal action can be implemented successfully, safely and affordably, before they consider this element in their regulation. Once demonstrated, such a mission will not only add to the reduction of the risk level in space, but also constitute a new instrument to stimulate future regulation; active removal would then be a possible action to be requested, once the disposal action failed. This would not only trigger more rigorous implementation of mitigation measures, but also create a market for active removal services.[9]

Mitigation measures apply for individual objects only. In a scenario of increased space traffic, however, long-term environmental consequences can occur, even if individual missions comply with mitigation measures. Therefore, in the long run, space must be considered as a commonly

4 For an overview of space technology and orbital manoeuvres, see generally: F. Sellmaier, T. Uhlig, M. Schmidhuber, (eds), *Spacecraft Operations*, Second Editions, Springer 2022; further, B. Reihs, J. Rowland, O. Marshall, et al, *Increasing Capabilities in a Growing Radar Network*, Paper, IAC-22,A6,1,6,x72502, 73rd International Astronautical Congress (IAC), Paris, France, 18–22 September 2022; H. Krag, S. Janardhana Setty, A. Di Mira, et al, *Ground-Based Laser for Tracking and Remediation – An Architectural View*, Paper, IAC-18-A6.7.1, 69th International Astronautical Congress (IAC), Bremen, Germany, 1–5 October 2018.

5 C. R. Phipps, et al, *A Laser-Optical System to Remove Low Earth Orbit Space Debris*, Paper, 6th European Conference on Space Debris, Darmstadt, Germany, 22–25 April 2013.

6 The capabilities for debris removal under this mission have been purchased by European Space Agency (ESA) as services from the Swiss company Clearspace. This first mission, planned for 2026, will remove the Vespa upper stage rocket from orbit; for further details, see ESA's own website

7 Full information on the Astroscale technology is available on their website.

8 See the information published by the Japanese cabinet office on STM and sustainability available from the cabinet office, https://www8.cao.go.jp/space/english/stm/index.html; see *infra*. 27.3.2.

9 On the transition in space from originally public dominated, to private operated space-based services, see the first chapter in this same volume by Philippe Clerc, *Towards a new legal ecosystem for the exploitation of space*. For a review of the legal parameters for debris removal, see Williamson, Smith, (eds.), Orbital Debris Removal: Policy, Legal, Political and Economic Considerations, Study Group 5.10, International Academy of Astronautics, ISBN/EAN IAA: 978-2-917761-79-3; further L. J. Smith, R. A. Williamson, *Active Debris Removal: Legal, Policy and Economic Aspects*, Paper, IAC-19,E3,4,12,x55005, 70th International Astronautical Congress, Washington, United States, 21–25 October 2019.

used resource, with a limited capacity. International coordination of the space traffic and frequencies required for orbital operations would be required for an efficient and interference-free use of space. The coordinated use of the available radio-frequencies could serve as a template. This involves securing the interaction between national regulatory authorities (NRA) for radio frequencies, as well as overseeing the system by the International Telecommunications Union (ITU). Several approaches to making the "consumption of space" visible have been proposed, and are outlined below. While the term "global commons" is not viewed by all nations as the appropriate concept for management and use of the outer space environment, a coordinated approach to its use would provide a solid basis for consensus-building and fostering progress.[10] The spirit as well as the letter of the treaty-based principles governing the freedom of exploration and use of outer space, as well as its status as the province of mankind, are the foundations for securing international cooperation.[11] This chapter explains how the capacity of space can be determined, and how the environmental footprint of a mission can be used to coordinate the use of space, in a way similar to how the world's carbon-dioxide emission budget is shared.

27.1.2 Use of orbital capacity as a future tool for space debris mitigation

Space debris mitigation requirements, today, follow a "bottom-up" approach. They address a single object and the requirements imposed are independent of the criticality of a mission. As a consequence, a 10t object in 1,200km altitude is today following the same technical criteria as a small mission of 50kg mass in 650km altitude.

This can never be sufficient to control the overall environmental impact: the bottom-up approach only addresses individual missions. There is no control over the combined effect resulting from several equivalent individual missions or missions to be launched. Fulfilling requirements at an individual level is not sufficient to control the global space environment. The problem can be seen in the following: the control regime for a mission of 200kg in 1200km altitude with comparably stringent requirements on the post-mission disposal (PMD) success of 90% already reaches its limit under the current mitigation requirements. Taking this further: if in a given year, 1,000 objects are cleared at this requirement and launched in the same year (e.g., a mega-constellation), this would mean, from a global perspective, that 100 objects are bound to fail to properly dispose of themselves, although each individual object complies with the current requirements.

A greater, more coordinated, mitigation approach would require a more global view and a top-down approach. It would start from assessing how much capacity the environment offers. From there, it would look at how much capacity is consumed by planned individual missions, and then prescribe measures, ensuring that the actual consumption is compatible with the overall available capacity. Different approaches to defining the capacity are conceivable. A physical definition could identify the capacity limit with, for instance, a maximum collision rate, or a maximum spatial density. A more economically oriented definition could address the point of time when a

10 The term "global commons" is not formally binding, but as with the law of the sea, can support concepts of free passage and rights of transit within various categories of territorial waters and the high seas. For a critical assessment of national space policy in this regard and a proposal to enable a feasible compromise in practice, see J. S. Goehring, *Why isn't Space a Global Commons?* in: Journal for National Security Law & Policy 11, n. 3, 2021, 573–590, at 588.

11 Treaty on Principles Governing the Activities of States in the Exploration and Use of Outer Space, Including the Moon and Other Celestial Bodies, entered into force 10 October 1967, 610 U.N.T.S. 205, at Art. I "The exploration and use of outer space, […] shall be the province of all mankind"; Art. II "Outer space, […] shall be free for exploration and use by all States".

mission implementer would have to implement more collision avoidance than routine manoeuvres, or when the collision risk becomes the driver for the selection of the mission orbit. Several other justified metrics could be considered. These approaches all have in common that they are ultimately related to the individual perception of non-tolerable risk. This means, however, that a purely technical definition is unrealistic, and that what is required is rather human consensus on what is perceived as a critical environmental state.

A good example for consensus was established within the Inter-Agency Space Debris Coordination Committee (IADC) in 2002, with the development of the so-called "25 year rule". Consensus was achieved by comparing environmental trends predicted by independent tools, when assuming a "0 year", "25 year", "50 year", or "100 year" rule for the permitted post-mission disposal lifetime. Following this exercise, the trend associated with the "25 year" rule became considered "acceptable" in both risk and effort. This rule could be adopted as a widely agreed acceptable trend for the environment in LEO over the next 200 years.

Once a consensus on the acceptable environment (i.e. "capacity") is established, metrics are required that describe the consumption of this capacity by a space object. Several of these (indexes, footprints, schemes) have been developed.[12] Research on such indices and consensus-finding are taking place today with accelerating pace. The World Economic Forum has published an index scheme built by a global consortium, the Space Sustainability Rating (SSR).[13] These approaches make use of one or more of the following technical elements that can be attached to a space mission, i.e. on-orbit catastrophic collision flux that it is exposed to:

- its collision cross-section;
- its natural orbital lifetime;
- number of released fragments in case of a collision;
- fragment cloud decay time.

The resulting metrics could be used to scale the requirements for a mission such that acceptable environment capacity is still achieved. If consensus on such a computation scheme were established, it could be used to transparently break-down the available environment capacity to the individual objects.

While spacefarers would not accept a limitation on the principle of free access to space, it might well be acceptable to add a mitigation requirement on the individual level that is driven by the overall planned launch traffic and the available environment capacity. These additional constraints would automatically result from the transparent computational logic previously presented and would, thus, be scaled according to the actual environmental criticality of the mission.

In practice, with this approach, mission proposals would need to be collected before launch. The most relevant information source for this would be the ITU online register for frequency filing. Practically all missions, if they use a transponder, are required to follow this process prior to launch. This information could be retrieved and the resulting fragment-years computed. The cumulated fragment-years for a launch year can be compared with the capacity available in a year

12 F. Letizia, C. Colombo, H. G. Lewis, H. Krag, *Assessment of breakup severity on operational satellites*, in: Advances in Space Research, 58, n. 6, 2016, 1255-1274; A. Rossi, G. B. Valsecchi, E. M. Alessi, *The Criticality of Spacecraft Index*, in: Advances in Space Research, 56, n. 3, 2015, 449-460; J. Utzmann, M. Oswald, S. Stabroth, et al., *Ranking and Characterization of Heavy Debris for Active Removal*, Paper, IAC-12,A6,2,8,x14182, 63rd International Astronautical Congress (IAC), Naples, Italy, 1–5 October 2012.

13 Further details of participating institutions are available on the WEF website.

(2,000 fragment-years). Using the time period of a year as checkpoint for capacity control is a conscious decision. This leads to the apportionment of consumable capacity over time, and offers good granularity for the control of its usage.

This precisely replicates the approach used by the ITU for geostationary orbit (GSO) satellite. The problem of capacity in the frequency domain and environmental capacity are indeed of similar nature. The consumption of environmental capacity is real and needs to be reflected in the underlying computation method as accurately as possible. The coupling of frequency allocation and orbit usage has worked in geosynchronous Earth orbit (GEO) due to the coupling of a mission with a well constrained geostationary environment. The – effectively global – presence of LEO satellites has to date made it possible to apply this principle. However, the coupling of ITU registration, capacity, and the resulting mitigation requirements would establish a similar principle for LEOs. At the same time, this approach would have the positive side effect of encouraging timely ITU registration, while helping to enforce ITU policies.

It is important to recall that the current mitigation guidelines are not replaced, but only extended. This is absolutely necessary in order to prevent that missions which benefit from early registration relax their requirements up to the capacity ceiling for their launch year. In other words, the existing mitigation guidelines are essential to secure fairness among the missions in a launch year. Beyond this, the approach might trigger some form of "capacity trading" between the missions of a launch year to further optimise the share (similar to carbon emission trading).

The computation of the available capacity and the consumption by proposed missions should be entrusted to a credible and technical international body. The IADC, with its expertise in technical consensus-building on environmental questions, could be well-suited for this. Technically, implementation could be as simple as an open-access (web-based) tool that is synchronised with the ITU registry. The tool would have to make use of a database on the current environment, which has technical consensus and then constantly update the capacity gaps per year. A user can specify his mission (orbit, mass area, disposal plan, PMD success rate). The tool will output the environment criticality and return the resulting capacity consumption per proposed mission in fragment-years.

On the regulatory side, implementation should be equally simple. As regulation is currently governed by mitigation requirements (either by law, standards, or guidelines) at the level of individual missions, and since current requirements need to remain active, this approach can only be achieved by an additional requirement. This additional requirement should ask for demonstration that the space object fits within the overall capacity apportionment for the envisaged launch year.

27.2 Risk management and liability for activities in outer space distinguished: risk and insurance

Outer space activities are inherently dangerous, and the management of associated risk accompanies all phases of space operations, from pre-launch to launch and re-entry, including the in- (or on-) orbit activities.[14] The risks are not related to activities of the spacecraft alone, so other sources of risk such as the frequent, natural hazards related to space weather, space storms, and not least asteroid warnings, must be taken into account.[15] The assessment of risk and risk management are concepts that relate to the probability of a hazardous event and its consequences. Risk manage-

14 Until on-orbit services (OOS) are developed beyond trial stage, there will not be a clear picture of how the risks are to be assessed for insurance purposes.

15 Solar winds and geomagnetic storms are among the most serious space weather risks. See the annual reports from space insurers, such as the recent Zurich Insurance coverage of space weather and its impact on the loss of forty

ment therefore encompasses the full range of operational procedures for the launch and orbital activities, plus the accompanying dangers.[16]

Identifying the risk factors and hazards forms part of the exercise of mapping out operational responses, and obtaining the insurance coverage, as prescribed by national space law.[17] The practice of insurance in the space industry reflects the different risks applicable at the various operational stages, as well as the international treaty rules regulating state liability for damage. Liability, the legal obligation to pay compensation to a third party for loss of life and damage to property in the specific circumstances defined by the law, operates on the basis of the prerequisites for a claim to compensation. The Liability Convention (LIAB) contains two different forms of liability. The distinction between the liability rules reflects the policy decisions made at the time of drafting the treaty on how risk should be allocated, identifying launching states as the most suited to carry the financial burden.

Damage on earth and in airspace by a space object incurs absolute and unlimited liability under Art. II LIAB, the fullest and strictest form of liability that exists, to which there is no defence and no limitation.[18] Damage in orbit to a spacecraft by another spacecraft leads to liability in terms of Art. III LIAB, only if there has been fault. The principles on which outer space operations, and insurance cover, are based, reflect the principle of acceptance of risk for own-damage, with second parties (i.e. those parties within the same framework of contractual relations in a particular space programme) accepting their own particular losses.[19] The space industry and operators have developed a system that is best understood in combination with standard contractual practices and licensing conditions that have developed in the sector. The contractual rules provide generously for waivers and disclaimers along the contractual chain for parties developing, collaborating, and operating within programmes. The separate and relevant category of third party liability is one which is more significant from a debris congestion and traffic management perspective. However, it has neither led to formal development of state of the art rules for fault liability, nor accountability for PMD disposal management. The absence of operational standards, recognised as state of the art in law, and against which the fault-based liability for outer space operations could be imposed for orbital activities causing damage, is a recognised *lacuna* in the current system. It is also one where national space laws and licensing practice differ in their approach to the overall spread of liabilities of governments as launching states and indemnities to be contributed by operators.[20]

Starlink satellites: *What is space weather – and how does it affect us down on Earth?*, 5 July 2022, published on its website.

16 The insurance industry operates with various categories of risk assessments, whether for launch or satellite collision. For a discussion of the realistic disaster scenarios (RDS) developed by Lloyds of London for space activities, see K. Havlikova, Risk Management and Insurance of On-Orbit servicing, in: *On-Orbit Servicing: Next Generation of Space Activities*, A. Fröhlich, Springer, 2021, 13–33.

17 Id; further, M. Polkowska, *Space Traffic Management – Legal aspects*, Polish Political science Yearbook, Vol. 50(1), 2021, 159–169.

18 L. J. Smith, A. Kerrest, Commentary on the Convention on International Liability for Damage caused by space objects, *Art II Liability Convention*, in: S. Hobe, B. Schmidt-Tedd, K. Schrogl, (eds), *Cologne Commentary on Space Law Vol. 2, Rescue Agreement, Liability Convention, Registration Convention, Moon Agreement*, Köln, Heymanns, 2013, 86–87.

19 This has the advantage that the industry internalises its losses, and the market sector is not disrupted or blocked by complex international damage litigation disputes.

20 Under US and French space legislation, the states accept the upper stage of liabilities beyond the limited liability level of the operator, for which the operator is required to take out insurance (€60 million). The period during which liability insurance cover is required by statute varies from one year post launch (France) to one month after launch (US), to the full term of space operations (UK).

Developing a new STM regime could be a game change for the community. It would require full compliance by operators with technical standards. More importantly, it would enable a measurable allocation of responsibilities and liabilities against the public and private space operators, should failures to maintain accepted technical standards lead to third party losses. Any new system for STM will require the law and practice of the third party liability insurance requirement sector to be analysed more closely. The insurance industry has assisted a structured approach to outer space insurance, by which the launch insurance is the most significant, and third-party liability insurance requirement varies according to national statute. As considerations for STM develop, there is room for considering how the fault liability rule for damage in outer space can be applied in the context of maintenance of safety and collision avoidance.

27.3 Stakeholder initiatives towards defining norms for responsible behaviour in space

27.3.1 From space debris mitigation to long-term sustainability guidelines

The international community initially approached the subject of STM in various sets of high-level, institutional operational guidelines. These were technical responses to the call for securing debris prevention and mitigation, and imposed technical requirements relating to spacecraft, as well as a spacecraft's orbital lifetime. The guidelines were referenced to ISO technical standards or norms, notably ISO 24113, applicable to the de-orbiting technology on space systems, with standard(s) for the PMD operations.[21] The guidelines and ISO norms formed a first standard for establishing a technical state of the art to be followed during operations.[22] Despite this, their impact was not sufficient enough to counteract the growth of dysfunctional debris, and the compliance and enforcement remained an open issue.[23]

Currently, there are approximately nine separate institutional sets of space debris operational guidelines, ranging from the first IADC Space Debris Mitigation Guidelines,[24] through to handbooks or compendia on the best practices for the sustainability of space operations. These guidelines were authored by the various institutional stakeholders, IADC, the ITU,[25] the UN,[26] space agencies (ESA),[27] and defined parameters for PMD after 25 years of spacecraft mission life.[28] The

21 *Space systems – Space debris mitigation requirements*, ISO 24113:2019, International Organization for Standardization, Geneva, Switzerland, 2019.

22 The concept of "*state of the art*" is relevant in the general law of fault liability. Activities that result in damage following failure to maintain the standard can lead to claims for liability for the damage caused.

23 *Supra.* note 24.

24 IADC Space Debris Mitigation Guidelines, Revision 2, IADC-02-01, 2020, available online.

25 International Telecommunication Union, *Environmental protection of the geostationary-satellite orbit*, Rec. ITU-R S.1003-2 (December 2010).

26 United Nations, Committee on the Peaceful uses of Outer Space, *Space Debris Mitigation Guidelines of the Committee on the Peaceful Uses of Outer Space*, A/62/20, 2007, Resolution adopted by the General Assembly on 22 December 2007, U.N. Doc A/RES/62/217, 1 February 2008.

27 Italian Space Agency (ASI), British National Space Centre (BNSC), French Space Agency (CNES), German Aerospace Agency (DLR), European Space Agency (ESA), *European Code of Conduct for Space Debris Mitigation*, 2004, available at UNOOSA website.

28 IADC Guidelines, *supra* note 24, p. 12: "Spacecraft or orbital stages that are terminating their operational phases in orbits that pass through the LEO region, [...] should be deorbited (direct re-entry is preferred) or where appropriate manoeuvred into an orbit with an expected residual orbital lifetime of 25 years or shorter"; ISO 24113:2019, *supra.* note 21, at 6.3.3.1: "The orbit lifetime of a spacecraft or launch vehicle orbital stage shall be less than 25 years".

relevant technical rules were to be applied within the licensing process at national level;[29] they are contained in specific national formal documents.[30]

As indicated, the compliance with guidelines at national level was, in practice, under par. Now, with a major transformation underway in how space activities are undertaken, and more space traffic expected than in the first almost seventy years of outer space activities, there is agreement that sustainability of orbital activities cannot be managed on the basis of these guidelines alone.[31] The LTSG are relevant in this regard.[32] The 21 guidelines define four different dimensions needed to ensure long-term sustainability: establishing an appropriate policy and regulatory framework, improving the safety of space operations, increasing international cooperation and capacity-building, and furthering research and development. The need for the improved dissemination of space traffic data is addressed in the guidelines as well, both in the dimension of active space objects (*Guideline B.1*) and space debris (*Guideline B.3*). As indicated above, considerations and discussions now focus on developing an orbital traffic management system, with the various elements required to construct an orbital space data architecture that reflects the operations and systems in place for collecting, processing relevant data, and the various stakeholder communities participating within the platform.[33] Moreover, it requires thought on how to apply the international rules of space law, notably jurisdiction, non-interference, and collaboration, in a field where command structures may lead to debris removal. Meanwhile, various states have established their own air force space commands, in response to securing national space assets, and the inability of the US to continue delivering its voluntary warning scheme of notifying incidents and potential conjunctions.[34]

27.3.2 National legislation

The congested state of the orbital environment has already prompted national legislatures over the past years to implement the space debris mitigation guidelines into formal requirements under national law or regulation. Among the most prominent are France, Japan, and the US. Various

29 For an overview of national mechanisms regarding space debris mitigation, see United Nations, Office for Outer Space Affairs, *Compendium of space debris mitigation standards adopted by States and international organizations.*

30 National Aeronautics and Space Administration, *NASA Spacecraft Conjunction Assessment and Collision Avoidance Best Practices Handbook*, NASA/SP-20205011318, 2020.

31 Meanwhile, this is also recognised as regards the atmospheric contamination of the space environment, see E. Sirieys, C. Gentgen, A. Jain, et al., *Space sustainability isn't just about space debris: On the atmospheric impact of space launches*, in: MIT Science Policy Review, 3, 29 August 2022, 143–150; Issues of mega constellations on the dark skies and astronomer's concerns: United Nations Office for Outer Space Affairs, Annual Report 2021.

32 United Nations, General Assembly, *Guidelines for the Long-term Sustainability of Outer Space Activities of the Committee on the Peaceful Uses of Outer Space*, in: Report of the Committee on the Peaceful Uses of Outer Space, Sixty-second session, 12-21 June 2019, U.N. Doc A/74/20 (3 July 2019), Annex II; see further P. Martinez, *UN COPUOS Guidelines for the Long-Term Sustainability of Outer Space Activities: Early implementation experiences and next steps in COPUOS*, Paper, IAC-20-E3.4.1, 71st International Astronautical Congress (IAC), 12–14 October 2020.

33 Some thought had been given to compliance with ISO norms as part of the contractual basis for space operations, and the practice of naming and shaming for non-compliance was already known at IADC level.

34 The United States through its space command, reformed as the Combined Space Operations Center (CSpOC), provides debris tracking information using its US Space Surveillance Network (SSN). The US space force relies on US Space Force's "Spaceflight Safety Handbook for Satellite Operators", see 18th Space Control Squadron, *Spaceflight Safety Handbook for Satellite Operators, 18 SPCS Processes for On-Orbit Conjunction Assessment & Collision Avoidance*, California, United States of America, 2020. In the meantime, France, Germany, and the UK have followed suit and instituted tracking capabilities via their air forces which have equivalent dedicated space tracking command divisions.

smaller European countries have also made provision for these technical requirements. The national provisions all prescribe and require adherence to technical standards and requirements as part of national licensing requirements.[35] Under French law, launch and return operations and the procurement of launch or control of space objects are regulated by the French Space Operations Act (FSOA) of 2008.[36] Further provisions are in force in France under the technical regulations, existing since 2011, that formally relate to authorisations under a 2009 decree governing outer space activities; these cover, *inter alia*, limiting space debris, fragments, end-of-life operations, de-orbiting after 25 years, mitigation of risk collision, and reflect the IADC guidelines.[37] Post-lifetime disposal provisions impact on national licensing requirements, where technical compliance must be demonstrated. The national legislation in Japan includes almost all the LTSG, such as space debris mitigation or conjunction assessment, in the licensing system established by the Space Activities Act of 2016.[38] These include launch vehicle and spacecraft design and operation requirements, which contain details of debris mitigation, removal, prevention of interference or collision, measures for controlled re-entry and efforts of removal from LEO within 25 years.[39] The significance of these technical requirements is that they are legally binding national provisions. This counters any assertions that there are no binding rules calling for standards designed to ensure sustainability of the outer space environment.

27.3.3 Contribution to call for STM by the non-governmental stakeholder community

Various key members of the stakeholder community are involved in contributing to independent discussions and initiatives on how to approach the subject of STM that are currently at various stages of maturity.[40] The communities, generally private commercial stakeholders, are addressing sustainability in the context of developing standards or "*norms of behaviour*" for orbital operations. The international scientific, space agency and industrial communities, represented through their member associations, International Astronautical Federation (IAF), International Academy of Astronautics (IAA), and the International Institute of Space Law (IISL) are among those contributing to a joint effort on mapping out a potential architecture and accompanying elements and formal requirements for mitigation under the aegis of the annual International Astronautical Congresses (IAC).[41] Parallel initiatives, notably CONFERS, the US-registered industrial consor-

35 Further initiatives are underway, including the European Union, initially through its research and development funds, commissioning various studies on EU regional provisioning into a global system for STM. The studies examine the technical requirements and legal competences of the EU in providing a regional EUSTM element to complement existing STM measures.

36 See Loi no 2008-518 du 3 juin 2008 relative aux opérations spatiales.

37 See France, Arrêté du 31 mars 2011 relatif à la réglementation technique en application du décret n° 2009-643 du 9 juin 2009 relatif aux autorisations délivrées en application de la loi n° 2008-518 du 3 juin 2008 relative aux opérations spatiales, The provisions were subsequently modified by art 11 of Decree of 2017, available online with identifiers, NOR: ESRR1720433A, ELI: JORF n°0181 du 4 août 2017.

38 Japanese Act on Launching of Spacecraft, etc. and Control of Spacecraft (Act No. 76 of 2016), available online.

39 Id., §6, 7, 22.

40 See G. Pavesi, *Private and Public Cooperation in SST in support of an effective STM system*, Paper, IAC-19-E3.4,9x54206, 70th International Astronautical Congress (IAC), Washington DC, United States, 21–25 October 2019.

41 The IAC is an annual forum for the stakeholder community, organised by the IAF as a membership association. Input on the subject of STM is being delivered from all three associations – IAF, IAA, and IISL – within the IAF Technical Committee 26.

tium that brought together members of the space industry interested in improving the stability of outer space and delivering the first operational technologies for OOS, have drafted an exemplary set of self-binding operational rules for the future. These are formulated as "norms of acceptable behaviour".[42] These efforts highlight the form and method of developing a consensual basis for securing greater international collaboration towards the development of ISO standards to manage potential, and not infrequent orbital conjunctions, and false communications.[43] Among more recent stakeholders within the community, the American Institute of Astronautics and Aeronautics, (AIAA) published a short guide entitled Satellite Orbital Safety Best Practices,[44] in conjunction with Iridium, OneWeb, and SpaceX. These initiatives are taking place out of the sheer necessity to ensure sustainability. The international community is looking to move this forward after mapping out the best format for managing the challenges of manoeuvres, collision avoidance and operational command behaviour.[45]

27.4 Rules for sustainable outer space missions – from guidelines to a code for space traffic management

27.4.1 Evolution of technical capabilities and orbits they serve

The systematic monitoring of all artificial space objects is not possible. There is a lower limit to the object size and altitude in which objects can be detected from ground. Because of their high sensitivity at short ranges, radars are mostly used for the LEO region. Systematic surveillance and tracking are possible with current radar systems for objects as small as approximately 10cm in LEO. Sporadic detections can detect as small as 1cm in LEO for specialized radar systems. The information gathered during short detection periods is not sufficient to follow the object. However, statistical counts of detections can provide insight into the number and distribution of those objects.

Telescopes rely on the objects being illuminated by the Sun, and usually cover the higher orbital regions with low angular velocity, making optical exposures more efficient. With today's surveillance and tracking telescope network, the lower size limit is about 70cm for GEO objects. Specialised telescopes can do sporadic detections of objects as small as 10cm.

Today, smaller objects can only be detected by in-situ sensors in space. These are sensitive surfaces in Earth orbit that register impact numbers and (typically also) impact energy. The larger the surface, the more meaningful the sample of impacts that are collected. Since large objects are less numerous than smaller ones, and impacts in orbit are still rare, most of the detected objects by *in situ* sensors are below 0.1mm in size. This leaves the regime of 1mm–1cm objects almost unobserved today.

42 CONFERS is a US-registered corporation composed of currently 52 industrial partners and academic institutions from the field of international satellite services.

43 CONFERS, *Guiding Principles for Commercial Rendezvous and Proximity Operations (RPO) and On-Orbit Servicing (OOS),* revised October 2021.

44 American Institute of Aeronautics and Astronautics (AIAA), *Space Traffic Management (STM): Balancing Safety, Innovation, and Growth, A Framework for a Comprehensive Space Traffic Management System*, Institute Position Paper, November 2017.

45 Air traffic management (ATM) developed beyond national borders in line with the development of cross-border civil aviation, with a clear focus on operational and human safety. The competence for securing and coordinating safe spaceflight remains formally with the state responsible at national level under Art. VI of the Outer Space Treaty (*supra* note 11).

Space surveillance networks make use of radar and telescope systems for systematic surveillance of objects in Earth-bound orbits in an operational manner. They provide full orbital information on the object they monitor, and usually update this information in a regular manner. They have become an important source of information for space operations.

The most prominent example is the US Space Surveillance Network, which has grown from ballistic missile defence systems that were built up in the 1960s. An important element has been the NAVSPASUR Space Fence, consisting of two transmitting and three receiving stations aligned with a fixed latitude on American ground. Individual, powerful radar and optical instruments deployed worldwide complement the system. The system is coordinated and controlled by the US Space Force (18th Space Control Squadron), and the data is shared with spacefarers worldwide.[46] The number of space objects regularly updated in a space object catalogue amounts to about 20,000 objects. The NAVSPASUR fence which was operating in VHF band has retired today, and powerful phased-array radars like Eglin (Florida), Cobra Dane (Aleutes) and Fylingdales (UK), all operating in L-band, deliver most of the radar observations. In the future, a new phased array system will be deployed on the Kwajalein Islands. Following the trend towards higher frequencies for the detection of ever smaller objects, this system will operate in S-band. In the past and in the near future, this system will be the prime source of space object data for research and operations.

In Russia, a military-run radar surveillance system called Outer Space Control System also exists. The full capability of this system is not known and data is not shared with other spacefarers. The Russian-led ISON (International Space Observation Network) is the largest network for surveillance telescopes so far, spreading over several continents, and is run by academics (Keldysh Institute of Applied Mathematics of the Russian Academy of Sciences). Data access is organised through active participation with telescope observations.

In Europe, ESA has set up a programme that, *inter alia*, pursues the development of space surveillance and tracking technology (ESA SSA Programme). In parallel, the EU is funding a consortium of member states to use existing sensors for the provision of operational space object data. Existing sensors are mainly the German TIRA L-band mechanical tracking radar/Ku-band imaging radar, the French GRAVES VHF surveillance phased array radar, and the Spanish S3T L-band surveillance radar. In 2020, the German GESTRA (German Experimental Space Surveillance and Tracking Radar), an L-band phased array, mobile unit, was handed over to the user (*Bundeswehr*). The networking and expansion of these systems and a full pooling of European resources are in progress.

In the meantime, also privately run systems emerge. A powerful example is the LeoLabs phased array radar in Texas (2017) and its companion in New Zealand (2019), followed by units in Costa Rica and more. A number of European start-ups follow this path. On demand precise orbit information and other services are sold to paying users such as state authorities and operators. On the optical side, companies such as ExoAnalytics, Deimos, and also academic (quasi-open source) networks are formed and prepared to provide data services. Some private approaches (e.g., the Canadian Northstar company, or Vyoma) also set up space-based optical assets to provide their services. Other companies (e.g., Comspoc, Okapi) focus on data services on the downstream of this data (e.g., to generate conjunction analysis or other services).

Laser tracking of orbital targets is a well-established technology in the scientific community (geodesy, space radar/optical imagery) with precision ranging to operational satellites equipped

46 18th Space Control Squadron, *Spaceflight Safety Handbook for Satellite Operators: 18 SPCS Processes for On-Orbit Conjunction Assessment & Collision Avoidance*, California, USA, 2020.

with retro-reflectors as well as to the Moon. For a few years, the use of this technology was also pioneered for the tracking of defunct objects, e.g., in order to identify its attitude motion from range residual analysis. After introduction of more sensitive receivers, more powerful transmission systems and improvement of track initialisation techniques, it became possible to receive and process echoes from uncooperative targets. Still, accurate *a priori* pointing information is required and the tight constraints on the observation conditions must be met if they are to be successful.

Presently, a new generation of pulsed lasers is being deployed with the prospect of achieving a power density at target that is higher by several factors than before. This will allow to track even smaller uncooperative targets, while challenges to initialise tracks will grow and require further maturing in the area of tracking in daylight, stare and chase, and networking technology.

The application of laser tracking in this domain will most likely be limited to the tracking of "known" targets. Hence, the size of the tracked objects will always be limited by the supporting (radar-based) surveillance system. Laser tracking will eventually develop as a cost-efficient alternative method for all target sizes in a catalogue, e.g., providing orbit refinement prior to conjunctions to a level that reduces false alerts dramatically.

27.4.2 An integrated STM regime

The call for an integrated STM regime is not new, and spans the transition to the new millennium. UNISPACE III in 1999 had set the barometer of concern for sustainability of the outer space environment, a subject that was thereafter pursued in the new millennium in the context of various technical reports and international instruments.[47] The drafting and subsequent revisions of the IADC Space Debris Mitigation Guidelines was an early contribution towards achieving this goal. Combatting the challenges of debris mitigation received further resonance in the wake of the Paris Agreement,[48] with the subject gaining further impetus within UNISPACE+50.[49] The goal of sustainable space was also addressed in the context of the United Nations Sustainable Development Goals 2030 (UNSDG), adopted in 2015,[50] as well as in the Report of the UN Secretary-General, published in 2021.[51] Meanwhile, the absence of a dedicated STM regime is perceived as a major

47 See K. Schrogl, C. Jorgenson, J. Robinson, A. Soucek, (eds), *Space Traffic Management, Towards a road map for implementation*, Cosmic Study Report, International Astronautical Association (IAA), 2018; R. S. Jakhu, T. Sgobba, P.S. Dempsey, (eds), *The need for an integrated regulatory regime for aviation and space: ICAO for space?,* Studies in Space Policy, Springer, Wien, New York, 2018.

48 *Paris Agreement to the United Nations Framework Convention on Climate Change*, entered into force Dec. 12 2015, T.I.A.S. No. 16-1104.

49 See United Nations, General Assembly, *Fiftieth anniversary of the first United Nations Conference on the Exploration and Peaceful Uses of Outer Space: space as a driver of sustainable development*, UN. Doc A/RES/73/6 (31 October 2018). The Resolution reflects sustainability as follows: "Stressing the need to ensure the long-term sustainability of outer space activities and, in particular, the need to address the significant challenge posed by space debris, and convinced of the need to strengthen, through the Committee on the Peaceful Uses of Outer Space, international cooperation to achieve those goals and contribute to realizing a shared vision for the future in the exploration and use of outer space for peaceful purposes and for the benefit and in the interest of all humankind", see further: United Nations, General Assembly, *Transforming our world: the 2030 Agenda for Sustainable Development*, U.N. Doc A/RES/70/1, 25 September 2015.

50 See United Nations, General Assembly, *Transforming our world: the 2030 Agenda for Sustainable Development*, U.N. Doc A/RES/70/2, 21 October 2015; for details of the Long-term Sustainability Guidelines (LTSG), see below p. 11.

51 United Nations, *Our Common Agenda – Report of the Secretary-General*, United Nations, New York, United States of America, 2021, p. 48.

risk, adding to the pressing need to secure the safety of outer space and the resilience of critical space-based services.[52] This became more evident during the period of discussion on the LTSG, which concluded in 2019 after eight years.

With the large numbers of satellites scheduled to be launched in LEO increasing rapidly and collision risk at its greatest, high-altitude platforms providing broadband as of 20 miles, other stratospheric activities such as launches from hot air balloons, outer space activities are becoming lower and more accessible, while aircraft activities are moving higher towards space, to provide point-to-point technologies and new routes.[53] As shown in the development of other major regulatory regimes, most recently, the law of the seas, mapping out and achieving consensus on an international model for STM will require time. Some inspiration can, however, be taken from the Paris Agreement which commenced in 2011, and concluded in 2015, entering thereafter into force in 2016. Developing an integrated and operational global system for STM is markedly different from considerations about air or maritime traffic management and control. Unlike air and maritime traffic, outer space is free from concepts of territoriality and appropriation, and jurisdiction over space assets and international responsibility of states are the determinant factors for all space operations.[54] STM requires a new look at cooperation models for tracking and identifying spacecraft and orbital positions, data cataloguing, and thereafter how access to this data is to be shared. This means defining the categories and acceptable parameters for gathering data, whether civilian or military, the development of data repositories, their management as well as access for the users.[55] STM is therefore addressed in the context of an architecture, with processes to be mapped out, international standards to be applied, and a solution to be agreed for coordinating space traffic.

27.4.3 Space traffic coordination centre – a new regulatory authority?

This part of the chapter discusses whether a new supervisory authority is required, or whether a coordination body can be integrated within existing relevant institutions such as, e.g., the ITU.

The issue of collision alerts between two active spacecraft will be enhanced in the future and will become a significant burden to operators. Coordination is necessary to clarify among the two involved operators, among others, the following issues:

- if the understanding on the criticality of the situation is the same;

52 The annual AMOS conference held on Maui, Hawaii, brings together the community of technical specialists in the field. It describes itself as the "top scientific conference in the field of space situational awareness (SSA)/space domain awareness (SDA)".

53 While not formally defined in international law, the Fédération Aéronautique Internationale, FAI, chose von Karman line to define boundary between airspace and outer space at 100km, '100km Altitude Boundary for Astronautics | World Air Sports Federation' (1 August 2017). Some national legislations follow this definition, e.g., the Danish Outer Space Act 2016: its Section 4(4) defines space as "space above the altitude of 100km above sea level".
For a summary of the discussion in international fora, see: United Nations, Committee on the Peaceful Uses of Outer Space, *Historical summary on the consideration of the question on the definition and delimitation of outer space*, Report by the secretariat, U.N. Doc A/AC.105/769/Add. I, 3 February 2020.

54 Outer Space Treaty, *supra* note 11, Art. II: "Outer space, including the Moon and other celestial bodies, is not subject to national appropriation by claim of sovereignty, by means of use or occupation, or by any other means".

55 For further information on the accompanying requirements for data cataloguing, data fusion, data sharing, see National Aeronautics and Space Administration, *Space Traffic Management (STM) Architecture, Highly scalable, decentralized, open-architecture data exchange platform for STM*, Newssheet, Moffett Field, United States of America 2015.

- if the other object is maneuverable;
- if a manoeuvre was already planned;
- what the manoeuvre capability and agility is (time to plan a manoeuvre, size of a manoeuvre); and
- who would take the action in the end.

This coordination is, therefore, highly iterative. Furthermore, no data standards exist for the information to be exchanged. While the latter can be overcome rather quickly by the rapidly developing landscape of space data standards (e.g., CCSDS), the automation of the process, in view of several events of this type per day and per spacecraft (for some operators), remains a challenge. The safe automation of this task could be an interesting challenge for the growing community of start-up companies. A good solution will be used and accepted by spacefarers and could be promoted to a *de facto* standard. Such developments could kick-start the process, while the establishment of a publicly controlled space management system for manoeuvre coordination will take much more time. It has been frequently demonstrated that a good working standard is then often adopted later by regulators. The necessary "rules of the road" could then emerge from the working practice.

27.5 Conclusion

One of the greatest advantages or benefits to be derived from a future system of STM would be the ability to use the STM rules (off the road) as indicators for technical operations and manoeuvers that accord and comply with acceptable standards. One of the major issues as regards the LIAB is in reality that the failure of states to remove or contribute to the reduction of dysfunctional debris, not to mention clear tracking of functional orbital spacecraft, has led to a situation in which no launching state's liability has become subject to litigation or dispute relating to orbital damage. The unspoken common interest has, at least until now, been rather to ignore than pursue alternative mechanism for ensuring better post-mission management, with known outcome. Events around us demonstrate vividly how fragile both earth and outer space environments are, and how essential it is to secure a safe, secure access to and autonomous return from space.[56]

STM has been welcomed as a new concept, as it would enable a much more efficient means of notification of pending collisions and dangers, as well as providing a more objective system of tracking and tracing spacecraft. However, it is a totally new regulatory system, the likes of which have never existed before; despite its attractiveness, achieving international agreement on such a system is not expected to be a fast process. The community nevertheless welcomes thought on regulatory input into an STM structure. Various projects are underway at regional and international levels with a view to pursuing both the technical and legal issues surrounding the subject.[57] At the time of writing, events are starting to overtake those responsible for security, and what is required to guarantee sustainable space is happening in reality.

56 This is most evident on the case of uncontrolled re-entries of rockets or upper stages, where air traffic services are put on alert and the sense of data sharing is most keenly felt.

57 Some examples are CONFERS and STM at the University of Texas at Austin; at EU level, see European Parliament Resolution of 6 October 2022 on an EU approach for space traffic management – an EU contribution addressing a global challenge (2022/2641(RSP)).

28

FUTURE REGULATORY AND LICENSING TRENDS FOR ACTIVE DEBRIS REMOVAL AND ON-ORBIT SERVICING IN THE UK AND US

Jason Forshaw and Laura Cummings

28.1 Introduction

On-orbit servicing (OOS) is the capability that unlocks the next chapter of what is possible in space. Also captured under terms such as in-space servicing, assembly, and manufacturing (ISAM),[1] and on-orbit servicing, assembly, and manufacturing (OSAM),[2] on-orbit servicing can be defined as the "on-orbit alteration of a satellite after its initial launch, using another spacecraft to conduct these operations".[3] Broadly, some subcategories of "servicing" emerge, including: (1) remote survey and/or inspection, (2) relocation, (3) refuelling, (4) repair, (5) replacement of parts, and (6) recharge.[4]

Prior to diving into conversations about OOS, it is key to introduce two terms that will be used throughout this chapter.

Servicer. The satellite doing the servicing (performing the servicing action).

Client. The satellite being serviced.

For example, in the case of active debris removal (ADR), the servicer is the one that rendezvouses with and removes the failed client from space. In the case of refuelling, the servicer is the one that

1 This name for OOS was recently proffered by the US Executive branch. *See* NAT'L SCI. & TECH. COUNCIL, EXEC. OFF. OF THE PRESIDENT, IN-SPACE SERVICING, ASSEMBLY, AND MANUFACTURING NATIONAL STRATEGY (2022) [hereinafter ISAM National Strategy].

2 Jill McGuire, *On-Orbit Servicing, Assembly, and Manufacturing*, NASA.

3 Benjamin A. Corbin et al., *Global Trends in On Orbit Servicing, Assembly, and Manufacturing (OSAM)*, INST. DEF. ANALYSIS iv (Mar. 2020). *See also CONFERS Lexicon*, CONSORTIUM EXECUTION RENDEZVOUS & SERV. OPERATIONS (Apr. 2022) (defining "on-orbit servicing" as "activities by a servicer spacecraft or servicing agent on a client space object which require rendezvous and/or proximity operations").

4 Benjamin A. Corbin et al., *supra*. note 3, at vi.

DOI: 10.4324/9781003268475-42

rendezvouses with and refuels the client that needs more fuel. It is important to note that in ADR missions – as opposed to other missions such as refueling, the client has failed and is thus non-functioning.

This chapter will explore several on-orbit servicing missions that have occurred to date, as well as those in the licensing process, to overview the many different threads an operator of an on-orbit servicing spacecraft must keep track of.[5] Additionally, as examples of OOS missions existing in both the UK and US, this chapter will compare the licensing procedures of the two nations. This comparison will inform comments, and questions of further inquiry, for nations designing or modifying national licensing regimes in order to facilitate the development of OOS missions.

28.2 Key OOS missions from a regulatory perspective

The following comprises a short rendition of key OOS missions that have happened to date, or are currently in development, and which lend insights to the regulatory regimes under which they operate. These missions, and the case studies that they represent, will be referred to throughout the chapter. Out of the UK, *RemoveDebris*, *ELSA-d*, and *ELSA-M* will be discussed. From the US, *MEV-1* and *MEV-2* will also be explored, as well as the updated regulatory regime and its projected impacts on the LEXI mission. RemoveDebris, ELSA-d, MEV-1, and MEV-2 are past missions (completed), whilst ELSA-M and LEXI are upcoming missions.

28.2.1 RemoveDebris

RemoveDebris (shown in Figure 28.1) was one of the world's first missions to test debris removal technologies, and the first key OOS mission in the UK.[6] RemoveDebris was a European Commission (EC) FP7[7] funded mission which drew on the expertise of some of Europe's most prominent space institutions to demonstrate key ADR technologies in a low-cost, ambitious manner. The mission was led by Surrey Space Centre (University of Surrey) and was a consortium partnership project.[8]

5 It should be noted that this chapter will focus on *servicing* operations; the following information may be a place to start when consideration in-space assembly and manufacturing operations. However, this is by no means holistic in addressing unique aspects of in-space assembly and manufacturing.

6 See Jason L. Forshaw et al., *Final Payload Test Results for the RemoveDebris Active Debris Removal Mission*, 138 Acta Astronautica 326 (Sept. 2017); *see also* Jason L. Forshaw et al., *RemoveDEBRIS: An In-orbit Active Debris Removal Demonstration Mission*, 127 Acta Astronautica 448 (Oct.–Nov. 2016).

7 FP7 is the "Seventh framework programme of the European Community for research and technological development including demonstration activities." "The framework programmes have been the main financial tools through which the European Union supports research and development activities covering almost all scientific disciplines". See *Seventh Framework Programme of the European Community for Research and Technological Development Including Demonstration Activities (FP7)*, Eur. Comm'n (29 June 2015); *Research Projects Under Framework Programmes*, Eur. Comm'n (15 Aug. 2022).

8 RemoveDebris consortium consisted of: Surrey Space Centre, Surrey Satellite Technology Ltd. (SSTL), Airbus Defense and Space GMBH, Airbus Defense and Space SAS, Airbus Defense and Space Ltd., ISIS, CSEM, Inria, Stellenbosch University. See *A Low Cost Active Debris Removal Demonstration Mission*, Eur. Comm'n (15 Feb. 2022).

Figure 28.1 RemoveDEBRIS, during assembly at SSTL, December 2017. Credit: SSTL/Max Alexander.

The mission consisted of a microsatellite platform (servicer) that ejected two CubeSats (clients). For mission purposes, the ejected CubeSats were used as clients instead of real space debris, enabling important testing in work towards a fully operational ADR mission. These clients assisted with a range of strategically important ADR technology demonstrations including net capture, harpoon capture, and vision-based navigation using a standard camera and LiDAR. The servicer also hosted a drag sail for orbital lifetime reduction.[9]

RemoveDebris launched in April 2018 from the International Space Station (ISS). At approximately 100 kilogrammes, RemoveDebris was the largest satellite to have ever been deployed from the ISS.[10] It went on to successfully complete demonstrations with a net, a harpoon, and vision-based navigation throughout 2018 and early 2019. RemoveDebris re-entered in December 2021, roughly three-and-a-half years after it was launched.

At the time of the mission, UK licensing of spacecraft came under the UK Space Agency (UKSA), which granted the mission licence. This was the first time a complex ADR mission was licensed by the UKSA and thus a test case for future missions in OOS.

28.2.2 ELSA-d

Since 2013, the Japanese-headquartered private company Astroscale has been a market leader in developing innovative and scalable solutions across the spectrum of on-orbit servicing. Astroscale has a strong international presence, with subsidiaries in the UK, US, and Israel; each office is innovating in a different field of on-orbit servicing, including life extension, end of life, and active debris removal.

9 *See RemoveDebris Satellite Overview*, SPACEFLIGHT101.
10 *Nanoracks Deploys Largest Satellite From International Space Station To Date*, NANORACKS (20 June 2018).

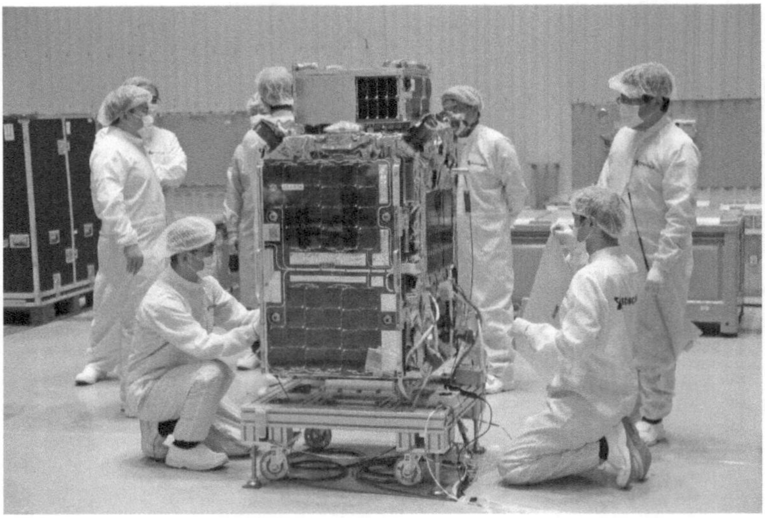

Figure 28.2 ELSA-d, pre-launch tests at Baikonur Cosmodrome, February 2021. Credit: Astroscale.

ELSA-d (shown in Figure 28.2),[11] which stands for End of Life Services by Astroscale (-demonstration), is an in-orbit demonstration for key end-of-life technology and capabilities of future debris removal missions. ELSA-d consists of two spacecraft, a servicer (~175kg) and a client (~17kg), launched stacked together. The servicer is equipped with proximity rendezvous technologies and a magnetic capture mechanism, whereas the client has a docking plate which enables it to be efficiently captured. With the servicer repeatedly releasing and capturing the client, a series of demonstrations could be undertaken.[12]

In March 2021, Astroscale launched the ELSA-d mission. In August 2021, the first test phase was completed, demonstrating release and rapid re-capture of client. This was the world's first time a magnetic capture system has docked with a docking plate for the purposes of debris removal.[13] On 25 January 2022, the ELSA-d servicer space craft successfully released its client spacecraft and began autonomous relative navigation, maintaining a constant and safe distance from the client spacecraft for several hours, over multiple orbits, as designed. Unfortunately, ELSA-d suffered from some technical propulsion-related issues in early 2022. Despite these, in May 2022, ELSA-d successfully completed a complex rendezvous operation, approaching from a far-range and switching to local relative sensors and navigation, which are key sequences in orbital rendezvous.[14]

11 Chris Blackerby et al., *The ELSA-d End-of-life Debris Removal Mission: Preparing for Launch*, in 70th International Astronautical Congress, IAC-19.A6.5.2(49982) (Oct. 2019); Jason Forshaw et al., *ELSA-D ADR Mission – Operations Setup & Post-Launch Update*, in 11th Int'l Assoc. Advancement Space Safety at 432 (Oct. 2021).

12 *See ELSA-d Press Kit 2022*, Astroscale (2022).

13 Jason L. Forshaw et al., *ELSA-d: A Case Study of ADR Mission Operational Practice*, in 72nd Int'l Astronautical Cong., IAC-21.A6.10-B6.5.1(64392) (Oct. 2021).

14 See *Astroscale's ELSA-d Mission Successfully Completes Complex Rendezvous Operation*, Astroscale (May 4, 2022).

ELSA-d is operated by Astroscale UK from the In-Orbit Servicing Control Centre, developed by primary contractor (lead) Astroscale and embedded in the Satellite Applications Catapult in Harwell, UK ELSA-d was licensed through the UKSA during the "authorisation" phase prior to launch. However, recently, UK space operations licensing has been handed over to the Civil Aviation Authority (CAA) for all future satellite missions; appropriately, the CAA has taken over the licensing and "continuous monitoring" aspects of the mission.

28.2.3 ELSA-M

Astroscale has been working with the European Space Agency (ESA) and the constellation operator OneWeb since 2018 towards an in-orbit demonstration mission, set to launch in 2024. The collaboration, termed Project Sunrise,[15] is maturing debris removal technologies and capabilities. Astroscale is continuing to build off of the Project Sunrise collaboration towards a future service family: ELSA-M.[16] ELSA-M will be the commercialised form of ELSA-d, designed for multi-client removal of magnetically prepared clients.[17] Although developed with OneWeb, ELSA-M is designed for a range of commercial constellation operators.[18]

ELSA-M will be the first commercialised Astroscale ADR mission to be licensed in the UK under the CAA. Additionally, ELSA-M will push even further than ELSA-d in terms of removal capabilities.[19]

28.2.4 MEV-1 and MEV-2

In the US, the aerospace and defence technology company Northrop Grumman has two successful OOS missions to date. Developed by the wholly owned subsidiary SpaceLogistics, the first Mission Extension Vehicle (MEV-1) should be recognised as an unprecedented push to evolve the US regulatory environment and enable commercial OOS missions. It took MEV-1, and its developing company, approximately *nine years* to secure the regulatory and policy approval for the first US commercial OOS mission.[20]

MEV-1 was launched in October 2019, entered into a geosynchronous transfer orbit, and proceeded to orbit-raised to 300 kilometres beyond the geosynchronous (GSO) belt.[21] The selected client for MEV-1 was Intelsat 901, another US-owned satellite. Intelsat 901 was also raised out of the GSO ring to rendezvous with MEV-1 in a graveyard orbit. To dock, MEV-1 inserts a retract-

15 See *First Leap for Beam-Hopping Constellation*, ESA (24 May 2021).

16 Jason L. Forshaw et al., *Towards Commercial ADR Services: The ELSA-d Mission*, in 72ND INT'L ASTRONAUTICAL CONG., IAC-21.A6.6.3(64394) (Oct. 2021).

17 *Id.*

18 See generally *OneWeb, Astroscale, and the UK and European Space Agencies Partner to Launch Space Junk Servicer ELSA-M With € 14.8 Million Investment*, ASTROSCALE (May 27, 2022) (discussing the development of ELSA-M).

19 See 28.3.2.7, *infra.* (discussing technical due diligence and the ELSA-M programme).

20 See the Federalist Society, *Modernizing American Space Policy*, THE FEDERALIST SOC'Y (26 July 2018) (Jim Armor noted working for seven to eight years on the policy and regulatory environment for MEV-1 and still not having all necessary permissions for launch of MEV-1); see also Application of Space Logistics, LLC., Authority to Launch and Operate a Mission Extension Vehicle, IBFS File No. SAT-LOA-20170224-00021 (grant in part, defer in part 5 Dec. 2017).

21 The geostationary belt is defined to be at 35,786 km, while "graveyard" is the region 200 kilometres or more beyond GSO, where satellites are commonly retired to. See Inter-Agency Space Debris Coordination Comm., IADC-02-01 (Rev. 2), *IADC Space Debris Mitigation Guidelines* at 7, 11-2 (Mar. 2020) [*hereinafter* IADC Mitigation Guidelines].

able capture mechanism into the liquid apogee motor of the client, and then stanchions provide a mechanical interface between MEV and the client's launch adapter ring.[22]

MEV-2 quickly followed upon the success of MEV-1. MEV-2's client was another Intelsat satellite – Intelsat-1002. However, unlike the concept of operations (CONOPS) of MEV-1, MEV-2 completed rendezvous and docking with Intelsat-1002 while the client was *still located* within the GSO arc.[23]

28.2.5 LEXI

Astroscale US, in conjunction with its wholly owned subsidiary Astroscale Israel, is also developing a geostationary servicing spacecraft – the Life Extension In-orbit (LEXI) vehicle shown in Figure 28.3. Beyond offering life-extension as a servicer, LEXI will also be capable of inclination correction, and will be refuelable – allowing it to sustainably extend its lifetime or conduct depletive manoeuvrers that may not otherwise be considered for traditional fixed-fuel satellites. LEXI is projected to launch in late 2025 and is intended to service US-flag or foreign satellites alike.[24]

While MEV-1 and MEV-2 were the first commercial US geostationary servicing satellites, LEXI will offer additional insights as a case study. First, both MEV-1 and MEV-2 serviced US clients, avoiding messy problems about international consent, spacecraft docking as an export, liability questions, and more. Additionally, the regulatory US environment has changed significantly since the MEV vehicles were licensed, making LEXI the first geostationary servicer that

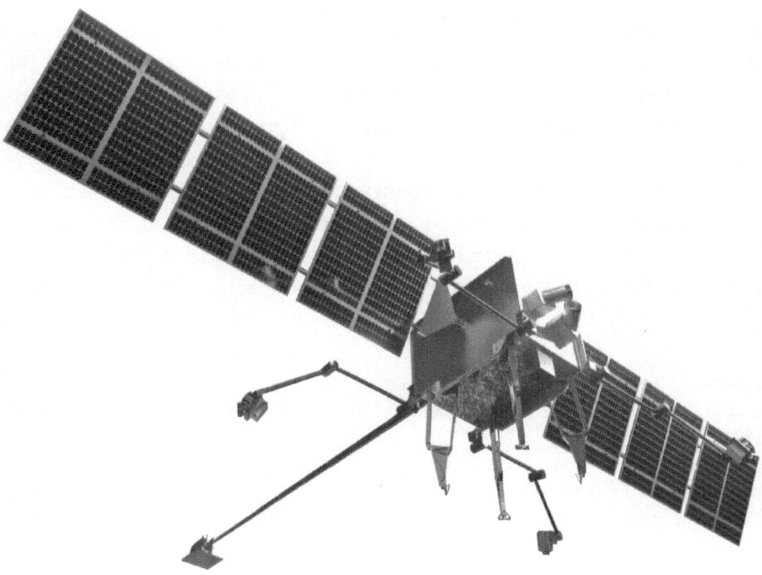

Figure 28.3 LEXI (Life Extension In-orbit) vehicle concept. Credit: Astroscale.

22 MEV-2 performs capture in a similar way.

23 See *Northrop Grumman and Intelsat Make History with Docking of Second Mission Extension Vehicle to Extend Life of Satellite*, NORTHROP GRUMMAN (12 Apr. 2021).

24 Rob Staples, *Key Capabilities of Our Life Extension In-Orbit (LEXI) Servicer*, ASTROSCALE US (Oct. 5, 2021).

will navigate these new regulatory regimes. Finally, while any rendezvous, proximity, and docking (RPOD) manoeuvre raise orbital debris questions, the added aspect of re-fuelability will increase the novelty and CONOPS investigation that must be done.

28.3 Insight into the UK licensing procedure

As noted in descriptions of UK missions above, formerly the UKSA was responsible for licensing of spacecraft, but this has recently been handed over to the CAA in July 2021.[25] Unlike the US,[26] UK licensing is handled through a single body which checks all the necessary permits are in place before issuing an Orbital Operator Licence ("space licence").

In the following description we introduce the key considerations needed to obtain a UK space licence. We start with the basic steps required under previously the UKSA and now the CAA. As OOS is an emerging market, regulatory aspects are consistently evolving to keep up with technological innovation, and it is possible that there are major changes in regulatory policy in the next decade as OOS services evolve and become more routine in nature. Later sections will postulate topics that licensing may evolve to cover in the future.

Two pieces of legislation – the Outer Space Act 1986 (OSA)[27] and the Space Industry Act 2018 (SIA)[28] – domestically enact international legal obligations from the UN space treaties[29] and establish the framework for licensing and regulation of activities.[30] The following activities in space require a space licence: (1) launching or procuring the launch of a space object; (2) operating a space object; and (3) any activity in outer space.

Activities which are conducted in the UK fall under SIA, and those outside the UK fall under OSA. For example, if the mission operations were to be conducted in the UK, this would fall under SIA. However, if the mission launch is to be conducted abroad, then that activity would fall under OSA. An application under both SIA and OSA can be submitted together.

The SIA 2018 sets out the high-level framework for commercial spaceflight operations, and the *Space Industry Regulation 2021* provides the specific regulations to implement the SIA. The SIA 2018 became law in March 2020,[31] however, many of the Act's provisions only came into force in July 2021, when the Space Industry Regulations came into force.

In the case of RemoveDebris and ELSA-d, both missions were operated from the UK – by Surrey Satellite Technology Limited (SSTL), and Astroscale respectively – and thus the UK operator needed to have applied for a space licence with the UKSA. Note that the satellite owner and satellite operator may be different entities.

28.3.1 Pre-application stage and traffic light system

A space licensing *Traffic Light System* (TLS) was being originally formalised back in the days of RemoveDebris (2016–2018). A TLS assessment is initiated by an applicant by making a short pre-assessment application to the CAA, through which CAA provides feedback to the applicant on

25 See *CAA Becomes UK Space Regulator and Launches Licensing Regime*, UK Civ. Aviation Auth. (July 29, 2021).
26 See 28.4, *infra*.
27 Outer Space Act 1986, c. 38 (Eng.).
28 Space Industry Act 2018, c. 5 (Eng.).
29 *See* Off. Outer Space Aff., U.N., International Space Law: United Nations Instruments (2017).
30 *See The Outer Space Act*, UK Civ. Aviation Auth. (2022).
31 This is when royal assent was given.

the likelihood that a proposed operation presents an acceptable level of risk. There are no specific metrics defined for what an applicant is assessed against, as this is an optional informal stage to provide feedback on what might or might not be acceptable to CAA prior to a full submission as explored in the sections below.

Following submission of a TLS, CAA returns to the applicant a non-binding Red, Amber, or Green rating. The function of the TLS is to: (1) help less experienced operators understand the need for safety, security, and sustainability; (2) advise operators of the likelihood of application success before they submit a full application; and, (3) where possible, to advise operators on what modifications would be required to bring their proposed mission in line with the licensing requirements. Neither RemoveDebris nor ELSA-d formally went through the TLS system; however, guidance was provided as to whether these missions were considered licensable. The TLS system is currently being re-termed a pre-application stage.

28.3.2 Licensing process

CAA is expected to follow four core principles in assessing an application for an orbital operator licence: safety, security, sustainability, and responsibility.[32] Figure 28.4 shows the licensing process under OSA.[33] The key aspects that will be considered as part of a licensing application including technical due diligence, financial due diligence, safety (including cyber), insurance, and spectrum. Each of these assessment areas does not correlate one for one with the core principles – in fact an assessment stage could overlap multiple core principles. All of these aspects will be addressed in the sections below.

28.3.2.1 Mission safety

ADR missions are examined for safety assurance at multiple stages, including during mission design and operations, insurance arrangements, and mission licensing. OOS missions often involve rendezvous and proximity operations (RPO), up to docking. Practically, this means that a servicer spacecraft must approach, and potentially dock to, the client spacecraft. This is a complex process for which significant design and testing effort is undertaken to ensure safe operations and to prevent accidental collision between the servicer and client. OOS missions with RPO phases differ greatly from conventional missions, where satellites often are very far away from each other, and the risk of accidental collision is minimal.[34]

Companies that offer OOS services are often guided in mission design, implementation, and operations by relevant international norms and standards – including the UN Long-term Sustainability Guidelines, the Inter-Agency Space Debris Coordination Committee (IADC) Guidelines, ISO standards, and CONFERS, NASA, and ESA best practices or guidelines.[35] An

32 UK Civ. Aviation Auth., CAP 2224 (Issue 01), Guidance for License Applicants: Outer Space Act 1986 (July 2021) [hereinafter CAP 2224].

33 SIA have a slightly different process where order in which items are considered may differ, but core areas of analysis are similar.

34 Nonetheless, collision avoidance maneuvers are still required for most satellites as discussed in 28.3.2.2, *infra*.

35 Rep. of the U.N. Committee on Peaceful Uses of Outer Space of Its Sixty-Second Session, Annex II, *Guidelines for the Long-term Sustainability of Outer Space Activities*, U.N. Doc. A/74/20 (June 12-21, 2019); Inter-Agency Space Debris Coordination Comm., IADC-02-01 (Rev. 2), IADC Space Debris Mitigation Guidelines at 7, 11-2 (Mar. 2020) [hereinafter IADC Mitigation Guidelines]; see generally Int'l Standards Org., Standards By ISO /TC 20/SC 14, Space Systems and Operations; *Guiding Principles for Commercial Rendezvous and Proximity Operations (RPO)*

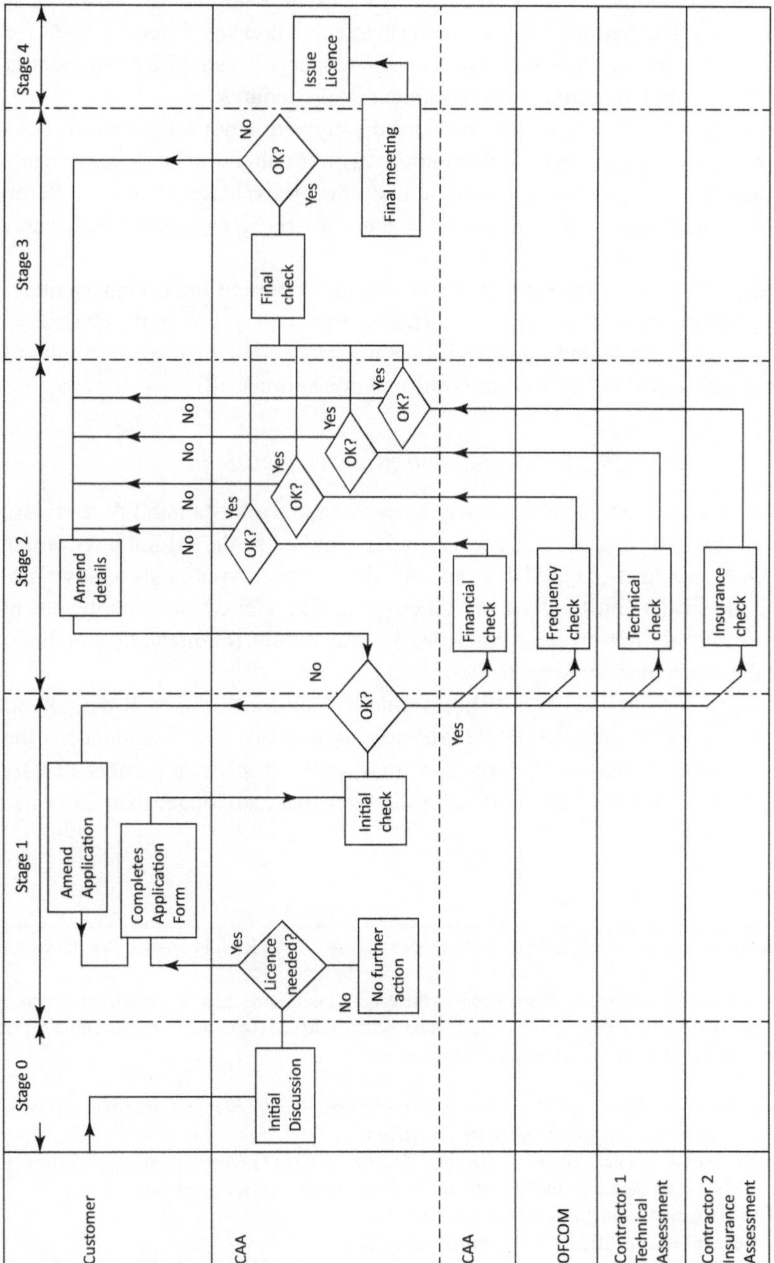

Figure 28.4 Outer Space Act Guidance – CAP 2224, 2021 (CAP 22224, *supra*. note 32.)

example of this is ELSA-d complying with the 25-year de-orbit guidance from the IADC (see 28.3.2.2 for more information).

While orbital operators are not required to provide a "safety case" during mission licensing, there is an expectation that safety due diligence is conducted and exhibited.[36] The SIA notes, "[Orbital operator license] applicants will be expected to demonstrate how they will work to ensure their operations are safe and that the risks are as low as reasonably possible and at an acceptable level".[37] At present in the UK, voluntary operator adoption of a wide range of standards – such as those listed above – could be considered to help present a safety case; however, none of the standards are binding. Furthermore, CAA may wish to delve into any aspects that impact on-board safety, which include aspects, such as mission design (especially reliability, redundancy, and fault tolerance), CONOPS, and operational and contingency procedures.

In the case of RemoveDebris, arrival at – and deployment from – the ISS necessitated a full NASA safety review to ensure that the spacecraft was not dangerous to the astronauts that were deploying the servicer (e.g., no sharp edges, no toxic materials, battery safety).[38] Safety information used for the NASA review was then used in the UK licensing process to give confidence on safety.

With respect to insurance, mission safety is also an important area. Underwriters determine how much they can insure a mission for – or whether they will insure at all – based on how risky a mission is perceived.[39] OOS missions are inherently more risky than conventional missions, as they involve multiple satellites in close proximity to one another.

28.3.2.2 Sustainability and responsibility

Two key factors determinative in licensing assessments are sustainability and responsibility. Sustainability is ensuring that the mission minimises impact to the orbital environment. For the case of some OOS missions (e.g., ADR), the sole aim of the mission is to remove orbital debris, thus improving the sustainability of the orbital environment. Nonetheless, applicants must ensure that in doing so they do not create further debris (preventing fragmentation or break-ups) and should ensure there is a plan for servicer de-orbiting.[40]

A key document for satellites is a disposal plan.[41] A disposal plan will demonstrate through simulations the number of years a satellite will take to de-orbit. IADC guidance is that satellites should de-orbit within 25 years of end of their mission,[42] but this is a number that frequently is under discussion in many fora. Low-earth orbit satellites that take longer than 25 years to de-orbit

and On-Orbit Servicing (OOS), CONSORTIUM EXECUTION COMMERCIAL RENDEZVOUS & SERVICING OPERATIONS (7 Nov. 2018).

36 "Unlike applications for a launch operator licence, there is no requirement for an applicant for an orbital operator licence to provide a safety case." UK Civ. Aviation Auth., CAP 2210, Guidance for Orbital Operator Licence Applicants and Orbital Operator Licensees (29 July 2021).

37 *Id.*

38 See, e.g., Tereza Pultarova, *Launch of Space-Debris-Removal Experiment Delayed Amid Safety Reviews*, SPACENEWS (26 May 2017) (discussing the delays from NASA's review).

39 See generally Rebecca Reesman, *Assurance Through Insurance and On-Orbit Servicing*, AEROSPACE CORP. (Feb. 2018) (discussing the considerations that go into insuring an on-orbit servicing mission).

40 See, e.g., IADC Mitigation Guidelines, *supra*. Note 36, at 11-2.

41 Alternative names are "end-of-life" or "decommissioning" plan.

42 IADC Mitigation Guidelines, *supra*. note 36, at 12.

are expected to use propulsion to move to a lower altitude to meet such criteria at end of life.[43] Recently, there has been more of a global push to reduce end-of-life de-orbiting guidance to five years. In September 2022 the FCC adopted a five-year standard for this.[44] End-of-life plans also may examine collision avoidance manoeuvre strategy – i.e. plans for how a satellite operator will respond to a third-party collision warning and move a spacecraft to avoid debris or other spacecraft when a conjunction is statistically probable.

Responsibility aspects aim to ensure that a satellite operator of an OOS mission behaves responsibly in space. This includes demonstrating to CAA that all international obligations can be met,[45] and being proactive in keeping the regulator in the loop during operations to ensure compliance with licensing conditions.

28.3.2.3 Security and cybersecurity

As part of every licensing application, under the SIA, an applicant must fulfil key roles. For the case of performing operations in the UK, one of the key roles is an "Accountable Manager" that must be assigned.[46] National security is another factor, with applications being checked to ensure they don't impair national security of the UK or contract to national interest; if there are national security implications, a "Security Manager" is also required personnel.[47]

Cybersecurity is a domain which has gained international attention recently and is an area highly relevant to satellite space and ground segment. Missions for OOS are frequently considered dual-use – in that they could be used for both commercial and military or proliferation applications. Firstly, with respect to cybersecurity, there is a risk that an OOS satellite could be hacked, or commandeered for nefarious purposes. As part of licensing procedures, organisations such as the NCSC (National Cyber Security Centre) may audit a company, ground segment or space segment design to ensure that a mission is secure.[48] This would happen in the post-application stages prior to any licence being issued. Examples of where interests lie include aspects such as whether a satellite has authentication or encryption, or whether a ground segment can be hacked.[49]

With respect to dual-use, engaging in transparency and international confidence and trust-building mechanisms helps indicate to external entities, such as governments or other commercial actors, what the missions plans are for an OOS mission. In the case of both RemoveDebris and ELSA-d, extensive briefings to government, the UN, policy groups, and at international conferences were undertaken to give clear guidance on what the objectives and plan for the mission were.[50]

Export control issues are complex and need to be examined with UK export control experts. The UK also has an export regime which controls how and where commodities are transferred.[51] Additionally, as satellite fabrication and operation is often international in nature, export consid-

43 See IADC Mitigation Guidelines, *supra.* note 36, at 12 (Guideline 5.3.2).

44 "FCC Adopts New '5-Year Rule' For Deorbiting Satellites To Address Growing Risk Of Orbital Debris", Federal Communications Commission, September 2022.

45 See UK Civ. Aviation Auth., CAP 2209, Applying for a Licence Under the Space Industry Act 2018 (July 29, 2021).

46 *Id.*

47 *Id.*

48 *Id.*

49 Ground segment considerations include which users can access the satellite operations, how the operations system can be accessed, and how secure the access link is.

50 See, e.g., *Showcasing ELSA-d to Japanese Prime Minster Abe*, ASTROSCALE (May 15, 2018).

51 CAP 2209, *supra.* note 45.

erations can flow from the home nation *or* implicated foreign nations. For example, parts coming from US suppliers often will require US export clearances, as US export controls follow the commodity.[52] The regulator may request copies of the granted export licences and would request this post-application prior to any licence being issued.

28.3.2.4 Financial due diligence

As part of a licensing application, the CAA will undertake financial due diligence checks on the applicant.[53] These include providing information about their business structure and foreign ownership or participation of foreign entities, assessing financial status to ensure that the applicant has adequate resources to carry out the proposed activity and to ensure that the applicant is sufficiently sound to enable a licence to be issued.[54] This includes the delivery as required of company accounts and parent company accounts where requested.[55]

28.3.2.5 Insurance, liability, indemnity

The UN Convention on the International Liability for Damaged Caused by Space Objects[56] specifies that a Launching State shall be liable for damage due to its faults in space. A Launching State is one which "launches or procures the launching of a space object" or one "from whose territory or facility a space objects is launched". In the case of RemoveDebris, Launching States were the UK, and US (SpaceX launch). In the case of ELSA-d, the Launching States were Japan, Russia (Soyuz, Baikonur). One of the Launching States will be considered the State of Registry, which will be coordinated between regulators to ensure there is a UN filing for the mission.[57]

To note, that if an in-space collision occurs the two entities will both have multiple launching states, which presents a complex legal case. The following Swiss Re resource discusses a hypothetical scenario which may result due to an in-space collision.[58] The SIA places a liability on persons carrying on spaceflight activities to indemnify the Government for any claims brought against the UK government for loss or damage caused by those activities.[59]

A range of insurance coverage exists for different aspects of a mission. It is mandatory to purchase third-party liability (TPL) insurance with the TPL insurance and indemnity scope being agreed with CAA. Other types of space insurances include launch insurance, transport to launch site insurance, mission insurance or mission-success insurance.

28.3.2.6 Ofcom spectrum filings and ground station licensing

In order to communicate with a satellite in space, the correct ITU (International Telecommunication Union) filings must be made. The ITU manages global spectrum filings and will facilitate coor-

52 See, e.g., Bureau Sec. & Indus. *Frequently Asked Questions to Export Licensing Requirements*, DEP'T COMM. (Nov. 2018).

53 CAP 2209, *supra*. note 46.

54 *Id.*

55 *Id.*

56 Convention on the International Liability for Damage Caused by Space Objects (1972) 961 U.N.T.S. 2389.

57 Convention on Registration of Objects Launched Into Outer Space (1974) 1023 U.N.T.S. 15.

58 *Space Debris: On Collision Course for Insurers?* SWISS RE (May 26, 2011).

59 *Guidance on Liabilities Under the Space Industry Act 2018.*

dination of frequencies for use in a satellite mission. An ITU spectrum filing can take up to two years to acquire, so this is one of the earliest steps in the licensing process. Ofcom (Office of Communications), is the government-approved regulatory and competition authority for the broadcasting, telecommunications industries in the UK.

In addition to core spectrum allocation, licences must be obtained for local ground stations communications. This is needed for each satellite to communicate with a ground station as it passes over that ground station (similar concept to an aircraft flying over an air traffic control). Each ground segment provider will work with the company and respective government to obtain the necessary licences.

In the case of some OOS missions, multiple ground passes, one after the other, are required in order to create sufficient communications time in order to execute complex space operations. ELSA-d needed a series of chained ground passes, meaning that Astroscale had to work with several ground station companies to acquire up to ten ground stations for usage on the mission in over six countries. This process can become complex. In the case of one US ground station, successive licensing work eventually required many of the separate US entities to be briefed.[60]

The regulator, CAA, will check with Ofcom that ITU spectrum filings have been granted and will also require evidence of local ground station licences from the applicant.

28.3.2.7 Technical due diligence

As part of a licensing application, the following technical information will be required:

Full details on the mission design (e.g., satellite and ground segment specifications), copies of the launch services contract, CONOPS, emergency procedures, radio frequencies and powers used during the mission, orbital location information.

One key area is the CONOPS. The high level CONOPS for one of Astroscale future missions ELSA-M (which stands for End of Life Services for Astroscale – Multi-client) is shown in Figure 28.5. This figure also indicates generically the steps which a servicer must go through operationally in space to perform its ADR mission. Firstly, the servicer will be launched into an insertion orbit. At some point it will orbit-raise to the operating orbit using long range navigation to find the client. After closing it, it will perform a diagnosis (or inspection) to check the craft for damage. After all checks have been satisfied, the servicer will capture the client and start the de-orbiting process. In the case of a multi-client mission (one in which the servicer can do more than one removal), the servicer will "drop-off" the client at a lower altitude for it to naturally re-enter and burn up, before heading back up to the next client to be serviced.

The way in which a mission CONOPS are designed has implications on all aspects of the licensing process – from mission safety, to how and where one communicates with the servicer (e.g. what spectrum allocation and what ground stations are needed), to implications on definition of mission insurance.

To note, that as part of the regulatory regime in the UK, CAA will not just assess the satellite once at the application stage, but post-launch the CAA is still involved in the continuous monitoring aspects of the mission. For example, operators will be expected to keep CAA informed

60 See, e.g., Denali 20020, Application for Special Temporary Authority, IBFS File Nos. SES-STA-20200113-00043 (granted Nov. 17, 2021) (listing, in license condition #7, the four Federal operators that ELSA-d passes had to be de-conflicted with).

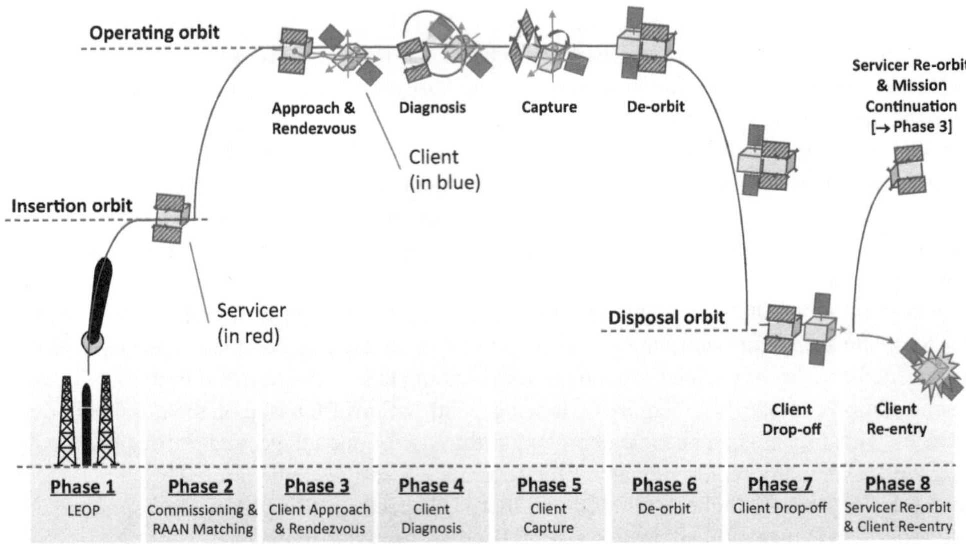

Figure 28.5 ELSA-M, Commercial Service CONOPS. Credit: Astroscale.

throughout the mission on mission progress – if CONOPS change, then this needs to be discussed with the CAA (and most probably insurer too).

28.4 Insight into the US licensing procedure

The US licensing environment for on-orbit servicing space missions is an environment in flux. The first Mission Extension Vehicle (MEV-1) launched in October 2019 and docked in February 2020, marking the first time two commercial satellites (both US) docked in orbit, and the first time mission extension services were offered in geosynchronous orbit.[61] Since this historic achievement, two major US space-licensing agencies have issued new regulations modifying previous regimes,[62] and the US Government has become more interested in the possibilities of OOS.[63]

There are three primary administrative agencies within the US from which a commercial space operator may need to obtain a licence. For OOS missions, an operator should plan on engaging, in at least some capacity, with the following: (1) the office of Commercial Remote Sensing Regulatory Affairs (CRSRA), under the Department of Commerce (DOC); (2) the Office of Commercial Space Transportation (AST), under the Department of Transportation (DOT); and (3) the International

61 Vicki Cox, *Northrop Grumman Successfully Completes Historic First Docking of Mission Extension Vehicle with Intelsat 901 Satellite*, Northrop Grumman (26 Feb. 2020).

62 The FAA created Part 450, *Streamlining of Launch and Reentry Licensing Requirements*, in a final rule released December 2020. See FAA & DOT, Final Rule, *Streamlined Launch and Reentry License Requirements,* 85 Fed. Reg. 79566 (10 Dec. 2020) (to be codified at 14 C.F.R. Part 450) [hereinafter Streamlined Launch]. NOAA re-did their remote sensing regulations as well, releasing updated regulations in May 2020. See NESDIS & NOAA, Final Rule, *Licensing of Private Remote Sensing Space Systems*, 85 Fed. Reg. 30790 (20 May 2020) [hereinafter Remote Sensing Order 2020].

63 See, e.g., ISAM National Strategy, *supra*. note 1 (laying out a national strategy for supporting and accomplishing ISAM missions).

Bureau (IB), under the Federal Communications Commission (FCC). While other executive agencies are involved in the licensing process through inter-agency consultations,[64] only the DOC, the DOT, and the FCC hold licensing authority for US commercial space missions.[65]

28.4.1 Department of Commerce – imaging

No person subject to jurisdiction and control of the United States may operate a private remote sensing space system without a licence.[66] In the United States, the Secretary of Commerce is the official authorised to license private remote sensing space systems.[67] This licensing power is delegated to the National Oceanic and Atmospheric Administration's (NOAA) Assistant Administrator for Satellite and Information Services, and carried out by the office of Commercial Remote Sensing Regulatory Affairs (CRSRA).[68]

28.4.1.1 US remote sensing regulatory jurisdiction

A company should first evaluate whether they fall under the jurisdiction of the US's remote sensing regulations. As a threshold, "remote sensing" is the "collection of unenhanced data by an instrument in orbit of the Earth which can be processed into imagery of the surface features of the Earth".[69] US jurisdiction over remote sensing activity can attach in one of two ways: (1) the operation of a remote sensing system occurs within the US, and/or (2) a US person operates a remote sensing system.[70]

First, to operate a system "means to have decision-making authority over the functioning of a remote sensing instrument. If there are multiple entities involved, the entity with the ultimate ability to decide what unenhanced data to collect with the instrument and to execute that decision, directly or through a legal arrangement with a third party such as a ground station or platform

64 See, e.g., 15 C.F.R. § 960 Appendix D (2022) (the MOU between the Department of Commerce and other USG. agencies involved in intergovernmental review of commercial remote sensing authorizations); 14 C.F.R. § 450.43(e) (2022) (relaying instances in the FAA's payload review when consultation with other agencies is undertaken).

65 Cong. Rsch. Serv., R45416, Commercial Space: Federal Regulation, Oversight, and Utilization 1 (2018).

66 51 USC. § 60122 (2022).

67 *Id.* § 60121 (2022). The empowerment of the Secretary of Commerce dates to the first remote sensing legislation in the US, the Land Remote Sensing Commercialization Act of 1984. Land Remote-Sensing Commercialization, 98th Cong., 98 Stat. 451 § 101(5) (1984). The subsequent Land Remote Sensing Policy Act of 1992, and its amendments, did not alter this structure. *See* Land Remote Sensing Policy Act of 1992, H. R. 6133, 102nd Cong. (1992); Commercial Space Act of 1998, H.R. 1702, 105th Cong. (1998) (changing the requirement that commercial sensing licensees notify the Secretary of Commerce of "any agreement entered into with foreign entities" to "any significant or substantial agreement intended to be entered into with a foreign entity"); Enactment of Title 51 – National and Commercial Space Programs, H.R. 3237, 111th Cong., 124 Stat. 3328 (2010) (relocation within the USC. and change to "positive law"; no alternation of legal obligations).

68 See Department Organization Order 10-15, Under Secretary of Commerce for Oceans and Atmosphere and Administrator of the National Oceanic and Atmospheric Administration § 3.01(qq) (effective Dec. 12, 2011); Nat'l Envtl. Satellite Data & Info. Serv, *Licensing*, NOAA (noting that "responsibilities have been delegated from the Secretary of Commerce to the Assistant Administrator for NOAA Satellite and Information Services (NOAA/NESDIS) for the licensing of operations of private space-based remote sensing systems").

69 15 C.F.R. § 960.4 (2022).

70 *Id.* § 960.2 (2022). A private "remote sensing space system" is "an instrument…capable of conducting remote sensing" with all additional components to support "operating the remote sensing instrument, receipt of unenhanced data, and data processing". *Id.* § 960.4 (2022).

owner, is considered to be operating that system".[71] The definition is designed to capture an entity with decision-making authority over a remote sensing instrument, and is not intended to capture entities engaging in limited capacities, such as operating a ground station as a service.[72]

Second, the definition of "US person" has been expanded to include citizens, lawful permanent residents, and "any corporation, partnership, joint venture, association, or other entity organized or existing under the laws of the United States or any State ... and any other commonwealth, territory, or possession of the United States".[73]

Finally, it should be noted that there is a "mission assurance" carve-out from the definition of a remote sensing system that is important for OOS. Under "mission assurance," instruments used *primarily* for mission assurance are not considered remote sensing instruments.[74]

28.4.1.2 Remote sensing licensing process

All entities are encouraged to initiate contact with CRSRA through submission of the Initial Contact Form,[75] whether they already know a remote sensing licence may be required or not. CRSRA will respond to the Initial Contact Form submission with a formal letter indicating whether the office believes the filer must submit a remote sensing system application.

If a remote sensing licence is needed, the applicant will begin an application and submit it for review.[76] CRSRA has seven days to consult with the Secretaries of Defense and State to determine whether the application is complete.[77] If the supplied information is complete, CRSRA will inform the applicant.[78] If the supplied application is deemed incomplete, CRSRA will inquire for the additional necessary information.[79] The applicant may submit additional information, or correct any previously incorrect submissions.[80]

Upon confirmation of a complete application, CRSRA will consult with the Department of Defense (DOD) and Department of State (DOS) to classify the applicant's system in the appropriate Tier.[81]

71 *Id.*

72 See Remote Sensing Order 2020, *supra.* Note 62, at, 30796.

73 15 C.F.R. § 960.4 (2022); see Remote Sensing Order 2020, *supra.* note 62, at 30795 (noting that the definition was and added lawful permanent residents).

74 *Id.* § 960.2(b) (2022); see Com. Remote Sensing Regul. Aff., Guidance Circular No. 960.2-1, *Instruments Used Primarily for Mission Assurance or Other Technical Purposes* (1 Apr. 2022) (discussing the "mission assurance" carve-out and balancing test for an instrument of remote sensing versus other purposes).

75 Nat'l Envtl. Satellite Data & Info. Serv, *Licensing*, NOAA (a link to the "Initial Contact Form" can be found under the "License Application Process" heading). As noted, the form is used for information purposes only and is considered non-binding. *Id.*

76 See 15 C.F.R. § 960 Appendix A, *Applicant Information Required* (2022); *see also* Com. Remote Sensing Regul. Aff., *Application Guide* (document from CRSRA containing prompts and further information to support completion of the remote sensing system application).

77 15 C.F.R. § 960.b(c) (2022). Note that the regulations reference the Secretary of Commerce in place of CRSRA. This section references CRSRA for continuity, and because the government employees an applicant will regularly interact with throughout the process are nominally CRSRA staff.

78 *Id.*

79 *Id.*

80 *Id.* § 960.5(d) (2022).

81 The 2020 rulemaking for remote sensing regulations moved to a Tier-based approach for classification of licenses, with Tier categorisations based on "the degree to which the unenhanced data to be generated by their proposed systems are already available (rather than based on the amount of risk they pose to national security)". Remote Sensing Order 2020, *supra.* note 62, at 30792.

- Tier 1 – A system capable of collecting unenhanced data *substantially the same* as unenhanced data available from unregulated sources (ex. foreign providers).[82]
- Tier 2 – A system capable of collecting unenhanced data substantially the same as unenhanced data already available *from entities or individuals licensed under US commercial remote sensing regulations*.[83]
- Tier 3 – A system cable of collecting unenhanced data *not* substantially the same as unenhanced data available from domestic or foreign sources.[84]

The tiered system was instituted to promote flexibility in categorisation, and systems may move between Tiers during the lifetime of the system.[85] Also beginning upon notification of a complete application, CRSRA has 60 days to determine whether an applicant will comply with requirements of applicable law and grant or deny the licence.[86] If a licence is granted, a licensee has continuing statutory obligations, as well as any terms contained in the licence.[87]

28.4.1.3 Remote sensing licensing and on-orbit servicing considerations

There are several aspects of remote sensing licensing in the US that OOS operators should pay attention to. First, a licensee must state the orbital characteristics of their satellite(s).[88] For OOS missions, this information may either be unknow until a customer contract is signed (prior to or after deployment) or may change per mission design. In the application phase, an unknown orbital location may constitute an incomplete application, and stall consideration of the licence application. If an operator already has a licence and would like to change orbits, this should be requested as a modification and change in "material fact".[89] A modification request starts the clock on another 60-day consideration phase for the modification,[90] and may change the Tier of the licensee's system.[91]

OOS operators should also remain aware of the regulatory treatment for imaging of "artificial resident space objects" (ARSO). Under current guidance, the imaging of ARSOs is still remote sensing, and not exculpated under the "mission assurance or other technical purposes" exemption, because "the imaging is done as service for another operator rather than to assure the safety of the mission".[92] A Tier 2 or Tier 3 system that wishes to conduct resolved imaging (resolution 3x3 pixels or greater) or an ARSO must: (1) have the written consent of the registered owner, and (2)

82 15 C.F.R. § 960.6(a)(1) (2022); see *id.* § 960.8 (standard licence conditions applicable to Tier 1 systems).

83 *Id.* § 960.6(a)(2) (2022); see *id.* § 960.9 (licence conditions applicable to Tier 2 systems).

84 *Id.* § 960.6(a)(3) (2022); see *id.* § 960.10 (licence conditions applicable to Tier 3 systems).

85 Remote Sensing Order 2020, *supra.* note 62, at 30798. It should be noted that a licensee will only move *up* in Tiers if a modification is requested by the licensee. See 15 C.F.R. § 960.13 (2022).

86 15 C.F.R. § 960.7(a), (b). Applicable law includes the Land Remote Sensing Policy Act of 1992, as amended, regulations for the Licensing of Private Remote Sensing Space Systems, and any terms contained within a licence. "The Secretary will presume that the applicant will comply, unless the Secretary has specific, credible evidence to the contrary." *Id.* § 960.7(a).

87 See 51 USC. § 60122(b) (2022).

88 See 15 C.F.R. § 960 Appendix A, *Applicant Information Required* (2022).

89 A "material fact" includes "a fact an applicant provides in the application". 15 C.F.R. § 960.4 (2022).

90 *Id.* § 960.13(d).

91 *Id.* § 960.13(b), (c).

92 Com. Remote Sensing Regul. Aff., Guidance Circular No. 960.2-1, *Instruments Used Primarily for Mission Assurance or Other Technical Purposes* at 4 (1 Apr. 2022).

notify the Secretary at least five days prior to imaging.[93] However, there are hopes that these constraints may be removed in the future. When the remote sensing regulations were redone in 2020, it was indicated that reconsideration of the Tier 2 and Tier 3 constraints related to ARSO imaging should be revisited in "approximately two years".[94] It is unknown whether this future rulemaking could also be used to challenge the conception that imaging related to OOS is "remote sensing" within the statutory definition.[95]

Finally, and as alluded to above, instruments for on-orbit servicing *may* fall under the "mission assurance" exemption depending on their primary purpose. An OOS operator should clearly distinguish which sensors are used for what purposes, and for how long. For instance, sensors used only for RPO phases and to ensure the safety of both spacecraft during a docking are arguably "mission assurance" sensors, and may not require an operator to obtain a private remote sensing system authorisation.

28.4.2 Federal Aviation Administration – launch and re-entry licensing

Within the DOT, the Federal Aviation Administration's (FAA) Office of Commercial Space Transportation (AST) is delegated[96] the authority to issue licences or permits related to commercial launch and re-entry operations, as well as license spaceports.[97] Specifically, the following activities – collectively referred to a spaceflight activities – fall under AST's jurisdiction: launch[98] of a launch vehicle,[99] operation of a launch site[100] or re-entry site,[101] or the re-entry[102] of a re-entry vehicle.[103] If the spaceflight activities occur within the US, an licence or permit will be required.[104] Additionally, if the spaceflight operations are conducted outside of the US by a US citizen or corporate entity organised or existing under US laws, a licence or permit will be required.[105]

93 15 USC. § 960.9(b), § 960.10(c) (2022).

94 Remote Sensing Order 2020, *supra*. note 62, at 30792.

95 See 51 USC. § 60101(4) (2022) ("The term 'land remote sensing' means the collection of data which can be processed into imagery of surface features of the Earth from an unclassified satellite or satellites, other than an operational United States Government weather satellite").

96 See 49 C.F.R. § 1.83 (b) (2022) (delegating the Secretary of Transportation's commercial space activities to the Federal Aviation Administrator); see also 14 C.F.R. § 401.3 (2022) (stating that the Office of Commercial Space Transportation is headed by an Association Administrator "to exercise the Secretary's authority to license or permit and otherwise regulate commercial space transportation and to discharge the Secretary's responsibility to encourage, facilitate, and promote commercial space transportation by the United States private sector").

97 51 USC. § 50901(b)(3),(4); *Id.* § 50903(a); *see* Fed. Aviation Admin., *Vehicle Operator Licenses & Permits*, Dep't Transp. (12 Apr. 2022).

98 51 USC. § 50902(7) (2022); 14 C.F.R. § 450.3(b) (2022).

99 51 USC. § 50902(11) (2022).

100 *Id.* § 50902(10).

101 *Id.* § 50902(18).

102 *Id.* § 50902(16).

103 *Id.* § 50902(19).

104 *Id.* § 50904(a)(1).

105 *Id.* § 50904(a)(2)–(4). Note, the statute requires a *foreign* corporate entity to obtain a licence for spaceflight activities conducted outside the US *if* a US citizen or corporate entity holds a controlling interest. Nominally, a licence or permit will be required absent "an agreement between the United States Government and the government of the foreign country providing that the government of the foreign country has jurisdiction over the launch or operation or reentry". *Id.* § 50904(a)(4); see *id.* 50902(1)(C) (defining "citizen of the United States" for entities organised or existing under the laws of a foreign country); see also 14 C.F.R. § 413.3 (2022) (delineating who must obtain a licence or permit).

Activities are regulated "to the extent necessary ... to ensure compliance with international obligations of the United State and to protect the public health and safety, safety of property, and national security and foreign interests of the United States".[106] Following these statutory considerations, the parts of a vehicle operator licence are: (1) policy approval, (2) payload determination, (3) safety approval, (4) environmental review, and (5) maximum probable loss analysis.[107] Flexibly, the various parts of a licence may be submit for approval and determination separately.[108]

28.4.2.1 OOS and the FAA

As noted above, the various parts of a vehicle operator licence can be applied for separately. Unless a launcher and OOS provider are vertically integrated, it may facilitate OOS mission licensing in the US to apply for a payload review and determination in advance of launch.[109] In this way, time for review and approval can be front-loaded; a launcher (licence applicant) can incorporate the favourable payload review as part of the ultimate application.[110]

As a payload review includes consideration of whether payload launch or re-entry would jeopardise US national security, foreign policy interests, or international obligations, the process has also been a beneficial process for green-lighting otherwise regulatory questionable missions.[111] However, the payload approval process may be daunting for foreign operators seeking US-provided launch as the regulations are not clear in what may affect payload review.[112] While the FAA regulations remain broad, the FAA has stated that it will release guidance – in the form

106 51 USC. § 50901(a)(7) (2022).

107 14 C.F.R. § 450.31(a)(2)–(6) (2022).

108 *Id.* § 450.31(b) (2022).

109 Traditional commercial space activities – specifically, telecommunication satellites and remote sensing satellites – fall under the jurisdiction of other US agencies (the FCC and NOAA, respectively). In the instances where a payload falls under jurisdiction of separate US agency, the payload is exempt from review. Additionally, when the payload is owned or operated by the US Government, it is exempted from review. 14 C.F.R. § 450.43(b) (2022); see *Starships and Stripes Forever – An Examination of the FAA's Role in the Future of Spaceflight: Remote Hearing Before the Subcomm. On Aviation Before the H. Comm. on Transp. & Infrastructure*, 117th Cong. X (2021).

110 14 C.F.R. § 450.43(h) (2022).

111 See Streamlined Launch, *supra.* note 62, at 79589 ("The FAA has not specified a timeline to complete payload reviews independent of a license application because, historically, payload owners or operators have requested such reviews for unique missions that have raised novel concerns regarding public health and safety, safety of property, or national security or foreign policy interests of the United States. Because independent payload reviews often raise complex issues and often require extensive interagency consultation, the FAA cannot anticipate a standard timeline for payload reviews conducted independently from a license application...Applicants are encouraged to discuss timelines to review their particular proposals during pre-application consultation."); Jeff Foust, *FAA Rejects Payload Review for Momentus,* SpaceNews (11 May 2021) (noting that AST denied Momentus's application for payload review due to Defense Department concerns about national security and foreign ownerships concerns raised during interagency review); Jeff Foust, *Moon Express Wins US Government Approval for Lunar Lander Mission*, SpaceNews (3 Aug. 2016) (discussing Moon Express's application for payload review, which included a broader "mission approval" request for the interagency to consider); Jeff Foust, *FAA Review a Small Step for Lunar Commercialization Efforts*, SpaceNews (6 Feb. 2015).

112 See Streamlined Launch, *supra.* note 62, at 79589–79590 (noting a comment from NZSA requesting that the final rule include "all legislative or regulatory standards by which the FAA will assess payloads at the application stage").

of an Advisory Circular – to increase transparency of the interagency process and help operators prepare to address any potential issues.[113]

A final issue to be aware of is orbital debris regulation. The FAA is preparing to release a Notice of Proposed Rulemaking in end 2022/early 2023 to discuss orbital debris mitigation guidelines during launch and re-entry, including risk to persons on the ground and aviation.[114] Sources indicate that the rule will seek to align FAA regulations with the Orbital Debris Mitigation Standard Practices.[115] Currently, regulation is largely focused on collision avoidance during orbital (or sub-orbital) launch or re-entry,[116] including during payload separation.[117]

28.4.3 Federal Communications Commission – spectrum

In the US, oversight of spectrum use is bifurcated between the Federal Communications Commission (FCC) and the National Telecommunications and Information Administration (NTIA).[118] The FCC oversees authorisation and use of commercial spectrum,[119] while NTIA is the authorising body for Federal spectrum use.[120] The FCC's authority includes oversight and regulation of spectrum used by satellites.[121] Within the FCC, the majority of commercial satellite works happens before the Satellite Division of the International Bureau.

28.4.3.1 Satellite spectrum licensing process

For US commercial operators, a spacecraft spectrum licence begins by submitting technical information to the FCC for its communication to the ITU.[122] This can be done prior to, or in tangent with, submitting an application to the FCC for a licence.

The FCC has three different licence regimes that an OOS operator may consider: (1) Part 5 – authorising experimental and proof-of-concept satellites that will *not* be providing commercial services;[123] (2) Part 25 – the normal pathway for commercial operations;[124] or (3) Streamlined Part 25 – a pared-down version of Part 25 licensing, with eligibility constraints based on size, lifetime,

113 *Id.* at 79590. However, no Advisory Circular is yet forthcoming, as of the time of writing. See Fed. Aviation Admin., *14 C.F.R. Part 450 Subpart C Accepted Means of Compliance Table*, Dep't Transp. (22 Apr. 2021) (listing topics and date of planned issuance for Advisory Circulars and Means of Compliance; does not include reference to Payload Review).

114 Off. Info & Reg. Aff., *View Rule – DOT/FAA, RIN 2120-AK81*, Off. Mgmt. & Budget (2021); see *Starships and Stripes Forever – An Examination of the FAA's Role in the Future of Spaceflight: Remote Hearing Before the Subcomm. On Aviation Before the H. Comm. on Transp. & Infrastructure*, 117th Cong. 16 (2021) (statement of Wayne R. Monteith, Associate Administrator, Commercial Space Transportation, Federal Aviation Administration).

115 *Starships and Stripes Forever*, supr.a note 118 (statement of Heather Krause, Director, Physical Infrastructure, US Government Accountability Office).

116 See 14 C.F.R. § 450.169 (2022).

117 See *id.* § 450.171(a)(1) (2022) (regulating "unplanned physical contact" between the launch vehicle and payload after separation); see also *id.* § 450.171(a)(2) (prohibiting debris generation from conversion of energy sources of the launch vehicle or components).

118 See 47 C.F.R. § 2.106 (2022) (the US Table of Frequency Allocations, noting US spectrum is split between "commercial" and "Federal").

119 See Telecommunications Act of 1996, Pub. L. 104-104., 110 Stat. 56 (1996).

120 See Pub. L. No. 102-538, 106 Stat. 3533 (1992) (codified at 47 USC. §901 *et seq.*).

121 See Communications Satellite Act of 1962, Pub. L. 87-624, § 201(c), 76 Stat. 419, (1962).

122 47 C.F.R. § 25.111 (2022).

123 *Id.* pt. 25, subpt. B (2022); *id.* § 5.64 (2022) (containing special satellite licensing provisions).

124 See *id.* part 25 (2022).

and several other factors.[125] The ELSA-d supporting US ground stations were authorised under a Part 5 experimental licence, as the demonstration was not for a commercial service.[126] In juxtaposition, both MEV-1 and MEV-2 applied for full Part 25 licences.[127]

As part of a licence application, an OOS applicant should prepare to provide the following information. First, as the FCC's regulation of spectrum is predicated on the "public interest", applicants should include language addressing how the satellite operation will benefit and serve the public. Second, an applicant will need to provide technical showings about the system, including which spectrum is desired, information on beams, power limits, etc. Finally, an applicant will be required to make an orbital debris mitigation showing.[128]

28.4.3.2 FCC consideration of ISAM

This text will not dive too deeply into considerations for OOS operators before the FCC, as this is an environment in flux. In-line with the US Executive's focus on In-Space Servicing, Assembly, and Manufacturing (ISAM),[129] the FCC Commissioners voted in August 2022 to adopt two new dockets – "Space Innovation" and "Facilitating Capabilities for In-space Servicing, Assembly, and Manufacturing".[130] The present action is a Notice of Inquiry (NOI), but it can be anticipated that a Notice of Proposed Rulemaking to update the regulatory environment would follow the NOI.

28.5 Future trends: predicting evolutions in OOS licensing

As the OOS market evolves, the licensing regime will also evolve to reflect such missions which may become more routine. RemoveDebris, then ELSA-d, were both major benchmark missions in the UK that set precedents in how OOS missions were licensed. Each mission that moves forward sets new precedents. Based on the new class of missions upcoming, there is already an understanding of what evolutions there could be in licensing:

- ***Multi-removal missions***. Missions such as ELSA-M, discussed above, aim to remove multiple clients. This naturally makes the licensing regime more complex. If the satellites being removed in future have different owners, different operators, or different launching states, this makes the licensing process much more complex.
- ***Spectrum access***. Few OOS operators currently recognise the pressing need for spectrum access to perform servicing. To date, it appears operators largely avoid spectrum questions by pre-identifying clients and matching a client's spectrum, foregoing complex coordination. However, this situation in not sustainable for an environment evolving to have servicers on-orbit *in advance* of client needs. Work at both the international level, before the ITU, and national level must be undertaken to identify spectrum for space-based services.

125 47 C.F.R. pt. 25, subpt. B (2022); *id.* 25.112-25.123 (2022).

126 See IBFS File Nos. SES-STA-20200113-00043, SES-STA-20200811-00859, SES-STA-20200117-00055.

127 *Space Logistics LLC,* IBFS File No. SAT-LOA-20191210-00144 (granted 25 Mar. 2020) (authorising Mission Extension Vehicle 2); *Space Logistics LLC,* IBFS File No. SAT-LOA-20170224-00021 (granted 20 June 2019) (authorising Mission Extension Vehicle 1).

128 47 C.F.R. § 25.114(d)(14) (2022).

129 ISAM National Strategy, *supra* note 1.

130 See *Space Innovation; Facilitating Capabilities for In-space Servicing, Assembly, and Manufacturing,* IB Docket No. 22-271 & 22-272 (released 15 July 2022).

- ***Space situational awareness (SSA) evolutions***. SSA is an evolving area, with more and more SSA service providers coming to the market. In future very accurate third party satellite location and analysis data could become available which could be used by regulators during the continuous monitoring stages of a mission. As noted, the US commercial imaging regime currently imposes restrictions on ASRO imaging, and it remains to be seen if anyone will challenge their exertion of authority over this matter as exceeding their statutory bounds.
- ***Mandatory ADR services***. Currently there is no regulation that mandates an ADR service must be used if a satellite fails and can't be removed. However, there are numerous steps towards this and already wording in the US Orbital Debris Mitigation Standard Practices – which apply to USG. missions – that retrieval is a method to comply with disposal for final mission orbits.[131] What is known is that in order to keep space clean, there must be a range of removals of existing assets in space plus 95 – 99% post-mission disposal compliance. These are also factors that may play into future licensing. For example, there has been advocacy before the FCC for regulators to consider an operator employing ADR in an end-of-life plan as a form of risk mitigation when looking at overall mission safety. Various agencies are taking space sustainability more seriously and the European Space Agency (ESA) in September 2021 became the first space agency to introduce a "net-zero" space debris policy with the ambitious goal of "inverting Europe's contribution to space debris by 2030", meaning if debris is generated it should be removed one way or another – while this doesn't mandate ADR services, it takes Europe one step closer to needing them if debris can't be removed through other methods.[132] Additionally, the US recently introduced draft legislation for an ADR mission.[133]
- ***Service ratings or kitemarks***. There are a range of efforts to introduce service ratings on to future satellites to determine whether a satellite or constellation passes certain criteria with respect to sustainability. One such rating is the Space Sustainability Rating (SSR) which originally was started by a World Economic Forum (WEF)/MIT collaboration.[134] This aims to give ratings to satellites of constellations on how sustainable they are. Future regulatory bodies could use such kitemarks as part of the licensing process (either mandate them, or use the rating as part of their assessments). In the UK the concept of a kitemark is being developed as part of some new type of Space Sustainability Standard by the CAA in collaboration with industry – however, this is something that is being evolved at present and the mechanism of how it would work is under discussion.[135]
- ***Preparing clients for servicing***. One key area in which might evolve is in the area of devices that prepare satellites for servicing. Docking Plates (DPs) are devices that can be fitted to a satellite before launch. If a satellite then fails, or requires servicing in some form, there is a standardised interface on the client that enables a servicer to more efficiently and easily dock with the client to remove or service it. DPs have been discussed in a range of policy fora, and may in future become key to future regulatory processes (for example, maybe in future it is

131 US Government, Orbital Debris Mitigation Standard Practices (Nov. 2019 Update) at 4-1.f (2019).

132 *When Debris Disaster Strikes*, ESA (18 Nov. 2021).

133 Orbital Sustainability Act of 2022, S. 4814 117th Cong. (referred to S. Comm. on Com., Sci., & Transp., 12 Sept. 2022).

134 See *The Space Sustainability Rating*, MIT Media Lab.

135 *Government Announces Package of New Measures to Drive Space Sustainability*, GOV.UK (23 June 2022).

easier for an operator to convince regulator how sustainable they are and their commitment to keeping space clean if they elect to fit a DP).

- ***Mission authorisation***. Overall, from the US side, there may also be an evolution towards a mission authorisation structure. Unlike the UK, where activities are clustered before one regulator, the US patchwork regime leaves gaps or vagueness for upcoming operations.[136]

28.6 Conclusion

This textbook chapter cannot definitively answer how to license an OOS mission in a world where the landscape is changing so rapidly. Through technology transfer, increased commercialisation and international activity, and the rapid innovation of technology, nothing in the future is certain. However, what this chapter hoped to do is demonstrate the various systems that must be considered when designing or working through an OOS licensing regime. Additionally, through comparison, there is hope that regulators and the commercial industry alike may come as close as possible to converging on an optimal way to license OOS missions, and in doing so, enable the future.

136 *See* Marcia Smith, *White House Wants DOT in Charge of Commercial Space "Mission Authorization"*, SPACEPOLICYONLINE.COM (2 May 2016).

29

LEGAL ASPECTS OF GROUND-BASED INFRASTRUCTURE FOR SPACE SITUATIONAL AWARENESS

Olga Batura and Regina Peldszus

29.1 Introduction

Across the past decade, the outer space environment has been undergoing unprecedented change. A growing number of space-faring actors, ever smaller satellites, large fleets or mega-constellations, and an increase in debris resulting from accidents and intentional destruction have resulted in so far unseen levels of proliferation of space objects. Currently, there are over 6,000 operational satellites in orbit,[1] with tens of thousands proposed to the US Federal Communications Commission,[2] and additional hundreds of thousands potentially foreseen,[3] in addition to over 32,000 trackable debris, and orders of magnitude smaller objects.[4] Future space operations will be characterised by this increase in objects, but also their novel ways of operation through greater manoeuvre capabilities for in-orbit servicing or active debris removal. At the same time, development of new sensor technologies and innovation in processing capabilities allow for greater levels of detection and awareness.[5]

Managing the resulting traffic and interaction among objects, and detecting evolving developments require an awareness of the situation in space, or space situational awareness (SSA). This awareness relies on data derived either from the objects themselves (i.e. ephemeris of spacecraft) or through space- or ground-based sensors. Ground-based sensors include, for instance, surveillance and tracking radars that can detect and follow objects to measure and refine their orbit, optical telescopes and lasers. These feed a catalogue of data that can be used for anticipating conjunctions and avoiding collisions. A comprehensive activity and capability of SSA relies on

1 Union of Concerned Scientists, UCS Satellite Database, 2022. As of 24 October 2022, the number was at 5,500; ESA counts 6,800 functioning objects on 7 November 2022, see ESA, Space debris by the numbers.
2 Lifson, M. & Linares, R., *Is there enough room in space for tens of billions of satellites?*, SpaceNews, 4 January 2022.
3 Hollinger, P., *OneWeb founder plans to launch 100,000 satellites in space comeback*, Forbes, 6 February 2022.
4 ESA Space Debris Office, ESA's Annual Space Environment Report. Darmstadt: European Space Agency, 2022.
5 Ailor, W., *Space Traffic Management*, in: Handbook of Space Security: Policies, Applications, Programs, Schrogl, K.-U., Hays, P. L., Robinson, J., Moura, D. & Giannopapa, C. (eds.), Vol. 1, New York: Springer, 2015, pp. 231–255; Pelton, J. et al., *Space Safety*, in: Handbook of Space Security: Policies, Applications, Programs, Vol. 1, pp. 210–214.

 DOI: 10.4324/9781003268475-43

extensive resources. Their set-up and design must take into account operational, technological, geographical, and infrastructural requirements and limitations, and may have geopolitical or policy constraints or implications.

This chapter presents an overview of the legal considerations of ground-based sensor architecture for future space operations. With a focus on the operational capability for SSA and Space Traffic Management (STM), the chapter describes existing SSA networks and those under development. It highlights legal considerations in view of future multi-stakeholder cooperation and offers considerations on implications of sensor ownership, tasking, dual use, and data policy in collaborative efforts in SSA and STM.

29.2 Current and emerging SSA capabilities

One of the fundamental requirements for space safety and the resilience of space infrastructure, including safety of operations and the coordination or management of space traffic, is the monitoring and understanding of activity in various orbital regimes in the form of SSA. To gain this awareness, space surveillance and tracking (SST) sensors such as radar, telescopes, or lasers, provide measurements on the location and vector of objects in orbit, such as satellites or debris. Fed into a database, this allows the correlation of known objects as part of a catalogue, the detection of unknown objects, and the prediction of an expected location of an object. Based on this information, products for conjunction warnings and collision avoidance can be computed.

Several state and non-state actors today maintain and develop SSA capabilities to varying degrees of maturity, either as standalone networks – for state-actors on and beyond their own territory, for non-state actors on or beyond the territories of the state they are operating from – or in cooperation with – others. Beyond the needs of the evolving space environment, some of the drivers shaping developments for SSA beyond the traditionally active actors include a growing recognition of the need for SSA and a desire for autonomy and collaboration, changing commercial motivations and the growing functional modularisation of the SSA system; however, increasing cooperation also requires increased oversight, coordination, and data sharing across state actors or aggregation of actors.[6]

The most advanced space surveillance capability today is operated by the United States through the US Space Command.[7] The US Space Surveillance Network has the largest number of sensors,[8] includes sensors in the United Kingdom and Australia[9] and is currently being enhanced with further sensors in the Southern Hemisphere.[10] A dedicated programme is in place for data sharing with over 100 other state and commercial actors.[11] From 2018, the shift from military SSA missions to a civilian-led effort has gained traction in the US through the formulation of Space

6 Lal, B., Balakrishnan, A., Caldwell, B. M., Buenconsejo, R. S. & Carioscia, S., *Global Trends in Space Situational Awareness (SSA) and Space Traffic Management (STM): IDA STPI Report*, April 2018. Washington, D.C.: Institute for Defense Analyses, Science and Technology Policy Institute.

7 West, J., *Space security index 2018*, Project Ploughshares, Waterloo, 2018.

8 In addition to ground-based sensors of the US SSN, additional space-based assets of the Geosynchronous Space Situational Awareness Program (GSSAP) are in operation.

9 West, J., *Space security index 2018*, Project Ploughshares, Waterloo, 2018, pp. 175 and 148.

10 Weeden, B. & Samson, V. (eds.), Global Counter Space Capabilities: An Open Source Assessment. Washington, D.C.: Secure World Foundation, 2022, p. 62.

11 Singer, K., *100th space sharing agreement signed, Romania Space Agency joins*, US Strategic Command, 29 April 2019.

Policy Directive 3 (SPD-3).[12] SPD-3 foresees a transition from the paradigm of a predominantly governmental approach to SSA with a military legacy, towards cooperation with international partners and, crucially, integration of commercial sector contributions in a diversifying ecosystem of SSA providers. STM, here, is understood as the "planning, coordination, and on-orbit synchronisation of activities to enhance the safety, stability, and sustainability of operations in the space environment".[13] By facilitating and enhancing data sharing, a range of new services are enabled, with measures to be put in place to forge "best practices, technical guidelines, safety standards, behavioural norms, pre-launch risk assessments, and on-orbit collision avoidance services"[14] that address novel operational practices including increase in manoeuvres.

Russia maintains the second most advanced SSA capability in the world with its Military Space Surveillance Network, including comprehensive capabilities for space surveillance such as radars and telescopes. Mainly confined to territory of Russia and former Soviet Republics, it has increasingly complemented its sensor locations by civilian partnerships in other geographical regions across the globe.[15] Russia's Automated Warning System is operated by the space agency Roscosmos with data from the International Scientific Optical Network (ISON) and other Russian sensors.[16]

China has been developing and maintaining increasingly comprehensive space capabilities including space situational awareness,[17] which includes sensors mainly within its borders, but also tracking ships.[18] It will be expanding its ground- (and space-) based infrastructure for telemetry, tracking, and command providing comprehensive global coverage, as well as enlarging its space surveillance database in view of enhancing collision avoidance, debris monitoring, event detection, and "space traffic control". It has installed ground stations in Bolivia, Indonesia, Namibia, Thailand, and South Africa[19] and as part of its efforts, cooperates on SSA infrastructure with other states of the Asia-Pacific Space Cooperation Organisation (APSCO), including in Pakistan and Peru,[20] and with other partners such as Chile.[21]

As part of the European Union space programme,[22] since 2021 a dedicated SSA component is primarily consisting of space surveillance and tracking. Borne out of an effort that became operational from 2016, this component makes use of the increasing capabilities in with capabilities particularly in France,[23] Germany, Spain, and Italy: in recognising the need for an advanced capability and the opportunity to pool existing SSA resources, first five, then seven, and soon 15 EU

12 Space Policy Directive-3: National Space Traffic Management Policy. Washington: The White House, 2018.

13 Ibid.

14 Ibid.

15 Global Counter Space Capabilities: An Open Source Assessment, p.105.

16 SSI, Space Security Index: Issue Guide Space Situational Awareness, Waterloo: Ploughshares, 2020, p. 5.

17 Harrison, T. et al., *Space Threat Assessment*, Washington DC: CSIS, 2022, p. 10.

18 Global Counter Space Capabilities: An Open Source Assessment, p. 131.

19 Articles 3(5), 5(2), 6 and 7 of China's Space Program: A 2021 Perspective, The State Council of the People's Republic of China, 28 January 2022.

20 Young, M., *Trends in Global Space Situational Awareness*. Proceedings of the 22nd AMOS Conference, Wailea, 2021.

21 Robinson, J., *State Actor Strategies in Attracting Space Sector Partnerships: Chinese and Russian Economic Footprints*. PSSI: Prague, 2019.

22 Regulation (EU) 2021/696 of the European Parliament and of the Council of 28 April 2021 establishing the Union Space Programme and the European Union Agency for the Space Programme and repealing Regulations (EU) No 912/2010, (EU) No 1285/2013 and (EU) No 377/2014 and Decision No 541/2014/EU, OJ L 170, 12.05.2021.

23 Global Counter Space Capabilities: An Open Source Assessment, p. 152.

Member States[24] cooperate as part of the EU SST Consortium.[25] EU SST maintains its own growing catalogue and currently serves 300 European spacecraft with its collision avoidance service.[26] Its globally distributed network of currently over 40 sensors (radars, telescopes, lasers), uses locations accessible to Europe in overseas territories or locations of partners of the specific Member States that operate a sensor asset (see Section 29.3). The EU proposes an approach of regional and multilateral cooperation for space surveillance in the context of STM, seeking complementarity and partnerships with the US and other states, while EU SST will serve as the operational capability of STM in the EU.[27]

India is expanding its efforts, including cooperation with the US.[28] Australia has made SSA capabilities part of their strategic priorities both from civilian[29] and military perspective.[30] Japan's SSA efforts have been mainly civilian so far, but expanding as part of space defence developments and in cooperation with the US to complement Indo-Pacific coverage, with a ground-based radar and space-based sensors.[31] Thailand is planning to expand its capabilities,[32] and cooperate with the US on data sharing.[33] Indonesia operates radar capabilities on its territory[34] and has expressed interest in pursuing a data-sharing agreement with the US Space Command.[35] Iran has limited capabilities and is developing more,[36] including some optical and radar SSA capabilities in cooperation with APSCO.[37] South Korea is developing its own capabilities as a priority for space

24 Commission Implementing Decision (EU) 2022/1245 of 15 July 2022 laying down rules and procedures for the application of Regulation (EU) 2021/696 of the European Parliament and of the Council as regards the participation of Member States in the SST sub-component, the establishment of the SST Partnership and the development of the initial key performance indicators, OJ L 190, 19.07.2022.

25 Peldszus, R. & Faucher, P., *European Union Space Surveillance & Tracking,* in: Handbook of Space Security: Policies, Applications and Programs, 2nd Ed. K.-U. Schrogl et ald (eds.), Heidelberg: Springer Nature, 2020, pp. 883–904.

26 EU SST, *EU Space Surveillance and Tracking Service Portfolio*. EU SST: Brussels, 2022.

27 European Commission & High Representative for Foreign Affairs & Security Policy, Joint Communication to the European Parliament and the Council: An EU Approach for Space Traffic Management – An EU contribution addressing a global challenge, JOIN(2022) 4 final of 15.02.2022.

28 Chaturvedi, A. & Khajuria, A., *India and US have signed a Space Situational Awareness Agreement*, SpaceWatch. Global, 25 April 2022.

29 Vignelles, A., Le Pellec, M. & Gallagher, F., *The Australian Space Agency's inaugural Space Situational Awareness technology roadmap: Context, methodology and learnings*. Proceedings of the 22nd AMOS Conference, 2021.

30 Royal Australian Airforce, Defence Space Power Manual, Defence Space Command, 22 March 2022.

31 Global Counter Space Capabilities: An Open Source Assessment, p. 163; Koshino, Yu., *Japan's new Space Domain Mission Unit and security in the Indo-Pacific region*, International Institute for Strategic Studies, 1 May 2020.

32 The Statement of Thailand to the 64th COPUOS, Agenda Item 4: General exchange of views, 27 August 2021, Vienna, Austri; Saperstein, H. T. & Cera, L., *Thailand's Smaller-State Space Power Amid Great-Power Competition in the Space Domain*. Paris: Asia Centre, 2021, p. 14.

33 USAF, *USSTRATCOM, Thailand sign agreement to share space services*, 16 October 2018.

34 Bahar, A., Dear, V., Husin, A., Faturahman, A., Jiyo, Pradipta, R., *Exploring an Extension of Space Situational Awareness in Southeast Asian Region Utilizing EAR Observation Data*, in: Yulihastin, E., Abadi, P., Sitompul, P., Harjupa, W. (eds.) Proceedings of the International Conference on Radioscience, Equatorial Atmospheric Science and Environment and Humanosphere Science, 2021. Springer Proceedings in Physics, Vol 275, Singapore: Springer.

35 IDP Forum, *Indonesia opens door for cooperation on space defense*, US Space Command, 28 September 2022.

36 Global Counter Space Capabilities: An Open Source Assessment, p. 160; Malekos Smith, Zh., *Iran's Space Programme and the Wall between "Peaceful Purposes"*, Washington DC: CSIS, 2020.

37 Harrison, T. et al., *Space Threat Assessment*, Washington DC: CSIS, 2022, p. 17.

operations,[38] in close cooperation with the US.[39] Other state actors are developing capabilities, including South Africa and Canada,[40] while others, such as Brazil, have signed data sharing agreements with the US.[41]

In the private sector, developments have been accelerated both through policy changes on the US-side (SPD-3) and the sharp increase in objects across the past five years. Particularly in the US, commercial actors have deployed and operate their own sensor networks, or have expanded their portfolios to offering SSA data or products in the US to domestic or international users. These include for instance Analytical Graphics who cooperate with the Space Data Association convening operators and fusing data from different sources; ExoAnalytic, who operate a growing network of over 350 geographically distributed telescopes; and LeoLabs, who operate ground-based radars in Costa Rica, New Zealand, and the US, with the aim of a network of 20 across different locations.[42] Other companies such as L3 Harris, Numerica, Kratos, ArianeGroup and Elecnor Deimos, or Share My Space operate their own networks, while others, such as Lockheed Martin build and operate sensor systems for governmental customers, or like GMV, Okapi, or Vyoma, offer processing tools or expertise.[43]

Commensurate with the proliferation of objects, the need for accurate and timely data has grown. Ground-based space surveillance sensors benefit from being operated in a networked distributed architecture, in view of covering the entire sky and allowing regular revisits of objects in various orbits. The considerable cost-intensity, technological sophistication, and complexity of operations of SSA sensors or a sensor network mean that cooperation with partners (i.e. distributed state-actors) constitutes an advantage – both to share the financial and operational burden, and to exploit geographical opportunities for sensor location.[44] Despite the potential for international cooperation, while partnerships across different state and non-state actors are forging ahead,[45] and new actors enter the field either in the operation of space assets or the provision of SSA services in a bottom-up way, the elaboration of norms has arguably been more stagnant.[46]

29.3 Legal aspects of SSA infrastructure

SSA/SST systems need access to ground-based optical sensors and radars. In order to provide effective coverage of complete orbits, the sensor and radar network should – ideally – be distributed around the globe. No jurisdiction alone can achieve extensive coverage of space. Hence

38 Global Counter Space Capabilities: An Open Source Assessment, p. 173.

39 Park, S., *U.S., South Korea agree to cooperate on space situational awareness for military purposes*, SpaceNews, 26 April 2022.

40 *Space Security Index: Issue Guide Space Situational Awareness*, p. 5.

41 Young, M., *Trends in Global Space Situational Awareness.*

42 LeoLabs, Global Phased-Array Radar Network, 2022.

43 Young, M., *Trends in Global Space Situational Awareness.*

44 McCormick, P. K., *Space debris: conjunction opportunities and opportunities for international cooperation.* Sci Public Policy 40(6), 2013, pp. 801–813.

45 DalBello, R., *SSA Policy Forum Keynote on Space Traffic Management*, 23rd AMOS Conference, Wailea, US, 27–30 September 2022; Commission Implementing Decision (EU) 2022/1245 of 15 July 2022 laying down rules and procedures for the application of Regulation (EU) 2021/696 of the European Parliament and of the Council as regards the participation of Member States in the SST sub-component, the establishment of the SST Partnership and the development of the initial key performance indicators, OJ L 190, 19.07.2022.

46 Verspieren, Q. & Aliberti, M., *International norm promotion strategies for space traffic management.* 73rd International Astronautical Congress, Paris, France, 18–22 September 2022.

international exchange and cooperation is necessary to secure access to various locations suitable for SSA/SST sensors and radars.

This is a non-trivial task, considering SSA/SST equipment and components not only often require optimal climatic and geographic conditions (e.g., on elevated surfaces, with suitable precipitation, wind and cloud-cover conditions), but can be also considered dual-use items. Dual-use items are subject to a special trading regime. Instead of being traded freely across borders, export and import of components for SSA/SST systems can be (or is) restricted in most jurisdictions, based on the security exception of Art. XXI of the General Agreement on Tariffs and Trade (GATT).[47] This makes international cooperation in the field of SSA sensor operations a complex matter.

In the absence of international rules or standards for the regulation of trade in dual-use items, each country decides unilaterally on the items that are restricted, the uses that are restricted and conditions with which the uses must comply. By way of example, the largest jurisdictions the EU and the US define dual-use items as tangible and non-tangible commodities that can be used for military and civil purposes. The former category of commodities includes components, materials, and systems, while the latter includes software and technology in the form of technical assistance or technical data.[48]

There is a growing tendency by jurisdictions to use the export control regime to advance economic and human rights objectives,[49] which expands the scope of application of trade restrictions. For instance, the new dual-use export control rules by the EU cover potentially non-military use of such items that may violate human rights and international humanitarian law. The 2021 EU Dual Use Regulation[50] requires authorisation for the export of cyber-surveillance items that are normally not restricted if there is a risk that they may be intended, in their entirety or in part, for use in connection with internal repression and/or the commission of serious violations of human rights and international humanitarian law. It also allows the EU Member States to prohibit completely or impose authorisation requirements on the export of other dual-use items due to reasons of public security or human rights considerations.

The above considerations limit the choice of locations for placing SSA/SST components. Yet, because a broad distribution of sensors is desirable, countries have developed various approaches. In the first line, some states use their own overseas territories and dependent territories. For example, one of the telescopes for the French TAROT (Télescope à Action Rapide pour les Objets Transitoires) network is situated in Réunion – the French department in the Indian Ocean.[51] Countries also conclude bilateral and multilateral cooperation agreements with like-minded part-

47 General Agreement on Tariffs and Trade of 1947.

48 See US Export Control Reform Act of 2018. Regulation (EU) 2021/821 of the European Parliament and of the Council of 20 May 2021 setting up a Union regime for the control of exports, brokering, technical assistance, transit and transfer of dual-use items (recast), OJ L 206 of 11.6.2021; Commission Recommendation (EU) 2021/1700 of 15 September 2021 on internal compliance programmes for controls of research involving dual-use items under Regulation (EU) 2021/821 of the European Parliament and of the Council setting up a Union regime for the control of exports, brokering, technical assistance, transit and transfer of dual-use items, OJ L 338 of 23.09.2021, pp. 12–13.

49 Joint Statement on the Export Controls and Human Rights Initiative by the governments of Australia, Denmark, Norway, and the United States of 10 December 2021; The White House, Fact Sheet: Export Controls and Human Rights Initiative Launched at the Summit for Democracy, 2021.

50 Articles 5(1) and 9(1) of the Regulation (EU) 2021/821 of the European Parliament and of the Council of 20 May 2021 setting up a Union regime for the control of exports, brokering, technical assistance, transit and transfer of dual-use items (recast), OJ L 206, 11.06.2021.

51 Boër, M. et al., *TAROT: a network for space surveillance and tracking operations.* 7th European Conference on Space Debris ESA/ESOC, Darmstadt/Germany, ESA, April 2017, Darmstadt, Germany.

ners. For instance, the Thule Air Base of the US in Greenland is used by the NATO allies Denmark, Canada and the US, and SSA/SST radars were tested there by NASA.[52] The atoll Diego Garcia in the Indian Ocean belongs to the UK and hosts a joint UK-US military base with a satellite tracking station.[53]

Countries also explore the possibilities of accessing sensor and radar capabilities through membership in international organisations. For instance, the World Meteorological Organisation (WMO) uses its capabilities and supports its members solely for civilian space use, in particular the observation of space weather and Earth weather, climate, and environment.[54] In addition, the capacities of private actors can be used to enhance the network coverage (see *supra*. 29.2). One public-private example is the Small-Aperture Robotic Telescope Network (SMARTnet) that was established by the research facilities and governments of Germany, Switzerland, the United States, Spain, South Africa, and Australia in a public-private partnership. The network organised by the German Aerospace Centre (DLR) and the Astronomical Institute of the University Bern has five telescope stations in said countries,[55] for civilian debris tracking.[56]

As access to suitable locations is limited, a well-functioning effective SSA/SST system needs access to data from various radars and sensors that are often located in different jurisdictions. Currently, there are no international multilateral agreements or standards for data exchange and sharing, but experts and governments advocate for increased data sharing. In particular, in 2019, the UNCOPUOS adopted Guidelines for the Long-term Sustainability of Outer Space activities that call for enhancing the practice and utility of sharing orbital information on space objects and debris as well as operational data on space weather and forecasts.[57]

In the absence of binding international rules or settings, national rules and policies on data sharing apply. For some countries (e.g., Russia), it is not entirely evident to external observers what SSA data are shared, with whom and on what conditions.[58] Others have a layered data sharing model: certain categories of data remain classified, while others are available to all users or upon signing a special data sharing agreement. The US employs this approach: for instance, two-line element (TLE) data are available freely, but only for the own use of registered entities, and almost any redistribution would be in violation of sharing agreements. More advanced data are available to commercial companies that enter special data sharing agreements. High accuracy data are available only to US allies that enter special bilateral data sharing agreements. For data sharing with commercial operators and security partners, the US has concluded agreements with over 30 nations, intergovernmental organisations and over 100 commercial operators.[59] As

52 Meiman, L., *NASA testing new radars at Thule, press release of the Air Force Space Command*, Air Force Space Command (archived), 28 May 2009; USSPACECOM, *USSPACECOM command team visits Thule Air Base, site of North American Air Defense, space tracking*, 2021.

53 Schriever Space Force Base, *21st Space Operations Squadron*, July 2020.

54 See WMO, Space Weather.

55 UN Doc. A/AC.105/C.1/2022/CRP.11, Research on space debris, safety of space objects with nuclear power sources on board and problems relating to their collision with space debris, 7 February 2022, pp. 3–4.

56 Fiedler, H. et al., *SMARTnet™ – Evolution and Results*. Paper presented at the 69th International Astronautical Congress, Bremen, Germany, 1–5 October 2018.

57 UN Doc. A/74/20, Report of the Committee on the Peaceful Uses of Outer Space Sixty-second session, 2019, Annex II, see Guidelines B.2, B.3, and B.6.

58 Global Counter Space Capabilities: An Open Source Assessment, pp. 31–34.

59 "USSPACECOM and Sweden sign a Space Situational Awareness sharing agreement, April 7, 2022" See https://www.spacecom.mil/Newsroom/News/Article-Display/Article/2992854/usspacecom-and-sweden-sign-a-space-situational-awareness-sharing-agreement/

part of the transition from US Department of Defense to the US Department of Commerce of sharing space safety-related information, a data sharing platform is currently in development that will enable institutional and commercial actors to share data for the development of STM services.[60] On the European side, EU SST has been operating a data sharing platform amongst its participating partners for their sensor measurements as part of the data processing function for SST services, which serves as the basis for the SST catalogue.[61] Additionally, there are a few networks of amateurs and enthusiasts collecting and sharing SSA-related data (e.g., SeeSat-L,[62] SatNOGs[63]).

In some jurisdictions, SSA/SST systems – as a part of space infrastructure – can be considered critical infrastructure or essential services and therefore are subject to special security rules. SSA/SST data are indispensable for the effective operation of thousands of assets already in space and thousands of others to be launched. If the networks handling SSA/SST information are breached and the data become corrupted, it would have serious consequences for security and resilience. The US is currently discussing a Space Infrastructure Act that will direct the Secretary of Homeland Security to issue guidance on designating space systems, services, and technology as critical infrastructure and how to protect them.[64] In the EU, SSA/SST could fall under the general definition of critical infrastructure or essential services,[65] though the ultimate designation is left to the EU Member States. The EU Security Strategy of 2020[66] indicates that essential space-based services and critical space infrastructure must be protected against current and anticipated threats of physical, cyber, and hybrid nature. If SSA/SST systems are designated as critical infrastructure or essential services, they are subject to higher security standards and their providers must introduce certain security policies and practices. For instance, they may need to use special data encryption technologies to ensure data integrity, conduct vulnerability and incidents/scenarios assessments, or obtain cybersecurity certificates.[67]

SSA/SST is particularly important in the context of responsibility and liability for space activities. Under the existing international legal rules, only states and intergovernmental organisations can be held responsible for space activities attributed to them and liable for damages caused by such activities.[68] They are obliged to supervise and monitor their national space activities, in which

60 Howard, D., Open Architecture Data Repository: Statement of the United States Department of Commerce Office of Space Commerce before the UN Committee on the Peaceful Uses of Outer Space Scientific and Technical Subcommittee, 58th Session, 28 April 2021; Erwin, S., *Office of Space Commerce rolls out prototype space catalog for traffic management*, SpaceNews, 12 February 2022.

61 EU SST, *EU Space Surveillance and Tracking Service Portfolio.*

62 See SeeSat-L home page.

63 See Libre Space Foundation, SatNOGS.

64 Bill of the Space Infrastructure Act, H.R.3713 – 117th Congress (2021–2022).

65 See Art. 2(a) of the Council Directive 2008/114/EC of 8 December 2008 on the identification and designation of European critical infrastructures and the assessment of the need to improve their protection, OJ L 345 of 23.12.2008; Article 5 of the Directive (EU) 2016/1148 of the European Parliament and of the Council of 6 July 2016 concerning measures for a high common level of security of network and information systems across the Union, OJ L 194, 19.7.2016.

66 Communication from the Commission to the European Parliament, the European Council, the Council, the European Economic and Social Committee and the Committee of the Regions on the EU Security Union Strategy, COM(2020) 605 final, 24.07.2020.

67 For example, the EU cybersecurity agency ENISA is completing its work on the cybersecurity certification scheme for cloud services, which are used for data sharing. See ENISA, EUCS – Cloud Services Scheme, 22 December 2020.

68 See Art. VI Outer Space Treaty and Arts II, III, and XXII Liability Convention.

SSA/SST plays a central role in ensuring the safety and security of, and in preventing possible damage from, space operations. Developing SSA/SST capabilities, designing and implementing effective requirements for (cyber) security of SSA/SST systems and ensuring data sharing with other countries could be considered necessary and even indispensable steps for states to fulfil their international obligations.

While certain issues can be handled by jurisdictions individually (e.g., developing national SSA/SST capabilities, national standards, and requirements for physical and cyber security), others need coordinated or cooperative efforts (e.g., developing data standards to ensure cross-border exchange, interoperability, data sharing framework).[69] The progress at the international level has been modest so far. Technical rules (standards) were developed at the international and regional levels (e.g., ISO with a proposal for STM and CCSDS for data messaging).[70] However, the development of the International Code of Conduct for Outer Space Activities was not successful as countries could not agree, in particular, on the type of legal instrument and the forum to negotiate it.[71] However, the activities related to Transparency and Confidence-building Measures in Outer Space Activities resulted in a widely supported UN Resolution[72] but did not bring about binding rules on information sharing, notifications of risk reduction efforts and other issues.[73]

29.4 Perspectives

Intensification of space activities by public and private actors, emergence of new space-faring nations and the resulting proliferation of space objects, including space debris, will continue to increase the need for effective STM. SSA/SST systems are indispensable for STM providing data and information, on the basis of which operational decisions can be made. Hence, more space-faring actors and satellite owners and operators will seek access to existing and emerging SSA/SST networks for data or rely on the products provided by them. Due to the unprecedented number of space assets and novel ways of operations, higher accuracy of data and data analysis as well as real-time data sharing will likely be necessary.[74]

New technologies (e.g., artificial intelligence, machine learning, quantum computing) may enhance SSA/SST allowing for more accurate big data analytics regarding the identification and analysis of risks and enabling advanced data sharing in real-time.[75] However, regulatory con-

69 Becker, M. & Faucher, P., *Recent developments in the implementation of European Space Surveillance & Tracking (EU SST) – Security and data policy*, Journal of Space Safety Engineering 8, 2021, p. 180.

70 ISO/CD 9490: Space systems — Space Traffic Coordination; ESA, Space Situational Awareness - Space Weather System Requirements Document, 2013; for discussion of several CCSDS standards that can be used see Berry, D.S., *Using CCSDS standards for Space Situational Awareness*, SpaceOps 2014 Conference, Pasadena, US, 5–9 May 2014.

71 Vazhapully, K., *Recent Efforts on Developing New Norms for Space Security: A Brief Overview*, CESL/NUJS, 2022; Beard, J. M., *Soft Law's Failure on the Horizon: The International Code of Conduct for Outer Space Activities*, University of Pennsylvania Journal of International Law, Vol. 38, No. 2, 2017.

72 UNGA Resolution 75/36, Reducing space threats through norms, rules and principles of responsible behaviours, 7 December 2020.

73 Vazhapully, K., *Recent Efforts on Developing New Norms for Space Security: A Brief Overview*.

74 Muelhaupt, T. J., Sorge, M. E. Morin J. & Wilson, R. S., *Space traffic management in the new space era*, Journal of Space Safety Engineering 6:2, 2019, pp. 80–87.

75 Barnes, C. et al., *Space Situational Awareness (SSA) and Quantum Neuromorphic Computing*, 2022 IEEE International Conference on Imaging Systems and Techniques (IST), 2022, pp. 1-6; Kyriakopoulos, G. D., Pazartzis, P., Koskina, A. & Bourcha, C., *Artificial intelligence and space situational awareness: Data processing and sharing in debris-crowded areas*, Proceedings of the 8th European Conference on Space Debris, Darmstadt, Germany, 2021.

cerns pertinent to such technologies (e.g., ethical use, data sharing, liability regimes) should be addressed by individual jurisdictions and internationally, and the question of technology transfer ought to be resolved.

In this context, international cooperation that includes all relevant stakeholders from the public and private sectors will become crucial, both for access to locations and for data sharing. Traditional institutional structures of international organisations, fragmentation of legal frameworks, and lack of international standards are likely to render such cooperation challenging. Hence, new multi-stakeholder formats for the discussion of solutions should be promoted at the international level that actively engage a variety of actors (e.g., institutional, commercial, and civil society). In the absence of binding international legal norms, policy and legal efforts of states need to be coordinated with each other and with regional or international efforts to ensure legal certainty and safety and security of space operations for all space-faring actors and those who depend on space services or who may wish to be active in space in the future. At the same time, efforts in the central international fora should continue to provide for a normative framework either for STM or for the enabling building blocks (e.g., data sharing, cybersecurity standards). While cooperation will be the single most effective approach to ensuring space safety through SSA as a shared goal, its specific mechanisms, rules, and infrastructure will require dedicated efforts across the coming decades in view of a highly dynamic and rapidly evolving orbital environment. Today's changing geopolitical landscape with new economic partnerships and strategic constellations has already shaped space cooperation and will likely result in new challenges and opportunities for collaborative infrastructure for SSA.

C

Long-term sustainability and the changing nature of space law (cybersecurity)

30

SPACE CYBERSECURITY AND US LAW

P. J. Blount

Introduction

Cybersecurity has become a critical issue in the space domain over the past decade. Traditionally, space operations were insulated from threats in the domain based on the unique nature of space technology and the attributes of its placement in orbit. Simply stated, satellites were far far away from cyberspace. This has changed. As space operations began to take advantage of the same network technologies that were underpinning the global "network of networks" comprising the internet, space assets became increasingly exposed to threats from that same network. As the space industry has awakened to these issues, the legal community has also taken notice, and the intersection of cybersecurity, law, and space operations has become a significant area of inquiry. Despite this, the bounds of what constitutes cybersecurity law applicable to the space domain is ambiguous at best.

This chapter will engage with this question within the context of the United States legal system. This is apropos, because the United States has, arguably, been a leader in the area of developing cybersecurity standards applicable to space operations. Even before the prominent release of "Space Policy Directive 5 on Cybersecurity Principles for Space Systems",[1] the Committee on National Security Systems (CNSS) had developed a policy for cybersecurity in space systems used in national security[2] and a Space Platform Overlay[3] that selects cybersecurity controls for national security space operations using the NIST SP 800-53 control list.[4] Currently, the United States Space Force's (USSF) Infrastructure Audit Pre-assessment (IA-Pre) programme has adopted a similar approach for commercial satellite communications providers that wish to bid on military

1 Space Policy Directive 5: Cybersecurity Principles for Space Systems (4 September 2020).

2 Committee on National Security Systems, *Cybersecurity Policy for Space Systems Used to Support National Security Missions*, CNSSP No. 12 (February 2018).

3 Committee on National Security Systems, *Security Categorization and Control Selection for National Security Systems*, CNSSI No. 1253 (27 March 2014) Attachment 2 Appendix F: Space Platform Overlay.

4 National Institute of Standards and Technology, *Security and Privacy Controls for Information Systems and Organizations*, rev. 5, SP 800-53 (September 2020).

DOI: 10.4324/9781003268475-45

contracts. These approaches to cybersecurity in space all flow from the US Government's broader approach to cybersecurity.

Lost yet? This chain of esoteric and technical documents, often denoted by generic strings of letters and numbers that define what constitutes "cyber secure" is interesting in both its complexity and in its distance from formal regulatory processes. These documents tend to describe processes that organisations can use to increase the security of their networked operations, yet they do not mandate specific action from an actor in a legal sense. It is this distance from law and regulation that leads to the question of "what is cybersecurity law?"[5] and how do lawyers "do" cybersecurity law. This chapter aims to answer that question by building a narrative around US cybersecurity practices for the space industry. Though the focus of this chapter is on the US, similar paradigms will likely be seen in other jurisdictions due to the nature of the cybersecurity enterprise.

This chapter is divided into three sections. First, it attempts to give a picture of a US perspective on cybersecurity law generally. Second, it seeks to construct a narrative that illustrates how cybersecurity standards become legally operational through the contracting processes with particular reference to the functioning of these processes as they function in the space domain. Finally, this chapter will briefly discuss the lawyer's role within the cybersecurity enterprise to give a better understanding of the nature of cyber "law".

30.1 Whither US cybersecurity law

The concept of cybersecurity law is a slippery one. Actors often find that so-called "cybersecurity laws" give them little guidance as to what constitutes a legally required level of cybersecurity. This is further complicated by the fact that there are scads of laws that impact an organisation's cybersecurity stance but never use the word "cybersecurity". Indeed, there are few laws in the US that directly mandate specific cybersecurity practices for organisations. Instead, cybersecurity law in the formal sense is most often concerned with how government institutions maintain security over their information. For instance, the Federal Information Security Management Act (FISMA)[6] and the Federal Information Security Modernization Act[7] both articulate a need for information security in federal information systems. These laws do not define what constitutes adequate security for these systems nor are they applicable to private information systems that do not store or process federal data and information. It is worth noting at this point that the above laws refer to "information security" rather than "cybersecurity". These are separate concepts, but they overlap substantially.

Information security refers to the security of information, including information that is not stored in a digital format. This is defined in US law as "protecting information and information systems from unauthorized access, use, disclosure, disruption, modification, or destruction" in order to provide for the confidentiality, integrity, and availability of the information.[8] Cybersecurity refers to the security of digital and networked systems including the information held on these systems.[9] US law does not directly define "cybersecurity", but the Cybersecurity Information Sharing Act[10] does define "cybersecurity purpose" as "the purpose of protecting an

5 See generally, Jeff Kosseff, "Defining Cybersecurity Law," *Iowa L. Rev.* 103 (2017): 985.
6 107 Pub. L. 347, Title III (2002).
7 113 Pub. L. 283 (2014).
8 107 Pub. L. 347, Title III (2002) §301.
9 See generally, ENISA, *Definition of Cybersecurity: Gaps and Overlaps in Standardisation*, v. 1.0, 2015.
10 114 Pub. L. 113, Division N (2015).

information system or information that is stored on, processed by, or transiting an information system from a cybersecurity threat or security vulnerability" and "cybersecurity threat" as "an action, not protected by the First Amendment to the Constitution of the United States, on or through an information system that may result in an unauthorized effort to adversely impact the security, availability, confidentiality, or integrity of an information system or information that is stored on, processed by, or transiting an information system".[11] Consistent with the closeness of these definitions, this chapter will not make much distinction between these terms as, from a legal perspective, the distinction is not significant and these processes will generally be managed by the same team within an organisation. At the same time, it should be remembered that in different contexts, such as the diplomatic debates concerning cybersecurity, the differences between these terms can have significant impact.[12]

There are, of course, other laws that define the types of information and systems that an organisation must keep secure. For instance, the International Traffic in Arms Regulations (ITAR) impose a duty to keep defence-related technical data and information secure, but ITAR does not define the specifications for this security.[13] Similarly, US policy imposes an heightened responsibility on operators of critical infrastructure, which are "systems and assets, whether physical or virtual, so vital to the United States that the incapacity or destruction of such systems and assets would have a debilitating impact on security, national economic security, national public health or safety, or any combination of those matters",[14] to keep these systems secure. However, neither policy nor law defines with any specificity what requirements such security entails. Indeed, at best the standard of security for protected data and systems is that of "adequate security". In other words, an operator must be able to show that it was engaged in adequate security practices to protect the system in order to avoid civil, administrative, or criminal sanctions in cases where there has been a breach. It should be noted that there are other factors than the law that impact an organisation's security stance. These will all play a part in developing a cybersecurity plan, but this chapter will focus solely on the legal factors.

The lack of specification in law and regulation may at first seem somewhat odd or even unjust, but it should not be surprising. The quickly changing nature of the cybersecurity landscape means that law and regulation are poor tools for addressing these issues. Law and regulation lack the agility and flexibility of governance mechanisms that sit below the level of legal prescription, whereas sub-statutory mechanisms, such as standards, gain in agility and flexibility what they trade off in terms of compulsoriness. The staticness of law means that it cannot be responsive to the quickly changing nature of cybersecurity where new threats and vulnerabilities emerge on a daily basis. Interestingly, this issue has been taken up in the judicial system. In the US, the Federal Trade Commission (FTC) is a significant enforcement agency with regards to cybersecurity. The FTC uses its authority over "unfair or deceptive acts or practices"[15] to pursue enforcement actions against commercial actors that have experienced data breaches that expose customer data.[16] In

11 6 U.S. Code §1501.

12 See for example, Dennis Broeders, Fabio Cristiano, & Daan Weggemans, "Too Close for Comfort: Cyber Terrorism and Information Security across National Policies and International Diplomacy," *Studies in Conflict & Terrorism* (2 June 2021).

13 22 C.F.R. §§120–130.

14 42 U.S. Code §5195c.

15 15 U.S. Code §45.

16 Lawrence J. Trautman and Peter C. Ormerod, "Corporate Directors' and Officers' Cybersecurity Standard of Care: The Yahoo Data Breach," *Am. UL Rev.* 66 (2016): 1237–1238.

FTC v. Wyndham Hotels,[17] Wyndham hotels challenged this authority, in part claiming that if the FTC was going to require security, they should "provide clear data security standards with 'ascertainable certainty'".[18] The Third Circuit rejected this argument, stating that all that was necessary was that the commercial actor only needed to have notice that they were subject to a requirement to be secure.[19]

Laws that create obligations for federal systems to be secure do result in substantive requirements that can be imposed on commercial actors. As noted above federal information systems are subject to federal cybersecurity law and are required to maintain adequate cybersecurity for their purposes. Thus, a threshold question for a lawyer operating in the space industry is whether the organisation that they represent manages a "federal information system"? A federal information system is defined as "an information system used or operated by an executive agency, by a contractor of an executive agency, or by another organization on behalf of an executive agency".[20] Thus, an organisation, especially one that is dealing with the transmission and storage of data, must consider not only whether it is a federal government owned operator, but also whether it would like to be a potential contract partner with the federal government. The word "potential" here is important as it indicates a possible future intent to bid for these contracts, meaning that design decisions made during development should take into account cybersecurity requirements even before bidding on contracts, Similarly, an organisation should also consider whether it could potentially be a subcontractor to a federal government contractor, which will also likely require the implementation of these cybersecurity standards and controls. Within the space industry, the US Government is a major customer of commercial space capabilities for both civil and military uses, meaning that a majority of US operators have a high potential to be in the chain of contract with the US Government as a prime contractor. Not every supplier will handle federal information, so not every subcontractor will be subject to cybersecurity requirements, but awareness of that potential is key.

The actual cybersecurity requirements for federal information systems flow from statutory language, but are not defined therein. FISMA requires federal agencies to provide "information security protections commensurate with the risk and magnitude of the harm resulting from unauthorized access, use, disclosure, disruption, modification, or destruction" of federal information or information systems.[21] These plans in turn are built on standards. Under FISMA, the National Institute of Standards and Technology (NIST) is tasked to "develop standards and guidelines, including minimum requirements, for information systems used or operated by an agency or by a contractor of an agency or other organization on behalf of an agency".[22] NIST has become the primary source for cybersecurity standards relevant to US federal information systems, and it has developed a large body of technical documentation covering a wide range of applications and issues within cybersecurity and information security. Though developed for federal information systems, this documentation is open access and can be applied to any system. However, these standards are not applicable to national security systems, which are overseen by the CNSS.

17 *FTC v. Wyndham Worldwide Corp.*,799 F.3d 236 (3d. Cir. 2015).

18 Jeff Kosseff, "Positive Cybersecurity Law: Creating a Consistent and Incentive-Based System," *Chapman Law Review* 19 (2016): 410.

19 *Id.*

20 107 Pub. L. 347, Title III (2002) §302.

21 107 Pub. L. 347, Title III (2002) §301.

22 107 Pub. L. 347, Title III (2002) §302.

In this context, the NIST developed its Cybersecurity Framework (CSF), which is a high-level process document for risk management in the context of critical infrastructure.[23] The CSF is complemented by the NIST Risk Management Framework (RMF), which articulates a similar approach for information security processes for federal information systems more generally.[24] Both of these documents set out non-linear processes for managing risk that emanates from cyberspace. These processes are non-linear because cybersecurity is not a finite process. It is constant, and the cybersecurity stance of an organisation must be constantly evaluated and updated as new technologies, threats, and vulnerabilities emerge. The idea of a non-linear process exposes the significant connection between cybersecurity and governance processes. For instance, the popular conception of cybersecurity professionals sitting at terminals and pounding on keyboards to thwart cybercriminals obscures the more realistic picture of the professional ensuring that systems are patched and updated subject to an internal policy that structures the decision-making around the timing of such patches.

This section will focus on the RMF process rather than the process under the CSF. This is because the RMF process is central to federal information systems and therefore plays a critical role in the narrative of legalisation of cybersecurity standards. Though the CSF was developed for application to critical infrastructure, it might be more attractive to some private operators as it is significantly less complex in its scope. Additionally, the CSF does not have its own control catalog and can be adapted to draw from a number of different control sets including the RMF catalog[25] or the commercially popular ISO/IEC 27001 catalog.[26] Regardless of the adopted process, both the CSF and the RMF function in substantially the same manner as tools that guide an organisation in developing robust methodologies for managing risk connected to digitized and networked technologies, and it is likely that some operators will employ a mix of these two frameworks. Despite the significant overlap, it should of course be remembered that these are not interchangeable and categorisation of the system being protected will be critical in making a determination as to which framework is best suited.

The RMF articulates a seven-step, non-linear process that organisations can employ to properly manage their risk. These steps are: Prepare, Categorise, Select, Implement, Assess, Authorise, and Monitor, and each step has a number of tasks associated with it.[27] In the Prepare step an organisation prepares itself to apply the RMF by "establishing a context and priorities for managing security and privacy risk".[28] The Categorise step requires the organisation to categorise the information systems and information held by the organisation "based on an analysis of the impact of loss"[29] using NIST standards.[30] In the Select step, the organisation chooses specific technical controls from a control catalog and tailors the selected controls to the identified systems and pro-

23 National Institute of Standards and Technology, *Framework for Improving Critical Infrastructure Cybersecurity*, ver. 1.1 (16 April 2018).

24 National Institute of Standards and Technology, *Risk Management Framework for Information Systems and Organizations: A System Life Cycle Approach for Security and Privacy*, rev. 2, NIST SP 800-37 (December 2018).

25 NIST SP 800-53 (2020).

26 ISO/IEC 27001:2013: Information technology – Security techniques – Information security management systems – Requirements (2013).

27 NIST SP 800-37, 23–83. As a comparison, the tasks that provide the core of the CSF are Identify, Protect, Detect, Respond, and Recover. NIST, *Framework for Improving Critical Infrastructure Cybersecurity*, 7–8.

28 *Id.* at 8.

29 *Id.*

30 *Specifically*, National Institute of Standards and Technology, *Standards for Security Categorization of Federal Information and Information Systems*, FIPS PUB 199 (February 2004).

cesses.[31] The next step is to Implement these controls so as to mitigate the identified risks to these systems and information and document the implementation of the selected controls.[32] The Assess step requires the organisation to evaluate the implementation of the security controls to ensure that they are "implemented correctly, operating as intended, and producing the desired outcomes".[33] This assessment is important as it emphasizes security over mere compliance.[34] If controls are working properly then the system can be Authorised for operation "based on a determination that the risk to organizational operations and assets, individuals, other organizations, and the Nation is acceptable".[35] Finally, there must be ongoing Monitoring of the system and controls to ensure that the security stance of the organisation is up to date and responsive to changing situations. This includes "assessing control effectiveness, documenting changes to the system and environment of operation, conducting risk assessments and impact analyses, and reporting the security and privacy posture of the system".[36]

It is worth investigating, in more detail, the Select step, as the controls that are selected present another level of documentation in the cybersecurity process. Important to the narrative being pursued in this chapter, it is the controls themselves that are the items that become "legalised" through procurement and contracting processes. In the Select step, the organisation should select specific security controls from NIST Special Publication 800-53.[37] NIST SP 800-53 is a catalog of more than 1000 governance and technical controls across 18 control families.[38] These controls can be selected from in order to meet the security requirements of a specific system. The idea of "select" is important here, as the control catalog is not a list of items that must be implemented to achieve cybersecurity. Implementing all controls for any system would be unnecessary and inefficient. Instead, the organisation must decide which controls best fit the system it is seeking to protect. The adaptability of cybersecurity standards to a specific system or organisation is at the core of the cybersecurity enterprise, and it is also one of the reasons why cybersecurity law and regulation often *seem* lacking. The cybersecurity governance process must be specifically tailored to each system giving the organisation flexibility in how it configures systems to best meet its goals, business or otherwise.[39] From this perspective, processes like those found in the RMF and CSF present structured paths in helping make these decisions, but at the end of the day cybersecurity is bespoke to each organisation and system.

Controls can be technical or governance related. Indeed, the first control in each control family in NIST SP 800-53 requires an organisation to develop policies to govern that control fam-

31 NIST SP 800-37, 9.

32 *Id.*

33 *Id.*

34 Eduardo Takamura and Kevin Mangum, "Tailoring NIST Security Controls for the Ground System: Selection and Implementation-Recommendations for Information System Owners," in *AIAA SPACE 2016*, (2016): 2.

35 NIST SP 800-37, 9.

36 *Id.*

37 NIST, *Security and Privacy Controls for Information Systems and Organizations*, rev. 5, NIST SP 800-53 (September 2020).

38 These families are Access Control; Awareness and Training; Audit and Accountability; Assessment, Authorisation, and Monitoring; Configuration Management; Contingency Planning; Identification and Authentication; Incident Response; Maintenance; Media Protection; Physical and Environmental Protection; Planning; Program Management; Personnel Security; PII Processing and Transparency; Risk Assessment; System and Services Acquisition; System and Communications Protection; System and Communication Protection; System and Information Integrity; and Supply Chain Risk Management. NIST SP 800-53, 8.

39 On tailoring see Takamura & Mangum, "Tailoring NIST Security Controls for the Ground System."

ily. For instance, the first control family is Access Control (AC), which is a set of controls that governs how organisations grant and manage access to their systems to both internal and external individuals and systems. Control AC-1: Access Control Policy and Procedures lays out the need for an organisation to develop, document, and disseminate "[a]n access control policy that addresses purpose, scope, roles, responsibilities, management commitment, coordination among organizational entities, and compliance; and … [p]rocedures to facilitate the implementation of the access control policy and associated access controls".[40] This illustrates the emphasis on the role of internal governance in cybersecurity processes. Like any other matter of corporate governance, cybersecurity requires proper documentation that shows internal compliance with adequate standards. Such governance-oriented controls are complimented by technical controls. For example, AC-3: Access Enforcement specifies that the organisation should "[e]nforce approved authorizations for logical access to information and system resources in accordance with applicable access control policies".[41] This is a system level control that requires technical implementations to limit users and systems to accessing only information, applications, and systems for which they have been authorised, for example, by associating access limitation with the users account. Importantly, though, these controls work in concert as the policy defines what needs to be done and the technical implementation ensures that the policy is properly followed.

This section has discussed US cybersecurity law generally, and it shows a clear path from law as a general statement of a need to be cyber secure to the development of detailed technical standards that can be applied in this enterprise. It has also sought to illustrate why legal mechanisms are ill suited to the task of identifying what constitutes adequate cybersecurity. The next section will turn to cybersecurity law as applicable to space assets and infrastructure.

30.2 Space and US cybersecurity law

As emphasised above, not all controls apply to all systems, but instead should be selected with the requirements of the specific system being protected. This is particularly pertinent in the space context where systems operate in a unique environment, which imposes a variety of challenges and limitations in securing those assets. This section will discuss this idea in more detail and construct a narrative around the legalisation of cybersecurity standards as applicable to space systems.

Space systems have unique characteristics and operate in a unique environment. This means that cybersecurity processes must be tailored to fit these systems. Attributes such as the payload and system design can create risks and vulnerabilities. For example, a system that can have its operating system updated has increased potential for a longer life and the ability to patch discovered vulnerabilities, but at the same time might be more vulnerable to attackers that could exploit this capability to upload malware.[42] The operational environment of space also affects the cybersecurity stance of satellites. Space is a strategic domain with extensive military uses and applications. This means that space assets could be valued targets for state actors seeking to disrupt space operations.[43] In particular, an attack on a space system through cyber capabilities could deny an

40 NIST SP 800-53, 18.

41 NIST SP 800-53, 23–28.

42 David Livingstone and Patricia Lewis, "Space, the Final Frontier for Cybersecurity?" (London: Chatham House. The Royal Institute of International Affairs, 2016): 4.

43 See generally, James Pavur and Ivan Martinovic, "The Cyber-ASAT: On the Impact of Cyber Weapons in Outer Space," in *2019 11th International Conference on Cyber Conflict (CyCon)* (NATO CCD COE, 2019), 1–18.

adversary the use of that asset and at the same time avoid creating unwanted debris.[44] There are myriad ways in which space operations impact how a space operator should evaluate cyber risks and vulnerabilities, and cataloging these is beyond the scope of this chapter. What is important at this juncture is that it is understood, first, that space systems create unique issues for cybersecurity and these must be taken into account when engaging in the risk management process. At the same time, it must be remembered that not all space systems are equivalent, and different types of operations will require different approaches and implementations. For these reasons, it is very difficult to describe cybersecurity for "space", because this will be a bespoke process for each system. Such a stance is consistent with the cybersecurity principles discussed in the previous section.

This is not to say, however, that cybersecurity in space is a free for all. Baselines for cybersecurity of space systems can be developed and used, and these baselines play an important role in developing a culture of security within the space industry. For example, one way of doing this is through the development of an overlay for particular systems engaged in particular activities. A prime example of such an overlay, is the CNSS overlay for space systems engaged in national security activities.[45] This overlay defines baselines and controls that must be adopted by national security space systems whether they are government owned or privately owned and procured by the government.[46] This overlay makes space specific adjustments to the controls selected from the NIST 800-53 control catalog for implementation on national security systems.[47] The CNSS overlay, though, is very specific to national security systems and implements a high level of security that will not be appropriate, efficient, or economical for operators that are not engaged in these types of activities. However, similar processes are at work that are pushing forward cybersecurity governance in space.

For a more complete narrative of the legalisation of cybersecurity standards within the space domain, one should begin with Space Policy Directive 5: Cybersecurity Principles for Space Systems. This directive is executive level policy that was adopted in September 2020 by the Trump Administration. Executive policy, generally, does not make law in the United States, but it sets out an administration's approach to a particular subject and the law surrounding that subject – in this case cybersecurity for space operations. The policy requires that "executive departments and agencies … will foster practices within Government space operations and across the commercial space industry that protect space assets and their supporting infrastructure from cyber threats and ensure continuity of operations".[48] It further states that the general principles that the policy outlines should be implemented through "rules, regulations, and guidance, [and] should enhance space system cybersecurity, including through the consideration and adoption, where appropriate, of cybersecurity best practices and norms of behavior".[49] What is evident from this policy is that the executive branch views cybersecurity in space as a critical goal of the government, but that this goal extends past government systems and to commercial systems. The principles that it adopts

44 P. J. Blount, "That Escalated Quickly: The Cyber-ASAT Conundrum," *Proceedings of the International Institute of Space Law 2017* 61 (2018): 701–707.

45 Committee on National Security Systems, *Security Categorization and Control Selection for National Security Systems*, CNSSI No. 1253 (27 March 2014) Attachment 2 Appendix F: Space Platform Overlay.

46 Committee on National Security Systems, *Cybersecurity Policy for Space Systems Used to Support National Security Missions*, CNSSP No. 12 (February 2018): Sec. III (5) ("This policy is applicable to all space NSS that are developed, owned, operated, controlled, or leased either by the USG or for the benefit of the USG by commercial entities (domestic and foreign) or foreign governments under bilateral or multilateral agreements").

47 *See* CNSSI No. 1253 and Attachment 2 Appendix F.

48 Space Policy Directive 5, s 3.

49 *Id.*, s 4(c)

are, consistent with the nature of the policy, high level and broad, but they do suggest that operators should develop "cybersecurity plans" that help protect these systems and to regain control of these systems in cases of breaches of that system.[50]

SPD-5 admonishes operators to adopt and follow rules, regulations, guidelines, and best practices, but it does not identify what these may be. There is, of course, no need for these operators to reinvent the wheel and develop a new set of standards specific to space operations in light of the frameworks developed by the NIST, which are intentionally flexible and adaptable to a wide range of systems. There is, though, still a need for these processes to be tailored to space operations "to avoid force-fitting them to support the unique environment and operations" in the space context.[51] The NIST's CSF and RMF provide frameworks that private and commercial entities can use to develop their cybersecurity plans regardless of their intent to contract with the government. At the same time, the impact of these frameworks is heightened because of the role they play in federal procurement of services and goods that have an impact on federal information security. The procurement process can result in the NIST framework, and the cybersecurity plans developed from the framework, becoming an integral part of the contract between the federal government and an organisation. In the space context, this is particularly powerful as the US Government is a significant player in the space marketplace. Further, as noted in SPD-5, the US Government treats the space economy as a critical issue, and the government "must manage risks to the growth and prosperity of our commercial space economy".[52]

To this end, the NIST has released NISTIR 8270(Draft): Introduction to Cybersecurity for Commercial Satellite Operations.[53] This publication, still in draft form at the time of this writing, explains a high-level methodology for applying the CSF to space operations.[54] Its guidance is still high level, and it does not create an overlay for space operations. Rather, it discusses the overall process in assessing the risks and vulnerabilities for space systems and how an organisation should move through the process of developing cybersecurity plans.[55] The document itself stays clear of detailing specific applications to specific operations outside of an illustrative example of a small-sat remote sensing system, but when the final version is adopted, it will nevertheless be an important touchpoint for operators beginning this process.

A more detailed approach can be found in the USSF Infrastructure Asset Pre-approval (IA-Pre) programme.[56] This programme applies to commercial satellite operators that wish to compete for military satellite communications contracts. Operators that wish to compete for these contracts will need apply a set of predefined controls from the NIST 800-53 catalog. They will then go through a third-party audit to confirm that they have achieved an adequate level of security through their implementation of these controls. Only after successfully passing this third-party "pre-assessment", will a provider be allowed to compete for these military satellite communication contracts.[57] When a provider is selected for such a contract, this predefined level of cybersecurity will become part of that contract, requiring the provider to maintain this security stance throughout the

50 *Id.*, s 4(b)

51 Takamura & Mangum, "Tailoring NIST Security Controls for the Ground System," 4.

52 Space Policy Directive-5, s 3.

53 National Institute of Standards and Technology, *Introduction to Cybersecurity for Commercial Satellite Operations*, NISTIR(draft) (25 February 2022).

54 NISTIR(draft), iv.

55 *Id.* at 11.

56 Space Systems Command, "SSC CSCO reaches critical milestone for IA-Pre, roll-out begins today" (26 May 2020).

57 *Id.*

lifetime of the contract. A few things are worth noting about this programme. First, it shows a clear connection between cybersecurity and the government procurement process, especially for space-related procurement. Second, it is detailed in nature (unlike SPD-5 and NISTIR 8270(Draft)), but limited in scope to a specific type of activity by a specific type of operator. Third is the ability of this programme to have a wider effect on cybersecurity for space operations as most of the potential providers will be applying these standards to space assets that serve a variety of customers aside from USSF.

Cybersecurity through contracts can have a ripple effect. A provider bound by cybersecurity standards in a procurement contract will of course need to control its exposure within its own contractual trail to its suppliers. Thus, cybersecurity requirements can ripple down the supply chain, via contract, and become a powerful legal force without ever being legislated as law or promulgated as regulation. However, law and regulation can certainly impact these contracts. For instance, US law prevents federal agencies from procuring certain brands of Chinese telecommunication equipment.[58] As a result, satellite providers will need to ensure that their systems are free of these technologies, which will require them to pass this obligation on to their suppliers. Such restrictions may in practice be limited to operators providing services and equipment to the US Government, but as these restrictions propagate throughout the supply chain they can have a significant effect on what technologies are available within the supply chain. Cybersecurity by contract is not unique to the procurement process and is common within commercial contracts among operators that are concerned with proper cybersecurity. However, the market force of a customer like the United States government within the space industry, helps to push these requirements into the supply chain, giving them significantly more force and shaping a set of common practices that can better protect all systems. This of course has limitations. For example, the alienation in US law of Chinese technologies means that these cybersecurity processes will not find their way into supply chains that serve different markets. The decision to exclude these technologies is, of course, connected to an assessment that there is inherent insecurity in these technologies to begin with, so this is not offered as a critique of the US law but as a salient example of the limits of cybersecurity by contract.

Contracts provide a flexible legal mechanism for managing cybersecurity risks among participants. Since there can be significant loss from a cybersecurity incident, parties need to manage and assign risk among themselves up and down the contractual ladder. The assigning and acceptance of obligations through private law mechanisms currently represents the most significant locus of cybersecurity *law*. More importantly, it shows how technical standards that are not on their face legally binding become implemented as legal obligations, and how government action outside of the legislative branch can promulgate rules through private law.

30.3 "Doing" cybersecurity law

While the application of cybersecurity standards is not a legal function in the sense that the law prescribes how these standards need to be applied to systems and organisations, there are still clear legal functions within this process, and a lawyer advising an organisation will play a critical role in the cybersecurity process. This section will discuss what it means to *do* cybersecurity law. It is important to understand that the role of the lawyer is just one of many since cybersecurity is

58 John S. McCain, National Defense Authorization Act for Fiscal Year 2019, 115 Pub. L. 232, s 889. See also Congressional Research Service, *Huawei and U.S. Law* (23 February 2021).

an organisation-wide endeavour, and numerous functions will exist outside the competence of the legal professional. At the same time, the connection of the lawyer to cybersecurity is constant and broad as will be discussed in this section.

A primary role of a lawyer in an organisation is to inform when legal risk results from law and regulation as in the examples of ITAR, US restrictions on Chinese technology, or privacy legislation, among many others. While law does not generally prescribe cybersecurity standards as such, it still has a significant impact on operators through laws and regulations that have an indirect effect on an organisation's cybersecurity plan. A good example of this is the European Union General Data Protection Regulation (GDPR), which provides for the protection of personal data of European residents but has implications for organisations globally.[59] While not a cybersecurity law, *per se*, this regulation does require regulated entities to pursue "data protection by design" when developing systems.[60] Such provisions will need to be interpreted by the lawyer and communicated to the team in charge of cybersecurity to ensure that the system is not just secure but also compliant with the operative regulation.

A second function is related to the cybersecurity obligations that an organisation incurs through contractual relations. Contracts can pass along cybersecurity obligations, which can flow down through the supply chain. As examples, a contract could require a party to maintain certain accreditations with regards to its cybersecurity or it could include clauses denoting specific security surrounding data transferred pursuant to the contract. As noted above, the bulk of American cybersecurity law flows from the procurement processes of the Federal Government. In this respect, the lawyer's role is connected both to advising on the negotiation of the contract itself, as well as continuing advice related to compliance and potential breaches of a contract. While a variety of parties within an organisation may have responsibility for activities connected to the contract, the lawyer has a primary role in managing the contract as a source of legal obligation for an organisation.

Finally, the lawyer has a significant role in ensuring that there is documentation of adequate evidence of compliance with the cybersecurity plan adopted by the organisation and its associated policies and procedures. The evidence-based posture of cybersecurity can be seen in the processes discussed above, which require documentation of steps and actions taken. The organisation's policy serves as evidence of how an organisation will implement cybersecurity. Technical implementations that provide compliance with the policy and the selected controls, as a result, should be documented and this documentation managed. The lawyer is not responsible for generating this documentation, but needs to be aware of the processes that create this documentation and advise on how it should be managed as a body of evidence. This body of evidence is critical in cases where there has been an incident or a breach. The evidence of compliance with internal governance generated through the cybersecurity process will be central to the legal response to claims against the organisation whether they be civil, administrative, or criminal. In such proceedings, an organisation need not show that it was impervious to cyber-attacks, but rather that it maintained an adequate security posture that properly and reasonably managed and mitigated risks.

30.4 Conclusion

Cybersecurity law, and specifically in the space context, is a growing field with significant discourse across a number of legal systems. This chapter addresses this topic within the framework

59 General Data Protection Regulation, EU Reg. 2016/679 (2016).
60 *Id.* Art. 25.

of US law, based on the significant steps taken towards establishing a strong cybersecurity posture within the US space industry. This is not to suggest that the approaches of other systems are insignificant. Quite the contrary, the development of cybersecurity standards, rules, and guidelines across jurisdictions will be a positive force in advancing the project of preventing catastrophic cyber-attacks in the space domain. There should be recognition within this industry though that cooperative efforts are the most effective in advancing security for all. As an example, the Space Information Sharing and Analysis Center (Space ISAC) is an industry-led effort to establish a mechanism for sharing information on threats and vulnerabilities that could be suffered by a variety of operators. There is a need for transnational capacity-building and efforts to better understand how operators should behave with regards to cybersecurity in space. While much of this discussion will be substantively technical in scope, law and governance processes will continue to play a significant role. The US system, in which the legalisation of technical standards through contract mechanisms can be observed, will likely be mirrored in other jurisdictions. This is not due to any sort of primacy in the US system, but more connected to the dictates of the cybersecurity enterprise itself, which resists hard legal rules in favor of flexibility. Lawyers functioning in this space will need to approach cybersecurity from a governance perspective and adapt legal responses to the unique characteristics of space operations. To this end, the US frameworks present useful tools even for operators that may not enter into the supply chain connected to a US federal procurement.

31

NEWSPACE AND ENSURING LONG-TERM SUSTAINABILITY OF THE SPACE ENVIRONMENT[1]

Gina Petrovici and Ulrike M. Bohlmann

31.1 Introduction

Despite major economic challenges, space endeavours continue to flourish and expand their role as a global cross-industry growth and innovation driver. The number of registered objects in the United Nations (UN) Register of Objects Launched into Outer Space *per annum* has increased almost tenfold since 2011.[2]

Space is a significant growth market, with opportunities for traditional players as well as those newcomer, non/traditional space-related ventures and start-up companies. This sector is delivering new technologies, and providing solutions that offer decisions makers, *inter alia*, accurate and timely data sets to manage global challenges such as disaster management. The political, socioeconomic, and cultural significance of space activities for states and other stakeholders is undeniable. As the benefits delivered by space activities continue to expand, it will become equally important to ensure that the outer space environment and its benefits remain available for future generations.

Since the start of the space age in 1957, the number of non-functional objects that remain in orbit has been increasing, bringing the total number of space objects in densely populated orbits, such as Low Earth Orbit (LEO). The volume of space debris, together with their combined mass, is one of the greatest challenges to the long-term sustainable use of outer space; it impedes the safe use of the orbital environment, a global common and an increasingly scarce resource. Collisions between space objects lead to increased conjunction events, which may eventually generate additional collisions and chain reactions (Kessler syndrome[3]), posing a constant threat. Space debris generates immense associated costs, impacting negatively on socio-economic benefits on a global

1 The views expressed are purely personal and do not necessarily reflect the views of any entities with which the authors may be affiliated.

2 Statement UNOOSA Director Di Pippo, LSC 2021.

3 Donald J. Kessler, Collisional cascading: the limits of population growth in low Earth orbit, 11 Volume of ADVANCED SPACE RESEARCH, 1991, at 63–66 [hereinafter Kessler (1991)].

DOI: 10.4324/9781003268475-46

scale. The goal is to prevent such negative impacts and the irreversible pollution. Yet there is a need for sufficient legal certainty to allow for innovation to flourish. Rules and regulations need to strike a balance between the general freedom to explore and use outer space by current space actors, and the ethical obligation to safeguard those same freedoms for future actors. This mixture creates important discretionary prerogatives for policy- and lawmakers around the globe, in responding to different political impulses when shaping national space legislation and other means of ensuring responsible and sustainable space activities.[4]

31.2 NewSpace

As emphasised by the German Coordinator for Aerospace Policy:

> The important thing is that we have an ecosystem composed by both sides: the classic space companies that we have – that are strong and important for the European ecosystem – but also smaller companies, startups and new firms, as it brings a kind of dynamic into the whole sector. [...] both sides together are a big chance for Europe to really have good and successful technologies and very new developments in the space sector that make us able to be an important partner for international cooperation.[5]

These developments facilitate disruptive innovation and technology in the space sector, allowing cheaper and faster access, also for less experienced actors and developing countries. Some impacts of this process are highlighted in the following sections.

31.2.1 Trends

Start-ups, including subsidiaries of traditional aerospace firms, are increasingly integrated within the traditional space economy to support public space activities and conduct their own, financed through either public private partnership, public sector orders, or venture capital. The industrial landscape now exceeds the traditional large system integrators and suppliers (LSI). Numerous NewSpace companies, particularly in the United States, have an IT background, and their expertise from previous ventures a distinct business advantage. NewSpace activities are often characterised by private entrepreneurs' assumption of risk and financing models primarily based on private capital, supplemented through government funding. States are increasingly supported by private entities in their space missions. These contribute significantly to key programmes, such as launch services to the International Space Station (ISS). Governments often act as anchor customers, purchasing services from private actors. This requires a high-level of reliability of industry partners, and suitable governance mechanisms.

In a similar vein, it is foreseen that there will be successful efforts to launch and operate commercial space stations when the ISS is taken out of use, scheduled for 2030. The United States have already signed an agreement with the commercial operator Axiom to build a first commercial space station. Japan also cooperates with this US-based company to gain access to the intended commercial space station modules. Developments in providing space services include the use of private crew launch vehicles (e.g. SpaceX Crew Dragon Module), and the launch of satellite

4 Dr. Ulrike M. Bohlmann, Global Space Governance, IISL Knowledge Constellation, 04 May 2021.

5 Luisa Low, Space Café Webtalk with Dr. Anna Christmann: Green Space is not an oxymoron, 22 February 2022.

constellations. These constellations bring a wide range of opportunities, remote sensing, national security and telecommunications, including broadband internet connection to underserved rural areas, also for the Internet of Things. The European Union (EU) acknowledged these opportunities in its initiative, "Proposal for a Regulation establishing the Union Secure Connectivity Programme for 2023–2027".[6]

Multiple NewSpace companies recognise the need to facilitate those space activities contributing to sustainability in space or on Earth. The support of NewSpace entities and business models is a much-declared objective, as seen by the European Space Agency (ESA), EU, Germany, Finland, and the United States. Attractive business models for sustainable space activities can become a competitive advantage.

31.2.2 Chances of and challenges for sustainability

NewSpace plays a decisive role within overarching sustainability objectives, like the UN Sustainable Development Goals (SDGs). Satellite-based services and technologies contribute directly to the availability of continuous, accurate and largely free, Earth observation data. They facilitate monitoring of atmospheric and climate changes, as well as sustainable use of resources. The goal of protecting space as a scientifically and economically promising environment, can be vehicle of innovation. A range of companies address challenges of the sustainable use of outer space. For example, LeoLabs, ExoAnalytic Solutions, and the German start-up OKAPI:Orbits offer space situational awareness (SSA) and space surveillance tracking (SST) services to operators monitoring the need for collision avoidance (CA) in the densely populated LEO. A further example is the private company, Astroscale, which develops innovative solutions, ranging from on-orbit servicing to *in situ* space situational awareness. At European level, D-Orbit and ClearSpace contribute to space debris remediation missions.

Other companies focus on sustainability on Earth by supporting the monitoring and realisation of the 17 SDGs, through Earth observation services, e.g. in the field of sustainable farming, water management climate, and disaster monitoring. Smart farming from space is one classical user field of sustainable NewSpace activities. It enables farmers to often increase yields, while managing their crops in a resource-saving and climate-friendly manner. ConstellR is such a start-up. It received a grant from the German Federal Ministry for Economic Affairs and Climate Action (BMWK) and the Fraunhofer AHEAD programme, after successfully competing in a competitive tender issued by ESA in 2017 on "Satellite missions with an important social impact".[7] Another outstanding mission is conducted by the Environmental Mapping and Analysis Program (EnMAP). The hyperspectral satellite collects data on the state of our home planet, by analysing the solar radiation reflected from the Earth's surface. Its spectrally high-resolution images can play an important role in tackling climate change and environmental destruction, as it provides valuable information for countermeasures. The mission is led by the German Space Agency on behalf of BMWK.[8]

According to an analysis of the United Nations Office for Outer Space Affairs (UNOOSA), 65 of 169 SDG indicators are based on satellite-based Earth observation and navigation. This equals

6 EU Secure Connectivity Proposal (2022).

7 For more information, please consult the Constellr Website.

8 For more information, please consult the dedicated DLR Website.

an amount of just under 40%. Space activities have the capabilities to address the challenges of our time, whether climate change, disaster management, or sustainable economic growth.

Another notable challenging development is the mass production of small satellites by new space actors, such as SpaceX, Amazon, and OneWeb. These companies are launching and operating thousands of broad-band satellites as constellations,[9] in the already densely populated LEO. At the same time, the exponentially rising number of satellites[10] in an orbit that is already populated by numerous functioning and non-functional space objects raises pressing issues.

On 8 February 2022, the US National Aeronautics and Space Administration (NASA) reacted to a SpaceX proposal for a second-generation Starlink constellation, with additional 30.000 satellites, expressing its concerns as follows: "With the increase in large constellation proposals to the FCC, NASA has concerns with the potential for a significant increase in the frequency of conjunction events and possible impacts to NASA's science and human spaceflight missions".[11]Accordingly, NASA publicly articulated the risk potentially leading to the Kessler Syndrome.[12] Large satellite constellations in LEO pose a further challenge to astronomy through the light pollution they cause. The International Astronomical Union has addressed this internationally at the Scientific and Technical Subcommittee (STSC) of the UN Committee on the Peaceful Uses of Outer Space (COPUOS), which agreed that "Dark and Quiet Skies" becomes a temporary STSC agenda item in 2022 and 2023.[13] Potential recommendations on the registration of large and mega-constellations have been discussed for the first time during the 61st COPUOS Legal Subcommittee in its Working Group on the Status and Application of the Five UN Treaties on Outer Space (Five-Treaty WG).[14]

Multilateral cooperation continues to be key in tackling such challenges to the long-term sustainable and safe use of outer space. A high level of legitimacy can be achieved through the process of involving multiple actors at COPUOS, as the primary forum for deliberating the peaceful uses of outer space. Dialogues among states and non-state actors can provide additional perspectives and outline industry needs, all of which are important indicators in reaching common understanding. This provides common ground for best practices combining legal, regulatory, technical, and economic perspectives. Recent examples, such as the Guidelines for the Long-term Sustainability of Outer Space Activities (LTS Guidelines or Guidelines),[15] show that this approach can be successful.

31.3 Public international law framework for sustainable NewSpace activities

Since the launch of the first artificial satellite in outer space, Soviet Sputnik 1 in 1957 and the establishment of NASA in 1958, the variety of space actors has changed. It is clear from the space treaties' *travaux préparatoires*[16] and the final provisions that the carrying out of space activities

9 For more information related to the topic of satellite constellations, see also Annette Froehlich (ed.), Legal Aspects Around Satellite Constellations, in: Studies in Space Policy Vol. 19, 2019, Springer Nature Switzerland.

10 See e.g. European Space Agency, ESA´s Space Environment Report 2022 available on the ESA Website.

11 Jeff Foust, NASA outlines concerns about Starlink next-generation constellation in FCC letter, 09 February 2022.

12 Kessler (1991).

13 This decision was taken by consensus and particularly welcomed by e.g. CHE, ESP, GER, UK, FRA, AUT, USA, RUS, ITA, CAN, FIN, und CHN; see: A/AC.105/C.1/L.394/Add.7, para. 13-27.

14 Report of the Chair of the Five-Treaty WG, para. 14, as contained in Annex I to the Report of the Legal Subcommittee on its sixtieth session, held in Vienna from 31 May to 11 June 2021, A/AC.105/1243 of 24 June 2021.

15 Guidelines for the Long-term Sustainability of Outer Space Activities, UN document A/74/20, Annex II.

16 For more details, please consult the dedicated UNOOSA Website section.

by private entities was part of the drafting process. Article VI Outer Space Treaty (OST)[17] *verbatim* refers to activities of non-governmental entities in outer space. This secures a dual-system, whereby non-state actions in space are considered permissible, on condition that states adopt measures for their authorisation and control.[18] The following sub-sections of this chapter explore the particular impacts on the sustainability of space activities by public and private actors.

31.3.1 Space treaty law

"The substance of the diplomatic dialogue [during the 1960s and 1970s] was characterized by the search for answers to basic questions related to the use of outer space".[19] The environmental law framework for outer space (see below, 31.3.2) was codified only after the successful negotiation of the main *corpus iuris spatialis*, the unanimously adopted 1961 Resolution on International Cooperation in the Peaceful Uses of Outer Space. That Resolution acknowledged the benefits and challenges associated with an increase in launch activities, focussing attention on the potential of international cooperation through expert fora. The UN bodies and the World Meteorological Organisation (WMO), with its related World Weather Watch (WWW) programme as well as the WMO – International Council for Science Global Atmospheric Research Programme, are all examples.

Those drafting the OST took environmental impact assessments into consideration, as contained in the *travaux préparatoires*. The STSC recognised that the conduct of space activities should avoid potentially harmful interference. An additional source of support in this direction were the proposals made by the Committee on Space Research (COSPAR[20]) Council in May 1964.[21] As a result of these deliberations, the space treaties and principles now contain implicit regulations and references to environmental considerations. Article III OST in particular requires treaty parties to carry on activities in the exploration and use of outer space in accordance with international law, thereby encompassing international environmental law.

Sedes materiae on the protection of the space environment is Art. IX, 2nd sentence OST, according to which it, states must conduct their space exploration activities in such a manner as to avoid harmful contamination and adverse changes in the environment of the Earth resulting from the introduction of extra-terrestrial matter. This provides a legal reference for the prevention of forward contamination of outer space and backward contamination of the Earth environment. Of interest is also that the Liability Convention (LIAB),[22] as *lex specialis* to the OST, does not exclude

17 1967 Treaty on Principles Governing the Activities of States in the Exploration and Use of Outer Space, including the Moon and other Celestial Bodies, 610 U.N.T.S. 205 (Outer Space Treaty, OST).

18 "States Parties to the Treaty shall bear international responsibility for national activities in outer space, including the Moon and other celestial bodies, whether such activities are carried on by governmental agencies or by non-governmental entities, and for assuring that national activities are carried out in conformity with the provisions set forth in the present Treaty."

19 Kai-Uwe Schrogl "Space Law and Diplomacy", Keynote speech on the occasion of the Nandasiri Jasentuliyana Keynote Lecture 2016.

20 The Committee on Space Research (COSPAR) was founded in London in 1958 by the then International Council of Scientific Unions (ICSU), which is now the International Science Council (ISC). COSPAR is tasked to promote and enhance scientific research in space and provide a forum for discussion for the international scientific community.

21 UN document A/5549, Annex II.

22 Convention on International Liability for Damage Caused by Space Objects, entered into force 9 Oct. 1973, 24 U.S.T. 2389, 961 U.N.T.S. 187.

environmental damage from the types of damage covered by Art. I(a). This provision cannot be interpreted to address environmental damage outside the surface of the Earth.

It is arguable that the absolute liability in Article II establishes an Earth-centric stamp in the *corpus iuris spatialis*. The Moon Agreement (MOON)[23] even if it has only now secured 18 signatory states, was negotiated in 1979 as the last of the five core space treaties, a time when environmental considerations gained importance in international discussions. Article 7.1 MOON introduces the concept of intergenerational equity in the context of space activities. Article 7 MOON refers to the *in situ* resource utilisation, a promising endeavour of commercial NewSpace and state actors alike for the use in additive manufacturing, such as 3D printing. This is already used aboard the ISS and intended for further use in deep space exploration. The following sub-paragraph will now shed light on significant developments in international environmental law.

31.3.2 International environmental law

At the first world environmental conference, the 1972 UN Conference on the Human Environment (Stockholm Conference), the participants decided upon the creation of the UN Environment Programme (UNEP), adopting a series of principles for sound management of the environment, including the Stockholm Declaration[24] and an Action Plan for the Human Environment. The Plan was divided in three main categories: global environmental assessment programme, environmental management activities, international measures to support assessment and management activities carried out at the national and international levels. In a similar vein, the Stockholm Declaration as the first significant legal statement with fundamental international principles for environment protection contains 26 principles. It marks the starting point of the ongoing dialogues between industrialised and developing countries on the well-being of society, by facilitating economic growth and reducing environmental pollution. Principle 21 Stockholm Declaration, obliges states in accordance with the UN Charter and the principles of international law, to take "the responsibility to ensure that activities within their jurisdiction or control do not cause damage to the environment of other states or of *areas beyond the limits of national jurisdiction*" (emphasis added). Considering outer space is one of these areas, it becomes apparent that the outer space environment is imminently protected by this principle. UN General Assembly Resolution 2996 (XXVII) 1972 on the International Responsibility of States in Regard to the Environment asserts in its preamble that Principle 21 and 22 Stockholm Declaration provide the fundamental rules governing the matter of environmental protection.

On the 20th anniversary of the first Human Environment Conference, the UN Conference on Environment and Development (UNCED), the "Earth Summit" – *supra* – was organised in June 1992 in Rio de Janeiro, Brazil. The 179 representatives involved focused on the impact of human socio-economic activities on the environment, with a view to developing a broad international agenda on environmental and development issues. This Conference concluded with the Rio Declaration on Environment and Development,[25] with its 27 universal principles; the UN Framework Convention on Climate Change (UNFCCC);[26] the Convention on Biological Diversity;

23 Agreement Governing the Activities of States on the Moon and Other Celestial Bodies, entered into force 11 July 1984, 1363 U.N.T.S. 3.

24 Declaration of the United Nations Conference on the Human Environment, U.N.Doc.A/Conf.48/14/Rev.1 (1972).

25 Rio Declaration on Environment and Development, U.N.Doc.A/Conf.151/26 (1992).

26 FCCC/Informal/84.

and the Declaration on the principles of forest management.[27] Principle 2 Rio Declaration and Art. 3 Convention on Biological Diversity repeat the responsibility to ensure that activities within a state's jurisdiction or control do not cause damage to the environment of other states or of areas beyond the limits of national jurisdiction. The due diligence principle provides for a liability regime, based on a state's general duty of care. First introduced by the International Court of Justice in the *Corfu Channel Case*,[28] and reiterated in the *Barcelona Traction Case*,[29] this notion has a direct effect on international state responsibility, particularly for environmental law. Principle 15 Rio Declaration takes it further:

> To protect the environment, the *precautionary approach shall be widely applied* by States according to their capabilities. Where there are *threats of serious or irreversible damage*, lack of full scientific certainty shall not be used as a reason for postponing cost-effective measures to *prevent environmental degradation* (emphases added).[30]

In its Advisory Opinion on the Legality of the Threat or Use of Nuclear Weapons[31] the International Court of Justice reaffirmed that notion, as was to be seen in the emphasis on the responsibility and liability of states for transboundary harm in the *Trail Smelter Arbitration*.[32]

31.3.3 Additional soft law instruments for environmental protection

The pattern by which states preferred the path of negotiating non-legally binding instruments and guidelines within COPUOS, for adoption by the UN General Assembly after the MOON agreement, to govern those aspects not covered by the traditional *corpus iuris spatialis* is known. The outcome can be seen in various soft law instruments on space activities,[33] such as the LTS Guidelines,[34] Safety Framework for Nuclear Power Source Applications in Outer Space,[35] and Space Debris Mitigation Guidelines of the Committee on the Peaceful Uses of Outer Space.[36] "Soft law" is used to describe instruments bearing legal and practical effects, but while not entailing jurisdictional control. These can range from recommendations to guidelines and principles. A similar development has been recognised in the field of environmental law since the 1970s. While environmental soft laws are often developed on a smaller scale, e.g., bilaterally or regionally, space soft law instruments are aiming to encompass a wide variety of aspects. Generally, soft

27 Report of the United Nations Conference on Environment and Development.

28 Corfu Channel Case (*U.K. v. Alb.*) (Judgment), 1949 I.C.J. 4 (April 9).

29 *Barcelona Traction, Light and Power Co., Ltd. (Belg. v. Spain)*, 1970 I.C.J. 3 (Feb. 5).

30 Declaration of the United Nations Conference on the Human Environment, U.N.Doc.A/Conf.48/14/Rev.1 (1972) [hereinafter 1972 Stockholm Declaration].

31 Legality of the Threat or Use of Nuclear Weapons (Advisory Opinion) 1996, I.C.J. 226 (8 July) [hereinafter Legality of the Threat or Use of Nuclear Weapons].

32 *Trail Smelter Arbitration (US v. Canada)* 1938/1941, R.I.A.A.1905 [hereinafter Trail Smelter Arbitration].

33 Fore a detailed discussion on the topic of soft law for space activities, see among others Walter et al (2011); and Freeland (2011).

34 Report of the Committee on the Peaceful Uses of Outer Space, U.N. GAOR, 62nd Sess., U.N. Doc. A/74/20, Annex II (2019) [hereinafter UN document A/74/20, Annex II].

35 Jointly published by COPUOS and the International Atomic Energy Agency (IAEA), UN document A/AC.105/934.

36 Adopted by the STSC of COPUOS at its 44th session in 2007, UN document A/105/890, para. 99, and endorsed by the United Nations General Assembly in UN document G.A.Res.217 (LXII), UNGA, 62nd Sess., U.N. Doc. A/RES/62/217* (2007) [hereinafter UN document A/RES/62/217*].

law comes into play if technical, scientific or extremely sensitive areas are concerned and also in situations when the desired outcome has to be rapidly adaptable to environmental or technological developments. As will be demonstrated in section 4.2.1. below, soft law instruments bear not only the opportunity to reach faster agreement and have a more flexible character than hard law instrument but in particular can also involve or consider various actors and societal circumstances.[37]

It is worth noting that soft law instruments mainly recall verbatim the *corpus iuris spatialis* as its basis, e.g. the LTS Guidelines underline: "nothing in the guidelines should constitute a revision, qualification or reinterpretation of those principles and norms. Nothing in the guidelines should be interpreted as giving rise to any new legal obligation for states".

This position in law is not totally replicated at all levels, but finds some support in statements by leading judiciary that soft law can still bear some legal effect, as seen in Council of Europe's Recommendations' impact on the Court´s institutional structure. Jörg Polakiewicz, legal adviser of the Council of Europe stated: "[T]he effectiveness of soft law standard depends not only on the authority and collective wisdom of the women and men who draft them, but also on the international environment, which may be more or less receptive to the new standards".[38] Some of the above non-legally binding instruments play a significant role in the conduct of space activities. The unique benefit of these instruments is their procedural legitimacy achieved at COPUOS through the consensus decision-making basis. States are more willing to transpose these rules at national level. It could be argued that the leading soft law norms become *opinio iuris sive neccessitatis*, signalising the acceptance by multiple state actors of the norm(s) having an implied mandatory effect, enhancing the overall effectiveness of these instruments towards broader implementation by the stakeholders.

31.4 Latest discussions on sustainability at COPUOS level

UNCOPUOS, supported by UNOOSA, continues in its decisive role to provide a unique multilateral platform fostering inclusive international dialogue and cooperation in the peaceful uses of outer space. This ranges from discussion on emerging chances and challenges for the safe and sustainable use of space as elaborated (discussed above at 31.2.2 and 31.2.3), as well as guiding member states on space object registration and a wide range of capacity and partnership building measures.

31.4.1 Sustainability through space – Space 2030 Agenda

As a means to raising awareness for the decisive contributions of space activities to the SDGs, and with this, sustainability on Earth through space, the UN General Assembly adopted the Space2030 Agenda: Space as a driver of sustainable development ("Space2030" Agenda) and its implementation plan in autumn 2021.[39]

37 See in this context also: Arthur Benz, Nicolai Dose, Governance – Regieren in komplexen Regelsystemen – Eine Einführung, 2010, at 253–256.

38 European External Action Service, Roundtable on Soft Law (2021).

39 The "Space2030" Agenda: space as a driver of sustainable development UN document G.A.Res.3 (LXXVI), UNGA,76th Sess. U.N.Doc.A/RES/76/3 (2021) [hereinafter UN document A/RES/76/3].

31.4.1.1 Background and negotiation process

The agenda traces back to the UNISPACE+50 resolution,[40] containing COPUOS Member States' objectives until 2030. It references the three specific development agendas: Sendai Framework for Disaster Risk Reduction,[41] the 2030 Agenda for Sustainable Development,[42] and Paris Agreement on Climate Change.[43] It reiterates fundamental principles of space activities, among them the aim to promote access to space for the benefit of all countries, to increase awareness and capacity building, and to strengthen the overall global governance of space activities. The resolution was adopted in the aftermath of a three-year process involving exchanges of UNOOSA with representatives of governments, industry, academia and civil society on the matters ranging from space industry to space diplomacy.[44] One of the outcomes of this process, was the proposal to improve the contributions of space activities to the realisation of the 2030 Agenda for Sustainable Development,[45] through the "Space2030" Agenda under a dedicated agenda item and within a respective Working Group (WG). The mandate, terms of reference and work plan were agreed upon by the required consensus in 2018. On the occasion of the UN General Assembly High-Level Week, the UNOOSA joined the UN Office for Partnerships and SpaceTrust to co-host the event "Space2030 Agenda: Space as a driver for peace" on 25 September 2018, which can be considered as first public event on the "Space2030" Agenda. It also involved a broad range of space actors, from the public and private sector including civil society, to discuss the role of international cooperation in the peaceful uses of outer space, as well as its potential as a vehicle for peace.

31.4.1.2 Adoption and the way ahead

COPUOS adopted the "Space2030" Agenda on 25 October 2021, as a long-term vision for delivering the full potential that space can deliver for sustainable development. This lists the goals to be achieved in the next ten years, categorised into four overarching objectives. The main pillars are:[46]

- **Space economy**, recognising the role of space activities for sustainable economic growth and new markets;
- **Space society**, acknowledging the benefits of space for society, sustainable lifestyle and resilient cities and communities. It is centered around how space-derived information can be applied world-wide to improve quality of life at all levels of society;
- **Space accessibility**, facilitating capacity-building and enhancing orbital access, frequencies, space data, and services for everyone, including without limitation to developing countries and emerging space-faring nations; and
- **Space diplomacy,** stressing the establishment of knowledge-based international partnerships and appropriate national and international mechanisms for effective governance.[47]

40 UN document A/RES/73/6.

41 https://www.undrr.org/publication/sendai-framework-disaster-risk-reduction-2015-2030 March 2015.

42 UN document A/RES/70/1, https://sustainabledevelopment.un.org September 2015.

43 http://unfccc.int/files/essential_background/convention/application/pdf/english_paris_agreement.pdf December 2015.

44 UN document A/AC.105/1137.

45 UN document A/AC.105/1166.

46 UN document A/AC.105/C.1/L.372.

47 UN document A/RES/76/3, Part B Ch. II, para. 10.

Implementation of the Agenda can be realised in various ways, such as existing regional and international fora, programmes, and initiatives, including UNISPACE+50, UN-SPIDER, the international Space Climate Observatory, the Access to Space for All initiative, Space Law for New Space Actors, UN-affiliated regional centres for space science and technology, Space4Water, and more.

It is for the international community now to deliver the tangible output and practical solutions called for by the unanimously adopted resolution. Promising reports are already being published on the numerous projects that Member States are successfully implementing.

31.4.2 Sustainability in space – Long-Term Sustainability Guidelines

The need to ensure sustainable conduct in outer space is recognised. It is UNOOSA that has facilitated the decisive exchange between COPUOS Member States on what constitutes sustainable space activities. The following sheds light on the negotiation process and current status of the follow-up Working Group (WG), also known as the WG on the Long-term Sustainability of Outer Space Activities 2.0 (LTS WG).

31.4.2.1 Negotiation process

Following decisive inputs of the Canadian delegate and former Chairman of the STSC, Karl Doetsch (2005)[48] and the French COPUOS chair Gérard Brachet, two years after the "Paris Informal Working Group" in 2008, followed by a conference room paper[49] submitted by France in 2010, a WG was establishment under the chairmanship of Peter Martinez (South Africa) to address the long-term sustainability of outer space activities. The unanimous agreement on the mandate, terms of reference and methods of work in the 54th session of the Committee,[50] enabled the WG to begin its substantial work on a set of voluntary, non-legally binding, guidelines covering the entire mission life cycle of space objects, with the objective of facilitating sustainable and safe space operations for future generations.[51]

From the outset, the WG rejected the development of new legally binding instruments in this context and referred to the existing treaties and principles governing the activities of states in the exploration and use of outer space as the legal framework for the guidelines. Committee delegations nominated their own experts from the governmental and private sphere to serve together with those intergovernmental bodies with permanent observer status, in four dedicated expert groups,[52] in an *ad personam* capacity, providing expert input not necessarily influenced by the official national governments' positions. Additional input was provided by, *inter alia* the ESA,

48 See also: Karl Doetsch, Gérard Brachet, Peter Martinez, Kenneth D. Hodgkins, Richard Buenneke and Amer Charlesworth, and Theresa Hitchens in Part I: The Multilateral Effort to Assure Space Sustainability in SPACE FOR THE 21ST CENTURY – DISCOVERY, INNOVATION, SUSTAINABILITY (Michael Simpson, Ray Williamson and Langdon Morris eds., 2016.

49 UN document A/AC.105/C.1/2010/CRP3.

50 UN document A/66/20, Annex II, pp. 51–57.

51 See also e.g. Peter Martinez, Development of an international compendium of guidelines for the long-term sustainability of outer space activities, 43 Volume of SPACE POLICY, 2018, at 13–17 [hereinafter Martinez (2018)].

52 The expert groups were focused on: (a) Sustainable space utilisation supporting sustainable development on Earth; (b) Space debris, space operations, and tools to support collaborative space situational awareness; (c) Space weather; and (d) Regulatory regimes and guidance for actors. Joint meetings served as platform for exchange about interconnected topics.

International Academy of Astronautics, and Inter-Agency Space Debris Coordination Committee (IADC).

The 62nd session of the Committee finally adopted the preamble and the 21 guidelines following the end of the WG's mandate.[53] This landmark agreement led to an accessible compendium of best practices for sustainable space activities, containing a commonly agreed definition of the term "space sustainability", which reiterated the UN Brundtland report:[54]

> [Space sustainability is] the ability to maintain the conduct of space activities indefinitely into the future in a manner that realizes the objectives of equitable access to the benefits of the exploration and use of outer space for peaceful purposes, in order to meet the needs of the present generations while preserving the outer space environment for future generations.[55]

The Guidelines address state and private space actors and include recommendations for all phases of a space mission, including the development, launch, operation, and disposal of a space object.

31.4.2.2 LTS follow-up

With the adoption of LTS Guidelines, a new WG under the long-term sustainability agenda item (A/74/20, para 165) was established with a three-fold mandate:

(i.) identification and study of challenges, as well as potential development of new guidelines;
(ii.) sharing experiences from the implementation of the Guidelines; and
(iii.) raising awareness and capacity building in particular among emerging space nations and developing countries.[56]

Growing international acceptance of the guidelines and the multifaceted commitments towards their implementation proves that multilateral consensus and international cooperation, combined are effective tools to facilitate long-term sustainable and safe space environment. The follow-up WG provides an opportunity to intensify this work towards responsible, sustainable, and safe space activities at international level. Considering the exponential growth of the space debris population in LEO[57] and the increasing number of collision avoidance manoeuvres, the WG carries particular importance. It is unquestionable that there is a need for urgent action to ensure equitable access to the exploration and benefits of the use of outer space for peaceful purposes. This is underlined in the UN Secretary General report "Our Common Agenda"[58] focusing on sustainable use of outer space and international Space Traffic Management (STM). It was prepared in response to the General Assembly Resolution 75/1 adopted in 2020 on the occasion of the 75th UN anniversary. It envisages an inclusive consultative process and a high-level, multilateral "Summit for the Future"

53 UN document A/74/20, Annex II.

54 1987 Report of the World Commission on Environment and Development.

55 UN document A/AC.105/C.1/2018/CRP.18/Rev.1.

56 UN document A/AC.105/C.1/2018/CRP.18/Rev.1.

57 As of 5 January 2022, around 130 million space debris objects from greater than 1 mm to 1 cm, 1,000,000 objects from greater than 1 cm to 10 cm and 36,500 objects greater than 10 cm are estimated by statistical models to be in orbit, see ESA, Space debris by the numbers. For more detailed statistics on the space environment, please consult e.g. the ESA's Annual Space Environment Report.

58 Our Common Agenda – Report of the Secretary-General (2021).

to advance governance arrangements for the aforementioned matters of concern. The Guidelines will remain a living document open for adaptations in the form of a "continued institutionalised dialogue"[59] if so required to keep outer space a peaceful, sustainable, responsible, and promising area of human exploration.

31.5 National measures for sustainable space activities

There is clearly a growing interest in sustainable space activities. The consensual adoption of the Guidelines, which must be considered as the first building blocks for a future STM regime, and under the Space2030 Agenda, highlight the recognition of sustainability as a key element of space activities for the international community. National space strategies and legislation increasingly emphasise the significance of sustainable space activities, in space and on Earth. For a variety of clear reasons, latterly emphasised by the immediate Director of UNOOSA, governments are keen to ensure responsible conduct – and unimpeded access and use of outer space:

> The democratization and intensification we see in the space sector represent encouraging news for the future. The sustainability challenges this new era creates must be addressed as a priority to ensure that the space sector can thrive. We must look at every action we take in space through the lens of sustainability, for which the LTS Guidelines provide an outstanding framework.[60]

The Guidelines call upon states to identify ways to implement these soft law instruments at national level to becoming fully effective. The means of doing so are multifaceted. Some states implement these soft law instruments through soft use in their national space strategies, others adopt project specific and/or general actor-related licensing or authorisation requirements. The unanimously adopted Guidelines and Space2030 Agenda Resolution call upon the international community to monitor these implementation practices, to provide guidance, support, and fora for exchange in this respect, as well as to raise awareness for the need of sustainable practices. Implementation serves the interests of states, space agencies, and private operators in keeping the relevant orbits accessible and useable. The development of sustainable business models and responsible norms of behaviour should be considered an opportunity, and not a burden. These developments ensure the continuation of far-reaching space missions, as well as the advance of innovate business solutions that provide the required services to public or private actors. Sustainable value creation has already been identified as an emerging concept in the field of corporate governance.[61]

The World Economic Forum, ESA, the Space Enabled Research Group within the MIT Media Lab, BryceTech and the University of Texas at Austin, have all initiated the Space Sustainability Rating (SSR) as an additional instrument to reduce space debris and ensure safe and sustainable management of rapidly increasing space exploration missions. This could become an instrument providing space service providers with future benefits in terms of lending or insurance, subject to their demonstration of certain standards in the project implementation. Participation in the rating is on a voluntary basis for spacecraft operators, launch service providers and satellite manufacturers. In

59 See the Preamble of UN document A/74/20, Annex II.

60 United Nations Office for Outer Space Affairs, UN Office for Outer Space Affairs and United Kingdom reinforce cooperation to promote space sustainability – Press release, UNIS/OS/560, 27 October 2021.

61 Beate Sjåfjell, Sustainable Value Creation Within Planetary Boundaries—Reforming Corporate Purpose and Duties of the Corporate Board Sustainability, SUSTAINABILITY 12, no. 15, 6245, 2020.

terms of the rating process, stakeholders can receive one out of four certification levels to prove the sustainability level of their missions. The Space Center at the Swiss Federal Institute of Technology Lausanne (EPFL) has been selected to lead and operate the SSR. Among those companies already expressing support are, for example, Airbus, Astroscale, SpaceX, Planet and Lockheed Martin.[62]

31.5.1 National implementation of international guidelines

National implementation of soft law norms does not only lead to the desired effect in reaching out to a broader range of actors beyond the initial addressees; it also provides for a predictable and certain framework for commercial operators. The text of the Guidelines makes clear that it is up to the discretion of states if and how an implementation can be realised.[63]

Even though such instruments are by nature voluntary, the necessary highest level of compliance can only be achieved through their implementation. The importance of national implementation is reiterated through the establishment of a follow-up WG, mandated to work on three pillars, one of which is the sharing of experiences, practices and lessons learned from voluntary national implementation of the adopted Guidelines.[64]

In this exercise, states are requested to assess their own capabilities of implementing these norms. Paragraph 17 of the Guidelines, addressing those states with greater capabilities to put enhanced efforts into implementation, is worth recalling. This is not an obligation, but rather an appeal to the collective and individual interest of all space actors. While states may freely decide for or against the whole or to only partly implement certain guidelines, they may also opt to reference the guidelines as a minimum standard or a basis for stronger national regulation.[65]

The two main categories of implementation are (i) hard and (ii) soft implementation. Both consist of a toolbox with different measures to ensure high compliance levels to turn political willingness into concrete action. In case of the LTS Guidelines the implementation toolboxes translate into the following concrete measures:

a) **Recognition of the Guidelines and/or its objective** to conduct space activities in a manner as to ensure equitable access to the benefits of the exploration and use of outer space for peaceful purposes, in order to meet the needs of the present generations while preserving the outer space environment for future generations. This can be realised through formal government statements at COPUOS level;
b) **Active contribution to development and evolution of the Guidelines** through active engagement in the work of the WG by sharing implementation experiences, associated chances and challenges;

62 For more information on the SSR, please consult the SSR Website.

63 UN document A/74/20, Annex II, para. 16.

64 Terms of reference, methods of work and workplan of the Working Group on the Long-term Sustainability of Outer Space Activities, para. 4(b)) as appended to the Report of the Working Group on the Long-term Sustainability of Outer Space Activities, UN document A/AC.105/C.1/LTS/2022/L.1 and UN document A/AC.105/L.318/Add.4, para. 6, 9, 15, 16–20.

65 See: UN document A/74/20, Annex II, para. 11; in a similar vein, s 3 of the COPUOS Space Debris Mitigation Guidelines entail a similar possibility, i.e. "It is also recognized that exceptions to the implementation of individual guidelines or elements thereof may be justified, for example, by the provisions of the United Nations treaties and principles on outer space", see UN document A/RES/62/217*.

c) **Soft implementation** through the adoption of national policies, standards, codes of conduct, and guidelines;
d) **Hard implementation** through national legislation and related references of courts to these legislations.

The most prominent implementation tool might be letter (d). While it can be argued that it has a stronger enforceable effect on a wider range of actors, including private industry, one also has to consider its underlying complex and time-consuming legislative processes. Furthermore, the in contrast to other soft law, the Guidelines address an extensive variety of topics, ranging from radio frequency (A.4) and conjunction assessments to space debris management (B.4), capacity building (C.4), and (D.2) new measures to manage the space debris population in the long-term. As such, they cover different technical and political objectives at the same time. Hence, they require dynamic assessment of the current state of the art and respective modifications of national requirements to keep up with ongoing developments in the space sector. According to Tapio and Soucek: "It is equally evident that much of the LTS Guidelines content [...] due to their heterogenous nature [...] will require different types of State action, and at appropriate level".[66]

National space legislation typically provides, among others, requirements for authorization and continuous supervision, space debris mitigation,[67] registration, and safety considerations. Since private actors are bound by the respective national jurisdiction, space legislation provides the respective state with strong enforcement mechanisms in case of non-compliance. This can result in the denial of a launch authorisation or even in court proceedings. In contrast, standards as contained, e.g. in product assurance and safety requirements may only be applicable to a limited number of addressees, namely those conducting projects procured by governments and/or space agencies. However, these soft instruments tend to be more specific than the aforementioned legislative acts. A comparison can be made with the example of space debris mitigation. While national space acts usually contain wording like "the operator shall seek to ensure that space activities do not generate space debris [...] reduce the risks of in-orbit break-ups and in-orbit collision",[68] implementing rules and space sustainability requirements for space projects tend to set forth concrete design and operational measures (e.g., reducing mission-related debris), passivation measures (e.g., discharging batteries), disposal measures (e.g., through controlled re-entry of LEO satellites and transfer of GEO spacecrafts into graveyard orbit after mission completion), and re-entry safety measures.[69]

66 Jenni Tapio and Alexander Soucek, National Implementation of Non-legally Binding Instruments: Managing Uncertainty in Space Law?, Volume 44, no.6 of AIR & SPACE LAW (2019), at 580.

67 In these cases, often complemented by more concrete technical parameters set forth in mission safety requirements.

68 See only as an example of the different national space laws: s 10 of the Finnish Act on Space Activities.

69 Germany e.g. reported on the adaptation of very specific project requirements with respect to space debris mitigation in the frame of its "Product Assurance and Safety Requirements for DLR Space Projects" on the recent example of the EnMAP Earth observation mission. Compliance with these requirements is ensured through monitoring and formal verification by the German Space Agency. In the particular case of the EnMAP mission the applicable space debris mitigation requirements were decided to be adapted when the project had already well progressed to ensure compliance to the latest internationally agreed standards and guidelines and to better reflect the current space debris situation. Recently, the German Space Agency further improved space debris mitigation in DLR supported small satellite projects at universities and research institutes by ensuring that the mitigation measures are implemented as mandatory requirements also in research grants for space missions, see Promoting Space Sustainability Case Studies.

It is important to reiterate, that the purpose of this chapter is not to give preference to one or the other means of national implementation. As indicated above, different levels of implementation are very often used in a complementary fashion to facilitate the desired effect of the Guidelines.

Member States have already started to exchange information on their implementation practices through various channels. The Committee's Member States, observer organisations, and private entities have actively contributed to the UNOOSA Promoting Space Sustainability Project.[70] This is strongly supported by the United Kingdom and aims to showcase implementation of the guidelines through a multi-stakeholder approach. Stakeholders are also invited to contribute case studies reporting on specific steps of implementation. As a second phase of the project, anonymous interviews with Member States, served as the basis for a report by UNOOSA and the United Kingdom to support Member States in their WG discussions. The foregoing already gives a clear indication that actors are highly interested and actively engaged in implementing all four chapters of the Guidelines timely and to a greatest extend.

31.5.2 Implementation through multilateral cooperation

Long-term sustainability cannot be ensured by a single state alone; international cooperation is the key to spreading the benefits of space to everyone, and requires each and every space-related actor to contribute to this end.

The text of the Guidelines booklet itself reiterates this, stating that:

> *International cooperation is required to implement* the guidelines effectively, to *monitor* their impact and effectiveness and to *ensure that*, as space activities evolve, *they continue to reflect the most current state of knowledge* of pertinent factors influencing the long-term sustainability of outer space activities (emphasis added).[71]

States are actively using international channels for a continued coordination and exchange on pressing issues, such as sustainability in space. As discussed below, states can use these to further develop measures for sustainable space activities, by providing (regulatory) framework conditions for private operators.

31.5.2.1 European fora

Space Summit to confirm their commitment towards safe, sustainable, and economically successful European space endeavours. The ESA Director General presented his vision for Europe of revolutionising space activities, to facilitate a green, digital, safe, and inclusive environment, whilst cooperating closely with industry. Based on recommendations by a High-Level-Advisory Group, the Space Summit endorsed the three "accelerators", i.e. Space for a Green Future, Rapid and Resilient Crisis Response, and Protection of Space Assets. In addition, two "Inspirators" are intended to substantiate new European exploration ambitions. The focus on sustainable activities

70 The UNOOSA/UK Promoting Space Sustainability project addresses Category C of the Guidelines aiming at capacity-building and awareness raising in the field of sustainable space activities. In general, UNOOSA is increasingly building up several initiatives with international partners for this purpose, such as Space4SDGS, Space Law for New Space Actors Project, the Access to Space for All initiative, the Space Economy Initiative, and the space debris infographics and podcasts.

71 See LTS Guidelines Booklet, UNOOSA (2021), p. 5.

was repeatedly emphasised. ESA's ClearSpace-1 mission[72] will be a clear case of realisation of the future green objectives, mandated for a pioneering mission to clean up space with technologies needed for future commercial debris removal. The mission is intended to be conducted by the spin-off company ClearSpace, established by an experienced EPFL researcher team under a contract for services. ESA Member States have endorsed a mission that contributes to a more sustainable space environment in line with Guideline D.2, while supporting new business models and innovative technologies. In general, Member States can contribute to the implementation of numerous Guidelines through their ESA funding involvement, e.g. Guidelines A.2, B.1, B.2, B.4, B.5, B.7, B.8, B.9, C.1, D.2.[73]

In the field of collision avoidance services, the European Space Surveillance and Tracking (EU SST) was established in 2014 by Decision 541/2014/EU of the European Parliament and the Council. The SST Consortium is composed of seven Member States, namely Germany, France, Italy, Romania, Poland, Portugal, and Spain. Starting in 2016, the Consortium, together with the European Union Satellite Centre (SatCen) joined forces for the SST Cooperation. Meanwhile, it is providing SST services for risk assessment of in-orbit collisions, fragmentations, and uncontrolled re-entries, to all EU countries, institutions, operators, and civil protection authorities. EU industry is not only benefitting from the SST services, but also directly involved in the capabilities required through participation in EU SST call for tenders. As an outcome, almost three-quarters of the EU funds for this purpose are sub-contracted to industry, while only around one-fourth is accounted to the EU SST consortium.[74]

The last example provided in this section is the European Cooperation for Space Standardization (ECSS), established in 1993, to develop a coherent, single set of user-friendly standards covering all European space activities. It is a collaboration of ESA, numerous national space agencies and the European industry representative, Eurospace. Industry representatives initiated ECSS as a follow-up to ESA's "Procedures, Specification and Standards (PSS)" systems to harmonise European space product assurance standardisation.[75] This highlights industry's willingness to take an active role in shaping standardisation processes, which have a big impact on their daily work. The four space companies currently possessing voting rights within ECSS are Airbus Defence and Space, Ariane Group, OHB System, and Thales Alenia Space, all of them private commercial actors with extensive experience in the field of space activities. ECSS documents are applicable through bilateral legal agreements, such as business contracts.[76] Awareness-raising measures are another important part of the ECSS efforts to promote the standards within Europe and on a global scale.

31.5.2.2 International fora

COPUOS Member States are actively involved in UNOOSA initiatives and programmes through the Committee's and both Subcommittees' sessions and WGs. Recognising the international

72 European Space Agency, ESA commissions world's first space debris removal, 9 December 2019.

73 For more details relating to the ESA implementation practice, see: UN document A/AC.105/C.1/2022/CRP.14/Rev.1.

74 High Representative of the Union for Foreign Affairs and Security Policy, An EU Approach for Space Traffic Management - An EU contribution addressing a global challenge, 15 February 2022, JOIN(2022) 4 final, p. 8.

75 W. Kriedte, Y. El Gammal, A New Approach to European Space Standards, Volume 81 of ESA Bulletin, 1995, at 38–43.

76 European Cooperation for Standardisation, ECSS-S-ST-00C, Rev.1, Descriptions, implementation and general requirements, 15 June 2000.

nature associated e.g. with the risks resulting from space debris, a number of states is also actively involved through diverse representation in international fora, including the IADC through agencies, the International Organization for Standardisation (ISO) through national standardisation organisations and/or academic committees, like the International Academy of Astronautics space debris committee and the International Astronautical Federation's security committee. The IADC might be one of the most prominent examples of these fora. It recently issued three updated documents, including its worldwide recognised IADC Space Debris Mitigation Guidelines. Moreover, it updates COPUOS on its activities through technical presentations and informed the International Committee on Global Navigation Satellite Systems (ICG) about study results on disposal options for satellites in Medium Earth Orbits. The IADC Guidelines provide one of the fundamental inputs to the ISO space debris mitigation requirements, which is a top-level standard, i.e. ISO 24113 (space systems – space debris mitigation requirements). The ISO WG in charge of this, "WG7", formerly entitled "Orbital Debris Coordination Working Group", continues to review and amend these requirements to ensure their validity given the fast pace of developments in the global space industry. It gathers members of commercial space industry, governments, space agencies, academia, and the ECSS.

Additional international dialogue on aspects of long-term sustainability is conducted, *inter alia*, in the COSPAR, the International Asteroid Warning Network (IAWN) and the Space Mission Planning Advisory Group (SMPAG) on Near Earth Objects (NEO) matters and in the Pan-European Consortium for Aviation Space Weather User Services (PECASUS) consortium, which supports civil aviation with space weather information.

31.6 Closing comments and outlook

Over the years, space activities have become indispensable for society. The provision of space-based data, services, technology and applications fosters industrial progress, provides the backbone of the information age, and bears tremendous relevance in tackling challenges of our time. An encouraging sign for the great potential of driving innovation, technical progress, and prosperity from space activities are indicators of how the benefits of space are brought closer to society. At the same time, the number of human-made objects orbiting in already densely populated Earth's orbits, has been increasing since the beginning of the NewSpace era. As space debris accumulates in certain orbital regions, the number of close encounters between operational space objects and space debris is rising. Collision avoidance manoeuvres are happening on a more regular basis than ever before. Ensuring the long-term sustainability of space activities concerns public and private actors alike. It is not only an ethical or idealistic question, but also one that secures massive investments in space upstream and downstream infrastructures. Each and every stakeholder should feel encouraged by the common efforts to promote international cooperation for socioeconomic development and for addressing global challenges. Space is international by legal status and by actual use. We know from experience that effective steps can only be achieved in this direction on the basis of close multilateral cooperation, dialogue, and awareness raising. It is in the collective interest of all peaceful space-faring and space-using nations to encourage the long-term sustainable, safe and responsible use of space. This chapter calls on all parts of space actors for:

- implementation of the Guidelines and the Space2030 Agenda to the greatest extend feasible and practicable – hard and soft law alike can influence the effectiveness of the instruments in different, but mutually influencing manner;

- sincere, intelligent, and visionary multilateral dialogue between all stakeholders, including governments, space agencies, science, and economy, at the appropriate level, with a view to enabling the huge benefits from space activities to be harvested, while avoiding legal *lacunae*;
- a coherent global approach, based on the UN space treaties and developed at the UN level in order to ensure that all space actors play by the same rules, and enjoy the benefits of space in the long-term; and
- raising awareness for what the required measures are to secure the benefits for private actors and the society as a whole. This is an important step towards acceptance and visible commitment of the private industry to contribute pro-actively to the implementation processes.

A common legal framework, with clear, transparent, and predictable measures applicable at national level, as well as responsible entrepreneurial action by all satellite operators along with the technical solutions available, can enable the space industry to grow in an ecologically and economically sustainable manner.

32

ENSURING SPACE SUSTAINABILITY THROUGH NATIONAL SPACE LEGISLATION

Ingo Baumann and Erik Pellander[1]

32.1 Introduction

In order to comply with their obligations under Art. VI of the Outer Space Treaty, states may adopt national space legislation ensuring that space activities of non-governmental entities are undertaken in conformity with obligations on the protection and preservation of the Earth and outer space environment. States may not only ensure compliance with binding obligations through national space legislation. National space legislation may also be used to give international guidelines and/or non-binding recommendations on space sustainability binding force towards commercial operators. Further, national space legislation may promote the progressive development of space and environmental law by setting requirements on space sustainability which are more ambitious than at international level. Taking into account that the sustainable use of outer space may limit the liability risk exposure of a state, national space legislation may set incentives for such sustainable use through special conditions on liability and insurance.

Potential environmental hazards caused by space activities which may be addressed by national space legislation include adverse effects on the Earth environment on ground and during the launch and re-entry phase, as well as adverse effects on the outer space environment during in-orbit operations.

Environmental hazards to the Earth environment mainly concern toxic substances in fuels, as well as effects on the Earth environment by emissions during launch and re-entry, namely global warming and ozone depletion.[2] Whilst environmental impact of fuels may be decreasing through newer and greener fuels, the growing number of launches may have increasing effects on global warming and on the ozone layer. Environmental hazards to the outer space environment mainly

1 The authors would like to thank Louise De Keghel and Katharina Prall, Research Associates at BHO Legal, for their contributions to this chapter.

2 *Erik J. L. Larson, Robert W. Portmann et al.*: Global atmospheric response to emissions from a proposed reusable space launch system, in Earth's Future, Volume 5 Issue 1, 2017, pp. 37–48.

DOI: 10.4324/9781003268475-47

concern space debris. The development of a lunar economy or space resource exploitation may create impacts on the environment of celestial bodies.

This chapter analyses whether and to what extent national space legislation may serve as a tool to address these concerns by

- flowing down international obligations to non-governmental entities (32.2),
- giving non-binding instruments at international level binding force towards non-governmental entities at national level (32.3),
- setting requirements at national level which are more ambitious than at international level (32.4),
- setting incentives for the sustainable use of outer space (32.5).

32.2 National space legislation as a tool to implement obligations under international law to protect and preserve the Earth and outer space environment

Bearing in mind that states are, according to Art. VI of the Outer Space Treaty, responsible for the space activities of their non-governmental entities and that they are under the obligation to ensure that such activities are undertaken in conformity with international law, there is a need to flow down international obligations on the protection and preservation of the Earth and the outer space environment to non-governmental entities. This is usually implemented through conditions on authorisation and by supervising compliance therewith. Relevant obligations may either derive from international environmental law or from international space law, both including international treaty law as well as customary international law.

32.2.1 Environmental law

32.2.1.1 Specific treaty law

As for effects of launch and re-entry on the Earth environment, the United Nations Framework Convention on Climate Change,[3] as well as the underlying Paris Agreement[4] are generally applicable. This framework sets long-term goals to guide all nations in reducing global greenhouse gas emissions to limit global warming. It is up to the parties to specify emission targets – so called nationally determined contributions. Whether and to what extent a state takes measures to reduce emissions from launch and re-entry of space objects within the framework of such nationally determined contributions is left to the discretion of the respective contracting party.

As regards potential ozone depletion, the applicable treaty law – the Vienna Convention for the Protection of the Ozone Layer[5] and its underlying Montreal Protocol[6] – does not yet cover emissions during launch and re-entry. Accordingly, states are not yet under obligation to limit such emissions through measures at national level. However, the Montreal Protocol provides a flexible legal framework that is regularly adapted to new emission sources. There are growing claims

3 United Nations Framework Convention on Climate Change, 9 May 1992, 1771 UNTS 107.

4 Paris Agreement to the United Nations Framework Convention on Climate Change, 12 December 2015, T.I.A.S. No. 16-1104.

5 Vienna Convention for the Protection of the Ozone Layer, 12 March 2015, T.I.A.S. No. 11097.

6 Montreal Protocol on Substances that Deplete the Ozone Layer, 16 September 1987, 1522 UNTS 3.

that launch and re-entry emissions causing ozone depletion should be added to the scope of the Montreal Protocol.[7]

In relation to environmental hazards during in-orbit operations, states have not yet adopted any particular treaties in the area of environmental law.

32.2.1.2 Principles of customary international environmental law

For hazards to both Earth and outer space environment, several principles of international environmental law acknowledged under customary international law may become relevant.

Under the general obligation not to cause transboundary harm, states are obliged to ensure that activities within their jurisdiction or control do not cause damage to the environment of other states or of areas beyond national jurisdiction.[8] In the context of space activities, this implies that states should ensure that space activities under their jurisdiction and control (including those undertaken by non-governmental entities) do not cause damage

- to the terrestrial environment of other states,
- to areas beyond national jurisdiction on Earth such as the high seas, or
- to the outer space environment.

Under the principle of sustainable development, development shall meet the needs of the present without compromising the ability of future generations to meet their own needs.[9] In order to comply with this principle, states shall ensure development of a space industry in a way so as to equitably meet developmental and environmental needs of present and future generations.[10] As regards emissions during launch and re-entry, this implies the obligation to limit global warming and ozone depletion caused thereby. In relation to the environmental hazards during in-orbit operations, the principle of sustainability implies the obligations

- to limit space debris so as to make orbits accessible for future generations,
- exploit space resources in a way so as to ensure that future generations may use such resources,
- undertake exploration and use of celestial bodies so as to ensure accessibility for future generations.

The precautionary principle establishes the obligation to adopt precautionary measures when scientific evidence about an environmental or human health hazard is uncertain and the stakes are high.[11] For space activities, this principle becomes in particular relevant for novel space activities

7 *Martin Ross*: Implications of a Growing Spaceflight Industry: Climate Change, Aerospace, 15 June 2022.

8 Declaration of the United Nations Conference on the Human Environment (Stockholm Declaration), 16 June 1972, Principle 21; Rio Declaration on Environment and Development (Rio Declaration), UN Doc. A/CONF.151/26 (Vol. I), 14 June 1992, Principle 2.

9 Stockholm Declaration, Principle 1; Rio Declaration, Principle 3; Legality of the Threat of Nuclear Weapons, Advisory Opinion, I.C.J. Rep. 1996, p. 226, para. 29.

10 Id.

11 Rio Declaration, Principle 15; Treaty on the Functioning of the European Union (TFEU), OJ C 326, 26.10.2012, pp. 47–390, Art. 191(2); European Parliament, The precautionary principle – Definitions, applications and governance, December 2015; recognised by the International Court of Justice as "a trend towards making this approach part of

for which environmental impacts cannot yet be fully assessed. Taking into account the ultra-hazardous nature of space activities, states may not avoid adopting precautionary measures in relation to novel space activities or requiring non-governmental to adopt such measures, respectively, on the grounds that the effect of such space activities on the Earth or the outers space environment are not yet fully clear.

Under the obligation to undertake an environmental impact assessment, states are obliged to assess adverse impacts to the environment of industrial activities which pose a risk of significant environmental damage.[12] States may adhere to this principle by undertaking such assessments with a view to effects on the Earth and the outer space environment in the course of authorisation procedures under national space legislation. Non-governmental entities may be required to conduct such assessments in advance of their planned space activities.

32.2.2 International space law

Regarding the protection of the terrestrial environment, Art. IX sentence 2 of the Outer Space Treaty stipulates that states should avoid "adverse changes in the environment of the Earth resulting from the introduction of extraterrestrial matter and, where necessary, shall adopt appropriate measures for this purpose".

As for the protection of the outer space environment, Art. IX sentence 2 of the Outer Space Treaty provides that "States Parties to the Treaty shall pursue studies of outer space, including the moon and other celestial bodies, and conduct exploration of them so as to avoid their harmful contamination [...] and, where necessary, shall adopt appropriate measures for this purpose". It is however rather difficult to derive legally binding obligations of states from this wording. At best, this article provides for a general obligation of due diligence to avoid the contamination of the outer space environment, e.g., through space debris.[13] The scope of this duty of due diligence is unclear. It needs to be determined according to the state of the art in science and technology as reflected in various international recommendations, guidelines, and technical standards.[14]

Under Art. IX sentence 1 of the Outer Space Treaty, states shall "conduct all their activities in outer space, including the moon and other celestial bodies, with due regard to the corresponding interests of all other States Parties to the Treaty". This implies the obligation not to impair the corresponding interests of other states by causing damage to the Earth or the outer space environment.

32.2.3 Implementation through national space legislation

States may implement the international obligations highlighted above by setting conditions for granting an authorisation in their national space legislation. They shall supervise compliance with such obligations once an authorisation was granted.

There are several potential approaches in this respect. States may

customary law" in *Pulp Mills on the River Uruguay (Argentina v. Uruguay)* Judgment, I.C.J. Reports 2010, p. 14, para. 135.

12 *Pulp Mills, supra.* note 10, para. 204.

13 *Sergio Marchisio*, "Article IX" in Stephan Hobe, Bernhard Schmidt-Tedd & Kai-Uwe Schrogl (eds.), Cologne Commentary on Space Law Volume I, 2009, p. 177.

14 *Alan Boyle*, "Outer Space and International Environmental Law" in Stephan Hobe & Steven Freeland (eds.), In Heaven as on Earth? The Interaction of Public International Law on the Legal Regulation of Outer Space, 2013, p. 359.

- set the general condition that non-governmental entities shall comply with the international obligations of the state regarding protection and preservation of the Earth and outer space environment,
- refer to particular treaty provisions or principles in conditions for authorisation, or
- prescribe detailed measures of implementation.

These approaches do not necessarily exclude each other, they may also be employed in parallel.

In the following, selected state practice is highlighted. This does not aim to provide a comprehensive overview, but rather to illustrate different approaches how to ensure that non-governmental entities comply with international obligations of a state on the protection and preservation of the Earth and the outer space environment.

Almost all national space laws set the condition for authorisation that non-governmental entities shall comply with international obligations of the state granting the authorisation. In principle, this requires also compliance with the treaties and principles on the protection and preservation of the Earth and the outer space environment highlighted above. Several laws describe which treaties and/or principles are of particular relevance.

A quite common condition for authorisation is the requirement to undertake an environmental impact assessment. For example, the UK's Space Industry Act 2018 provides, under Section 11(2), that the regulator may not grant an application for a licence unless the applicant has submitted an assessment of environmental effects. This is defined in Section 11(3) as "an assessment of the effects that launches of spacecrafts or carrier aircrafts from the spaceport in question, or launches of spacecraft from carrier aircraft launched from the spaceport, are expected to have on the environment".

Under the Finnish Act on Space Activities,[15] an applicant for an authorisation is required to submit an environmental impact assessment, as well as "a plan for measures to counter and reduce adverse environmental impacts".[16] The Finnish act serves as a rare example for explicit references to the principle of sustainable development. Article 10 of the Act on Space Activities provides that operators shall carry out their space activities in an environmentally sustainable manner and promote the sustainable use of outer space.

According to Section 7 of the Danish Executive Order on Requirements in Connection with Approval of Activities in Outer Space, which specifies the general obligation under Section 6(5) to carry out space activities in an environmentally safe manner, the licensing authority "may stipulate requirements, and request a description of: 1) the environmental impact of the space activity on the Earth and the atmosphere, e.g. specifying the technology, components, manufacturing processes and products applied; 2) the potential environmental impact in outer space of the space activity, and 3) the operator's measures to minimize the impact on the environment on the Earth, in the atmosphere and in outer space".

Many national space laws specify that the international obligations to be complied with in particular concern the UN space treaties (or some of them). Some laws explicitly refer to Art. IX of the Outer Space Treaty. France, for example, requires adherence with certain planetary protection standards "for the implementation of Article IX of the Treaty on Principles Governing the Activities of States in the Exploration and Use of Outer Space", under Art. 26 of the Arrêté on

15 Act on Space Activities (63/2018).
16 Id., s 10 sentence 2.

technical regulation.[17] Austria does not explicitly mention Art. IX of the Outer Space Treaty, but uses nearly the same wording: authorisation of space activities requires that "the space activity does not cause harmful contamination of outer space or celestial bodies or adverse changes in the environment".[18]

32.3 National space legislation as a tool to give guidelines and standards binding force towards commercial operators

Apart from implementing international obligations of states on the protection and preservation of the Earth and the outer space environment, national space legislation may serve as a tool to give relevant non-binding international guidelines, recommendations and technical standards binding force towards commercial operators.

32.3.1 Existing international guidelines and technical standards

International guidelines and standards pertaining to aspects relevant for space sustainability mainly concern the IADC Space Debris Mitigation Guidelines, several sets of UN Guidelines, technical standards by the International Organization for Standardization (ISO), and the COSPAR Policy on Planetary Protection.

32.3.1.1 IADC Space Debris Mitigation Guidelines

In 2002, leading space agencies in the Inter-Agency Space Debris Coordination Committee (IADC) developed guidelines for space debris.[19] The IADC Space Debris Mitigation Guidelines apply to mission planning as well as to the design and operation of satellites and upper stages.[20] They describe existing practices that are appropriate for reducing the generation of space debris. Emphasis is placed on limiting debris released during normal operations (Section 5.1), minimising the potential for orbital abortions (Section 5.2), post-mission disposal of space debris (Section 5.3), and orbital collision prevention (Section 5.4).

The committee developed the concept of "protected regions" in space. These regions include the low-Earth Orbit (LEO) and the geostationary Earth orbit (GEO). Efforts to mitigate space debris are intended to relieve and protect in particular these orbits. In GEO, spacecrafts that have terminated their missions are to be maneuvered into orbits outside the protected region. These are also known as graveyard orbits. In LEO, a spacecraft or orbital stage terminating their operational phases should be de-orbited or, where appropriate, maneuvered into an orbit with an expected residual orbital lifetime of 25 years or shorter. The probability of success of disposal should be at least 90%. For certain missions, such as large constellations, a shorter residual orbital lifetime and/

17 Arrêté du 31 mars 2011 relatif à la réglementation technique en application du décret n° 2009-643 du 9 juin 2009 relatif aux autorisations délivrées en application de la loi n° 2008-518 du 3 juin 2008 relative aux opérations spatiales.

18 Austrian Federal Law on the Authorisation of Space Activities and the Establishment of a National Space Registry, adopted by the National Council on 6 December 2011, entered into force on 28 December 2011, § 4. (1) No. 5.

19 *Peter Stubbe*, "UN Space Debris Mitigation Guidelines" in Stephan Hobe, Bernhard Schmidt-Tedd & Kai-Uwe Schrogl (eds.), Cologne Commentary on Space Law Volume III, 2015, p. 624.

20 IADC Space Debris Mitigation Guidelines, IADC-02-01 Rev. 3, June 2021.

or a higher probability of success may be required. Retrieval is also acknowledged as a disposal option.

32.3.1.2 UN Guidelines

The UN has developed several sets of guidelines pertaining to aspects relevant for space sustainability, such as the UN principles relevant to the Use of Nuclear Power Sources in Outer Space, the UN Space Debris Mitigation Guidelines, and the UN Guidelines for the Long-Term Sustainability of Space Activities.

32.3.1.2.1 THE UN PRINCIPLES RELEVANT TO THE USE OF NUCLEAR POWER SOURCES IN OUTER SPACE

The UN Principles relevant to the Use of Nuclear Power Sources in Outer Space (NPS Principles) address the safe use of nuclear power sources in outer space, in order not to contaminate the Earth's environment.[21] These Principles were adopted in 1993, after the satellite Cosmos 954 of the Soviet Union had a malfunction during re-entry and scattered radioactive debris over northern Canada. According to these Principles, the launching state has to perform a safety assessment prior to the launch of a space object which uses nuclear power (Principle 4) and has to notify the international community in case of a re-entry of such space object (Principle 5). However, these Principles only apply to nuclear power sources that are used for electricity generation.[22] Space objects that use nuclear power sources for propulsion purposes are not covered by this framework.

32.3.1.2.2 THE UN SPACE DEBRIS MITIGATION GUIDELINES

In 2007, the United Nations Committee on the Peaceful Uses of Outer Space (UNCOPUOS) adopted Space Debris Mitigation Guidelines[23] which are based on the IADC Guidelines, but deliberately go into less technical detail.[24]

Like the IADC Guidelines, the UN Guidelines aim to limit debris released during normal operations,[25] minimise the potential for break-offs in Earth orbit,[26] dispose of space debris after the mission,[27] and prevent in-orbit collisions.[28] The guidelines also adopt the concept of protected regions in LEO and GEO.

21 *Marchisio, supra* note 12, p. 176.

22 Principles Relevant to the Use of Nuclear Power Sources in Outer Space, United Nations General Assembly Resolution 47/68: "this set of Principles applies to nuclear power sources in outer space devoted to the generation of electric power on board space objects for non-propulsive purposes".

23 Space Debris Mitigation Guidelines of the Committee on the Peaceful Uses of Outer Space, A/62/20, Annex, 2007,

24 *Lotta Viikari*, "Environmental Aspects of Space Activities" in Frans von der Dunk & Fabio Tronchetti (eds.), Handbook of Space Law, 2017, p. 742.

25 Space Debris Mitigation Guidelines of the Committee on the Peaceful Uses of Outer Space, *supra* note 22, Guideline 1 Limit debris released during normal operations.

26 Id., Guideline 2.

27 Id., Guideline 3.

28 Id., Guideline 6 and 7.

By Resolution 62/217 of 22 December 2007,[29] the UN General Assembly endorsed the guidelines and agreed that they reflect existing practices developed by a number of national and international organisations. It called on Member States to implement them through appropriate national mechanisms. It also recalled that international cooperation is needed to extend appropriate strategies for minimising the impact of space debris to future space missions.

32.3.1.2.3 THE UN GUIDELINES FOR THE LONG-TERM SUSTAINABILITY OF SPACE ACTIVITIES

The 2019 Guidelines for the Long-Term Sustainability of Space Activities,[30] adopted by UNCOPUOS, deal with environmental protection and sustainability in space in a much broader sense than the previous guidelines on space debris. The Guidelines address policy and regulatory frameworks for space activities, safety of space operations, international cooperation, capacity building and awareness, and scientific and technical research and development.

The guidelines are voluntary and not legally binding under international law, but any action taken to implement them should be consistent with applicable principles and norms of international law. Nothing in the Guidelines should constitute a revision, limitation, or reinterpretation of those principles and norms. Nothing in the Guidelines should be interpreted as creating a new legal obligation for states.

Guidelines A.1, 2, and 3 call upon states and international intergovernmental organisations to develop or adapt national regulatory frameworks for space activities. Guideline A.2 lists a number of provisions that states and international intergovernmental organisations should consider in developing these frameworks, such as the UN Space Debris Mitigation Guidelines and the Principles Relevant to the Use of Nuclear Power Sources in Outer Space.

Guidelines B.1, 2, and 3 provide detailed recommendations for improving the exchange of information and data on the space situation, space activities, aborts, collision hazards, or uncontrolled re-entry of objects, and for strengthening the coordination of actions.

Part C includes more general recommendations for improving international cooperation, building knowledge and capabilities, and raising awareness of space activities. Part D addresses research and development.

On their implementation, the Guidelines provide that states and international intergovernmental organisations should take voluntary action through their respective national or other applicable mechanisms to ensure that the Guidelines are implemented to the maximum extent possible, consistent with their respective needs, conditions, and capabilities, as well as their existing obligations under applicable international law, including the provisions of applicable United Nations treaties and principles on outer space. States and international organisations are encouraged to use existing procedures and, if necessary, to establish new procedures to meet the requirements associated with the Guidelines. In implementing the Guidelines, states should be guided by the principle of cooperation and mutual assistance and should conduct all their activities in outer space with due regard to the corresponding interests of other states.

29 United Nations General Assembly Resolution 62/217, International Cooperation in the Peaceful Uses of Outer Space.

30 Guidelines for the Long-term Sustainability of Outer Space Activities of the Committee on the Peaceful Uses of Outer Space, A/74/20, Annex II, 2018.

32.3.1.3 ISO Standards

The International Organization for Standardization (ISO) has developed several technical standards pertaining to aspects relevant for space sustainability.

32.3.1.3.1 ISO 24113 "SPACE SYSTEMS – SPACE DEBRIS MITIGATION REQUIREMENTS"

ISO standard 24113 "Space systems – Space debris mitigation requirements"[31] "defines the primary space debris mitigation requirements applicable to all elements of unmanned systems launched into, or passing through, near-Earth space, including launch vehicle orbital stages, operating spacecraft and any objects released as part of normal operations".[32] The technical requirements of the standard address the limitation of debris released during normal operations, the minimisation of break-offs, and the disposal of space debris after the end of the mission. For the design of the mission, the standard requires the establishment of a space debris reduction plan.

32.3.1.3.2 ISO STANDARD TR 16158 "SPACE SYSTEMS – AVOIDING COLLISIONS WITH ORBITING OBJECTS"

ISO standard TR 16158 "Space systems – avoiding collisions with orbiting objects"[33] describes some widely used techniques for sensing approaches, estimating collision probabilities, estimating cumulative survival probabilities, and performing manoeuvres to avoid collisions.

32.3.1.3.3 ISO STANDARD 24330 "SPACE SYSTEMS – RENDEZVOUS AND PROXIMITY OPERATIONS (RPO) AND ORBITAL MAINTENANCE (OOS) – PROGRAMMATIC PRINCIPLES AND PRACTICES"

ISO standard 24330 "Rendezvous and proximity operations (RPO) and orbital maintenance (OOS) – programmatic principles and practices" was published in August 2022.[34] Rendezvous, proximity, and maintenance operations have particular importance in combating space debris, since they enable the extension of satellite life or the disposal of satellites or debris. ISO 24330 is intended to establish responsible standards of conduct for RPO and OOS. It addresses a wide range of stakeholders, such as manufacturers, spacecraft operators, service providers or insurers.

32.3.1.4 COSPAR Policy on Planetary Protection

The Committee on Space Research (COSPAR) has, among others, the task to develop recommendations for avoiding interplanetary contamination. In accordance with this mandate, the COSPAR Policy on Planetary Protection imposes controls on interplanetary contamination in accordance with a specified range of requirements, based on the following policy statement:

> The conduct of scientific investigations of possible extra-terrestrial life forms, precursors, and remnants must not be jeopardized. In addition, the Earth must be protected from the potential hazard posed by extra-terrestrial matter carried by a spacecraft returning from an

31 ISO 24113:2019 Space systems – Space debris mitigation requirements, July 2019.

32 Id.

33 ISO/TR 16158:2021 Space systems – avoiding collisions among orbiting objects, October 2021.

34 ISO 24330:2022 Space systems – Rendezvous and Proximity Operations (RPO) and On Orbit Servicing (OOS) – Programmatic principles and practices, August 2022.

inter-planetary mission. Therefore, for certain space mission/target planet combinations, controls on contamination shall be imposed in accordance with issuances implementing this policy.[35]

32.3.2 Implementation through national space legislation

In contrast to treaty obligations, states are not bound by guidelines and standards. There is also no obligation to flow down such guidelines and standards to non-governmental entities by setting appropriate conditions for authorisation under national space legislation. However, several states (voluntarily) implement these guidelines and standards through their national space laws and thereby give them binding force towards commercial operators. In this regard, the various guidelines and standards serve as a tool for specifying the rather vague obligations under international law on the protection and preservations of the Earth and the outer space environment. On their basis, states may determine which measures are "appropriate" to avoid "harmful contamination" of the outer space environment and "adverse changes in the environment of Earth", in order to comply with their obligations under Art. IX of the Outer Space Treaty.

States may and, in practice, do employ various approaches for implementing guidelines and standards pertaining to aspects relevant for space sustainability. They may

- refer to internationally accepted guidelines and standards in general when setting requirements under national space legislation and in authorisations granted thereunder,
- explicitly refer to particular guidelines and standards,
- describe in national space legislation and authorisations granted thereunder which detailed measures are required to comply with internationally accepted guidelines and standards,
- develop their own policies, guidelines, or standards at national level.

As with the above overview on state practice on the implementation of treaties and principles through national space legislation (32.2.3), the following overview on state practice with regards to the implementation of guidelines and standards does not aim to provide a comprehensive overview, but to give some illustrative examples.

The Finnish national framework on the authorisation of space activities serves as an example for general reference to international guidelines. Under Section 10 of the Act on Space Activities, "[i]n accordance with generally accepted international guidelines, the operator shall seek to ensure that the space activities do not generate space debris". It further serves as an example for a national framework which describes detailed measures required to comply with such guidelines. Section 10 of the Act on Space Activities provides that "[i]n particular, the operator shall restrict the generation of space debris during the normal operations of the space object, reduce the risks of in-orbit break-ups and in-orbit collisions and, after the space object has completed its mission, seek to move it into a less used orbit or into the atmosphere". Section 3 of the Decree of the Ministry of Economic Affairs and Employment on Space Activities stipulates that "[t]he operator shall seek to ensure that, within 25 years from the end of the functional operating period of the space object, the space object moves or is moved into the atmosphere or is moved into an orbit where it is considered not to cause any danger or harm to other space objects or other space activities".

35 COSPAR Policy on Planetary Protection, prepared by the COSPAR Panel on Planetary Protection and approved by the COSPAR Bureau on 17 June 2020.

The national framework of the United Kingdom is another example for a generic reference to international guidelines. Under Section 2 of the Space Industry Act 2018, "[t]he regulator must exercise the regulator's functions under this Act in the way that the regulator thinks best calculated to take into account [...] any space debris mitigation guidelines issued by an international organisation in which the government of the United Kingdom is represented". Schedule 1 of the Space Activities Act 2018 provides that particular conditions may be included in licenses pertaining to "compliance with [...] space debris mitigation guidelines". From the perspective of the licensing authority, such generic approach brings the advantage of flexibility in considering developments on international level and in deciding on individual conditions of a license. From the perspective of an applicant, however, such an approach may cause uncertainty regarding the detailed implementation requirements.

France serves as an example for being more prescriptive in setting requirements on compliance with guidelines and standards on the protection of the outer space and Earth environment. Article 26 of the Arrêté on technical regulation[36] states that "[a]ny launch operator carrying out a launch to another celestial body, including or not a return of extraterrestrial matter, shall comply with the international standard "Planetary Protection Policy" published by the Committee on Space Research (COSPAR) for the implementation of Article IX of the [Outer Space Treaty], and provide evidence on its application in a planetary protection plan".

Belgium also employs a prescriptive approach to the extent that it requires that the environmental impact study to be submitted by an applicant for an authorization shall be composed, among other matters, of "a description of the technical and operational characteristics of the activity and purpose by which the operator demonstrates its compatibility with: the recommendations adopted by the United Nations Committee on the Peaceful Uses of Outer Space and published on the [Government's] website [...], insofar as these recommendations are applicable to the activities concerned".[37] At the same time, it employs a generic approach to the extent that, by such description, the operator shall demonstrate its compatibility with "where applicable, any other models or technical standards identified by the Minister prior to the application for authorization".[38]

The US serves as an example for a jurisdiction which has implemented guidelines and standards on the protection and preservation of the Earth and outer space environment through the adoption of its own policies at national level. Current FAA space debris mitigation regulations focus on end-of-launch safety. Under FAA regulations, there must be no unplanned physical contact between the vehicle or any of its components and the payload after payload separation, and the conversion of power sources to energy must not result in debris generation that could destroy the vehicle or its components.[39] The detailed regulations in the Code of Federal Regulations (CFR) also include provisions for reentry by reusable or nonreusable objects.

The FCC had already developed rules for dealing with space debris in 2004. Under those rules, applicants are required to submit detailed information about orbital use and space debris mitigation plans.[40] They required that geostationary satellites be placed in graveyard orbits at the end of

36 Arrêté du 31 mars 2011 relatif à la réglementation technique en application du décret n° 2009-643 du 9 juin 2009 relatif aux autorisations délivrées en application de la loi n° 2008-518 du 3 juin 2008 relative aux opérations spatiales.

37 Royal Decree implementing certain provisions of the Law of 17 September 2005 on the activities of launching, flight operations and guidance of space objects, Art. 8(1)(d).

38 Id.

39 14 CFR 415.39; 14 CFR 417.129 (a) and (b).

40 47 CFR 5.64; 47 CFR 25.114.

their mission in accordance with the IADC Space Debris Mitigation Guidelines, and that all satellites must unload stored power sources at the end of the mission.[41] The FCC rules on orbital debris were updated in 2020[42] and 2022.[43] The current rules are more ambitious than any internationally agreed guidelines and recommendations by requiring post-mission disposal of space objects in LEO within five years. Further details on this update are provided in the following section at 32.4.

The standard NOAA licensing conditions require that licensees must dispose of any satellite in a satisfactory manner.[44] In practice, NOAA refers in this regard to the FCC's licensing requirements regarding orbital debris and spacecraft disposal to avoid duplicative regulations, since nearly all commercial Earth observation systems also require licensing by the FCC and therefore are subject to the detailed regulations cited above.[45]

32.4 National space legislation as a tool for the progressive development of international law

States may contribute to the progressive development of international environmental and space law by setting pro-active requirements at national level that are more ambitious than internationally agreed guidelines, recommendations or standards.

The US serves as the main example in this regard. In November 2018, the FCC adopted a Notice of Proposed Rulemaking (NPRM) on a comprehensive update to its rules relating to orbital debris mitigation.[46] The introduction to the NPRM provides that "[t]he current period of innovation in the space industry has resulted and will likely continue to result in a significant increase in the number of satellites and types of operations in orbit, both of which have the potential to increase the amount of orbital debris" and that the NPRM is "designed to improve and clarify these rules based on experience gained in the satellite licensing process and on improvements in mitigation guidelines and practices, and to address the various market developments".

In April 2020, a Report and Order updating the existing rules regarding orbital debris of 2004 was issued.[47] These updates were published in the Federal Register in August 2020.[48] However, the FCC deferred adopting many of the more contentious proposed rules such as post-mission disposal timelines shorter than 25 years and was seeking additional comments through another NPRM.

In September 2022, the FCC issued a second report and order updating its rules on orbital debris through which the 25-year benchmark for post-mission disposal of space objects in LEO was shortened to five years. It elaborates that

> [w]e believe strong compliance with post-mission disposal guidelines is an effective tool that can help stabilize the orbital debris environment. Currently, it is recommended that operators

41 47 CFR 25.283.

42 Federal Communications Commission (FCC), Mitigation of Orbital Debris in the New Space Age, Report and Order and Further Notice of Proposed Rulemaking, IB Docket No. 18-313, 23 April 2020.

43 FCC, Second Report and Order, Mitigation of Orbital Debris in the New Space Age, IB Docket No. 18-313, 29 September 2022.

44 15 CFR 960.8 lit. d.

45 Department of Commerce, National Oceanic and Atmospheric Administration (NOAA), Request for comments on 15 CFR Part 960 for Licensing of Private Remote Sensing Space Systems, 20 May 2020.

46 FCC, Mitigation of Orbital Debris in the New Space Age, Notice of Proposed Rulemaking and Order on Reconsideration, IB Docket No. 18-313, 15 November 2018.

47 FCC, *supra*. note 41.

48 FCC, Mitigation of Orbital Debris in the New Space Age, Final Rule, 85 FR 52422, 25 August 2020.

with objects in LEO ensure that their spacecraft are either removed from orbit immediately post-mission or left in an orbit that will decay and re-enter Earth's atmosphere within no more than 25 years to mitigate the creation of more orbital debris. However, we believe it is no longer sustainable to leave satellites in LEO to deorbit over decades. Accordingly, in this Second Report and Order, as part of our continued efforts to mitigate the generation of orbital debris, we shorten the 25-year benchmark for post-mission disposal of space stations in LEO to five years. The regulations we adopt today are designed to ensure that the Commission's actions concerning radio communications, including licensing U.S. spacecraft and granting access to the U.S. market for non-U.S. spacecraft, promote the sustainable use of outer space without creating undue regulatory obstacles to new satellite ventures. This action by the Commission furthers the public interest in preserving viable options for future satellites and systems and the many services that those systems provide to the public.[49]

32.5 National space legislation as a tool to set incentives for the sustainable use of outer space

National space legislation regularly sets requirements on liability and insurance. While some legislations set pre-defined amounts, others foresee case-by-case decisions considering the individual liability risk exposures associated to a particular space activity. Generally speaking, liability risk exposure may be lower for space activities with special emphasis on sustainability. Special measures avoiding fragmentation, ensuring safety of operations, collision avoidance, or rapid de-orbiting can reduce the probability of damage to space objects of third parties and to the environment. At the same time, such measures may increase the costs for operators associated to the space activity.

Accordingly, States may not only set conditions for authorisation to comply with obligations under international law or non-binding guidelines and standards pertaining to aspects relevant for space sustainability. They may further set incentives to operators which take special measures regarding sustainability. One possibility for such incentives lies in applying comparably lower limits of liability and associated mandatory insurance coverage. Factors which may be taken into account for determining the individual conditions can include:

- colision-avoidance measures, including use of SST services,
- trackability and manoeuvrability of satellites,
- measures against debris propagation/malfunction during operations,
- measures ensuring rapid de-orbiting or other forms of post-mission disposal,
- on-orbit servicing such as refuelling or active debris removal.

So far, no state has implemented such approach. However, the United Kingdom is currently working on a liability and insurance scheme which acknowledges and incentivises actions taken to improve sustainability of space activities.

The Space Sustainability Rating (SSR) developed under the auspices of the World Economic Forum and activated since June 2022 may serve as a tool for lawmakers and licensing authorities in assessing the sustainability grade of a space activity. The SSR "provides a rating system

49 FCC, Mitigation of Orbital Debris in the New Space Age, Second Report and Order, IB Docket No. 18-313, 29 September 2022.

informed by transparent, data-based assessments of the level of sustainability of space missions and operations – without disclosing confidential mission data and proprietary information".[50] The rating is based on a tiered scoring systems which recognises efforts and incentivises sustainable manufacturing and operating practices. Points for this score are awarded based on the positive impact on the space environment. Accordingly, action which result in more sustainable impact receive more points. The score is based on factors such as readiness to share data, ability to verify information received, choice of orbits, collision avoidance measures, plans to remove satellites from orbit after mission completion, and launch service provider selection. Bonus points are awarded for additional measures such as de-orbit devices used to actively remove the object after its operational life has expired. Adherence to international guidelines pertaining to space sustainability is also taken into account.

Voluntary participation provides operators, launch service providers, and satellite manufacturers with an independent reference that describes the level of sustainability of their mission. By making their overall assessment publicly available, they increase transparency and highlight their approach to avoiding space debris without revealing mission-sensitive or confidential information. Such independent reference may be taken into account by lawmakers and licensing authorities when assessing the sustainability of a space activity for the purpose of determining conditions on liability and insurance for a particular space activity. Not to say that it may also be taken into account when assessing compliance with conditions for an authorisation on space sustainability.

32.6 Summary and outlook

At times when international law-making is confined to adopting non-binding guidelines, recommendations, and standards, national space legislation gains importance. Non-binding international instruments pertaining to space sustainability and environmental protection may become binding for commercial operators through provisions in national space law or through conditions in individual licenses. National space legislation may even promote the progressive development of international environmental and space law by setting requirements at national level which are more ambitious than at international level.

National law makers and licensing authorities may even consider setting incentives for more sustainable use of outer space, namely when determining individual conditions on liability and insurance. Operators implementing measures on space sustainability which go beyond the conditions for authorisation may be subject to lower liability burden and associated insurance obligations.

Ambitious requirements on space sustainability under national space legislation may, at least in the short term, increase mission costs. Industry representatives in some countries have also invoked potential competitive disadvantages. However, ambitious requirements on space sustainability may, at the same time, lead to technological advancement and new business models. Among others, this includes technologies and services for refuelling, repair, lifetime extension or active debris removal.

In the long term, the overall costs of non-compliance with requirements on space sustainability, i.e. that damage to the Earth and outer space environment hinders further economic development, are in any case much higher than the costs of compliance.

50 See the SSR's homepage.

D

Outlook

33

MISSION OFF-WORLD

A technology-enabled vision for reimagining our society on Earth and beyond

Adriana Marais

33.1 Introduction

We live in an unprecedented era of development in science and technology, and the window to expand our society beyond Earth is open. However, it may not be open forever. We face immense challenges here on our home planet Earth, with our rapidly growing population and increasing resource requirements. The industry that supports the technologically enabled lifestyles of some is having an impact on our life-support system, while much of the population lives in relative poverty without access to either clean water and air and nutritious food, or to the reliable power and communication systems essential to participate meaningfully in this era.

The focus of space exploration has to date been largely on developing the technologies required to get there and investigate. Escape from the gravitational field of Earth is resource intensive, and as our activity increases, the utilisation of space resources to maintain, repair, or develop technologies for use in space is a topic of discussion. Furthermore, our ability to establish human communities, with their own resource requirements, on the Moon, Mars, and beyond is within reach. Both of these scenarios open up a new set of challenges in terms of the frameworks required to regulate such resource extraction beyond Earth, as well as the systems according to which communities living beyond Earth may manage themselves and their resources. Thus far, we have extended national systems of regulation and governance into activities in space, with international treaties regulating some aspects of global significance.

However, our track record here on Earth of managing our resources and society begs the question, can we do better? Preparing to expand our society beyond Earth provides an invaluable opportunity to rethink the fundamental principles on which we have structured ourselves. Currently existing systems have enabled us to reach this point; they have resulted in the technological capabilities that have given birth to this era. At the same time, these technologies can enable new ways of understanding ourselves and the reality in which we find ourselves. Preparing to expand beyond Earth is an important opportunity to reimagine society.

DOI: 10.4324/9781003268475-49

33.2 Technologies for off-world habitation

33.2.1 Communication

In the 1860s, scientist James Maxwell predicted that the interaction between electricity and magnetism generates an electromagnetic wave. Astoundingly, he calculated the speed of this wave to correspond to estimates of the speed of light, revealing that light is an electromagnetic wave. By the turn of the 20th century, inventor Guglielmo Marconi was sending electromagnetic radio waves across the Atlantic Ocean, establishing the basis of modern communication systems. Optical systems using visible light have high bandwidth owing to high frequencies that overcome losses typical of lower frequency radio wave transmissions. However, radio remains the effective medium for long-distance communications such as with spacecraft or technologies beyond Earth's atmosphere, which is transparent to longer wavelengths.

Exploration involves investigating novel locations, and communicating what is discovered there. While humans have only travelled as far as the Moon, the Voyager missions launched in 1977 are now almost 20 billion kilometres away in interstellar space. In the past few decades, numerous space missions have sent information back to Earth from a range of planets and moons in our Solar System. If Earth is not in direct sight, then the data can be relayed via other spacecraft, for example rovers on the surface of Mars utilise spacecraft in orbit around the planet. On Earth, a range of extremely sensitive large receivers up to 70 metres across positioned in various locations around the planet transmits received signals to the various teams on standby to receive the data.

Space communications have to date essentially been point-to-point radio wave signalling. For a total of a few dozen space probes, this has been sufficient. Recently, more countries as well as private companies are developing space exploration capabilities, and various projects are aiming to send crews to the Moon, Mars, and beyond in the coming decades. The internet, our global communications system of interconnected computer networks that use standard protocols to link billions of devices worldwide, has revolutionised the way we communicate, operate and think here on Earth. Can we achieve such a network in space?

Local networks on the surface of, for example, Mars, would be able to run similar protocols to those on which the web functions on Earth. The near side of the Moon is close enough to Earth to consider integration with the internet here. However, for activities on the far side of the Moon, or for a network enabling data sharing between probes or communities on Mars or beyond with Earth, the primary limitations are unavoidable delays and disruption of communications owing to planetary rotation as well as the finite speed of light relative to the large distances in the Solar System. Building storage capability into each communications node is a potential solution, and the testing of such delay-tolerant networks in space is already underway. As well as local storage capability in space, local computing power at each site of activity is another critical capability as we think about crews living beyond Earth.

33.2.2 Computing

Based on principles developed over decades, the first transistor was demonstrated in 1947 by physicists John Bardeen, William Shockley, and Walter Brattain, later awarded the Nobel Prize in Physics for their discovery. A transistor is an electronic component containing a semiconductor material that can both conduct and insulate current, meaning it can be used as a switch in electrical circuits. Transistors are fundamental building blocks of computers: a transistor either prevents, corresponding to the logical bit "0"; or allows, "1", current to flow through. Modern processors contain billions of transistors to perform digital calculations on an input signal according to a program, as well as to store information.

The first transistor computer was completed in 1954. By the time we were ready to go to the Moon over a decade later, computing still left a lot to be desired by modern standards: physicist Katherine Johnson did the calculations by hand for the first landing in 1969. However, crews were equipped with computers that flew most of Project Apollo, except briefly during landing. Only in the 1970s, did first generation home computers reach comparable performance levels to the Apollo Guidance Computer, which although cutting edge at the time, had less computing power than a modern USB-C charger. And today, our best supercomputer is more than 30 trillion times faster.

Traditionally, data collected in space by satellites in Earth orbit, or more remote probes, is sent to Earth to be processed. More recently, commercial high-performance computers have been sent 400 kilometres up to the International Space Station (ISS) for the first long-term demonstrations of supercomputing capabilities in space. This enables activities on the ISS that require advanced data processing, such as DNA sequencing or satellite data analysis. These computers can also connect via satellite to data centres on Earth for more demanding analysis.

An extreme example of so-called "edge computing", where data is processed locally in a remote location, is on the surface of Mars in the active rovers deployed there: Curiosity, Perseverance (US), and Zhurong (China). Signals from Mars take on average more than 10 minutes to travel to Earth, so the rovers are equipped to make some decisions locally. Both NASA rovers use processors used in desktop devices from the late 1990s with about a thousand times fewer transistors than a modern smartphone, since robustness against radiation and reliable error correction to repair any damage to data are prioritised.

The number of transistors in processors has been increasing exponentially since the invention of computing. Moore's Law tracks the associated increase in computing power as a function of time: accordingly, the speed and capability of computers can be expected to double every two years. However, we are reaching a fundamental limit to the number of transistors we can pack in, not because of technological limitations, but rather because the laws of physics will prevent transistors functioning traditionally if they are any smaller and closer together.

Beyond this limit, quantum computing offers further speed-up for certain types of problems, including the ability to solve certain open problems. Potential applications include machine learning, drug design, and modelling of complex phenomena like protein folding or climate patterns. It has been shown that a universal quantum computer would be able to crack traditional encryption systems used to keep data private. However, in the drive towards the universal quantum computer, we have only recently achieved so-called quantum supremacy, which means that state-of-the-art quantum computers can only just outperform our best supercomputers, and only for certain specific tasks. To understand the role quantum computers may play off-world, we first need to realise more advanced systems here on Earth.

33.2.3 Propulsion

The first rockets are thought to have been deployed in China a thousand years ago; fire arrows propelled by a mixture of potassium nitrate, charcoal, and sulphur, or gunpowder. Centuries later, inspired by the novels of Jules Verne, rocket scientist Konstantin Tsiolkovsky established the field of astronautics, and pioneered ideas realised and yet fantasised about, including multistage boosters, airlocks, space stations, hovercraft, and space elevators. He calculated the speeds required to orbit Earth, and proposed how this could be achieved by means of a multistage rocket fuelled by liquid oxygen and liquid hydrogen. Just 22 years after his death in 1935, the Soviets did just that and achieved the unthinkable: an artificial satellite orbiting the Earth.

Fuelled by Cold War tensions, rapid developments in space exploration took place over subsequent decades, including crews landing on the Moon and living in space stations in Earth orbit, as well as landers revealing surface conditions on neighbouring planets Venus and Mars. In terms of spacecraft, however, tried and tested designs prevailed.

A rocket is currently the only technology with which to get to Earth orbit or beyond. Traditionally, chemical rockets are used for this purpose: either solid-fuel rockets providing powerful thrust with relatively simple design; or liquid-fuel rockets using liquid propellants such as hydrogen and oxygen requiring smaller volume tanks. To get back to Earth, either a winged vehicle like the Space Shuttle or a capsule like the Soyuz is typically employed.

Billionaire Elon Musk established SpaceX in 2002 with the goal of making spaceflight routine and affordable, in order to make humans a multiplanetary species. By pioneering reusable rockets, SpaceX has already cut launch costs by an order of magnitude. It is also the first private company to deliver crew to and from the ISS. With the fully reusable Starship currently being developed, capable of delivering over 100 tons of crew or cargo to the Moon, Mars, and beyond, and back, SpaceX is on track towards achieving Musk's ambitious vision.

With existing chemical rocket technology, it takes around three days to get to the Moon, seven months to Mars and around a year to the Asteroid Belt. A speed of over 40,000 kilometres per hour is required to escape Earth's gravity, at which point, limited by the mass of fuel, propulsion systems are typically disabled, and the spacecraft continues at constant velocity through the frictionless vacuum of space.

Beyond chemical propulsion, novel systems can achieve better fuel efficiency, however, they are either not powerful enough to launch from Earth or remain developmental. For example, VASIMR's experimental plasma rocket has vastly reduced fuel requirements; if it can continuously accelerate through space, we can get to Mars in just 39 days. Accelerating at Earth's gravity for the first half of the journey, reorienting the spacecraft, and decelerating at the same rate for the remainder, would enable crews to experience Earth gravity for long duration space flights throughout the Solar System.

The Voyager missions are our first technology to venture beyond the Solar System into interstellar space. Proxima Centauri is the closest star to Earth, yet at Voyager 1's current speed of over 60,000 kilometres per hour, it is more than 70,000 years away. Even at 300,000 kilometres per second, light takes more than four years to travel there. We will need a revolution in our understanding of space-time to travel to the nearest stars in a human lifetime. So, for now, we remain confined to our Solar System.

33.2.4 Life-support

Over the past 200,000 years, Homo Sapiens have migrated far and wide around Earth; through ice ages, over mountains, across deserts and oceans, with survival tools in hand. Our planet is at just the right distance from the Sun to support liquid water, and life is a tenacious phenomenon here on Earth. The breathable air and nutritious food produced by networks of various organisms were available in sufficient quantities to support human communities in most places we went. In environments not supporting normal human function, more advanced tools were required.

In the 1800s, centuries of designs for underwater exploration culminated in the first crewed submarines. Around the same time, the first steam trains were developed. People worried that they would not be able to breathe or withstand the vibrations at such speeds, but within the next 50 years, passengers were traveling at previously unbelievable speeds of 80 kilometres per hour. By 1938, passengers in commercial aircraft were breathing pressurised air 6,000 metres up at speeds of almost 400 kilometres per hour.

After successfully launching Sputnik into space in 1957, as per Tsiolkovsky's calculations reaching a maximum speed of nearly 30,000 kilometres per hour, no time was wasted in building an additional pressurised compartment. Later the same year, the second-ever orbiting spacecraft carried Laika the dog into orbit. In 1961, cosmonaut Yuri Gagarin became the first human in space. Gagarin orbited Earth once at an altitude of around 300 km in his five-ton spacecraft, before landing safely back in the Soviet Union by parachute almost two hours later.

The first Moon landings less than a decade later required further sophistication of life-support systems, with crews being away from Earth for just over a week. The Apollo spacecraft had three parts: a command module including a cabin where the crew would return to Earth; a service module providing propulsion, power, oxygen and water; and a lunar module consisting of a lander and an ascent stage to get the astronauts back into lunar orbit. During the journey, the crew breathed pressurised air from an on-board oxygen source, wearing space suits for launch, re-entry and on the lunar surface. Food and drink came freeze-dried, rehydrated by adding water. All waste was stored in bags with germicide to prevent gas production.

The first humans to walk on the Moon, astronauts Neil Armstrong and Buzz Aldrin, spent almost 22 hours on the surface of the Moon, during which time pilot Michael Collins circled the Moon, completely alone, once every two hours. The first layer of the space suits worn on the surface was water-cooled underwear, next an airtight pressure garment, then a multi-layer outer garment for protection from micrometeorites and radiation. The portable life-support system, sustaining four hours of activity before requiring recharge, was worn like a backpack over the suit, its functions including regulating suit pressure, providing breathable oxygen; removing carbon dioxide from air; cooling and recirculating oxygen and water; two-way voice communication; and display of astronaut and suit health parameters.

While we have not returned to the surface of the Moon in 50 years, since its launch in 1998, over two decades of human habitation of the ISS have provided an opportunity to further sophisticate life-support systems at a relatively safe distance from Earth, just 400 kilometres up. Life in the ISS has produced research and development in areas of solar technology, water filtration systems, LED lighting to grow food, additive manufacturing, remote healthcare, as well as communication and computing systems, to name but a few.

The leap of faith that pioneers in space exploration took decades ago is unimaginably greater than that required to return to the Moon or to visit the surface of Mars. In the meantime, the remote exploration of space has led to great progress in automation and robotics, data analysis and a host of other industries. Crewed missions to the Moon and Mars in the coming years promise to further revolutionise our capabilities.

33.2.5 Robotics

The word "robot", from the Czech word "*robota*" for forced labor, was first used in 1921 by playwright Karl Capek, in a play about mechanical factory workers that rebel against their human masters. The first modern machines in the form of humans were built in the 1950s by inventor George Devol, one of which he sold to General Motors in 1960 to lift hot pieces of metal for car production.

The field of robotics – the design, construction, and use of machines to perform tasks done traditionally by humans – was established to replace people in performing simple repetitive tasks, and in industries where work is performed in environments hazardous to humans.

Space is a notable example of an extreme environment, and while humans have only been as far as the Moon, our direct knowledge of a range of locations in the Solar System is thanks to robotic missions that have travelled there. Sputnik was the first robot in space, while the Voyager missions achieved the milestone of taking a robot out of the Solar System into interstellar space. Robots do not require the complex resources that humans do, and as long as their power, controls, sensors, and communication systems are functional, they continue working in all kinds of harsh environments reliably and without rest. Largely because of the data acquired on the surface of Mars by more than two decades of roving by remotely operated vehicles, can we begin planning the first crewed missions there.

33.2.6 Manufacturing

As humans, our use of tools has defined us. Historically, tools were produced and used by individual artisans. Then the invention of engines, first powered by steam and then by internal combustion, culminated in the Industrial Revolution in the UK, continental Europe, and the US. This era saw a transition to mass production of goods using recently invented engine machinery, and was facilitated by the new economic concept of manual labour – long, repetitive hours of human work – as well as by the colonisation of various other parts of the world for raw materials. People began to move to cities to get paying jobs in industry in order to buy the goods being produced, and public transportation, communication and banking systems emerged. Thus, with manufacturing, capitalism was born.

In 1913, Henry Ford implemented the first moving assembly line for the mass production of an entire automobile, pioneering automation in manufacturing and reducing the time to build a car from over 12 hours to one hour and 33 minutes. The resulting production of millions of affordable cars for the public created thousands of jobs and revolutionised the way we travel.

Transportation systems are fundamental to space exploration, and our remote investigation of the Solar System has resulted in continued rapid development in automation and robotics. The manufacturing industry has simultaneously enjoyed reduced costs and improved efficiencies of increasingly mechanised production. A culmination of this mechanisation is "additive manufacturing" or 3D printing.

The 3D printing process builds parts layer by layer by depositing material according to digital 3D design data. Plastic and more recently metal 3D printers were deployed in the ISS, meaning that repair or replacement of certain parts of equipment can be done locally in Earth orbit. While manufacturing may require less and less human labour, we cannot do away with the requirement for raw materials. The production of 3D printing input materials, or feedstock, from recycled materials in space is an area of investigation.

Local and in particular additive manufacturing will be a critical capability of communities in remote locations, to enable emergency maintenance and repair of infrastructure according to design data sent at light speed from Earth, and eventually to produce all kinds of technologies, from data storage devices and processors to 3D printers themselves, using recycled as well as *in situ* resources.

33.2.7 Data analysis

In 1884, statistician Herman Hollerith invented an electromechanical tabulating machine for punched cards to store data, establishing the foundations of digitisation and data processing. The first network email was sent in 1971 by computer engineer Ray Tomlinson to a computer next to his; it said, "something like QWERTYUIOP". Today, over 10 billion devices are online. This means anyone with an internet connection can achieve amazing feats like accessing supercomputing resources remotely or zooming down to a recent street view of almost any city on the planet.

To date, we have created, communicated, and consumed over 600 billion gigabytes of data. This is predicted to double in the next couple of years. Almost half of the data we currently produce comes from machines; devices that are able to sense the environment, from microphones to satellites in Earth orbit. With the help of our personal devices, we generate the rest.

The benefit of all this information is determined by our, or increasingly our machines', ability to analyse it. Data processing is the task of converting raw data into more meaningful information that can then become knowledge. Current state-of-the-art machine learning algorithms, often referred to as artificial intelligence, can be automated such that we are typically not aware of the actual algorithms being employed. Nonetheless, through repetition and large data sets, underlying patterns embedded in the data can be uncovered.

The combination of sensors and predictive data processing techniques are particularly useful in the context of extreme environments on Earth or beyond: from air or spacecraft functionality; to resource or life-support system health; to physiological indicators, monitoring a plethora of parameters to build large sets of data allows the prediction of errors before they occur, for vastly increased safety of people and performance of the equipment keeping them alive.

33.2.8 Encryption

The benefits of connectivity come with the associated risk around how the information that we create, communicate and store can be intercepted, sometimes with malicious intent. Cryptography is the ancient art of achieving confidentiality by transforming a message such that it is only intelligible to someone in possession of a key. Since the emergence of the internet, a multitude of algorithms for data security have been developed, and global standards for encryption protocols provide some level of communications security over computer networks. Satellite data transfers are typically encrypted, and communications with the ISS are protected. Data relating to life-support systems in the extreme environment of space in particular needs to be safeguarded.

33.2.9 Blockchain

Just months after the financial crash of 2008, triggered by increasing deregulation of the industry, the first digital currency to employ cryptography to solve the problem of "double spending" without the requirement for a central trusted third-party regulator was proposed. That currency was Bitcoin, now valued at over a trillion US dollars. Since then, thousands of other cryptocurrencies have been established. The technology underlying this decentralised capability is a distributed ledger, or blockchain. Transactions are recorded in blocks that are linked and secured by cryptography; these records are verified and stored across a network making the ledger, as well as the rules governing the transactions, resistant to modification.

While adding new information to the Bitcoin network is energy intensive, high energy-consumption is not intrinsic to blockchain technology in general, and novel consensus mechanisms determining how information is added to the ledger achieve significant reductions. This combination of capabilities in computing, connectivity, and cryptography has applications not only in the financial world, but also in any transactional environment, including for decentralised data management systems requiring transparency and immutability.

One compelling application of blockchain is in securing online identity. How to verify, secure, and manage identity and personal data online is a major challenge of the current era, while an estimated 1.1 billion people worldwide do not have any formal identification whatsoever. In this context, blockchain enables individuals to own and control their identities online in a decentralised personal data management system where records are verified and stored across a network making the ledger resistant to modification. Irrespective of the nation they happen to be born in, with an Internet connection, they can access the service.

Another application of blockchain is for management of critical resources. Billions of humans on Earth live without access to adequate shelter and nutrition, clean air and water, and also the reliable power and communications systems that have become important tools to participate in society. Neither governments, nor the corporations they increasingly answer to, appear to be equipped or inclined to deal with this issue. In fact, inequality and the number of people living in extreme poverty has increased of late, fuelled by the COVID-19 pandemic, climate change, and an ever-increasing population of humans confined to a planet no longer able to replenish the natural resources their society consumes. A decentralised system of monitoring resource consumption may be a start towards addressing these issues.

The Outer Space Treaty of 1967 outlines noble aspirations that the exploration and use of outer space shall be carried out for the benefit and in the interests of all countries, and that those going there shall be regarded as envoys of all humanity. In this spirit, decentralised systems to manage life-support systems, resources, and even personal identity, that do not rely on record-keeping and regulation by a central (terrestrial) authority, seem particularly attractive.

33.3 Off-world outlook

33.3.1 Earth orbit

33.3.1.1 Resources

The space above Earth's surface between altitudes of 160 and 36,000 kilometres is a shared resource for communication and observation, as well as research and development in the micro-gravity environment there. Since the launch of Sputnik in 1957, there are now thousands of artificial bodies in orbit around Earth; both operational and defunct satellites owned by almost 100 different nations on Earth, as well as space stations for human habitation launched and operated by a handful of national governments.

The vantage point from above the surface of the Earth provides convenient monitoring and signal transmission capabilities, and typically satellites are equipped with sensors to collect data on atmospheric or surface conditions of our planet, or are relaying signals where point-to-point propagation of electromagnetic waves is obstructed. The benefits on the ground of satellites in orbit are huge; from providing reliable connectivity, in particular for communities disconnected from the world due to conflict, natural disasters or a lack of infrastructure, navigation systems, as well as monitoring systems collecting big data on climate and weather patterns, the Sun's activities, or natural resource management.

There are currently just two inhabited space stations in Earth orbit, the ISS and the recently launched Chinese space station. For the past 20 years, the ISS has been the soccer field-sized platform facilitating our entire planet's research into scientific fields ranging from human physiology in microgravity, Earth observation, high-energy astrophysics, to the development and sophistication of life-support systems necessary to sustain life in space. Owing to aging after 20 years in service, coupled with government budget cuts, it was recently announced that the ISS will be decommissioned by 2031, deorbited and plunged into the Pacific Ocean. There is discussion of transitioning habitation of Earth orbit to commercial operations, but plans to launch further space stations remain to be confirmed.

On the other hand, the almost US$300 billion global satellite economy, including telecommunications and internet infrastructure, the Global Positioning Service, Earth observation capabilities, national security satellites and more, continues to experience massive growth. Decreasing launch costs have enabled a variety of industries to benefit from satellite technologies to drive innovation and efficiency in their products and services. For example, SpaceX plans to launch in excess of 40,000 satellites to complete its Starlink constellation, which at full capacity could provide the company with tens of billions of US dollars annually from millions of internet subscribers all over the planet, thereby funding its Mars missions.

By the end of 2021 there were around 5,000 active satellites in orbit. If SpaceX, Amazon, Boeing, China, and others achieve their ambitious constellation plans, there could be tens of thousands of additional satellites in Earth orbit within the next decade. As usual, these advances come at a price.

The accumulation of space debris, or artificial objects in Earth orbit that no longer serve a function, poses a risk to our activities in space. Space debris includes defunct satellites and spacecraft, abandoned launch vehicles, mission-related debris and fragments thereof. Of the Starlink satellites launched by SpaceX, over 1,000 are no longer functional; further contribution to the almost 30,000 pieces of debris larger than 10 centimetres currently orbiting the Earth.

Collisions between debris and operational satellites can disrupt observation and communication capabilities, threaten the safety of people in orbit, or in the long term, trigger chain collisions that could spell the end of our ability to explore space altogether. Our current economic system creates incentive for companies to innovate in areas where there is money to be made. However, hoping patiently that cleaning up Earth orbit, or indeed the continued presence of people there, will eventually be profitable and pursued commercially, seems counterproductive.

Additional regulation by international organisations could mitigate the negative impact of a free-market system in Earth orbit. However, existing space treaties do not provide explicit mandates for orbital debris removal, and moreover international space law has not been significantly amended in decades. But yet space debris is an untapped resource in itself.

33.3.1.2 Infrastructure

There is currently as much as 10,000 tons of junk in Earth orbit. By comparison, the ISS weighs 450 tons. Space "debris" typically consists of components that could be repaired or harvested for reuse, or contains rare metals – all of which have been extracted, processed, and launched from Earth in resource intensive processes. There are proposals under development to remove debris from Earth orbit by retrieving old equipment and fragments thereof via magnetic effects, harpoons, claw-like structures, or sticky robotic arms, then typically pushing them towards Earth to burn up in the atmosphere. From a resource efficiency perspective, can we do better?

Mechanised and crewed on-orbit servicing infrastructures could provide maintenance, refuelling or repair services for failed satellites in orbit; furthermore, component and material recycling coupled with 3D printing technologies could enable the production of satellites in orbit. Space manufacturing is within reach: enabled by developments including the increasing miniaturisation and modularisation of many satellite technology components; developments in additive manufacturing including the demonstration of 3D printing in the ISS; as well as impressive advancements in robotics and automation particularly on the surface of Mars. Decentralised and immutable satellite tracking from launch through to repair or repurposing of hardware including for sensitive applications like defense, can be achieved through blockchain, already applied similarly as a single source of truth in supply chain management and property ownership transfer.

Another orbital resource useful for production is the lack of gravity: crystals grown in the microgravity of Earth orbit contain fewer imperfections than those grown on the surface, with applications in materials science and healthcare research, drug production as well as technologies such as radiation monitoring devices. Beyond the studies typically performed by just six people in the ISS, with bigger teams and more facilities, research and innovation in the microgravity environment of space could be extended to include the development of novel propulsion systems, new materials, modular life-support systems to be serviced and maintained in space, robotic manufacturing and assembly, off-world supercomputers to support this activity, or design spacecraft, to name but a few.

33.3.1.3 Society

Our activities in Earth orbit have thus far provided a good precedent for international cooperation amongst crews representing a (small) range of countries. While nearly half of the countries on Earth have their own satellites in orbit, just a few regions on Earth have access to the research and development, and more recently tourism, taking place in the microgravity environment of Earth orbit through human presence there. Canada, Japan, Russia, the United States, the European Union, and more recently with their own space station, China, currently fund and access facilities in orbit, and with the rise of space tourism, more citizens who are wealthy enough to afford it, mostly from these same regions, are joining in.

We have been launching things into space since the 1950s. We have been living in space for the past 20 years. What is next? It is time we advance to being able to produce space technologies in space, from resources we extract there. To utilise space debris, we will need more diverse crews as well as robotic support in orbit, which will require space station facilities. At a relatively safe distance of a few hundred kilometres above home, where resupply and evacuation are just hours away, more people living and working in the microgravity environment of Earth orbit will provide crucial data for the teams and the technology that we will need to explore further beyond Earth in the coming years.

With the current state-of-the-art technologies discussed in previous sections, we have the tools at our disposal to develop the infrastructure required for our sustainable use of Earth orbit. Assuming we want to continue advancing in our exploration of the space beyond our planet, we need to reflect on whether the economic and regulatory systems that drive and manage activities in Earth orbit are aligned with this objective. Our very ability to leave the surface of Earth in the future depends on our ability to successfully manage the space above our planet.

It's unlikely that new economics prioritising efficient resource utilisation or exploration ahead of profits will emerge as a result of activities in such close proximity to the largely capitalist surface of Earth. So for now, we can only hope that the commercial value of data obtained in Earth orbit, as well as potentially reduced costs of repurposing space debris for satellite manufacture coupled with revenue from space technology innovation in orbit, will suffice to support our continued activity there.

Beyond Earth orbit, there's a place that may advance our understanding of resources, infrastructure and society at a more rapid rate: the brightest object in the night sky.

33.3.2 The Moon

33.3.2.1 Resources

Our natural satellite, the Moon, orbits Earth at a distance of around 400,000 kilometres, and has a total area just bigger than the continent of Africa. With temperatures ranging over 300 degrees

Celsius during fortnight long days and nights, no atmosphere, gravity just one sixth, and surface radiation over 200 times that of Earth, the harshness of the environment on the Moon is rivalled by few other places in the Solar System. It is therefore a convenient resource for off-world exploration, research and innovation just three days travel from Earth.

So far, it has been underutilised. With only four American men still alive who have walked there, over a half-century ago, plans to return to the lunar surface in the next few years and build habitable bases there have been announced by the US, China, and Russia, and are finally underway. While we do not need a revolution in propulsion systems to get to the Moon and back, human presence there will require resources. The equipment required for shelter, power, mobility, communications, and to produce oxygen and water on the surface of the Moon will initially come from Earth; the ability to maintain, repair, or augment this infrastructure locally with lunar resources is an active area of investigation.

Before we set foot on the Moon, we were not sure what it was made of. Local analysis by Apollo crews as well as samples brought back to Earth finally shed some light on its surface composition. In 2019, China became the first nation to investigate the surface of the far side of the Moon, the following year becoming the third country to achieve lunar sample return from the near side, for the first time since the Soviet Union in 1976. Our data and samples show that the Moon contains volatiles, minerals and metals, some of which may also be useful on Earth.

The elemental composition of the lunar surface is largely similar to the Earth, dominated by oxygen and silicon, except that there is more iron and titanium, while carbon, nitrogen, and alkali metals like sodium and potassium are less abundant. Our knowledge of what lies below the surface is limited; a Japanese mission has detected the presence of the heavier radioactive elements uranium and thorium in lunar dirt.

Helium-3 is thought to occur in greater abundance on the Moon than on Earth, and is an appealing candidate for nuclear fusion fuel, as a stable isotope of helium that does not produce dangerous waste products. However, the feasibility of scalable fusion power generation, for the time being, remains uncertain.

There is evidence of water ice in the permanently shadowed craters on the Moon's surface. Water supports life, in liquid form as well as owing to its oxygen content. Through the process of electrolysis, the hydrogen and oxygen atoms in water can be split apart, providing fuel in the form of hydrogen burned in oxygen. Decades of innovation in air and water management as well as radiation protection for the crews in the ISS will provide an important basis for the life-support infrastructure on the Moon. With the technological innovation that has taken place since last we were there, grand visions for infrastructure on the Moon are within reach.

33.3.2.2 Infrastructure

Lunar bases could include modular shelters with panels produced from lunar regolith; power production redundancy through periodically abundant solar energy, together with hydrogen fuel cells and radioisotope thermoelectric generators; waste water processing to produce hydrogen and nutrients for lunar food production; indoor agriculture and cultured meats from stem cells; solar and hydrogen powered pressurised rovers, the list goes on. Besides extracting lunar ice for water, hydrogen and oxygen, or uranium or thorium as fuel for nuclear devices, proposals to extract metals like titanium as well as silicon from the surface of the Moon and vacuum-deposit these materials to produce solar cell or even telescope components locally, are also under development.

The near side of the Moon is in permanent line of sight with some part of Earth and at just a couple of light seconds away, is close enough to consider integration with the existing internet.

Connectivity on the far side will require lunar satellites, which can also be deployed for signal transmission between distant locations on the surface. There are currently a handful of active satellites in lunar orbit, launched by the US and also India. Future lunar communication satellites and local networks, computing power, surface mobility vehicles, healthcare facilities and so on, could become an opportunity for joint use and collaboration between the nations and private companies that are active there.

Lunar cryptocurrencies and locally implemented cryptocurrency mining could form part of the lunar economy, facilitate trade between outposts on the Moon, as well as provide the financial infrastructure for lunar-based transnational projects to trade resources or information with organisations back on Earth.

33.3.2.3 Society

So, who on Earth will pay for all of this? Of late, and accelerated by the COVID-19 pandemic, our economic system is producing greater numbers of billionaires, wielding net worths exceeding many national space budgets. A new era of public-private partnership in the space industry is stimulating activity the likes of which we have not seen since the Cold War. Commercial resource utilisation is central to the US endeavour to return to the Moon; NASA has announced that it will buy resources such as ice, rocks, dirt, and other lunar materials to stimulate private extraction of off-world resources for its use in space. China, on the other hand, is making rapid progress towards the utilisation of space resources towards its own national economic development.

Just how profitable could lunar resources be? In the past few years, launch costs from Earth have dropped significantly, but it is still a million dollars to get a ton to orbit. The value of extracting water on the Moon, whether for local lunar use or for refuelling within the Earth-Moon system, will be determined in relation to such costs. Beyond water, here on Earth a range of factors from environmental to societal can result in shortages in metal and mineral supplies, and disruptions in technology supply chains. For example, the economic lockdowns associated with the COVID-19 pandemic played a central role in the global semiconductor chip shortage crisis. It is not impossible that resource shortages fuelled by a combination of international conflict, sanctions, extreme weather, a consumerist culture and ongoing shortcomings in waste management, could result in it becoming cost efficient to deliver certain resources from the Moon to Earth.

Besides mining, there is commercial opportunity for the information produced on the Moon; from documentary footage to research data to technology innovation. Private companies are also developing capabilities to take people to the Moon, raising questions about how restrictions on tourist activities on the lunar surface could be enforced.

Similarly to Antarctica, activity on the Moon is governed by international treaties. With line-of-sight communication and accessibility all year round, the Moon is arguably less remote than Antarctica; another difference is that commercial activities in Antarctica are in general explicitly not permitted, and perhaps as a result, the continent has never seen large-scale conflict. Once it has been established that there is money to be made on the Moon, will regulation keep up? The unchecked accumulation of debris in Earth orbit as the result of an emerging trillion-dollar industry does not bode well.

The Moon Agreement of 1979 disallows states to conduct commercial mining on celestial bodies until there is an international regime for such exploitation; however, it has not been ratified by any nation able to launch crews. The Outer Space Treaty on the other hand has been signed by most countries on Earth, limiting the use of the Moon and other celestial bodies to peaceful purposes for exploration and utilisation by all nations. But, it is largely silent or ambiguous on commercial activities on the Moon, including resource extraction such as lunar mining. Whether national or private, when large profits are at stake, international agreements can be deprioritised, and the outcome can be conflict.

If we get it right, human presence on the Moon will be an opportunity for collaboration-driven innovation in an extreme environment; a laboratory for space exploration in relative proximity to Earth. The data we collect from wearables, surface exploration, subsurface investigation and the performance of innovations in life-support systems increasingly fuelled by *in situ* resources, will enable us to prepare for establishing off-world communities throughout the Solar System.

The proximity of the Moon to Earth will likely preclude any radical rethinking of terrestrial economics or governance systems. While the Earth-Moon system will likely remain united as one, and potentially become a flagship for international cooperation beyond Earth, there is another candidate for off-world habitation that is just far enough for things to get really interesting.

33.3.3 Mars

33.3.3.1 Resources

Assuming that the development of SpaceX's Starship continues successfully, a few 100-ton cargo deliveries are all that stand between us and the first crews' arrival on Mars. But what then? Unlike our ancestors who set off towards the horizon without knowing what lay in store, we have detailed knowledge of the surface of Mars owing to decades of data acquired from Earth-based and orbital observations, as well as landers and rovers with direct experience of the conditions. While we have not yet brought back any samples from Mars, hundreds of meteorites retrieved on Earth have been identified as Martian, further contributing to our knowledge of the planet.

Mars is just over half as wide as Earth; its rust colour comes from the iron oxide content in the sand. The atmosphere is unbreathable at a pressure of less than one percent of sea level pressure on Earth, containing 96% carbon dioxide, and traces of argon and molecular nitrogen. In spite of the thin atmosphere, winds can stir up the fine dust, which falls back down in a gravitational field 38% of Earth, or more than double of the Moon. The surface sand contains a few percent by mass water ice, or as much as 50 percent a couple of feet down, depending on the location, remnants of a warmer and wetter times around four billion years ago when Mars had a global magnetic field that maintained a thicker atmosphere and oceans. Now, temperatures are typically well below zero, with a global average of around -63 degrees Celsius. Due to its atmosphere, conditions on Mars are less extreme than the Moon, with temperatures ranging from -150 to 20 degrees Celsius, and surface radiation levels less than half. The day-night cycle is remarkably similar to Earth, at 24 hours and 39 minutes.

Mars is currently around seven months away by spaceflight, and whether we should go there at all tends to be a controversial topic. One argument is that the resources required would be better spent on solving problems on Earth. However, investments here continue to have no overall impact on the way we manage our resources or on addressing global issues like poverty. Furthermore, states of emergencies as a result of pandemics or extreme weather events serve to enhance consumption and inequality. For example, the COVID-19 pandemic and associated economic lockdowns, coupled with climate change, have pushed hundreds of millions more people into extreme poverty, while billions of single-use facemasks discarded daily has significantly contributed to global plastic waste pollution.

The infrastructure we need to inhabit the surface of Mars will be focused on technology-enabled resource efficiency due to harsh conditions and distance from Earth; living on Mars necessitates the transformation of "waste" into resources. Human settlement of our neighbouring planet will be an important demonstration of community resilience in resource-constrained conditions. The tools and the mindset to achieve this are just as critical for survival on Mars as for a sustainable future here on Earth, where a growing population of humans competing for Earth's finite resources in the face of extreme weather events, pandemics and resulting conflict, is facing increasingly uncertain times.

33.3.3.2 Infrastructure

The technology we require to inhabit Mars already exists; living in the ISS or even on the Moon is more challenging from an engineering perspective than setting up camp on a rocky planet with significant gravity and an atmosphere. Much of the thinking towards lunar settlement can be copy-pasted here. However, unlike Earth orbit or the Moon, at on average over 200 million kilometres away from Earth, the remoteness will define an approach to infrastructure choices focused on circular resource utilisation and sustainability.

After securing an expandable shelter, with connected landers, inflatable modules or sealed lava tubes, or all of the above, the most fundamental step towards establishing a community on Mars is power production. Energy availability enables all other functionalities of the settlement. If power systems fail, within minutes, so does life; hence redundancy is critical.

Radioisotope thermoelectric generators fuelled by radioactive materials, some of which may be locally available, for example thorium-228, have no moving parts, and with appropriate shielding, are reliable sources of heat and energy that could be functional on arrival. Solar irradiance on the surface of Mars is at best around half of that on Earth, and while laying out a solar array and connecting batteries brought from Earth is a good start, their limited lifetime in the harsh surface conditions as well as the challenge to manufacture such technologies locally, means that supporting or replacement systems need to be considered.

Fuel cells utilising local resources are good candidates for a Martian settlement not only for their energy generation and storage capabilities, but because of their by-products. For example, a regenerative solid oxide cell system can store energy via the electrolysis of water to produce molecular oxygen and hydrogen, with the energy generation phase producing water via a reaction between these gases.

While water will need to be extracted from surface soil using rovers and heating procedures, carbon dioxide is easily pumped from the Martian atmosphere. With oxygen produced by electrolysis from either of these molecules, creating pressurised breathable air additionally requires an inert gas like nitrogen, which makes up a few percent of the Martian atmosphere. Another source of nitrogen is from wastewater processing, managed through the controlled use of specific microbes employed to retrieve both pure water as well as resources like fuels and nutrients from the digestion of organic waste.

Critical for the transformation of resources is the oldest living process on Earth, photosynthesis. Food for the community can be grown inside agricultural units and photobioreactors optimised for biomass production. A lively ecosystem can be supplemented with insects and fish, conveniently transportable in eggs and sources of agricultural nutrients and dietary protein; algae, rich in a range of essential vitamins and minerals; also a range of medicinal plants, fungi and bacteria as a source of biomolecules for healthcare applications amongst others.

In the longer term, a settlement would need to locally manufacture the infrastructure to produce power and cycle resources as outlined above; 3D printing is a critical starting point for such manufacturing capabilities. *In situ* manufacturing may lead to unexpected paradigm shifts. For example, graphene is a material consisting of a single layer of carbon atoms arranged in a lattice.

It conducts electricity better than copper, is stronger and lighter than steel, can replace indium in touch screens, a range of rare metals in solar cells, provide radiation shielding, and has a plethora of other applications in various industries. New methods to mass produce graphene, like combining hydrocarbon gas, oxygen and a spark plug inside a chamber, could mean that the momentum to innovate using graphene may be greater on Mars than Earth, where profitable legacy systems and their custodians impede progress.

33.3.3.3 Society

At ten light minutes from Earth, remote resource management and governance will be impractical. Not unlike the compact for self-governance drawn up by the male pilgrims on the Mayflower, considered by some to have laid the foundation for the independence of the New World, we can expect that local systems of regulation will emerge.

A notable characteristic of Mars is that is has no current commercial value. A leap of imagination greater than that required to imagine lunar resources having value on Earth, is to imagine that a rocky planet like Mars, similar to Earth in composition but on average more than 200 million kilometres away, could any time soon be of economic value for Earth. However, conversely, this could prove to be a critical reason why our expansion there is important. It gives us an opportunity to rethink the function and structure of an economic system.

A data-driven economic system designed for an extreme and resource-constrained environment would prioritise efficient, and likely also equitable, resource utilisation. In such an environment, energy availability provides an indicator of the fundamental health of the system since energy is required for any transformation of resources from one form to another. Therefore, power production capability would provide a useful standard of value. A secure, connected system to monitor power production would provide data on which to base subsequent decisions on power allocation for all other operations.

For example, assuming life-support systems are functioning normally, a community on Mars may want to stockpile fuel. Each step in the process of extracting carbon dioxide from the atmosphere, introducing it into a photobioreactor where it is converted by cyanobacteria into sugars, feeding these sugars to E. coli who then produce a kind of fuel called 2,3-butanediol, will have an energy price tag. Optimisation of such resource transformations can be implemented by comparison, for example, to methane production via the Sabatier process involving the reaction of hydrogen with carbon dioxide to produce methane and water, to arrive at the best way to produce fuel given current energy availability. Blockchain could be a suitable platform to scale such a resource ledger for a city on Mars. And this is the tip of the iceberg of what is possible when we think about the fundamental principles on which we would build a society from scratch.

We have been sold the idea that life on Earth is about competition, that evolution is driven by survival of the fittest. While this thinking has played a role in achieving our current level of technological development, the question we need to ask ourselves is whether the centralisation of power and resources that has resulted, is serving our best interests going forward. A system that drives consumerism only makes sense in the context of Earth's current economic system, and only for a few. In a world of finite resources, for an ever-expanding population inculcated in a culture of materialism, things do not end well.

A far more fundamental natural theme than competition is cooperation. Ten percent by mass of our bodies, the hydrogen content, is as old as the Universe itself, produced in the Big Bang; around half of our cells are not human but microbes that evolved billions of years ago on which we depend for essential functioning. There is no such thing as a single living organism. Life on Mars will be a fragile resource; collaboration and an attitude of appreciation for life and all that is needed to sustain it will likely characterise early regulatory systems there.

To be self-sufficient in the longer term, a society on Mars will need significant amounts of resources. A terraforming initiative, to transform the surface into a place more comfortable for terrestrial life, will require vast amounts of resources, and likely collaboration with Earth. The beauty of exploration is that once we are able leave the limited environment on Earth, resources are more abundant than we think. And to extract these resources, we do not need to disrupt the only thriving biosphere that we know of; the living ecosystem unique to Earth. The answer to our future resource requirements, whichever planet we are on, may lie in a region just beyond Mars: the Asteroid Belt.

33.3.4 Asteroid Belt

33.3.4.1 Resources

Too small to be planets, too big to be ignored, asteroids have been the cause of the extinction of many a species here on Earth due to global environmental changes that can result when a big enough impact with the surface of our planet takes place. The characterisation of asteroids is therefore a critical first step towards mitigating extinction level impacts; there are many near-Earth asteroids traversing the Solar System that are as yet uncatalogued. A perhaps more tangible reason to be interested in asteroids is for the resources they contain.

Just a few generations ago, less than a dozen materials were in wide use, among them wood, brick, iron, copper, gold, silver, and a few plastics. By contrast, a single modern computer chip uses more than 60 different elements of varying scarcity. The Earth is largely a closed system, loosing just heat, hydrogen, and helium to its surroundings. Bar very few extremely rare metals, the notion that we are "running out" of certain resources is true only in the economic sense that extracting or recycling these resources is not cost-efficient.

Increased societal demand coupled with our failure to implement suitable waste management strategies may result in it becoming profitable to return certain off-world resources to Earth. While the Moon and Mars have compositions comparable with Earth, Asteroid Anteros, for example, is a two-kilometre wide lump of rock estimated to contain rare metals and minerals worth more than five trillion US dollars.

There is in fact correlation between locations where significant amounts of heavy metals and rare minerals have been extracted on Earth, and meteor impact sites. When a large body, typically an asteroid fragment or a comet, crashes into Earth, it deposits its contents near the surface. Additionally, the immense amounts of energy transferred to the crust of the Earth during a collision can produce minerals. For example, around two billion years ago, a meteorite ten kilometres wide smashed in an area just south of Johannesburg in South Africa. The 300-kilometre wide impact site, the Vredefort dome, is co-located with the Witwatersrand region, where the largest deposit of gold and the largest rough diamond ever found on the planet were extracted. Today, this region is home to all four of the deepest mines on Earth, with operating depths of up to four kilometres, as we exhaust the gold conveniently deposited near the surface.

The resources required to prepare a typical space mission are comparable with those required to establish a terrestrial mine: teams of experts working for typically over a decade, with costs running into the billions of dollars. Furthermore, what is left of potential locations for mining, are mostly already home either to humans or increasingly shrinking natural ecosystems. The total mass of a collection of rocks in orbit between Mars and Jupiter, the so-called Asteroid Belt, is estimated to be around four percent of the mass of the Moon, however, this region likely contains more metals and minerals than what is left of Earth's surface reserves, because amongst these rocks are fragmented planetesimal cores, containing the same stuff we have been mining on Earth. It is time to go directly to the source: the Asteroid Belt.

33.3.4.2 Infrastructure

Thus far, government agencies have launched a number of missions to asteroids and comets: a European mission was first to land on a comet; Japan has twice retrieved asteroid samples; and the US has samples currently en route back to Earth. Commercially, private space mining companies, including Planetary Resources and Deep Space Industries, were established a couple of decades ago with the aim to extract resources from asteroids. The passing of legislation in the US and then in Luxembourg allowing companies ownership of what they extract from celestial bodies did not, however, enable these two companies to succeed. Perhaps because the leap of imagination from mining the surface of the Earth, to drilling, blasting, cutting, and crushing in the vacuum of space hundreds of millions of kilometres away, was too much.

More successful ventures may be those that have application somewhere closer to home, like Earth orbit. Furthermore, we may need to rethink traditional mining methods. A candidate concept for asteroid resource extraction involving the encapsulation of the entire target goes by the acronym SHEPHERD (Secure Handling by Encapsulation of a Planetesimal Heading to Earth-moon Retrograde-orbit Delivery). The concept involves sealing a target, anything from a defunct satellite to a planetesimal, within a gas-filled enclosure, and redirecting it to the required orbit using gas flow.

Owing to the minimal interaction of the method, sensitive items like satellites could be targeted: data stores retrieved; refuelling or maintenance performed; or repurposing or recycling of defunct components achieved. Further away, many asteroids are well-described as weakly consolidated rubble piles, and their encapsulation for resource extraction would provide protection for spacecraft hardware from loose debris and dust disturbed on the target's surface, enable the acquisition of volatiles from icy objects through heating, as well as enabling processing of material enroute to the desired destination. Processing methods could include electroforming; the use of gases to differentiate metals from volatiles which burn off so that the metals can be collected. During processing, spectral analysis of the composition of the target can be performed, and subsequent decisions to abort or continue the mission made.

33.3.4.3 Society

While bringing resources back to Earth could contribute to the cost-effectiveness of initial missions, the real potential of asteroid mining is in realising humanity's ambition to explore and settle space. Launch from Earth is getting cheaper, but the cost of getting large amounts of resources off Earth's surface remains prohibitive. So finding and extracting useful materials in space could turn asteroids into fuel stops. Resources like water, organic compounds, minerals, and metals extracted in space will not only extend the range of crewed space exploration; in combination with technologies such as 3D printing, resources extracted from asteroids can be used to create tools, machines, and even habitats, making crewed space exploration and the establishment of off-world settlements throughout the Solar System feasible.

Once we have demonstrated asteroid resource extraction and utilisation, and have tested the basic infrastructure required to support human communities on the surface of the Moon, harsher than many other environments in the Solar System, then the illusion of scarcity that we have been sold here on Earth falls away. We live in a vast universe, containing plenty of the hydrogen, oxygen, carbon, nitrogen, and other atoms of which we are made and on which we depend to maintain our state of living.

Once we have developed the tools to travel beyond Earth, as well as manufacture infrastructure off-world with *in situ* resources, we can start thinking about interplanetary trade. Blockchain-based systems are an existing platform on which this could be achieved. A natural standard of value in the Martian context is power production capability, which determines the allocation of resources to all other activities. However, as we begin to understand that decentralised systems can withstand multiple failures in the network, we may want to move away from centralised notions of value altogether. Can we imagine a world where all exchanges of resources take place for whatever reasons the involved parties feel like?

33.4 Conclusion

The projections outlined here may seem idealistic, however well-motivated and supported by logic and existing technologies. So what is holding us back? We cannot ignore the global economic system.

Perhaps we do not realise that our money does not mean anything. Since the gold standard, which tied currency value to gold, was dropped in 1971, the value of money is solely in accordance with a government's declaration of its value. Hence the term *fiat* which means "by decree". The entire monetary system is upheld simply because we buy into it, literally. When the financial system faced collapse in 2008, bank bailouts occurred perhaps because the idea that the system should fail was unimaginable – especially to those benefiting most from that system. We missed an opportunity to reimagine economics. Our next opportunity may be off-world.

Preparing to build communities beyond Earth is minimally a powerful thought experiment: if we could discard the layers of legacy, containing some systems we would like to retain, but also those that are no longer serving us, on what fundamental principles would we establish a society? What systems will we use to realise these principles?

A greed-based system is not likely to be sustainable in a resource-constrained environment like a single planet. We are at risk of irreversibly destabilising the only life-support system we currently have, Earth, through our incessant pursuit of economic growth. Living systems all require resources to survive. And efficient resource management is a characteristic of a viable society. Advancing beyond Earth is an opportunity to reimagine suboptimal systems that have emerged here on Earth, and demonstrate what is possible when we put collaboration rather than competition at the heart of human endeavour.

Living on more than one planet avoids a single point of failure for our species, and is an essential aspect of becoming a more advanced society. Through technological innovation and an enhanced perspective of reality and our place in it, expanding beyond Earth will encourage new ways of thinking, enable us to become better stewards of Earth, and equip us for the beginning of our journey into the stars. From a vantage point beyond Earth, we may be able to achieve the noble aspirations of the Outer Space Treaty, and explore and use space for the benefit, and in the interests, of all humanity.

INDEX